The Russian Patriotic War of 1812 is the only publicly available translation into English of Bogdanovich's official history of the Russian forces' involvement in the fight against Napoleon and his allies in Russia in 1812. This translation also includes extracts from Ivan Liprandi's critique of Bogdanovich's work.

Volume 1 of *The Russian Patriotic War of 1812* includes the causes of the war and an account of the operational planning by Russian forces for their retreat from the borders into the Empire, dispelling the myth of the non-existence of any premeditated plan. The logistics of the forces on both sides are examined, along with highly detailed descriptions of the operations from Russia's western borders to beyond Smolensk and operations on the northern and southern flanks. Outstanding feats were performed not only by prominent personalities but also by others who participated in this war. The composition of the forces are shown as clearly as possible, as are force numbers, casualties on each side, and so on. The maps attached to this work were drafted in such a way that they might serve to explain entire phases of the war. The battle plans show the locations of dominant terrain according to detailed state surveys, while villages, forests and roads have been copied from previously published plans.

Born in Sumy, Ukraine, in 1805, Modest Ivanovich Bogdanovich was initially educated in the Noble Regiment, being commissioned into the artillery in 1823. Bogdanovich saw combat in the Polish campaign of 1831 and upon his return in 1833, he entered the Imperial Military Academy, becoming its Director of Operations until 1839. Thereafter, he served on committees of the General Staff. He died in August, 1882 in Oranienbaum. General Bogdanovich is famed for a number of major works, making an invaluable contribution to Russian military historiography. His History of the Patriotic War of 1812 won the Demidov Prize for History in 1861.

Peter G.A. Phillips is a veteran of 27 years in the British Army Intelligence Corps, including working as a Russian, German, and Serbo-Croat linguist, thereafter spending five years as part of a Civil Service team training British Armed Forces personnel to serve in UK diplomatic missions. He is now retired and spends his time translating Russian military histories of the Coalition Wars. His published translations include: Mikhailovsky-Danilevsky's histories of the wars of 1805 and 1806-1807; a collaboration with renowned Napoleonic historian Dr Alexander Mikaberidze of Ilya Radozhitskii's trilogy of memoirs covering 1812-1814; and numerous articles for the Waterloo Association's www.napoleon-series.org archive website. Peter now lives in the Philippines with his Filipina wife of 34 years. They have two adult daughters.

The Russian Patriotic War Of 1812 Volume 1

The Russian Official History

Modest Ivanovich Bogdanovich

Translated by Peter G.A. Phillips

Helion & Company

Helion & Company Limited
Unit 8 Amherst Business Centre
Budbrooke Road
Warwick
CV34 5WE
England
Tel. 01926 499619
Email: info@helion.co.uk
Website: www.helion.co.uk
Twitter: @helionbooks
Visit our blog at http://blog.helion.co.uk/

Published by Helion & Company 2024
Designed and typeset by Mach 3 Solutions (www.mach3solutions.co.uk)
Cover designed by Paul Hewitt, Battlefield Design (www.battlefield-design.co.uk)

Original text published as *History Of The Patriotic War Of 1812 According To Reliable Sources.*
Compiled in accordance with Supreme orders, St Petersburg, 1861
Translation © Peter Philips 2024
Maps and diagrams by George Anderson © Helion & Company 2024

Cover: The Battle of Mir. Oil on canvas by Wiktor Mazurowski. (Borodinskaya Panorama Museum)

ISBN 978-1-804514-32-0

British Library Cataloguing-in-Publication Data.
A catalogue record for this book is available from the British Library.

For details of other military history titles published by Helion & Company Limited, contact the above address, or visit our website: http://www.helion.co.uk

We always welcome receiving book proposals from prospective authors.

Contents

List of Maps

Translator's Foreword

The inspiration for this translation of Bogdanovich's History Of The Patriotic War Of 1812 came from Dr. Alexander Mikaberidze during a video call between us in 2020. Coming from a professional background in British Defence Intelligence where collaborative working is a First Principle, I was keen to deconflict those Russian works that might already be getting translated with him, such that I would not end up clashing with the projects of other historians. We agreed that Bogdanovich's works covering 1812-1814, and Milyutin's covering 1798-1799 deserved to be presented to the English speaking world and, with good fortune, they should now all see the light of day, and not before time!

Modest Ivanovich Bogdanovich was born in Sumy, Ukraine in 1805. Descended from the nobility of Kharkov Governorate, he received his initial education in the Noble Regiment, from where in June 1823 he was commissioned as an ensign into the 1st Grenadier Artillery Company of the reserve corps in the force commanded by Tsarevich Konstantin Pavlovich.

Four years later, Bogdanovich was sent to serve in the 24th Artillery Brigade, with which he took part in the Polish campaign of 1831 and was in combat at Wawer, at Grochów and Dębe Wielkie. For distinction in these battles, he was awarded the Order of St. Anna, 4th class with the inscription 'for valour' and the rank of lieutenant. In this campaign, in an action at Rogoźnica, he suffered such a severe contusion to his right leg that he was left for dead on the battlefield and was captured by the Poles, being held prisoner until August.

Upon his return to Russia in November 1833 he entered the Imperial Military Academy (later the Nikolaev Academy of the General Staff), from where, after completing a course of sciences in 1835, he was appointed to serve in the Third Department of the former office of the Quartermaster General of the General Staff, but remained in this position no more than a year and, by Supreme Command, was assigned to the Military Academy for training as an assistant professor.

Appointed shortly thereafter as Head of Chancellery of the academy, Captain Bogdanovich in September 1838 was approved as an assistant professor in the Department of Military History and Strategy and, in his spare time, taught tactics to the Noble Regiment, and also took part in the publication of the Military Journal and the Military Encyclopaedic Lexicon. He remained in the position of Director of Operations until 1839, after which in 1841, with the rank of lieutenant colonel, he was appointed as field officer supervising the officers studying at the academy; in February 1843 he was granted the status of professor; in 1847 he was appointed a member of the military-scientific committee for the Department of the General Staff and in September 1855 he was promoted to major general.

In 1863, Bogdanovich was appointed to be at the disposal of the Minister of War and Quartermaster General of the General Staff, with the rank of honorary member of the conference of the Academy of the General Staff and Honoured Professor, and in the same year he was promoted to the rank of lieutenant general. Following that, he was co-opted as a member of the advisory committee of the General Staff, and in June, 1873, on the 50th anniversary of his commissioning, he received the Order of St. Alexander Nevsky. In 1881, Bogdanovich was appointed a member of the military council. He remained in the latter position until his death in August 1882.

General Bogdanovich is known for a number of major works, which are a valuable contribution to Russian military historiography. Numerous works by the talented and prolific historian remain without general critical evaluation, with the exception of a pedantic critique by Ivan Petrovich Liprandi, an eyewitness of the military campaigns during the reign of Alexander I; Bogdanovich's History Of The Patriotic War Of 1812, in 3 volumes, the first of which was published in 1859, was awarded the Demidov Prize in 1861.

Dr. Mikaberidze also suggested to me that Liprandi's criticism of Bogdanovich deserves consideration, having served as Chief Quartermaster in General Dokhturov's VI Corps throughout 1812 and been an eyewitness to many events, keeping a detailed diary and notes from his interviews with many fellow veterans regarding their experiences of the Patriotic War of 1812. His conflict with Bogdanovich came to a head when the latter published an article in 1858 proposing that General Raevsky's name ought to be applied to the great redoubt at the centre of the Borodino position. Liprandi described this article (by a man who was only a boy when these momentous events were being played out) as pompous, while Bogdanovich appears to have likened Liprandi's eyewitness accounts of the battle of Borodino to Baron von Münchausen's tall stories, thus Liprandi responds with similar references to the legendary Baron to hint at fabrications in a number of cases, and suggested that Bogdanovich was not above appropriating the arguments of others as his own!

Mikhailovsky-Danilevsky had published an official history of the Patriotic War of 1812 in 1839, during the reign of Nicholas I, under strict censorship. Bogdanovich's history of 1812, however, being first published between 1859 and 1861, came out under the moderately more liberal regime of Alexander II, which may have been less censorious at that time. In response, Liprandi published his lengthy critique of Bogdanovich in 1869, questioning his reasons for producing another version in such great haste, making it inferior, in Liprandi's opinion. At one point, Liprandi asks (somewhat sarcastically, one feels) 'On the other hand, is it possible, in all fairness, to demand, as already noted, that this enormous work must not contain any kind of failing when it took only three years to produce?' Curiously, he does not rebut Bogdanovich's assertion that Danilevsky was guilty of omitting significant detail and of confirmation bias, but notes that Bogdanovich makes similar errors, further suggesting that Bogdanovich's work, despite being twice the size of Danilevsky's, added very little to the sum of knowledge of this war, largely due to the inclusion of lengthy passages from already available publications by foreign historians, mostly giving context on enemy activity and that the inclusion of so much foreign material diluted the Russian nature of the history.

Some of Liprandi's criticisms are wholly justified – notable from Volume 1 alone: picking Bogdanovich up for factual errors regarding, for instance, Bagration's career; failing to provide references for several contentious events and for including unsubstantiated legend. He is also critical of Bogdanovich's frequent and seemingly gratuitous mentions of Ivan Onufrievich Sukhozanet, a mere lieutenant colonel of artillery at the time (they had both seen action at Grochów in 1831, where Sukhozanet lost a leg). Sukhozanet was commandant of the Imperial Military Academy from 1832 until 1854, and was thus Bogdanovich's boss and had provided Bogdanovich with access to his personal papers (Sukhozanet died in 1861, shortly after the publication of Bogdanovich's history) – Liprandi's inferences of cronyism and of inflating Sukhozanet's contribution to the war are therefore hard to refute! Another serious accusation stems from an anecdote referenced to 'Nikitin's papers.' Liprandi mentions that these papers had never been published and could not be found in the archives; that the anecdote was implausible, trivial and uncharacteristic of Nikitin and that the whole matter was suspicious and deserved further investigation!

Others of Liprandi's fault-finding are less fair. At one point, Liprandi pedantically describes at length (what we might today refer to as 'mansplaining') the application of left and right regarding orientation to the enemy versus direction of travel and I found myself reminiscing on my time on the parade square executing counter-intuitive yet technically correct drill commands such as 'Change direction, left. Right form!' None of which was necessary, since Bogdanovich's technically incorrect application was not misleading and a glance at the map makes everything plain. He is, in a similar vein, critical of Bogdanovich's anachronistic use of the term 'battery' to describe artillery companies; technically, the only such sub-units so designated in 1812 were in the Lifeguard Horse Artillery.

Nevertheless, where Liprandi makes valid points, I have included them as footnotes in square brackets. Similarly, anything that I have added to the original text, such as dates using the modern calendar, alternative spellings of place names and surnames, are also in square brackets. I have also maintained from the original the Russian practice of applying an ordinal number to namesakes in order to help distinguish them from one-another.

Peter G.A. Phillips
2023

Author's Foreword

In submitting my description of the Patriotic War of 1812 to review by my peers, I consider it necessary to say a few words about my work. Three years have passed since I began to put in order the material I was collecting related to the war of 1812; by Supreme command, all the State Archives were opened to me at that time in order to find information on this subject. Paying due justice to the works by the historians of the Patriotic War, generals Buturlin [Dmitry Petrovich Buturlin (b. 1790)] and Mikhailovsky-Danilevsky [Alexander Ivanovich Mikhailovsky-Danilevsky], I was convinced, however, that many of the most fascinating documents of the war of 1812 were not known to them. In addition, in the last twenty years, Military History has been enriched with works that may, in all fairness, be considered exemplary. Smitt [Friedrich von Smitt], Höpfner [Friedrich Eduard Alexander von Höpfner] and Milyutin [Dmitry Alekseevich Milyutin] have shown in practice that a history of war, based on a critical study of events, may be more useful and entertaining to military and non-military readers than a narrative in which one cannot see either the character of the participants or the reasons that prompted them to take the given actions. Despite the multitude of foreign works on the war of 1812, none of them match either the importance of the subject or the current state of the art. Thus, there is a gap in our Military Historiography that our military authors must fill.

In particular, a description of this war, drawn up with proper impartiality, is necessary at the present time when works have appeared that contain an investigation of the events of 1812 which are not always based on fact. Of all the foreign descriptions of our Patriotic War, the following are mainly noteworthy: Prinz von Württemberg's 'Erinnerungen aus dem Feldzuge des Jahres 1812 in Russland,' Mr. Bernhardi's [Felix Theodor Bernhardi] 'Denkwürdigkeiten des Grafen von Toll,' and Chambray's [Georges de Chambray] 'Histoire de l'expédition de Russie.' But the last two, despite their undoubted merits, do not always contain reliable evidence. As for Wollzogen's [Ludwig Freiherr von Wollzogen] notes (Wollzogen Memoiren), these were published solely to glorify the author himself and his exploits in the war of 1812, and not to clarify the truth. All this notwithstanding, however, foreign works, documents and private letters must certainly be taken into account when studying the war of 1812: General Mikhailovsky-Danilevsky fell into many errors due to the fact that he completely rejected them, or used only those publications that confirmed his own preconceptions. When describing the war, one cannot do without comparing the evidence from both sides, which is the only way it may serve as an impartial investigation of the truth. The extent to which I was guided by these statements will be explained at the end of my work, when listing material that served as sources for the History Of The Patriotic War Of 1812.

Likewise, when compiling my book, I used a great deal of memoirs, letters and manuscripts, some of which were not known to generals Buturlin and Mikhailovsky-Danilevsky at all, and others remained unknown to the public, because our historians had not used them. Among these manuscripts, pride of place is occupied by extracts from A.P. Yermolov's papers, for which I owe his benevolent attention to me, and Depiction Of Operations By First Western Army, compiled by Barclay de Tolly [Mikhail Bogdanovich Barclay de Tolly]. I also had the following papers: A.A. Shcherbinin's [Alexander Andreevich Shcherbinin], who served as a General Staff officer in the war of 1812; General Maevsky's [Sergey Ivanovich Maevsky], who held the appointment of Auditor-General in Prince Kutuzov's army; generals: Chaplits [Yefim Ignatiev Chaplits]; Raevsky [Nikolai Nikolaevich Raevsky] (with a letter to General Jomini [Antoine Henri, baron de Jomini]); Löwenstern [Woldemar Hermann von Löwenstern] (a famous partisan in 1813 and 1814); Saint-Priest [Guillaume Emmanuel Guignard, vicomte de Saint-Priest]; information: from the records of I.O. Sukhozanet [Ivan Onufrievich Sukhozanet]; from the notes by P.A. Tuchkov [Pavel Alexeevich Tuchkov 3rd]; from the History Of The Russian Guards Artillery, compiled by V.F. Ratch [Vasily Fëdorovich Ratch]; information regarding partisan operations by D.V. Davydov [Denis Vasilevich Davydov], sent by his son; information provided by P.D. Leslie [Pëtr Dmitryevich Leslie]; letters from generals Konovnitsyn [Pëtr Petrovich Konovnitsyn] and Baggovut [Karl Gustav von Baggehufwudt].

Despite the abundance of official material (Military journals, Returns on the composition and numbers of troops, etc.), it was rather difficult to state the composition of the detachments and the strength of the forces at each of the events described. In this respect, I had a great deal of work to do — to determine according to partial data or from others that had hitherto remained unknown. The readers will decide to what extent I have achieved this aim.

An explanation of the means for provisioning the Russian army was extracted by me from papers submitted by Kankrin [Yegor Frantsevich Kankrin] to Barclay de Tolly, various memoirs, official papers and private correspondence, and information on the provision of supplies to the enemy army – from the correspondence of Napoleon, the works of Roos, Lemazurier [Pierre-David Lemazurier], Chambray, etc.

With all the quality materials that served as the basis for my work, I am fully aware of the difficulty of being a historian of the Patriotic War of 1812. On the one hand, it was necessary to depict the lofty image of the Monarch, confident in the physical and moral strength of the Russian people and having won the upper hand over an enemy genius at the cost of incredible labour and sacrifice; on the other hand, to present a picture of the formidable invasion of Russia by an army made up of almost every European nation and the struggle of the Russian people against it. With all the vastness of the work ahead of me, I must not lose sight of a single feat, nor a single characteristic feature of the gigantic-commanders of the war of 1812. It was necessary to explain the innermost reasons for the actions that remained obscure, mysterious, solely because the lamp of Truth was sometimes overshadowed by bias. It was necessary to show the influence of the elements, heat and cold, hunger and thirst, and finally – events, which play such an important role in military affairs.

In order to satisfy all the calculations and many other scholarly requirements, I had to study the historians of the war of 1812, re-read many memoirs and letters, listen to the assessments by the witnesses of this era. Some of the material was known to me previously; others I found in various archives; I owe a lot of information to the persons who have honoured my work with their attention and who have passed their papers to me, or who have made comments on the events I have described. The footnotes to my History of the War of 1812, numbering more than one and a half thousand in general, indicate the sources for the facts I have described, and, in addition, the appendices contain many interesting documents that were not included in my narrative.

In this way, readers can trace the truth of my historical narrative, trusting it through the reliability of the sources that serve as its foundation. As for the conclusions I made, on the basis of a critical study of the events, then, taking full responsibility for them, I can only say that my pen led me to be impartial both to my own and to my enemies.

I think it is not superfluous to explain, in a few words, what exactly new readers will find in my work:

1. Regarding an account of the operational planning for the Russian forces, once they had retreated from the borders inside the Empire, some historians of the war of 1812 deny the existence of any premeditated plan; others talk about it in passing, or distort the truth.

2. The means for supplying the troops on both sides with food and military supplies are set forth in more detail than in all previous works on the war of 1812.

3. The *opolchenie* [militia] and donations in 1812 are detailed. Readers will also find many interesting details in the narrative of the People's War and Partisan Operations.

4. Much hitherto unknown information is contained in the chapters: the meeting in Abo between Tsar Alexander I and the Crown Prince of Sweden; the mobilisation of the western regions of the Empire, which remained behind enemy lines.

5. Descriptions of the battles are much more detailed than any of those that were published in previous works about the war of 1812.

6. The glorious feats committed not only by the main personalities, but also by others who participated in this war are not forgotten. If anything is missing in this respect, then it happened solely due to a lack of information on which it might be possible to base a description of the exploits.

7. The composition of the forces is shown as clearly as possible everywhere. Anyone familiar with military-historical research knows how difficult it is to describe the composition of the various army formations down to the last battalion and squadron. It is no less difficult to determine the number of troops, the casualties on each side, and so on. I hope that in this respect, too, I have been able to clarify and correct many of the mistakes by historians of the war of 1812.

8. The maps attached to this work have been drafted in such a way that they might serve to explain entire phases of the war. The battle plans show

the locations of dominant terrain, according to detailed state survey, and villages, forests and roads have been copied from plans made in the past.

In drafting some of the drawings, plans from the Military Atlas, drafted by Lieutenant Colonel of the General Staff, Poltoratsky [Vladimir Alexandrovich Poltoratsky], served me in good stead.

In conclusion, I will say that I have used the works of former historians of the war of 1812 only to indicate to whom exactly that which I owe. The readers of my book may decide to what extent my work stands alone.

1

Tsar Alexander's First Wars against Napoleon

Tsar Alexander I and Napoleon. – The war of 1805. – The war of 1806-1807. – The Treaty of Tilsit. – The situation in Prussia and Austria after the treaties of Pressburg and Tilsit. – The war of 1809 between France and Austria. – The Treaty of Schönbrunn.

At the beginning of this century, Tsar Alexander I and Napoleon became the rulers of great monarchies; no one could have foreseen then that they would decide the fate of all of Europe through the struggle between themselves. Alexander, destined for royal purple from the cradle itself, the beloved grandson of Catherine the Great, who saw the brightest hopes of Russia in him, Alexander, whose handsome features expressed earthly greatness and heavenly goodness, mild, adored by his subjects, began his reign with words of peace, had ended the war with Britain, and remained on friendly terms with their enemies. Napoleon, a fortunate warrior who had blazed his way to the throne with the sword, seemed at the time to be content with the laurels earned in Italy and in distant Egypt. Comprehending the difficult art of governance by the power of genius, in a few years he had blotted out the traces of the stormy revolution, restored the domain of religion, gave force to the law, and reconciled France with Britain and Turkey. But Napoleon's beneficent striving for good deeds soon gave way to an insatiable lust for power; the genius, carried away by passions, contemptuous of his high calling, aspired to the dominance of Europe.

The spread of French power and influence to neighbouring countries, from the very beginning of Napoleon's empire, was accompanied by assurances of the firm determination of its master to respect the rights of other rulers.

The situation for Russia, separated from France by vast distance, secured our Fatherland from the hostile interests of Napoleon; but Tsar Alexander, having perceived the plans of the French ruler, decided to forestall him in good time. The surest means for this was the formation of a coalition of the foremost European states: Britain, facing an existential threat and concerned about a landing by Napoleon's legions on the British coast, formed the first link of the coalition, to which Russia and Austria joined. The allies hoped for the support of the Prussian government; but Prussia, in spite of the persuasion of Tsar Alexander, remained neutral, waiting in inaction for the consequences of the struggle for European independence. This war was unsuccessful: the Austrian army, having advanced to Ulm and thus deprived itself of the opportunity for timely reinforcement by Russian forces, laid down its weapons almost without a fight; while Kutuzov's auxiliary army [Mikhail Illarionovich Golenishchev-Kutuzov], yielding every step at a cost in blood, retreated from the Inn to Moravia, where the Russian force, put in a hopeless position by the senseless orders of our allies, was defeated at Austerlitz [Slavkov u Brna]. Austria, completely losing hope of success through continued resistance to Napoleon, hastened to conclude the Peace of Pressburg [Bratislava] on very difficult terms for them.

In the course of this war, misunderstandings arose between the French and Prussian governments. The conqueror, recognising no rights except the right of might, insulted Prussia through the advance of Bernadotte's corps [Jean-Baptiste Jules Bernadotte] through Ansbach, one of the Prussian provinces. This state, raised to a high status through the genius of Frederick the Great and flourishing under the paternal rule of King Friedrich Wilhelm III, could not bear this blood grievance. The whole of Prussia resounded to the cry: to arms! Tsar Alexander sent a Russian force to the Vistula. It seemed as though the recollection of the victories won by the Austrians at one with the Russians on the Trebbia and at Novi would prompt the Viennese cabinet to a new uprising against Napoleon; but the Austrian government, in turn, responded neither to the persuasion of Tsar Alexander, nor to the appeals by their fellow Teutonic neighbours. Napoleon took advantage of Austria's inaction and the negligent deployment by the Prussian forces. On the fields of Jena and Auerstedt, in one day, Frederick the Great's majestic, outmoded creation was crushed; almost all of Prussia was conquered within a few weeks. But after that, the Napoleonic hordes met with more resolute resistance; in the battles of Pułtusk and Preußisch Eylau [Bagrationovsk], the foundations of the military brotherhood between the two great nations were laid. The victories won by Napoleon had cost him dearly, and the harsh climate delayed the success of the French army for a long time. This was the first hint of the fickleness of Fortune towards its favourite; Napoleon understood this and, despite a decisive victory at Friedland [Pravdinsk], he hastened to make peace with Tsar Alexander.

The reason that prompted Russia to make peace was not the loss of the battle of Friedland, but the refusal of the British ministry to land a British force on the coast of northern Germany or France, or to grant the subsidies that our government was requesting at the time.[1] As far as Russia was concerned, the Treaty of Tilsit [Sovetsk, Kaliningrad Oblast] was not an expression of terms dictated by a victor to the vanquished at all. At Tilsit, the former foes, having personally acknowledged each other, became friends. Tsar Alexander possessed the skill of capturing the hearts and minds of everyone with whom he happened to engage; while Napoleon would have a strong influence on Alexander I's mind, him being receptive to everything extraordinary. The gracious genius and the genius of war had a meeting of minds. Prussia, already condemned to destruction by Napoleon, was saved at the insistence of Tsar Alexander.

But despite the fact that the Treaty of Tilsit was necessary, in order to reform the armed forces of Russia, weakened by the bloody struggle in the west with France and in the south with Persia and Turkey, despite the acquisitions of the Białystok *Oblast*

---

1   *Histoire abrégée des traités de paix, etc. par C.G. de Koch, augmentée et continuée, par F. Schoel. Ed. de Bruxelles, 1838,* III, pp. 37-39.

and Finland, which were the consequences of this treaty, it did not appeal to Russian hearts. The Treaty of Tilsit was concluded under the shadow of the defeat we suffered at Friedland, and therefore could not but offend Russian national pride; moreover, seeing the oppression that the other powers had been subjected to by the proud conqueror, we feared that his hand weighing over them would also reach out to us with similar intrusions and assertions; while the subsequent actions by Napoleon not only failed to dissipate the painful impression made upon Russia by the Treaty of Tilsit; but justified our fears. With reverence – with humility – we accepted the treaty given to us by Tsar Alexander, but deep down we remained foes of the French and were aggrieved about the breach with Britain.

The Treaty of Tilsit, between Russia and France, was decided on the basis of the terms of the peace and secret treaties of alliance concluded on 25 June (7 July) and ratified on 27 June (9 July); the relationship between France and Prussia was decided by a peace treaty concluded at Tilsit on 27 June (9 July) and at the Königsberg [Kaliningrad] Convention on 30 June (12 July).

According to the Tilsit Peace Treaty, between Russia and France, the political existence of Prussia was secured, albeit with heavy reparations from this power. It was determined: to form the Duchy of Warsaw from a large part of the Polish provinces that had belonged to Prussia, giving it to the King of Saxony [Friedrich August I]; to delimit the natural boundaries of the duchy with Russia, wherever possible, to annex the Białystok *Oblast* to the Russian territories; while Danzig [Gdańsk] was declared a free city, under the protection of Prussia and Saxony. To return the dukes of Oldenburg, Mecklenburg-Schwerin and Saxe-Coburg to their territories, such that the harbours of the first two would be occupied by French troops until the conclusion of peace between France and Britain. Tsar Alexander recognised Napoleon's brothers as the kings of Naples, Holland and Westphalia, expressed his consent to all orders by Napoleon, regarding the Confederation of the Rhine [Rheinbund], and ceded the Jever *Herrschaft* on the eastern border of Friesland under full ownership to Louis [Louis Bonaparte], King of Holland. Tsar Alexander took up the mediation for a reconciliation between Britain and France, while Napoleon did likewise for a reconciliation between Russia and the Ottoman Porte, furthermore it was necessary for the Russians to evacuate the Danubian principalities, while the Turks would not allow their troops to enter until the conclusion of peace with Russia. Both monarchs vouched for the mutual integrity of the territories of both Powers and their allies. The protocol for both Courts was established on the basis of perfect equality between them.

On the basis of the secret articles of this same treaty, it was laid down that the Bay of Kotor [Bocche di Cattaro] and the Ionian Islands would come into Napoleon's possession, such that the French government would leave the Montenegrins alone, who had participated alongside the Russians in the last war; such that the German princes, deprived of their lands by Napoleon – the Elector of Hesse-Kassel [Wilhelm I], the Duke of Brunswick [Friedrich Wilhelm von Braunschweig], as well as the Prince of Orange [Wilhelm Friedrich von Oranien-Nassau], would receive certain compensations from those who had taken their lands, King Jérôme [Jérôme Bonaparte] of Westphalia and Murat [Joachim Murat], the Grand Duke of Berg.

Finally, according to the secret treaty of alliance concluded in Tilsit between Tsar Alexander and Napoleon, it was decided: to fight as one in all the wars involving Russia or France, determining, in such eventualities, the number of auxiliary troops and the location of their operations; while should the need arise, to help each other with full strength and not conclude peace otherwise than by the mutual agreement of both Powers. Should Britain not agree to recognise the freedom of navigation at sea of all fleets and return the colonies it had seized since 1803 from France and the powers allied with it by 1 November, then Russia undertook to declare war on the British by 1 December. At the same time, it was agreed that Russia and France would invite Denmark, Sweden and Portugal to declare war on Britain, and if any of these powers refused to do so, they would themselves declare war on them. Should Britain immediately conclude peace, then Hannover was to be returned to them, in exchange for French, Spanish and Dutch colonies. Should the Porte not conclude peace with Russia within three months, then Tsar Alexander and Napoleon pledged to wage war as one against Turkey and agreed to divide among themselves all the European possessions of this power, with the exception of Constantinople [Istanbul] and Rumelia.[2]

On the basis of the peace treaty concluded between France and Prussia in Tilsit on 27 June (9 July), it was decided that Prussia should cede: at Napoleon's disposal, all their territories between the Elbe and the Rhine; in favour of Saxony, the Cottbus *Kreis* [district] and all lands acquired from Poland since 1772, with the exception of Ermland [Warmia], parts of western Prussia and Graudenz [Grudziądz], which remained in Prussia, Danzig, declared a free city, and the Białystok *Oblast* ceded to Russia. In general, Prussian losses since 1805 extended, together with Ansbach, Neuchâtel and Kleve, some 2,693½ square *Meilen* with 4,800,000 inhabitants. Thereafter, just 2,877 square *Meilen* with 5,000,000 inhabitants remained in their possession.[3]

King Friedrich Wilhelm recognised Napoleon's brothers as the kings of Naples, Westphalia and Holland, as well as all orders by Napoleon for the Confederation of the Rhine. It was deemed necessary to convene a dedicated convention in order to determine the terms for the return of Prussian fortresses and the withdrawal of French troops from Prussia. This convention, concluded in Königsberg, on 30 June (12 July), ruined Prussia with sums of money and all kinds of reparations taken from them by Napoleon, and gave him an excuse to maintain French garrisons in Prussian fortresses, and was just as disastrous for Prussia as the treaty concluded at Tilsit. Napoleon took advantage of errors by Field Marshal Kalckreuth [Friedrich Adolf von Kalckreuth], a brave warrior but a poor diplomat, who signed a convention so vaguely worded that any interpretation might be given to it. Napoleon was well aware that a devastated Prussia could not pay the enormous reparations of 112 million francs (about 28 million silver roubles [over 500 tonnes of pure silver]) immediately agreed upon by the convention, but he found it more advantageous, under the pretext of non-payment of the sums due to him, to occupy Prussian provinces with his troops, a total of 150,000 men, to provide them with food at Prussian

---

2   *Mémoires tirés des papiers d'un homme d'état,* IX, pp. 429-432.
3   Höpfner. *Der Krieg von 1806 und 1807,* III, pp. 707-709 & 712.

expense, to monitor the implementation of the prohibitive measures taken by him against British trade, and have, in any case, a strong army in the vicinity of the borders of Russia and Austria. Napoleon knew that the Prussian people, deeply offended in the person of their government, could not harbour feelings of sympathy for France, and therefore, wishing to weaken Prussia and make it harmless to themselves, agreed, according to a secret clause of the Paris Convention, of 8 September, 1808, such that the Prussian government, for a period of ten years, should have no more than: 6,000 men in the *Leibgarde*, 22,000 line infantry, 8,000 cavalry and 6,000 men in the artillery, sappers and miners, for a total no greater than 42,000 men.[4]

Thus, Prussia, being in a constrained situation, dependent on Napoleon, declined to the status of a secondary power; but not for long. The nation, led by a wise government, did not lose confidence in their own forces, and soon, with the care and the husbandry of men forever in the memory of Prussia, Stein [Heinrich Friedrich Karl Reichsfreiherr vom und zum Stein] and Scharnhorst [Gerhard Johann David von Scharnhorst], a mighty armed force was formed among the Prussian people, which remained covert until the time when the hour of Germany's liberation struck. Having established the military system that served as the basis for their current one, for six years, from 1807 to 1813, Prussia prepared a formidable army, the existence of which Napoleon had suspected, but about which he had no accurate intelligence. These suspicions were enough to induce Napoleon to take the most hostile measures against Prussia, but, fortunately, he, putting faith in his abilities, did not see the danger that threatened him.

The situation in Austria during this era was incomparably less painful than that in Prussia. Although the losses suffered by the former of these powers according to the Treaty of Pressburg were very raw, nevertheless, huge resources still remained in the hands of the Austrian government, and even more so since in the war with Napoleon, in 1805, Austria had not exhausted all its means for resistance to this conqueror. The Austrian government, realising its strength, was waiting for a favourable moment to harm Napoleon, and was actively preparing for war. Napoleon knew about this rearmament and took precautions for his part, reinforcing the French forces in Prussia and putting the contingents from the Confederation of the Rhine on a war footing. Meanwhile, after the conclusion of the Treaty of Tilsit, Napoleon's attention was mainly focused on matters in the Iberian Peninsula. Knowing the breakdown of all government institutions in Spain, under the control of an incapable courtier, Godoy [Manuel Godoy y Álvarez de Faria], Napoleon considered the Spanish kingdom to be easy prey; but this calculation turned out to be erroneous, because very important factors had not been taken into account: the character of the people, ready to die in defence of their independence; the nature of the terrain in the country, extremely beneficial for defence while hindering the success of offensive operations; the self-sufficiency of the provinces, from which each could conduct a defensive war independently, despite the occupation of the capital of the kingdom by enemy forces; finally – the accessibility of the Iberian Peninsula to the British, which helped them to take an active part in the Spanish war.

---

4   For details of additional bi-lateral treaties between France and Prussia, see Appendix I.

The cumulative effect of all these factors was not slow in becoming apparent. The British, who had long been unable to celebrate victories on land over their centuries-old enemy, defeated Junot's [Jean-Andoche Junot] force and forced them to abandon Portugal, on the basis of the Convention of Cintra [Sintra]; not long before that – Napoleon's legions, surrounded by discordant hordes of Spanish insurgents, had been forced to lay down their arms at Bailén. Napoleon, intending to go to Spain the following year (1809) and take command over the troops there in order to lend the war a more decisive character, wanted to secure himself in Germany, which endured his yoke with impatience. Fearing Prussia, despite the occupation of the Prussian fortresses and lands by French troops, not trusting Austria, despite the friendly messages from the Austrian government, Napoleon wanted to seal the alliance with Russia by meeting with Tsar Alexander. In addition to the Russian Monarch and Napoleon, the Kings of Saxony, Bavaria [Maximilian I. Joseph (Bayern)] and Württemberg [Friedrich Wilhelm Karl von Württemberg], the King of Westphalia, Grand Duke Konstantin Pavlovich, Prince Wilhelm of Prussia, the Grand Duke of Baden [Karl Friedrich von Baden], the Crown Prince of Bavaria [Ludwig Karl August], the Duke of Saxe-Weimar [Carl August von Sachsen-Weimar-Eisenach], the father in law of Grand Duchess Maria Pavlovna, many other rulers and diplomats from every Court that was in alliance with France and Russia; at this congress, the main issues of European politics were resolved personally by Tsar Alexander and Napoleon. Their activities had prepared a vast field of action for themselves at opposite ends of Europe: Russia was already fighting two wars: in the north, against the Swedes, and in the south, against the Turks; while France was involved in the war against the Spaniards and was in hostilities with Britain. With this state of affairs, it was not difficult for Tsar Alexander and Napoleon to agree on their outlook, without an obvious conflict of interests for either state.

During their three-week stay in Erfurt, Tsar Alexander and Napoleon vied with each other for friendship and attention. Not to mention the important concessions made by them to one another, which were the result of mutual calculations, the monarchs seized the opportunity to please each other even in less important matters. On one occasion Napoleon, in the presence of Tsar Alexander, let slip that he would be pleased if someone else were to be appointed as the Russian representative in Paris to replace Count Tolstoy [Pëtr Alexandrovich Tolstoy]. Tsar Alexander immediately ordered the Russian representative at the Viennese Court, Prince Kurakin [Alexander Borisovich Kurakin], to be ambassador to the Court of Emperor Napoleon in Paris.

A consequence of the meeting in Erfurt was the conclusion of a secret (*secretissime*) convention on 30 September (12 October), 1808, which was intended to:

1. Open negotiations with the British government, on the basis of each of the contracting powers keeping their present territories (*uti possidetis*).
2. Napoleon agreed to the annexation of Finland, Moldavia and Wallachia to the Russian Empire; while Tsar Alexander would recognise Napoleon's brother as King of Spain.
3. The contracting powers mutually vouched for the integrity of all other territories of the Ottoman Porte.

4. In the event of a war between Austria and Russia or France, both Powers pledged mutual assistance.
5. The convention was to be kept secret for ten years.

Witnesses at the Erfurt Congress noticed that, despite the vocal expressions of mutual friendship between the great monarchs, there was no longer the sincerity between them that had distinguished their meeting in Tilsit. Napoleon's lust for power would not entertain the idea that: 'in order for his plans to succeed, he needed the consent of Tsar Alexander.' But the time had not yet come for a breach between the mighty rivals. Each of them went about his business: Napoleon went to Spain; Alexander reinforced his forces operating in Finland and on the Danube.[5]

Meanwhile, clouds were gathering on the horizon of Europe, ready to burst into a thunderstorm over Germany. The Treaty of Pressburg had deprived Austria of many provinces, weakened it, but did not deprive the Austrian government – either of the desire – or of the opportunity to chance their luck in a new war with Napoleon. Cash and troops were needed for this: Britain supplied the former, while troops were mobilised in large numbers and in a short time, thanks to the general preparedness to rearm the nation, and the measures taken by the Austrian government. Soon, the militia, given the name of *Landwehr*, was increased to 200,000 men; the regular army was manned to some 400,000; the cavalry, artillery and transport were supplied with horses, and all Austrian troops in general were put on war establishment. Political means were not overlooked either: in every part of Germany, the population, enthusiastic for revolt, were covertly preparing to arm themselves against the French; Tyrol was flooded with skilled men, devoted to the House of Austria: there were sparks smouldering everywhere, threatening to burst into flames; the Spanish insurgents even looked to Austria for assistance, separated from them by a great distance, but sympathetic to their efforts, and the first proof of this was the refusal of Kaiser Franz to recognize Joseph Napoleon as King of Spain.

Tsar Alexander, being aware that all Austria's attempts to overthrow the yoke that weighed Germany down could not achieve anything at that time, except an even greater elevation of Napoleon's power, proposed to conclude a convention, together with Napoleon, through the Minister of Foreign Affairs, Count Rumyantsev [Nikolai Petrovich Rumyantsev], to the Austrian envoy in Paris according to which all three Powers would mutually vouch for the integrity of their territories. But the Viennese Court rejected this offer, out of distrust of Napoleon.[6]

The 1809 war, between France and Austria, was fought with varying degrees of success. Tsar Alexander, having exhausted all means to divert Austria from its stated intention to wage war against Napoleon, took part in it, assisting the French army with a 30,000 man Russian force. Napoleon was not pleased with the operations by our corps, accusing us of indecision; but if Tsar Alexander had really spared his former ally, then the influence of our Tsar did a great service to Napoleon, in pushing Austria towards peace, which had been prepared to continue the war, to the

---

5   *Hist. générale des traités de paix, par M. le comte de Garden.* X, pp. 283-290.
6   *Mémoires tirés des papiers d'un homme d'état,* X, 297.

ruin of both sides and very problematic for the ruler of France, at a time when he was being forced to commit huge forces to the Iberian Peninsula.

Under the terms of the Treaty of Schönbrunn, signed on 28 September (10 October), 1809, Austria was forced to make the following concessions:

1. In favour of Bavaria: Salzburg, Berchtesgaden, Innviertel and part of Hausruck: the first three areas having formerly belonged to Bavaria; the latter was one of the oldest territories of the House of Habsburg.
2. In favour of Napoleon: Austrian Friaul; Trieste with its surroundings, the only harbour in Austria; Carniola [Kranjska] with the rich mines of Idrija; the Villach district in Carinthia [Kärnten]; parts of Croatia and Dalmatia, on the right bank of the Sava.
3. Western Galicia including Kraków; the salt mines in Wieliczka were placed under the joint control of the Emperor of Austria and the King of Saxony.
4. In favour of Russia: a small part of eastern Galicia.

In general, according to the Schönbrunn Treaty, Austria lost 2,150 square *Meilen* with 3,500,000 inhabitants, while 9,350 square *Meilen* with 20,740,000 inhabitants remained under their control.[7] Under the secret terms of the same treaty, Austria undertook to reduce its army and pay 55 million francs in order to secure Napoleon's evacuation of Vienna; it has been said that Napoleon's marriage to the Archduchess Marie Louise [Marie-Louise von Österreich], so flattering to his ego, was resolved at the same time.[8]

The conclusion of the Schönbrunn Treaty marked the beginning of the disagreements between the palaces of St Petersburg and the Tuileries. Napoleon was the first to give grounds for this, including in the treaty the terms: 'such that the section of eastern Galicia, ceded by the Austrian government to Russia, does not include Brody.' the only location of any importance due to its significant market. But Tsar Alexander was even more displeased about the expansion of the Duchy of Warsaw, which might arouse the unrealisable dreams of the Poles. The disagreements that arose on this subject gave rise to other controversial issues and, eventually, to an open breach. And it could not have been otherwise: Tsar Alexander would not subjugate his Power to such dependence on Napoleon, to whom almost all the states of Europe were then subordinated, while Napoleon wished to be the sole ruler.

---

7   *Hist. abrégée des traités de paix, par Koch, 1838*, III, 139-144.
8   *Mémoires tirés des papiers d'un homme d'état*, X, 480-481.

Causes of the War of 1812

The convention on Poland. – Napoleon's refusal to ratify the convention. – Annexation of the Duchy of Oldenburg by France. – Protest from Tsar Alexander. – The Continental System and the Trianon Decree. – New Russian tariffs.

With the conclusion of the Tilsit and Vienna treaties, most of Europe had become dependent upon Napoleon. From that time on, he began to conceal his encroachments on the rights of the states neighbouring the French empire even less than before. But his relationship with Tsar Alexander, for several months, remained unchanged, or – at least – appeared to be the same as it had been at the conclusion of the Treaty of Tilsit.

The French Foreign Minister, the Duc de Cadore [Jean-Baptiste Nompère de Champagny], in response to a letter from the Chancellor, Count Rumyantsev, on the conclusion of the Treaty of Fredrikshamn [Hamina] with Sweden, reporting after the ratification of the Vienna Treaty on 14 October, 1809 [new style], wrote:

It would have been easy for Emperor Napoleon to take all of Galicia from Austria, instead of the regions ceded by this power in Germany and Italy; but he was unwilling to incur the displeasure of his friend and ally. He could not betray the inhabitants of western Galicia as a sacrifice to Austria, who had so eagerly rebelled in his favour. But in order to support Tsar Alexander's views, this region was handed over to the King of Saxony, whose character and way of thinking might serve as a guarantee of the inviolability of the peace and security of the neighbouring territories. Emperor Napoleon not only wanted to avoid seeding hopes for the restoration of Poland, but is ready to help to do anything to blot out its memory. His Majesty agrees that the words Poland and the Poles should disappear not only from every treaty, but also from History. The current Duchy of Warsaw comprises no more than a tenth of the former Poland. Is it possible that a vast state might rise from such a small area?

Napoleon, in a speech delivered to the legislative assembly (*corps législatif*) on 3 December, 1809 new style, said himself:

My ally and friend, the Russian Emperor, has annexed Finland, Moldavia, Wallachia and a section of Galicia to his vast Empire.[1] I shall not contend against anything that may serve to benefit this Empire. My feelings in relation to its renowned Monarch agree with my political opinions.[2]

In a report by the French Minister of Foreign Affairs, for 1809, the explanations for the causes prompting the Emperor of the French to expand the Duchy of Warsaw were most explicit, and at the same time – as if to reject the idea of a rapprochement between France and Austria – the most unfavourable review was made about Archduke Ferdinand [Ferdinand Karl Joseph von Österreich-Este], who commanded the Austrian troops in Galicia during the 1809 campaign:

'qui aussi arrogant qu'ignorant dans l'art de la guerre, n'a sû avec quarante mille hommes que se faire battre par le prince Joseph Poniatowsky [Józef Antoni Poniatowski] qui en a commandé treize mille.'[3]

Tsar Alexander, for his part, did not express displeasure – neither for the expansion of the boundaries of the duchy, nor for the meagre compensation for Russia for the costs of the war with Austria, the Tarnopol [Ternopil] Oblast, which was not at all consistent with the wishes submitted to Napoleon.[4]

Tsar Alexander only hoped that Napoleon would pledge that Poland should never be restored, in order to prevent the unrealisable dream that might be aroused in Poland by the expansion of the Duchy of Warsaw. To that end, a convention was drafted and signed in St Petersburg by the French envoy on 24 December, 1809 (5 January, 1810), and had Napoleon ratified it, the question of Poland would have been resolved in accordance with the wishes of the Russian government. But together with the ratification of the convention, in the form in which it had been drafted in St Petersburg and signed by the French representative, Napoleon expressed his readiness to undertake that he would never contribute to any enterprise tending towards the restoration of Poland. At first glance, it would appear that such terms completely ensured Russia in relation to Poland, but to anyone who is at all knowledgeable in matters of diplomacy, it was obvious that the convention drafted in St Petersburg, giving no grounds for any twists or turns, was much more definitive than the one that Napoleon proposed. If he really had the intention of complying with the treaty being concluded, then it should have been drafted in such a way that did not permit any grounds for violating the terms contained therein. Napoleon, having been dissuaded from ratifying the convention signed by Caulaincourt [Armand Augustin Louis, marquis de Caulaincourt], stated that: 'it is impossible to

---

1   At the time it appeared to be a fait accompli.
2   Discours au Corps législatif, prononcé le 3 Déc. 1809. From the Russian ambassador to Paris, Prince Kurakin's report.
3   Moniteur. 1809. No 348.
4   Napoleon, in a conversation with cavalry Captain Chernyshev, on 15 (27) September, 1809, said that, according to the peace treaty with Austria: 'Lemberg [Lviv] avec encore quelque chose sera le lot de la Russie.' From minutes kept in the Archive of the Ministry of Foreign Affairs [M.F.A.].

vouch for the future.' But his actual guarantee was limited to the fulfilment of that which was solely dependent on the French government and did not go beyond the limits of the possible.

Tsar Alexander, still keeping his hopes alive of settling the question of Poland, in agreement with Napoleon, gave orders for the Russian envoy in Paris, Prince Kurakin, to inform the French Minister of Foreign Affairs, the Duc de Cadore (Champagny) of the draft convention on Poland, (*Contreprojet*) with an explanation of the reasons for the basis on which the Russian government had proposed to amend the convention drawn up in Paris. The most important of these amendments were the following:

On the first point, instead of an obligation not to contribute to the restoration of Poland:

> His Majesty the Emperor of the French, King of Italy, meaning to take away any hope of breaching the general peace of the continental powers from their enemies, pledges, as does the Emperor of All Russia, that the Kingdom of Poland shall never be restored.

On the third point, instead of not issuing the former Polish Orders in the future:

> Abolish the former Polish Orders and all the awards and distinctions associated with them.[5]

Napoleon never gave a definitive response to this proposal, nor to any of the precepts and subsequent reminders to ratify the convention. Thus a whole year passed; and in the meantime the French government continued to encroach on the rights of its neighbours: 1810 began with the annexation of Hannover to the Kingdom of Westphalia; on 16 February new style Napoleon established (*érigea*) the Grand Duchy of Frankfurt in favour of the primacy [*Staat des Fürstprimas*] of the Confederation of the Rhine; on 9 July, the independence of the Kingdom of Holland was extinguished, and thereafter it was annexed to the French Empire; on 12 November, Kanton Wallis (*le Valais*) was annexed under the name *Département Simplon*; by decree (*senatus-consulte*) dated 13 December, the Hanseatic cities, the Duchy of Lauenburg [*Herzogtum Sachsen-Lauenburg*] and the North Sea coast between the lower reaches of the Ems and the Elbe were annexed. The method of these accessions was very simple: the minister of foreign affairs presented a report to the emperor, in which the necessity of the proposed acquisition was justified; whereupon this report was submitted to the Senate, which, without any formalities, announced the annexation of new territories to the empire. In a report to Napoleon from the French Foreign Minister, it stated: 'the annexation of the Hanseatic cities, Lauenburg and all towns from the Elbe to the Ems is demanded by the circumstances (*la réunion est commandée par les circonstances*).'

---

5   Chancellor Count Rumyantsev's memo to Prince Kurakin dated 4 [16] March 1810, from documents kept in the Archive of the M.F.A.

To give an idea of the painful impression made not only in Germany, but throughout Europe, by these orders from Napoleon, it is sufficient to quote the following words from the manifesto promulgated in 1813 by Tsar Alexander:

> This act of aggression was carried out without any cause, without entering into discussion with any of the powers, under an arbitrary empty pretext, as if the war against Britain demanded it. This decree subjecting coastal Germany to French dominion, naming it the thirty-second military district, aroused the fears of all neighbouring states, not only because of the orders contained in it, but even more because it was quite rightly considered a harbinger of other – even greater – aggressions. This decree violated the system proclaimed by the French government itself, the system determining the so-called natural borders of France. Napoleon did not spare even the territories that owe their existence to him. Neither the lands of the Confederation of the Rhine, nor the Kingdom of Westphalia, nor of any other country, were protected from predation: borders, drawn by an unaccountable whim, without principle, without a plan, without any respect for age-old or modern political association, stretched across lands and rivers, deprived Germany of communications beyond the Elbe, reached the Baltic and – it appears – were aimed at the line of Prussian fortresses on the Oder, occupied by French troops. And these acts of aggression, violating – both the rights of the people – and property rights, these invasions across boundaries designated by the political and military relations between states, had so few signs of a definitively agreed system that they could have been considered the beginning of an even greater aggression that threatened Germany with complete subjugation.

The area of land annexed to France by the decree of 13 December, 1810 was more than 600 square *Meilen*, with 1,173,550 inhabitants, of which 561½ square *Meilen* with 926,550 inhabitants were taken from rulers who belonged to the Confederation of the Rhine. The Kingdom of Westphalia was deprived of a quarter of its lands. The Grand Duchy of Berg, which lost a fifth of its territory, received some of the land taken from the Duke of Arenberg [Prosper Ludwig von Arenberg], etc.[6]

Tsar Alexander could not look at such acts of aggression by his ally dispassionately, both from a sense of justice and so as to prevent danger from being a neighbour of Napoleon's, which, judging by his *modus operandi*, was very possible. So thought the Russian ambassador in Paris, Prince Kurakin: as soon as he learned about the new acquisitions made by France, he hastened to inform the Duc de Cadore that:

> Although Russia's friendly relations with France suggest that His Majesty the Emperor Napoleon had informed my Emperor of his intention to annex the Hanseatic cities to France, this event is so important for Russia that

---

6   *Hist. générale des traités de paix, par M. le comte de Garden.* IX, 279-281.

I consider it my duty to bring it to the attention of His Majesty the Tsar Alexander, etc.[7]

Among the rulers who suffered as a result of the decree of 13 December was the uncle of Tsar Alexander I, the Duke of Oldenburg [Peter Friedrich Wilhelm von Oldenburg], whose territories were located inside the lands annexed to the French Empire. It seemed that Napoleon, out of respect for the Russian Monarch, intended to deal with the duke infinitely more leniently than with other German princes. The Emperor of the French, having annexed all the coastal areas of Germany between the lower reaches of the Ems and Elbe to his domains, let the Duke know that he left it completely to his discretion – to preserve his territory, or to receive another region as compensation for it; except that, in the first case, he would be subject to some inconveniences, namely, the passage of French troops through the lands of the duchy and the establishment of French customs.[8] The Duke of Oldenburg replied that he preferred to retain his territories, which had belonged to his ancestors for almost a thousand years, to which he was bound by feelings of sincere fellowship and duty; at the same time, the Duke informed Tsar Alexander, as head of the House of Holstein [Romanov-Holstein-Gottorp], of the unexpected proposal from the French government.

But no sooner had the Tsar received the Duke's letter, than matters took a sharp turn: French officials who had arrived in the duke's territories announced that they had been ordered to freeze all treasury assets and form an internal administration for the duchy, as a region already annexed to France, and that Erfurt and its environs had been assigned to the duke in exchange for Oldenburg. Tsar Alexander initially attributed the actions of the French commissars to a misunderstanding at the fault of the instructions issued to them, and ordered Count Rumyantsev to write a response to the Russian envoy in Paris in this regard and to report this to the French government.[9] The Tsar, wishing to convince Napoleon of the legality of the Duke of Oldenburg's rights, ordered Prince Kurakin to press the Duc de Cadore:

1. That, according to Article 12 of the Treaty of Tilsit, the duke had been guaranteed the preservation of his territories.
2. That the duchy owed its existence to Russia and after the extinction of the dominant House it would belong to the Russian Empire: hence – the duke has no right to dispose of these provinces.

---

7   Prince Kurakin's letter to the French Minister of Foreign Affairs (in the Archive of the M.F.A).

8   Prince Kurakin's memo to count Rumyantsev dated 12 [24] December 1810 (from the minutes kept in the Archive of the M.F.A.).

9   'Par suite de la réunion de la Hollande, des villes hanseatiques et d'une partie de l'Allemagne septentrionale à la France le duché d'Oldenbourg devient l'enclave de cette puissance. L'Empereur Napoléon a declaré néamoins, que le Duc d'Oldenbourg conservera la souveraineté de ses états. La déclaration de Sa Majesté est violée par les autorités Françaises. S.M. Impériale désire que cette méprise de la promesse soit reparée et que le Duché d'Oldenbourg recouvre son indépendance.'
Count Rumyantsev's dispatches to Prince Kurakin, dated 5 [17] January 1811.

3.   That Erfurt and its surroundings cannot be considered sufficient compensation for the Duchy of Oldenburg.

At the same time, he was ordered to report that if, beyond all expectations, the duke was deprived of his territories, the emperor would be forced to make a formal protest to protect both his uncle's and his own rights.

To all these arguments, personally presented by Prince Kurakin to the French Minister of Foreign Affairs, Champagny the response was:

Emperor Napoleon, proposed to the Duke of Oldenburg either to retain his territories, or to receive others in return, and did not expect the duke to decide to stay in Oldenburg, retaining imaginary dominion in a country, surrounded on all sides by French provinces. By remaining in Oldenburg, the duke could no longer be the sovereign prince, but would become a subject of France, which, without any doubt, did not coincide with his views. The attention shown by His Majesty to the duke, and the desire to compensate him in a most generous manner, are based on the feelings of respect for your Sovereignty, fostered by Emperor Napoleon.

It is true that Erfurt, with its environs, is not sufficient to compensate Oldenburg, that the area of the former is barely a fifth of the latter – that the number of its inhabitants is less; but having said that the soil of Erfurt is more fertile, the inhabitants are richer than those of Oldenburg, and the income from both estates is almost the same. There is no palace in Erfurt, but as far as I remember, there is a large house which, for the meantime, may suffice.

Emperor Napoleon has tried to compensate the duke; he did not stand on ceremony with the Salm princes [Konstantin Alexander Joseph Johann Nepomuk 3. Fürst zu Salm-Salm and Friedrich IV. Ernst Otto Philipp Anton Furnibert Fürst zu Salm-Kyrburg], whose territories were annexed to the empire, and they became French subjects themselves, retaining only their princely dignity. That the Emperor acted differently with the Duke of Oldenburg, was simply out of respect for your Sovereignty.

To a remark by the Russian envoy that: 'The territory of Oldenburg has been held for almost a thousand years by this House, whose senior branch reigns in Russia.' Champagny stated that:

Charlemagne had owned Hamburg and all the surrounding lands for a thousand years before then.

One must submit to the inevitable force of circumstances. Small states cannot preserve their independence, so long as they do not coincide with the interests of the great powers, which, like raging torrents, sweep away everything they encounter in their path.

At the end of this meeting, the French Foreign Minister promised Prince Kurakin that he would bring everything he had heard from him to the attention of Emperor

Napoleon.[10] A few days later, the Duc de Cadore gave the Russian envoy, on behalf of his sovereign, the reply that: 'His Majesty cannot amend the Senate decree, which is now being carried out.' Prince Kurakin noted that: 'such a decision, if unchanged, is completely contrary to one of the terms of the Treaty of Tilsit, and that the Russian government will find itself compelled to protect its rights through a formal protest.' The French minister, for his part, expressed the hope that our envoy, being convinced by the arguments set out to him, would abandon his intention to file a protest, which would give cause for a cooling off of the alliance between courts of the Tuileries and St Petersburg without resolving the matter at all.[11] Prince Kurakin replied that: 'he could not do this,' and after that he sent him a declaration on the Oldenburg affair; but the French minister would not accept it, saying that:

Emperor Napoleon, having learned of your determination to file a protest, finds such an intention completely inconsistent with the feelings of friendship he has for your Tsar. Such a protest, together with the new Russian tariffs, which are clearly hostile to French trade, cannot, in His Majesty's opinion, serve anything but confirmation of rumours about an approaching breach between Russia and France, meanwhile, the emperor wants all of Europe to be convinced of the inviolability of the alliance of both empires, and their actual interests demand it. In any case, your protest would only be a pointless formality, because it is already impossible to change what has been done. Emperor Napoleon, guided by feelings of friendship for your Sovereign, is ready to fully compensate the Duke of Oldenburg and transfer his rights and those of the Russian Imperial House to a new territory. His Majesty, in observing the duties imposed on him by the alliance with Russia, has never allowed himself to rebel openly against the actions of the Russian government, even when he had a right to do so: he did not protest – neither against acts hostile to French trade interests – nor on the occasion when Russian troops, despite the clear terms of the Treaty of Tilsit, continued to occupy Moldavia and Wallachia.

To this accusation, Prince Kurakin noted: 'that the Russians had remained in the principalities -in all probability – was not without the knowledge of Emperor Napoleon. The Duc replied to that: 'Of course, our government knew about that, but has never expressed its consent to it.'

In conclusion, the French minister urged Prince Kurakin to appreciate the importance of the arguments inspired by a desire to preserve the alliance with Russia, and to abandon his willingness to file a protest so unpleasant to Emperor Napoleon, the Duc added, as he placed the file on the desk: 'and therefore I am returning it to you unopened.' The consequence of this was a dispute between the diplomats, neither of whom, not one nor the other, wanted to take the file. Finally, Prince Kurakin,

---

10   Prince Kurakin's dispatches to Count Rumyantsev, dated 27 January (8 February) 1811, from documents kept in the Archive of the M.F.A.

11   His dispatches, dated 3 (15) February 1811, from documents kept in the Archive of the M.F.A.

seeing the Duc's stubbornness and not being able to forcefully hand him the protest, remembered (as he put it in his response to Count Rumyantsev) *qu'à l'impossible nul n'est tenû*, and was forced to leave the declaration on his desk.[12]

Tsar Alexander expressed his displeasure to Prince Kurakin for the fact that he had not conveyed the protest on the Oldenburg matter to the French Minister of Foreign Affairs.[13] After that, the following note was sent to all our residents, to inform the Courts to which they were accredited:

> His Imperial Majesty of all the Russias has learned with surprise that H.M. the Emperor of the French; the King of Italy, his ally, in setting new borders for his Empire, is including the Duchy of Oldenburg, through a *senatus-consultum*. His Majesty has brought to the attention of the Emperor, his ally, as he does to the whole of Europe, that the Treaty of Tilsit, explicitly, guarantees the peaceful possession of this Duchy to its legitimate Sovereign.
>
> His Majesty has reminded this monarch and every power of the fact that Russia, by the provisional treaty of 1767 and that of 1773, abandoned to the King of Denmark all that they held in the Duchy of Holstein, and received in exchanges the Counties of Oldenburg and Delmenhorst, which by known transactions, in which several powers must necessarily have taken part, were formed into a sovereign Duchy in favour of a cadet branch of this same house of Holstein-Gottorp, to which His Imperial Majesty belongs by the most direct ties of blood.
>
> The Emperor considers that this state, created through the generosity of his empire, cannot be annulled without injuring every justice and its rights. He is therefore obliged to use the right of reservation, and to protect, as he does by this office, in his own name and that of his heirs to the throne in perpetuity, all the rights and obligations that derive from of the above-mentioned treaties.
>
> What value is there to keeping alliances if the treaties on which they were founded are not kept? But His Majesty, so as not to give rise to any misunderstanding, declares here that great political interest has produced his alliance with His Majesty the Emperor of the French; that this interest survives, and that he therefore proposes to see to the preservation of this alliance, and expects the same and reciprocal care from a monarch to which he is entitled.
>
> This union of the interests of the two empires, conceived by Peter the Great, and which since then has encountered so many obstacles, has already provided advantages for His Majesty's empire, just as it has for France.
>
> It therefore appears to be useful for the two empires to endeavour to preserve this alliance, and His Majesty will devote all his care to it.'[14]

---

12   His dispatches, dated 8 (20) February 1811, from documents kept in the Archive of the M.F.A.

13   Count Rumyantsev's dispatches to Prince Kurakin, dated 11 [23] March 1811, from documents kept in the Archive of the M.F.A.

14   For the original text of this note, in French, see Appendix II.

The presentation of the protest had been distinguished by its moderation, but Napoleon, accustomed to the unquestioning obedience of sovereigns, was very disappointed with the Russian note. Subservience to the conqueror extended to the point that our residents could only fulfil the orders given to them – to hand over the protest to the Courts at which they were accredited – with great difficulty.

Simultaneously with the matter of the Duchy of Oldenburg, another dispute arose between the Russian and French governments – over trade, closely connected with the continental system. Napoleon, not possessing the kind of fleet that he needed to deliver a decisive blow to Great Britain, hoped to destroy the trade and maritime strength of the British by blocking access to all their agricultural and manufactured goods throughout the continent of Europe. To that end, wherever Napoleon's influence reached, decrees were promulgated and enforced the cessation of trade and that which was expected of them in anticipation of the ruin of Britain, and had direct consequences throughout the rest of Europe through high prices and a decline in social welfare.

The continental system was based on a decree signed by Napoleon in Berlin on 21 November, 1806 [new style], which contained the following orders:

1. The British Isles are declared to be under blockade.
2. Both trade and any communication with the British are prohibited, and, consequently, letters and parcels addressed to Britain, or to the name of a British subject, may not be mailed and are subject to confiscation.
3. Any British subject detained in an area occupied by French or allied forces shall be regarded as a prisoner of war.
4. Any property belonging to a British subject shall be confiscated.
5. All goods pertaining to Britain and anything from its factories or colonial products thereof shall be confiscated.
6. Half of the sums received from the sale of confiscated property shall be used to compensate those merchants whose ships have been captured by British cruisers.
7. Ships arriving from Britain or British colonies shall not be admitted into any harbour.
8. Vessels that violate this regulation shall be confiscated along with their cargo.
9. The final decision on all matters which may arise from the execution of this decree, are subject to the prize commissions established in Paris and Milan.
10. The Minister of Foreign Affairs shall inform the kings of Spain, Naples, Holland and Etruria, and our other allies, whose subjects, like the French, must endure oppression from the injustice and barbarism of British maritime regulations.[15]

---

15   *Hist. générale des traités de paix, par le comte de Garden.* X, 307-308.

In response to this decree, on 7 January, 1807, (new style) orders by the British Council of Ministers [Orders in Council] were issued, on the basis of which it was forbidden for neutral ships to trade in the harbours of France, or their allies. On 11 November (new style) of the same year, another order followed, by which all the harbours in Europe and the colonies, from which the British flag had been excluded, were announced to be under a state of blockade, and, as a result, any ships previously in those harbours were subject to inspection by British cruisers, could be withdrawn to Great Britain and the payment of a set fine.

Napoleon learned about these orders by the British ministry during his stay in Milan and on 17 December, 1807 (new style) promulgated a new decree, which ordered neutral ships not to act in compliance with British demands and completely destroyed all maritime trade. It was decided that all vessels, whatever nation they might belong to, which obeyed the Orders in Council promulgated on 11 November, were announced to have been 'owned' by Britain (*denationalisés*) and would be confiscated. In this same decree, the British Isles were declared to be under a state of siege by land and sea, such that any ship sent from Britain, from the British colonies, or from places occupied by British troops, as well as ships visiting British harbours, or in their colonies and regions occupied by British troops, were subject to confiscation.[16]

The orders adopted by the belligerent governments were so incompatible to their own interests that both sides also considered it necessary to cancel some of the steps they themselves had just taken, and the example was set by Britain: on 26 April, 1809, ships from the United States of America were permitted to trade through any harbours that were not under close blockade, such as: with any of the coastal parts of Spain not occupied by the French army; with Russia, and in general with any of the ports on the Baltic.

Napoleon, for his part, on 5 August, 1810, issued a decree known as the Trianon Tariff. Up to this point, the continental system had aimed at the destruction of British trade, both in colonial goods and in the agricultural and manufacturing produce of the British Isles. But upon discovering that there was no way to replace colonial products with French ones, through the Trianon and subsequent decrees of 12 September and 19 October, 1810 (new style), Napoleon stated:

1. That the import of colonial goods was allowed, upon the payment of customs duties of 40 or 50 percent of their value.
2. That all British manufactured products and goods found in France, Holland, Northern Germany, Italy, Illyria, the Kingdom of Naples, Spain and in all places occupied by French troops were to be burned.

Meanwhile, as the fires of the commercial inquisition burned in all the countries mentioned, Napoleon and many persons acting upon his authority enriched themselves through the introduction of the sale of so-called exclusive licenses, on the basis of which it was permitted to import a certain amount of colonial goods into

---

16   *Hist. générale des traités de paix, par le comte de Garden.* X, 312-313.

France, upon condition of exporting French manufactured products of a similar value, and including at least a third of silk products. Thus, anyone who acquired a permit had to pay a set fee for it, and, in addition, customs duties for the import of goods, in accordance with the Trianon Tariff, and for export, in compliance with the general provisions. It was impossible to make any profit on goods exported from France, because their import into Britain was associated with huge taxes and great difficulties, and therefore speculators who traded by means of permits sold French products to smugglers and customs almost for nothing, or even ditched them in the sea. Consequently, colonial goods had to be sold at such a price that would cover the enormous duty imposed on them and the losses of products purchased in France. However, in order to avoid these losses, speculators resorted to various tricks, such as the export of faulty products, the compilation of cargo manifests for imaginary export items, etc. To prevent the smuggling trade, strict countermeasures were introduced.[17] But the government itself facilitated the evasions, without which the sale of exclusive licenses would have been impossible.[18]

The consequences of such measures were: on the one hand – the cessation of fair trade, and on the other – the development of a huge amount of smuggling and extortion. In addition, the main aims of the continental system, the destruction of Britain's trade and of its economy, were not, and could not be achieved. Britain, having temporarily lost communications with mainland Europe, acquired a monopoly of trade in every other part of the world; the destruction of British products ruined not the British, but those merchants who had bought their goods; finally, the introduction of the continental system aroused general displeasure in every country and was one of the reasons for Napoleon's breach with Tsar Alexander.

Russia, upon the conclusion of the Treaty of Tilsit, being in alliance with France, adopted the continental system as a hostile measure against Britain, but had not completely abandoned trade with neutral states: American ships had free access to our harbours, while any British, who attempted to trade in the guise of neutral ships, were impounded. The consequences of these strict measures were: a decrease in the export of Russian raw materials, an unfavourable state of the balance of our trade and, finally, a decline in the exchange rate and value of bank notes.

These were the concessions made by Tsar Alexander to preserve the alliance with France, already very unreliable, as it turned out due to many actions by the French government. From the moment the path to succession to the Swedish throne was opened to Marshal Bernadotte, Paris had no doubts about the impending breach

---

17   The following Decree was attached to Count Nesselrode's dispatches to Chancellor Count Rumyantsev, dated 25 July (6 August): 'Décret Impérial, du 5 Juillet 1810. Trente à quarante bâtimens américains pourront importer en France du coton, huiles de poisson, bois de teinture, poissons salés, morues, cuirs en poil et pelleteries. Ils pourront exporter des vins, eaux de vie, soieries, toiles, draps, bijoux, meubles et autres produits de nos manufactures. Ils ne pourrons partir que de Charlestown ou de New-York, avec obligation de porter une gazette de jour de leur départ (gazette américaine) ainsi que plusieurs certificats, d'origine des marchandises, delivrés par le consul Français et contenant une phrase en chiffres. Les négociants Français, qui feront venir les marchandises par les navires américains, devront prouver qu'ils sont associés avec les chefs des manufactures de Paris, Rouen ou autres villes.'

18   Hist. génér. des traités de paix, par le comte de Garden. X, 313-319.

with Russia. From that time on, articles hostile to our country began to appear in French periodicals, which, judging from previous experience, served as a precursor to war. At the same time, orders were issued for the call up of the conscription class of 1811, which would boost the French army by 120,000 men, and orders were issued to transport the parks that had been stationed in Ulm and Augsburg since the late Austrian war, to the fortresses of Glogau [Głogów], Küstrin [Kostrzyn nad Odrą] Stettin [Szczecin] and Danzig.[19] By the middle of 1810, Napoleon's dislike for Russia was already becoming apparent, either through his affectionate treatment of Polish immigrants, or by his efforts to sow discord between the Russian and Austrian governments. To that end, he occasionally exaggerated our successes in the war against the Turks and, in conversation with Graf Metternich [Klemens Wenzel Lothar von Metternich], condemned the annexation of Moldavia and Wallachia to Russia. He said: 'As for me, I have never entered the territory of a conquered province before the formal cession, at the conclusion of peace, made me their rightful owner.'[20] At the same time, Napoleon, on every occasion, continued to express his sincerity and friendship for Russia, saying that he did not need to resort to any twists and turns. He once said to *Flügel-Adjutant* [Equerry] Chernyshev [Alexander Ivanovich Chernyshev]:

> I am so strong that I don't need to. If the annexation of Moldavia and Wallachia to Russia were contrary to my interests, then I would prevent you from doing so by open force. This acquisition will put Russia in a formidable position with regards to Austria, but my business lies in this direction: this is an Austrian question, not a French one. I am firmly sticking with the alliance with you, and only in two eventualities would I break it: firstly, if you were to make peace with the British, and secondly, if you were to expand your borders beyond the Danube. The existence of the Porte is so important to the preservation of the political balance in Europe that I cannot allow any further separation of provinces from Turkey.[21]

Napoleon was hostile towards Russia, but preoccupied with the indecisive war in Spain, he was reluctant to break with Tsar Alexander, and, in all likelihood, would have postponed it for a long time if the Russian Monarch, like many European rulers, had fulfilled the whims of the conqueror. Napoleon wanted the Trianon Tariff that he had introduced to be enforced throughout continental Europe with the same or even greater severity as in France. Italy, Germany, Holland, Denmark, unquestioningly fulfilled the will of the strongman. Sweden, unable to exist without sea trade, was forced to conduct it covertly. Napoleon expressed a desire for the tariff promulgated by the French government to be introduced in Russia as well, seeking to prevent neutral shipping from entering Russian harbours, and thereby a complete cessation of our maritime trade.

---

19   *Flügel-Adjutant* Chernyshev's letter to Count Rumyantsev dated 5 (17) September 1810.
20   Count Nesselrode's letter to Count Rumyantsev dated 28 June (10 July) 1810.
21   *Flügel-Adjutant* Chernyshev's letter to Count Rumyantsev sent during October 1810.

Tsar Alexander gave orders to respond to this inappropriate demand that he intended to inviolably maintain the alliance with France and inflict all kinds of harm on the common enemy, but at the same time, guided by the frankness that had always served as the basis for his actions, he would present to the French government that tariffs and other internal regulations went beyond the obligations of the international alliance and constituted an internal matter, which each state controlled, paying attention exclusively to the interests of its subjects. Furthermore, it was stated that the Russian government could in fact prove how vigilantly it was observing the prevention of British contraband trade, and that the confiscation of 96 British ships we had captured demonstrated the strictness of Russian customs.[22] After Napoleon, in conversation with *Flügel-Adjutant* Chernyshev, insisted on the adoption of new decrees issued in France by the Russian government, the Chancellor, Count Rumyantsev, by Supreme Orders, was to write the following response for Prince Kurakin:

> As for the adoption of trade laws for a foreign tariff without considering their application to the sources and the course of one's own national wealth, His Majesty could never permit himself.
>
> It would be showing too little concern for the fortunes of one's subjects. One would thereby weaken the love to which one aspires and persuades oneself to have the right. A great Empire has great interests to spare; within the limits of one's own borders and in the relations of the most extreme friendship one must set one's own course.[23]

Moreover, it was presented to the French government that Emperor Napoleon had considered it necessary to ease the severity of those very decrees on his own territory that he sought to make binding on other states, and that colonial goods, formerly doomed to destruction, had now appeared across France, in every continental market, and had even been set free from the imposition of high duties, declaring themselves to have arrived from Ile-de-France [Mauritius], Batavia [Indonesia] and other colonies governed by France. As for the destruction of British manufactured goods, such a measure, in the opinion of Tsar Alexander, could lead, upon the conclusion of peace, to an even greater enhancement of British industry, and in general all the decrees that obstructed sea trade were more harmful to the continental powers than to Britain.[24]

---

22 Count Rumyantsev's dispatches to Prince Kurakin, dated 25 September [7 October] 1810.

23 Extract from Count Rumyantsev's dispatches to Prince Kurakin, dated 24 November [6 December]: '*Quand à l'adoption des loix commerciales d'un tarif étranger sans en examiner l'application aux sources et à la marche des richesses de sa propre nation, Sa Majesté ne se le permettra jamais.*
Ce serait montrer trop peu de sollicitude pour la fortune de ses sujets. Elle en affaiblirait par là l'amour auquel Elle aspire et se persuade avoir des droits. Un grand Empire a de grands intérêts à ménager; dans l'étendue de ses propres limites et dans les rapports de la plus extrême amitié il doit garder sa propre marche.'

24 Extract from Count Rumyantsev's dispatches to Prince Kurakin, dated 24 November [6 December].

These same convictions were expressed by the Emperor in a conversation with Caulaincourt. He said:

> I shall try to harm the British, but I do not consider myself obligated to take measures that go beyond the terms of the agreement I concluded with Emperor Napoleon. He disposes of everything as he pleases, whichever is more consistent with his own interests.[25]

Napoleon, accustomed to unconditional obedience from other European sovereigns, expressed his indignation with petty measures against Russian trade: to that end, the duty was raised on potash, tea, rhubarb, fish oil and other items exported by Russia. Prince Kurakin initially petitioned for a decrease in duties on Russian goods, but later left this matter hanging, believing that it was more profitable for the Russian government to take advantage of the opportunity to raise duties on luxury goods imported into Russia from France.[26]

The disagreement between the Emperors Alexander and Napoleon, on the subject of trade, increased even more with the introduction in Russia, in December 1810, of a new tariff, the purpose of which was to reduce the export of hard currency to France, for luxury goods, in exchange for Russian goods which could not be exported overland. To ameliorate this inconvenience, which led to the devaluation of bank notes, along with the restriction of sea trade, some products from French factories were prohibited, while others had a high duty imposed. Napoleon, as we have already seen, had set a precedent for such orders himself, raising the customs duty on many products exported by Russia, but despite this, he gave orders to express his displeasure at the introduction of a new tariff by us, supposedly beneficial to the British and completely depriving France of opportunities to trade with Russia. In response to these complaints, it was explained that our relations with the British were still hostile, and that the only purpose of the new tariff was: to buy less and sell more than previously. Prince Kurakin, in a conversation with the Duc de Cadore, confessed that:

> The import of French goods into Russia would decrease, but that such a restriction on imports applied not only to France, but to the whole of Germany, with which you are also in the most friendly of relations.

To the Duc's objection that this measure was contrary to the conditions of the Treaty of Tilsit, the Russian envoy replied:

> The treaty states that the subjects of both states, in trade relations, would respect the existing tariffs, or those that should exist afterwards.

---

25   Caulaincourt's dispatches to the Duc de Cadore, sent during November 1810, from minutes kept in the Archive of the M.F.A.

26   Prince Kurakin's dispatches to Count Rumyantsev, dated 30 November (12 December) 1810.

When the Duc de Cadore noted that Emperor Napoleon had not been previously informed about the intention of our government to introduce a new tariff, Prince Kurakin thereupon said that His Majesty did not consider it necessary to notify Emperor Napoleon about measures related to the internal administration of his state, furthermore, he noted, Emperor Napoleon also had not considered it necessary to notify Tsar Alexander in advance of his intention to annex the Hanseatic cities and other provinces of northern Germany to France.[27]

Napoleon, wishing to take revenge on our government for the introduction of the new tariff, ordered the naval department not to buy any materials for the fleet from Russia; but this order would be harmful to France itself, because they were forced to obtain these necessary materials from Russia as before, but buying them in Germany through middle-men, and paying more for them than previously.

By the beginning of 1811, Napoleon no longer concealed his displeasure at the independent actions of the Russian government. But as he cooled towards Russia, he tried to show benevolence and affection to the Polish immigrants who lived in Paris. Wanting to win Sweden over to his side, he suggested that the Swedish government supply a 20,000 strong corps to assist French forces in the event of a war with Russia, and he hoped not only to return Finland, but to annex Livonia [Livland] and Courland [Kurland] to Sweden.[28] At the same time, he replenished his army, sent artillery and a significant number of muskets to the Duchy of Warsaw, fortified Danzig, strengthened the garrisons there and ordered the members of the Confederation of the Rhine to maintain their troops at full readiness. Many believed that these formidable preparations would lead to war breaking out in 1811. But the Emperor of the French postponed the execution of his hostile plans against Russia for a while in order to prepare even greater forces and war resources, whose importance could not be hidden from his eagle eyes.

---

27   His dispatches dated 28 January (9 February) 1811.
28   Prince Kurakin's dispatches to Count Rumyantsev, dated 9 (21) February and 2 (14) March 1811.

3

Preparations for War

Napoleon's preparations. – The conscription of 1811. – Gradual strengthening of troops in northern Germany. – The conscription of 1812. – Orders for Davout. – Diplomatic relations between Napoleon and the Russian government. – Conversations between Tsar Alexander and the French ambassadors Caulaincourt and Lauriston. – Conversation between Napoleon and Prince Kurakin. – Activities by Alexander I fostering peace. – Napoleon's mistrust. – Stockpiling supplies in Danzig; transport means; pontoons. – Assembly of the *Grande Armée*. – Collection of intelligence on Russia.

Tsar Alexander's preparations. – Fortification of the most important locations in the western regions. – The gradual reform of the Russian army from 1810 to 1812. – Reserves for the field armies. – Artillery parks. – Magazines. – The concept for means of provisioning the Russian army in the war of 1812.

At the present time, after almost half a century has passed since the struggle for the independence of Russia, the question of who was the instigator of this war has been finally resolved. History has already paid tribute to the moderation of Tsar Alexander, no one doubts that he did everything that the dignity of a Russian Monarch permitted him to do in order to deflect the thunderstorm that had gravitated towards our fatherland for two years. The best evidence of his concern for maintaining peace with Napoleon is the testimony of the French ambassador to St Petersburg, the Duc de Vicence (Caulaincourt), who constantly assured his government of the pacific nature of Tsar Alexander. Napoleon, who wanted to absolve himself of violating the peace, recalled Caulaincourt (who, according to him, had become a Russian), and, in the spring of 1811, appointed General Lauriston [Jacques Jean Alexandre Bernard Law, marquis de Lauriston] as envoy to the Russian Court.

Tsar Alexander wanted to preserve the alliance with France, but could not achieve this great objective, and with faith in God, relying on the loyalty of his subjects, which never changed in times of danger, began to actively prepare for a life and death struggle with the arrogant conqueror. Thus, preparations for war on both sides began and continued almost simultaneously: Tsar Alexander preparing defensive measures in order to counter the aggressive steps taken by Napoleon.

In order to draw a picture of the gradual development of forces and resources that served as tools in the hands of the powerful rivals, we shall outline the preparations – first by Napoleon and then by Tsar Alexander.

The beginning of Napoleon's preparations for war against Russia was the call up of the conscription class of 1811, in December 1810, a total of 80,000 men.[1] After that, the fortification of Danzig and the strengthening of the garrison there began under the pretext of defending against a landing by the British.[2] At the end of June [early July] 1811, Davout's [Louis Nicolas Davout] so-called Corps of Observation of the Elbe, which was stationed in northern Germany and had its headquarters in Hamburg, was increased to 51,337 men; in July, an order was issued to re-role four dragoon and two *Chasseur à cheval* regiments into eight lancer regiments, each with 1,000 horses, and even before that, an elite Polish Lancer regiment had been formed in Warsaw by Colonel Łubieński [Tomasz Andrzej Łubieński] (*régiment de lanciers d'élite polonais* [actually: *2 Pułk Ułanów Nadwiślańskich*]); by August it had reached the following: Davout had some 70,000; there were 22,000 in the Saxon *7e Corps* while the Duchy of Warsaw contingent reached 60,000; while by October the number of French troops in northern Germany, together with the garrisons of the fortresses on the Oder, had reached 89,850; in addition, in the camps at Utrecht and Zuidlaren there were 23,981 men, of whom no less than 20,000 had been sent at the same time to reinforce Davout; the Danzig garrison consisted of 17,482 men: therefore, in the north of Germany there were more than 130,000 French troops, which in a short time could be reinforced by contingents from the Confederation of the Rhine, numbering more than 100,000 men, and even by the end of 1811, Napoleon could send up to 240,000 men against Russia, in addition to the garrisons of Stettin, Küstrin and Glogau, totalling more than 20,000 men.[3] In December a decree was issued for the call up of 120,000 conscripts for the army and 12,000 for the navy.[4]

The artillery parks that had been stationed in Augsburg and Ulm since the Austrian War of 1809 were transported to Danzig and the fortresses on the Oder: Glogau, Küstrin and Stettin, were occupied by French garrisons.[5] As early as the spring of 1811, 60,000 muskets and a significant number of artillery pieces had been sent to Warsaw.[6]

The foundations of the *Grande Armée*, assigned for the invasion of Russia, were intended to be the corps under Marshal Davout (Corps of Observation of the Elbe), which, in administrative terms, could, in all fairness, be considered exemplary. Napoleon informed the marshal that: 'they would have to operate in a poor country, which, in all likelihood, would have been devastated by the enemy, and that they should be ready to move around under their own resources,' whereupon

---

1   *Moniteur du 4 février 1811.*
2   Prince Kurakin's dispatches dated 17 (29) March 1811. For the French explanation of these measures, see Appendix III.
3   Prince Kurakin's dispatches dated 28 and 29 October (9 and 10 November) 1811. *Tableau général de la dislocation de l'armée française et de ses alliés à l'époque du 1 novembre 1811.* Archive of the Military Topographic Depot [M.T.D.] No. 22,638.
4   Prince Kurakin's dispatches dated 8 (20) December 1811.
5   *Flügel-Adjutant* Chernyshev's dispatches dated 5 (17) September 1811.
6   Prince Kurakin's dispatches dated 17 (29) March 1811.

the experienced warrior answered the emperor with a calculation of all his assets, writing:

> My 70,000 men are equipped with everything they need; they will have a 25 day supply of rations. In every company there are tailors, cobblers, masons, bakers, armourers, in a word – every kind of tradesman. My corps, having everything with it, is a proper colony. We will also have hand mills with us.[7]

Napoleon, finding the annual conscriptions insufficient for the manning of his armies, set out to collect the men from previous conscription classes who had not yet served in the ranks of the forces. The numbers evading conscription by hiding in the mountains and forests reached 60,000. Napoleon, knowing that they were evading their duty with the assistance of the local population, held the entire family of a deserter responsible for their escape. Mobile columns were established to pursue the evaders (réfractaires), racing across the country in various directions. Their commanders had the right to post soldiers within the families of deserters, who had to feed their guests and pay them a set penalty. The mobile columns consisted of old soldiers who considered evasion to be as shameful as it was criminal, and therefore it is not surprising that they allowed themselves to behave very cruelly towards the townsfolk and that this extreme measure in a short time delivered many thousands of fugitive conscripts to the army.[8]

Thus, the entire year of 1811 was used by Napoleon to prepare the resources for waging war with Russia, and if hostile operations were not opened in this year, then the only reason for this was Napoleon's desire to increase his strength. Meanwhile, he tried to lull the vigilance of the Russian government with incessant assurances of his peacefulness and loyalty to Tsar Alexander. It goes without saying that Napoleon's objective could not be achieved: it was impossible to hide the huge preparations clearly directed against Russia. Our envoy in Paris, Prince Kurakin, and his Equerry Chernyshev, sent to Napoleon on instructions from the Emperor, followed all the actions of the French government: we were quite familiar with both Napoleon's mobilisation and his diplomatic duplicity. The Emperor of the French, wishing to divert our forces to the south and exhaust them in a war against Turkey, criticised our government for the withdrawal of some of the troops from Moldavia and Wallachia and lured us back there with the hope of annexing the principalities to Russia, meanwhile advising the Turks not to agree to the cession of these provinces. His actual enforcement of the continental system was intended to aggravate the disruption of our finances, which was quite clearly revealed on one occasion by the words of the Duc de Bassano [Hugues-Bernard Maret], saying to Prince Kurakin: 'You no longer adhere to the continental system at all. This was the reason for raising tariffs against you.'[9]

In such circumstances, once war had already been decided upon in Napoleon's plans, the negotiations between Russia and France could not lead to a sincere

---

7   Ségur. *Histoire de Napoléon et de la grande armée en 1812*. I, 122.
8   Thiers. *Histoire du Consulat et de l'Empire. Edition de Bruxelles*. XIII, 13-15.
9   Prince Kurakin's dispatches dated 25 July (6 August) 1811.

renewal of friendly relations. On the question of Poland, nothing was done; in the case of the Duchy of Oldenburg, Napoleon confined himself to vague promises to compensate the duke; and when the Russian government asked him to express more clearly the intended compensation, then they demanded that we say exactly what we want in return for Oldenburg from France; our refusal to comply with this demand gave Napoleon the excuse to conclude that Tsar Alexander was trying to get the Duchy of Warsaw. In relation to the continental system, having severed all relations with Britain, and, thus, having fully satisfied the terms concluded with France, our government did not consider itself obligated to be stricter than Napoleon himself, at the cost of our trade with neutral Powers. Napoleon's preparations for war and the defensive measures taken by Tsar Alexander served as a new pretext for arguments and mutual recriminations by both sides.

During a later visit by Caulaincourt to our Court, in conversation with the Emperor, he could not help but confess to the significant mobilisation of France, but attributed it to that which was done in Russia. Tsar Alexander, not seeing a great need to hide the truth, and perhaps wanting to show that he would not be taken by surprise, replied to the French envoy that he was actually preparing for war. The Tsar said:

> But I did not begin this before having received accurate information about bringing Danzig into a defensive state, about strengthening Thorn [Toruń], about completing Modlin's fortifications, about increasing Davout's army and the Danzig garrison; about the orders given to the Poles and Saxons to be ready to march. Having received all this intelligence, I directed the building of fortifications, but not well forwards, rather behind the borders of my empire on the Dvina [Daugava] and Dnieper: in Riga, Dünaburg [Daugavpils], Bobruisk, Kiev, that is, almost the same distance from the Neman [Niemen] as Paris is from Strasbourg. If your sovereign should take it into his head to fortify Paris, should I complain about it? I have not withdrawn whole divisions from Finland, but only returned those regiments operating against the Swedes to their divisions located in Lithuania, converted garrison battalions into troops of the line, reformed the organisation of my depots and strengthened the Lifeguard to make it worthy of comparison with Napoleon's. Finally, I pulled five divisions out of Turkey; you yourselves are the reason for this, preventing me from reaping the agreed fruits of our alliance, very meagre in comparison with your conquests. In a word, I shall not allow myself to be attacked by surprise. My generals are inferior in quality to yours; I cannot equal Napoleon in the skill of commanding troops, or in experience, but I have good soldiers, my subjects are loyal to me, and we are all ready to die under arms rather than to allow ourselves to be treated like the Dutch and the citizens of Hamburg. But, I give you my word of honour that the first shot will not be mine. I shall allow you to cross the Neman first. I repeat to you, I do not want war and my people do not want it; but if you attack us, we shall stand up for ourselves.[10]

---

10   Thiers, XIII, 60-62.

The Emperor received the new French ambassador, Lauriston, who arrived in St. Petersburg on 9 [21] May, 1811, with the same frankness. The Emperor did not hide from him that rearmament was taking place in Russia, but added that the only cause for our preparations was those that Napoleon had threatened:

> I am not looking for war at all and will not start one, unless you force me to do so: I give you my word that I shall not do otherwise. The Americans have access to my harbours, because I cannot do without trade, and even that is in accordance with the terms of the Treaty of Tilsit, which I am obliged to observe, not the Berlin and Milan decrees, but the statutes governing relations with neutral states; I abide by these statutes more precisely than France; as for these preparations of mine, I am ready to cancel them, if only we can mutually agree to stop mobilising.

Whereupon, the Tsar, bidding goodbye to Caulaincourt, asked him to bring the whole truth to Napoleon's attention. He told Lauriston: 'And you must repeat, in turn, everything that you have heard from me. But they will not believe you, just as they did not believe your predecessor. They will say that I have deceived and subverted you, and that you have turned from a Frenchman into a Russian.'

And Lauriston, just like Caulaincourt, reported to his government that Tsar Alexander did not want war at all and in no case would be its instigator; that he was ready, in exchange for Oldenburg, to accept any compensation, even Erfurt, although he would have preferred something better; that, with regard to trade, even the strictest measures would be taken in our country, but that Russia cannot manage without trading with neutral states completely. Lauriston wrote:

> I can only observe and convey what I have seen. I am presenting matters in their present form, and if we are not satisfied with the concessions that are possible, then we shall fight, because we ourselves are looking for war, and – as far as I can tell – this war will be hard.

All these assurances could not shake Napoleon's resolve to wage war with Russia, and merely convinced him that the Russians would not act offensively, and that he could postpone the opening of hostilities until the following year. During this time, he intended to strengthen his army and prepare everything related to the logistics for the force on a lavish scale.[11]

To that end, while continuing to play for time in fruitless negotiations with the Russian government, Napoleon was actively preparing for war. Its inevitability was already obvious to the whole of Europe, which was waiting anxiously for the clash of powerful rivals, and therefore Napoleon, wishing to lay the blame for the upcoming struggle in advance, took advantage of the opportunity for that, and on his birthday, 3 (15) August, during a larger congress at the French Court, he subjected our envoy, Prince Kurakin, to a long diatribe. At this point, many of the invited diplomats

---

11   Thiers, XIII, 67-72.

had already left and, except for Kurakin, only the Austrian, Spanish and Neapolitan residents remained with Napoleon. Napoleon expressed his displeasure to the Russian envoy as a result of the contents of the latest dispatches he had received from Lauriston. He stated:

> We have been negotiating for six months now; but matters have not advanced a single step; six months have passed since I proposed to compensate the Duke of Oldenburg. By allowing smuggling onto his territory, he was clearly violating his obligations to me, protector of the Confederation of the Rhine; I could, on the basis of old German law, take the territory from him (*le mettre au ban*). Is it worth it to have a quarrel between the great powers, who have found so many benefits in friendly relations with each other, over a small duchy, bringing in half a million francs of income? I have asked your Tsar several times already to appoint compensation for the duchy somewhere in Germany himself; I can attribute his silence only to the view that he wishes for the acquisition of Danzig, or part of the Duchy of Warsaw; but I shall not give up a single foot of land belonging to a territory that counts upon me for its existence. Despite all your assurances, Russia is striving to swallow it up (*elle veut l'engloutir*), but I shall give up nothing of Poland... nothing.
>
> I do not want to fight with you, but you are challenging me yourselves. Where has the protest sent by your government to every European Court led? I do not comprehend your policy: Russia is at war with Britain, at war with Turkey and in conflict with France. Tsar Alexander himself announced to Count Lauriston that you were preparing for war, and announced it at a time when I was not even considering a breach with you. When in doubt, and against my will, I must take precautions. I have also put the army on a war footing; it has cost me a hundred million already, but I will not stop my preparations this year, or for two, or three, until I have resolved all the controversial issues with you.
>
> You harm yourselves by reducing the field army in Turkey, and remove thereby the opportunity to conclude a profitable peace with the Turks. Having weakened your army by the withdrawal of five divisions from Wallachia, you can neither operate offensively, nor even successfully defend the long line along the Danube from Vidin to the Black Sea. Why did you evacuate Ruschuk [Ruse], the occupation of which in the form of a bridgehead, and manoeuvring on both sides of the river were the only means to defend Wallachia? The true art of defence lies in the ability to switch to the offensive.
>
> I repeat again that I do not wish to fight with you, nor to restore Poland. But, in the event of a war, if success is on my side, then the first consequence of it will be the independence of Poland.
>
> I have called up conscripts, reinforced my regiments with new battalions, and increased the Danzig garrison. By November I shall have 200,000 men, over and above the 80,000 sent to flesh out the army in Spain; next year I shall call up 200,000 conscripts, not counting the troops of the

confederation of the Rhine and the Duchy of Warsaw: within two years, I can put 600,000 up against you. You place hope in your allies... Where are they? It cannot be from the Austrians, with whom you waged war in 1809 and from whom you took a province at the conclusion of the peace? Is it from the Swedes, from whom Finland was taken away? Is it from Prussia, from whom part of their territory was torn away, in spite of the fact that you were in alliance with them? It's time for us to end our arguments. Tsar Alexander and Count Rumyantsev will answer before the world for all the disasters that might befall Europe in the event of war... It is easy to start a war, but difficult to determine when and how it will end. Write to your emperor about everything you have heard from me. I am sure that he will consider our common cause, as he should.[12]

Tsar Alexander, having received word of Napoleon's duplicity, ordered the chancellor to write to Prince Kurakin that these events could not cool Russia's friendly relations with the French government, which would remain unchanged; but that the Tsar had taken note of Napoleon's expressions with surprise and sorrow: suggesting that His Majesty wanted to acquire Danzig, or part of the Duchy of Warsaw. Tsar Alexander ordered it to be declared, in the most emphatic manner, that he did not consider acquiring any part of the duchy at all, and that, in not striving to expand the boundaries of his empire, he was concerned solely with maintaining general peace and tranquillity.[13]

At the same time, instructions were passed to the Russian ambassador, which serve as evidence of the inclination of Tsar Alexander to avoid anything that could give rise to an acceleration of the breach with Napoleon. Count Rumyantsev, in announcing the usual recruitment in the imperial empire, wrote that it was not being carried out to increase the armed forces, but out of a need to fill the shortfall in the forces resulting from the war with the Turks and Persians and from diseases endemic in the theatres of military operations. and that these circumstances had forced them to make a recruitment of four recruits per 500 souls, which, although more than previous year, would not increase the established numbers of our forces at all, but serve only to fill the ranks of the army.

Another snippet of information sent, at the behest of Tsar Alexander, to Prince Kurakin, to be passed to the French government, was that the British ministry, probably having learned of an order placed with one merchant to supply saltpetre for the Russian gunpowder factories, had sent a transport loaded with saltpetre to St Petersburg. The Tsar gave orders for it to be sent back immediately and informed Count Lauriston.[14]

The Russian Monarch acted in exactly the same manner in relation to the Powers allied to Russia. The King of Prussia, alarmed by the mobilisation on the borders of his territories, offered his mediation to resolve the misunderstandings between

---

12   Prince Kurakin's dispatches dated 3 (15) August 1811. Thiers, XIII, 203-210. For the full text, in French, see Appendix IV.
13   Count Rumyantev's instructions to Prince Kurakin, dated 25 September [7 October] 1811.
14   Count Rumyantev's instructions to Prince Kurakin, dated 25 September [7 October] 1811.

the Russian and French governments. Tsar Alexander gave orders to inform the Tuileries Cabinet that he would not – and could not – recognise the assumption of a difference of opinions between Russia and France as sound, and therefore rejected the mediation of Prussia. The Austrian government offered its services for the same purpose, but the Tsar refused this offer, as incompatible with His friendly relations with Napoleon.[15] Unfortunately, this frank explanation would not defuse Napoleon's suspicions with regard to the fitting out of the Prussian fortresses, which he attributed to Prussia's hostile intent towards him.[16]

Meanwhile, as the negotiations continued, which on the part of Napoleon had the sole purpose of gaining time, meanwhile, behind the so-called Corps of Observation of the Elbe, the Army of the Rhine was being formed, which was intended to be split into two corps, having been reinforced with some of Davout's troops, whereupon these were to be entrusted to Ney [Michel Ney], summoned from Spain, and Oudinot [Nicolas Charles Marie Oudinot]. Prince Eugène [Eugène Rose de Beauharnais] in Italy, Poniatowski in the Duchy of Warsaw, the King of Saxony and other princes of the Confederation of the Rhine were ordered to hold their troops at full readiness to march. Napoleon, concerned about a sudden Russian invasion of the Duchy of Warsaw, ordered the Saxon King and his governor in Poland Poniatowski to gather all the artillery, military stores and provisions into the fortresses on the Vistula, Danzig, Thorn and Modlin. Thus, on the part of Napoleon, measures had been taken to prevent our attempts at an offensive.

He was no less actively engaged in the arrangement of the logistics units, which presented extreme difficulties, because it was a question of supplying everything necessary for a half-million man army. Napoleon had in mind to collect a year's supply of food for 400,000 or even 500,000 men in Danzig, not counting those stores that were required, at the same time, for the 20,000 man garrison of this fortress. To achieve this aim, General Rapp [Jean Rapp] was ordered to monitor the delivery of bread, and as soon as war had become inevitable, in Napoleon's opinion, he was to proceed to purchase between 600,000 to 700,000 *Zentner* [1 *Zentner* = 50 kilogrammes] of wheat, a huge amount of oats and all the hay that could be obtained. To cover these costs, funds were assigned, located in Danzig, Magdeburg and Mainz and known only to the Emperor of the French.

Thus, Napoleon managed to collect very large supplies of provisions and fodder at the points closest to the intended theatre of military operations; but he was faced with an even more difficult task – to look for resources to transport these supplies after the army. In addition to several transport battalions, with one and a half thousand hard-tack wagons, which were driven by four horses, they required two drivers each and contained a three-day supply for one battalion, there were also hard-tack carts with the troops, lighter, containing a one-day supply of hard-tack for one battalion. Napoleon, not content with that, considered it necessary to introduce light one-horse carts as used in Franche-Comté (*chars à la comtoise*), and bullock wagons, and therefore, in addition to the eight transport battalions assigned for the campaign in Russia, he added four battalions of one-horse carts and five battalions of

---

15   Count Rumyantsev's dispatches to Prince Kurakin, dated 11 [23] October 1811.
16   Prince Kurakin's dispatches dated 8 (20) November.

bullock wagons: the former were formed in Franche-Comté, while the latter formed up in Lombardy, Germany and Poland. The advantages of one-horse carts were that they were very light and required a single driver for several horses trained to follow one after the other; and ox wagons could move along the worst roads, and besides, oxen required almost no supervision and could, upon delivery of provisions, serve as food for the troops. This total of seventeen battalions, with five or six thousand wagons, were sufficient to transport two months' supply of provisions for 200,000 men. Napoleon limited himself to this supply, intending to float the provisions and fodder collected in Danzig along the Vistula via the Vistula Lagoon [Frisches Haff], and from there to the Pregel [Pregolya] and to the Neman. He hoped that, having arrived with 500,000 or 600,000 men on the Neman, he would lead no more than three hundred thousand to the internal provinces of Russia, and that then, having with him a forty-day supply of food and using some of the resources of the country, he could feed his army.

But five or six thousand carts required 8 to 10,000 drivers and 18 to 20,000 horses and oxen; and with more than 100,000 cavalry and artillery horses, one can understand how difficult it was to feed so many animals. Napoleon hoped to increase his chances by opening the campaign not before the appearance of summer pasture.

As the supply of bread to the troops, rather than hard-tack, causes more difficulties with grinding grain into flour than with baking, Napoleon ordered most of the grain stock in Danzig to be ground and to fill the barrels adapted to the new carts with flour. Bricklayers were hired for the construction of the ovens.

Finally, the pontoon parks were again improved in the second year of preparation for war. Napoleon ordered the construction of two parks in Danzig, one hundred pontoons each, which were busy with standard carts. As the timber needed for the construction of bridges can be found almost everywhere, and especially in the terrain where the war was intended to be waged, while, on the contrary, it was much more difficult to get the necessary iron and hemp, Napoleon found it useful to take ropes and anchors with him. and all other iron and hemp fittings for the construction of a third bridge. For the construction of permanent bridges, fittings for piles, drivers for driving them in, and so on were directed to Danzig. All of this equipment was supposed to follow the army in wagons, for which two thousand horses were assigned. General Éblé [Jean-Baptiste Éblé] was appointed commander of the pontoon parks, who was distinguished by his skill in this area. Napoleon wrote: 'With such resources, we shall overcome all obstacles (*nous dévorerons tous les obstacles*).'

While the French troops under Davout, Oudinot and Ney, and the allied troops from the Confederation of the Rhine and the Duchy of Warsaw completed their preparations and were supplied with everything necessary for the difficult campaign ahead, Napoleon ordered Prince Eugène to prepare to cross the Alps with the Army of Italy. Relying on the friendship of Austria, he transferred almost all the troops stationed in Illyria and the Kingdom of Naples to Lombardy. Three selected battalions were taken from each of the best regiments, and thus an army of 40,000 French troops was formed, which, having been reinforced with 20,000 Italians, Napoleon assigned them to march into Russia. The remaining (4th and 5th) battalions of the regiments, along with some entire regiments and Murat's Neapolitan army were left to protect Italy from the British and the hostile population. In addition, a reserve army was made up of some Italian and Illyrian regiments, which were intended to replace the *Garde impériale* in Spain and the Polish troops who had been assigned to go to Russia.[17] Among the military preparations by Napoleon, we note the formation of 214 companies of coastal customs guard, these were intended to replace some of the troops guarding the coastline of France.[18]

Preparing for a campaign in a little-known country, Napoleon tried to acquire all possible information about Russia and gave orders for a hundred-sheet, or, so-called, detailed map of our western provinces to be engraved with a translation of the inscriptions into French; this map was distributed to many of his generals. French agents in Russia, including the embassy secretary, Prevost, were instructed to collect: 'detailed statistical information about the governorates: Estland, Livonia, Courland, Pskov, Vitebsk, Mogilev, Minsk, Vilna [Vilnius], Grodno, Białystok [Białystok], Volhynia, Kiev, Podolsk and Kherson.'[19]

The five years that elapsed after the conclusion of the Treaty of Tilsit were used by Tsar Alexander to great advantage. After the struggle with Napoleon in 1805-1807, our army was in disarray and was weakened; but, in spite of this, Alexander found the means: to wage war against Persians and Turks at the same time; to curb the rebellious highlanders in the Caucasus; force Sweden to concede Finland; to increase the numbers of troops significantly and improve their tactical training; to strengthen the militarily important locations of his state; prepare all the necessary stores in abundance. And all this was done within a little over four years, in the course of incessant wars, without burdening the subjects with taxes and without large loans weighing down the future of the state. Such a feat, in all fairness, gives Tsar Alexander I the inalienable right to the glory of a wise administrator – the guardian of the people's welfare.

Tsar Alexander's preparations for war against France began as soon as doubts arose about Napoleon's intentions, but the measures taken by Russia to repel the enemy were delayed by the war that we had been waging against the Turks for several years. This situation did not allow the Russians to fully develop all their military resources and forced them to abandon offensive operations initially, and thereafter, from the defence of the western borders of our homeland.

Our preparations for war consisted of the study of the area which was to serve as the theatre of war; in strengthening the most important locations through innovative means; in the manning of the forces, the formation of reserves, the arrangement of depots, magazines, hospitals and parks, in accordance with the wartime needs.

To investigate the properties of the theatre of war, officers of the Quartermaster's Department were sent out in 1811, who surveyed the western border area of Russia, and provided highly satisfactory descriptions of this region.

In relation to the strengthening of the most important locations on our western border, it was decided: to fortify Riga, Bobruisk, Kiev; to fortify Dünaburg and

---

17   Thiers. *Hist. du Consulat et de l'Empire. Ed. de Brux.* XIII, 214-226.
18   *Flügel-Adjutant* Chernyshev's letter to Count Rumyantsev dated 6 (18) December 1811, from memos in the Archive of the M.F.A.
19   From intercepted dispatches in the Archive of the M.F.A.

Sebezh, where it was intended to collect large stores of rations and fodder; to build fortified camps on the Dvina at Drissa [Verkhnyadzvinsk], and on the Dnieper at Kiev, and a bridgehead on the Berezina, at Borisov. Most of these works, as well as the fortification of the town of Mosty [Masty] on the Neman and the construction of a *Tête de pont* near the town of Selets [Sialiec] on the Yaselda [Jasiołda] river, which were intended to secure mutual communications between the separate formations of our army, were carried out in the spring of 1812. The population in the immediate vicinity of these locations were employed to work in Riga, Dünaburg, the Drissa camp and Kiev. There was not enough time to complete all the works planned by the Department of Engineering, however, Riga and Bobruisk were brought to a state to withstand a siege and subsequently influenced operations.[20]

Let us turn to the gradual transformation and strengthening of the Russian forces, from the moment a breach between Russia and France became inevitable, specifically from 1810.

After the reform of the line infantry, on the basis of a Supreme Rescript to Barclay de Tolly dated 12 [24] October, 1810,[21] the Russian army had the following composition:

Infantry	Battalions
Lifeguard: four regiments, two battalions (Lifeguard Finland, Lifeguard Marines)	15
Line: 141 regiments, two (training) battalions	425
Total:	440
Cavalry	Squadrons
Lifeguard: six regiments, one Sotnia	29
Line: 58 regiments	370
Total:	399
Artillery	Companies
Lifeguard: Foot Battalion, Horse Artillery	6
Line: 26 brigades, 130 artillery companies, 20 pontoon companies	150
Total:	156
Engineering Troops	Battalions
Two pioneer regiments	6

The infantry regiments were on a three-battalion establishment, with the exception of the Lifeguard Preobrazhensky, which had four battalions. Each battalion consisted of four companies. In the event of war, only the 1st and 3rd (field) battalions were to be sent on campaign from the line regiments; the 2nd (replacement) battalions were to be left in quarters to provide replacement manning to the field battalions, with the exception of the grenadier [flank] companies of the 2nd battalions, from which it was intended to form combined grenadier battalions (two

---

20   For a description of the theatre of operations, see Appendix V.
21   Complete Collection of Laws of the Russian Empire, Vol. XXXI, p. 420.

battalions on a three-company establishment in each division). Of the cavalry, all the Lifeguard regiments had a five-squadron establishment, except for the Lifeguard Cossacks, which had three squadrons. In the line cavalry, the cuirassier and dragoon regiments consisted of five squadrons, while the ulans and hussars had ten squadrons. The latter were divided into two battalions each. In the event of war, it was intended to send four squadrons from each of the Lifeguard, cuirassier and dragoon regiments, and from each lancer and hussar battalion; the remainder, nominated as replacements, were intended to remain in quarters and send drafts to the field squadrons.[22] Each battery [heavy] company had four half-*Pud* [18-pounder] Licornes [gun-howitzers], four 12-pounder cannon of medium weight and four of light weight; in light companies: four 12-pounder Licornes and eight six-pounder cannon; in horse companies: six 12-pounder Licornes and six six-pounder cannon.

On the basis of the establishment tables, in the Lifeguard infantry, the total number of men in a battalion was 764, while in the line it was 738; in the Lifeguard squadrons 160; in the line 150. The total numbers in the regular forces of the Russian army, at the end of 1810 stood at 400,000 to 420,000 men with 1,552 guns.

In 1810 and 1811, our armed forces were increased with newly formed units: the Lifeguard Finland Battalion was transformed into a three-battalion regiment.[23] One of the battalions of the Lifeguard Preobrazhensky Regiment became the cadre for the Lifeguard Lithuania Regiment.[24] A third training battalion, for grenadiers, was formed.[25] Thirteen new line regiments and several internal garrison battalions and half-battalions were formed from 52 garrison battalions;[26] the 27th Infantry Division was re-constituted with six regiments;[27] in general, the line infantry was increased by 23 regiments (including the regiments of Marines). The Lifeguard cavalry was increased by the formation of the Lifeguard Black Sea *Sotnia*;[28] two line cuirassier regiments were re-established.[29] The Lifeguard Horse Artillery was divided into two batteries;[30] the Lifeguard Artillery Battalion was renamed the Lifeguard Artillery Brigade;[31] the Lifeguard Reserve Artillery Company was renamed 1st Training Company,[32] and in 1812 a second training company was formed. Finally, the field artillery was greatly increased through the formation of new companies.

Thereafter, at the beginning of 1812, the Russian army had the following strength:

---

22 Complete Collection of Laws of the Russian Empire, Vol. XLIII, Pt. II, p. 153.
23 19 [31] October 1811. Complete Collection of Laws of the Russian Empire, Vol. XXXI, p. 876.
24 7 [19] November 1811. Complete Collection of Laws of the Russian Empire, Vol. XXXI, p. 903.
25 16 [28] July 1811. Complete Collection of Laws of the Russian Empire, Vol. XLIII, Pt. II, p. 278.
26 17 [29] January 1811. See Supreme Orders
27 6 [18] November 1811, Supreme Decree addressed to the War Ministry.
28 18 [30] May 1811. Schedule of forces.
29 12 [24] October 1811.
30 2 [14] September 1811. Schedule of forces.
31 In October 1811. Schedule of forces.
32 22 February [6 March] 1811. Complete Collection of Laws of the Russian Empire, Vol. XXXVII, p. 198.

Infantry	Battalions
Lifeguard: six regiments, one battalion (Lifeguard Finland, Lifeguard Marines)	19
Line: 164 regiments including Marines	492
Grenadier training battalions	3
Total:	514
Cavalry	Squadrons
Lifeguard: six regiments, two *Sotnia*	30
Line: 60 regiments	380
Total:	410
Artillery	Companies
Lifeguard: four foot companies, two horse companies	6
Line: 27 field brigades	81
Ten reserve brigades	40
Four replacement brigades	32
Total:	159[33]
Engineering Troops	Battalions
Two pioneer regiments	6

The grand total of all these troops, by 11 [23] June, 1812, according to the establishment tables, not counting training and garrison troops, and twelve infantry regiments re-formed from recruits by Supreme command dated 1 [13] May, 1812, some 480,000 men with 1,600 guns. They were composed of: Lifeguard infantry and cavalry divisions and a Lifeguard artillery brigade; 27 infantry, two cuirassier and eight cavalry divisions; 27 field, ten reserve and four replacement artillery brigades. The training troops and pioneer regiments were not subordinated to divisions.

A significant part of the Russian forces were deployed throughout the entire area of the empire's borders. Thus, at the very moment when Napoleon was ready to invade our lands, the Army of Moldavia (later Army of the Danube), under General Kutuzov's command, consisted of 6th Division and 7th Cavalry Division; 8th Division, 9th Division, 10th Division, 15th Division, 16th Division and 22nd Division, with the exception of eight battalions from 9th Division, and contained 87,000 men. In the Crimea and the Novorossiya sectors, under the command of the duc de Richelieu [Armand-Emmanuel-Sophie-Septimanie de Vignerot du Plessis, duc de Richelieu], there were: 8th Cavalry Division, 13th Division and eight replacement battalions from 9th Division 19,500 men, in total. On the Caucasus Line, under the command of Lieutenant General Rtishchev [Nikolay Fëdorovich Rtishchev], was a single dragoon regiment and four infantry regiments from 19th Division, with a total of 10,000 men (within this formation there were garrison regiments on field establishment: Vladikavkaz, Astrakhan, Kizlyar and a battalion of the Mozdok). In

---

33   Of these, only 133½ companies had managed to form up in 1811. A brief overview of the state of Russian artillery from 1798 to 1848. Artillery Journal, 1852.

Georgia, under Lieutenant General Marquis Paulucci's [Philip Osipovich Paulucci] command were, two dragoon regiments, 20th Division and part of 19th Division for a total of 24,000 men. In Finland, under Lieutenant General Steinheil's [Faddey Fëdorovich Steinheil] command, two dragoon regiments, 6th Division, 21st Division and 25th Division, with a total of 30,000 men. In Moscow, the 27th Division was being reformed, with a total of 8,000 men. The training troops, pioneers and reserve artillery, not subordinated to divisions, had 12,000 men. Therefore, there were 280,000 men assembled near the western borders of Russia, or 200,000 men, not including replacement battalions and squadrons.

These troops were intended to form two armies: First and Second Western (First Army and Second Army), while from the replacement (2nd) and reserve (formed in recruitment depots) battalions and squadrons three armies were to be formed: First Reserve Army, Second Reserve Army and Third Army of Observation. The latter plan could not be executed, and therefore the replacement and reserve battalions and squadrons were either incorporated or used at various locations within the empire. Part of Second Army was detached in order to form Third Army, which was intended to cover Volhynia.

Reserves For The Field Armies:
The replacement (2nd) battalions of infantry regiments and replacement (5th or 9th and 10th) squadrons of cavalry regiments of the field armies, excluding 12 battalions and 16 squadrons forming General Saken's Corps [Fabian Wilhelmovich Osten-Saken], served as the foundation of the reserves (some 35,000 men in total). These troops were located along the Western Dvina [Daugava], Berezina, Dnieper and at Mozyr on the Pripet.[34]

The second element of the reserves were recruitment depots. This part of the armed forces was established in 1808 and reformed in 1811, when the latest recruits were housed in these depots. Subsequently, all the depots of the field army were arranged in three lines: the first, which consisted of 19 depots, stretched from Staraya Russa through Toropets, Vyazma, Roslavl, Starodub and Konotop to Olviopol [Pervomaisk, Mykolaiv *Oblast*]; on the same line, artillery depots were established, additionally at Starodub and Konotop, and in Pskov and Smolensk. The second line of nine depots, proceeded from Petrozavodsk, via Novgorod, Tver, Moscow, Kaluga, Orël, Kursk and Kharkov, towards Yeketerinoslav [Dnipro].[35] In addition to these depots, five more were established: in Kargopol and Olonets to provide manning for units in Finland; in Ivanovsk, near Slovyanoserbsk, supporting 13th Division, stationed in Odessa and the Crimea; in Taganrog and Azov, for the troops deployed along the Caucasus Line and in Georgia. From the recruits gathered at the depots, the following were formed: 4th (reserve) battalions for infantry regiments, of three companies each, numbering 500 men; 6th (reserve) squadrons for cuirassier and dragoon regiments, 11th and 12th squadrons for regiments of light cavalry, of 150 men, and 29 artillery companies; in March 1812 orders were issued to form 18 new

---

34   Bernhardi. *Denkwürdigkeiten des Grafen v. Toll*, I, 238-239.
35   10 [22] September 1811. Complete Collection of Laws of the Russian Empire, Vol. XXXI, p. 835 and 836, Vol. XLIII, Pt. II, p. 359.

infantry divisions from the 2nd or replacement battalions (less flank companies) and the 4th or reserve battalions, and eight new cavalry divisions from the replacement and reserve squadrons; throughout 1812, the artillery of the field army was increased by 25 companies formed by the four artillery depots.[36]

The replacement and reserve battalions and squadrons for the most part served, as already mentioned, to supply drafts to the battalions and squadrons of the field army, which, before retreating to the Tarutino position, had received 46,000 infantry and 9,300 cavalry from all the aforementioned and newly established depots.[37]

Reserve Artillery Parks:
To supply the troops with ammunition, 58 reserve parks were established, located in three lines, as follows:

1st Line Parks	2nd Line Parks	3rd Line Parks
Supporting Count Wittgenstein's I Corps 1st & 2nd in Dünaburg.	8 parks (21st – 28th) in Pskov (with ½ 15th Pontoon Coy)	8 parks (40th – 47th) in Novgorod (with ½ 15th Pontoon Coy)
Supporting First Army 3rd, 4th, 5th, in Dünaburg (with these five parks were 12th & ½ of 13th Pontoon Companies). 6th, 7th, 8th, in Vilna (with ¾ of 19th Pontoon Coy). 9th in Nesvizh (with ¼ of 19th Pontoon Coy). 10th & 11th in Bobruisk (with ½ 13th Pontoon Coy).	29th & 30th in Smolensk (with the garrison coy). 31st from Bryansk.	48th & 49th in Smolensk from Moscow (with a garrison coy). 9 parks (50th – 58th) in Bryansk & Shostka from Kaluga.
Supporting Second Army & Third Army of Observation 12th, 13th, 14th in Poland (with 20th Pontoon Coy). 15th, 16th, 17th, 18th, 19th, 20th, in Kiev (with 14th & half 22nd Pontoon Coys).	32nd, 33rd, 34th from Bryansk (with a garrison coy). 35th, 36th, 37th, 38th, 39th in Shostka (with ½ 22nd Pontoon Coy) & powder mill.	
1st line total of 20 parks.	19 parks in the 2nd line.	19 parks in the 3rd line.

The parks of the 1st line (mobile) contained a complete load of charges, cartridges, spare flints and laboratory supplies and were equipped with carts and horses; while

---

36   Complete Collection of Laws of the Russian Empire, Vol. XXXII, p. 229 and 231. Schedule of forces for 1812.
37   Bernhardi, I, 239.

the 2nd and 3rd lines (static) had no carts or horses. The charges, cartridges and laboratory supplies for the first-line parks were replenished from the second-line ones, where there were teams of artillerymen preparing charges and cartridges from laboratory materials, and there were ready-made shells, spikes, coats and ignition tubes. Finally, the parks of the 3rd line contained just the raw materials. Horses for the parks of the 1st line (534 for each) were collected before the start of hostilities, 500 from each recruiting site, in each of the Governorates: Ostsee, Belorussia, Western and Malorussia. The transportation of ammunition from the parks of the 2nd and 3rd lines was intended to be carried out on peasant carts.

In addition to these 58 parks, there were also those belonging to the Army of Moldavia (Danube), in Finland, on the Caucasus Line and in Georgia.

From a report by the Inspector of Artillery, Baron Meller-Zakomelsky [Pëtr Ivanovich Meller-Zakomelsky], from a directed Supreme order, dated 22 July [3 August], 1812, No. 1313, it is clear that there was gunpowder in parks, at recruitment depots and in fortresses at that time, in the following amounts:

In the parks of all three lines, together with the parks in Moldavia and Finland: 296,580 prepared artillery charges and 44 million live cartridges, in which there was some 50,362 *Pud* [1 *Pud* = 16.4 kilogrammes or 36.1 pounds] of gunpowder.

Gunpowder: in Siberia 15,458 *Pud*, in Kazan 5,243 *Pud*, in other locations 293,516 *Pud*, for a total of 314,217 *Pud*.

Throughout the summer, it was intended to prepare: at state-owned gunpowder factories, 47,000 *Pud*, while in Moscow, in private factories, 8,659, all in all 55,659 *Pud*.

Consequently, by November 1812, there would have been, all in all, 420,238 *Pud* of gunpowder.[38]

During the initial deployment of the Russian armies on the western borders of the Empire, the main magazines were located in Vilna, Sventsiany [Švenčionys], Kołtyniany [Kaltanėnai],[39] Grodno, Slonim, Slutsk, Pinsk, Mozyr, Brest, Kovel, Lutsk, Dubno, Zaslavl [Zaslawye], Stary Konstantinov [Starokonstantynów] and Ostrog; and later in Riga, Dünaburg, Drissa, Sebezh, Velizh, Bobruisk, Rogachev, Zhytomyr, Kiev, Novgorod, Velikiye Luki, Kaluga, Trubchevsk and Sosnytsia. In general, the magazines were arranged along the routes leading from the Neman to St Petersburg, Moscow and Kiev. In the first instance there was prepared: more than 600,000 *Chetvert* [1 *Chetvert* = 110 litres or 5¾ bushels] of flour; more than 56,000 *Chetvert* of groats; some 800,000 *Chetvert* of oats.[40]

---

38 Extracted from General Buturlin's papers. Archive of the M.T.D. No. 32,417. Orders from the Minister of War to the Inspector General of Artillery, General Meller-Zakomelsky, dated 29 May [10 June], 1811 No. 477. Report on directed Supreme order to the Inspector of Artillery, dated 22 July [3 August] 1812, No. 1313. Information held in the Archive of the M.T.D. No. 46,692.

39 15 *Versts* north-west of Sventsiany

40 'A summary of stocks by Supreme Command,' signed by *Proviantmeister-General* Laba [Nikolay Osipovich Laba]. In the Archive of the M.T.D. No. 32,417. Report by Field Marshal

The rations for the Russian army, at the time of the impending war, were expected to be provided by reserve magazines established in the border governorates, on probable lines of operations, every eight stages. This method of positioning the magazines was absolutely fundamental, because, in anticipation of a hostile invasion, it was necessary to keep the forces constantly concentrated. But in the detail of the location of the magazines, one cannot fail to notice important mistakes: the magazines were too large and were very far from one another, which, on the one hand, made it difficult to deliver supplies to the troops, while on the other hand, the potential loss of any one of these magazines would have harmful consequences. In addition, we lacked bakeries and did not issue any advance orders regarding the baking. In order to form a mobile magazine, it was intended to collect carts from the countryside, but there was not enough time for this, and some of the collected carts went to the enemy. Thereafter – some time later – a mobile magazine was arranged from tent carts and other regimental transport and from pontoon wagons. Our biggest mistake was the lack of procurement along the upper reaches of the Dvina and Dnieper, also in Smolensk and on the road to Moscow; even on the road to St Petersburg, little was found at full readiness. It had been arbitrarily decided to continue the retreat, once started, only as far as the Dvina; but once we were forced subsequently to retreat further, then the resources gathered to provision the army were insufficient. Even before the enemy invasion crossed our borders, due to the high cost of stores, it was intended to collect them by requisitioning methods in our own provinces, while it also allowed the troops to take the necessary supplies against a receipt. Of these two measures, requisitioning was unsuccessful, due to the novelty of the system, due to a host of opposition and due to a lack of the necessary energy in its execution; and therefore the troops, on the retreat to Drissa, mostly contented themselves with taking supplies from the population, against receipts, without any assistance from the quartermasters.

In general, all our initial preparations were of little use once operations began, precisely because they had been collected at too few locations, in too large amounts. Fortunately, a significant portion of the stores were used up by the troops even before the start of the war; some magazines were removed during the retreat; the rest were burned. Only the loss of the magazine established in Kołtyniany was painful.

From the time of the retreat from Drissa, our troops were content initially with supplies drawn from the magazines there, and later with provisions originating from suppliers on the enemy bank of the Dvina. But once the army moved further up the Dvina, to block the route to Moscow, then rather painful shortages were suffered for some time, because there were no magazines along this route, and there was no way to collect supplies from the countryside. It was necessary to resort to all sorts of improvised measures, and the countryside suffered greatly, although the Commander-in-Chief had not intended its deliberate devastation.

In the meantime, they began to work on another, highly effective measure, which may be referred to as a universal levy on food supplies. Every inhabitant around Smolensk was obliged to provide a set amount of hard-tack, cereals and, for some,

---

Count Barclay de Tolly for the war of 1812-1814. For more detail, see Appendix VI.

oats: all this was transported to the army on local carts, transferred into larger carts, which, from time to time, received latest orders on where they should go. Such extraordinary alternative methods brought tangible benefits from the time of the Battle of Borodino and gave the army the opportunity to remain for so long at Tarutino, without suffering shortages, because by then the resupply had become very successful. As the army approached Moscow, then supplies were sent from there to meet the troops. Moreover, local requisitions were made and large carts drawn by horses and oxen arrived in time, sent from distant governorates and loaded with supplies for the army. At the same time, herds of cattle, assigned for slaughter, had arrived; but despite this, the troops mainly used meat from local cattle. Green fodder and hay were obtained, for the most part, through foraging, as it was difficult to get it by other means. In the opinion of Count Kankrin, if our army had been concentrated near Tarutino other than in the summer or autumn, when it was possible to get grass, and the peasants reserves had not yet been depleted, then we could not have stayed for so long at this strategic point.

Independent corps and detachments were resupplied in a similar manner. However, the army that arrived from Moldavia, which was subjected to fewer difficulties, had a large mobile magazine (made up of local carts), which lagged behind the troops initially, but later brought great benefits.

This state of affairs changed completely once the retreating enemy was pursued. The path of their retreat ran through devastated countryside, where the strong vanguard, assigned to the direct pursuit, could barely find even the poorest food. The main Russian army, although in a single column alongside roads parallel to the enemy's retreat, nevertheless, the diminishing number of troops and the freshness of the countryside, which was poor only in bread, but did not suffer a shortage of either meat or forage, eased the difficulty. At the beginning of the pursuit, the military authorities strongly insisted on the rapid advance of the resupply convoy, but it soon fell far behind the army. Whereupon requisitions were made in neighbouring significant towns and orders were issued to deliver the collected supplies to the army via converging routes; but many places were poor, and the carts could not keep pace. The main obstruction to all the other carts was the excessively large artillery reserve, which followed along with the army to the Dnieper.

Subsequently, orders were sent, forwards and to the flanks, for the villagers to hold a certain amount of grain in readiness in each house, which was of great benefit. Eventually, as the army lagged behind the enemy and spread out to the flanks, then officials were sent ahead with teams to procure bread baked by the inhabitants, which was also successful.

The enemy magazines captured in Vilna and the deployment of troops into quarters in the neighbouring countryside ended this extremely difficult situation for our army.[41]

---

41   Count Kankrin, *Über die Militar-Öconomie*, I, 84-87.

4

The last moments before the War

Continuation of Napoleon's military preparations. – Kutusov's success on the Danube. – Armistice with the Turks. – Political attitudes towards Russia and France by other European states: the Treaty of Alliance between Russia and Sweden; treaties of alliance between Napoleon and Prussia and Austria. – Napoleon's decree on the *Garde nationale*. – The formation of Russian armies on the western borders of the empire. – Instructions given by Napoleon to Chernyshev. – Napoleon's conversation with Prince Kurakin regarding demands to withdraw French troops from Prussia. – Napoleon's departure from Paris for Dresden. – Arrival of Tsar Alexander in Vilna. – The mission given by Napoleon to Comte de Narbonne. – Napoleon's stay in Dresden and Tsar Alexander's in Vilna. – Napoleon's departure from Dresden to the army. – Measures taken by him on the way to the Neman. – His appeal to the troops. – Contemporary rumours regarding Napoleon in Russia.

By the end of 1811, the Emperor of the French was just completing his preparations for the campaign in Russia. The army assembled in northern Germany had been reinforced to 125,000 men. Napoleon could, at this time, put 350,000 men against us. But he postponed the opening of hostilities until the following summer, in order to further strengthen his mobilisation and wait for the grazing needed for the many horses in the French army.[1]

Napoleon hoped that Russia, forced to keep significant forces in the theatre of war in Turkey far from the western borders, would exhaust its resources and would not be able to resist his invasion. But this hope did not come true. Kutuzov, taking advantage of an oversight by the Turks, surrounded their army at Slobodzia, near Ruschuk, and thus forced the Porte to conclude an armistice and open negotiations for peace. Upon being informed of this event, Napoleon lost his temper. He asked: '*Conçoit-on ces chiens, ces gredins de Turcs, qui ont eu le talent de se faire battre de la sorte! Qui est-ce qui aurait pu le prévoir?*'[2] Couriers were immediately sent with dispatches to Constantinople in order to encourage the Porte to continue the

---

1   *Flügel-Adjutant* Chernyshev's report to Count Rumyantsev dated 6 (18) December 1811, in the Archive of the M.F.A.

2   'Can you believe it these dogs, these scoundrels of Turks, who had the talent to be beaten like this! Who could have foreseen it?'

war at all costs, but the Turks, taught by experience, had no intention of fighting as one with the French, but they wished and hoped to take advantage of the tempest coming from the west to make peace with Russia without major concessions.[3] In France, many anxiously awaited the news of the conclusion of peace between Russia and Turkey, believing that this event might prevent a war in the north.[4]

By embarking on the expedition against Russia, Napoleon was trying to win over all the European states neighbouring his homeland to his side. But persuasion by the formidable conqueror was not entirely successful. Sweden, instead of an alliance with France, took the side of Russia; Prussia and Austria acted as could have been expected, as Powers allied to Napoleon by compulsion, while Turkey calmly observed the struggle of the great states, not taking the slightest part in it.

Back in November 1810, Napoleon had forced the Swedish government to declare war on Britain. But not content with this, and wishing to put Sweden under the same dependency on France as the Confederation of the Rhine and Denmark, he demanded that six thousand Swedish sailors be placed at his disposal; King Charles XIII rejected this intimidation, referring to the laws of his state. Thereafter, the French government forced Sweden to introduce the Trianon tariff and to accept French customs officers in Gothenburg. The British, ignoring the declaration of war by the Swedes, did not take any hostile action against their trade; on the contrary, Napoleon, although he was in an alliance with Sweden, nevertheless allowed French privateers to intercept Swedish ships not provided with permits (licenses), to confiscate vessels loaded with food supplies and products of native factories from the Sound, under the pretext that they were intended to be exported to Britain, and to detain Swedish sailors in German harbours. All this aggression was topped off by the invasion of Pomerania and the island of Rügen by a 15,000 strong French corps, in February 1812. Napoleon, hoping by these means to coerce the Swedish government into unconditional obedience, proposed, in a note dated 7 [19] March, to return Pomerania to the Swedes but demanded on their part that they:

1. Sever all communications with the British with the strictest enforcement.
2. Place a 30,000 or 40,000 strong army facing Russia, simultaneously with operations by French troops.

In return, Napoleon promised that Sweden would get Finland back.[5] The response to this note was the conclusion of an alliance between Russia and Sweden, in St Petersburg, on 24 March (5 April):

1. Both Powers vouched for the mutual integrity of their territories.
2. It was agreed to send a corps of troops, numbering from 25,000 to 30,000 Swedes and from 15,000 to 20,000 Russians to the coast of Germany, opposing France and their allies.

---

3   Chernyshev's report, dated 6 (18) December 1811. Thiers, *Histoire du Consulat et de l'Empire*. *Ed. de Brux*. XIII, 113.
4   Chernyshev's report, dated 6 (18) December 1811.
5   General Sukhtelen's report to the Tsar, dated 18 [30] March 1812.

3. This landing was to be preceded by the annexation of Norway to Sweden, by agreement with the Danish government, or by force of arms: in the first case, they intended to offer the Danish king compensation in Germany; in the event of his refusal, hostilities would be opened against Denmark using combined forces.
4. Upon the annexation of Norway to Sweden, the allied army was intended to invade Germany.
5. The King of Great Britain would be invited to take part in the alliance by the Contracting Powers.[6]

The situation in Prussia since the Treaty of Tilsit had been disastrous. This state, surrounded on three sides by Davout's forces, Saxony and the Duchy of Warsaw, containing strong French garrisons in its three fortresses, disarmed by the mistrustful conqueror and devastated by innumerable extortions and reparations, throbbed for its independence. Napoleon more than once expressed his intention to weaken Prussia even more. The French foreign minister, speaking on one occasion with the Prussian resident in Paris, General Krusemark [Friedrich Wilhelm Ludwig von Krusemarck], about the difficulties the Prussian government had regarding the payment of the indemnity imposed by Napoleon, hinted at the cession of Silesia.[7] Then, in a report to Emperor Napoleon by the Minister of Foreign Affairs, Champagny, it was claimed that an alliance with Prussia might deliver no more than 30,000 or 40,000 unreliable troops for France; whereas the occupation of Prussia by armed force would make it possible to exploit the rich resources of the best provinces of this state.[8]

The King of Prussia expected salvation for his monarchy to come solely from Tsar Alexander. Back in July 1811, General Scharnhorst had been sent to St Petersburg, with a proposal – to conclude a defensive treaty of alliance between Russia and Prussia. The King hoped that his determination would force the Russian government to immediately conclude peace with the Porte, send all armed forces to our western borders and draw closer to Austria: these measures would completely protect Prussia from attempts by Napoleon on their existence; but as current circumstances did not allow us to end the war with the Turks, nor to induce Austria into an alliance with Russia, Friedrich Wilhelm, was troubled by justified fears for the future of his state, and terrified by the invasion of Swedish Pomerania by French troops, did not dare to take the side of Russia. As Napoleon and Tsar Alexander were mobilising, the situation for Prussia, squeezed by huge forces from all sides, became more and more dangerous. The King of Prussia, foreseeing that it was impossible for him to remain neutral in the clash between his powerful neighbours, offered Tsar Alexander his mediation; but the Tsar rejected this, not wanting to give grounds to thoughts of a cooling of the alliance between Russia and France, and notified the French government of the proposal made to him. Napoleon, in gratitude for such

---

6   *Hist. génér. des traités de paix, par Garden*. XIII, 214-215.
7   Prince Kurakin's dispatches dated 8 (20) February 1810, in the Archive of the M.F.A.
8   The Duc de Cadore's report dated 16 November (new style) 1810, in the Archive of the M.F.A.

a frank revelation, expressed his displeasure to the Prussian resident in Paris. He remarked: 'I do not understand why Tsar Alexander did not agree to your mediation. Your king's letter was shown to my representative with disdain.'[9]

Napoleon, by acting in this manner, had the intention of embroiling Tsar Alexander with the King of Prussia, but did not achieve his aim. The mutual trust and friendship between the Monarchs remained unchanged. Nevertheless, the King, seeing himself and his subjects in the hands of Napoleon, invited him to conclude a treaty of alliance, on the basis of which Prussia undertook to put an auxiliary corps at the disposal of the French government, such that Napoleon would vouch for the integrity and independence of Prussian territory. Napoleon, concealing his intent, replied that the king's proposal was incompatible with the relationship between France and Russia. Friedrich Wilhelm was forced to plead, as a favour, until Napoleon agreed to his assistance in the war against Tsar Alexander. Napoleon hesitated a long time before responding, and the king, in despair, was already preparing to mobilise against the French himself; but, in the meantime, the French government became more accommodating towards Prussia. The consequence of this was the conclusion, on 12 (24) February, 1812, of several treaties between the French and Prussian governments, in Paris.

On the basis of the first defensive treaty, both Powers pledged to provide each other with assistance in any war, mutually vouched for the integrity of their territories and closed their harbours to neutral shipping that had any kind of contact with the British.

Under a secret treaty, a defensive and offensive alliance was concluded for any war, except in those cases where France might conduct a war beyond the Pyrenees, in Italy, or in Turkey.

According to a secret convention signed on the same day, 24 February [new style], it was decided that Prussia, in the event of a war with Russia, by 15 March, would deploy an auxiliary corps of 20,000 men, with 60 guns, a double issue of ammunition and 10 or 20 days' supply of food. It was agreed that Prussia should have 18,000 troops garrisoned at Kolberg [Kołobrzeg], Potsdam, Graudenz and fortresses in Silesia, independently of this corps. The Prussian government pledged not to begin any conscription, or any troop concentrations and military movements, while the French army was in Prussian or in enemy territory. Finally, in the event of success in a war against Russia, Napoleon pledged to reward Prussia with an increase to their territory.

We consider it not superfluous to note that Napoleon, in addition to the three fortresses on the Oder, which he occupied with his troops on the basis of previous treaties, ordered the establishment of French garrisons in the fortresses of Pillau [Baltijsk] and Spandau, only because they had been omitted when calculating which fortresses were to be occupied by the Prussian army.

At the same time, two more conventions were concluded: in the first, measures were agreed for planning against Britain, while in the second, Prussia was assigned

---

9   Count Lieven's dispatches dated 20 January (1 February) 1812. *Flügel-Adjutant* Chernyshev's letter dated 12 January (new style) 1812, in the Archive of the M.F.A.

and entrusted to issue significant provisioning to the French army as it moved through their territory.[10]

Although Austria had suffered significant losses under the treaties concluded in Pressburg and Vienna, they were in an incomparably more advantageous position than Prussia. Without a doubt, the Austrian government could remain neutral, not taking part in the struggle between the two Powers, to whom they had been obliged to take repeated assistance from one in the wars, while being united to the other through the alliance of Napoleon and the daughter of the Austrian Emperor. But Austria, in its political relations, was guided neither by chivalrous feelings of gratitude for services rendered, nor by the family ties of its sovereigns. Convinced of Napoleon's invincibility through their own experience, the Austrian government did not doubt he would triumph over Russia and did not dare to deny him their assistance; on the other hand, accepting the possibility that Napoleon might fail, it was not difficult to foresee that Tsar Alexander's own interests would force him, in the event of success against Napoleon, to seek an alliance with Austria.

On the basis of such considerations, which were later justified in fact, Kaiser Franz found it more advantageous to act in alliance with Napoleon against Russia than to remain neutral. On 2 (14) March 1812, a treaty was signed with the following content: the allied Powers mutually vouched for the integrity of their territories; pledged to support one another with a 30,000 strong corps of troops with 60 guns; undertook to protect the integrity of the Ottoman Porte's territory; the Austrian Kaiser renewed the terms of observing the prohibitive system against Britain; finally, this treaty of alliance could neither be made public, nor be made known to any of the Courts, without the consent of both contracting Powers.

On the basis of the specific secret treaty, Austria was exempted from an obligation to participate in wars between France and Britain or beyond the Pyrenees, but made a promise, in the event of a war with Russia, to call up the aforementioned auxiliary corps, which was intended to come under the command of an Austrian general and, acting on the basis of orders from His Majesty the Emperor of the French, was to remain at full strength. Napoleon pledged to keep Galicia for Austria, even if Poland were to be restored. If the Austrian Kaiser found it more advantageous to return part of Galicia to any Polish kingdom in exchange for the Illyrian provinces, the Emperor of the French pledged to agree to that. In the event of a successful end to the war, Napoleon promised to deliver such an increase in territory to the Austrian Kaiser that it would not only compensate him for the sacrifices and losses associated with war, but would also serve as a reminder of the sincere and permanent alliance between the two sovereigns. Finally, it was agreed to invite Turkey to participate in the alliance.[11]

It is quite remarkable that neither Prussia nor Austria declared war on Russia.

Meanwhile, negotiations between Russia and the Ottoman Porte continued without a definitive outcome. Tsar Alexander, wishing to hasten the conclusion of peace with the Turks, in order to direct all his armed forces to the western borders of the Empire, through a Supreme Rescript dated 18 February [1 March], 1812, ordered

---

10   *Hist. génér. des traités de paix, par Garden*. XIII, 220-238.

11   Garden, XIII, 244-245.

the duc de Richelieu to sail from Odessa to Constantinople with a powerful landing force. To that end, 9th Infantry Division, 12th Infantry Division and 13th Infantry Division were to concentrate around Odessa. But shortly thereafter, the danger to our fatherland from the west forced all the troops assigned for the landing to move towards this threat. Russia was forced to moderate its demands and concluded the Peace of Bucharest, on 16 [28] May, 1812, on the basis of which the borders of the empire were moved from the Dniester to the Prut and the Danube.

Napoleon, having turned almost all of Europe against Russia, realised that the usual measures for manning the army through annual conscription were insufficient and resorted to an emergency remedy. The entire population of France capable of military service, formed a *Garde nationale* for the empire, divided into three categories (*bans*): firstly, from all men from 20 to 26 years of age left over from the conscription; secondly, from all healthy males aged 26 to 40, and thirdly (*arrière-ban*), from healthy males aged 40 to 60. One hundred cohorts from the first category, numbering about 112,000 men, were immediately placed at the disposal of the Minister of War.[12]

By the end of February [early March], the Russian troops located on our western borders were divided into two armies (First Army and Second Army) and two independent corps (Right Flank and Observation), which later became I Corps of First Army while Third Army was formed in April.

On our side, it was intended to launch offensive operations by crossing the borders of the empire, as soon as enemy troops crossed over to the right bank of the Oder; but this plan was abandoned as soon as intelligence was received about the treaty of alliance between France and Austria.[13]

Simultaneously with the troop movements by Tsar Alexander and Napoleon, negotiations continued.[14]

The Emperor of the French, having summoned *Flügel-Adjutant* Chernyshev on 13 (25) February, expressed his displeasure at the failure of the Russian government to fulfil their Treaty of Tilsit obligations; he criticised our Tsar for hostility towards France, regretted Count Nesselrode's [Karl Vasilevich Nesselrode] failure to visit Paris for negotiations (as agreed between the two governments), assured him that he did not want war, and, in conclusion, sent Chernyshev to St Petersburg with a proposal to renew friendly relations on the following terms:

1. The precise execution of the Treaty of Tilsit and all measures against British trade, facilitating only the export of native products, in exchange for imported goods, that is, by adopting a system of permissions (licenses) which would not be beneficial to the British, but would help the Poles and other Powers, which is not at all contrary to the objectives implicit in the introduction of the continental system.

---

12 Prince Kurakin's dispatches dated 1 and 4 (13 and 16) March 1812, in the Archive of the M.F.A.
13 Tsar Alexander's handwritten orders to Barclay de Tolly, dated 7 [19] April 1812, in the Classified Archives of the General Staff Department.
14 For the personal correspondence between Alexander and Napoleon, see Appendix VII.

2. The conclusion of a commercial treaty or convention, which, in accordance with the tariff introduced in Russia, would eliminate everything that is offensive to the French government.
3. An agreement on the Duchy of Oldenburg, which would wipe away the unpleasant perceptions produced by the protest, and would consist either in a refusal of any compensation, or by defining it, to the exclusion of Danzig or any other part of the Duchy of Warsaw.[15]

These proposals were made by Napoleon solely in order to gain the time necessary for the completion of his military preparations. Even on the eve of the conversation with Chernyshev, as has already been mentioned, an agreement was concluded with Prussia. The Russian ambassador in Paris, in his report to Tsar Alexander, speaking of the inevitability of war with Napoleon, considered it useful for us to conclude an alliance with Sweden and to make peace with Britain, which would not only bring us important benefits in relation to trade and raise our exchange, while, through the actions of its fleet, would induce Turkey to make peace with Russia.

It is quite remarkable that in this dispatch, Prince Kurakin's opinion regarding the method of waging war against Napoleon is the same. Whereas Russia was protected from enemy invasion solely by the chests of its defenders; while Napoleon was preparing to wage a war 2,000 *Versts* [1 *Verst* = 1,067metres or ⅔ Statute Mile] from his borders, covered by several lines of fortresses, Prince Kurakin suggested: act with all possible caution, avoid decisive battles, restrict ourselves to a *guerilla* war, exactly as in Spain, and wipe out the huge masses directed against us by denying them provisions.[16]

Such an opinion, expressed by a person who was not a military man and who had only a general, superficial understanding of the conduct of a war, most convincingly shows that the need to retreat inland, when acting against the huge forces led by Napoleon, had been recognised by many in our country even before the start of the war, while it was by no means a consequence of suggestions by Wollzogen and Knesebeck [Karl Friedrich von dem Knesebeck], as some foreign authors have tried to assert.

Throughout April, Napoleon's corps which had been held back, were sent to reinforce the troops at the front. *1er Corps, 2e Corps, 3e Corps, 6e Corps, 7e Corps* and *8e Corps*, as well as *1er Corps de Cavalerie* and *2e Corps de Cavalerie*, were directed through Prussian territory and crossed the Oder; *4e Corps* and *3e Corps de Cavalerie* proceeded from Italy via Tyrol and Austrian territory, into the Duchy of Warsaw, where the Polish troops of *5e Corps* and *4e Corps de Cavalerie* also gathered on the Vistula. *10e Corps* was deployed between Danzig and Königsberg. The Austrian Corps was concentrated in Galicia. Napoleon's *Garde* was directed to march from Paris to Dresden. *9e Corps* remained in reserve between the Elbe and the Oder. *11e Corps* was forming up in the area of Mainz. In early [mid] May the French *Grande Armée* arrived on the Vistula.

Tsar Alexander, wishing to preserve the peace and deciding to make new proposals to achieve this aim, ordered Prince Kurakin to hand Napoleon a letter

---

15   *Flügel-Adjutant* Chernyshev's report to Tsar Alexander in the Archive of the M.F.A.
16   Report to Tsar Alexander dated 19 (31) March 1812, in the Archive of the M.F.A.

from Him, in which he expressed his consent to the Duke of Oldenburg's acceptance of another territory and to lower our tariffs in favour of French trade, but at the same time demanded that Napoleon's troops should be withdrawn from Prussia and the garrison in Danzig be reduced in order to avoid any grounds for a clash between Russia and France.

Napoleon, having received the Russian ambassador, told him that he regretted the time that was lost in vain discussions, solely because our resident did not have the authority to conclude an agreement. Napoleon continued: 'Instead of agreeing with me, you armed yourselves and forced me to do likewise. I shall not conceal from you that I am completely prepared. My troops are on the Vistula... The Duc de Bassano told me that you want to force me to evacuate Prussia. I cannot do that. Your demands are insulting. You are coming at me with a knife. My honour will not allow me to grant your wish. You, a noble man, make an offer such as this!.. Let us negotiate. Let us agree among ourselves on our mutual requirements.'

Prince Kurakin replied that, before any discussions, we had to ensure that the primary condition proposed by the Tsar would be fulfilled, the evacuation of Prussia and the reduction of the Danzig garrison.

Napoleon interrupted: 'You behave like the Prussians before the Battle of Jena: they demanded that I withdraw my troops from Germany. And now, as then, I cannot agree to the evacuation of Prussia. This is a matter of my honour.'

Our ambassador continued: 'But Your Majesty, you yourself admitted, together with Tsar Alexander, that for the strength of the alliance between Russia and France, it was necessary to preserve independent territories in the space between them: Prussia had to comply with these terms, and the Duchy of Warsaw was given to Saxony for the same reason. Do we not have the right to demand that which, in your Majesty's own opinion, substantially contributes to the preservation of the alliance between the empires: namely, that Prussia would preserve its independence and that the convention concluded with them by Your Majesty would be carried out.'

Napoleon replied: 'I cannot agree to this. We shall negotiate, but do not talk about such demands.'

Prince Kurakin insisted on the need to fulfil the will of his Tsar, and mentioned the tremendous preparations for war by the French government, which had forced Tsar Alexander to take precautions, without any intent towards France.

The Russian ambassador went on: 'But your latest convention with Prussia, a convention whose conditions are no doubt repugnant to the Poles in Russia, because they were not communicated to our government; but the consequences of this convention, evidently revealed by the movement of your armies to the Oder and your advanced troops to the Vistula, place you in a hostile position in relation to us. I have received an order to announce to Your Imperial Majesty's Ministry that the passage of significant forces of the French army across the Oder will be taken as a declaration of war, and that, in this case, offensive operations may be launched by our side, without any other hostile purpose, than solely to occupy positions advantageous for defence.'

Napoleon replied that Davout's corps was already on the Vistula and went on: 'My situation is completely different from yours. My troops are located in lands belonging to me or my allies, the Duchy of Warsaw, as a member territory of the Confederation

of the Rhine, is under my protection. The King of Prussia is my ally. I have a responsibility to protect them. On the contrary, you cannot cross the line of your borders
without breaching the inviolability of other nations' territories... Having received
no reply from Tsar Alexander to my letter sent through Colonel Chernyshev for so
long, I have ordered Davout to be ready to repulse force with force, and Lauriston to
leave St Petersburg with all the residents of the Confederation of the Rhine, at the
first news of the opening of hostilities.'

Whereupon Napoleon said that Marshal Davout had received orders to halt on
the left bank of the Vistula, but then let slip that his troops had moved beyond the
Passarge – as if to exploit the most convenient food supply.

The Russian ambassador noted that: 'It will indeed be difficult to supply a half-
million man army in this country with provisions and fodder, which, according to
Your Majesty, has been assembled against us.'

Napoleon objected: 'Oh! I shall not encounter any difficulties as far as that is
concerned. I have foreseen everything and set up huge magazines in Thorn and
Danzig well in advance. I have nine thousand wagons ready for transporting provisions, and forage will grow under the feet of the horses (*le fourrage naitra sous les
pieds des chevaux*) wherever my cavalry goes... You are unhappy with my agreement
with Prussia. They offered you their mediation; you rejected it. The Prussian king
had no choice but to draw closer to me. Austria also offered you its services and
received a refusal in response...'

Kurakin interjected: 'What! Should I conclude from this speech by your Imperial
Majesty that Austria is also against us?'

Napoleon's response was: 'Yes, without a doubt, if war breaks out, the Austrians
will act in concert with my troops.'

Subsequently, Napoleon criticised our government for not being able to take
advantage of the alliance with France, as it should; he asked if the rumours about
the departure of Tsar Alexander to Vilna were true, and ended the audience,
repeating that he could not meet our demands, adding: 'However, if you have been
ordered to solicit their execution at all costs, turn things around such that I can
accept your terms.'[17]

These last words from Napoleon gave our ambassador some hope for the preservation of peace. But to all his demands for a definitive answer, when meeting with
the Duc de Bassano, he constantly received the same reply, that: 'instructions from
Emperor Napoleon have not yet been issued.' The only consequence of Napoleon's
conversation with Prince Kurakin was the departure of one of the Emperor of the
French's Adjutants-General, Comte de Narbonne [Louis-Marie-Jacques-Amalric de
Narbonne-Lara], from Berlin to St Petersburg, with Napoleon's own handwritten
letter to Tsar Alexander and with a note from the Duc de Bassano, in which the
French minister, outlining the course of misunderstandings between the empires
from his point of view, and offered the means for a mutual agreement. The real
purpose of Narbonne's journey was to observe the actions of the Russian government. Maret wrote to him: 'Your mission has a political and a military objective.

---

17   Prince Kurakin's report dated 15 (27) April 1812 in the Archive of the M.F.A.

To achieve them, you must remain with Tsar Alexander for as long as possible.'
Meanwhile, Napoleon's imminent departure was already well known in Paris, and
therefore Prince Kurakin, wishing to draw a definitive answer from the French
Minister of Foreign Affairs, decided to send a note to him on 25 April (7 May), in
which he wrote that if by the following day consent to the proposals by our government was not received, then he would find it necessary to consider his residence in
Paris completely unnecessary and would be forced to demand his passports in order
to leave France.[18]

But this policy, like all the previous ones, was not successful. The Duc de Bassano
left Paris for Dresden without seeing Prince Kurakin or giving him the required
passports, and on 27 April (9 May) left Saint-Cloud for Dresden as did Napoleon
himself.

Meanwhile, Tsar Alexander, having received news of the advance to Königsberg
by French troops, had gone to the headquarters of First Army, located in Vilna.
After a prayer service by Metropolitan Ambrose [Andrey Ivanovich Podobedov] in
the cathedral of Our Lady of Kazan, on 9 [21] April, at two o'clock in the afternoon,
the Emperor, accompanied by the fervent prayers of thousands of subjects who had
gathered in front of the cathedral, left the capital and arrived in Vilna on 14 (26)
April.

With the person of His Majesty in Vilna there were: princes George von Oldenburg
[Peter Friedrich Georg von Oldenburg] and Alexander von Württemberg, Chancellor
Count Rumyantsev; generals; Count Arakcheev [Alexey Andreevich Arakcheev],
Bennigsen [Leonty Leontevich Bennigsen], Balashev [Alexander Dmitryevich
Balashov], Prince Volkonsky [Peter Mikhailovich Volkonsky] and Count Armfeldt
[Gustav Moritz Armfeldt]; Active Privy Councillor Prince Kochubey [Viktor
Pavlovich Kochubey], Secretary of State Nesselrode and, formerly in Prussian
service, Baron Stein and Major General Phull [Karl Ludwig August Friedrich von
Phull (Pfuel)].[19]

The first two weeks of the Tsar's stay in Vilna, from mid to late April [late April to
early May], were spent reviewing the troops and discussing forthcoming operations;
moreover, Prince Volkonsky was always an active assistant in the Emperor's work.
At the end of April [early May], the Comte de Narbonne appeared, who, instead
of travelling to St Petersburg, arrived in Vilna, on the occasion of the arrival of
Tsar Alexander there. The note delivered to him by the French Foreign Minister
contained the same criticism of the Russian government, on account of alleged non-
compliance with the terms of the Treaty of Tilsit, the protest over the Oldenburg
affair, the concentration of our armed forces on the western border of the empire
and our refusal to continue negotiations, which, allegedly, on the part of Napoleon,
were intended to prevent a hostile clash between Russia and France. In conclusion, it
was said that the Emperor of the French, seeing the failure of his attempts to reconcile with Russia, had been forced to send a note to the British government with a
proposal to open peace negotiations, and that if the note should have favourable
consequences, then Tsar Alexander could take part in negotiations, on the basis of

18   Garden, XIII, 314-316. Prince Kurakin's report dated 26 April (8 May) 1812.
19   Brief Notes by Admiral Shishkov, 2nd Ed. 1832, p. 6-7.

the terms of the Treaty of Tilsit, or as an ally of Britain, if Russia had already entered into relations with them.[20]

Narbonne's visit to Vilna did not manage to achieve the objectives proposed by Napoleon: he was unable to distract the attention of Tsar Alexander, nor to find out anything except that which was given to him intentionally. But Narbonne's mission led many to believe that he would be sent a second time with more definitive proposals. Returning to his master, who, meanwhile, had already arrived in Dresden, Narbonne was forced to admit that the Russians were preparing to repel the attack, were not prematurely triumphant, but also not wallowing in despondency.[21]

Napoleon arrived in Dresden, together with Empress Marie-Louise, on 4 (16) May. The following day, the Austrian Kaiser arrived with his wife, almost all the rulers who belonged to the Confederation of the Rhine, many other noble persons and diplomats, including Metternich and Hardenberg [Karl August von Hardenberg]. The King of Prussia, who was preparing to receive Napoleon in Berlin, received, instead, an invitation to join the throng of crowned guests of the King of Saxony and arrived in Dresden on 14 (26) May. The time Napoleon spent in Dresden was the most glittering period of his reign. Surrounded by rulers who gathered at his call, he was the focus of the hopes and fears of almost all of Europe. Was it possible for him not to get carried away by the dazzling brilliance of the gifts of Fortune, which had subjugated these sovereigns to his whims, whose ancestors had ruled the fate of Germany for several centuries.[22]

At that moment Napoleon and Alexander I presented a great, instructive spectacle! Napoleon, surrounded by German rulers, obedient to his will out of compulsion, until a twist of fate might allow them to turn the weapons honed against Russia, against him. Napoleon, who left France behind him, weary, weakened by victories acquired with the rich blood of their best sons, could not, with all his intuition, see the danger of his situation. It seemed that nothing could resist him; having gathered enormous forces in order to crush the last obstacles to world domination, he threatened Russia with subjugation; as Britain had the conquest of India. Europe, in the expectation of new successes by the brilliant commander, silently awaited the outcome of its fate. Meanwhile, Tsar Alexander, at the head of his people, was preparing to accept Napoleon's challenge, as a test sent down by Providence. Indeed, the war of 1812, having tempered the hearts of the Russians in love for the fatherland, instilled confidence in our own strength in us for a long time.

Tsar Alexander, during his short stay in Vilna, impressed the inhabitants of Lithuania with the graciousness and kindness that were the hallmarks of his character. Many Polish magnates, enchanted by the friendly treatment of the Russian Monarch, suggested that he declare himself the ruler of Poland. Napoleon, fearing that the moral power of Alexander might spread to Warsaw, decided to send a resident there who could oppose the influence of the Russian government with eloquence, splendour, and especially – activity and all kinds of intrigues. Napoleon's choice fell on Pradt [Dominique Frédéric Dufour de Pradt], archbishop of Mechelen

---

20   The Duc de Bessano's note to Count Rumyantsev dated 15 April (new style) 1812.
21   *Mémoires tirés des papiers d'un homme d'état.*1836, IX, 375.
22   Garden. XIII, 358-359.

(Malines). Among the instructions given to him it was stated: 'lead the Poles towards delight, not towards madness.' Almost at the same time (20 May new style), orders were issued to Count Lauriston to go from St Petersburg to Vilna to negotiate, but Tsar Alexander did not give his consent. Neither the orders given to Narbonne by Napoleon, nor Lauriston's proposed visit to the headquarters of the Russian troops, would have been of any consequences: war had already been decided upon in the mind of the Emperor of the French. Immediately upon the Comte de Narbonne's arrival in Dresden, before the courier sent to Lauriston had even reached St Petersburg, Napoleon ordered the advance of his troops to the Russian borders to be accelerated while he left Dresden (28 May new style) himself, via Glogau and Poznań, to Thorn, visited Danzig, where he stayed from 7 to 12 June, announcing that this city was annexed to the territory of the French Empire and moved the *État-major général de la Grande Armée* to Königsberg on 31 May (12 June). Napoleon stayed there for four days, and then continued on his way, through Insterburg [Chernyakhovsk] and Gumbinnen [Gusev, Kaliningrad], to Wilkowischken [Vilkaviškis], where he arrived on 9 (21) June.

Napoleon, in the course of his journey through Prussia and the territory of the Duchy of Warsaw, saw traces of the disasters suffered by the inhabitants of this country from the troops passing through it, and especially from those who, having made the long march from Italy and from the Rhine, suffered shortages of everything and could not survive otherwise than at the expense of the provinces they passed through. The mass of field and regimental artillery assigned to the troops made it extremely difficult to provide forage; while the heavy wagons, introduced instead of the former infantry carts (*caissons d'infanterie*), turned out to be unsuitable for the marshy plains of Poland and therefore were replaced partly by one-horse carts (*voitures à la comtoise*), partly by local carts, bought or taken by force on the way, on the orders of Marshal Davout. The drivers of these carts, from the population of the country, for the most part fled; fighting men were used in their stead, which, from the first step towards the Russian borders, had significantly weakened the army. The bullock carts did not deliver the benefits that were expected of them, due to the slowness of their movement and the huge losses of oxen, which was the result of general illnesses and lack of care. Finally, the transport battalions, composed of recruits who had barely finished their basic military training, were not at all fit for purpose. A straggling multitude of carts blocked the roads, bogging down in the deep ruts carved out by overloaded vehicles, and littering the verges with horse cadavers. In exchange for the dead horses, others were taken from the inhabitants by force, issuing receipts, which had to be redeemed by the Prussian government. Thus, the countryside through which the *Grande Armée* passed was completely devastated, while the cavalry, artillery, and especially the vehicles were already in disorder and had not yet reached the Neman.

To somehow alleviate these disasters, Napoleon took measures to reduce the number of vehicles. Rules were drawn up regarding the number of carts that each of the officials with the army had a right to have with them; reduced headquarters staff and sending many members of the diplomatic corps to Warsaw and Dresden. Orders were issued to prioritise green fodder for all transport horses; the majority of the carts were assigned for the transportation of provisions; finally, all the remaining oxen were distributed to various parts of the force to supply the soldiers with a meat ration.[23] But all these means turned out to be insufficient to provide food for the half-million man army in a sparsely populated country.

Upon arrival in Königsberg, Napoleon completed the orders issued by Marshal Davout for the arrangement of inland navigation, for about 800 *versts*, from Danzig, along two branches of the Vistula, to Elbing [Elbląg], from there through the Frisches Haff to Königsberg, then up the Pregel to Tapiau [Gvardeysk, Kaliningrad], along the Deime [Deyma] to the Kurisches Haff and towards Memel [Klaipėda], and finally up the Neman to Kovno [Kaunas] and along the Viliya [Neris] to Vilna. Orders were issued to dispatch the first cargo immediately, consisting of 20,000 hundredweight of flour, 2,000 hundredweight of rice, 500,000 hard-tack rations, and all materials required for the building of six bridges, the supervision of which was entrusted to the famous engineer General Éblé. This cargo was to be followed by others with provisions, fodder, clothing, footwear and one of the siege parks designated for the advance on Riga. At the same time, hospitals for 20,000 patients were established in Königsberg and on the lower Vistula.[24]

During Napoleon's stay in Gumbinnen, the secretary of the French embassy, Prevost, arrived there from St Petersburg with the news that Lauriston had not received permission from Tsar Alexander to go to Vilna. Napoleon immediately recalled his envoy, gave orders to issue passports to Prince Kurakin, and on the following day upon his arrival in Wilkowischken, 10 (22) June, announced the following appeal in orders for the troops:

> Soldiers! The second Polish war has begun! The first ended at Friedland and at Tilsit, where Russia vowed to maintain an eternal alliance with France and to be at enmity with Britain. They have broken their vow! They do not want to give any explanation for their strange actions until the French Eagles retreat beyond the Rhine, giving them our allies as a sacrifice. Russia is flirting with fate! They shall not escape their destiny. Do they think we have changed? Are we not still the warriors of Austerlitz? They place us between dishonour and war: the choice is beyond question. And so – forwards! Let us cross the Neman, bringing arms into Russia! The second Polish war will be as glorious for France as the first, but the peace that we will conclude will be lasting and put an end to the arrogant five-year influence of Russia on European affairs.

This appeal was issued to all the troops of the *Grande Armée*, with the exception of MacDonald's [Étienne (Jacques-Joseph-Alexandre) Macdonald] Corps, made up mostly of Prussian troops, and the Austrian Corps, which were informed of the opening of hostilities in special orders.[25]

Napoleon did not doubt the complete success of his enterprise; almost everyone around him shared the arrogance of their master; all the generals and officers were

23   Thiers. *Hist. du Consulat et de l'Empire. Ed. de Brux.* XIII, 598-599.
24   Thiers, XIII, 608-611.
25   Garden, XIII, 362-373. Chambray. *Histoire de l'expédition de Russie*, I, 165-167.

looking for an appointment to the *Grande Armée* as a special favour, whose intended exploits were to surpass anything that had been done before. Almost no one gave a thought to the difficulties, the hardships. 'We are going to Moscow, see you soon!' said thousands of those who were destined never to see their homeland again. Only a few expressed their alarming concerns; but these few were: Ségur [Philippe-Paul de Ségur], Caulaincourt, Duroc [Géraud Christophe Michel Duroc] who had studied Russia; they also included: Talleyrand [Charles-Maurice de Talleyrand-Périgord], Cambacérès [Jean-Jacques-Régis de Cambacérès], Daru [Pierre Daru] and some other personalities who foresaw a dark future on the basis of their profound experience in state service. But the voices of the opponents of the war were drowned out by the stormy cheers of the majority of the men who made up the *Grande Armée*, of whom many, hoping for a share of rich booty, dreamed of becoming sovereign princes. The conviction of Napoleon's invincibility, based on his constant successes, prevailed not only in France, but also in Germany; it was even shared by many in Russia. The contemporaries of 1812 testify that the name of Bonaparte at the time instilled in our common people a mysterious dread, like the name of a demonic spirit. With the approach of war, every fire, every natural disaster, was attributed to the influence of Napoleon and his agents, who were allegedly sent out by the French government, in large numbers, to collect intelligence and to stir up faint-hearted people to rebellion and betrayal. In 1811, a comet appeared. 'This star is an ill omen. It will scour the Russian earth.' they said of us. The vast field of imagination was opened: they spoke of heavenly signs that foreshadowed something extraordinary; they believed that the time of the Final Judgment of God was already at hand. In the name of Napoleon itself, transliterated into numbers, according to Hebrew calculations, they thought to find the beast (the Antichrist) revealed in the Apocalypse by the number 666; and as in another place in the Apocalypse the extent of the glory of this beast was determined by the number 42, it was hoped that 1812, in which Napoleon would reach 43 years of age, would be the time of his fall.[26] These rumours are mentioned solely in order to present an accurate image of the times. It may serve to give a clearer understanding of the spirit of the Russian people. Few in our country could hope for victory in the war against Napoleon, but all were ready to arm themselves, according to the Tsar's words, in defence of our insulted fatherland.

---

26 For the numerology derived from the apocalypse of St John the Evangelist, see Appendix VIII.

5

The Initial Operational Plan by the Russian Forces

Various courses of action, compiled before the war of 1812. – D'Allonville's plan. – Toll's plan. – Phull's plan. – Barclay de Tolly's opinion on the best course of action against Napoleon. – The gradual change in the original plan of action by the Russian forces.

The suggestion that operations by the Russian armies in the first half of the 1812 campaign, from Napoleon's invasion of Russia to the French occupation of Moscow, were carried out without any definite plan is quite groundless. But it would be just as unfounded to assert that the phases included in the original plan of action for the Russian forces were executed exactly in the form in which they had been proposed. At the moment when Napoleon was preparing to invade Russia, no one in our country could determine exactly – either a course of action for our armies, or the direction in which we should move in the event of a retreat, or the final point to which we must retreat. All this depended in the war of 1812 – as in all wars – on many factors inaccessible to human foresight. Napoleon, just like us, could not have known at the beginning of the war in which direction he would have to lead his troops throughout the duration of operations and how far he would have to push into Russia; upon reaching Smolensk, he hesitated in indecision himself – whether to go forward, or stop on the Dnieper and overwinter in Lithuania and Belorussia.[1]

All this is so obvious that it does not require further proof, but there is also no doubt that the plan for the retreat of our armies within the country belongs not just to foreigners (as Wollzogen was eager to prove), and that the main executor of this consideration, Barclay de Tolly, compiled it himself long before the war of 1812.

This is proved by both historical facts and documents held in our state archives.

Before the war of 1812, when the thoughts of the Russian and French governments predicted an imminent struggle, many plans of action were presented to Tsar Alexander.[2]

---

1 Chambray. *Expédition de Russie. 3me ed.* 1839, II, p. 14.
2 Comte d'Allonville's memoirs, Archive of the M.T.D. No 43,096. Graf von Toll's memoirs, Archive of the M.T.D. No 29,199. Councillor of State Fanton-de-Verrion's memoirs, Classified Archive of the General Staff.

Among them is a remarkable memo by a French emigrant, Comte d'Allonville [Armand François d'Allonville], presented to Tsar Alexander, in January 1812, by Admiral Count Nikolay Semënovich Mordvinov, acknowledged by the Tsar and reported at the same time to Barclay de Tolly.[3] The author, at the beginning of his memo, outlining the relative situations of Russia and France, and giving factual evidence of the hostile views of Napoleon and the danger that threatened Russia, proposes, politically and militarily, the mission to determine the surest way to guarantee the independence of our fatherland. Whereupon d'Allonville, considering Napoleon's courses of action, states that:

> he, possessing large resources for the conduct of war, but not being able to maintain enormous armies, due to the fragility of French finances, would be obliged by the very force of circumstances to wage an offensive war, to quickly invade an enemy country, to provision his troops through requisitioning, lacking the convenience of magazines, to seek decisive battles and rush quickly towards the enemy capital, with the aim of occupying it, dictating terms for peace and acquiring the resources that France is deprived of, due to the disorganised state of its industries and trade.
>
> How should one operate against such an enemy? He has indicated what should be done himself: his objective is to act quickly and to exploit every advantage from the war; therefore we must involve him in a long and ruinous war; in particular, general battles should be avoided, retreating to the interior, dragging the enemy along with us, keeping their forces constricted as much as possible, flood the provinces that the enemy must leave in their rear with Cossacks, to operate against the French detachments sent to get food. The enemy must be kept in constant fear; restricting them to local engagements, which, while maintaining the self-confidence of our own troops, tire the enemy, weaken them, and, in any case, are more harmful for an army that has moved 500 leagues (2,000 *versts*) from its borders than for an army waging a war in its own country. In order to counter those bold envelopments which Napoleon has used to decide the outcome of wars, one should have another army behind the active army – a reserve army that could support the main forces and secure their lines of communications.
>
> By waging this form of war, one may play for time, and meanwhile endure four or five summer months, the most convenient for operations by the enemy army, in terms of the abundance of forage, the length of the days and the nature of the climate; with the onset of autumn and winter, long nights will contribute to the raids by Russian light troops and hinder French operations, who, being accustomed to a temperate climate, will suffer due to the bad weather and cold more than the Russians.

---

3   *Mémoire politique et militaire sur les circonstances présentes (janvier 1811)*. Compiled by Comte d'Allonville, author of *Mémoires tirés des papiers d'un homme d'état*, works that have long been attributed to Count Hardenberg. The defensive measures proposed in d'Allonville's plan of action were endorsed by Barclay de Tolly, as recorded in the work *Mémoires tirés des papiers d'un homme d'état*, XI, 284.

Politically, in order to succeed in operations against Napoleon, it follows to:

1. Conclude an alliance with Britain, which may offer a financial advantage to Russia.
2. Conclude an alliance with Spain, as guarantors of their political independence.
3. Make peace with Turkey, on the most moderate terms, in order to take advantage of the assistance of Turkish troops invading Illyria, or, in the case of an alliance between Austria and France, to threaten Austrian territory.
4. Try to conclude an alliance with Austria, who has everything to fear from France and everything to hope from Russia; in the event of an alliance between Austria and Napoleon, operate in unison with the Turks against the Austrians.
5. Send an auxiliary corps to Prussia in order, with the assistance of this Power, to initiate an uprising against Napoleon in northern Germany, who are completely ready to rise in arms against the French, which is evidenced convincingly by the events of 1809. Sweden and Denmark must also be severed from their alliance with France. The latter would join Russia, in order to avoid the harmful consequences that threaten them from an unsustainable increase in their armed forces and the suspension of maritime trade.
6. Restore, by all possible means, the alliance between Sweden and Britain, which alone could ruin or enrich the Swedes, devastate or protect the Swedish coast, and even elevate one of the legitimate heirs of the royal House to the throne.
7. Arouse the royalists in France, which will force Napoleon to use some of the troops to keep his own provinces under subjection and to resort to oppressive measures that will increase displeasure against the government in France and hasten the fall of its ruler.
8. Finally, in order to induce Napoleon into developing enormous forces, disproportionate to his resources, we must carry out several diversions, for example, into Dalmatia, for which one may use Greek and Albanian militias; into the Kingdom of Naples, where ten or fifteen thousand Russian troops, with the help of the British and the population of Sicily and Calabria, may, exploiting the local character of the region, operate successfully against significant enemy forces; into Pomerania, Hannover, the Netherlands, to assist the Prussian army; finally – into Brittany, or into Bayonne, to support the royalists, to instigate an uprising in the Pyrenees and to facilitate the expedition proposed by the Duc de Orleans to Roussillon.

Although it is possible to be accused of arrogance, setting out in advance a military plan of action and indicating the locations for the forces, one cannot fail to notice that, in all likelihood, militarily, we shall have to:

1. Open offensive operations by invading the Duchy of Warsaw and, if possible, Silesia, so that, having occupied the Oder line together with Prussian troops, initiate an uprising in northern Germany and secure ourselves from the left flank with the assistance of the Austrians, or through our own observation corps and Turkish troops, who must, in the event of a breach between the Porte and Austria, invade Hungary.
2. Disband the Polish forces, or exile them to Russia.
3. If necessary, evacuate the Duchy of Warsaw, devastating it in order to deny the enemy the opportunity to provision the army from the country's resources. The retreat of the main forces should be directed towards Moscow, the location at which the main depots and warehouses should be established. The army should gradually fall back on the following defensive lines: the Oder, the Vistula and the Dnieper, occupying favourable positions, strengthening them with fortifications and abatis, destroying bridges and spoiling roads, while Cossack flying columns should devastate provinces in the rear of the enemy, harass them with incessant raids, cut off supplies and hinder the enemy's offensive.
4. Place reserve armies near Kiev and Smolensk, equipped with everything they need and capable of rapid movements.
5. Keep the enemy inactive, or to involve them in such operations, which, even if successful, would cost them dearly, bringing limited advantages; and, meanwhile, to go over to the offensive only when we have a decisive superiority in troop numbers on our side, or when advantageous circumstances favour us.

To carry out this plan of action, we must have the following troop numbers: a field army from eighty to one hundred thousand men; a corps, thirty to forty thousand, on the Austrian border; another corps, from twenty to thirty thousand, to assist the Prussian army; two reserve armies, from forty to fifty thousand men each, at Kiev and Smolensk; ten thousand men for an expedition to Naples; a similar number for diversions into France; from twenty to thirty thousand men to occupy fortified locations, escort supplies, form flying detachments, etc. Consequently – a total of two hundred and fifty to three hundred and twenty-five thousand men.[4]

As he was presenting this memo to Tsar Alexander, Admiral Mordvinov cited two historical events in support of the plans contained therein: the retreat by Peter the Great, who lured the army of Charles XII into the country and defeated the Swedes at Poltava, and the retreat by Wellington [Arthur Wellesley, 1st Duke of Wellington] to Torres Vedras, at Lisbon, which resulted in huge losses to the French army and the retreat of the French to Spain.

The documents bequeathed by Graf von Toll [Karl Wilhelm von Toll] also include a draft of a military plan of action conceived by him. This project was presented to

---

4   Extracted from a draft drawn up by Comte d'Allonville, entitled: *Mémoire politique et militaire sur les circonstances présentes (janvier 1811)*. For the complete text, see Appendix IX.

Tsar Alexander by Prince Peter Mikhailovich Volkonsky, shortly after the arrival of His Majesty in Vilna, namely, on 29 April [new style], 1812.[5]

Toll's memoir leaves no doubt that in our headquarters at that time they did not have accurate intelligence on the location of the French forces, and therefore the conclusions drawn by Toll themselves were based on very inaccurate assumptions; but it deserves attention as an expression of the concepts of military affairs by one of Russia's remarkable generals and as new evidence that the war of 1812 was fought on the basis of considerations discussed in advance.

But Toll's opinion was that the Russian armies at this time should limit themselves to defensive operations, because the favourable moment for the offensive had already been missed, and Napoleon, taking advantage of this, had managed to concentrate 220,000 men at Warsaw (sic). Thereafter Toll condemns the deployment of the Russian armies stretched across 800 versts, which could only have been determined by the economic needs of the troops, but by no means corresponded to the military objective. According to Toll, the enemy, having separated two corps, each with a force of 30,000 men to cover their flanks, could send a 160,000 strong army between our armies, separate them completely from one another and defeat them in detail.

To counteract the enemy, Toll proposed: to station I Corps, comprising 18,000 men, at Kovno, to shield Courland from an invasion by the enemy left flanking corps; the main body of First Army (II Corps, III Corps, IV Corps, V Corps and I Cavalry Corps) was to be located in concentrated quarters along the Neman, from Grodno to Mosty, while VI Corps, comprising 18,000 men, was to assemble at Pruzhany, while the II Cavalry, maintaining communications between VI Corps and the main body of First Army, was to be stationed at Wołkowysk [Vawkavysk]. At the opening of hostilities, VI Corps was to advance, in the role of vanguard, to Drohiczyn on the Bug, the main body of First Army was to stand between Białystok and Grodno, while Second Army was to stand between Siemiatycze and Brest, and thus establish communications with each other. Overall, their locations, from one flank to the other, as Toll proposed, stretched for 176 versts; while, in order to concentrate both armies at a single location, it would take from 25 to 70 hours.

Thus, according to Toll, it was necessary to operate with concentrated forces, being careful, above all, to avoid the separation of First Army from Second Army by the swamps of the Pripet River.

Even before this plan of action outlined by us, another had been drawn up by General Phull, a Prussian officer who had transferred into Russian service. He was considered a genius in the Prussian General Staff.[6] In reality, although neither his intelligence nor education could be denied, his information was very limited, or, better said, one-sided. Immersed in a study of the operations by Julius Caesar and Frederick the Great, he did not submit it to critical research and assimilated this knowledge literally, without understanding its principles. All the events of the latest wars remained alien to him; moreover, in avoiding society and leading a philosophical life, he not only appeared to be eccentric, but was one in reality. Faint-hearted, characterless, he was confounded by any unexpected occasion, and yet he showed

---

5   For the text of von Toll's plan, see Appendix X.
6   *Hinterlassene Werke des Generals Carl. v. Clausewitz.* VII, p. 6.

a kind of false decisiveness, which was unnatural for him. Practising occupations that were not applicable to anything practical all his life, during the six years he spent in Russia, not only did he not bother to learn the Russian language, he did not even think about acquiring any idea of the personalities who occupied the most important roles with us, or even about the state and military institutions of our fatherland. However, justice requires that it be noted, for all these shortcomings, for all his inability, Phull was distinguished by directness and nobility of character.

To investigate the foundations of Phull's plan, one must not lose sight of the fact that his constant occupation was the study of the Seven Years War, and the only fruit of this obsession was the conclusion of several mechanical principles from the operations of Frederick the Great and Prince Henry [Friedrich Heinrich Ludwig von Preußen], the chief of which was that a defensive war should be waged by two armies, one of which should fix the enemy frontally, while the other would operate on their flanks and rear. Phull then expanded on Bülow's idea that the best way to hold off an advancing enemy was to position one's army to one side of the protected route, taking up a so-called flanking position.

Neither Barclay de Tolly, nor any of our famous military men, was involved in drawing up Phull's plan. Barclay, the Minister of War, who was at the same time Commander-in-Chief of First Army, not only did not approve of this plan of action, but had to execute it against his will.

This notorious plan was drawn up in St Petersburg, and preliminary orders for its execution were made mostly before Barclay had learned of its existence.[7]

To draw up a plan of action, it is necessary to have, if possible, accurate intelligence on the intentions of the enemy. This intelligence can almost never be obtained directly, but it can be deduced quite definitively from some information, such as from the preliminary location of the enemy forces, the location of their headquarters, the location of the main magazines and other enemy stores, finally, from what is most profitable for them to attempt under certain circumstances. As far as can be judged from the actual disposition of our armies before the opening of hostilities, it emerges that we remained in the dark about the current dispositions of the enemy forces. In our headquarters, everyone was sure that Napoleon's army was assembling near Warsaw and that the main line of French operations would be in the direction of Białystok, or Grodno, from where the enemy could turn left to Vilna, or go to Slonim and Nesvizh [Nyasvizh], towards Smolensk.

According to Phull's plan, it was necessary to wage a defensive war, in an area limited on the one hand by the western borders of the Empire, and on the other by the Dvina and the Dnieper, operating with two armies, one of 120,000 and the other of 80,000 men. Believing it most likely that Napoleon would head from Grodno towards Vilna, Phull based his defence system predominantly on this assessment. But how was it possible to know where the enemy would go beyond Vilna, i.e.:

1. To Druya and Pskov towards St Petersburg.
2. To Smolensk towards Moscow.

---

7   Bernhardi. *Denkwürdigkeiten des Grafen v. Toll.* I, 258-259.

Whereupon First Army was to assemble at Sventsiany, behind Vilna, in three stages and retreat to the fortified camp at Drissa. According to Phull, this position, located at a distance of one stage from Druya, two stages from Polotsk, and five or six stages from Vitebsk, could serve as a flanking position to shield the routes leading from Vilna:

1.   Via Druya towards St Petersburg.
2.   Via Polotsk, towards St Petersburg.
3.   Via Vitebsk, towards Moscow.

By concentrating at least 120,000 men in the Drissa fortified camp and holding both banks of the Dvina, we hoped to obtain important advantages in operations against the enemy, forced to divide their forces on both sides of the river, in order to invest our camp; and in the meantime, it was proposed to send Second Army, reinforced by Platov's Cossacks [Matvey Ivanovich Platov], towards the enemy army's lines of communications, which, being in devastated countryside, could not remain in this position for any length of time and would have to retreat. It is impossible not to notice that many of the assumptions upon which Phull based the success of his plan existed only in his imagination: Second Army, instead of 80,000 men, after the detachment of almost half of the troops assigned to it in order to form Tormasov's [Alexander Petrovich Tormasov] Third Army, was only 40,000 strong; at Dünaburg, where it was intended to collect large stores of provisions, under the protection of fortifications, there was no fortress at the time; Sebezh, another location which was also supposed to be a storehouse in a fortified city, was neither supplied with stores, nor skilfully fortified. The camp at Drissa (as will be described later) was located in a very unfavourable area for defence and had been fortified (in accordance with Phull's own project) extremely poorly: consequently, it did not satisfy the main condition of any fortified camp – to serve as a secure refuge for the army.

These were the shortcomings of our original plan of action. The Commander-in-Chief of First Army, which constituted the most significant part of our armed forces, did not share the conviction of the merits of this plan. For a long time he had already been convinced of the need to retreat in order to weaken the enemy army, and this is convincingly proved by the words he said to the famous historian Niebuhr [Barthold Georg Niebuhr], at the time when Barclay, having been wounded in the battle of Preußisch Eylau in 1807, was lying on his sick bed in Memel. Barclay said at the time: 'If I had a chance to fight against Napoleon in the role of Commander-in-Chief, then I would avoid a general battle and retreat until the French faced, instead of a decisive victory, another Poltava.'[8]

Thereupon Niebuhr brought Barclay de Tolly's comments to the attention of the Prussian minister Stein, who reported them to General Knesebeck, and Knesebeck to Wollzogen and Phull. Wollzogen, who possessed extraordinary erudition, not only assimilated Barclay's thoughts as sent to him, but, supplementing them with his own assessment, drawing up a plan of action against Napoleon, which was presented

---

8   Dumas. *Précis des événements militaires.* XIX, 447-448. *Souvenirs du lieutenant-général Dumas.* III, 416. For an extract from Barclay de Tolly's notes, see Appendix XI.

by him to Quartermaster General, Prince Volkonsky, in August 1810.[9] For his part, Knesebeck, having been sent to St Petersburg at the beginning of 1812, on the instructions of the Prussian government, conveyed this idea to Tsar Alexander. But from what we have said before, it is clear that neither the Tsar nor Barclay learned anything new from Knesebeck. Wollzogen, in his notes published in 1851, vainly suggests that he was the director of the Russians in the war of 1812; Barclay, taking advantage of his extraordinary memory and topographic information, used him for information, in the form of a living encyclopaedia, and by no means as an adviser.[10]

Five years had passed since the conversation with Niebuhr before Barclay de Tolly got the opportunity to actually execute his plans.

Having accepted the plan proposed by Phull, we fell into a mistake, but managed to correct it in time, and the erroneous movement towards Drissa was the beginning of the retreat of the Russian troops towards Moscow, which resulted in the weakening of Napoleon's formidable army.

Before the outbreak of the war of 1812, many of our generals, including Bennigsen and Prince Bagration [Pëtr Ivanovich Bagration], did not recognise the need for

---

9   The essence of the plan presented by Wollzogen is as follows:
Napoleon's genius in the art of war gives him such superiority over all his opponents that, in order to oppose him, the only means remains – to have the advantage of strength on one's side, that is, a decisive superiority in the number of troops, sufficiently supported by reserves, to take an advantageous position and secure a line of retreat for the troops in the event of a reverse. To overcome Napoleon, it is necessary to oppose his skill with all the means that knowledge can provide, that is:
Thoroughly established foundations.
The direction of the courses of action consistent with the objective.
Selection of excellent positions for them.
The construction of fortified camps and the skilful use of fortresses to achieve the aims of the war.
Having explained all these subjects more from a hypothetical than from a practical point of view, the author quite rightly rebelled against the idea of covering the country with border fortresses. He stated: 'The defence of the country is achieved solely by the destruction of the enemy army, and for this it may be necessary, perhaps, to retreat a hundred *Meilen* inland. Therefore, in order not to weaken the forces operating in the field and not to waste state funds, I propose to confine ourselves to a few fortresses in the interior *Oblasts*. But these few fortresses must be reinforced with all the aids of science and, with the fortified camps built with them, must provide shelter and support to the troops operating in the field. The resistance that the fortresses have should offer the opportunity to gain time to launch powerful raids behind enemy lines. To that end, in addition to the army operating against them from the front, there must be another army, and it must be established at the very beginning of operations, in accordance with its mission, such that the extent of the frontage of both armies forms a re-entrant angle: thereafter their lines of retreat would have divergent directions towards the main base; while the lines of operation serving for their offensive would converge in the rear of the enemy army. Our method of operations should consist of retreating with the army against which the main enemy forces would be directed, from one strong position to another, delaying and weakening it gradually, at the same time, sending our other army to the rear, to operate with partisan detachments...' etc. *Memoiren des Königlich Preuss. Generals der Infanterie, Ludwig Freih. V. Wollzogen. Erste Beilage.* V-XVI.

10   From the notes by Major General Baron Löwenstern, the former senior aide de camp at the headquarters of First Army, in 1812. The comments made to Niebuhr were conveyed to Löwenstern by Barclay de Tolly himself.

the retreat of the Russian forces into the interior of the Empire and even had a completely opposite opinion, believing that an enemy invasion could be prevented by an invasion of the Duchy of Warsaw. Before Barclay de Tolly's arrival in the army, everyone in our headquarters was confident that we would operate on the offensive, and in this respect, instructions had been given to generals: Essen 1st [Ivan Nikolaevich Essen], Prince Bagration, Count Wittgenstein [Pëtr Khristianovich Wittgenstein] and Lavrov [Nikolay Ivanovich Lavrov],[11] and Intendant-General Kankrin.[12] On the arrival of Barclay, in order to take command of First Army, the principles for military operations, approved by the Tsar, were communicated, on the basis of which any of the Russian armies, attacked by superior forces, was to retreat, while the other army, which was not facing such superior forces, was assigned for a decisive attack on the enemy flanks and rear.[13] Subsequently, when the huge superiority in the number of enemy troops was no longer subject to doubt, it was necessary to unite both Russian armies and operate with combined forces. At first, the city of Sventsiany was designated as the point for the concentration of our forces; then the fortified camp at Drissa; later Orsha; finally, the army was actually united at Smolensk, but as, at this time, the decisive superiority in forces still remained on the side of the enemy, our troops continued to retreat. This was the gradual change in our general plan of action in the first half of the war of 1812.

---

11   The Minister of War's instructions dated 1 [13] March 1812.
12   The Minister of War's secret instructions dated 1 [13] April 1812.
13   The Minister of War's instructions dated 10 [22] April 1812.

6

The retreat of the Russian Armies
First Army to Drissa and Second Army
to Nesvizh

The composition and location of the Russian armies on the western borders of the Empire. – The composition of Napoleon's *Grande Armée*. – Napoleon's plan of action. – The movement of enemy troops up to the Russian border. – Napoleon's crossing of the Neman and the offensive towards Vilna. – Orders for the Russian troops and the letter from the Tsar to Count Saltykov. – Instructions given to Balashev. – Barclay de Tolly. – The retreat of the Russian troops to Sventsiany and Wiłkomierz. – Napoleon in Vilna. – Conversation between Napoleon and Balashev. – Measures taken by Napoleon to split the Russian armies. – The action at Dziewałtów. – The retreat of First Army from Sventsiany to Drissa. – The retreat of Dorokhov, Kreutz, Dokhturov. – The action at Kochergishki. – The arrival of First Army at the Drissa camp. – The concurrent direction of enemy troops.

Operations by Second Army. – Prince Bagration. – Bagration's movement towards Slonim, while Platov moved on Lida. – Bagration's move towards Nikolaev and Nesvizh, Platov's to Iwje, while Dorokhov moved to Kamen, and on towards Nesvizh. – The action at Mir. – Operations by King Jérôme and his departure from the army.

Before the opening of the war of 1812, our troops and the entire Russian people were confident that we would go on the offensive. The idea of admitting the enemy within the frontiers of the Russian domain would not find a place in the thoughts of our nation: since the invasion of Charles XII, for more than a hundred years, the sounds of battle had not been heard in the Russian *Oblasts*: against Frederick the Great we fought in his domain; against Napoleon – on the territory of our allies. Despite the unsuccessful outcome of our latest wars against France, Russian soldiers, along with Austerlitz [2 December 1805] and Friedland [14 June 1807], remembered with pride Krems [Dürenstein, 11 November 1805], Hollabrunn [Schöngraben, 16 November 1805], Czarnowo [23 December 1806], Pultusk [26 December 1806], Eylau [7 to

8 February 1807] and Heilsberg [10 June 1807]. And therefore it is not surprising that many of the personalities from these battles, and among them those who had acquired their renown, Bagration and Bennigsen, were convinced of the need for offensive operations. Others, more familiar with the precise information on the relative strengths of Russia and France, believed that the surest way to crush the enemy, who decided the fate of wars by swift, bold operations, was to retreat into the interior of the country, evade a general engagement and inflict creeping exhaustion on the enemy through a *guerilla* war. Among the proponents of this *modus operandi* –as we have already had occasion to say –was the Minister of War, Barclay de Tolly, who, by the very nature of the duties he performed, perfectly understood the military forces and resources of Russia. But neither he nor anyone else dared to voice the need to retreat from the borders, or, in other words, the need to sacrifice several *Oblasts* to save the state. Anyone who expressed such an opinion at that time would have been considered a traitor, and therefore Barclay had no choice but to hide from everyone, and even from our senior generals, the need to retreat. From this came a kind of indecision, a kind of hesitancy in all our initial military orders, and especially before the retreat of Russian forces from Vilna. It should also be noted that the reasons for such hesitancy could be, in addition, the adoption for the first time of a plan of action by Phull consistent with Barclay's convictions, and the very extended deployment of our troops, which did not allow either their quick concentration, or the precise execution of orders received from headquarters.

We have already noticed, when setting out the initial plan of action of the Russian forces, that the reason for overextending their deployment was the lack of accurate intelligence about enemy intentions. Napoleon, spreading false rumours, managed to convince us that his main forces were concentrated in the Duchy of Warsaw and that Austria was preparing to direct a significant army against us from Galicia. This made us split our forces into three distinct formations: First Western Army (First Army), Second Western Army (Second Army) and Third Reserve Army of Observation (Third Army), with the following composition:

Order of battle of First Army, under the command of Minister of War, General of Infantry Barclay de Tolly.

Corps	Division	Bns	Sqns	Coss Regts	Arty Coys
I Corps. Lieutenant General Count Wittgenstein	**5th Infantry Division.** Major General Berg 1st [Grigory Maksimovich Berg]	14	–	–	3 Foot
	14th Infantry Division. Major General Sazonov [Ivan Terentevich Sazonov]	14	–	–	3 Foot 1 Pioneer
	1st Cavalry Division. Major General Kakhovsky [Pëtr Demyanovich Kakhovsky]	–	16	–	–

Corps	Division	Bns	Sqns	Coss Regts	Arty Coys
	1st Reserve Artillery Brigade				2 2 Pontoon 1 Pioneer
	Cossacks	–	–	3	–
	TOTAL	28	16	3	12
II Corps. Lieutenant General Baggovut	4th Infantry Division. Major General Prinz Eugen von Württemberg	12	–	–	3 Foot
	17th Infantry Division. Lieutenant General Olsufiev [Zakhar Dmitryevich Olsufiev]	12	–	–	3 Foot
	Yelisavetgrad Hussar Regiment	–	8	–	1 Horse
	TOTAL	24	8	–	7
III Corps. Lieutenant General Tuchkov 1st [Nikolay Alekseevich Tuchkov]	1st Grenadier Division. Major General Stroganov [Pavel Aleksandrovich Stroganov]	12	–	–	3 Foot
	3rd Infantry Division. Lieutenant General Konovnitsyn	12	–	–	3 Foot
	Lifeguard Cossack Regiment & Black Sea Sotnia	–	4	–	1 Horse
	Cossacks	–	–	1	–
	TOTAL	24	4	1	7
IV Corps. Lieutenant General Count Shuvalov [Pavel Andreevich Shuvalov]	11th Infantry Division. Major General Bakhmetiev 2nd [Nikolay Nikolayevich Bakhmatiev] (later Major General Choglokov [Pavel Nikolayevich Choglokov])	12	–	–	3 Foot

Corps	Division	Bns	Sqns	Coss Regts	Arty Coys
	23rd Infantry Division. Major General Bakhmetiev 1st [Alexey Nikolayevich Bakhmatiev] (later Major General Laptev [Vasily Danilevich Laptev])	11	–	–	3 Foot
	Izyum Hussar Regiment	–	8	–	–
	TOTAL	23	8	–	6
V Corps. His Imperial Highness, Grand Duke Konstantin Pavlovich	**Lifeguard Infantry Division.** Major General Yermolov [Alexey Petrovich Yermolov]	18	–	–	4 Foot
	Lifeguard Marines	1	–	–	–
	Combined Grenadier Division	7	–	–	1 Pioneer
	1st Cuirassier Division Lieutenant General Depreradovich [Nikolay Ivanovich Depreradovich]	–	20	–	2 Horse
	TOTAL	26	20	–	7
VI Corps. General of Infantry Dokhturov [Dmitry Sergeevich Dokhturov]	**7th Infantry Division** Lieutenant General Kaptsevich [Pëtr Mikhailovich Kaptsevich]	12	–	–	3 Foot
	24th Infantry Division Lieutenant General Likhachev [Pëtr Gavrilovich Likhachev]	12	–	–	3 Foot
	Sumy Hussar Regiment	–	8	–	–
	7th Horse Artillery Company	–	–	–	1 Horse
	TOTAL	24	8	–	7
I Cavalry Corps. Lieutenant General Uvarov [Fëdor Petrovich Uvarov]	**Major General Chalikov's Division** [Anton Stepanovich Chalikov]	–	12	–	–

Corps	Division	Bns	Sqns	Coss Regts	Arty Coys
	Major General Chernysh's Division [Ivan Ivanovich Chernysh]	–	8	–	–
	5th Horse Artillery Company	–	–	–	1 Horse
	TOTAL	–	20	–	1
II Cavalry Corps. Major General Baron Korf [Fëdor Karlovich Korf]	**Colonel Davydov's Division** [Nikolay Fëdorovich Davydov]	–	8	–	–
	Major General Panchulidzev 2nd's Division [Semën Davidovich Panchulidzev]	–	16	–	–
	6th Horse Artillery Company	–	–	–	1 Horse
	TOTAL	–	24	–	1
III Cavalry Corps. Major General Count Pahlen 2nd [Pëtr Petrovich Pahlen]	**Major General Skalon's Division** [Anton Antonovich Skalon]	–	8	–	–
	Colonel Klebeck's Division [Yegor Yermolaevich Klebeck]	–	8	–	–
	Mariupol Hussar Regiment	–	8	–	–
	9th Horse Artillery Company	–	–	–	1 Horse
	TOTAL	–	24	–	1
Light Force. General of Cavalry *Ataman* Platov [Matvey Ivanovich Platov]	**Cossacks**	–	–	14	1 Horse
	Reserve Artillery				3
	TOTAL	–	–	14	4

Overall, First Army consisted of 149 battalions, 132 squadrons, 18 Cossack regiments, 49 artillery companies (16 heavy companies, of twelve-gun establishment, 22 light companies, some of twelve, some of ten-gun establishment, and 11 horse companies, each with 12 guns, except for the Lifeguard batteries, which had eight guns each), two pioneer and two pontoon companies.[1] According to the works by

---

1   The remaining two pontoon companies were directed to the establishment of mobile magazines under First Army (Supreme Orders to the Minister of War dated 28th June [10th July]).

Buturlin and Mikhailovsky-Danilevsky, this gave a total strength of 127,000, while the works by Prinz Eugen von Württemberg and Toll, have no more than 110,000 men, with 558 guns.[2]

Order of battle of Second Army, under the command of General of Infantry, Prince Bagration.

Corps	Division	Bns	Sqns	Coss Regts	Arty Coys
VII Corps. Lieutenant General Raevsky [Nikolay Nikolayevich Raevsky]	**26th Infantry Division.** Major General Paskevich [Ivan Fëdorovich Paskevich]	12	–	–	3 Foot
	12th Infantry Division. Major General Kolyubakin [Pëtr Mikhailovich Kolyubakin]	12	–	–	3 Foot
	Akhtyrka Hussar Regiment	–	8	–	–
	8th Horse Artillery Company	–	–	–	1 Horse
	TOTAL	24	8	–	7
VIII Corps. Lieutenant General Borozdin [Mikhail Mikhailovich Borozdin]	**2nd Grenadier Division.** Major General Prinz Karl von Mecklenburg–Schwerin	12	–	–	3 Foot
	Combined Grenadier Division. Major General Count Vorontsov [Mikhail Semënovich Vorontsov]	10	–	–	2 Foot
	2nd Cuirassier Division. Major General Knorring [Otto Fëdorovich Knorring]	–	20	–	–
	TOTAL	22	20	–	5
IV Cavalry Corps. Major General Sievers [Karl Karlovich Sievers]	**Major General Panchulidzev 1st's Division.** [Ivan Davidovich Panchulidzev]	–	8	–	–

2   In the returns on the troop states of First Army, dated 2 [14] July, 1812, signed by Colonel Stavrakov [Semën Khristoforovich Stavrakov], who held the appointment of Duty General, the number of troops in First Army less III Cavalry Corps was 106,111 men.

Corps	Division	Bns	Sqns	Coss Regts	Arty Coys
	Colonel Emmanuel's Division. [Georgy (Yegor) Arsenevich Emmanuel (Manuilovich)]	–	8	–	–
	Lithuania Ulan Regiment	–	8	–	–
	10th Horse Artillery Company	–	–	–	1 Horse
	Engineers	–	–	–	1 Pontoon 1 Pioneer
	TOTAL	–	24	–	3
Reserve Artillery.		–	–	–	4
Light Force. Major General Ilovaisky 5th [Ivan Dmitryevich Ilovaisky]	Cossacks	–	–	9	1 Horse

Overall, Second Army consisted of 46 battalions, 52 squadrons, nine Cossack regiments, 18 artillery companies, one pontoon and one pioneer company. In addition, they were to be joined by 27th Infantry Division under Lieutenant General Neverovsky [Dmitry Petrovich Neverovsky], consisting of 12 battalions, which was on the march from Moscow. The number of troops in Second Army, excluding the yet to arrive 27th Infantry Division, came to 37,000, but with the active battalions of this division, would reach 45,000 men, with 216 guns.

Order of battle of Third Army of Observation, under the command of General of Cavalry Count Tormasov.

Corps	Division	Bns	Sqns	Coss Regts	Arty Coys
General of Infantry Count Kamensky's Corps. [Sergey Mikhailovich Kamensky]	18th Infantry Division. Major General Prince Shcherbatov [Alexey Grigorevich Shcherbatov]	12	–	–	3 Foot
	Combined Grenadier Brigade.	6	–	–	–
	Pavlograd Hussar Regiment.	–	8	–	1 Horse

Corps	Division	Bns	Sqns	Coss Regts	Arty Coys
Lieutenant General Markov's Corps. [Yevgeny Ivanovich Markov]	**15th Infantry Division.** Major General Nazimov [Fëdor Viktorovich Nazimov]	12	–	–	3
	9th Infantry Division. Major General Udom [Yevstafy Yevstafovich Udom]	12	–	–	3
	Alexandria Hussar Regiment	–	8	–	1
Lieutenant General Baron Saken's Corps.	**36th Infantry Division** (replacement battalions of 15th Division & 18th Division). Major General [M.M.] Sorokin	12	–	–	–
	11th Cavalry Division (replacement squadrons of 4th Cavalry Division, 5th Cavalry Division & 2nd Cuirassier Division).	–	16	–	2
	Lubny Hussar Regiment	–	8	–	–
Major General Count Lambert's Cavalry Corps. [Karl Osipovich Lambert]	**Major General Berdyaev's Cavalry Brigade.** [Alexander Nikolayevich Berdyaev]	–	8	–	–
	Major General Khrushchev's Cavalry Brigade. [Ivan Alexeevich Khrushchev]	–	8	–	–
	Knorring's Tatar Ulan Regiment. [Karl Bogdanovich Knorring]	–	8	–	–
	Vladimir Dragoons, Taganrog Dragoons, Serpukhov Dragoons	–	12	–	–
Light Force.	Cossacks	–	–	9	–
Reserve Artillery		–	–	–	1 Foot 1 Pontoon 1 Pioneer

Overall, Third Army of Observation consisted of 54 battalions, 76 squadrons, nine Cossack regiments and 14 artillery companies, for a total of 46,000 men, with 164 guns.

Consequently, the number of Russian troops located on the western borders, together with the Cossacks, reached some 193,000 men, while without the Cossacks, there were some 175,000 fighting men in the regular armed forces.[3]

Behind these forces were two reserve corps, made up of reserve battalions and squadrons.

I Reserve Corps, under Lieutenant General Baron Meller-Zakomelsky, consisting of 32nd Infantry Division under Major General Gamen [Alexey Yurievich Gamen], 33rd Infantry Division under Major General Ulanov [Gavrila Petrovich Ulanov], and 9th Cavalry Division under Major General Prince Repnin-Volkonsky [Nikolay Grigorevich Repnin-Volkonsky].

II Reserve Corps, under Lieutenant General Ertel [Fëdor Fëdorovich Ertel], of 34th Infantry Division, 35th Infantry Divisions and 10th Cavalry Division.

I Reserve Corps was quartered in Toropets, and II Reserve Corps in Mozyr. Both changed as the war continued, both in their composition and in the number of troops.

First Army under General of Infantry Barclay de Tolly, on 11 (23) June, on the eve of the opening of hostilities, was located along the Neman, between Rossieny [Raseiniai] and Lida as follows:[4]

Headquarters in Vilna

I Corps, under Lieutenant General Count Wittgenstein, at Kiejdany [Kėdainiai]; Colonel Vlastov's detachment [Yegor Ivanovich Vlastov] at Rossieny; the vanguard of I Corps, under Major General Kulnev's command [Yakov Petrovich Kulnev], at Jurburg [Jurbarkas].

II Corps, under Lieutenant General Baggovut, at Orzhishki, where a bridge of rafts had been built on the river Viliya under the control of the Lifeguard Marines; the vanguard, under Major General Vsevolozhsky's command [Alexey Matveevich Vsevolozhsky], was at Janau [Jonava].

III Corps, under Lieutenant General Tuchkov 1st, at Novy-Troki [Trakai]; the vanguard, under Major General Prince Shakhovskoy's command [Ivan Leontievich Shakhovskoy], was at Wysoki Dwór [Aukštadvaris].

IV Corps, under Adjutant General Count Shuvalov, at Olkieniki [Valkeninkai]; the vanguard, under Major General Dorokhov's command [Ivan Semënovich Dorokhov], was at Orany [Varėna].

VI Corps, under Lieutenant General Dokhturov,[5] was at Lida; the vanguard, made up of elements of III Cavalry Corps, under Major General Count Pahlen's command, was at Lebioda [Žaludok].

---

3   Army orders of battle as kept in the Archive of the Department of Inspections and M.T.D. Bernhardi. *Denkwürdigkeiten des Grafen v. Toll.* I, 238. Returns attached to Gen Buturlin's work. For the full order of battle, see Appendix XII.

4   See Map of Significant Movements by the Russian and French armies from the beginning of the war to the battle of Smolensk.

5   [I.P Liprandi notes that Dokhturov had long since been promoted General-of-Infantry and was not a Lieutenant General. He also notes that the corps was still on the march from Antopol and had not reached Lida].

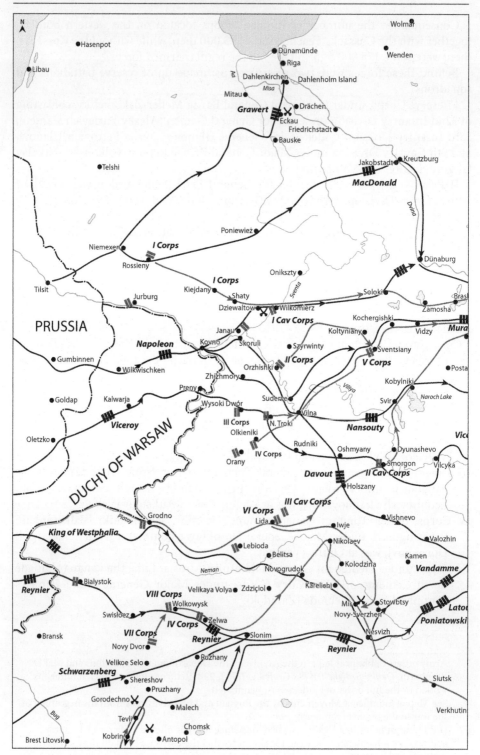

Map of significant movements by the Russian and French Armies, from the borders to Smolensk.

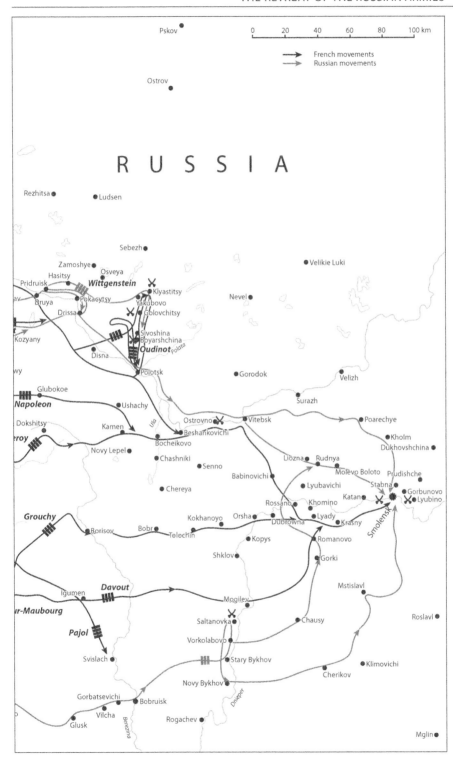

V Corps, under His Imperial Highness, Tsarevich Konstantin Pavlovich, at Sventsiany, I Cavalry Corps, under Adjutant General Uvarov, at Wiłkomierz [Ukmergė]; and II Cavalry Corps, under Adjutant General Baron Korf, was at Smorgon [Smorgonie], forming the second echelon of First Army.
General Platov's Light Corps had been pushed forwards to Grodno.

Second Army, under General of Infantry Prince Bagration, was deployed between the Neman and the Bug:

The headquarters was at Wołkowysk.
VII Corps, under Lieutenant General Raevsky, was at Novy Dvor.
VIII Corps, under Lieutenant General Borozdin, was at Wołkowysk.
IV Cavalry Corps, under Major General Sievers, was at Zelwa.
The Light detachment under Ilovaisky 5th was at Białystok.

Finally, Third Army of Observation, under General of Cavalry Tormasov, was deployed in Volhynia, with his headquarters at Lutsk.
The enemy army assigned to invade Russia consisted of the following:
Order of battle of the *Grande Armée*.

Corps	Division	Bns	Sqns
Garde impériale	One division of *Vielle Garde*, Marshal Lefebvre [François Joseph Lefebvre].	10	–
	Two divisions of *Jeune Garde*, Marshal Mortier [Adolphe Édouard Casimir Joseph Mortier].	32	–
	Légion de la Vistule	12	–
	Cavalerie de la Garde, Marshal Bessières [Jean-Baptiste Bessières].	–	35
	Artillerie de la Garde, Comte Sorbier [Jean Barthélemot de Sorbier].	–	–
	TOTAL	54	35
1er Corps. Marshal Davout	Morand's Division [Charles Antoine Louis Alexis Morand]	18	–
	Friant's Division [Louis Friant]	17	–
	Gudin's Division [César Charles Étienne Gudin]	18	–
	Dessaix's Division [Joseph Marie Dessaix]	13	–
	Compans' Division [Jean Dominique Compans]	23	–
	Girardin's Cavalry [actually Pierre Claude Pajol's]	–	16
	TOTAL	88	16

Corps	Division	Bns	Sqns
2e Corps. Marshal Oudinot	Legrand's Division [Claude-Juste-Alexandre Legrand]	17	–
	Verdier's Division [Jean Antoine Verdier]	15	–
	Merle's Division [Pierre Hugues Victoire Merle]	19	–
	Light Cavalry Brigades under Castex [Bertrand Pierre Castex] and Corbineau [Jean-Baptiste Juvénal Corbineau]	–	20
	TOTAL	51	20
3e Corps. Marshal Ney	Ledru's Division [François Roch Ledru des Essarts]	17	–
	Razout's Division [Louis-Nicolas de Razout]	17	–
	Württemberg Division, under Marchand [Jean Gabriel Marchand]	14	–
	Württemberg Light Cavalry, Wohlwart [*sic*]	–	24
	TOTAL	48	24
4e Corps. Prince Eugène, Viceroy of Italy	**Guardia Reale Italiana** Lechi [Giuseppe Lechi]	5	8
	Delzons' Division [Alexis Joseph Delzons]	19	–
	Broussier's Division [Jean-Baptiste Broussier]	18	–
	Pino's Division [Domenico Pino]	15	–
	d'Ornano's light cavalry [Philippe Antoine d'Ornano]	–	16
	TOTAL	57	24
5e Corps. Prince Poniatowski	Zajączek's Division [Józef Zajączek]	16	–
	Dąbrowski's Division [Jan Henryk Dąbrowski]	16	–
	Knyazhevich's Division [actually Ludwik Kamieniecki's]	12	–
	Kamieński's cavalry [Michał Ignacy Kamieński]	–	20
	TOTAL	44	20
6e Corps **(Bavarian).** Saint-Cyr [Laurent de Gouvion-Saint-Cyr]	Deroy's Division [Bernard Erasme von Deroy]	15	–
	Wrede's Division [Carl Philipp Joseph von Wrede]	13	–
	Two light cavalry brigades	–	16
	TOTAL	28	16

Corps	Division	Bns	Sqns
7e Corps (Saxon). Reynier [Jean-Louis- Ébénézer Reynier]	Le Coq's Division [Karl Christian Erdmann von Le Coq]	9	–
	Funck's Division [Karl Wilhelm Ferdinand von Funck]	9	–
	Gablenz's **leichten Kavalleriebrigade** [Heinrich Adolph von Gablenz]	–	16
	TOTAL	**18**	**16**
8e Corps (Westphalian). Duc d'Abrantes (Junot)	Tharreau's Division [Jean-Victor Tharreau]	9	–
	Ochs' Division [Adam Ludwig von Ochs]	7	–
	Hammerstein's **leichten Kavalleriebrigade** [Hans Georg von Hammerstein-Equord]	–	12
	TOTAL	**16**	**12**
9e Corps. Marshal Victor [Claude-Victor Perrin]	Partouneaux's Division [Louis de Partouneaux]	21	–
	Daendels' Division [Herman Willem Daendels]	13	–
	Girard's Division [Jean-Baptiste Girard]	20	–
	Fournier's cavalry [François Louis Fournier-Sarlovèze]	–	16
	TOTAL	**54**	**16**
10e Corps (Prussian). Marshal MacDonald	Grandjean's Division [Charles Louis Dieudonné Grandjean]	16	–
	Yorck's Division [Johann David Ludwig von Yorck]	20	–
	Massenbach's cavalry [Eberhard Friedrich Fabian von Massenbach]	–	16
	TOTAL	**36**	**16**
11th Corps (Reserve). Marshal Augereau [Charles Pierre François Augereau]	Heudelet's Division [Étienne Heudelet de Bierre]	18	–
	Loison's Division [Louis Henri Loison]	12	1
	Durutte's Division [Pierre François Joseph Durutte]	18	–
	Detrès' Division [François Detrès]	12	4
	Morand's Division [Joseph Morand]	23	–
	Cavaignac's cavalry [Jacques-Marie Cavaignac de Baragne]	–	32
	TOTAL	**83**	**37**

Corps	Division	Bns	Sqns
Austrian Corps. Prinz Schwarzenberg [Karl Philipp Fürst zu Schwarzenberg]	Bianchi's Division [(Vincenz Ferrer) Friedrich von Bianchi]	10	–
	Siegenthal's Division [Heinrich Freiherr Bersina von Siegenthal]	11	–
	Trauttenberg's Division [Leopold Freiherr von Trauttenberg]	6	–
	Frimont's cavalry [Johann Maria Philipp Freiherr Frimont von Palota]	–	54
	TOTAL	27	54
1er Corps de Cavalerie Nansouty [Étienne Marie Antoine Champion de Nansouty]	Bruyère's light cavalry [Jean Pierre Joseph Bruyère]	–	28
	St Germain's cuirassiers [Antoine Louis Decrest de Saint-Germain]	–	16
	Valence's cuirassiers [Jean-Baptiste Cyrus Adélaïde de Timbrune de Thiembronne de Valence]	–	16
	TOTAL	–	60
2e Corps de Cavalerie Montbrun [Louis Pierre de Montbrun]	Sébastiani's light cavalry [Horace François Bastien Sébastiani]	–	28
	Wattier's cuirassiers [Pierre Wattier]	–	16
	Defrance's cuirassiers [Jean-Marie Antoine Defrance]	–	16
	TOTAL	–	60
3e Corps de Cavalerie Grouchy [Emmanuel de Grouchy]	Chastel's light cavalry [Louis Claude du Chastel]	–	28
	Doumerc's cuirassiers [Jean-Pierre Doumerc]	–	16
	La Houssaye's dragoons [Armand Lebrun de La Houssaye]	–	16
	TOTAL	–	60
4e Corps de Cavalerie Latour Maubourg [Marie Victor Nicolas de Faÿ de Latour Maubourg]	Rożniecki's light cavalry [Aleksander Antoni Jan Rożniecki]	–	24
	Lorge's cuirassiers [Jean Thomas Guillaume Lorge]	–	20
	TOTAL	–	44

Overall, Napoleon's *Grande Armée* consisted of 604 battalions and 530 squadrons,[6] with 1,242 field guns and 130 siege artillery pieces, for a total of 492,000 infantry, 96,000 cavalry, and 20,000 men in the siege park, engineering troops and transport: all in all, 608,000 men. There were more than 180,000 war horses and draught animals.[7] The contingents of this myriad army were troops from: France, Lombardy, Illyria, Tuscany, Naples, Holland, Austria, Prussia, Bavaria, Württemberg, Saxony, Westphalia, Baden, Hesse-Darmstadt, Berg, Mecklenburg, Spain, Portugal and Poland.

Nothing reliable can be said about the reasoning behind Napoleon's initial plan of action, because, by personally directing the operations of his army, he did not feel the need to draft definitive instructions, which would have been the sole explanation of his plans. But from letters by Napoleon to his brother Jérôme and the operations themselves it turns out that, by directing the main mass of his forces over the Neman against our First Army, he intended to push it back, and then to send one part of the force after First Army, and the other into the rear of Second Army. The troops assigned for operations from the front against Second Army, under the command of King Jérôme, were to advance a few days later, with the aim of keeping Prince Bagration fixed in anticipation of his defeat;[8] in the interval between these elements of the *Grande Armée*, a third was to proceed, under the command of the Viceroy of Italy, in order to separate our armies and assist the main forces under Napoleon, in the event that we were to give battle. In addition to each of these armies, in order to threaten the flanks of the general deployment of our forces, corps were directed as follows: MacDonald's *10e Corps* towards the lower Neman, and Schwarzenberg's Austrian Corps towards the Bug.

On 11 (23) June, the main body under Napoleon, consisting of Davout's *1er Corps*, Oudinot's *2e Corps*, Ney's *3e Corps*, Nansouty's *1er Corps de Cavalerie*, Montbrun's *2e Corps de Cavalerie* and the *Garde*, totalling about 220,000 men, approached the Neman in the vicinity of Kovno, while MacDonald's *10e Corps*, numbering 32,500 men, went to Tilsit.[9]

At the same time, the following were approaching our borders: the Viceroy, with his *4e Corps*, Saint-Cyr's *6e Corps* and Grouchy's *3e Corps de Cavalerie*, numbering around 80,000 men, at Kalwarja [Kalvarija] towards Preny [Prienai], King Jérôme, with Poniatowski's *5e Corps*, Reynier's *7e Corps*, Vandamme's [Dominique Joseph René Vandamme] *8e Corps* and Latour Maubourg's *4e Corps de Cavalerie*, also numbering around 80,000 men, moved towards Białystok and Grodno; while

---

6   In Schreckenstein, *17 Pułk Ułanów* is shown as part of 4e *Corps de Cavalerie*, which increases the number of cavalry by four squadrons. *Die Kavallerie in der Schlacht an der Moskwa.* 162.

7   For the full order of battle, see Appendix XIII.

8   Napoleon wrote to his brother Jérôme: 'Order 100,000 rations of hard tack to be prepared in Lublin and spread rumours about your move there with a 100,000 strong army. Make every possible indication to reassure everyone that you have been ordered to link up with the Austrians; in fact, you are to go in the opposite direction completely; but I am writing this for your eyes only, and I don't want even your chief of staff to know about it. Position and move your light cavalry as if you are making for Volhynia. Send spies there and order them to prepare quarters for themselves in Lublin. I repeat to you that you must not tell anyone about this – not even your chief of staff.' Dresden, 26 May (new style) 1812.

9   Chambray, I, Table II.

Schwarzenberg, with 34,000 men of the Austrian Corps moved towards Drohiczyn, on the Bug.[10]

Consequently, the total number of troops from Napoleon's *Grande Armée*, which was initially to invade Russia, reached 446,500, and together with the headquarters staff some 450,000 men, against whom we could bring no more than 200,000, or even 175,000 men.[11]

On the morning of 11 (23) June, a road carriage pulled by six horses quickly drove up to 6 *Pułk Ułanów*, which was stationed in outposts in the vicinity of the banks of the Neman, it was accompanied by several *Chasseurs à cheval de la Garde*, whose gasping horses were blown with fatigue. Napoleon and Berthier [Louis-Alexandre Berthier] got out of the carriage. The commander of *1er division de cavalerie légère*, General Bruyère, then galloped up, and several Lancer officers came running up. Napoleon, turning to their most senior, Major Suchorzewski [Tadeusz Suchorzewski], asked him about the routes leading to the Neman, about the locations of the outposts, etc. meanwhile he expressed a desire to change into Polish uniform. Several officers took off their uniforms. Napoleon put on Colonel Pogowski's jacket and cap; Berthier also disguised himself as a lancer, and both of them, with one of the Polish officers, set off on horseback to the outposts, to the village of Alexoten, which lies opposite Kovno, thereafter Napoleon, accompanied by General Haxo [François Nicolas Benoît Haxo], who had previously surveyed the area, rode upstream along the Neman to the village of Panemunė, where Haxo had found a very convenient crossing point: at this point the river forms a large loop, conducive to the concentrated fire of batteries placed on the left bank. Napoleon surveyed the area without being noticed; on the opposite bank of the Neman no troops were seen, except for Cossack patrols. Returning from the reconnaissance, Napoleon was very cheerful and on this day he repeatedly sang an old song: '*Marlbrough s'en va-t-en guerre.*' Then, having changed back to his original uniform, he went to Nogaryshki [*Narsiečiai*], a village located six *versts* from Kovno, a little to the right of the main road leading there from Wilkowischken [*Vilkaviškis*].

Upon arrival in Nogaryshki, to where the *État-major général* [headquarters] had been moved that day, Napoleon ordered the drafting and issue of a disposition for crossing the Neman to the troops, on the basis of which, the *commandant en chef des équipages de pont* [Chief of the Pontoniers], General Éblé, was to construct three pontoon bridges at Panemunė, each of 75 pontoons, such that the distance between the bridges was at least 150 paces. In addition, a fourth bridge of a similar type was ordered to be sent to Alexoten, where the pontoons were to remain until the occupation of Kovno by French troops, and then serve as the crossing on the highway between this city and Alexoten. The disposition indicated the deployment of troops before the crossing and upon its completion in detail, the location of the batteries, which were intended to provide security for the construction of the bridges and the order of march for the columns to the opposite bank of the river.[12]

---

10   Chambray, I, Table II.
11   Chambray, I, Table II. Bernhardi, I, 238.
12   Chambray, I, 171. Sołtyk, *Napoléon en 1812*, 8-11. *Ordre pour le passage de Nieman* (M.T.D. No 47,352).

At nine o'clock in the evening, Napoleon, with a very small retinue, went to the place chosen for the crossing at Panemunė once more, where, in his presence, work began. Several boats, found on the left bank of the river, were used to ferry three companies of *13e Légère*, which immediately occupied a nearby village; a Lifeguard Cossack patrol, having exchanged several shots with the enemy, retreated on the orders of the regimental commander, Orlov-Denisov [Vasily Vasilievich Orlov-Denisov]. At the same time, reports were issued about the crossing by the French. Meanwhile, the enemy began building the bridges; the pontoons were lowered into the Neman and by one o'clock in the morning the French army was already moving across the bridges to the far bank of the river; as they reached the right bank, the troops formed deep columns. Davout's corps was to advance along the road leading via Zhizhmory [*Žiežmariai*] directly towards Vilna, and following him, Murat's cavalry crossed over to the right bank of the Neman.

The die was cast! From the first steps of the enemy army on Russian soil, terrible devastation began along its route – the inevitable consequence of the concentration of a huge mass of troops in a small area. In the orders given on behalf of Napoleon, any pillaging was strictly prohibited; but there was no way to enforce the execution of these orders: everywhere one could see the trampled fields, which had promised a rich harvest the day before, the age-old trees stripped to feed bivouac fires, the ruins of villages that had been evacuated a few hours before; frightened inhabitants were visible in all directions, abandoning their hearths and fleeing. The neighbouring countryside could not meet the needs of this new migration of peoples; the resources in it not used by the troops were plundered, scattered, destroyed, while the carts with stores could not keep up with them. There was a lack of forage. The cavalrymen were forced to feed their horses unripe oats, which is why they became exhausted and dropped.[13]

During the course of 12 (24) June, the main body of the *Grande Armée* managed to cross at Panemunė and occupied Kovno, to where Napoleon moved his *État-major général*. During his stay in Kovno, he ordered the pontoon bridges at Panemunė to be raised and sent them after the army; General Éblé was instructed to build permanent bridges over the Neman and the Viliya. Napoleon several times inspected the work on the construction of the bridges himself and of the ships loaded with food and military stores. Magazines, bakeries and hospitals were established in the city, and the construction of fortifications was ordered along all routes leading there. The next day, 13 (25) June, the troops moved forward in three columns: the first, consisting of the *Réserve de cavalerie*, *Garde* and Davout's *1er Corps*, with which the *État-major général* was located, proceeded along the Vilna turnpike to Zhizhmory; the centre, consisting of troops from Ney's *3e Corps*, moved up the left bank of the Viliya, to Skoruli; in the left column, Oudinot's *2e Corps* with Doumerc's *3e division de cuirassiers*, having repaired the bridge over the Viliya, which had been burned down by our troops, crossed to the right bank of this river and proceeded, some upstream to Janau, some to Babtai.[14]

---

13   Sołtyk, 20-24.
14   Chambray, I, 179. Thiers, *Edit. de Brux.* XIV, 7.

The news of the enemy crossing of the Neman arrived in Vilna during the night of 12 to 13 (24 to 25) June. The governor of Kovno, Bistrom, was the first to break the news, before a report arrived from the vanguard on command. Tsar Alexander was at a ball prepared by His Majesty's adjutants general in Zakret [Vingis Park], General Bennigsen's country house at the time. The Minister of Police Balashev quietly reported about the news he had received to the Tsar. The Emperor ordered Balashev to keep the terrible news a secret, remained at the ball for about an hour, and then spent most of the night at work. In accordance with the original plan of action, each corps of First Army was ordered to retreat to Sventsiany, while Prince Bagration and Platov were to operate decisively on the enemy flank.[15] Whereupon, summoning Secretary of State Shishkov [Alexander Semënovich Shishkov], the Tsar told him:

> We must now write orders for our troops and for St Petersburg to Field Marshal Count Saltykov [Nikolay Ivanovich Saltykov] about the enemy invading our borders, and by the way, say that I shall not make peace for as long as at least one enemy soldier remains on our soil.[16]

These documents, signed by the Tsar on the same night, read as follows:

> Order for the army:
> For a long time now we have noted the hostile actions of the Emperor of the French towards Russia, but always hoped to deflect them with mild and peaceful measures. Finally, seeing the incessant repeat of obvious insults, with all Our desire to maintain silence, We were compelled to take up arms and mobilise Our forces; but even then, still offering reconciliation, we remained within the boundaries of Our Empire, not violating the peace, but being only ready for defence. All these methods of mildness and peacefulness could not maintain the tranquillity We desired. The Emperor of the French, attacking our troops at Kovno, opened hostilities first. And so, having seen that he is by no means adamant for peace, there is nothing left for Us but to call upon the help of the Witness and Intercessor of truth, the Almighty Creator of heaven, to pit Our forces against the forces of the enemy. I do not need to remind our leaders, commanders and soldiers of their duty and courage. Since ancient times, the blood of the Slavs has coursed resoundingly with their victories. Soldiers! You are defending Faith, Fatherland, freedom. I am with you. For God the creator.
> (signed in original) Aleksandr.
> Vilna, June 13 [25] 1812.

---

15   Barclay's message to Prince Bagration and his instructions to Platov and the corps commanders, dated 12 [24] June 1812.
16   Admiral Shishkov's Brief Notes, 7-8.

To Field Marshal Saltykov:

> Count Nikolay Ivanovich! French troops have invaded the borders of Our Empire. This most treacherous attack is the reward for our strict observation of the alliance. I have exhausted every means compatible with the dignity of the Throne and the welfare of My people for the preservation of peace. All My efforts have been unsuccessful. Emperor Napoleon has firmly set out to destroy Russia in his name. The most moderate proposals were left unanswered. This unexpected attack has revealed in an obvious way the falsity of the peaceful promises reaffirmed in recent times. And therefore, there is no other choice for Me but to rise up in arms and use all the methods entrusted to Me by Providence to meet force with force. I am reliant on the fervour of My people and the courage of My armies. Being threatened in the bosom of their homes, they will protect them with their characteristic firmness and courage. Providence will bless Our righteous work. The defence of the Fatherland, the preservation of our independence and the honour of the nation has forced Us to gird ourselves for battle. I shall not lay down my arms until not a single enemy warrior remains in My Domains. I remain grateful to you.
>
> (signed in original) Aleksandr.
> Vilna. June 13 [25] 1812.

Tsar Alexander, in undertaking a life and death struggle with the mighty conqueror, grieved over the disasters that would inevitably befall His subjects and had not rejected any means of averting war, even at a time when there was no longer any hope of maintaining peace. On 13 (25) June, at nine o'clock in the evening, the Tsar, having sent for Adjutant General Balashev, said to him:

> You surely do not know why I have summoned you: I intend to send you to Emperor Napoleon. I have just received a report from St Petersburg that a note has been sent to our Ministry of Foreign Affairs from the French embassy, in which it is explained that as our ambassador in Paris, Prince Kurakin insistently demanded passports to leave France twice in one day, then this is interpreted as a breach and has equally also commanded Count Lauriston to ask for passports and to leave Russia. And so, although it is very weak, even I see the reason, in the first instance, which Napoleon uses as a pretext for war; but that alone is insignificant, because Kurakin did it by himself, while he had no command from Me; he saw that everyone was leaving Paris, not only Napoleon, but also Bassano, and considered that he would have no one to ask for his passport for himself thereafter, and to that end he insistently demanded them before they left. And as, meanwhile, there had been a dispatch to Me from Napoleon, his adjutant general, the Comte de Narbonne, who had also been minister of war previously, then in accordance with this I have decided to send you. Although, by the way, between you and I, I do not expect the end of the war from this premise, but

let it become known to Europe and serve as further evidence that we have not started it.[17]

Whereupon the Tsar said that He would write to Napoleon; he ordered Balashev to prepare for departure that same night, and having sent for him a second time at two o'clock, he read him the letter that was to be delivered by him. Upon releasing him, the Emperor instructed him to tell Napoleon that: 'if he intends to enter into negotiations, then they can begin now, on one condition, but immutable, that is, that his armies re-cross the border; otherwise, the Tsar gives his word, as long as one armed Frenchman is in Russia, he will neither speak nor accept a single word about peace.'

The enemy crossing of the Neman should not have been unexpected for us, but in our headquarters it was not believed that Napoleon would undertake it so soon; even less was it thought that he would be able to transfer more than 200,000 men in a few hours. Overall, our orders at this time were hesitant and untimely: not before 3 [15] June were the corps commanders ordered to take measures for the evacuation of stores, or for the destruction of those that, in the event of a retreat, could not be taken away with them; not before 12 [24] June, were orders issued to evacuate the archives, treasury, etc. from Vilna.

The Commander-in-Chief of First Army, Minister of War, Barclay de Tolly was distinguished by experience in battle and the assertive reform of military and administrative departments; the main features of his character were straightforwardness, composure and resolve. The desire to eliminate the shortcomings and abuses that existed in military management prompted him to introduce reforms that brought undoubted benefits, but caused the displeasure and anger of his powerful predecessor, Count Arakcheev, who tried to undermine him at every opportunity. Mistrust was one of the distinctive features of his character; this forced him to strive to carry out many duties that he should have entrusted to his subordinates, and made it difficult to manage the troops. His loyalty to the Tsar and to Russia was limitless. But he lacked the ability to speak to Russian soldiers; the troops and people considered him a foreigner, which, in a national war, was a misfortune for Barclay himself and an obstacle to the overall cause. For all the firmness of his character, Barclay was forced to disguise his intentions out of fear of displeasing popular opinion, and sometimes declare in orders not at all what was required by the circumstances and necessity. At a time when we had just been forced to abandon offensive operations and when our extended deployment did not allow us to think about defending our borders, Barclay wrote to Prince Bagration: 'I hope that God will have mercy on us for retreating.' The consequence of this was the distrust of the troops towards their Commander-in-Chief; few, only those closest to him more than any others, could appreciate this superior quality of his.

Despite his conviction of the need to avoid combat with superior enemy forces, Barclay reluctantly proceeded to retreat. In the note he sent to Prince Bagration on the morning of 12 (24) June, he wrote:

---

17   Extracted from a handwritten note by Adjutant General Balashev.

If First Army does not have the opportunity to give battle to advantage near Vilna, then, having united with the corps under Wittgenstein and Dokhturov at Sventsiany, we may give battle there, while if circumstances permit, I shall advance from Sventsiany to attack the enemy.[18]

Upon the departure of the Tsar from Vilna for Sventsiany on the 14 (26 June), Barclay concentrated III Corps and IV Corps in Vilna, but hesitated to implement his intent to retreat, remaining in Vilna until the last moment. This cool-headed, unflappable warrior did not want to yield Vilna, without giving the enemy a fight; two or three successful clashes by our rearguard would reassure him of his chosen decision, and all the more so as an untimely retreat might shake the courage and resolve of the participating Russian soldiers. He remained in Vilna throughout 15 (27) June, joining the infantry of III Corps' rearguard and leaving his cavalry on the river Verkė; Baggovut's II corps was ordered to halt at Szyrwinty [Širvintos].[19] But when, after that, on 16 (28) June, the enemy vanguard began to press our troops closest to them, then Barclay was forced to retreat. The day before, he had sent his aide de camp, Captain Seslavin [Alexander Nikitich Seslavin], to the commander of IV Corps' vanguard, Major General Dorokhov, who was in danger of being cut off when the enemy moved towards Troki, with orders to retreat from Orany to Mikhalishki [Smolzavod].[20] General Platov was ordered to retreat from Grodno, through Lida and Smorgon, to Sventsiany, also to join First Army, attempting to harass the enemy day and night, delaying them and destroying stores and means of transportation along the way.[21]

At the same time, Barclay de Tolly, informing Prince Bagration of his march with III Corps and IV Corps from Vilna to Sventsiany and about Napoleon's offensive with his main force from Kovno against First Army, and informing him of the orders given to Platov to retreat to Sventsiany, Barclay wrote: 'here we will give general battle to Napoleon; and then your Excellency, with these movements in mind, try to prevent the enemy from cutting off your route through Minsk to Borisov and protect your right flank.' At the same time, the Minister of War asked Prince Bagration to maintain links with Platov and Tormasov.[22] Notifying General Tormasov of the orders for both Western armies, Barclay suggested that he stay in constant communication with Prince Bagration.[23]

Simultaneously with these orders from the Minister of War, Tsar Alexander sent his equerry, Benckendorf [Alexander Khristoforovich Benckendorf], to Prince Bagration, with orders to move to join First Army with the troops entrusted to him, through Novogrudok or Belitsa, to Vileyka [Wilejka], having sent 27th Infantry Division thence, marching from Minsk towards Novogrudok at the time. If it was

---

18   Minister of War's note to Prince Bagration, dated 12 [24] June 1812, No 292.
19   Bernardi, I, 280-281.
20   Barclay de Tolly's report to the Tsar dated 16 [28] June 1812, No 322.
21   Minister of War's instructions to General of Cavalry Platov dated 15 [27] June 1812, No 321.
22   Minister of War's note to Prince Bagration dated 15 [27] June, No 320.
23   Minister of War's note to General of Cavalry Tormasov dated 15 [27] June, No 319.

impossible to execute this movement, orders were issued to retreat to Minsk and Borisov.[24]

In the meantime, the Commander-in-Chief of First Army, having sent out instructions to his corps to retreat to Sventsiany, sent his heavy baggage there from Vilna, on the evening of 15 (27) June, and set out with III Corps and IV Corps himself, on 16 (28) June, at four o'clock in the morning, in three columns: on the right (turning to face the enemy) was 3rd Infantry Division, directed via Zeleny Bridge [Žaliasis tiltas], Verki [Verkiai] and Lyubovo [Liubavas]; in the centre was 1st Grenadier Division, moving along the left bank of the Viliya, towards Antovil and Britanishki [Bratoniškės], where a bridge of rafts had been built; on the left was the whole of IV Corps, moving towards Antovil and Punzhany [Punžonys], where another bridge of rafts had been built.[25] At six o'clock in the morning, the enemy, driving in our outposts, attacked the rearguard of III Corps, swiftly pursued it through Vilna and started a rather heated exchange of fire with the Lifeguard Cossack and Teptyar regiments at Antokol [Antakalnis]. Several men were killed or wounded on each side in this action. The Cossacks captured Captain Comte Ségur [Octave-Henri Gabriel, comte de Ségur] and seven privates of *8e Hussards*. During the retreat from Vilna, our troops managed to take everyone with them, except for 85 sick. The ration magazine located in the city was burned down. The bridges over the Viliya were demolished during the retreat by our troops as they crossed this river.

Simultaneously with the retreat by III Corps and IV Corps, I Corps withdrew from Kiejdany to Wiłkomierz, where they joined up with I Cavalry Corps; II Corps retreated from Orzhishek via Szyrwinty and Giedroyćy [Giedraičiai]; II Cavalry Corps proceeded from Smorgon to Mikhalishki; VI Corps from Lida to Holszany [Halshany] and onwards in two columns, to Dyunashevo and Smorgon; III Cavalry Corps moved in the same direction. The Lifeguard remained at Sventsiany.[26]

Meanwhile, Napoleon's troops were rapidly moving towards Vilna. On the 13th (25 June), Murat and Davout reached Zhizhmory, where the *État-major général* was transferred the next morning; On the 14th (26 June) the enemy reached Jewie [Vievis], and on the 15th (27 June) Murat's cavalry stayed overnight at Rykonta [Rykantai]. The next day [28 June], after a minor clash between the French *7e Hussards* and *8e Hussards* and our Lifeguard Cossacks, Napoleon occupied Vilna.[27]

He made a ceremonial entrance to this city. The streets and squares were filled with people, many of the houses were decorated with expensive tapestries, women

---

24 Supreme Orders to Prince Bagration dated 16 [28] June 1812.
25 In general, during the retreat from the western borders, the Lifeguard Marines were obliged to build bridges for First Army, who carried out this work under the guidance of road engineers.
26 Reports to the Tsar in the name of the Minister of War, dated 16 [28] June, No 326 and 17 [29] June, No 334. War Diary of First Army, from the frontier to Drissa, kept by Major General Mukhin. Information about the places where the temporary bridges were built was obtained from Vice-Admiral Lermontov, who built one of them himself, namely at the village of Punzhany. The bridges were built from dismantled peasant huts; and barrels were placed under them so that they could take the weight of artillery.
27 Thiers, XIV, 12-13. Sołtyk, 35.

were visible at every window, expressing a most animated delight; loud cheering was heard everywhere;[28] among the Poles, indulging in noisy joy at the supposed liberation of their homeland, there were probably many who, not long before that, had greeted their legitimate Emperor with enthusiasm.

Upon entering Vilna, Napoleon went to inspect the outskirts of the city with a small detachment of his *cavalerie de la Garde*, ordered a battery to be set up on Zamkovaya Hill [Gediminas' Tower] before descending from there to the bridge over the Viliya, set on fire by the Russian troops during their retreat. There he dismounted, sat on a log near the bank, summoned several lancers to swim across the river to inspect the suburbs, and immediately ordered three bridges to be built, one of which, on rafts, was completed in his presence. Whereupon Napoleon went to the same house in which, a few days before, Tsar Alexander had been resident.

Napoleon stayed in Vilna for 18 days: he spent this time, for the most part, in studies with the main aim of acquiring information about the theatre of operations and inciting Lithuania and Poland to revolt against Russia. The so-called one hundred-sheet map[29] of our western *Oblasts* turned out to be so inaccurate that it was impossible to rely on it for the movement of troops. In particular, the transliteration of place names were distorted to the point that even the inhabitants of the country could not always guess about which location they were being asked. The French tried to supplement the lack of topographic information with inquiries, but did not have time to find out anything reliable, except for fragmentary statements that would not bring the slightest benefit.

A few days after the French troops occupied Vilna, Napoleon received the Vilna nobility and clergy at a public audience. At the same time, turning to some of the most important personalities, he asked about many subjects related to the state of Russia and Lithuania, and, it seemed, was not happy with the answers. The next day the university presented itself to him. Napoleon talked with the professors about the subjects of their studies, and in particular talked at length with the rector Śniadecki [Jan Śniadecki], who extolled the virtues of Tsar Alexander, recounting everything that this enlightened Tsar had done for public education, and in conclusion said that the University of Vilna owed its flourishing fortune to the patronage and favour of this Monarch. Napoleon, after listening to this review, replied: 'Indeed, Tsar Alexander is an excellent Tsar!'

Napoleon, wishing to draw the inhabitants of Lithuania to himself, devoted his leisure time to receiving the most honourable personalities and appeared at balls, where he tried to appear friendly and talkative with everyone who was honoured with his conversation, but at times he involuntarily lapsed into thoughtfulness. A few days after his arrival in Vilna, a deputation of Poles, which had arrived from Warsaw, presented themselves to him. On the way from there to Vilna, they had been exposed to great danger from French marauders who were plundering and devastating the countryside in the rear of the *Grande Armée*. The deputies hoped that Napoleon would express to them his intentions regarding the fate of Poland;

---

28   Sołtyk, 36.
29   Or Detailed Map.

but, instead, they heard a call to universal mobilisation and the promise of protection, in general indefinite terms.[30]

Among the concerns regarding the movement of the huge forces of the *Grande Armée*, in a country through which only a few routes lay, about the measures to supply the troops with food, regarding the structure of government in Lithuania, about the war in Spain, about affairs in France and in all states subject to it at that time, Napoleon could not strive for the execution of his proposed plan with the total unity of effort aimed at achieving the common objective, which had been the hallmark of his operations.

Early on in his stay in Vilna, Napoleon received Adjutant General Balashev, who had been sent – as already mentioned – by Tsar Alexander from Vilna, at the time when the headquarters of the Russian army was located there. General Balashev, setting out on the night of 13 to 14 [25 to 26] June, arrived in the village of Rykonta at dawn, where the enemy outposts were already stationed. With him were two Cossacks and a trumpeter, with whom, having approached the enemy vedette, Balashev received an invitation to stay. Colonel Julner, who commanded the forward outpost screen, having received information about the arrival of a Russian *parlementaire* from an hussar who had galloped to him, arrived at the screen and, having heard Balashev's explanation, he sent a report to Murat, who immediately sent one of his aides de camp to escort our general to Marshal Davout. On the way, Balashev met Murat, who was surrounded by a large retinue and was wearing a rich, somewhat remarkable costume. The King jumped off his horse; as did Balashev. Murat greeted him with the words: 'I am very glad to see you and to meet you, General! It seems that everything here portends a war.' Balashev responded: 'Indeed, your majesty, it seems that Emperor Napoleon wants to lead that way.'

'And so – you, do you not think that the instigator of the war is Tsar Alexander?'

'Not at all; and I have proof of it with me.'

'Yet there is a note with which you imperatively demanded that French troops evacuate Prussia without entering into any explanation.'

'As far as I know, Your Majesty, that requirement is not the most important of the terms of this note.'

Murat continued: 'But still we could not accept it. However, I sincerely wish the emperors could get along with each other, and that the war that began against my will be ended as soon as possible. I shall not detain you any longer, General! You may continue on your way. I don't know for sure where the Emperor is, but he's probably not far from here.'

Upon arrival at Davout's command post, Balashev was greeted with incredulity by the stern Marshal. 'I do not know where the Emperor is right now,' said Davout: 'Give me your package; I shall forward it.' Balashev took the letter out of his pocket, but at the same time noted that he had been ordered to hand the Tsar's letter to Emperor Napoleon personally.

'That does not matter!' objected the Marshal: 'you are nobody here; do what is asked of you.'

---

30   Sołtyk, 53–63.

'Here is the letter,' Balashev replied with indignation: 'I grant that you pay no attention to my person, but I ask you to remember that I have the honour to bear the status of Adjutant General of His Imperial Majesty Tsar Alexander.' Davout replied that he would be given all due respect, and after that, ordering dinner to be served, he said little, as if reluctant. The next day, at lunch, the Marshal told Balashev that, having received orders to go on, he was granting him quarters, baggage and his aide de camp de Castries [Edmond Eugène Philippe Hercule de La Croix de Castries]. 'I ask you, only one thing' added Davout, 'do not speak to anyone except my aide de camp, and do not go beyond the screen of sentries.' Balashev remained under these conditions until 18 [30] June, when the order was received to send him to Napoleon in Vilna. He was brought to Berthier's quarters, and the next day, Napoleon, having sent his chamberlain, Comte Turenne [Henri Amédée de Turenne], for him, received our general in his office, the very room from which he had been sent, five days previously by Tsar Alexander.

Napoleon, having greeted Balashev amicably, explained the reason for his displeasure at the Russian leadership and tried to present us as the instigators of the war. To this Balashev replied that the Tsar was most astonished at the invasion by the French army across our borders without a declaration of war, under the excuse that Prince Kurakin had demanded his passports, and that Tsar Alexander himself, in this case, had not approved of the actions of his ambassador. 'The Tsar has instructed me to report to your Majesty,' continued Balashev, 'that now, as before, He is ready for peace, with only one condition, but this being an indispensable condition, that the French immediately cross back beyond our borders. At the same time, I am commanded to assure your Majesty that our government has not entered into any relations with Britain.'

Napoleon, continuing to list the perceived reasons for war, to the proposal by Tsar Alexander, stated in response to Balashev:

'Eighteen months have already passed since I demand that you explain yourselves to me. Did you not ask me to evacuate Prussia? Such notes cannot be borne by even the smallest Powers in relations – not even by Sweden; and no one has ever dared to make such a proposal to a French government. I could not accept it even in the event of you giving me St Petersburg and Moscow for that. Were you not the first to mobilise? Your Sovereign arrived with his army before me. I was forced to cancel my visit to Spain. You have saddled me with a greater cost. I know that war between France and Russia is not a trifle – neither for me, nor for you. But I have made better preparations, I am twice as strong as you; I know your strength as well as you; maybe even better. Tsar Alexander is surrounded by inferior people: Armfeldt, Stein, Bennigsen are with him! Armfeldt is a depraved, shameless, sly man; Stein is a scoundrel, expelled from his fatherland; Bennigsen, who showed his incompetence in 1807. I do not know Barclay de Tolly, but judging by your initial deployment, his talents are very limited: your troops move without a definite objective; you yourselves have burned many of your magazines; it would have been better not to establish them at all. Do you really think that I came all this way just to look at the Neman. No enemy has crossed your borders since the time of Peter I, while now – I am already in Vilna. You vainly rely upon your soldiers; before Austerlitz they considered themselves invincible; now they certainly know in advance that my troops will beat them.'

'I dare to assure your Majesty' interrupted Balashev 'that the Russian troops, instead of doubting their strength, are eagerly keen to fight, and especially since our borders are under threat. This war will be terrible; you will be dealing not with troops alone, but with the entire Russian nation, which is loyal to the Tsar and the Fatherland.' Napoleon disagreed with Balashev, said that no one in Russia wanted war, and again he listed his huge resources, assuring him that there were 80,000 Poles in his army, and that he would recruit some 200,000 of them. He stated:

'And they fight like lions, if you continue the war, then I shall take the Polish *Oblasts* from you. I assure you that you could never have started a war under more unfavourable circumstances.'

'We hope to finish it with success,' Balashev answered.

'You could do nothing,' Napoleon continued, 'even when Austria was on your side, and now, when all of Europe is with me, who are you relying on?'

'We will do whatever we can,' Balashev said.

'You don't have enough men; where will you recruit? And what value does your recruit have? How long does it take to make a soldier out of him? They say you have made peace with the Turks; is it true?' And having received an affirmative answer, Napoleon continued: 'If you renounce your claim to Moldavia and Wallachia, then the Sultan will make peace with you; however, I have very little respect for either Turks or Swedes.' He then expounded on the benefits that Russia could derive from an alliance with France, threatened that he would destroy Prussia, and ended his speech with an expression of inclination towards peace.

'Assure Tsar Alexander on my behalf that I am as devoted to him as before; I know him perfectly and appreciate his superior qualities. Oh God, my God! How wonderful his reign could have been if he had not fallen into trouble with me! I shall not detain you any longer, General. You shall receive a letter from me for your Tsar.'

Having bowed to Napoleon, Balashev, upon leaving him, was invited to dine at seven o'clock by Duroc, on behalf of the Emperor.

Throughout this dinner, at which, in addition to the Emperor of the French and Balashev, were Berthier, Bessières and Caulaincourt, Napoleon was much more arrogant than before. Among the questions he put to Balashev, he expressed a wish to get an impression of Moscow. He asked: 'how many inhabitants are there?'

'300,000.'

'And dwellings?'

'10,000.'

'And churches?'

'More than 240.'

'Why so many?'

'The Russian people are devout.'

'Completely, what kind of piety is that now?'

'Excuse me, your majesty,' said Balashev, 'maybe there are few pious people in Germany and Italy, but there are still many of them in Spain and Russia.'

Napoleon, dissatisfied with this allusion to the resistance he was meeting in Spain, fell silent, but suddenly, turning to Balashev, asked: 'Which route might one take to Moscow?'

'Your Majesty has put me in great difficulty,' he replied: 'the Russians, like the French, say that all roads lead to Rome. Many routes also lead to Moscow. Charles XII moved in that direction to Poltava.'

Thereupon Napoleon went back into the office with everyone sitting at the table with him and began to criticise Tsar Alexander with venom: 'He has taken my personal enemies into his confidence; he has personally insulted me. I have the right to do likewise. I shall expel all his relatives from Germany, Württemberg, Baden, Weimar. Let him prepare a sanctuary for them in Russia! I was told that your Tsar has taken command of his troops. What for? War is my profession; I am accustomed to it. Tsar Alexander is not needed at all; his business is to reign, not to command troops. It is pointless for him to take on such responsibility.' Then, pacing several times across the room, Napoleon went up to Caulaincourt and, touching him lightly on the cheek, said to him: 'Well, why do you not say something, apologist for Tsar Alexander? Are the horses ready for the general; give him mine; he has a long way to go.'[31]

The mission assigned to Balashev by Tsar Alexander was the last interaction between the Tsar and Napoleon. Having run out of time to prevent a bloody war, He decided not to halt the struggle until the complete triumph over his arrogant rival.

After the occupation of Vilna, Napoleon continued to pursue First Army: Oudinot, as has already been mentioned, moved towards Wiłkomierz following Count Wittgenstein's I Corps; Ney, before reaching Vilna, crossed the Viliya, near the town of Sudervė, and moved towards Molėtai; Murat, with Montbrun's 2e Corps de Cavalerie and with two divisions from Davout's Corps (Friant's Division and Gudin's Division) followed the main body of First Army, towards Sventsiany; Nansouty, with his 1er Corps de Cavalerie, less Valence's 5e division de cuirassiers, and with a single infantry division (Morand's Division) from Davout's 1er Corps, was sent to cut across Dokhturov's line of retreat, towards Mikhalishki; while Davout himself, with the remaining two divisions from his corps (Dessaix's Division and Compans' Division), Grouchy's 3e Corps de Cavalerie (less Doumerc's 3e division de cuirassiers attached to Oudinot's 2e Corps), two light cavalry brigades (Pajol's and Bordesoulle's [Étienne Tardif de Pommeroux de Bordesoulle]) and Claparède's [Michel Marie Claparède] Polish Division [Légion de la Vistule], moved towards Valozhin, in order to sever the line of retreat of Second Army.[32]

On the same day as the French occupation of Vilna, 16 (28) June, there was an action at Wiłkomierz, between the leading troops under Oudinot and Wittgenstein. Upon the arrival of I Corps at Wiłkomierz, on 15 (27) June, Count Wittgenstein halted there to rest the troops, following three forced marches, and to link up with Vlastov's detachment retreating from Rossieny, via Remigale, to the town of Onikszty [Anykščiai]. A rearguard was located, six versts in front of Wiłkomierz in order to shield the main body of the corps and to observe the roads leading from Shaty [Šėta] and Janau towards this town, under the command of Major General Kulnev, consisting of 23rd Jägers, 25th Jägers, four squadrons of Grodno Hussars, three Sotnia of Platov 4th's Don Cossacks and six guns from 27th Light Artillery Company.

31   All the details of Balashev's mission have been extracted from his own handwritten notes.
32   Buturlin. Hist. milit, de la campagne de Russie, I, 172-173.

On 16 (28) June, one of the patrols sent out by General Kulnev discovered the enemy on the road from the town of Shaty, seven *versts* from Dziewałtów [Deltuva]. Having received this report, Kulnev dispatched Captain Kempfert, with his squadron from the Grodno Hussar Regiment and a *Sotnia* of Cossacks, to scout out the enemy force. Captain Kempfert held the French cavalry back with local attacks until infantry arrived to help them, and then, on Kulnev's orders, he retreated through the forest and joined the vanguard, and was wounded by a bullet in the leg. Once the enemy, pursuing Kempfert, emerged from the forest with several squadrons and battalions, then Kulnev, to whom six horse artillery guns had been sent not long before, under the command of Colonel Sukhozanet 1st [Ivan Onufrievich Sukhozanet], to relieve the light artillery in his detachment, he pushed forward two guns, under escort by jägers and hussars, and, letting the enemy cavalry column moving along the highway close to cannon range, gave orders to open fire. The enemy troops, who did not have artillery with them, were thrown into disorder and disappeared into the forest. Meanwhile, Lieutenant General Uvarov, who had remained in Wiłkomierz with I Cavalry Corps, anticipating a new enemy assault, dispatched the Nezhin Dragoon Regiment to support Kulnev.

At one o'clock in the afternoon, the enemy renewed the attack with six infantry and four cavalry columns and forced Kulnev to retreat beyond the village of Dziewałtów. Our troops, having occupied an advantageous position there, held on for about two hours with cannon fire from skilfully placed artillery and cavalry attacks. Meanwhile, the main body of the corps managed to cross the Sventa [Šventoji (Neris)]. Kulnev, having learned of this, also began to retreat, covering his movement with cavalry across open ground, and with infantry in the brush; on reaching Wiłkomierz, having made one last cavalry charge, gaining time for all remaining troops to pass through the town and cross the Sventa; whereupon the cavalry also retreated under cover of musket fire from jägers stationed behind the hedges on the left bank of the river.

With this retreat, Count Wittgenstein's horse artillery was in great danger. At the moment when the rearguard, falling back, was just approaching Wiłkomierz, Kulnev, keeping Lieutenant Colonel Sukhozanet with six horse-artillery guns with him, ordered the horse-artillery echelon, which was waiting in front of the town, to follow after Count Wittgenstein's troops. The officer of the General Staff appointed to indicate the route, due to ignorance of the Wiłkomierz area, instead of leading the artillery across the bridge over the Sventa, led them to the left, through the middle of the town, to a bridge over a minor tributary of the Sventa: thus, the horse-artillery echelon was sent in a direction that separated it from the rest of the corps troops.

Meanwhile, Lieutenant Colonel Sukhozanet, remaining with Kulnev's rearmost troops, occasionally exchanged cannon fire with the enemy; once our infantry occupying the town opened fire, then Kulnev sent his cavalry back with the last six guns, Sukhozanet, also not knowing the Wiłkomierz area at all, galloped with his guns in the footsteps of the retreating echelon, but emerging from the town up onto high ground, was left by his commander, Prince Iashvili [Levan Mikhailovich Iashvili], who, without realising the direction his horse artillery had taken, pointed out the masses of Wittgenstein's Corps, in the valley, on the far bank of the Sventa. Sukhozanet, realising the mistake, explained to Prince Iashvili that he could make his way through the town to the bridge over the Sventa himself albeit at great risk, or cross by swimming; but that reversing the movement was impossible for the artillery, because the French had already charged into Wiłkomierz. 'Don't waste a minute, Prince, you may rely on my good fortune with horse artillery,'[33] he said. Iashvili galloped into the town, where the musket fire continued unabated, and, meanwhile, Sukhozanet, with the entire horse artillery, trotted up the Sventa; but as soon as French cavalry appeared from the town, he placed the 12 guns from his battery on high ground, showing the enemy his readiness to wait for their attack; he formed two half-squadrons using the gunners from the other battery; while the guns without their mounted gunners were ordered to move back with all possible speed and to find the crossing over the river Sventa, to which the carts of the entire corps had also been sent before dawn, in accordance with the general disposition.

The French cavalry, noticing our supposed readiness for battle, stopped at the exits from the town, and it was also evident that the cavalrymen were dismounting from their horses. Lieutenant Colonel Sukhozanet, taking advantage of the indecision by the enemy, began to retreat very slowly by bounds, until he received news of the discovery of a crossing point; whereupon they went at a trot and, having crossed the Sventa, re-joined the corps.

In the action at Dziewałtów, Kulnev's vanguard lost about 100 men killed and wounded. The enemy losses are not known precisely; 20 men were captured by our troops.[34]

On this day, 16 (28) June, Count Wittgenstein reached the village of Perkele with the main body of I Corps, and on the next day, 17 (29 June), continuing to retreat further, he picked up Vlastov's detachment and a convoy from the Telschi [Telšiai] and Schaulen [Šiauliai] magazines, with the arrival of which he had some 8,000 *Chetvert* of grain with the corps.[35] The movement of the troops, and in particular of the convoys, was hampered in the extreme by inclement weather, which began on 17 (29) June, the day after the French occupied Vilna.[36] On 19 June (1 July) I Corps was in Sołoki [Salakas]; II Corps was at Kołtyniany; V Corps was at Daugieliszki [Senasis Daugėliškis] behind Sventsiany, while III Corps and IV Corps and II Cavalry Corps had concentrated at Sventsiany,[37] less the rearguard of IV Corps, under Major General Dorokhov's command,[38] which, having earlier been stationed at Orany, on the route between Grodno and Vilna, had become isolated from IV Corps by

---

33   [Liprandi believed that this phrase was 'borrowed' from Yermolov at Borodino, arguing that Sukhozanet, as a junior commander in his first combat, had no established good fortune to fall back upon, however, Sukhozanet had served in East Prussia in 1806-1807, thus Liprandi's criticism seems a little unjust].

34   Count Wittgenstein's report to the Tsar dated 30 June [12 July] 1812. The number of killed and wounded is from a return signed by Wittgenstein. Count Wittgenstein's War Diary, in the archive of the M.T.D. No 29,200.

35   Count Wittgenstein's report dated 18 [30] June 1812.

36   Lieutenant General Uvarov's reports to the Tsar dated 18 and 19 June [30 June and 1 July] 1812.

37   Commander-in-Chief's and Corps Commanders' reports to the Tsar in the archive of the M.T.D. No 32,415.

38   1st Jägers, 18th Jägers, Izyum Hussars and two Cossack regiments, with a single light artillery company.

the enemy. General Dorokhov, having not received any orders from headquarters and already knowing of the enemy crossing of the Neman,[39] decided, on 15 (27) June, to march to Olkieniki, where he hoped to find IV Corps, which at that time had already reached Vilna. Then, having received the Commander in Chief's orders from Seslavin during the night of 16 to 17 (28 to 29 June), to go to Mikhalishki, Dorokhov hurriedly diverted, and arrived at Soleczniki [Šalčininkai] on the 17th [29 June]; but as his patrols encountered enemy on every route leading towards First Army, he was forced to try to link up with Second Army. To that end, marching to Dziewieniszki [Dieveniškės], Holszany and Valozhin, he established communications with Platov's Cossack detachment on 23 June (5 July), and then, reaching the town of Novy-Sverzhen [Świerżeń Nowy], on the 25th (7 July) joined the troops under Prince Bagration. This forced march, made in the midst of enemy troops, was very painful. 'Some of the soldiers, and even some officers, carried three or four muskets, taken from the exhausted, putting the backpacks of those drained of strength on their riding horses. Not only sweat, but blood flowed from the armpits from unbearable chafing.[40] Yet in spite of all this and the loss of men in several skirmishes with the enemy, Dorokhov lost, in the course of the nine-day march, no more than 60 men, some even re-joined whom he had already considered dead.

During the retreat by our troops to Sventsiany and onwards, several magazines had been burned; in particular, the loss of the larger magazine in Kołtyniany, where provisions worth 1,000,000 roubles were destroyed, was especially painful.[41]

General Dokhturov, having received orders from Barclay de Tolly to march to join First Army at Sventsiany, assembled VI Corps at Holszany, on 15 (27) June, and the next day marched with them in two columns to the crossings on the Viliya, at Smorgon and Dyunashevo; on the 18th (30 June), the entire corps assembled at the latter location. Meanwhile, Count Pahlen's III Cavalry Corps, managed to concentrate near the town of Lida and was reinforced there by 19th Jägers and 40th Jägers (from VI Corps) on 14 (26) June. Having received orders to cover the flanking march by Dokhturov, Count Pahlen sent all the heavy wagons to Vileyka, towards Polotsk, and dispatched Colonel Baron Kreutz [Kiprian Antonovich Kreutz], with the Siberia Dragoon Regiment and two squadrons of Mariupol Hussars (six squadrons in total), to Oshmyany [Ashmyany], in order to cover his corps from the left flank, while he [Pahlen] took the shortest route to Smorgon himself in order to cross the Viliya there. General Dokhturov, for his part, wishing to secure communications with Count Pahlen, left one battalion and two guns each at both crossings at Smorgon and Dyunashevo, with orders to wait for the arrival of the troops of III Cavalry Corps.[42]

Meanwhile, Colonel Kreutz, upon approaching Oshmyany at dawn on 17 (29) June, found the town in French hands, taking them by surprise, he drove them out,

---

39   The Minister of War's aide de camp, Guards Captain Seslavin, had been sent to Dorokhov with orders to go to Mikhalishki on 15 (27) June.
40   Mikhailovsky-Danilevsky's History of the Patriotic War of 1812, I.
41   Active Privy Councillor Tuchkov's notes. Kankrin, in his work *Über die militair Öconomie*, also mentions the loss of the Kołtyniany magazine.
42   Dokhturov's report to the Tsar dated 16 [28] June 1812.

took several prisoners, freed many of ours captured on the Vilna road, and, setting up outposts in the direction of Vilna, settled with his dragoons outside the town, on the route leading to Smorgon. Colonel Kreutz, intending to slow down the enemy advance as much as possible in order to gain time for Count Pahlen to forestall the French in Smorgon, ordered all the exits from the town to be barricaded with logs; at the same time, an order was issued that the Mariupol men, who were stationed on the Vilna road, in the event of an attack on them, were to retreat not along the Smorgon road, but to the left, towards Narbutovshchizna [Narbuty] (15 *versts* from Oshmyany), where they were to rendezvous with the dragoons. Thereafter, the enemy drove in our forward outposts, which withdrew in the indicated direction. Some of the French cavalry raced off to pursue the hussars; others broke into Oshmyany; but the enemy infantry, bypassing the town, headed for the forest, which lay three *versts* behind our dragoons. Whereupon Kreutz, having detached Lieutenant Baron Offenberg 2nd [Ivan Petrovich Offenberg] with one squadron, ordered him to occupy the forest with marksmen, while he held the enemy as they were leaving the town himself, attacking them by squadron three times, and, having captured a field officer and more than 40 lower ranks, retreated to the forest and beyond; the French pursued him to Narbutovshchizna, where the hussars joined the dragoons, crossed the river and dismantled the bridge, fighting with enemy flankers until evening. At night, having received news of the arrival of Count Pahlen in Smorgon, Kreutz re-joined him and assumed command of the corps rearguard.

Upon arrival at the Viliya river, Count Pahlen did not find detachments from VI Corps there, which had already retreated after Dokhturov's main body. The bridge at Smorgon was half destroyed by them, probably in order to leave just one crossing over the Viliya at Dyunashevo. Upon the hasty repair of the Smorgon bridge, III Cavalry Corps moved to join VI Corps, while Dokhturov, having learned about movements towards them by Nansouty's Corps, through Mikhalishki, on 19 June (1 July), marched 42 *versts* from Dyunashevo to Svir, forestalling Nansouty there, who had given his troops a rest at Mikhalishki, and continued onward through Kozyany towards Drissa. Count Pahlen, first moving to the right of Dokhturov, and then, behind him, also passed Kozyany and left Adjutant General Baron Wintzingerode [Ferdinand Fëdorovich Wintzingerode] with the Mariupol Hussar Regiment in outposts at this town.

In all likelihood, our outposts were very careless, because on the very next night the enemy cavalry caught the hussars by surprise and quickly pursued them until Colonel Kreutz arrived in time to help. Wintzingerode himself and the regimental commander, Colonel Prince Vadbolsky [Ivan Mikhailovich Vadbolsky], with two squadrons, were brushed aside and only managed to re-join their own with great difficulty, three days later; the other six squadrons were rallied by Colonel Kreutz. In this action, we lost about 40 men; among the seriously wounded was the valiant Lieutenant Figner.[43]

---

43   The namesake of the famous partisan, who was serving in the artillery at the time. From Kreutz's notes in the M.T.D. No 47,352. Minister of War's report to the Tsar dated 24 June [6 July] 1812, No 384.

The Tsar himself, noting the movements of the troops and realising the danger to which the left flank corps of First Army had been exposed, ordered them to speed up their retreat. To ease conditions for the men, Generals Dokhturov and Count Pahlen were ordered to take peasant horses for the supply of ammunition and give the troops daily rations of meat and wine, taking cattle and wine from the inhabitants against receipts.[44]

These rapid marches, necessary in order to concentrate forces spread over a large area at one location, were associated with extreme fatigue for the men and entailed the loss of much transport that had lagged behind the army and was captured by the enemy.[45]

The retreat of the main body of First Army from Sventsiany, where the troops had a rest day on 20 June (2 July), was begun the following day without any losses. Only Captain Galev 1st, with a single squadron of Poland Ulans, detached for a reconnaissance of the enemy at Mikhalishki and returning from there to Sventsiany, was surrounded near this town by three enemy cavalry regiments, but he cut his way through them, for the loss of one non-commissioned officer and 46 privates. Among the enemy dead were two field officers.[46] As a reward for this feat, the brave Galev was awarded the Order of St George, 4th class.

During the retreat beyond the river Disna by First Army, the rearguard of the main column, under General Korf's command, was attacked near the village of Starye-Daugieliszki on 23 June (5 July) by General Subervie's [Jacques-Gervais Subervie] light cavalry brigade, which formed the vanguard of Murat's *Réserve de cavalerie*. General Korf went into battle at the village of Kochergishki [Kačergiškės], then withdrew across the Disna River, holding there all day and retreated at night on the orders of the Commander-in-Chief. Our losses that day were quite significant (236 men); among the wounded was Colonel Rakhmanov [Pëtr Alexandrovich Rakhmanov] of the Lifeguard Preobrazhesnky Regiment. The enemy losses are not precisely known. A colonel of the Württemberg contingent, Prince Hohenlohe and 30 lower ranks were captured by our troops.[47]

The further retreat by First Army to the river Dvina was made in three columns: the main body proceeded along the road leading from Sventsiany, to Vidzy [Widze] and Belmont towards Leonpol; I Corps went from Soloki, to Braslav, towards Druya, where they crossed to the right bank of the Dvina; VI Corps and III Cavalry Corps went from Dyunashevo, via Kozyany, towards Stary-Kryuki near the Dvina.[48]

From 27 to 29 June (9 to 11 July), troops of First Army arrived at the camp at Drissa; of these, Count Wittgenstein's I Corps, crossing at Druya, on the 28th (10 July) via three bridges, received orders to dismantle two of them, made of pontoons, keeping the third in the event of a retreat by the Cossacks, left by Wittgenstein on the left bank of the river; whereupon I Corps was reinforced with reserves formed from

---

44   Supreme Orders to General of Infantry Dokhturov and Major General Count Pahlen dated 17 [29] June 1812.

45   Dokhturov's report to the Tsar dated 24 June [6 July] 1812.

46   Captain Galev 1st's report to the Minister of War. The Minister of War's notes about him.

47   Minister of War's report to the Tsar dated 24 June [6 July] 1812, No 384.

48   Commander-in-Chief's report to the Tsar. War Diary of First Army.

replacement units of the force, consisting of eight battalions and three combined regiments, some 2,200 infantry and 1,300 cavalry in total. On 29 June (11 July), Count Wittgenstein moved up the right bank of the Dvina and positioned himself opposite Leonpol, to the right of the Drissa camp; while Dokhturov's Corps, also crossing the Dvina, via the bridges at Drissa, stood at Prudinki, to the left of the camp. The remaining troops occupied the fortified camp in the following order: Baggovut's II Corps on the right wing; Tuchkov's III Corps in the centre; IV Corps on the left wing, under the command of Count Osterman [Alexander Ivanovich Osterman-Tolstoy] due to the illness of Count Shuvalov; the three cavalry corps formed the second line, while V Corps formed the third.[49]

Along the entire line of retreat by the Russian force from Sventsiany to Drissa, the enemy pursued them rather weakly. Murat, moving to Vidzy and Opsa, arrived at Zamosha [Zamosh'e] on 1 (13) July, and took under command the troops of Ney's and Nansouty's flanking columns, moving to Drysvyaty and Postawy, while Oudinot, proceeding via Sołoki, arrived at Dünaburg.[50]

Meanwhile, as Napoleon's main body, having passed Vilna, chased after our troops in various directions, the Viceroy, crossing the Neman on 18 (30) June, at Preny, marched to Novy-Troki with his *4e Corps*, and onwards via Rudniki [Rūdninkai] to Smorgon, on 30 June (12 July). On this march, along very bad country roads, many horses were lost, most particularly from the artillery. On 2 (14) July, the Viceroy continued to move in the direction of Vileyka and Dokshitsy [Dokšycy], where he arrived on 6 (18) July. Meanwhile, *6e Corps* under Saint-Cyr arrived in Vilna and set out from there behind the *Garde*, which had marched to Glubokoe [Głębokie], in early [mid] July.

Simultaneously with these forces, King Jérôme also advanced. Having occupied Grodno, on 18 (30) June, the King remained there for several days, and then on the 22nd (4 July), he sent *4e Corps de Cavalerie* under Latour Maubourg, Poniatowski's *5e Corps* and Vandamme's *8e Corps*, through Belitsa to Novogrudok, where Reynier's *7e Corps* also went via Białystok and Wołkowysk.[51] On 26 June (8 July), Latour Maubourg passed Karelichi. At the same time, the Austrian Corps under Schwarzenberg, having crossed the Bug at Drohiczyn, moved towards Slonim.

Thus, the troops under Murat, stationed at Zamosha, were facing First Army; Napoleon and the Viceroy, were proceeding in the direction of Glubokoe and Dokshitsy, and Davout, moving towards Minsk, separated our armies from each other, while King Jérôme pursued Second Army.[52]

Let us turn to operations by Second Army, and their retreat simultaneous with First Army's from the borders of the Empire towards the Dvina.

The Commander-in-Chief of this army, Prince Bagration, a warrior at heart, who developed his natural abilities under Suvorov's command, who was his protege, who

---

49   Reports by Count Wittgenstein, Dokhturov and reserve commanders Major General Gamen and Prince Repnin-Volkonsky, in the archive of the M.T.D. No 32,415. For the Tsar's rescript to Barclay de Tolly, regarding the appointment of Count Osterman, see Appendix XIV.
50   Chambray, I, 212-213.
51   Reynier, having reached Slonim, was ordered to turn to face Tormasov.
52   Chambray, I, 201-202 and 205.

fought with glory in the Caucasus, Turkey, Poland, Italy, Austria, Finland, wherever our Colours reached, he was adored by the Russian troops. His name, inseparable from the memories of Ochakov, Praga, the Adda, Trebbia, Novi, Saint-Gotthard, Schöngraben, Preußisch-Eylau, Heilsberg, Kvarken [Merenkurkku] and Brailov,[53] was repeated with respect in every part of Russia. Being constantly in the vanguard, or in the rearguard, paving the way to victory for the troops, or protecting them with his chest, entering the battle first and leaving it last, Bagration did not know fatigue in war: in the few hours that he rested, as soon as a report came to him, no matter how unimportant it was, he was immediately awakened: this was the standing order! Caring about others, strict with himself, he, like his famous patron Suvorov, knew how to appreciate the worthy diligence and abilities of his subordinates. Allowing them to share the military efforts and glory, Bagration considered it a pleasure to publicise their merits. Being around him was enchanting. All those around him were devoted to him; his trust towards his closest associates was unlimited and also sometimes gave them the opportunity to exploit their authority for evil. Yielding to Barclay in education, theoretical knowledge and administrative experience, Bagration surpassed him in his ability to animate the troops and speak to Russian soldiers.

The original mission of Second Army was to operate on the flank of the enemy in the event of an offensive by Napoleon's main body against First Army, supporting Platov's raiding detachment, which, at the same time, was intended to race into the rear of the enemy army. But these movements by Supreme orders were not to be executed before having received orders from headquarters, but in anticipation of further orders, the troops of Second Army,[54] consisting of VII Corps, VIII Corps and IV Cavalry Corps, had assembled in the vicinity of Wołkowysk by 8 (20) June; at the same time Platov's raiding corps was at Grodno.[55]

The invasion by Napoleon, blocking direct communications between Second Army and headquarters, made Prince Bagration concerned about being completely cut off. Remaining completely in the dark about both enemy operations and those of First Army, until on 16 (28) June, he received a note from Barclay de Tolly dated 15 (27) June, which ordered him to retreat to Minsk, while maintaining communications with Platov and Tormasov.[56] Prince Bagration set out on 16 (28) June from Wołkowysk, towards Slonim, and arrived at the town of Zelwa, where by 18 (30) June all the troops of his army had concentrated, with the exception of the rearguard made up of the Combined Grenadier Division, under Major General Count Vorontsov with two of Adjutant General Vasilchikov's [Illarion Vasilievich Vasilchikov] cavalry regiments. After the concentration of all the troops of Second Army, Prince Bagration issued the following order:

---

53   [Liprandi notes that Bagration did not take part in the crossing of the Kvarken Straits, as he was 267 miles away in the Aland Islands at the time, nor in the storming of Brailov, which took place in 1770 – when Bagration was just five years old].
54   See Map of Significant Movements by the Russian and French armies from the beginning of the war to the battle of Smolensk.
55   War Diary of Second Army, in the archive of the M.T.D. No 29,180.
56   Barclay de Tolly's message dated 15 [27] June, No 380.

Warriors of Russia! Do I need to stir up your passion for the Fatherland when the Tsar calls you to defend it? All that remains is for us to listen to His voice and, with faith in the help of Almighty God, unquestioning obedience to the commanders and fearlessness on the battlefield, we shall make the enemy rue the day they dared to set foot on Russian soil.[57]

General Platov, complying with orders he had received from the Minister of War, also set out on 17 [29] June from Grodno, to Szczuczyn, towards Lida.[58] Meanwhile, on 18 (30) June, *Flügeladjutant* Colonel Benckendorf visited Prince Bagration, in Zelwa, with Supreme orders – to march to join First Army, via Novogrudok or Belitsa, and onwards to Vileyka.[59]

Prince Bagration, arriving in Slonim on 19 June (1 July) (while Platov's raiding corps reached Lida on the same day), set out on 20 June (2 July) in the indicated direction and on 21 June (3 July) arrived in Novogrudok with his main body, where he took under command General Neverovsky's 27th Infantry Division, which had arrived from Moscow; on the same day, the cavalry of the rearguard, under the command of Vasilchikov, was stationed at Velikaya Volya, on the river Shchara; while Count Vorontsov's infantry stood in support of the cavalry at Zdzięcioł; in order to protect the army from the direction of Brest, there was a Cossack detachment in Slonim, under Major General Ilovaisky 5th, who had been instructed to move by forced marches to the left flank of the army, to cover its crossing over the Neman.[60] On 22 June (4 July), all the corps of Second Army had arrived at the place designated for crossing the Neman, at Nikolaev; in the absence of pontoons, a flying bridge and a ferry were soon built, along which, during the evening of the same day, the vanguard, VIII Corps and 2nd Cuirassier Division, crossed to the right bank of the river; the ration wagons and other heavy transport were assigned to cross opposite the village of Kolodzina. On 23 June (5 July), the rest of the army was supposed to cross. A survey of the routes leading to Vileyka, through forests and swamps, convinced the troops of the difficulties ahead; having said that, Prince Bagration, ignoring both the rising water levels in the Neman from heavy rains, which slowed down the transfer of troops to the right bank of the river, and the obstacles that awaited him on the onward march to Vileyka, was determined to carry on, but, meanwhile, he received a report from Platov about the occupation of Vishnevo [Wiszniew] by Davout's *1er Corps*, which, according to the interrogation of prisoners, consisted of 60,000 men. Indeed – Platov, who set out on 20 June (2 July) from Lida, after destroying the magazines located there, arrived in Iwje, on 21 June (3 July), and intended to go on to Vishnevo, to join First Army, but having received intelligence from patrols sent out by him regarding Davout's location overnight in Vishnevo, he decided to turn towards Bakshty in order to link up with Dorokhov, who, meanwhile, having also been cut off from First Army, had moved from Valozhin to the village of Kamen. After that, Bagration received information

---

57   Order of the day for Second Army dated 17 [29] June, No 65.
58   Prince Bagrations message dated 17 [29] June, No 337.
59   Supreme orders dated 16 [28] June.
60   Prince Bagration's report to the Tsar dated 20 June [2 July], No 349.

about the appearance of the enemy to the rear of Second Army, at Zelwa, as well as on the flank from the direction of Grodno.

This news prompted Prince Bagration to abandon the route to Vileyka, and, crossing back to the left bank of the Neman, to go through Novy-Sverzhen and Kaidanovo [Dzyarzhynsk] towards Minsk. He did not know that Davout's *1er Corps*, weakened by the detachment of three divisions, consisted of no more than 40,000 men at that time; in addition, Bagration hoped that Davout, convincing himself of his crossing at Nikolaev, would divert from the route to Minsk in order to counter him, and would thus give him the opportunity to forestall the enemy at this location and re-establish communications with First Army. On the basis of these considerations, Prince Bagration assembled his force on the left bank of the Neman and moved to Karelichi on 23 June (5 July), where he received a note from Platov about his liaison with Dorokhov's detachment that had arrived in Kamen. Taking advantage of this, Bagration ordered Platov, 'to occupy Valozhin together with Dorokhov and, holding there on the 26th [8 July], retreat to join Second Army, directed on Minsk, via Kamen and Stowbtsy.'[61]

The orders by Prince Bagration were based on exaggerated intelligence on the strength of Davout's Corps, which was blocking his way to Vileyka; but it is rather difficult to understand the orders issued to Platov – to occupy Valozhin, which could not have been carried out without pushing Davout back, and such an operation was obviously beyond the strength of Platov's and Dorokhov's formations. Perhaps, in issuing these orders, Bagration had in mind to incite Platov into a decisive attack on Valozhin, which would keep Davout's main body fixed at this location and slow down his advance towards Minsk.

On the evening of 23 June (5 July), Second Army was located at Karelichi; while on 24 June (6 July) they arrived in Mir. The Commander-in-Chief, having received a report from General Dorokhov there, regarding the appearance of significant enemy forces at Minsk, did not dare to clear the route by force himself, especially since he had received a Supreme order earlier via the Minister of War: 'to avoid decisive battles with a stronger enemy.' Prince Bagration, concerned about being held accountable in the event of a failure, decided to change the direction he had taken and go via Nesvizh and Slutsk towards Bobruisk.[62] On 25 June (7 July), VIII Corps was sent directly to Nesvizh, while the Commander-in-Chief, with the remainder of his force, proceeded to the town of Novy-Sverzhen in order to link up with Dorokhov's detachment; the next day, 26 June (8 July), the entire Second Army had assembled at Nesvizh, and during the night of 27 June (9 July), Platov's Cossack Corps arrived at Mir from Karelichi.

The Commander-in-Chief, intending to give the troops a rest, after the forced marches made by them along swampy and sandy roads, in hot and humid weather, and also to have time to withdraw the artillery parks and heavy baggage that were intended to proceed via Slutsk to Mozyr, ordered Platov to hold in Mir.[63]

---

61   Prince Bagration's report to the Tsar dated 24 June [6 July], No 372. Platov's report of 22 June [4 July] and his message of 28 June [10 July].

62   Prince Bagration's report to the Tsar dated 26 June [8 July], No 391.

63   War Diary of Second Army, in the archive of the M.T.D. No 29,180.

Even before receiving these orders, on 26 June (8 July), Platov was attacked by enemy cavalry near Karelichi and drove them back to Novogrudok. That night, the *Ataman* proceeded to Mir and, three *versts* short of this location, stopped to collect his detached regiments. Whereupon, having received orders from the Commander-in-Chief to hold on to Mir, Platov set up an area ambush: in front of the town, on the Karelichi road, an outpost of a hundred Cossacks was set up, both to monitor the enemy and to lure them towards Mir; off the verges of the road, in close country, there were ambushes of one hundred selected Cossacks each. The commander of the outpost was ordered to entice the enemy with a hasty retreat and then, once they had already passed the ambush, to strike at them simultaneously from all sides. Sysoev's [Vasily Alekseevich Sysoev] Regiment, located in Mir, was intended to support this attack, while the other regiments, remaining on full alert, were to await the orders of the *Ataman*. On 27 June (9 July), three regiments of Rożniecki's *4e division de cavalerie légère*, under General Turno's [Kazimierz Turno] command, were ambushed, and having suffered a complete defeat, were pursued 15 *versts* from Mir. The enemy, in addition to many killed, lost 248 men taken prisoner, including two field officers and four subalterns. The Cossack casualties were insignificant, because, as the *Ataman* reported: 'they did not engage in a firefight with the enemy, but happily charged with the lance.' The enemy defended themselves very fiercely and all the prisoners we captured had been wounded.

On the night of 27 to 28 June (9 to 10 July), the Commander-in-Chief dispatched Adjutant General Vasilchikov with 16 squadrons to support Platov. For their part, the enemy, wishing to avenge the defeat suffered, appeared in great strength in the same place where they had fought the day before. Six cavalry regiments launched repeated attacks on Vasilchikov for four hours; but meanwhile, quite by accident, Major General Kuteinikov [Dmitry Yefimovich Kuteinikov], who was returning from an expedition with part of a raiding detachment at the time, appeared on the enemy's flank; at that moment, the other Cossack regiments enveloped the Poles and struck them from behind. The enemy was smashed to pieces, but their losses are not known. Meanwhile, Second Army remained at Nesvizh until the evening of 28 June (10 July), and then marched towards Slutsk in two echelons. The raiding corps followed them as the rearguard, reinforced by the Combined Grenadier Division under Count Vorontsov.[64]

As our armies retreated from the borders of the Empire to the Dvina and Berezina, misunderstandings arose between the Commanders-in-Chief, Barclay de Tolly and Prince Bagration. Barclay was dissatisfied with the fact that Bagration had not joined him, and attributed it to Platov's involuntary deviation from the original plan of action –to march on the enemy's flank, while maintaining communications with First Army;[65] while Bagration, believing that Napoleon's main body was concentrated against him, expressed the opinion that Barclay should have attacked the enemy, and thus distracted some of the forces operating against Second Army.[66]

64   War Diary of Second Army, in the archive of the M.T.D. No 29,180. A description of the military operations of the Don Cossacks in 1812, in the M.T.D. No 47,352.
65   Barclay de Tolly's letter to the Tsar dated 17 [29] June 1812.
66   Prince Bagration's message to Barclay de Tolly dated 17 [29] June, No 337.

Both of them, only taking into account the difficulties they were facing and not considering each other's situation, confirmed the difficulties of operating with two separate armies in the same theatre of war. Tsar Alexander, being with First Army and being an eyewitness to the circumstances that prevented Barclay from operating decisively, was dissatisfied with Bagration's orders. The Tsar attributed his avoidance of Vileyka, and then from Minsk, to excessive caution.[67] Then, in his next letter to Prince Bagration, Tsar Alexander wrote:

> According to your report, you should have been in Minsk on the 27th (June) [9 July]; the enemy occupied it on the 26th [8 July] and, according to the most accurate intelligence, numbered no more than 6,000. Therefore, by continuing your swift march on Minsk, you would undoubtedly have ejected them... But now we should think about the future, not about the past.
>   ... Any day now we expect the most significant events. But do not forget that, up till now, we have had superior enemy forces against us everywhere, and because of this it is necessary to operate prudently and not to deny ourselves the resources to continue an active campaign for the sake of one day. Our sole objective should be to play for time.[68]

Indeed, in executing Kutuzov's orders at Schöngraben, Bagration had fought with 6,000 men against 40,000 enemy, now he did not dare to break through Davout's corps, of equivalent strength to his army, because he did not want to take responsibility for the outcome of this attempt. On the one hand, he was prepared to sacrifice himself and his detachment in order to save the army; on the other, he was obliged to realise what a harmful effect the loss of the troops entrusted to him would have, and especially at a time when the Russians had to fight the *Grande Armée* triple their strength.

Napoleon was most dissatisfied with the operations by his brother, Jérôme, who, according to his calculations, was to have caught up with and defeated Prince Bagration. But justice demands that we note that as soon as Jérôme, executing the orders of Napoleon himself, crossed our borders five days later than the main body of the French army, he no longer had the opportunity to make up for lost time. By 17 (29) June, only Poniatowski's light cavalry had arrived in Grodno, leaving more than a thousand cart horses and many young soldiers, exhausted from fatigue on the way; the following day Jérôme arrived himself with the rest of his cavalry; the infantry reached Grodno in several echelons, between 19 to 21 June (1 to 3 July). Meanwhile, the torrential rains that fell on 17 (29) June had completely ruined all the roads; the ration wagons lagged behind the troops; it was necessary to acquire not only grain, but also the means for transporting it up to the army in Grodno. King Jérôme hastened the advance of his infantry echelons from Grodno to Novogrudok, giving them only one rest day each, and hastened Reynier, who was proceeding via Białystok towards Slonim; but at the same time he had to keep his forces as concentrated as possible,

---

67   Handwritten letter from the Tsar to Prince Bagration dated 26 June [8 July].
68   Handwritten letter from the Tsar to Prince Bagration dated 5 [17] July.

because rumours had inflated Bagration's strength to 100,000 men. Jérôme, who did not have much military experience, could not distinguish between truth and lies and moved forward hesitantly, like a blind man. Emerging with the last infantry echelon from Grodno on 22 June (4 July), moving along bad roads in hot and humid weather, the diet for his soldiers was meat alone, without salt and without bread, he would be able to gather some 45,000 men of the main body of his army, already weakened by fatigue and shortage, in Nesvizh not before 28 June (10 July), because the distance from Grodno via Novogrudok to Nesvizh is about 200 *versts*. At this point, Prince Bagration, having managed to give his army a rest, could easily retreat further, or give battle in which, operating with 40,000 Russians against 45,000 allied troops, he would have the probability of success on his side.

Napoleon, who was unaware of these circumstances, wishing to give greater unity to the operations by the troops directed against Second Army, subordinated his brother to Marshal Davout. Jérôme, upset by this order, left the army for his capital, Kassel, on 4 (16) July.[69]

---

69   Chambray, I, 205-207.

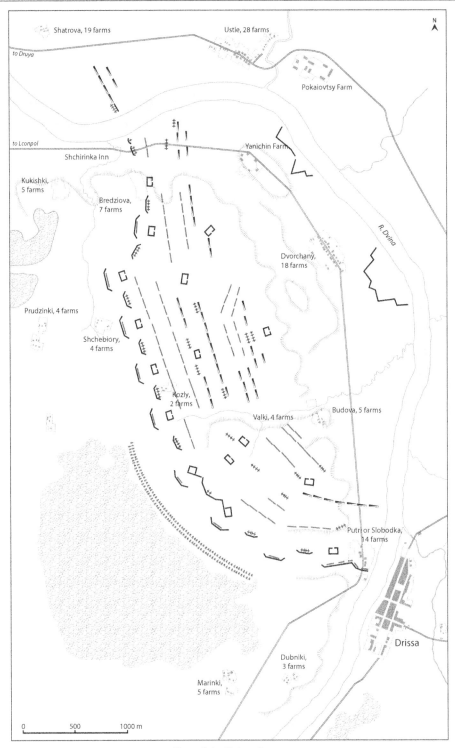

Plan of the Drissa Camp.

7

Tsar Alexander I in the Camp at Drissa and in Moscow

The fortified camp at Drissa. – Its disadvantages. – Orders for the troops. – The Tsar's intention to form a general *opolchenie*. – The withdrawal of First Army from the Drissa camp. – Kulnev's successful reconnaissance. – The movement of First Army from Drissa towards Vitebsk and deployment along the river Luchosa. – Napoleon's advance towards Vitebsk. – Departure of Tsar Alexander from the army. – The Appeal to Moscow and the Manifesto on the general *opolchenie*. The Tsar's stay in Smolensk. – His arrival in Moscow. – The enthusiasm of the Muscovites. – Donations by the noble and merchant classes. – Manifesto on the national *opolchenie* in the governorates closest to the theatre of war. – Administrative steps taken by the Tsar. – Formation of a corps for the immediate defence of St Petersburg. – Prayers for the repulse of the foe. – Diplomatic actions. – Letter from the Tsar regarding donations from the Smolensk and Moscow governorates. The Tsar's arrival in St Petersburg. – Orders for the manning of the army through new recruit selection.

Following the occupation of the Drissa camp by the troops of First Army between 27 and 29 June (9 and 11 July), they remained there for only a few days. The disadvantages of this camp were so obvious that no one doubted them, except for Phull himself. Away from all the main routes that lay inside the Empire, the fortified camp did not directly protect any of them. Tactically, it was also fatally flawed.

The Drissa fortified camp was located in a bend formed by the Dvina, between the town of Drissa and the village of Shatrova, with an area of about four *versts* in length and three *versts* in width.[1] The fortifications consisted of three lines of lunettes and redoubts. Ahead of the first line, a solid barrier was arranged, consisting on the right wing of a double row of palisades, and on the left – of unfixed abatis: the latter were intended to protect the position from the direction of the nearby forest and the high ground that dominated the closest fortifications. The redoubts of the second line were interconnected by a row of palisades, and, moreover, these fortifications,

---

1   See previous 'Plan Of The Drissa Camp' for the plan of the fortified camp at the town of Drissa.

as well as those in the third line, were protected with palisades. The redoubts had internal dimensions of some 30 *sazhen* [1 *sazhen* = 2.13m or 7'] long and some 15 *sazhen* wide, and were adapted only for defence with the musket; but between some of them there were batteries protected by demi-bastions. For communications with the opposite bank of the Dvina, four bridges had been built, of which two were behind the centre of the fortified camp with one each between the centre and the flanks of the camp: all of them were covered by bridgeheads.[2]

The fortifications of the Drissa camp, which cost considerable effort and money, could not serve the intended mission – for stubborn defence and for operations against enemy communications. On the contrary, the troops occupying the fortified camp were in danger of being defeated or besieged by an enterprising enemy. The forest, located half a *verst* from the left wing of our position, would assist an enemy approaching it to direct an assault with concentrated forces. The camp itself was intersected by deep ravines, which impeded communications between elements of the force and the movement of reserves; the descents to the bridges were extremely awkward. Some of the fortifications did not provide each other with mutual support and in general all had a weak profile. The three bridgeheads were very cramped and positioned so badly that one could observe the movement of every man inside from the high ground just a few hundred paces away. In addition, the location of the fortified camp, away from all the main routes, would allow the enemy to cross the Dvina upstream or downstream of Drissa and, enveloping the camp from the rear, besiege the troops located there and put them in a most dangerous situation.

The disadvantages of the Drissa camp were obvious to many. Barclay de Tolly himself expressed doubts about the value of the fortified camp,[3] while General Paulucci, who had held the appointment of Chief of Staff of First Army for a short time, quite clearly expressed his opinion, likening this camp to the camp at Pirna [siege of Pirna in 1756].[4]

Among those who doubted the usefulness of the positioning of the army in the Drissa fortified camp was Colonel Michaud [Alexander Frantsevich Michaud de Beauretour], a very knowledgeable Sardinian engineer who had transferred to Russian service. Arriving in Drissa, on 26 June [8 July], on the eve of the Tsar's arrival there, Michaud examined the camp and the next day brought his conclusions to the attention of the Emperor, via Prince P.M. Volkonsky. The Tsar immediately went to the camp with his suite, which also included Phull. Noticing that none of the Russian officers shared Phull's beliefs about the benefits of the camp, Tsar Alexander lost confidence in him.[5] Nevertheless, however, on that same day, 27 June (9 July), on which Russia celebrated the anniversary of the victory at Poltava, the following Supreme Order was issued to the troops:

---

2   Plans for the Drissa camp, are kept in the archives of the Military Topographic Depot and the Department of Engineering. *Mémoires pour servir à l'histoire de la guerre en 1812. Par un officier de l'état-major de l'armée française (g-l Vaudoncourt). Londres 1815.* 95-96.

3   Barclay de Tolly's report to the Tsar dated 25 June [7 July] 1812, from Belmont.

4   From General Tuchkov 3rd's notes.

5   Bernhardi, *Denkwürdigkeiten des Grafen v. Toll*, I, 297-298.

Warriors of Russia! You have finally reached the objective towards which you were aiming. When the enemy dared to invade the borders of Our Empire, you were on the frontier to witness it. Until the complete union of Our army, your raging courage has been held back in a temporary but necessary retreat – to stop the bold steps of the enemy. Now each of the corps of Our First Army have united at the designated place. Now there is a new opportunity to demonstrate your well-known courage and to acquire the rewards for the efforts incurred. This day, the anniversary of the victory at Poltava, may serve you as an example! May the memory of your victorious ancestors inspire you to the most glorious deeds! They struck down their adversaries with a mighty hand; you, following in their footsteps, must strive to destroy the enemy assaults on faith, honour, fatherland and your families. God sees our truthfulness and will send His blessings on you.

Tsar Alexander's short stay in Drissa was marked by the adoption of many decisive measures to frustrate the enemy's plans. On 1 (13) July, a Manifesto on recruitment in the governorates of Vitebsk, Mogilev, Volhynia, Podolia, Livland and Estland was promulgated for five recruits per 500 souls.[6] The Army of the Danube was ordered to cancel the proposed campaign towards the Adriatic and move towards Volhynia to link up with Tormasov, who was ordered to launch offensive operations. To the twelve regiments that Prince Lobanov-Rostovsky [Dmitry Ivanovich Lobanov-Rostovsky] was forming in Vladimir, Kostroma, Ryazan, Tambov, Yaroslavl and Voronezh, six more new regiments were ordered to be added, whose formation from the recruitment depots was entrusted to Lieutenant General Kleinmichel [Andrey Andreevich Kleinmichel].[7] The Kiev military governor, General of Infantry Miloradovich [Mikhail Andreevich Miloradovich], was ordered to form a corps of 55 battalions, 26 squadrons and 14 artillery companies in Kaluga from the first line recruitment depots, to look for reliable assistants from among retired generals and officers, and to be ready to operate, on demand, towards Vyazma or Mozhaisk. In the Supreme Rescript sent to General Miloradovich, the Tsar's intention to form a general *opolchenie* in the state was first expressed. He wrote to Barclay de Tolly: 'I have made up my mind to call upon the nation to exterminate the enemy which has invaded Our borders, such is the kind of work that the faith itself demands. I hope that we shall become like the Spaniards in this respect.'[8]

Earlier, during the retreat of First Army from Vilna to Sventsiany, on 16 (28) June, Barclay de Tolly had sent Lieutenant Grabbe [Pavel Khristoforovich Grabbe] from Niemenczyn [Nemenčinė] with orders for Dokhturov, Dorokhov and Platov, who were in danger of being cut off by the enemy. Having found Dokhturov and Count Pahlen (Pëtr Petrovich) on the way, Grabbe found Dorokhov during a skirmish with the enemy near Soleczniki and, having confirmed his intention to go to Valozhin, went to find Platov, who, being cut off from First Army, had gone to join Second Army. Thereafter, finding Count Sievers in Nikolaev on the Neman and

---

6   Complete Collection of Laws, XXXII, 384.
7   Supreme Orders directed to the Minister of War, dated 27 June [9 July]
8   The Tsar's handwritten letter to Barclay de Tolly, dated 27 June [9 July] 1812.

learning from him about the direction taken by Prince Bagration, Grabbe returned, via Minsk, to headquarters First Army on 2 (14) July, at a time when it was still in Drissa, and having had the good fortune to personally report to the Tsar about the outcome of his journey, he added that significant enemy forces were trying to move into the gap between First Army and Second Army. Tsar Alexander initially expressed doubts about the reliability of this intelligence, believing at the time that the majority of Napoleon's troops were moving towards First Army frontally, but later he was completely convinced of the accuracy of the intelligence provided by Lieutenant Grabbe.[9]

The unsuitability of the Drissa camp, recognised by Tsar Alexander, could have been partially eliminated if the troops of First Army were strengthened, as was intended, with significant reinforcements and had established communications with Second Army. But the reserves that arrived at the fortified camp barely made good the losses suffered since the beginning of the campaign, and meanwhile, the direction of Napoleon's troops towards Dokshitsy and Glubokoe revealed the enemy's intention to separate our armies from one another and to push First Army away from Moscow and from the southern governorates of the state. This was the situation of this army, when at a council of war, convened by the Tsar and consisting of Barclay, Count Arakcheev, Prinz Georg von Oldenburg, Prince Volkonsky and Wolzogen [Justus Philipp Adolf Wilhelm Ludwig Freiherr von Wolzogen], the abandonment of the Drissa camp was proposed, but it was not decided where exactly the army should be directed. Then, at the suggestion of *Herzog* Alexander von Württemberg, who was in the headquarters at the time, supported by Barclay, a route was selected towards Vitebsk, where First Army, having taken up an advantageous position, would link up with Second Army. The magazines in Velizh would be able to provide the ration supply for the troops.[10]

Thus, Phull's plan was rejected and instead of placing one of the armies in a forti-fied position, while the other would act on the enemy's communications, it became necessary to retreat in order to unite both armies.

On 2 (14) July, First Army crossed to the right bank of the Dvina, where it was positioned from the village of Baliny (opposite Leonpol) to the city of Drissa, with the exception of II Cavalry Corps and III Cavalry Corps, which remained on the left bank of the Dvina to observe the enemy. The vanguard of I Corps, under General Kulnev's command, was at Pridruisk [Piedruja]. Count Wittgenstein, wishing to obtain accurate intelligence about enemy strength and intentions beyond the high ground at Druya, ordered the bridge facing the town to be repaired during the night of 2 to 3 (14 to 15) July, and instructed Kulnev to carry out a detailed reconnaissance the following day; and moved some of his corps to Pridruisk in support. On the morning of 3 (15) July, Kulnev crossed the Dvina River with the vanguard of I Corps and sent the Cossacks forward, reinforcing them with the Grodno Hussar Regiment, under the command of Lieutenant Colonel Rüdiger [Fëdor Vasilevich Ridiger]. The Cossacks drove off the French outposts in Druya and pursued them to the village of Onikszty, where there were eight enemy squadrons from *11e chasseurs à cheval* and

9   From Adjutant General P. Kh. Grabbe's notes.
10   Bernhardi, I, 300-301. War Diary of First Army.

10 Putk Huzarów. The Cossacks went into action against them and continued the combat until Rüdiger arrived with his hussars, enveloped the enemy on both flanks, rolled them up and pursued them to the village of Chernevo, 15 *versts* from Druya. Meanwhile, Kulnev remained by the Dvina, to cover the advanced cavalry from the enemy who were opposite the Drissa camp. Having received intelligence from the dispatched patrols regarding an advance by strong French columns down the right bank of the river Druja and Rüdiger's report that there was no infantry anywhere in the sector between Druya and Chernevo, Kulnev withdrew his cavalry and crossed to the right bank of the Dvina with the entire force, except for the Cossacks, left on the left bank of the river.

This bold cavalry action cost us 75 men (12 killed and 63 wounded), including six officers. The enemy casualties extended to 300 men, as well as 144 prisoners, including *Général de brigade* Saint-Geniès [Jean Marie Noël Delisle de Falcon de Saint-Geniès] and three officers.[11]

Meanwhile, the Dünaburg garrison, for three days in a row, successfully repelled attacks by Marshal Oudinot.

As early as 19 June (1 July), Barclay de Tolly, while in Sventsiany, had ordered artillery Colonel Tishin [Vasily Grigorevich Tishin?] to go to Dünaburg and evacuate the gunpowder and other state property from there to Novgorod, leaving only what was necessary for the defence of the bridgehead. But any weapons and anything that could not be taken away was ordered to be prepared for destruction. Colonel Tishin, having arrived in Dünaburg, established communications with the local authorities regarding the collection of 5,000 peasant carts; and meanwhile invited the commandant of Dünaburg, Major General Ulanov, to convene a council of war on 21 June (3 July); at this council it was decided: to abandon the defence of the bridgehead; to remove the guns and ammunition from there and put them on barges so that, at the first sign of the enemy's appearance, they could be dumped into the Dvina; while the bridgehead would be demolished by mines. The evacuation of the sick and parks were also ordered, and wherever possible, flood or burn everything else, even including the treasury. Barclay de Tolly, not approving these measures,

---

11   *Précis de la campagne du 1 Corps de l'armée d'Occident pendant l'année 1812.* Archive of the
M.T.D. No 29,200. General Kulnev, in his report to Count Wittgenstein about this action, wrote: 'A defeat was suffered by two enemy regiments – *11e chasseurs à cheval* and 10th Polish Hussars. In addition to those taken prisoner, with whom I am attaching a return, the entire road is strewn with corpses all the way to Chernevo. In addition to those taken prisoner, 47 men died of wounds in Druya, and many, in the absence of carts, had been abandoned on the road. I am obliged, your Excellency, to recommend the particularly courageous Lieutenant Colonel Rüdiger, who commanded the Grodno Hussar Regiment entrusted to me, to whom I owe this glorious and complete victory, and if the authorities take this outstanding feat into account, then they should reward the worthy and brave Lieutenant Colonel Rüdiger, with a high honour, instead of me, and without whom I could not have won this complete victory,' etc. (extracted from Major General Kulnev's report dated 3 [15] July, No 284).
Count Wittgenstein, in his report to the Tsar, repeated Kulnev's statement regarding Lieutenant Colonel Rüdiger, and in his recommendation for an award he wrote: 'This worthy and brave lieutenant colonel has shown his great potential to be a good and reliable leader, for him to be promoted to higher rank.'

presented his opinion to the Tsar. Tsar Alexander, believing that it was possible to defend Dünaburg for some time, ordered the local garrison to be reinforced with four replacement battalions. Whereupon, by way of a Supreme command, Major General Prince Iashvili was sent to Dünaburg to put matters in order in the fortress there. Having arranged the evacuation of state property from the bridgehead fortifications and repulsing the most recent enemy attack, in early [mid] July, Prince Iashvili returned to I Corps headquarters. The command of the Dünaburg garrison was entrusted to Major General Gamen.[12]

In the camp at Drissa, a Supreme Order appointed: Major General Yermolov as Chief of Staff, First Army, in place of the temporary occupant of this post, Lieutenant General Marquis Paulucci, while Colonel von Toll was appointed Quartermaster General, in place of Major General Mukhin [Semën Alexandrovich Mukhin].

As a result of the change from the original plan of action, the troops of First Army, with the exception of I Corps left at Pokaevtsy in order to protect the route to St Petersburg, moved in two columns upstream on the right bank of the Dvina; II Cavalry Corps proceeded as the rearguard, which crossed over to the right bank of the river at Drissa, while III Cavalry Corps, crossed at Disna [Dzisna].[13] On 6 (18) July, the army reached Polotsk, while Korf's II Cavalry Corps remained at Drissa, and Pahlen's III Cavalry Corps was at Disna. The Commander-in-Chief, in agreement with the opinion of the Chief of Staff First Army, proposed to cross the Dvina between Polotsk and Vitebsk, at Budilovo, and march via Senno to Orsha, which would facilitate not only the unification of the Western armies, but also operations by a concentrated force against the left column under Marshal Davout, moving towards Orsha and Dubrowna. But Barclay cancelled this move, because there were no magazines in the sector between the Dvina and the Dnieper. On 8 (20) July, the troops of First Army marched in two columns to Vitebsk and united at this city on the 11th (23rd July). On that same day, III Corps, IV Corps, V Corps and I Cavalry Corps, having crossed to the left bank of the Dvina, camped along the river Luchosa, on the road to Beshankovichi [Bieszenkowicze]; II Corps and II Cavalry corps remained on the right bank of the Dvina near Vitebsk, while VI Corps was at Staroe-Selo, having III Cavalry Corps half a stage to their rear. The headquarters of First Army was located in Vitebsk.[14]

The French army was also moving towards Vitebsk. Murat was moving from Zamosha to the town of Disna with Ney's *3e Corps*, three divisions from Davout's corps, Nansouty's *1er Corps de Cavalerie* and Montbrun's *2e Corps de Cavalerie*, shifting Montbrun's corps to the right bank of the Dvina on 10 (22) July, and continued to move via the town of Ulla to Beshankovichi, meanwhile Oudinot's *2e Corps*, reaching Drissa that same day, destroyed the fortified camp there and

12   General summary of movements and operations by Russian forces in the war of 1812, compiled by General Khatov. Barclay de Tolly's report by Supreme direction. Minutes of the council of war in Dünaburg, 21 June [3 July]. Barclay de Tolly's message to Count Wittgenstein dated 1 [13] July. Chambray, I, 218.
13   War Diary of First Army, compiled by Colonel von Toll.
14   General Yermolov's letter to the Tsar dated 16 [28] July. War Diary of First Army, compiled by von Toll.

moved towards Polotsk. To the right of Murat, the *Garde* proceeded to Glubokoe and Dokshitsy, while *4e Corps* under the Viceroy, having crossed the Ula at Bocheikovo, arrived at Beshankovichi on 12 (24) July, at the same time as Murat's force. Napoleon arrived there himself on the evening of the same day. Meanwhile, the Bavarian *6e Corps* under Saint-Cyr, which had remained in the rear, was moving towards Ushachy.[15]

Not long before that, Tsar Alexander, taking into account the necessity of His presence within the state, in order to rouse the general efforts of the nation to revolt against the enemy, decided to leave the army. Without a doubt, the Tsar's presence among the troops who adored him would increase their enthusiasm; but Tsar Alexander, convinced of the benefits of unity of command, wished to give the commander he had chosen complete freedom to direct his operations; in addition, any failure by the troops, suffered in the presence of the Emperor, would have a very unfavourable effect on the morale of the nation and would allow Napoleon to exaggerate his success.[16]

Tsar Alexander, before his departure from the army, on 6 [18] July, sent Adjutant General Prince Trubetskoy to Moscow with an appeal to the ancient capital and a Manifesto on the general *opolchenie*, with the following content:

> To the ancient capital of Ours, Moscow.
> The enemy has invaded the borders of Russia with huge forces. They have come to destroy our beloved Fatherland. Although the mobilised Russian army, burning with courage, stands ready to meet and overthrow their insolence and malice; however, due to our paternal compassion and concern for all our faithful subjects, We cannot leave them without warning about this danger that threatens them. May our indiscretion not gift an advantage to the foe. For this cause, with the intention to raise new forces in the interior for a most reliable defence, we turn firstly to the ancient capital of Our ancestors, to Moscow. It was always the foremost of other Russian cities: it has always poured a deadly force from its depths on our foes; following their example, from every other district the sons of the Fatherland flowed thence like blood to the heart in order to protect it. It has never felt that lofty need more than it does now. The Faith, the Throne, the Kingdom, demand it. And so, may the spirit of that everlasting warfare which God and our Orthodox Church bless, spread in the hearts of our famous nobility and in all other classes; Yes, to building up this general eagerness and enthusiasm for new forces, and let them multiply, starting with Moscow, throughout vast Russia? We shall not hesitate to stand ourselves in the midst of Our people in this capital and in other cities of Our State, for the guidance and leadership of all Our *opolchenie*, both blocking the foe's path now, and again arranged to defeat them wherever they appear. Let destruction rain down

---

15   Chambray, *Expédition de Russie*, I, 222 and 226. Denniée, *Itinéraire de l'empereur Napoléon pendant la campagne de 1812. Tableau des opérations de la Grande armée*, in the archive of the M.T.D. No 3,909.

16   Admiral Shishkov's brief notes, 13-27.

upon whomever thinks to bring us down, upon their heads, and Europe, freed from subjugation, shall exalt the name of Russia.

Supreme Manifesto.

The enemy has invaded our borders and continues to carry their weapons into Russia, hoping to shake the peace of this great Power by force and subversion. They have in their minds the malicious intent of destroying our honour and prosperity. With guile in their hearts and flattery in their mouths, they bring us eternal chains and fetters. We, having called upon God for help, have placed Our troops as a barrier to them, seething with courage to scourge, overthrow them, and shall drive whatever remains alive from the face of Our land. We rely upon the strength and fortitude of your firm faith, but we cannot and should not hide from our faithful subjects that the forces of the various powers that have gathered are great, and that your courage requires constant vigilance against them. For this purpose, with every firm hope in our brave army, we believe that it is necessary to gather new forces within the state, which, inflicting new horrors upon the enemy, would constitute a second wall to reinforce the first, and to protect the homes, wives and children of each and every one.

We have already appealed to Our first city, Moscow, and now we appeal to all of Our loyal subjects, to all of the spiritual and secular classes and ranks, inviting them together with Us, unanimous in a common uprising, to help against every enemy intention and assault. May they find at every step the faithful sons of Russia, striking them with every resource and strength, heedless of any of their cunning and deceit. Yes, let them encounter a Pozharsky in every nobleman – a Palitsyn in every priest – a Minin in every citizen [militia leaders during the 'time of troubles']. Gracious nobility! You have been the saviours of the Fatherland at all times. Holy Synod and Clergy! You have always called benevolence upon the leaders of Russia with your warm prayers. People of Russia! Courageous descendants of the brave Slavs! You have repeatedly smashed the teeth of the lions and tigers rushing at you; unite all: with the cross on your heart and with a weapon in your hands, no human force shall prevail against you.

For the initial compilation of the intended forces, it is given to the nobility in all provinces to assemble the men supplied by them for the defence of the Fatherland, electing a commander over them from among themselves and informing Moscow about their number, where an overall commander is to be elected.

Departing Polotsk during the night of 6 to 7 (18 to 19) July, the Tsar only stopped for a single day in Smolensk on the way. There, the nobility, inspired by the age-old valour of their ancestors, had pre-empted the will of the Monarch, through the governorate leader Leslie [Dmitry Yegorovich Leslie], expressed their readiness to raise 20,000, or more, soldiers to defend the fatherland. Many retired military men also openly offered to go with the peasants to face the common foe. At the request of the nobility in the Name of the Sovereign it was stated:

These defenders of the Fatherland, appointed in cities and *Uezds*, may remain in their homes until called up to whichever place in the Smolensk Governorate, that need or danger might dictate, where they may arrive in time from nearby *Uezds* in the shortest time, and from distant ones by their own transport within three days, each one with provisions, which they have prepared for a month in hard tack and cereals of their own, while at the request of the *Uezd* they are to protect them from small enemy patrols. If muskets with bayonets, bullets and gunpowder are issued, then skilful and courageous field officers and subalterns who live in the governorate and in their villages may, in their free time, teach proper marksmanship, bayonet fighting, effective and rapid movement, while before receiving muskets, allow them to drill, even just with pikes remaining from the militia, however many of them are in the cities under the jurisdiction of the mayors.

Whereupon, the Tsar went to the Uspensky Cathedral [Dormition Cathedral], and from there – to the square, where he inspected the troops, consisting of 27 battalions and eight squadrons, which, by Supreme command, along with the four artillery companies that were being formed at that time in Smolensk, formed a detachment under Adjutant General Wintzingerode, which was initially intended to assist with the unification of the Western armies, while thereafter being used as replacements.[17]

On the morning of 11 (23) July, news spread in Moscow about the imminent arrival of the Tsar, perhaps on the same day. Every square, every street was full of people. The Muscovites, grieving over the success of the enemy invasion, instantly cheered themselves up, congratulated each other on their common joy, and conspired to meet their beloved guest. 'Let's go to the House of the Lord; let us pray for the Tsar, and from there go to the city gates,' they said. Many went to Poklonnaya Hill, wanting to beg permission to unhitch the horses from the royal carriage and draw it themselves. Thousands of people of every status moved along the Smolensk road with loud singing and cheers of hurray! By sunset they were already 17 *versts* away. Finally, at ten o'clock, the news came that the Tsar was staying in Perkhushkovo (the first stage from Moscow), where Count Rostopchin [Fëdor Vasilevich Rostopchin] was at the time. The people dispersed, but the peasants of the village of Pokrovskoye near Moscow, impatiently awaiting the procession of the Tsar, sent two messengers to Perkhushkovo, who, galloping back at full speed, informed their fellows about the departure of the Tsar's carriage from the village of Perkhushkovo. Indeed, Tsar Alexander, hoping to avoid a ceremonial welcome at a time of distress for the fatherland, wished to enter the capital at night.

The village priest from Pokrovskoye, hearing the welcome news, hastened in his vestments to Poklonnaya Hill, with a silver dish on which lay a cross; the aged deacon was holding a candle that shed a flickering glow in the gloom of a moonless night. The Tsar got out of the carriage, bowed down to the ground, and, sighing from the depths of his soul, kissed the Saviour's cross.[18]

---

17   Admiral Shishkov's brief notes, 31. Original request from the Smolensk nobility dated 7 [19] July, signed by the governorate leader, Leslie.

18   S.N. Glinka's notes, 6-12.

Tsar Alexander arrived in Moscow at about midnight; accompanying His Majesty were: *Oberhofmarshal* Count Tolstoy [Nikolay Alexandrovich Tolstoy], Count Arakcheev, Adjutants-General: Balashev, Prince Volkonsky and Count Komarovsky [Yevgraf Fedotovich Komarovsky], Vice-Admiral Secretary of State Shishkov. On the eve of the Tsar's arrival, some of the Muscovites had already found out about the Manifesto to the former capital. We, Russians, reading it even now – after half a century – with tenderness and trembling in our hearts, can comprehend how it changed minds, how the inhabitants of Moscow felt at that time, always unchanging both in love for the fatherland and in devotion to their Tsars.

On 12 (24) July, as soon as dawn began to break, the people rushed into Red Square like a wave. Nobody had heard an announcement, but everyone already knew about the arrival of the Tsar. With the rising of the sun, which shone brightly on this state occasion, the entire Kremlin was filled with Russians, eager to see their Tsar. Alexander the First left the palace at nine o'clock in the morning, and at the same instant the tolling of bells rang out, hurray! Thousands of people exclaimed: 'Lead us wherever you want; lead us, our Father! Let us win or die!' If Napoleon could have witnessed the greeting of the Russian Emperor by the people in Moscow, then, of course, he would have doubted his hopes of subordinating this blessed country to his will, where devotion to the Tsar, the representation of God on earth, united the striving of many millions towards a benevolent outcome. Alexander, touched by a spectacle reminiscent of the times of Minin and Pozharsky, stopped for a few moments on the Red Barbican; it seemed that His bright gaze reflected the love of the multitudes of people for Him. Meanwhile, the bell ringing continued. The Tsar walked to the Uspensky Cathedral, accompanied by shouts of: 'Our Father! Our angel! May the Lord God keep you!' At the gates of the cathedral, the Right Reverend Vicar of Moscow Augustine [Alexey Vasilievich Vinogradsky], greeting the Monarch with a short speech, concluded by saying: 'God is with us! Understand the tongues and obey, for God is with us!' At the end of the Mass, a thanksgiving service was performed with kneeling and a cannon salute, on the occasion of the news of the ratification of peace with the Turks, received by the Tsar during his visit to Smolensk.[19]

---

19   In front of the doors of the cathedral, His Grace Augustine, the vicar of the Moscow Metropolitanate, gave a welcoming speech with the following content: 'August Emperor! Most Merciful Tsar. Incense is still being smoked on these altars, the candle flames of thanksgiving prayers are still burning for those glorious victories with which the Almighty has crowned Thine armed forces. And finally, the proud Ottomans bow their defeated heads before Thee: in the south, covered by the clouds of battle, the light of a blessed peace shines forth. This capital, its head held high, covered with grey hair, admires, looking to the extent of the borders of Russia; amazed, heeding the thunder of Thy glory. Russia is ready to sing a song of praise to the Lord of Hosts – and to Thee, Christ the Lord.
But behold, in the West, storms ring out, and Thou, like a giant, proceed on the route to immortal deeds and glory. Thine exit is from the edge of heaven, and Thy salvation is at the edge of heaven. There, among Thy powerful and brave *opolchenie*, Thou hast cast lightning bolts against the impudent enemy; here Thou dost kindle our souls with love for Thee and the Fatherland. Here Thou dost move thunder to defeat malice; there Thou dost excite and move our hearts to defend Thy beloved Russia. Execute here, rest there; here Thou dost kill, there Thou dost revive.

On 15 (27) July, on the summons of the Tsar, the noble and merchant classes gathered in the vast halls of the Sloboda Palace. Even before the arrival of the Tsar, the Commander-in-Chief, Count Rostopchin, appeared to both groupings, ordered the reading of the Supreme Manifesto and with a fiery speech summoned each and every person to an active participation in the great cause of defending the Fatherland. Immediately it was decided by the nobles, raising a tenth of the men, following the example of citizens of Smolensk, to assemble a militia of 80,000 men; the merchants pitched in to make a general collection and regardless of anything else, open a subscription to private donations. A common phrase boomed: 'Tsar! Take everything: our property and our lives!' Meanwhile, the Tsar was in the Sloboda Palace chapel, where a Mass was performed; and then, accompanied by the most distinguished persons of the clergy, he arrived in the hall where the nobility had assembled. Greeted there with enthusiasm, the Emperor briefly explained the position of the State, 'which the troops, for all their courage and sacrifice, could not defend themselves against the disproportionately superior enemy numbers,' recalled that the State owed its salvation to the efforts of the nobility, and concluded his speech, saying: 'I am determined to exhaust all the resources of My vast Empire, before submitting to the arrogant enemy.'

The Tsar's words found an echo in the hearts of the Moscow nobles. They expressed their readiness to send ten warriors from every hundred souls to form the *opolchenie* of 80,000 men; equip them, provide them with rations and even, if possible, with weapons. Tsar Alexander gratefully accepted this donation: 'I did not and could not expect otherwise from you; you have justified my opinion of you' he said. Then, going into the hall where the merchants and the bourgeoisie were gathered, the Tsar explained to them, like a father to devoted children, the danger that threatened the State; he did not hide from them that significant resources were needed to repel the foe who threatened the welfare of all; he announced the conclusion of an alliance with the Swedes and peace with Turkey; about the impending renewal of friendly relations with Britain, which was ready to reopen its harbours to Russian trade; he noted that every hope for the welfare of the country was threatened by the enemy invasion, and repeated that, being confident of the assistance of his loyal subjects, he would resist the enemy to the bitter end. The response to the Tsar were the words spoken from the heart by all who had the good fortune to hear His speech: 'We are ready to sacrifice our property to You, our father.' Upon the departure of the Tsar, a subscription for donations began and, after two hours, one and a half million roubles had been pledged. But this was only the beginning of the sacrifices made by the Muscovites to redeem the Fatherland.[20]

Tsar! Thou hast conquered thousands by force of arms, but with the blessing of humility. Our gratitude, our love for Thee has no limits: Thy fatherly love for us surpasses all our feelings of zeal and gratitude towards Thee. Thou art a victor over us too: Thou dost triumph over Thine own.

To the Tsar! The Lord is with Thee; He will command the storms with Thy voice, and stand in silence, and the waves of flood waters shall be silenced. God is with us; understand the tongues and obey, for God is with us!'

20   S.N. Glinka's notes. Bestuzhev-Ryumin's manuscript notes.

In general, the donations from Moscow's citizens were enormous. The anonymous author of the Book of 1812 (*Das Buch vom Jahr 1812*) called these donations 'statistically impossible.'[21] He spoke the truth, but had lost sight of the fact that at that time the Russians had no time to study the calculations. Everyone thought then only about how to bring all their property and themselves to the defence of mother Russia, who raised millions of heroes in her mighty hands for the destruction of her foes.

That the *opolchenie* of 1812 was not fielded on an even larger scale, and therefore did not fully reveal the entire defensive strength of our fatherland, then the main reason for this was the speedy resolution of the struggle, which decided the issue before the governorates far from the theatre of war could take part. The Moscow *opolchenie* itself was assembled in much smaller numbers than those offered by the nobles. The occupation of the capital by the enemy stopped the formation of the Moscow territorial forces at the very beginning; but, having said that, many of the *opolchenie*, not having time to join the ranks of the army, armed themselves spontaneously and operated independently against small groups of the enemy. Thus, at various locations in the theatre of war, a national war broke out, not with resounding victories, but disastrous for Napoleon's army.

Alexander, during his six-day visit to Moscow, was vigilantly engaged in orders aimed at the defence of the State. Considering the general mobilisation of all of Russia unnecessary, He put it into effect only in the 16 governorates closest to the theatre of war: on the basis of this, the following manifesto was promulgated on 18 (30) July:

> In an appeal to all Our loyal subjects regarding the compilation of territorial forces to defend the Fatherland and upon our arrival in Moscow, We found, to our complete delight, among all ranks and classes such zeal and enthusiasm that the voluntary offerings submitted to us far exceed the number of men required for the *opolchenie*. To that end, for the sake of accepting such enthusiasm with paternal affection and gratitude, We direct Our attention such that, having made up sufficient forces from a number of governorates, we do not disturb others unnecessarily. In order to do this we have established:
>
> 1. A District, consisting of the Moscow, Tver, Yaroslavl, Vladimir, Ryazan, Tula, Kaluga and Smolensk governorates, which is to take the swiftest and most active measures to assemble, equip and organise the territorial forces that are intended to protect Our capital city of Moscow as well as the boundaries of this District.
> 2. A District, consisting of the St Petersburg and Novgorod governorates, which is to do the same for the protection of St Petersburg and the boundaries of that district.

---

21   *Das Buch vom Jahr 1812*, 63.

3.   A District, consisting of the Kazan, Nizhegorod, Penza, Kostroma, Simbirsk and Vyatka governorates, which is to prepare to select and appoint men, but not to assemble them and not to take them away from agricultural work until ordered.

4.   All other governorates are to remain inactive in this regard, until there is a need to use them for equivalent commitments and services to the fatherland.

5.   The entire territorial force that is now being assembled is not a militia or a conscription of recruits, but a temporary volunteer *opolchenie* of the faithful sons of Russia, set up as a precaution, to reinforce the troops and to provide a most reliable shield for the fatherland.

Each of the commanders and soldiers, retains their existing status with their new rank, is also not forced to change their uniform, and after the necessity has passed, that is, after the enemy is driven out of Our land, everyone is to return with honour and glory to their previous state and to their former duties. State, economic and specific peasants, in those governorates in which the temporary territorial *opolchenie* has been established, are not to participate in it, but are subject to regular conscription according to the established regulations.

To increase the funds in the State Treasury, it was ordered:

1.   To halt all government building construction and works;

2.   Until permission is granted, to halt the issuing of loans to individuals from state institutions, and so on.

The head of the Tula arms factory, Major General Voronov [Fëdor Nikitich Voronov], was summoned to Moscow by Supreme will for a meeting on the means to increase the production of muskets, he received an order, under the Tsar's handwritten signature, to produce or repair from old weapons, 13,000 muskets monthly at the Tula arms factory. In the conclusion of the Supreme command to Voronov, it stated:

If you, by your prudent administration and the diligence of the free craftsmen, exceed the monthly production, then this will be accepted by Me as a special token of your zeal towards Me and the fatherland. I instruct you to declare to all factory master craftsmen and workshop owners who have factories of their own that no period in Our Fatherland has required more diligence and sacrifice from everyone than the present; consequently, I am sure that they will turn their entire workshops over solely to the arms business, and thus will find a way to pass their names on to the memory of posterity.

At the same time, a Supreme order was issued to form a corps to defend St Petersburg, notwithstanding Count Wittgenstein's force. The foundations of this formation, to be named Narva Corps, was intended to be provided by the Voronezh Infantry and two Marine regiments, one battery company and one light artillery company, located in St Petersburg. In addition, several 4th battalions, made up of recruits, and the Mitau Dragoon Regiment were ordered to be moved from Finland; as were eight replacement squadrons from the Starorussia and Podgoschino depots; four artillery companies from Pskov, and so on. More than 10,000 men in total. The defence of St Petersburg and overall command of all the troops in St Petersburg, Kronstadt and Finland was given to Kutuzov, who had just arrived from Bucharest.[22]

Tsar Alexander, in raising the resources of this great Power, granted to him by God, in arms, turned to his Source of Strength – God's help. The pious Tsar, going out at the head of His people to do deadly battle, commanded His Grace Augustine to compose a prayer to repel the foe, to be read with genuflection in the churches of the Moscow diocese. This prayer met with Supreme approval and was published.[23]

One of the subjects of this all-encompassing activity by Tsar Alexander in 1812 was the renewal of friendly relations with those Powers hostile to the French Empire – Spain and Britain. During the Tsar's visit to Moscow, the peace treaty concluded in Örebro on 6 (18) July, between Russia and Great Britain, and the treaty of alliance signed in Velikiye Luki, on 8 (20) July, were made by the representatives of Russia and the Spanish Cortes.

As early as 10 (22) June, Tsar Alexander, being in Vidzy, had instructed Count Rumyantsev to write the following dispatch to the Russian plenipotentiaries, Count Sukhtelen [Pëtr Kornilovich Sukhtelen] and Baron Nikolai [Pavel Andreevich Nikolai]:

> His Imperial Majesty, cherishing the interests of Sweden, has gladly decided on a new offering for them. The Emperor wants you, to sign the peace treaty with Britain, as soon as you are invited to by the King of Sweden, on the basis of the draft that you were sent with the last courier and attached herewith with the approval of His Majesty, without any further discussion in favour of Russia.
>
> I ask you to bring to the attention of the King and the Crown Prince the command you have received, which completely leaves it at their discretion to restore peace between Russia and Great Britain. Never before has either Sweden, or any other Power, received such great, such honourable evidence of respect and friendship.
>
> His Majesty has no doubt that the King will appreciate His loyalty and that the agreed assistance that forms the basis of our treaty of alliance shall be honoured completely. The consensus of the allied powers and their perseverance shall serve to convince the whole of Europe of the strength and real benefits of the new alliance.

The consequence of this dispatch was the reconciliation between Russia and Britain, according to the treaty signed by the representatives of both states in Örebro, on 6 (18) July. The return of the Russian squadron, detained by the British at the mouth of

---

22   Mikhailovsky-Danilevsky, Description of the war of 1812, I, 251-259.
23   Mikhailovsky-Danilevsky, I, 265.

the Tagus in 1808, and the payment of subsidies by the British government (£700,000 Sterling, or 4,200,000 silver roubles), were agreed upon by special, secret, clauses of the treaty. As the interests of both Powers demanded the immediate restoration of trade between them, Tsar Alexander I, by Supreme decree dated 4 (16) August, ordered the opening of Russian harbours to British merchant vessels, even before the ratification of the peace treaty had been exchanged. At almost the same time, Lord Cathcart [William Schaw Cathcart] arrived in St Petersburg as ambassador extraordinary.[24]

The treaty of alliance concluded between Russia and the Spanish government had neither military nor commercial importance, but it confirmed the determination of Alexander I – to overthrow the Napoleonic system based on the destruction of age-old statutes and to restore rights suppressed by the right of might.

Such were the successes of the various activities of the Tsar, blessed from On High. Having accomplished this great feat, but facilitated by general eagerness, having roused Moscow and Russia to an uprising against the formidable conqueror of kingdoms, Tsar Alexander expressed gratitude to His people, in a letter to Count Saltykov, dated 15 (27) July, as follows:

> My visit to Moscow was of real benefit. In Smolensk, the nobility offered me 20,000 men for mobilisation, which they immediately proceeded to do. In Moscow, this governorate alone had given me a tithe from each estate, which will amount to 80,000 men, not including those who come voluntarily from the bourgeoisie and commoners. The nobility have donated some three millions in cash; the merchants likewise have given ten. In a word, one cannot help but be moved to tears, seeing the spirit that animates everyone, and the zeal and readiness of everyone to contribute to the common good.

Tsar Alexander, having departed His own capital, during the night of 18 to 19 (30 to 31) July, stopped for a day in Tver, visiting Grand Duchess Catherine Pavlovna, and arrived in St Petersburg on 22 July [3 August] – the saint's day of Empress Maria Feodorovna [Sophie Dorothea von Württemberg].

Upon the arrival of the Tsar in the northern capital, new concerns awaited Him. The success of the enemy invasion demanded new sacrifices in order to save the fatherland. On 4 (16) August, a new conscription was ordered of two recruits from every 100 souls, from appanage and state peasants everywhere, and from landowners in all those governorates where the *opolchenie* had not been called up by the Manifesto of 18 [30] July 1812. The governorates of Pskov and Estland were also excluded from this conscription.[25] Thereafter it was ordered: from the specific estate of Grand Duchess Catherine Pavlovna, who expressed a desire to form an independent battalion, taking only one recruit per hundred, rather than two; not to collect conscripts in Georgia, while in Siberia, they were to conscript five men per

24   Garden, *Hist. génér. des traitès de paix*. XIII, 406-409.
25   Complete Collection of Laws, XXXII, 405.

500 souls.[26] Subsequently, on this matter, several more orders were promulgated, which will be presented in due course.

Let us turn to the battles that had been raging on the Dvina and Dnieper during the Tsar's visit to Moscow.

---

26 Complete Collection of Laws, XXXII, 406.

8

The Unification of the Western Armies at Smolensk

Barclay de Tolly's plans for the troops of First Army upon reaching Vitebsk. – Napoleon's arrival at Beshankovichi. – Count Osterman's detachment to Ostrovno. – The actions at Ostrovno and Kakuvachino. – Barclay's intention to accept a general battle on the Luchosa. – The cancellation of this plan. – Count Pahlen's detachment to engage the enemy. – The rearguard action on 15 (27) July. – The casualties on both sides in the action at Vitebsk. – The retreat of First Army. – Its deployment at Smolensk. – The deployment of Napoleon's troops upon reaching Vitebsk. – The order of battle of these troops. – The retreat of Second Army from Nesvizh towards Slutsk. – The action at Romanovo. – The advance of Davout's troops towards the Dnieper. – The capture of Mogilev by the French. – The arrival of Second Army at Bobruisk. – Sysoev's sweep to Mogilev. – Second Army's offensive along the Mogilev road. – Davout's deployment at Saltanovka. – The battle of Saltanovka. – Second Army's retreat towards Novy Bykhov. – Prince Bagration's move towards Smolensk, while Platov and Dorokhov moved to link up with First Army. – The causes of Marshal Davout's inaction. – Barclay de Tolly's greeting of Prince Bagration. – The deployment of Second Army at Smolensk. – The current state of both sides. – The reasons prompting our Commander-in-Chief to switch to the offensive.[1]

In accordance with the situation of the main body of First Army, on 11 (23) July, on the Luchosa river, Barclay de Tolly, misled by rumours about the occupation of Mogilev by Prince Bagration, not only considered the unification of both armies completely assured, that he even wrote to the governor of Smolensk that he, together with Bagration, would go over to the offensive.[2] In all likelihood, Barclay did not yet have accurate intelligence about the strength of Napoleon's army, or simply wanted to calm the citizens of Smolensk, who were threatened with an enemy invasion. Once it was discovered that Prince Bagration had not yet managed to reach Mogilev,

---

1   See Map of Significant Movements by the Russian and French armies from the beginning of the war to the battle of Smolensk.
2   Minister of War's letter dated 11 [23] July 1812.

then Barclay decided to halt for a while near Vitebsk to wait for the delivery of provisions from Velizh; while then trying to effect a union with Second Army via Senno or Babinovichi. To that end, on 12 (24) July, Major General Tuchkov 4th [Alexander Alekseevich Tuchkov] was sent to Babinovichi with a detachment of four Jäger battalions, 12 squadrons, a Cossack regiment and six guns, while Major General Orlov-Denisov set off for Senno with a Cossack detachment. But intelligence of an advance by Napoleon's army caused Barclay to abandon the proposed movement.[3] He decided to give battle forwards of Vitebsk. General Yermolov, who was completely familiar with this area, argued of the danger of a battle with an enemy superior in numbers, in an intersected position which greatly impeded the movement of troops, with the Commander-in-Chief, with his usual passion. Barclay, appreciating the thoroughness of his arguments, replied that he would order the troops to fall back.

Meanwhile, Napoleon was already in Beshankovichi with the main body of his force on 12 (24) July (a distance of about sixty *versts* from Vitebsk). Wanting to find out about the direction taken by the Russian troops, he ordered a reconnaissance. They immediately began building a bridge on the Dvina; but von Preysing's [Maximilian von Preysing-Moos] light cavalry brigade (from the Bavarian *6e Corps*), without waiting for the completion of this work, forded the river. Meanwhile, the bridge was completed and Napoleon himself followed our retreating troops with Preysing's Brigade for about eight *versts*. This reconnaissance convinced him that the Russian army had already managed to cross to the left bank of the river. Returning to Beshankovichi, Napoleon immediately sent Montbrun's *2e Corps de Cavalerie* along the right bank of the Dvina to pursue Dokhturov's VI Corps, while he sent the main body along the left bank of the river, towards Vitebsk.[4] Barclay, having received intelligence about the offensive by enemy troops along both banks of the Dvina, on 12 (24) July, dispatched Lieutenant General Osterman, with IV Corps, reinforced by the Ingermanland Dragoons, Nezhyn Dragoons, Sumy Hussars and Lifeguard Hussars, to Ostrovno [Astroŭna], to delay the enemy and gain time. Seven *versts* from Vitebsk, Count Osterman encountered Nansouty's leading troops, marching at the head of Napoleon's force. The Russian cavalry, having driven them off, pursued to Ostrovno, where Osterman's remaining troops then arrived.[5]

The next day, 13 (25) July, Murat, having assumed command of Nansouty's *1er Corps de Cavalerie*, to which the *8e Légère* from Delzons' Division had been attached, set out at dawn towards Ostrovno.[6] General Piré [Hippolyte-Marie-Guillaume de Rosnyvinen de Piré], who was advancing with the *8e Hussards* and *16e Chasseur à Cheval* in the vanguard of the French cavalry, ran into two squadrons of Lifeguard Hussars, accompanied by six horse artillery guns. The French, taking advantage of their superiority in numbers, scattered the Lifeguard Hussars and captured our guns. Murat arriving at the scene of the fighting himself, with the remaining brigades from Bruyère's *1re division de cavalerie légère* and with Saint-Germain's *1re division de cuirassiers*, moved on at the head of the column and, cresting the rise, at

3   Minister of War's report to the Tsar dated 12 [24] July 1812. Bernhardi, I, 312-313.
4   Chambray, *Expédition de Russie*, I, 226-227.
5   Minister of War's report to the Tsar dated 14 [26] July 1812.
6   See Plan of the Battle of Ostrovno, 13 (25) July 1812.

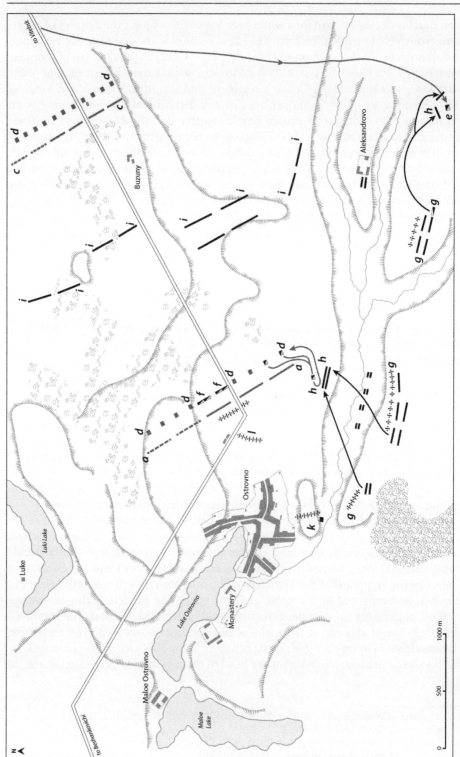

Plan of the Battle of Ostrovno, 25 July 1812.

Legend
a. First position of 11th Division.
c. Subsequent position of 11th Division.
d. 23rd Infantry Division.
e. Ingermanland Dragoon Regiment.
f. Sumy Hussar Regiment.
g. French positions.
h. French cavalry charges.
i. Subsequent positions of the French force.
k   Place where the Viceroy was located throughout the battle.
l. Place where six horse artillery pieces were captured by the enemy at the start of the battle.

the foot of which this engagement had taken place, he saw Count Osterman's force, located in readiness to fight for Ostrovno, across the highway, while his flanks were protected by swamps and woodland. 11th Division, deployed in line, formed the first wave; while 23rd Division, in battalion columns, and the cavalry formed the second; in front of the first wave were powerful batteries. On the enemy side, on the left wing, near Ostrovno, Saint-Germain's Cuirassier Division (16 squadrons) was formed in three waves; in the centre, the *8e Légère* had been scattered as skirmishers, behind whom some of Bruyère's cavalry (16 squadrons) had been placed in the second echelon; on the right wing were the rest of Bruyère's regiments: two Polish and one Prussian (12 squadrons). At the same time, the Viceroy was instructed to hurry up and arrive with Delzons' Division.

No sooner had Murat issued these orders than the Ingermanland Dragoons, emerging from the forest, which adjoined the left flank of our force, appeared on the right flank of the enemy cavalry; but, at that very moment, the *6 Pułk Ułanów* and *8e Hussards* executed a change of front to the right, struck the flank and rear of the Ingermanland Dragoons and drove them off, taking some 200 men prisoner. Having said that, Bruyère's other two regiments, which charged into the attack along the highway, were completely disordered by the fire of the Russian infantry. Count Osterman, wishing to push back the French skirmishes spreading out opposite our centre, ordered three battalions of the left wing to charge at them with fixed bayonets; but at the very moment that they were moving past the enemy cavalry, several squadrons moved towards their flank and forced them to return to the left wing of our position. Whereupon Osterman, intending to distract the enemy's attention and gain time, sent several battalions to envelope the right wing of Murat's force and two battalions to threaten his left wing. But both of these attacks were repulsed: the first by the Polish lancers and hussars, and the Prussian *2. Leib-Husaren-Regiment*; while the second was met by the *9e Chevau Légers*, supported by cuirassiers.

The bitter fighting had been going on for several hours, when the arrival of Delzons' Division gave the enemy an almost double superiority in numbers. Despite this, however, Count Osterman continued to hold his ground until evening. When he was informed that some of the regiments had suffered heavy casualties from enemy canister fire and was asked – what might his orders be? He replied: 'There is nothing to be done but to stand and die.' One of the battery commanders rode up to him and reported that many gunners had been killed in his company and that his guns were damaged. 'What are your orders, Your Excellency?' he asked Osterman. 'Keep firing those remaining,' the count answered abruptly. Meanwhile Barclay sent Uvarov's I Cavalry Corps to support him; but Count Osterman did not consider it necessary to bring them into action. Konovnitsyn's 3rd Division following Uvarov's Corps, which had been assigned to relieve the troops of IV Corps, was located behind them, eight *versts* from Ostrovno, near the village of Kakovyachino [Kukovyachino]; while at dawn on the 14 (26 July), IV Corps withdrew to this position and formed Konovnitsyn's reserve.

At eight o'clock in the morning, Murat approached the position occupied by the regiments of 3rd Division with Nansouty's and Delzons' troops. Their front was protected by a deep ravine: the right flank by the Dvina, which, however, was fordable at this point; the left was just a swampy dense forest. The enemy skirmishers of the *8e Légère*, approaching the lip of the ravine, started a firefight with our Jägers; while, in the meantime, Delzons issued orders for an attack: General Huard [Léonard Jean Aubry Huard de Saint-Aubin] was to move towards the right wing of Konovnitsyn's position with the *Régiment Croate*, supported by *84e Ligne*; General Roussel [Jean-Charles Roussel] was to march through the dense forest against our left wing with *92e Ligne* and one battalion of *106e Légère*; the remaining three battalions of *106e Légère* were held in reserve facing the centre of our position. A small part of Murat's cavalry was transferred to the far bank of the Dvina, in order to threaten to envelope Konovnitsyn's right wing.

As soon as the powerful batteries pushed forwards by General d'Anthouard [Charles Nicolas d'Anthouard de Vraincourt] opened fire, the enemy attacked both wings of our position simultaneously. The French attack on our left flank, protected by the forest, was repulsed; but, having said that, d'Anthouard pushed the battalions on our right wing back. General Konovnitsyn sent his entire reserve there, which, enveloping the enemy's left flank, pushed them back beyond the ravine; another attack by the Croats and the French at this point was also unsuccessful; one of our columns, emboldened by the pursuit, crossed the ravine; at this very moment, Murat himself charged into the attack with *8 Pułk Ułanów* and drove off the nearest Russian infantry, while the Viceroy, taking advantage of this success, ordered Delzons' Division to resume the offensive and brought the *106e Légère*, which was in reserve, into action. Roussel's troops eventually captured the large forest and enveloped Konovnitsyn from the left flank; the left wing of the enemy infantry also pressed forwards. The battery stationed in the centre of our position was under great threat when enemy cavalry attacked it, but was saved by the brave Pernov Infantry and Kexholm Infantry, under Major General Choglokov's command. The French, with shouts of: *'Vive l'Empereur!'* rushing forwards, captured three of our guns; the Chernigov Infantry charged with fixed bayonets and recovered the lost artillery. Eventually, Konovnitsyn ordered his troops to retreat. The enemy, seeing Osterman's columns behind Konovnitsyn's regiments, did not dare to pursue our division; but Napoleon himself, having arrived on the field of battle, ordered the offensive to continue. The Russian troops withdrew in perfect order, gradually, from one position to another as far as the village of Komary, where Konovnitsyn, with 9,000 infantry and 3,000 cavalry, held out against 20,000 men until five o'clock in the afternoon, and then retreated to Dobreika and joined up with the other divisions of Tuchkov 1st's III Corps, who, having taken command of the rearguard, pulled them back over the Luchosa river at night. Osterman's troops also retreated there and Dokhturov's and Pahlen's Corps arrived from the right bank of the Dvina.

Napoleon stopped for the night near the village of Kakovyachino, near the highway, where a tent was pitched for him; while Murat was at Dobreika with the vanguard, not quite eight *versts* from Vitebsk.

On our side, a new vanguard, consisting of eight battalions, almost all of the light cavalry that was with the army, and two Cossack regiments, under the command of Count Pahlen, was to move forward, during the night of 14 to 15 (26 to 27) July, to the left bank of the Luchosa and settled in position, just short of Dobreika.[7]

Our troops, in both actions on 13 and 14 (25 and 26) July, showed heroic fearlessness, but the bravest of the brave were their worthy commanders: Count Osterman and Konovnitsyn. We attach Konovnitsyn's note to his wife, sent by him a day after the battle:

16 [28] July 1812 at ten o'clock in the evening, from Surazh.

I have not disgraced myself in front of everyone; I was with the skirmishers at the front, had two corps facing me and Bonaparte himself; I even saw him – similar to the statements by the prisoners – on a small white horse, with a docked tail. From eight o'clock in the morning to five o'clock in the afternoon, I fought against – dare I say – 60,000 men with four regiments and two battalions of combined grenadiers. I will tell you, my friend, I was not ashamed; neither you nor my children will blush for me.

The whole day I kept Napoleon himself at bay, who had wanted to dine in Vitebsk, but did not get there even for the night – the next day, maybe. Our men have fought like lions. But we are not united. Bagration, Platov and Wittgenstein are separated from us.

We are in a bad situation. Maybe God unseen will deliver us. Don't think about it... I shall not put myself to shame and would willingly die for my Fatherland. God will not abandon our children or you, but my fatherland – perhaps – remember me.

Imagine, my friend, that two batteries were already taken from me, but I stayed in the front line: everything was also smashed – the cannon were targets... When a friend of mine lost six the day before. We are not thinking of awards... That is not our business.

But the superiority of the enemy numbers was too great. Despite the courageous feats by our troops and the skilful orders from their commanders, the enemy, using his double strength, managed to close on Vitebsk, where the main body of First Army was located. Barclay, still hoping for the arrival of Bagration at Orsha via Mogilev, from where Second Army could just establish communications with First Army,

---

7   The plan of the battle of Ostrovno is in the archive of the M.T.D. Travel notes of an artilleryman, I, 73-82. Buturlin, *Histoire militaire de la campagne de Russie en 1812*, I, 214-220. Chambray, I, 228-232. Thiers, XIV, 147-157. Konovnitsyn's notes.

decided to give battle on the Luchosa, although the position he took did not present defensive advantages. The reasons prompting him to do so consisted, according to his own statements:

1. The fact that the enemy had not yet managed to concentrate all their troops at Vitebsk.
2. The stubborn resistance to the enemy by our troops, in the actions on 13 and 14 (25 and 26) July, vouched for success in a battle against superior numbers.
3. By giving battle, Barclay would distract the attention of the enemy from Bagration, who, exploiting this, could more conveniently close the gap to First Army.

In all likelihood, the latter of these reasons – the desire to facilitate the union with Bagration, more than any other, prompted our Commander-in-Chief to give battle; in addition, the Russian troops longed for a decisive engagement with the enemy: was it possible to avoid it at a time when Prince Bagration, at the invitation of Barclay himself, must have been on the way to Orsha and, in the event of a retreat by First Army, was in danger of being attacked and defeated by Napoleon's main force? If this were to happen, then all responsibility for the defeat of Second Army would fall on Barclay de Tolly. Without any doubt, he could have made a flank march to meet Bagration, at Orsha; but such a movement in close proximity to the enemy army was even more dangerous than the acceptance of a battle on the position behind the Luchosa.

Having said all that, the disparity of his forces with the enemy's did not suggest the likelihood of success. On our side, no more than 80,000 men could be brought into action against the 150,000 of Napoleon's army. Such a significant superiority of enemy troop numbers would assist him in bypassing Barclay's position, cut off our line of retreat to Porechye [Demidov, Smolensk *Oblast*] and push First Army into the Dvina, flowing between high, steep banks along this stretch and providing possible crossings at only a very few points.[8]

Thus, a decisive battle seemed inevitable. Napoleon, from the very beginning of the campaign, sought for it: in our army – many wanted to fight, guided by instinctive courage and not reckoning on the consequences. But by the time the dispositions for the battle had already been issued – just after Barclay de Tolly had informed the Tsar about his intention and informed Bagration about the same, begging him to move to Orsha – at this very moment, during the night of 14 to 15 (26 to 27) July, Bagration's aide de camp, Lieutenant Prince Menshikov [Alexander Sergeevich Menshikov], arrived at the headquarters of First Army, with the news from Prince Bagration about the failure of his attempt to push through Mogilev.[9] At the same time, Bagration, notifying Barclay about the concentration of Davout's forces in Mogilev and about the movement of his right to this location, expressed doubts about the possibility of uniting our armies at Smolensk. Despite all this Barclay de

---

8   Clausewitz, *Der Feldzug von 1812 in Russland*, 101.
9   Minister of War's report to the Tsar dated 15 [27] July 1812, No 538.

Tolly, for all his steadfastness, was carried away by a simple urge and did not dare to retreat. General Yermolov hurried to him and predicted the inevitable demise of the army in the event of a battle in the position in front of Vitebsk. 'The only feature that might save us,' he said: 'is to protect the front of the position with the Luchosa, which is rather difficult to ford. While the enemy is looking for the fords, we must immediately withdraw from our position and begin to retreat; otherwise, our army will be defeated in detail.'

The Commander-in-Chief convened a council of war; everyone agreed with Yermolov's opinion; but General Tuchkov 1st suggested staying in the position until evening. 'Who can guarantee that we will not be broken before evening?' objected Yermolov: 'Would Napoleon undertake to leave us alone until nightfall?' The Commander-in-Chief, sharing General Yermolov's convictions, decided to retreat to Smolensk via Porechye. 'Under such circumstances,' he wrote in his notes, 'there could be no intention of fighting near Vitebsk: the victory itself would not have brought us any benefit if, meanwhile, Davout had occupied Smolensk. If I went into battle, I would sacrifice 20,000 or 25,000 men to no advantage, without having a way, even after winning a victory, to pursue the enemy; as Davout, having occupied Smolensk, could have got into the rear of First Army; and if I decided to attack him, then Napoleon would follow me and I would be surrounded by enemy troops. I could only retreat, even after a victory, and would have to direct it towards Velizh via Surazh, and, consequently, I would be moving even further away from Second Army. For all these reasons, I decided to proceed to Smolensk immediately. All transport and artillery reserves sent to Surazh were ordered to go to Porechye and Smolensk; and the care of the army's provisioning was entrusted to the local governor and the leader of the nobility.'[10]

Retreating in close proximity to an enemy army is very difficult. The Commander-in-Chief, wishing to mask his intentions, instructed Count Pahlen's detachment to delay the enemy along the route to Vitebsk, strengthened by reinforcements sent to him of some 14 battalions, 32 squadrons and two Cossack regiments with 40 guns.[11] To that end, Count Pahlen selected a position eight *versts* from the city, protected frontally by an insignificant stream flowing into the Dvina, while the right flank was anchored on the Dvina; the left flank was completely open; in addition, the extent of the position was disproportionate to the strength of our detachment: there were no more than 4,000 men in all 14 battalions, which forced the infantry to be deployed in two echelons, without a reserve, with very large intervals between battalions; the cavalry was formed up on a small plain at the confluence of the stream with the Dvina, but as this plain was constrained on one side by the Dvina, and on the other by high ground overgrown with forest, our squadrons were arranged in a chess-board pattern, in three and partly even in four waves, as a result of which there were huge casualties from the enemy cannonade.

---

10   Depiction of military operations by First Army (compiled by Barclay de Tolly).
11   Clausewitz (who was Chief of Staff in Count Pahlen's Corps at that time), *Der Feldzug von 1812 in Russland*, 102. [Liprandi states: 'There was an officer of the General Staff under Count Pahlen, Captain Dannenberg. Clausewitz, who did not speak a word of Russian, naturally could not hold the post of corps Chief of Staff, and did not hold it.'].

On 15 (27) July, at dawn, Napoleon directed his troops along the road to Vitebsk. Ahead went the light cavalry and Broussier's Division; behind them came the main body of the army. After proceeding about two *versts*, the enemy discovered our rear-guard; behind them, in the distance, they could make out, through the haze, the location of Barclay de Tolly's main force. The bell towers of Vitebsk rose opposite the French left flank. The enemy, approaching the river, proceeded to rebuild the bridge, which had been burned down by Russian troops the day before. This work, carried out under fire from our Lifeguard Horse Artillery, which operated excel-lently under Colonel Kosen's [Pëtr Andreevich Kosen] command, took a long time; thereafter, *16e chasseurs à cheval* moved across the bridge over the river; Broussier's infantry, having also crossed the bridge, formed up in squares, while one of the light regiments headed towards the wooded high ground, where the left wing of our detachment stood, while the *16e chasseurs à cheval*, with two *voltigeur* companies of *9e Ligne*, hurrying to the left, became significantly separated from the other troops. Count Pahlen, seizing the opportunity, sent the Lifeguard Cossacks facing them into the attack, supported by two squadrons of Sumy Hussars. The French *chasseurs à cheval* stood their ground, and as soon as our cavalry galloped up to them, they greeted it with a volley from their carbines; but this did not stop the Cossacks and hussars, who in a swift charge scattered the *chasseurs*, drove them into a ravine and charged at the *voltigeurs*. The two enemy companies, surrounded on all sides by our cavalry, nevertheless managed to retreat in small groups and reach the ravine, where they were rescued by the *53e Ligne*. Napoleon, following the progress of the action himself from a small hill, rode out to get behind the ravine and, drawing level with the skirmishers, asked: 'What regiment is this?'

'*9e Ligne* and all *Parisiennes*' they replied.

'You are fine fellows; every one of you is worthy of a cross!' said Napoleon, who was then escorted further along the entire line to cheers of: '*Vive l'Empereur!*' Broussier's troops, formed in regimental squares, with artillery in their intervals, pressed forwards, but were halted by decisive counter-charges by Russian cavalry. Napoleon was forced to commit all of Nansouty's cavalry and Delzons' infantry to battle, following which Count Pahlen, seeing the obvious impossibility of holding out against such overwhelming strength, retreated behind the Luchosa, at five o'clock in the afternoon. As the battle continued, the withdrawal by one of the French cavalry regiments, which had the intention of making room for Delzons' troops, caused a panic in the enemy train; service support troops and *Vivandières* fled along the road to Beshankovichi and spread rumours of the defeat of the French army.[12]

The fighting on 13, 14 and 15 (25, 26 and 27) July came at a heavy cost – both to us and to the enemy. On our side there were 827 men killed (including the death on the 13th [25 July] of Major General Okulov [Modest Matveevich Okulov]), 1,855 wounded (including Major General Kutaisov [Alexander Ivanovich Kutaisov] with a gunshot wound to the leg on the 14th [26 July]); there were 1,082 missing in action: in total, 3,764 men.[13] Enemy casualties reached 3,704 men, of whom 300 men

---

12   Condensed War Diary, compiled by von Toll. Chambray, *Expédition de Russie*, I, 229-234.
      Buturlin, I, 222-223. Thiers, *Hist. du Consulat et de l'Empire*, XIV, 149-161. Bernhardi, I, 313-320.
13   Returns for killed, wounded and missing from First Army, signed by Duty General Kikin.

were taken prisoner. Among those killed were *Général de division* Roussel and one *Général de Brigade*; another *Général de Brigade* was wounded.[14]

In Barclay de Tolly's report to the Tsar regarding the actions at Vitebsk, he stated:

> The forces of Your Imperial Majesty, during these three days, fought against superior enemy numbers with amazing courage and spirit. They fought as Russians should, ignoring the risk to their lives for their Tsar and the fatherland. I cannot decide whether to praise the vanguard troops, IV Corps or 3rd Division over any other: everyone vied in courage, diligence and bravery, the Lifeguard Hussar Regiment especially distinguished itself.
>
> Only unfavourable circumstances forced First Army into the necessity of this retreat, which it may be proud of, in the military sense, having performed it within sight of overwhelmingly superior enemy numbers held back by a small vanguard, constituted under the command of Count Pahlen.
>
> … The unshakable courage of the troops gives us certain hope for great successes.[15]

The commander of the rearguard on 15 (27) July, Count Pahlen, was promoted to Lieutenant General.[16]

Barclay had initially intended to remain on the Luchosa only until noon on 15 (27) July, and then to begin the retreat, but the stubborn resistance by our rearguard, giving him the hope of holding the enemy on the Luchosa until evening, stayed in place until four o'clock in the afternoon. Wanting to assist Pahlen in slowing down the French, the Commander-in-Chief dispatched some of the main body to support him and advanced his left wing, threatening the enemy with envelopment on their right flank.[17]

Napoleon had hoped to entice Barclay de Tolly into a decisive battle. The French troops, tired from the long marches, having almost no bread at all and having, for the most part, only under-cooked meat to eat without salt, wished for a fight, hoping for something better. But the Russian Commander-in-Chief was already preparing to continue the retreat.[18]

At exactly four o'clock our army withdrew from its position. The troops retreated in three columns: on the right (II Corps and IV Corps) took the Surazh road towards Agaponovshchino; the centre column (III Corps and II Cavalry Corps), with which the headquarters was located, took the route to Porechye, towards Veledichy; the left (V Corps, VI Corps and III Cavalry Corps) moved along the direct route towards Smolensk, heading towards Rudnya, reaching Korolevo. Count Pahlen's rearguard remained on the Luchosa until dawn the next day. Huge bivouac fires, blazing on the site of the army's former camp, assured Napoleon of the hope of fighting the main body of the Russian army.

---

14   Extracted from documents captured from the French in 1812.
15   Barclay de Tolly's report dated 15 [27] July 1812, No 538.
16   Supreme Orders dated 10 [22] August 1812.
17   Bernhardi, I, 319-320.
18   Thiers, XIV, 161.

On the following day, 16 (28) July, the right column, shielded by Pahlen's main rearguard, retreated to Janovichy [Janaviçy]; the centre, covered by Korf's rearguard, went to Kolyshki; the left, with Major General Shevich's [Ivan Yegorovich Shevich] cavalry forming the rearguard, went to Liozna. The enemy cavalry, inattentively pursuing Pahlen's rearguard, was defeated at Agaponovshchino.[19] The French troops, famished from a lack of provisions and forage, were exhausted by the heat, reaching 28 degrees (R) [35 degrees Centigrade] in the shade. Napoleon, having lost hope of keeping our armies apart, decided to call off the pursuit and give his troops a rest in order to allow the stragglers to re-join and to collect much needed supplies from the surrounding countryside.[20]

On 17 (29) July, II Corps and IV Corps joined up with III Corps at the town of Porechye, while V Corps and VI Corps had arrived in Rudnya. The onward movement proceeded in two columns. The troops, from their first steps into the Smolensk Governorate, were greeted with true Russian hospitality: the peasants brought food supplies to the camp and refused to take money for them, or accepted a token payment with gratitude. Many of them expressed their readiness to arm themselves and innocently asked: 'Would we have to answer for it if we killed a Frenchman?'

On 20 July (1 August), the main formations of First Army linked up at Smolensk and camped along the right bank of the Dnieper, on the roads leading from Porechye and Rudnya. The headquarters of First Army was in Smolensk. Count Pahlen's rearguard, reinforced by Korf's Corps, was located near Porechye; Major General Shevich's rearguard was at Rudnya. In Smolensk, the army was reinforced by the reserve battalions and artillery companies under Adjutant General Wintzingerode's command, who, having surrendered them to the force, received the Kazan Dragoons and four Cossack regiments to command for operations on the enemy army's left flank towards Vitebsk.[21]

From Napoleon's side, the troops operating against Barclay were located as follows: the *État-major général* was in Vitebsk, as was the *Garde*. The Viceroy's *4e Corps* was in Surazh on the Dvina, forming the army's left wing; the right, facing Rudnya had all of Murat's *Réserve de cavalerie*, with Ney's *3e Corps* behind them; while three of Davout's divisions were behind Ney, between Babinovichi and Vitebsk. Saint-Cyr remained, as before, at Beshankovichi. Napoleon's five-week campaign from the banks of the Neman to Vitebsk had no result, other than the swift occupation of several governorates, poor in resources and devastated by the troops from both sides. In particular, the destruction of the mills was harmful to the French, as it prevented them from using the bread-making grain found in the countryside. Russian magazines, captured by the enemy, were far from being able to meet the needs of Napoleon's huge army, and there was an extreme shortage of transport. A consequence of all this was looting and marauding, which developed initially in the foreign contingents, and then throughout the entire army. But in addition, there were other reasons for the weakening of the force: foraging, escorting the huge carts, caring for the herds that followed the army; regimental artillery, all of which

---

19   Condensed War Diary, compiled by von Toll.
20   Thiers, XIV, 168-169.
21   Condensed War Diary, compiled by von Toll.

diverted many infantry soldiers from their real duties and did not bring the slightest benefit; eventually forcing many horsemen to trudge on foot after the troops. From the cumulative influence of these factors, the army melted away noticeably, and this could not be averted by either Napoleon's genius or the experience of the French military administration. It was becoming apparent that the conduct of war in Russia was incomparably more difficult than operations in Italy or southern Germany – populous countries with abundant resources for maintaining troops and intersected in all directions by good roads. The troops, which were under the direct command of Napoleon at that time (Ney's, the Viceroy's, Saint-Cyr's, three of Davout's divisions, Murat's *Réserve de cavalerie* and the *Garde* Corps), in which there had been 220,000 men at the crossing of the Neman, counted no more than 150,000 in the ranks, upon reaching Vitebsk, and had therefore been, weakened by a whole third – 70,000 men, of whom a tenth had been put out of action in combat.[22]

Having outlined the operations by Barclay de Tolly and his colleagues before the arrival of First Army at Smolensk, I shall proceed to describe the retreat of Second Army, after their three-day rest in Nesvizh.

On 28 June (10 July), VIII Corps set out for Slutsk;[23] on the 29th [11 July], the rest of Prince Bagration's force followed; while Platov's Cossack detachment was located at Nesvizh as the rearguard. On 1 (13) July, the entire Second Army, with the exception of the rearguard, was located at Slutsk. There, intelligence was received of the appearance of Davout's troops in the town of Svislach, 40 *versts* from Bobruisk, which forced Prince Bagration, who was 120 *versts* from there, to speed up the pace. The next day, 2 (14) July, General Raevsky was sent to the village of Verkhutino with VII Corps. Meanwhile, the day before, Platov had gone to Romanovo [Lenino], leaving Major General Karpov 2nd [Akim Akimovich Karpov] at Nesvizh, with two Cossack regiments; whereupon Karpov's detachment proceeded after him. The enemy, noticing the retreat of the Cossacks, pursued them with three squadrons of lancers. Although our detachment was more than a match for them, nevertheless, Karpov, wishing to lure them further away from Nesvizh, ordered the Cossacks to speed up their retreat and set off four *versts* from the town, then, suddenly turned on the lancers and charged home, wiping out a whole squadron and pursued the remainder as far as Nesvizh, and then moved back to re-join the raiding detachment.

On 2 (14) July, Platov was attacked at Romanovo by seven cavalry regiments; the Cossacks, having driven them off, rode straight at the enemy infantry, located five *versts* from Romanovo. 'Two of the best regiments, *1er chasseurs à cheval* and a horse-grenadier regiment, were driven into the dust,' the *Ataman* wrote in his report. Following this, the enemy, strengthened by significant reinforcements, forced the Cossacks to retreat to join up with Adjutant General Vasilchikov's detachment at Romanovo; the two independent batteries of the Don Horse Artillery Company were stationed there, with an escort from 5th Jäger Regiment, under the command of Colonel Gogel [Fëdor Grigoryevich Gogel]; behind them, under the direct command of General Vasilchikov, there were: the Akhtyrka Hussars, Kiev

---

22   Chambray, I, 242-249. Thiers, XIV, 176-185.
23   See Map of Significant Movements by the Russian and French armies from the beginning of the war to the battle of Smolensk.

Dragoons and Lithuania Ulans; while major generals Krasnov 1st's [Ivan Kozmich Krasnov], Ilovaisky 4th's [Ivan Dmitryevich Ilovaisky], Kuteinikov 2nd's and Karpov 2nd's Cossack regiments were stationed on their flanks.

The enemy, closing up to our position, was greeted with cannon fire and was attacked several times by the Cossacks from the flanks. The action, which lasted for more than an hour, ended with the retreat of the enemy force to the town of Timkovichi. Judging from the course of the battle, their casualties were very signif-icant; 18 field officers and subalterns, and 360 lower ranks were captured by the Cossacks. Our casualties were moderate. Among those who distinguished them-selves, the *Ataman* named generals Vasilchikov, Count Vorontsov and all the main Cossack commanders; about General Kuteinikov 2nd he stated that: 'he participated in the most powerful attack and rout in the midst of fire and so on.' On that same day, Platov moved beyond the river Moroch.[24]

Following the action at Romanovo, the troops, formerly under the command of the King of Westphalia, stopped pursuing Second Army from behind and turned to the left: included in this was Tharreau, who had replaced Vandamme in command of the Westphalian *8e Corps*, moved from Nesvizh, via Minsk, towards Orsha on 4 (16) July; Poniatowski with the Polish *5e Corps*, from Romanovo, via Igumen [Chervyen], towards Mogilev; while Latour Maubourg, having reached Glusk, on 12 (24) July passed through the town of Berezino towards Mogilev. General Reynier's Saxon *7e Corps*, moved back to Slonim, from where they were to move against Tormasov.[25]

The troops under the direct command of Davout, also continued to advance towards the Dnieper. Having detached Pajol's cavalry brigade to Igumen (from where Pajol sent patrols to Svislach) in order to protect the Minsk depots, rein-forced by part of Bordesoulle's brigade and one infantry regiment, and leaving one of the regiments from Dessaix's division in Minsk, Davout set out from Minsk on 1 (13) July and arrived in Igumen on the 3rd (15 July), while Grouchy's *3e Corps de Cavalerie* seized the Borisov bridgehead, forcing Colonel Gresser [Alexander Ivanovich Gresser], who was in Borisov with three weak reserve battalions, with a total of some 400 men, to retreat to Mogilev. Whereupon Davout's corps, with a cavalry division from Grouchy's corps, moved on Mogilev, while the rest of Grouchy's force, marching from Borisov via Kokhanavo and Babinovichi, became part of Napoleon's main force.[26]

On 7 (19) July, the governor of Mogilev, Count Tolstoy [Dmitry Alexandrovich Tolstoy], having learned about the appearance of the enemy near the town of Knyazhitsy, ten *versts* from Mogilev, sent Police Chief Litvinov there with 30 privates from the Interior Guard, who attacked a forward enemy outpost and captured a single Frenchman; the next day, at four o'clock in the morning, Davout's vanguard arrived at the Vilna checkpoint, and after a bitter fight with the Mogilev Garrison Battalion, seized the city, from where at the same time the governor left and many residents fled. On the 8th (20 July), Davout entered via the Shklov gate.

---

24   Condensed War Diary, compiled by von Toll. Platov's report to the Tsar dated 3 [15] July 1812.
25   Chambray, I, 207.
26   Chambray, I, 273-274. Buturlin, I 229.

The enemy found significant stocks of provisions in the magazines, which had not been destroyed, in fact, because no one anticipated the seizure of the city by the French. In addition to those stores found in Mogilev, the enemy began to acquire an abundance of provisions, cattle and horses from the landowners, in accordance with a schedule drafted by the provisional government, compiled by order of Davout. But every attempt by this turncoat administration to form an armed force in favour of the French failed. Although the provisional government managed to recruit some 400 jägers from the gentry, who were designated the National Guard, they did not bring the slightest benefit and deserted without firing a single shot against the Russians. To their shame, Mogilev was destined to be the only example of contempt for sacred duty during the war of 1812. The Archbishop of Mogilev, Varlaam [Grigory Stepanovich Shishatsky], not only took the side of the enemy and commemorated Napoleon as the legitimate sovereign at litanies, but also roused his flock and swore a binding oath, which obliged everyone who belonged to his Eparchy to fulfil the orders of the enemy authorities to the letter.[27]

On 6 (18) July, all the troops of Second Army were assembled in Bobruisk. The advantages brought by this fortress in the circumstances of that time are beyond doubt: if we did not have a fortified point there that secured the crossing over the Berezina, then Davout, upon reaching Igumen, could have forestalled Prince Bagration on this river, or attacked him before Second Army could have the opportunity to cross the Dnieper. In the present day, when one of the most important and best lines of communication for the Empire passes through Bobruisk, the strategic importance of the Bobruisk fortress has increased even more so.

On 7 (19) July, during a rest day for Bagration's troops at Bobruisk, a Supreme Command was received, via *Flügel-Adjutant* Prince Volkonsky, for Second Army to march to join First Army via Mogilev and Orsha. But at the same time, intelligence was received of Davout's movement directly towards Mogilev.[28] On that same day, Prince Bagration, hoping to prevent the concentration of a significant enemy force in Mogilev and force his way through to Orsha, dispatched Raevsky's VII Corps from Bobruisk towards Mogilev (with the exception of 5th Jäger Regiment attached to Platov's raiding detachment) and some of Count Sievers' cavalry. On the following day, 8 (20) July, Borozdin's VIII Corps set out along the same route, followed by their rearguard under Count Vorontsov with the Combined Grenadier Division and Kharkov Dragoon Regiment. Before leaving Bobruisk, Bagration added six reserve battalions to his army from the local garrison, leaving the defence of the fortress to 12 battalions with a *sotnia* of Cossacks, a total of 5,000 men.[29]

On 9 (21) July, Raevsky reached Stary Bykhov [Bykhaw]; the remaining troops of Second Army remained behind but within a day's march. On the same day, Colonel Sysoev, moving with his Cossack regiment ahead of Sievers, on the way to Mogilev met Gresser's weak detachment, which, during its entire march, had been subjected to incessant attacks by a French *chasseur à cheval* regiment. The arrival of Sysoev forced

---

27 Extracted from information provided by the former commandant of Mogilev, Okunev.

28 Chief of Staff of Second Army, General Count Saint Priest's report to the Tsar dated 10 [22] July, from Stary Bykhov.

29 Condensed War Diary, compiled by von Toll. Buturlin, 230-231.

the enemy to call off the pursuit. Meanwhile, Count Sievers arrived in good time with two dragoon and two Cossack regiments, which made it possible for Sysoev to operate decisively; moving swiftly forward with his Cossacks, he caught up with the *chasseurs à cheval*, surrounded them on all sides and, routing them totally, pursued the enemy, but being greeted five *versts* from Mogilev by fire from a battery of six guns, located under escort by the *85e Ligne*, he returned to Sievers' detachment. In this action, all in all, the French lost 32 officers and 460 lower ranks, of whom: one colonel, eight field officers and more than 200 lower ranks were taken prisoner.[30]

Davout was convinced of the need to hold Mogilev to his rear, whence his main body had been directed; and in the meantime he managed to gather a maximum of 28,000 men at this location. As there were no good defensive positions in the vicinity of Mogilev, the Marshal decided to move those troops that were with him along the road towards Stary Bykhov. To that end, accompanied by General Haxo, he made a thorough reconnaissance of the area in this direction and, choosing a position near the village of Saltanovka [Soltanovka], behind one of the tributaries of the Dnieper, deployed a force totalling 28,000 men, on 10 (22) July.

Prince Bagration, having confirmed the enemy occupation of Mogilev, although he probably knew neither about the number of troops stationed there, nor about the strength of those who could reinforce them later, nevertheless he decided to advance to engage Marshal Davout and push his way through by armed force. In a report to the Tsar, he explained the reasons that prompted him to do so, as follows:

> For my part, achieving Your Majesty's objectives, to block the enemy's route to Smolensk and have the centre of Russia to the rear of Second Army, I must certainly proceed to Mogilev, as by the most direct route, and to cross the Dnieper only there, as all other crossings over it have been constructed on very distant routes; while what is even more important, in leaving the enemy in Mogilev, wherever the army crosses, it will always be in danger of being caught between two, as it must be assumed, rather strong corps moving from Orsha to Smolensk and located in Mogilev.[31]

In preparing to march against Davout, Prince Bagration, like a true military leader moulded in Suvorov's school, was to secure his retreat to the left bank of the Dnieper: to that end, he wrote to the governor of Mogilev about the availability of rafts and timber, down the Dnieper, from Stary Bykhov to Novy Bykhov, in order to construct a bridge there.[32] On 10 (22) July, Raevsky's leading troops, pushing back the enemy vanguard located near the village of Dashkovka, forced them to retreat to the position at Saltanovka.[33]

---

30   Description of the military operations of the Don Cossacks (M.T.D. No 47,352, folio 2). Thiers, XIV, 125. Information extracted from documents captured from the French. General Raevsky's letter to General Jomini, written in 1822 (M.T.D. No 47,352, folio 2).

31   Report dated 10 [22] July 1812, No 434.

32   Message dated 10 [22] July 1812, No 623 (in the collection of the Commander-in-Chief's chancellery).

33   See Plan of the Action at Saltanovka, 11 (23) July.

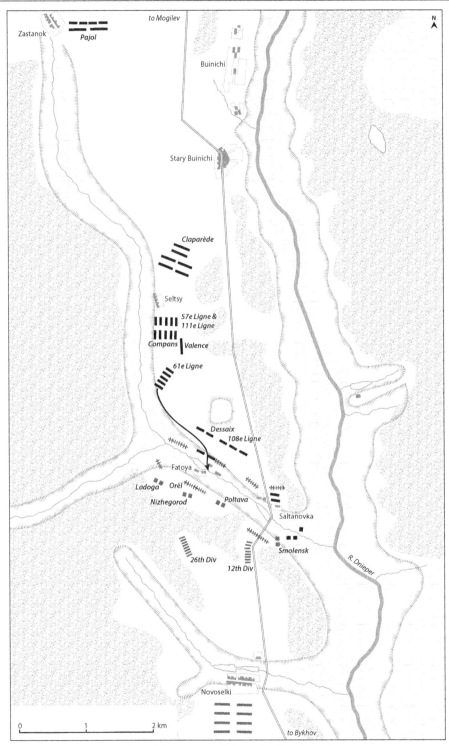

Plan of the Action at Saltanovka, 23 July 1812.

Marshal Davout's force was deployed in this position as follows: an inn near Saltanovka and a mill at Fatova had been prepared for defence, and were held by five battalions of the *85e Ligne*, under the command of General Friederichs [Jean-Parfait Friederichs]; behind them, in reserve, stood General Dessaix with *108e Ligne*; the bridge by the inn was barricaded and the mill dam breached; artillery was located at the most advantageous points for their operation. Behind these troops, at a distance of about three *versts*, near the village of Seltsy [Selets], were three regiments from Compans' Division (*61e Ligne* and behind them *57e Ligne* and *111e Ligne*) and Valence's *5e division de cuirassiers*, with some of the artillery; Claparède's Polish Division [*Légion de la Vistule*] was between Seltsy and Mogilev; finally, General Pajol had been assigned to guard the road leading from Mogilev to Igumen, with a light cavalry brigade and *25e Ligne* (from Compans' Division). The strength of all these troops came to 20,000 infantry and 6,000 cavalry.

On 11 (23) July, Bagration ordered Raevsky to attack the enemy, with his corps and part of Sievers' cavalry, numbering 15,000 men. The remaining elements of Second Army, at the same time, proceeded to Dashkovka. At eight o'clock in the morning, the action began between the leading troops of both sides, in the forest, just short of Saltanovka. The French, conducted a fighting retreat to their position; and our men, passing through the forest in two columns, settled in the tree line: Kolyubakin's Division was facing the bridge at Saltanovka, while Paskevich's Division faced the dam at Fatova. After a short cannonade and some skirmishing, our troops charged the bridge, but were greeted with withering canister and musket fire and they were forced to retreat.

Raevsky had sent Paskevich's Division to Fatova, hoping to find fewer terrain obstacles there; the Ladoga Infantry drove out one of the battalions of the French *85e Ligne*, which had been holding the buildings on the right bank of the stream, and under covering fire from a 12-gun battery moved to the far side, but were pushed back by the *61e Ligne*, which, in the meantime, had closed up to the forward edge of the defended position on Marshal Davout's orders. Here, in bloody combat, the Orël Infantry, which had rushed to the aid of the Ladoga Infantry, had its Colour taken by the enemy, but it was rescued by the regimental adjutant. One of the battalions from Dessaix's Division, carried away in the pursuit of the repulsed troops, crossed the ravine, but was driven off with heavy casualties. General Paskevich attempted to outflank the enemy; our skirmishing screen, proceeding through the forest, was already approaching the village of Seltsy, when the French, sending several battalions into the densest part of the forest and threatening to cut off our troops, forced them to retreat.

Meanwhile, a powerful cannonade continued on both sides. Raevsky, hearing the roar of guns in that direction, believed that Paskevich was pressing forwards, and noticing a wavering in the enemy line, sent 12th Division towards the Saltanovka bridge once more. Together with Vasilchikov and all the officers of his staff, including Raevsky's own sons, he dismounted and stood in front of the Smolensk Infantry, assigned to march at the head of the column.[34] This excellent regiment,

---

34   [Liprandi claims that, at this moment, one of Raevsky's sons said to his colleague, a 16-year-old Sub-Ensign: 'Let me carry the Colours!' and received the response: 'I know how to die myself!'].

on whose Colours is inscribed the evidence of their exploits 'for the capture of French Colours in the Alps,' raced towards the bridge; but at that very moment, seeing an enemy column that had made its way across the stream downstream of the bridge on his flank, he drove at it with bayonets fixed and hustled the French into the swamps. Raevsky was preparing to push across the bridge, when suddenly the news came from Paskevich that it had been impossible to outflank the enemy; at the same time, a number captured Frenchmen confirmed that Marshal Davout had three infantry and two cavalry divisions, and his remaining forces were assembled in Mogilev. General Raevsky, seeing the complete impossibility of breaking through this choke-point, behind which stood significant enemy forces, ordered the troops to retreat. The enemy pursued him rather weakly only as far as Novoselki and halted at the very location where their forward outposts had stood the day before; while Raevsky's troops settled at Dashkovka, where Prince Bagration and Platov arrived while the Combined Grenadier Division under Count Vorontsov and the remaining troops of Second Army arrived that night.[35]

The losses on both sides in the battle at Saltanovka were significant. The French lost some 3,400 men altogether, of whom about 500 were taken prisoner. On our side there were 16 field officers and subalterns, and 548 lower ranks killed; two generals, 35 field officers and subalterns, and 1,309 lower ranks wounded; two field officers and subalterns, and 592 lower ranks were reported missing; in total, we had lost 2,504 men.[36]

General Raevsky, reporting to Prince Bagration about this battle, wrote:

> The singular courage and eagerness of the Russian forces were able to save me from destruction facing a superior enemy in a position of great advantage to them. I myself witnessed that many officers and lower ranks, having suffered two wounds each and having had them dressed, returned to the fighting as if to a feast.[37] I cannot praise the courage and skill of the gunners highly enough: they were all heroes. This battle was the first combat for my corps in this campaign. The troops were motivated with exemplary courage and zeal, worthy of astonishment.[38]

On the following day, 12 (24) July, Davout, expecting a second attack from Bagration (whom he considered much stronger than he was in reality), held in place and concentrated all his attention on strengthening the position at Saltanovka. But, in the meantime, Second Army had retreated to Novy Bykhov, where a crossing point on the Dnieper had already been prepared; Raevsky's Corps remained at Dashkovka throughout the entire day in order to conceal this movement. The raiding detachment

---

35   General Raevsky's letter to General Jomini, written in 1822. General Mikhailovsky-
      Danilevsky's History of the Patriotic War of 1812, I. Buturlin, I, 232-237. Thiers, XIV, 224-232.
36   Information extracted from documents captured from the French. Casualty Return for the
      fighting troops, signed by Duty General Kikin (in Second Army's War Diary, our casualties
      are given as 3,000 men).
37   Raevsky also mentioned this, later, in a letter to General Jomini.
38   General Raevsky's report to Prince Bagration dated 20 July [1 August], No 196.

under Platov and Dorokhov, with 1st Jägers and the Izyum Hussars, were ordered to cross at Vorkolabovo [Borkolabovo] and march between the Dnieper and the Sozh, in order to join First Army; the 18th Jäger Regiment, which until now had been in General Dorokhov's detachment, was left with the main body of the army, due to the extreme fatigue of the men from previous marches.

On 14 (26) July, the main body of Second Army crossed the Dnieper at Novy Bykhov and in the following days continued to move via Mstislavl [Mscislau], shielded from the direction of the Dnieper by the vanguard, proceeding from Propoysk [Slawharad] to Chausy [Czausy], Drybin and Gorki [Horki], to Dubrowna [Dubroŭna], while Platov's raiding detachment, which, together with Dorokhov's, having crossed the Dnieper at Dashkovka and Vorkolabovo, moved via Chausy, Gorki and Dubrowna, to Lyubavichi, and, having reached the latter location, established communications with First Army. At this point, I think it is necessary to say a few words about how Dorokhov made the crossing using the high degree of military training of the Izyum Hussar Regiment through his care. Having approached the Dnieper with several Cossacks and a trumpeter from the Izyum Hussars, he found a convenient place for crossing, and partly by fording, partly by swimming, crossed to the far side of the river. There, after waiting for the arrival of Izyum Hussars at the Dnieper, he ordered the trumpeter to sound 'assembly.' As soon as the hussars heard the signal, they rushed into the river and, at the direction of the Cossacks sent to meet them, crossed to the left bank of the Dnieper.[39]

Throughout the duration of these movements by Prince Bagration and Platov, Davout, despite the reinforcements that had joined him, did not dare to cross the Dnieper, for fear of being caught between our Western armies. Such caution from an experienced campaigner was a necessary consequence of the weakening of his forces, under the influence of the same unfavourable circumstances that had exhausted the rest of Napoleon's troops. Instead of the 100,000 men who had crossed the Russian border, in those units of the force that were directed to the Dnieper, Davout could assemble no more than 70,000 on this river.[40]

On 21 July (2 August), on the day that Second Army was at a distance of one stage from First Army, Prince Bagration arrived in Smolensk and immediately went to Barclay de Tolly, who, upon learning of his arrival, put on his sash, took his hat and greeted him in the anteroom. 'Having learned of your arrival in Smolensk, I was already on my way to visit you,' Barclay told Prince Bagration. The meeting between the Commanders-in-Chief dispelled the misunderstandings that had arisen between them over the continuation of the retreat by the armies entrusted to them. It remained to decide to which of them the overall command of the entire force assembled in Smolensk belonged, as a Supreme command had not been issued in advance. Prince Bagration was the senior in rank; on the other hand, Barclay enjoyed specific authority from the Tsar, had commanded the majority of the army from the very beginning of the war, and, as Minister of War, had more up to date information on the administrative elements of the forces and about everything that had already been prepared and what still remained to be done for the defence of

---

39   Tsar Alexander and his Contemporaries. Biography of General Dorokhov.
40   Buturlin, I, 229.

the state. Prince Bagration subordinated himself to Barclay de Tolly, who had been under his command on more than one occasion. In their reports to the Tsar, both of them did each other justice. Tsar Alexander, for his part, expressed His complete satisfaction to them. He wrote to Barclay:

> I was very glad to hear about your good agreement with Prince Bagration. You have sensed the importance of the moment yourself, and that any egoism must be eliminated when it comes to saving the fatherland.

At the same time, he responded to Bagration:

> Knowing your eagerness to serve and love for the fatherland, I am sure that at present you have suppressed all personal motives, having the welfare and the glory of Russia, so important at this time, as your sole objective. You are to operate in unison towards this objective and with continuous consensus, thereby acquiring new rights to My gratitude.[41]

Following the unification of the Western armies, on 23 July (4 August), Prince Bagration dispatched General Neverovsky to occupy the town of Krasny with his division, reinforced by the Kharkov Dragoons and three Cossack regiments, with twelve heavy guns and a small element of the Smolensk *Opolchenie*, in order to support the Cossack patrols guarding the roads to Orsha and Mogilev; the sector on the right bank of the Dnieper, from Krasny to the Porechye road, was protected by the forward outposts of First Army, supported by their vanguards, under the command of Count Pahlen and Major General Shevich, of which the former was at Stabna, and the latter at the village of Bury.[42]

On the French side, at the end of July [early August], the troops of the main army were located between Surazh and Mogilev. General Latour Maubourg, upon arrival at Mogilev, on 24 July (5 August), was detached the next day to Svislach with his *4e corps de cavalerie* and with Dąbrowski's Division (Poniatowski's *5e Corps*), to monitor the Bobruisk fortress and Ertel's II Reserve Corps, which was stationed, as before, at Mozyr.[43]

The unification of First Army and Second Army at Smolensk had cost us the sacrifice of the area from the borders of the Empire to the Dnieper and the many magazines that had fallen into the hands of the enemy or were destroyed. But, on the other hand, our losses in personnel during the retreat were insignificant, despite the fact that Second Army was forced to march from Wołkowysk to Bobruisk about 600 *versts* in 20 days. The total non-battle casualties in both Russian armies did not exceed 10,000 men, so that, upon reaching Smolensk, the forces under Barclay de

---

41   Tsar's letter dated 28 July [9 August] 1812 (a copy is held in the classified archives of the Department of the General Staff).

42   Condensed War Diary, compiled by von Toll. Buturlin, 241.

43   Lt Gen Dąbrowski, *Mémoires concernant les opérations de la 17e division depuis le moment qu'elle reçut une destination separée le 23 aôut jusqu'au 28 novembre.* Chambray wrote that Dąbrowski moved from Mogilev to Rogachev, I, 280.

Tolly and Prince Bagration were 120,000 men, and, in addition, on the Dvina 25,000 and in Volhynia 30,000 men: hence, some 175,000, not including the garrisons of Riga and Bobruisk and Ertel's II Reserve Corps.[44]

On the other hand, the losses in Napoleon's army, of sick and stragglers, in the first five weeks of the campaign of 1812, had been enormous and amounted to almost a third of the force that had entered Russia. Of these 450,000 men, about 150,000 had been left on the Dvina, facing Riga and Count Wittgenstein; at Rogachev, facing Bobruisk and in Volhynia, against Tormasov: as a result, 300,000 men were directed towards Vitebsk and Mogilev, of whom, upon arrival at Smolensk, in early [mid] August, less than 200,000 were present.[45]

Prior to the unification of our armies near Smolensk, the Russian troops, although they wanted a battle, nevertheless had patiently endured the constant retreat. But eventually, once the long-awaited concentration of forces had taken place, everyone in our army from general to soldier was confident that the day of bloody reckoning for the devastation of their native country was at hand, and even those closest associates of Barclay de Tolly, Prince Bagration, Yermolov, von Toll, were convinced of the need for a decisive battle and its success was not in doubt. According to the somewhat inaccurate intelligence we had collected at the time, Napoleon had no more than 150,000 to oppose our 120,000 men. They hoped to compensate for this numerical superiority of the enemy force through the self-sacrificial nature of the Russian troops. In addition, the French army was stretched out over a considerable area and could be defeated in detail. The defence of Smolensk, one of the most important locations in the state, demanded a battle, further evasion of it would have a most harmful effect on the morale of the troops, especially since in First Army, since the very beginning of the war, the news of the accomplishments of other parts of the force resulted in extraordinary competitiveness. Platov's ambush at Mir was, in the general opinion, a brilliant feat; the action at Saltanovka was considered a victory, paving the way for Bagration to reach Smolensk; Tormasov's and Wittgenstein's successes were exaggerated in the retreating army. All this served to encourage the troops; but, any further evasion from battle would lead to discouragement and instil distrust of the Commander-in-Chief. Thus, until such time as he had united with Bagration, he could avoid a decisive battle, but as soon as the armies were united, then Barclay, with all his steadfastness, carried away by the general feeling, had no choice but to fight, despite the significantly superior numbers of the enemy.[46]

---

44   Strength returns dated 1 [13] August 1812.
45   Clausewitz, *Der Feldzug von 1812 in Russland,* 106-108.
46   Clausewitz, 109-111.

9

Offensive Operations by the Russian Armies at Smolensk

Initial steps taken after the unification of the Western armies at Smolensk. – Barclay de Tolly's predicament. – His intention to launch an offensive. – The Council of War. – The deployment of the French army. – Napoleon's plan of action. – Comparison of the strength of both sides. – The advance of the Russian armies. – Their flanking movement along the road to Porechye. – The action at Molevo Boloto. – Concentration of strength by the French army. – Reasons for Barclay de Tolly's indecision. – Bagration's retreat towards Smolensk and Barclay's deployment across the route to Rudnya at Volokova. – The French advance along the Smolensk road. – Napoleon's arrival at Rossasno. – The reasons that prompted Napoleon to envelope the left flank of the Russian army. – The French advance towards Krasny. – Neverovsky's feat. – Raevsky's arrival. – His intention to defend himself in Smolensk.

Following the unification of the Western Armies near Smolensk, the first three days were spent replenishing those regiments weakened by combat losses and the rigours of the campaign, and the production of hard tack. Of Wintzingerode's troops stationed in Smolensk, ten battalions were absorbed into First Army and the remaining seven infantry battalions into Second Army. Four artillery companies were also assigned to the field army. The cavalry, consisting of eight squadrons, were sent to Kaluga to train personnel in the reserve under General Miloradovich. Upon the completion of all the necessary administrative orders, it remained to decide on the mode of further operations, to that end, on 25 July (6 August), a council of war was assembled, at which, in addition to both Commanders-in-Chief, the following were present: His Imperial Highness, Grand Duke Konstantin Pavlovich, the Chiefs of Staff of both armies, Yermolov and Comte Saint-Priest, Quartermasters General von Toll, from First Army and Major General Vistitsky [Mikhail Stepanovich Vistitsky] from Second Army, and Colonel Wolzogen.[1] Even before the council had been convened, von Toll gave Barclay de Tolly a note, in which, stating the need to take advantage of favourable circumstances for a switch to offensive operations,

---

1   Bernhardi, *Denkwürdigkeiten des Grafen v. Toll,* I, 341. Barclay de Tolly's report to His Imperial Highness, dated 25 July [6 August], No 605

he proposed to move quickly and decisively along the route leading to Vitebsk via Rudnya: operating in this manner, it would be possible, according to von Toll, to split the enemy army into two isolated parts, to occupy a central position between them, to break them up with concentrated forces. It was subsequently discovered that at that time we did not have accurate intelligence either regarding the strength of Napoleon's forces or about their locations, and therefore it is very difficult to assess the balance of probability for the success for von Toll's proposal. The cautious, cool headed Barclay, although he considered the enemy weaker and more over-stretched than they were in reality, nevertheless remained convinced that the time was not yet right for a decisive counter offensive against Napoleon's troops. On the other hand, Barclay understood the universal fervent desire of the troops and their commanders – to measure themselves against the enemy and put a limit to their success. The Tsar had expressed His hope to him that the unification of our armies would be the beginning of a decisive turn of events. The Emperor wrote to Barclay de Tolly:

> I cannot remain silent that although, for many reasons and circumstances, at the start of hostilities it was necessary to abandon the frontiers of Our land, but it is only with regret that I have witnessed that these retrograde movements have continued as far as Smolensk. It is with great pleasure that I have heard your assurances about the good condition of Our troops, about their warlike spirit and their ardent desire to fight. I am no less pleased with the experience of their outstanding courage in all the battles that have taken place thus far and the fortitude shown by them on every arduous and long march.
>
> You are unrestricted in all your operations, without obstacle, and therefore I hope that you will not miss any chance to frustrate the intentions of the enemy and to inflict all kinds of harm upon them...
>
> I look forward to hearing of your offensive operations, which, according to your words, I regard as already underway...[2]

Thus, Barclay was in a most difficult situation: on the one hand, his own conviction that it was impossible to oppose an overwhelming enemy, prompted him to avoid a decisive engagement with them; on the other hand, everyone around him, the entire army, all of Russia, most of all, the Tsar himself, demanded that our armies protect their homeland from the enemy. It was impossible to stop the continuing French invasion by remaining inactive at Smolensk.

Such were the circumstances that forced Barclay de Tolly, in his discussion with von Toll, to express, against his better judgement, his readiness to undertake an offensive, but not before safeguarding the force's lines of communication with Smolensk and neutralising the danger of being attacked from both sides. To that end, according to Barclay, leaving Second Army at Smolensk, to protect the route to Moscow, it was necessary to move First Army against the enemy army's left wing, to seize the area between Surazh and Velizh using General Wintzingerode's

---

2   Handwritten orders from Tsar Alexander.

detachment. Once First Army had thus established itself on the enemy flank, then the troops of both armies were to march on Rudnya and operate with concentrated forces.[3]

On the same day as the unification of the Western Armies, 22 July (3 August), Barclay, reporting this to Tsar Alexander, wrote:

> I intend to go forward and attack the nearest of the enemy corps, it seems to me, Ney's *3e Corps*, near Rudnya. However, it appears that the enemy is preparing to envelope me from the right flank with a corps located near Porechye.[4]

At the council of war convened on 25 July (6 August), Colonel Wolzogen proposed: the fortification of Smolensk as much as possible and to wait for the enemy at this location. This course of action did not accord with the general opinion of our generals; moreover, Smolensk did not present an advantageous defensive position. As for von Toll's suggestion of moving towards Rudnya, Wolzogen assured that, according to his own research, the vicinity of Rudnya was completely inappropriate for the movement of significant forces, and that as soon as our army went deep into this impassable terrain, Napoleon would head from Porechye towards Smolensk and would sever our line of retreat. Colonel Toll, to whom the surrounding area was incomparably better known than to Wolzogen, argued that it did not present any great difficulties at all. With the exception of Wolzogen, the constant advocate of retreat, and Barclay de Tolly himself, every member of the council was in favour of decisive offensive operations, and therefore it was necessary to march with united forces towards the centre of the enemy deployment, towards Rudnya.

The factors that prompted us to do this were: firstly, the need to prevent the concentration of enemy forces, dispersed over a significant area; secondly, fixing the enemy in place in order to complete the mobilisation within the empire; thirdly, and finally, the fact that upon the success of our operations, the war would take a new, much more favourable turn for us, while in the event of failure there was the possibility of a trouble free retreat.[5]

On the evening of that same day, the Commander-in-Chief, having summoned von Toll and Saint-Priest, announced to them that he would launch an offensive towards Rudnya such that the troops would not move more than three stages away from Smolensk. Barclay de Tolly said in conclusion: 'We are dealing with an enterprising adversary who will not miss any opportunity to envelope us, and thus snatch victory from our grasp.' This remark, together with the conditions that put the offensive under such tight restraints, forecast a slow, hesitant execution for the proposed operation.[6]

During the retreat of First Army from Vitebsk to Smolensk and the halt by both Russian armies in the vicinity of this city, Napoleon made good use of his ten-day

---

3   Bernhardi, I, 339.
4   Barclay de Tolly's report dated 22 July [3 August].
5   Barclay de Tolly's report to the Tsar dated 25 July [6 August], No 605.
6   Bernhardi, I, 341-342. Thiers, XIV, *Ed. de Brux*, 220.

pause in Vitebsk. His troops, tired from their marches, spent this hottest period in the shelter of huts; many straggling soldiers had chance to re-join the army; the artillery parks and transport that had lagged far to the rear arrived in Vitebsk; the formation commanders, the Viceroy, Ney, Davout, gathered a seven-day supply of provisions from the countryside, over and above the transported supplies. Russian magazines captured in Surazh and Velizh served to the benefit of *4e Corps* and the *Garde*. In order to cross the Dnieper and maintain communications with Davout's force, Napoleon ordered the construction of four bridges of rafts at Rossasno.

The locations of the French forces, upon the retreat of the Western Armies to Smolensk, was as follows: the *Garde* and one of the divisions from *1er Corps* (Davout's) were at Vitebsk, where Napoleon was also resident with his *Maison*, and although his stay there would not be long, nevertheless he ordered the demolition of several houses and a church whose construction had just been started, in order to expand the square on which he conducted reviews of his troops. Two divisions from *1er Corps* were deployed at Pavlovichi, between Vitebsk and Babinovichi; *4e Corps* (the Viceroy's) was in Velizh, Surazh and Janovichy; Murat's *Réserve de cavalerie* (Montbrun's and Grouchy's Corps, less Doumerc's *3e division de cuirassiers*, located on the Dvina with Oudinot's *2e Corps*), was at Rudnya, with Sebastiani's *2e division de cavalerie légère* (*2e Corps de cavalerie*) forming the vanguard at Inkovo; *3e Corps* (Ney's) was behind the cavalry at Liozna. Davout's two remaining divisions, Claparède's, and Valence's cuirassiers were deployed in close quarters to the Dnieper, between Babinovichi and Dubrowna; the Westphalian *8e Corps*, now under Junot's command, were at Orsha; the Polish *5e Corps* (Poniatowski's) were in Mogilev; Latour Maubourg's *4e Corps de cavalerie* and General Dąbrowski's Polish Division had been detached from Mogilev in order to monitor Bobruisk and General Ertel's II Corps, stationed in Mozyr. The total strength of all these forces, on 22 July (3 August), came to 156,886 infantry and some 36,722 cavalry, making some 193,000 men altogether, while if we exclude those detached from the field army under Latour Maubourg and Dąbrowski, the main body of the French army had a total of 182,608 men.[7]

Napoleon, concealed behind the forests and swamps separating his troops from the Russians, planned to execute a flanking march to the right, cross the Dnieper at Rossasno, capture a weakly defended Smolensk and, enveloping our troops from the left flank, sever their line of retreat towards Moscow and inflict a decisive defeat on us. Whether this course of action was drawn up before the move by the Russians from Smolensk towards Rudnya, or whether it was inspired in Napoleon by our subsequent movements: this issue has not be resolved with absolute certainty.[8]

---

7   Bernhardi, I, 335-336. Chambray, I 297.
8   Historians of the war of 1812, for the most part, agree among themselves that the Russians, having undertaken the offensive towards Rudnya and Porechye, gave rise to the flanking movement that Napoleon made. Chambray states: 'However, notwithstanding the enemy (Russian) commander's course of action, Napoleon, having begun moving his troops, decided to launch the operation anyway: consequently, Barclay's offensive simply advanced the execution of the plan drawn up by his adversary by several days.' (I, 294). A more recent historian of the war of 1812, Thiers, believes that the course of action was drawn up by him before the Russian offensive could have been known to him. In presenting this view, Thiers

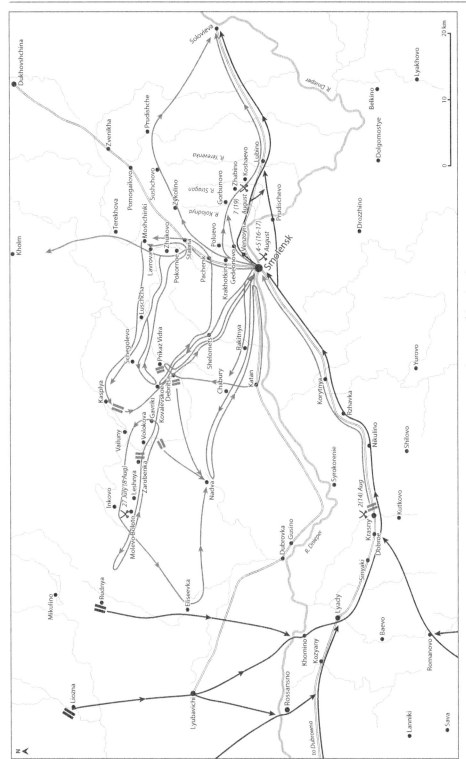

Map showing operations In the Area of Smolensk.

On our side, the total number of troops in both armies, at Smolensk, did not exceed 113,000 regular troops, while together with the Cossacks it reached some 121,119 men.[9]

I have already mentioned the case of Neverovsky's 27th Infantry Division, Kharkov Dragoons, three Cossack regiments and a small element of the Smolensk *Opolchenie*, which was under the command of Major General Olenin [Yevgeny Ivanovich Olenin], with fourteen guns that was located in Krasny in order to monitor the routes leading from Orsha towards Smolensk. As 27th Division was made up of recruits, in order to give it greater resilience, two of its regiments had been replaced by the Ladoga Infantry and Poltava Infantry regiments from 26th Division. Smolensk was held by a single infantry regiment. All the other troops of both armies moved forward on 26 July (7 August) in three columns.[10] Second Army with a total of 30,000 regular troops, having moved via Smolensk along the right bank of the Dnieper, proceeded as the left column, along the river bank, to the village of Katan, while First Army, with a total of 70,000 men (not including Cossacks or units left in the rear), advanced in two columns, of which the left (V Corps, VI Corps and III Cavalry Corps), under Dokhturov's command, marched along the Rudnya road towards Prikaz-Vidra [Bannyi Ostrov], while the right (II Corps, III Corps, IV Corps, I Cavalry Corps and II Cavalry Corps) under Tuchkov 1st's command, was directed initially along the Porechye road towards Zhukovo, and then to the left at Shchegoleva, towards Kovalevskoe. Each column formed their own vanguard. Bagration's vanguard was commanded by Vasilchikov; Dokhturov had Count Pahlen; Tuchkov appointed Major General Passeck [Pëtr Petrovich Passeck]. An independent detachment, under Major General Prince Shakhovsky [Ivan Leontievich Shakhovsky], marched to the right of Tuchkov to the village of Kasplya, and even further to the right was a Cossack detachment under Krasnov going towards Kholm. Finally, a detachment under Major General Baron Rosen [Grigory Vladimirovich Rosen?], made up of jäger regiments from both armies, maintained communications between Bagration and Dokhturov, moving towards the village of Chabury [Kuprino]. The forward troops under Platov remained at Zarubenka for the day, so as not to reveal the general offensive by the Russian armies to the enemy. It was planned that Platov, supported by regular cavalry under Count Pahlen 2nd would attack the leading enemy troops on the following day; he was to be followed by the main forces of both armies.

However, during the night of 26 to 27 July (7 to 8 August), Barclay de Tolly received intelligence of a concentration of significant enemy forces near Porechye from Adjutant General Baron Wintzingerode, who had been sent towards Velizh. According to the intelligence received, it could be concluded that the Viceroy was at this location with *4e Corps* and *1er Corps de cavalerie* and with Defrance's *4e Division de Cuirassiers*. Assuming that there was a large part of the enemy's reserves

---

refs to correspondence between Napoleon and Marshal Davout, but does not attach this
evidence of the fact he claims.

9   Bernhardi, I, 326. Buturlin gives the number of Russian troops as 120,000 men, *Hist. milit. de la campagne de Russie en 1812,* I, 245.

10   See Map illustrating operations in the vicinity of Smolensk.

behind this force, between Porechye and Vitebsk, and that Napoleon had the intention of moving from Porechye towards Smolensk, to sever our route to Moscow, Barclay abandoned the proposed offensive and focused solely on securing himself from the right flank. In his report to the Tsar regarding the cancellation of the proposed offensive, Barclay wrote:

> Having a skilful and cunning adversary facing me, who knows how to take advantage of every opportunity, I find it necessary to observe the strictest principles of caution.

Accordingly, on 27 July (8 August), elements of First Army (II Corps, IV Corps, V Corps and I Cavalry Corps) were directed along the Porechye road towards the villages of Lavrova [Dubrovo] and Stabna; the remaining formation (III Corps, VI Corps, II Cavalry Corps and III Cavalry Corps), under Dokhturov's command, was deployed at Prikaz-Vidra;[11] at the same time Barclay proposed to Prince Bagration that he direct Second Army to conduct a flank march towards Prikaz-Vidra, where, according to the Commander-in-Chief:

> The position was more advantageous than at Smolensk and from where he could monitor the enemy and reinforce his outposts, being closer to First Army and the detachment in Krasny.

In his report to the Tsar, Barclay de Tolly wrote:

> Both armies in their new positions will be at a range of one march from one another; the road to Moscow and the entire area between the sources of the Dvina and the Dnieper will be protected by them, and their food supplies will be completely secured by the convenience of delivering them from Velikiye Luki, Toropets and Bely.[12]

After taking the road to Porechye, Barclay wrote to the Tsar:

> From my new location, I can strike the enemy on the left flank with superior numbers, open communications with the upper Dvina and secure Count Wittgenstein's left wing. This situation has undoubted advantages and offers complete freedom of action in accordance with the circumstances.[13]

Barclay de Tolly's closest associates did not share his convictions about the benefits of the area he was holding, and some of them also did not disguise their opinions. Bagration himself believed that he should have had more concern about the left

---

11   Barclay de Tolly's report from Prikaz-Vidra dated 27 July [8 August], No 618. Condensed War Diary of First Army, compiled by Colonel von Toll.
12   Depiction of military operations by First Army (Note by Barclay de Tolly). Barclay de Tolly's report to the Tsar, from Prikaz-Vidra, dated 27 July [8 August], No 618.
13   Barclay de Tolly's report dated 28 July [9 August].

rather than the right flank of the army. Dissatisfaction spread among the troops regarding the Commander-in-Chief: it was believed that his indecision had deprived the army of the opportunity to win a certain victory, and they even dared to suspect the straightforward Barclay of betrayal.

The success achieved by our advanced troops served to complete the misunderstanding that arose in the army. On the same day that Barclay was moving elements of his army onto the Porechye road, on 27 July (8 August), *Ataman* Platov, still not having any information about this, attacked the enemy. While at Zarubenka, with seven Cossack regiments, 32 squadrons of light cavalry and a jäger brigade in reserve at Prikaz-Vidra under Count Pahlen 2nd's command, Platov received a report from Major General Denisov 7th [Vasily Timofeevich Denisov], who formed his vanguard with two Cossack regiments at the village of Kastritsyno [Kostricheno], regarding the appearance of an enemy detachment from the village of Leshnya consisting of nine cavalry regiments and one of infantry. Platov ordered Denisov to stand his ground as long as possible until the arrival of reinforcements, while he moved to their aid himself, with the remainder of his regiments and twelve guns of the Cossack horse artillery. Four enemy regiments, engaged at the village of Molevo Boloto by four Don regiments and two *Sotnia* of Bashkirs, under Denisov's command, were driven off and pursued until the rest of the detachment's troops arrived to rescue them. General Denisov then began to fall back to meet Platov, having been attacked by superior forces from Sebastiani's *2e Division de cavalerie légère*, which was following him, and, on the approach of the enemy, sent Major General Kuteinikov 2nd to the left flank with the *Ataman's* Cossacks, Kharitonov 7th's Cossacks and Simferopol Tatars, while a powerful cannonade was opened up on the French from the front. The enemy charged the battery and came so close that many of our gunners and horses were wounded by bullets from the marksmen of the *24th Légère*, who came running up behind the cavalry; but at this critical moment, the Don regiments under Melnikov 3rd and Kharitonov 7th arrived in time to save the battery, cut into the infantry and drove off the nearest of the enemy cavalry regiments. The courageous Melnikov was killed in this attack. Platov, noticing the disorder of the French troops, attacked the enemy with all the Cossack regiments, put them to flight and drove them for two *versts*. Further pursuit was entrusted to General Pahlen, who had arrived at the scene of the battle with the Izyum Hussars, Sumy Hussars and Mariupol Hussars, who continued chasing the French for about eight *versts*, until, when, having encountered the enemy in significant numbers, they received the order to fall back to the village of Leshnya. The French detachment's casualties were very significant; ten field officers and subalterns and more than 300 lower ranks were taken prisoner. On our side, the losses were incomparably fewer, but were not recorded anywhere.[14]

In his report to the Commander-in-Chief regarding this action, Platov wrote:

> The enemy did not ask for quarter, the Russian troops of His Imperial Majesty, being enraged, stabbed and beat them.

---

14   General of Cavalry Platov's report to Barclay de Tolly dated 27 July [8 August], No 110.

Indeed, the good-natured, pious men of the Don were annoyed to the point of being enraged by everything that they saw in the places where the enemy troops had been. Platov wrote to Barclay de Tolly:

> It is my duty to inform Your Excellency, of the extraordinary visions of war waged by the French, fitting only for barbarians. Not only do they rob the villages and landowners' homes, beating the inhabitants and raping their wives and daughters, they act unmercifully with the priestly dignity, beat them, bind them and extort money from them, even the most holy Orthodox churches cannot avoid the frenzy of the French. Holy vessels and utensils are plundered. In the churches in the village of Inkovo, they washed and hung their underwear on stolen holy images. Would it please Your Excellency to present this accurately described image of our enemy's warfare to the sight and information of the entire fatherland? Such an announcement would inflame every heart with a righteous zeal for revenge and to compete to make any sacrifice in order to expel the hard-hearted and unjust enemy from the borders of the fatherland.[15]

Among the documents seized by the Cossacks in Molevo Boloto, in General Sebastiani's quarters, there was an order from Murat, in which he, informing Sebastiani of the Russians' intention to send their main body towards Rudnya, ordered him to pull back to the infantry (as for the concentration of French troops on Porechye road, mentioned by some writers, this was out of the question). In the headquarters of the Russian army, they could not comprehend how the enemy could have obtained such accurate intelligence about our intentions; all foreigners were suspected of treason in general, and Wolzogen in particular. In fact, one of our officers was the cause of this, having had the imprudence to warn his mother, who lived on her own estate, near the town of Rudnya; thereafter Murat lodged with her, and the note accidentally came into his possession.[16]

Thus, the plan of action had been revealed to the enemy, much of the successful implementation of which depended on keeping the planned situation secret. On 28 July (9 August) the Russian troops continued the flanking movement they had already begun: Dokhturov moved from Prikaz-Vidra via Shelomets, towards Moshchinki with III Corps, VI Corps, II Cavalry Corps and III Cavalry Corps, to where the headquarters was also relocated; Platov pulled back to Gavriki; Second Army moved towards Prikaz-Vidra; their vanguard, under Major General Vasilchikov 1st's command, deployed to Volokova, to the left of Platov.[17]

Napoleon, having learned about Sebastiani's defeat at Molevo Boloto, took measures to quickly concentrate his army. To that end, Murat and Ney were ordered to pin the Russians to the Rudnya road for as long as possible; the three divisions from *1er Corps*, stationed near Vitebsk, and the Viceroy's *4e Corps*, were directed towards Liozna, to link up with Murat and Ney; Davout, with his composite corps,

---

15   Platov's report to Barclay de Tolly dated 26 July [7 August], No 109.
16   Bernhardi, I, 348.
17   Condensed War Diary of First Army, compiled by Colonel von Toll.

Junot with the Westphalians, Poniatowski with the Polish *5e Corps* and Latour Maubourg's cavalry, were to link up between Rossasno and Lyubavichi (only Saint-Cyr's *6e Corps* was detached to Polotsk to assist Oudinot; three battalions and eight squadrons remained with the Viceroy in Surazh, facing Wintzingerode; while Dąbrowski's Division, with a light cavalry brigade from Latour Maubourg's *4e Corps de cavalerie*, had been directed to the right of the main force in order to monitor Bobruisk and Ertel's detachment stationed in Mozyr). Thus, some 185,000, or, according to other sources, some 178,000 men could be assembled in an area of about thirty miles, between Liozna and Lyubavichi, or between Babinovichi and Dubrowna, within two days of receiving the first news of our offensive in Napoleon's *État-major général*, that is, no later than 30 July [11 August].[18]

The capability for such a rapid concentration of enemy forces proves that it was not at all as scattered as many of Barclay de Tolly's critics imagined. There is not the slightest doubt that in the state of affairs at the time it was impossible for us to stop the enemy invasion with a decisive defeat of their army. Had we continued the offensive through Rudnya to Babinovichi, or to Liozna, all our successes would have been limited to acquiring trophies and inflicting casualties on the enemy, bought at the price of weakening our own forces, which were the key to saving the fatherland. Barclay understood the situation in which we found ourselves very well, an offensive in which the initial successes could have carried him beyond the limits suggested by wise caution, especially since, despite the title he held as Commander-in-Chief of both Western armies, his power over the troops subordinate to Prince Bagration was very limited due to the relationship between both generals. If Barclay, like Napoleon, had been able to act with complete unity of command, he could have boldly raced to Rudnya, with the objective of inflicting all kinds of harm on the enemy, retreated in good time and continued the retreat into the countryside, which was weakening the formidable enemy army bit by bit. But the Russian Commander-in-Chief knew that, having won victories over the scattered formations of Napoleon's force, being subject to the influence of his closest associates and general opinion, he would be forced to continue offensive operations and would put the army entrusted to him at risk. These were the causes of Barclay de Tolly's alleged indecision: having undertaken an advance on Rudnya against his own wishes, he sought every plausible opportunity to suspend it and return to the previous *modus operandi*, which necessity subsequently demonstrated to have been the best course.[19]

Explaining his views to Prince Bagration, Barclay de Tolly wrote:

> The first priority of our operations should be to ensure the security of our flanks, and most of all the right, in order to maintain communications with Lieutenant General Count Wittgenstein. With our advance on Vidra, we distracted the enemy from this direction, which is why he is pulling his troops back and thereby diverting his forces from Oudinot's Corps, which

---

18   Bernhardi, I, 349.
19   Chambray, setting out all the reasons that prompted Barclay de Tolly to avoid a decisive battle, stated: 'Success would not secure him against further enemy attacks; while failure would put Russia on the brink of ruin.' (I, 292-294).

he could have strengthened. Moreover, both armies cannot remain in such a close connection as we are now, as they will absolutely need provisioning; but the movement of First Army to the right will open the shortest communications for the delivery of rations from Velikiye Luki, Toropets and Bely, and the army entrusted to Your Excellency will then be provided with rations from Vyazma, Dorogobuzh, Smolensk, Yelnya and Yukhnov...

Furthermore, in the same response to Prince Bagration, Barclay de Tolly, under the influence of his constant conviction of the need to avoid a decisive battle, wrote:

It would be all very well and useful to hold on to Smolensk; but this objective should not, however, deter us from the most important aim: which is the preservation of the army and the continuation of the war, in order, meanwhile, to prepare powerful reinforcements for these armies within the State; moreover, the will of the Sovereign Emperor is not that both armies should operate in unison, but should be in communications with each other such that one could provide assistance if need be, so that if one was forced to retreat facing superior enemy numbers, then the other must decisively operate offensively, always trying to envelope the enemy flanks, offering them unit level engagements and harassing them continuously with irregular troops.[20]

Meanwhile, as First Army remained on the Porechye road, a short march from Smolensk, Second Army, after a two-day halt at Prikaz-Vidra, moved towards Smolensk on 31 July (12 August). The reason for this movement, made by Prince Bagration without orders from Barclay de Tolly, and also without approval from him, was, according to Bagration, a lack of drinking water at Prikaz-Vidra. And indeed, during the hot, dry summer, the Russian troops more than once suffered extreme need of it, and the French were very often forced to be content with water from the bogs, and therefore were subjected to widespread disease. In addition, Prince Bagration had it in mind to secure himself from being enveloped from the left flank through the occupation of Smolensk. Only the vanguard of Second Army, under the command of General Vasilchikov, remained at Volokova as before; and to support it, a detachment under Lieutenant General Prince Gorchakov, made up of the Combined Grenadier Division and eight Ulan squadrons, was stationed at Debritsa.[21]

Bagration's retreat to Smolensk was made at the very moment that Barclay de Tolly was preparing to renew his offensive towards Rudnya. Having received intelligence from the forward detachments about a concentration of enemy troops in the vicinity of Lyubavichi and Dubrowna, Barclay believed: 'that he intended to attack

---

20   The Minister of War's note to General of Infantry, Prince Bagration, dated 29 July [10 August].

21   Bernhardi, I, 352. General summary of the movements and operations of the Russian army in the war of 1812, compiled by General Khatov (archive of the M.T.D. No 37,640).

us from this direction, hoping, perhaps, to cut off part of First Army, which was extended towards Porechye.'

In order to frustrate this plan, he decided: 'to combine the two armies in the position at Volokova, as it was one of the most advantageous among those found by us during this campaign, and to await a battle there.'[22]

On 2 (14) August, First Army deployed between the village of Volokova and Kasplya lake; Count Pahlen's detachment was stationed on the extreme right wing, close to the southern shore of the lake, at the village of Vailuny. Platov's Cossack detachment was pushed forwards towards Inkovo. The headquarters was moved to Gavriki. Of the troops from Second Army, VIII Corps moved from Smolensk to the village of Katan, while VII Corps was to follow them the next day.[23] Barclay believed that the French would attack him on 3 (15) August, Napoleon's birthday, and hoped to repel the enemy, despite the fact that the formations of the Russian armies were not concentrated. Barclay de Tolly wrote: 'It was desirable that the enemy attack us in this position, as all the advantages were on our side.'[24] Since no one in our headquarters wanted to think about a further retreat, until that point no contingencies had been made in the event of their advance along the route to Moscow. But as an engagement with the main enemy force already seemed imminent, it was then considered necessary to prepare provisions along the route to Moscow.[25]

Throughout the movements by the Russian armies described here, Napoleon was preparing to attack them with his main force. News of the offensive by our troops arrived in Vitebsk on 28 July (9 August). This news could not convey an accurate understanding, either of the direction of the Russian armies, or about Barclay de Tolly's intentions; nevertheless, Napoleon, who was looking for an opportunity to engage in a decisive battle, immediately took steps (as we have already had occasion to say) to concentrate troops in the very area to which the Russian armies had initially been sent. The inclement weather prevented the enemy troops from advancing to the general assembly areas earlier than 30 July (11 August), and the following day a significant part of the French army, assembled facing ours, was already prepared for a decisive engagement. Once Napoleon had become convinced that Barclay's offensive had been suspended, and the Russians were limited to occupying a position at Volokova, the enemy was then directed to envelope our left flank on the Dnieper, such that, having occupied Smolensk, they could drive the Russian army away from the Moscow road. To achieve this objective, the troops under the direct command of Napoleon made a flank march to their right to the crossings over the Dnieper, at Rossasno and Khomino, while the corps entrusted to Marshal Davout moved from Orsha and Mogilev towards Rossasno and Romanovo.[26]

Napoleon himself, on his way through the town of Babinovichi, stopped at the house of one of the local bourgeoisie, and from there visited the troops in Rossasno, where he arrived on the evening of 1 (13) August. Eyewitnesses of these events said

22   Depiction of military operations by First Army (written by Barclay de Tolly).
23   Condensed War Diary etc. compiled by Colonel von Toll.
24   Depiction of military operations by First Army (written by Barclay de Tolly).
25   Bernhardi, I 353.
26   Chambray, *Expédition de Russie*, I, 294-295.

that he rode on an English mare and was distinguished from the generals around him, who were in uniforms richly embroidered with silver and gold, by the simplicity of his dress. Upon arrival at Rossasno, Napoleon entered the house of the Jew, Hirsch Yudkin, but, noticing the untidiness of the rooms, he immediately went out and gave orders for his tent to be pitched in a pine forest, overlooking the left bank of the Dnieper. This marquee, as far as could be judged later on by the drainage ditches dug at this place, was three *sazhen* long and two wide; it was made of a striped (green and white) thick silky fabric and consisted of five rooms:

1. Reception room, which also served as a dining room.
2. Bedroom.
3. Ministerial room.
4. Berthier's chancellery.
5. Room for aides de camp and orderlies.

At the back of this tent, several huts and a kitchen were built from spruce. In the meantime, as they pitched the tent, Napoleon again mounted his horse, rode through the town, looked intently at the troops gathered around, dismounted his horse and entered his campaign dwelling with Marshal Davout, who had only just arrived in Rossasno. After a rather lengthy conversation, they sat down to dine together, in the marquee; being served by Rustan [Roustam Raza] the Mameluke. At the same time, for the generals and officers of Napoleon's Staff, a green Morocco leather ground-sheet was laid out with silver plates and gilded cups. In the evening, as the troops, located around the town in a vast area, indulged in rest and silence fell, Napoleon, bareheaded, walked alone along a path in the forest, and, from time to time, putting his hand to his head, was plunged deep in thought. In the vicinity of this place where the staff of the French *État-major général* spent the night, there were traces of a large pit, into which, after Napoleon's retreat from Moscow, many bodies of dead Frenchmen were thrown.[27]

On 2 (14) August, at sunrise, the enemy army moved and Napoleon left Rossasno, via Lyady, towards Krasny. Some military historians, including that most famous of French Marshals, Saint-Cyr, believe that Napoleon should have outflanked the Russian army not from their left, but from the right. Indeed, if he had gone from Vitebsk along the road leading via Porechye to Smolensk, he would have avoided having to make two crossings over the Dnieper, at Rossasno and Smolensk; but, in that case, judging from Barclay de Tolly's concerns for his right flank, he, in all likelihood, would have avoided battle and would have retreated along the Moscow road, not allowing himself to be encircled: consequently, Napoleon, by enveloping our right flank, would not have achieved the objective he had been striving for since the very beginning of the campaign. On the contrary, by heading towards Smolensk, a very important location, both for the magazines located there, and for its importance in Russian culture, Napoleon hoped that Barclay, despite all his desire to avoid a decisive denouement of the issue, would be involuntarily dragged into a general

---

27   Extracted from information delivered from the Mogilev Governorate to the Babinovichi *Uezd*.

engagement. In addition, Napoleon, by moving to Porechye, would have separated the French troops located in the vicinity of Vitebsk from Davout's force and would have been endangered from the combined forces of both Russian armies.

These were, in all likelihood, the reasons that prompted Napoleon to cross the Dnieper and race towards Smolensk. The pontoon bridges were ready as early as the afternoon of 1 (13) August – two at Rossasno and one at Khomino, built under the protection of Davout's composite corps, which had arrived on the left bank of the Dnieper at Dubrowna. During this and the following day, they managed to cross Grouchy's *3e Corps de Cavalerie*, three divisions of *1er Corps*, the Viceroy's *4e Corps* and the *Garde* at Rossasno, while Murat crossed at Khomino with Nansouty's *1er Corps de cavalerie,* Montbrune's *2e Corps de cavalerie* and Ney's *3e Corps*; at the same time, Davout's force, pushed forwards to Rossasno and Romanovo, had established communications with the corps that were crossing the Dnieper. On the other side of the river, only Sebastiani's *2e division de cavalerie légère* remained, under the command of Lieutenant General Pajol, directed towards Smolensk on the right bank of the Dnieper. Overall, Napoleon's forces, at this time, extended to 180,000 men.[28]

At the same time as the enemy army was moving up the left bank of the Dnieper, the Russian troops, as before, were on the right bank of the river. Only Neverovsky, with his small detachment, which consisted largely of recruits, was in the town of Krasny, 47 *versts* from Smolensk, which was held by a weak garrison. Neverovsky's force was initially located in front of Krasny, along the Lyady road, but once the Cossacks who had been stationed at Lyady informed him of an advance by a huge enemy force along the post-road and across the fields, then Neverovsky retreated behind the town of Krasny leaving a battalion of the 49th Jäger Regiment with two guns, and crossed the defile formed by a causeway to settle down with the rest of the force behind a deep ravine.

On 2 (14) August, Murat reaching the town of Lyady at dawn with the *Corps de Cavalerie* under Grouchy, Nansouty and Montbrun, some 15,000 horsemen, drove off the small detachment under Major General Olenin, and moved towards Krasny, appearing in front of the town at three o'clock in the afternoon; Ney was moving up behind them with some of the infantry from his *3e Corps*. Neverovsky, upon learning of the enemy approach, formed his regiments behind the ravine in battle order, placing ten guns on the left flank under the protection of the Kharkov Dragoons. At the same time, Nazimov's [Nikolai Gavrilovich Nazimov] 50th Jäger Regiment, with two horse-artillery guns, was sent back fifteen *versts* along the road to Smolensk, in the role of a backstop, with orders to hold the crossing over a minor river there.

As soon as Neverovsky's 27th Division had managed to take up new positions, the French attacked the battalion stationed in Krasny. Several companies of the *24e Légère*, under Ney's personal command, broke into the town, drove off our jägers and captured the two guns that were with them. After that, some of the French cavalry enveloped Neverovsky's positions from the left flank. Our dragoons charged into the attack, but were driven back and forced to abandon the place of battle; of the ten guns in this position, five were captured by the enemy; the remainder followed the dragoons

---

28   The total for Napoleon's troops, according to Chambray, reached 182,608 men. *Hist. de l'expédition de Russie*. I, 295-296. Thiers gives a total of 178,000.

along the Smolensk road. Whereupon Neverovsky, left with just infantry alone and seeing several infantry columns from Ney's Corps facing him from the front while the huge forces of Murat's *Réserve de cavalry* were moving into the rear of our detachment, decided to retreat towards Smolensk. Having formed his regiments into dense columns, Neverovsky reminded the soldiers of how they were expected to perform. He said: 'Lads, remember what you were taught; there is no cavalry that can defeat you: only do not rush your fire; shoot accurately, take your time. Nobody must start without my command.' These orders were carried out: as soon as the French cavalry flew in, Neverovsky halted his infantry; on his signal, the alarm was sounded; it was followed by the dense firing of battalion volleys; within moments the whole area around our columns was covered with fallen horses and horsemen. All the efforts by the French to break through the solidly united mass of infantry were in vain; their commanders, setting an example of courage, jumped at the closed squares with the bravest of their warriors and died on the Russians' bayonets, or, being turning away, they left under a hail of bullets in the greatest disorder. 'Well done, lads!' yelled Neverovsky after beating off the first attack. 'You see how easy it is to deal with cavalry; thank you... congratulations!' The men responded with 'It's our pleasure! Hurrah!' The wide post road, the verges cut by ditches and lined with two rows of large birches, contributed to the defence, making it difficult for cavalry attacks and preventing them from being carried out in proper formation on a wide front. It goes without saying that with such a retreat, carried out over the distance of an entire stage, there was no way to maintain the intervals between the retreating columns; the entire division moved in one dense mass, which could not be shaken by the attacks of the superior cavalry, led by the most famous cavalry commander of the Napoleonic era. Only once, at the entrance to a village, where the barrier formed by ditches and birch avenues was interrupted for some distance, did the enemy manage to snag a corner of the Russian column. In the evening our troops approached the village of Korotne [Korytnya], which our guns had earlier been sent to hold behind the river under the protection of a single battalion. Their fire halted the pursuit, and this allowed Neverovsky's weary infantry to recuperate. The overall losses of the Russian detachment reached 1,500 men, including eight hundred taken prisoner. On the French side, some five hundred men were killed or wounded.[29] Our foes themselves gave justice to Neverovsky's retreat. Chambray, describing the action, stated that: 'it presents a memorable example of the superiority of a well-trained and skilled infantry commander.' Another French historian, Comte Ségur, wrote: 'Neverovsky retreated like a lion.' Puybusque [Louis-Gullaume de Puybusque] stated: 'One cannot help but admit that although he (Neverovsky) was dealing with forces superior in numbers and perhaps more experienced, the Russians distinguished themselves by their steadfastness and courage.' The anonymous author who compiled *Das Buch vom Jahr 1812* wrote: 'This action, which was of little further consequence, demonstrated remarkable skill in the application of operations using the ground and with a force which consisted of infantry alone.'[30] Prince Bagration

---

29 Chambray, I, 302-304. Thiers, XIV, 227-228. Condensed War Diary etc. compiled by Colonel von Toll. Bernhardi, I, 356-357.

30 '*Je suis entré dans de plus grands détails que ne le comportait l'importanee de ce combat, parcequ'il offre un exemple mèmorable de la supériorité d'une infanterie aguerrie et bien conduite*

wrote in a report to the Emperor: 'One cannot praise the courage and firmness highly enough with which a completely new division fought against the overwhelmingly superior enemy forces. One might even say that such an example of courage has never been demonstrated by any army.' It should be noted that the successful retreat by the Russian detachment was greatly facilitated by Murat's excessive ardour, who seemed to have forgotten about his horse artillery, left it behind him and persisted in repeating attacks many times without preparing for success through the fire of artillery.

Throughout the duration of the action at Krasny, First Army remained in position at Volokova; from among the troops of Second Army, VIII Corps moved from Smolensk towards Nadva, where it arrived on the morning of 3 (15) August; 2nd Cuirassier Division, on 2 (14 August) in the evening, was stationed at Katan; while VII Corps, which had set out from Smolensk before noon, only managed to cover about 12 *versts* by evening. The news of the attack on Neverovsky by a superior enemy force was received by our Commanders-in-Chief on the night of 2 to 3 (14 to 15) August; but they did not know that Napoleon, in crossing to the left bank of the Dnieper, was moving towards Smolensk with all the forces of his army, and therefore the entire reaction made by our side was restricted to the movement of Raevsky's VII Corps to Smolensk, with orders to go from there, on the following day, by road to Krasny and to support Neverovsky. At the same time, Bagration drew Vasilchikov's detachment in from Volokova and Gorchakov's from Debritsa, to VIII Corps at Nadva. Platov's raiding detachment, reinforced with two jäger battalions and one dragoon regiment, was sent via Inkovo to Yeliseevo, towards Lyubavichi, while Pahlen was ordered to support them. Barclay de Tolly and Bagration agreed between themselves to operate in such a way that Second Army would cross to the left bank of the Dnieper at Katan and blocked the enemy's path; First Army was to support Second Army, by following the French army and guarding the sector between the Dvina and the Dnieper. In a report to the Tsar, Barclay de Tolly wrote:

> Although the movement by the enemy to the Dnieper and onto its left bank, through which he has abandoned almost the entire area between the Dvina and the Dnieper, gives us great cause for surprise; nevertheless until I am sure of his true intentions, I shall not depart from directing operations according to the existing circumstances, and I shall place the army in such a position that, being always able to support Second Army, I might at the same time hold the sector between the Dvina and the Dnieper.[31]

---

sur la cavalerie.' Chambray, I, 304. 'Newerowskoi fit une retraite de lion.' Ségur, I, 264. '… le général russe Newerowskoi perdit 8 canons et 2,000 hommes: on doit convenir, que quoiqu'il eut affaire à des troupes supérieures en nombre, et peut être plus exercées, il est impossible de montrer plus de fermeté et de véritable courage que n'en déployèrent les Russes dans cette rétraite, où ils furent poursuivis jusqu'à la fin de la journée.' Puybusque, Lettres sur la guerre de Russie en 1812, 72-73. 'Interessant ist dies übrigens einflusslose Gefecht als Beispiel weiser Benutzung des Terrains und des Truppencharakters (hier passive Zähigkeit) von Seiten des Führers einer ganz auf sich allein angewiesenen Infanterie.' Das Buch von Jahr 1812. II, 151-152.

31   Barclay de Tolly's note to Prince Bagration dated 3 [15] August, No 645. Barclay de Tolly's report to the Tsar dated 3 [15] August, No 648.

On 3 (15) August, with the arrival of VI Corps at Nadva, Prince Bagration set out with VIII Corps to Katan, where they immediately began building bridges. But in the meantime, the situation became completely clear, and our Commanders-in-Chief were forced to change their course of action.

We have already mentioned that on 2 (14) August, Raevsky, having managed to move out of Smolensk for some 12 *versts*, had received orders from Prince Bagration during the night to return to this city and go to Krasny in order to support Neverovsky. Setting off during the night of 2 to 3 (14 to 15 August) for Smolensk, Raevsky, at the same time, sent a report to Bagration, in which he asked for reinforcements for his VII Corps from the cuirassiers who were at Katan; at the same time, in the event of him encountering superior enemy forces, he asked for clarification: should he defend Smolensk, or should he retreat behind the Dnieper and defend the crossing points? Not having had time to receive a reply to his report, Raevsky was forced to operate at the dictates of his own experience. Upon arriving in Smolensk, at dawn on 3 (15) August, he learned, according to rumours, that Neverovsky had perished with his entire detachment. As Bennigsen was in the city at the time, Raevsky turned to him, asking for his advice. Bennigsen, confirming the fatal news of the destruction of Neverovsky's detachment, told Raevsky that he would be marching to certain destruction, and that the artillery should have been left on this side of the river in order, at least, to save the guns. Raevsky preferred to take the artillery with him, believing very professionally that the disruption of the enemy and the time gained for the concentration of the army were more important than the preservation of a few guns. Passing through the city and moving along the road to Krasny, at two o'clock in the afternoon, Raevsky linked up with Neverovsky, who, reporting on all the circumstances of the action at Krasny, said that his Cossacks had been left seven or eight *versts* from Smolensk, within sight of a significant enemy force.

Everything was quiet until five o'clock in the afternoon, when suddenly a cannon shot rang out, and, after that, a Cossack galloped up with the news of a huge French attack. Indeed, by nightfall, all Murat's cavalry and behind them a dense mass of infantry had settled down for the night opposite the positions of VII Corps, enveloping them from the left flank; the huge glow of bivouac fires illuminated a large section of the horizon.[32]

Raevsky's position was extremely precarious. Being 30 *versts* from the nearest support, he had with him, along with Neverovsky's troops, just 28 battalions.[33] The number of troops with which Raevsky absolutely had to halt Napoleon's 180,000 strong army and defend Bagration's and Barclay's communications with Moscow and the southern *Oblasts* of the Empire did not exceed 13,000. But to Raevsky, as one of the renowned personalities of 1812 said, it did not seem difficult to execute what few would dare to do. Napoleon himself, in the Notes written by Montholon [Charles-Tristan de Montholon], under his dictation on the island of Saint Helena, stated:

---

32   An extract from Raevsky's notes.
33   Two regiments from VII Corps were located with General Vasilchikov's vanguard; a few days earlier another two had been sent off in order to form cadres in the interior of the Empire.

This 15,000 strong Russian division, coincidentally located in Smolensk, managed to defend this city for 24 hours, which gave time for the arrival the following day of Barclay de Tolly.

Had the French army taken the opportunity to seize Smolensk by surprise, they would have crossed the Dnieper there and attacked the Russians from the rear, as they had not yet managed to concentrate their forces, etc.[34]

Raevsky intended to defend himself in a position in front of Smolensk, behind a ravine, where his VII Corps was stationed at the time. The generals summoned to a conference by him were of the same opinion, but Paskevich, who had arrived late having been with the vanguard, suggested pulling back into Smolensk and defending themselves in the city itself. He said: 'You are holding exactly the same sort of position as me, three *versts* to your front. The right flank is protected by the Dnieper; the left one is completely exposed; behind you – an obstacle, impassable to artillery. The enemy has outflanked me today, tomorrow they will outflank you, and even if you manage to repulse the French to your front, they will occupy Smolensk in your rear and cut you off. You will be forced to retreat into the clutches of the enemy; even if you break through to Smolensk, assaulting with infantry, and on to the bridges over the Dnieper, you will still not smuggle the artillery through. Better to give battle in Smolensk itself. Perhaps we can hold out there. In the event of a disaster, we would lose our artillery, but we would save the corps. In any case, we would win time and allow the army to come to the rescue.'

That night there was a full moon. Raevsky and Paskevich went to check on the situation around Smolensk; on their return, the infantry were immediately withdrawn into the city; the cavalry was left where it was until dawn, with orders to maintain the bivouac fires, and in the event of an offensive by the French, to retreat into Smolensk. By dawn, the infantry had occupied the places indicated for them for the defence of the city.[35] Such was the eve of the two-day battle under the walls of the ancient stronghold, which Godunov [Boris Fëdorovich Godunov] called 'the precious Russian gorget.' By leaving the left bank of the Dnieper unattended and directing our main forces along the right bank of this river, we exposed firstly Neverovsky's detachment, and then Raevsky's VII Corps to extreme danger; despite having a significant number of light troops, they lost sight of the enemy, allowed them to envelope us from the left flank and we were almost cut off from communications with Moscow and with the southern *Oblasts* of the Empire. All these errors were the inevitable consequence of the division of command between the two

---

34 '... *une division de quinze mille Russes qui se trouvait par hasard à Smolensk eut le bonheur de défendre cette place un jour, ce qui donna le temps à Barklay de Tolly d'arriver le lendemain. Si l'armée française eût surpris Smolensk, elle y eût passé le Borysthène et attaqué par derrière l'armée russe en désordre et non réunie.' Mémoires de Napoléon. Notes sur l'ouvrage intitulé: Considérations sur l'art de la guerre.* XII Note, *Moskow.*

35 This is how General Mikhailovsky-Danilevsky describes the contribution by Paskevich, in the Council convened by Raevsky, without however showing the source for the thoughts expressed by Paskevich. In the notes left by Raevsky it states: 'Sensing that I would have to fight at Smolensk, I carefully surveyed the position in front of the city and the suburbs and tried to take advantage of the benefits that they presented to me.'

Commanders-in-Chief, and although one of them had subordinated himself to the other, this ad hoc subordination was very restricted. The lack of unity of command for the armies was the cause of misunderstandings, which, despite the indisputable merits of the commanders and the courage of the troops entrusted to them, could have had the most disastrous consequences for us.

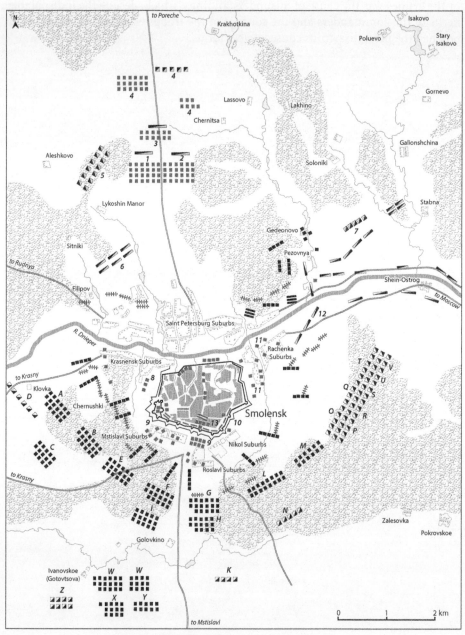

Plan of the Battle of Smolensk, 17 August 1812.

Plan of the Battle of Smolensk

Legend:

Russian Forces		**Enemy Forces**	
1.	II Corps	A.	Ledru's division
2.	IV Corps	B.	Marchand's division
3.	Stroganov's grenadier division	C.	Razout's division
4.	V Corps	D.	Wohlwart's division
5.	I Cavalry Corps & II Cavalry Corps	E.	Gudin's division
6.	Platov's Cossacks	F.	Morand's division
7.	III Cavalry Corps	G.	Friant's division
8.	Likhachev's division	H.	Dessaix's division
9.	Kaptsevich's division	I.	Compans' division
10.	6th Jäger Regiment	K.	Girardin's division
11.	Neverovsky's division	L.	Zajączek's division
12.	Dragoon regiments	M.	Knyazhevich's division
13.	Konovnitsyn's division	N.	Kaminski's division
		O.	Chastel's division
		P.	La Houssaye's division
		Q.	Pajol's division
		R.	Wattier's division
		S.	Defrance's division
		T.	Bruyère's division
		U.	Saint Germain's division
		V.	Valence's division
		W.W.	*Jeune Garde*
		X.	*Légion de la Vistule*
		Y.	*Vieille Garde*
		Z.	*Cavalerie de la Garde*

10

The Battle of Smolensk

A description of the terrain around Smolensk. – Raevsky's deployment on 4 (16) August. – The deployment of enemy forces. – The fighting on 4 (16) August. – The arrival at Smolensk of the main bodies of both Western armies. – The movement of Second Army along the Moscow road. – Dokhturov relieves Raevsky. – The deployment of Dokhturov's force on 5 (17) August. – The deployment of Napoleon's army. – The fighting on 5 (17) August. – The burning of Smolensk. – The losses on both sides. – An analysis of the fighting at Smolensk. – The withdrawal of Russian troops from Smolensk. – Events of 6 (18) August. – The reasons for the inaction of both sides throughout 6 (18) August.

The city of Smolensk lies on both banks of the Dnieper: the major part was situated on the left bank, which inside the city itself descends steeply to the river; the vast St Petersburg suburbs are located on the right bank, less steep than the left, but completely dominating it.[1] The city itself is surrounded by an ancient wall, constructed from stone and brick in the times of Godunov, which stretches five *versts* long and is 25 to 40 feet in height, and 10 to 18 feet thick. The upper part of it is crenellated, and behind it is a catwalk, five feet wide, with loopholes for firing muskets; in addition, the wall was reinforced on the inside with buttresses. In order to provide flank defences for the ditch, 36 quadrangular and polygonal towers had been built, with very shallow profiles, of which, in 1812, only 17 remained intact. Upon the capture of Smolensk by the Poles in 1611, King Sigismund III gave orders to build an earthen pentagonal fortification of limited size (the so-called Royal Bastion) on the western side of the city, between the present Krasnensk and Mstislavl suburbs. This fortification protrudes from the stone wall, such that three bastions face open ground, and two face the city. The moat in front of the former bastions was dry; while it was water-filled in front of the latter, over which a drawbridge had been built. In front of some parts of the city wall, a covered way had been built, most likely also in recent times. The ditch surrounding the wall was not deep and was dug only in order to get the soil needed for the construction of the glacis, which had a very low profile and did not protect the wall at all. Behind the stone wall, an earthen catwalk had been constructed level with it, with the intention of mounting guns

---

1   See Plan of the Battle of Smolensk, 5 (17) August 1812

there; but, having said that, the width of both catwalks combined was not enough for the suitable positioning of the artillery.

There were three gates to Smolensk: the first, at the junction of the roads leading from Krasny, Mstislavl and Roslavl, was known as the Malakhov; to the west of it lay the Mstislavl suburb; while the suburbs of Roslavl and Nikol stretch to the east of this gate and from the Mstislavl road; the latter has a link to the city through the Nikol Gate; further – on the northeastern side of the city, by the river itself, lies the suburb of Rachenka, via which the road from Smolensk passes through the village of Shein-Ostrog, to the village of Prudishchevo [east of Novoseltsy]. Near both of these locations there are fords on the Dnieper in shallow water: one four *versts*, and the other eight *versts* from Smolensk. The third gate, the Dnieper, facing the river, is famous for the chapel with the miraculous icon of the Madonna, which accompanied our troops as they marched from Smolensk to Tarutino and back. In addition to these gates, two breaches had been made in the city wall: one, to the left of the Dnieper Gate, known as the Dnieper gap, and the other, in the northeastern corner of the wall, near the river, known as the Rachenka gap. Both of them were made on the occasion of the visit to Smolensk by Empress Catherine II, as the Dnieper and Malakhov gates were too narrow for the passage of the State Carriage.

On the right bank of the Dnieper, by order of Peter the Great, a fairly regular earthen crown-work had been built with the role of protecting a wooden bridge that served to link the city with the right bank of the Dnieper. This fortification could put down fire from the dominant high ground on the right bank of the river.

The defences of Smolensk were strengthened on the eastern and western sides of the city by the Rachevka and Churilovka (Surganovka) rivers, flowing in deep and steep sided ravines and draining into the Dnieper near the suburbs of Rachenka and Krasnensk adjacent to the left bank of the Dnieper. In addition, in the city itself, three smaller streams flow in similarly deep ravines.[2]

In anticipation of the appearance of the enemy near Smolensk, General Raevsky had deployed his force to defend the city as follows: three regiments from 26th Division: Ladoga Infantry, Nizhegorod Infantry and Orël Infantry to the right of the Royal Bastion in the Krasnensk suburbs and in the covered way. Two guns were positioned to fire at the approaches to the Krasnensk suburbs. The remaining regiments from 26th Division: Poltava Infantry, 5th Jägers and 42nd Jägers with eighteen guns occupied the Royal Bastion. The Vilna Infantry from 27th Division and several hundred men from various regiments, released from convalescence, were posted along the walls. Four regiments from 12th Division: Narva Infantry, Smolensk Infantry, Novoingermanland Infantry and Alexopol Infantry with 24 guns held the Mstislavl suburbs. Two regiments from 27th Division, Odessa Infantry and Tarnopol Infantry, with twenty-four guns, were stationed in the Roslavl suburbs and in the cemetery in front of it. The 6th Jägers from 12th Division with four guns were in the Nikol suburbs. Two regiments from 27th Division, 49th Jägers and 50th Jägers were in reserve. The remaining regiment from this division, Simbirsk Infantry, with

---

2   History of the city of Smolensk, compiled by Nikitin. Information provided by local authorities from the Smolensk Governorate. Condensed War Diary of First Army. *Das Buch vom Jahr 1812*. II, 162-166 (extracted from Blessonov's description of Smolensk).

41st Jägers from 12th Division, with four guns, were stationed at the bridge over the Dnieper. Finally, regiments of IV Cavalry Corps, Novorossiya Dragoons and Lithuania Ulans (having a total of 12 squadrons), which had joined the corps during the night of 3 to 4 (15 to 16) August, were used, together with four Cossack regiments, commanded by Colonel Sysoev, to monitor the enemy on the left flank of our position – a very important location, because the Moscow road passed not far from it.

On 4 (16) August, at eight o'clock in the morning, Ney's *3e Corps* and Murat's *Réserve de cavalerie*, approaching Smolensk along the Krasny road, halted outside of cannon range; Ney's troops deployed facing the Krasnensk and Mstislavl suburbs, with their left flank on the Dnieper, and with their right flank on the Mstislavl road; Grouchy's cavalry lined up to the right of the infantry, attacking our cavalry and forcing it to retreat to the Nikol suburbs. Meanwhile, Napoleon himself, having spent the night in the bishop's dacha, known as Novy-Dvor, three *versts* from Smolensk, joined Ney's *3e Corps* at nine o'clock, and at the same time Davout's troops began to arrive.

At the very beginning of the battle, Raevsky received the following note from Prince Bagration: 'My friend! I am not walking, but running; I should like to have wings to more swiftly join with you. Hold on. May God be your helper!'

Then, 2nd Cuirassier Division arrived to the assist the defenders of Smolensk, but Raevsky, not being in a position to use cuirassiers for the defence of the city, ordered them to stay on the right bank of the river. The Russian troops, despite the vastly superior enemy numbers, managed to hold on to the positions they occupied in front of the city. The day was already fading towards evening, when Raevsky received news of the capture of the Royal Bastion by the enemy from an officer who had galloped to him, and at the very moment when he was preparing to go there with two battalions of the reserve stationed in the Mstslavl suburbs, a report came via another officer (who later could not be found) that the French had taken possession of the bridge on the Dnieper, where General Olenin had been stationed with four battalions. Having received this information, Raevsky immediately sent two battalions from the reserve from the Mstislavl suburbs to the Royal Bastion, while he rushed to the bridge himself, with two battalions of the reserve stationed in the city but upon arrival there he learned that there was no enemy there at all, and that Olenin's troops were waiting undisturbed. From there Raevsky rushed to the Royal Bastion with his reserve, which Ney himself had actually attempted to seize with the *46e Ligne*, but had been repulsed by one of the battalions of the Orël Infantry, under Paskevich's personal command. At seven o'clock in the evening, four regiments of 2nd Grenadier Division arrived to assist our troops, who took post with the reserves, by order of Raevsky. Soon after that, Prince Bagration and Prince Alexander von Württemberg arrived on the battlefield. On the right bank of the Dnieper, the main body of the Russian forces was approaching Smolensk; on the left bank, Napoleon's troops girded the city in a wide arc. But darkness was already falling; the firing subsided little by little, and eventually fell completely silent. The enemy, in preparation for a merciless struggle, moved away from our positions and settled down outside of cannon range.[3]

---

3   Raevsky's notes. Thiers, *Hist. du Consulat et de l'Empire*, XIV, 230-231. Description of the battle of Smolensk, compiled by von Toll.

Overall, throughout the whole day of 4 (16) August, the enemy restricted themselves to cannon fire on the suburbs and mostly probing attacks. General Raevsky, the hero of this memorable battle, noted: 'The Battle of Smolensk, with all its upheavals, in which I had to oppose huge forces, having insignificant resources at my disposal, is for me the most memorable of all the actions of my military career. Inscrutable Providence, taking me from the brink of death, and giving me the opportunity for survival. I fought with a firm resolve to perish in this post of salvation and honour; but, weighing, on the one hand, the importance of the action I have survived, and on the other hand, the insignificance of the losses suffered by my troops, I attribute the success not so much to my own considerations as to the weakness of Napoleon's attacks, who failed to seize the opportunity to decide the fate of the Russian army and the entire war.'[4]

Meanwhile, as Raevsky fought in Smolensk, both Russian armies were moving to his aid. Bagration, who was at Katan, having learned about the movement of the French army through Korytnya towards Smolensk, ordered the dismantling of the bridge he had built and moved his troops up the right bank of the Dnieper in several echelons. In the afternoon, his leading column, consisting of 2nd Cuirassier Division, soon appeared on the high ground beyond the St Petersburg suburbs; the remainder of Second Army assembled by evening. On that same day, 4 (16) August, First Army, setting off at dawn once more from Volokova and Nadva, moved by forced marches towards Smolensk and arrived there by nightfall. This movement was made in three columns, of which one, under the command of Tuchkov 1st (III Corps, IV Corps and I Cavalry Corps), proceeded from Volokova, through Lushcha [Zhornovka] and Lavrova, to the Porechye road and on towards Smolensk; Prince Shakhovsky's detachment moved from Kasplya along the same route; the second column under Grand Duke Konstantin Pavlovich (II Corps, V Corps and II Cavalry Corps), moved from Volokova along the direct route to Prikaz-Vidra and Shelomets; the third column (VI Corps) went from Nadva, via Chabury and Rakitnya, towards Smolensk; while Count Pahlen deployed at Prikaz-Vidra with the rearguard. On that day, the first column completed a march of 40 *versts*.[5]

It is rather difficult to understand why Napoleon, having had the opportunity to capture Smolensk on 4 (16) August, when there were only 13,000 Russian troops at the start of the battle, did not abandon his intention to attack this city the next day, once it was defended by large forces supported by the entire army. Had Napoleon sent part of his force to the crossing point at Prudishchevo, it would have been enough to force the Russians to evacuate Smolensk and abandon the locations occupied by us on the high ground outside the city and would have put us in danger of losing communications with Moscow. Instead, he undertook an operation that inevitably required huge sacrifice. In all likelihood, the reasons for this were: firstly, ignorance of the nature of the surrounding terrain, and secondly, the desire to force the Russians into a general battle at all costs. And indeed, if our commanders, encouraged by the success of the defence by Raevsky, had committed all their forces

---

4   Raevsky's notes.
5   General summary of the movements and operations of the Russian armies etc. compiled by General Khatov (archive of the M.T.D. No 37,644.

into action on the following day, leaving a large river to their rear, Napoleon could have taken advantage of this circumstance and, having defeated us in a general battle, would have been compensated in abundance for the losses suffered by him under the walls of Smolensk. Napoleon's hope to involve us in a decisive battle was partly fulfilled. And it could not have been otherwise: all of our main operational commanders, with the exception of Barclay de Tolly, believed that the time had now arrived to put a stop to the enemy's offensive. We cannot condemn the eagerness that led them to sacrifice themselves in defence of the fatherland, but, in giving everyone their due, let us say that Barclay had just reasons for abstaining from the general enthusiasm, and that the caution of his actions was most appropriate against a decisive commander who had almost all his forces at his disposal.

The defence of Smolensk brought us some benefits as long as the enemy limited themselves to a frontal assault on this location; but as soon as they, moving to their right, might envelope us from the left flank (which would have been especially facilitated by crossing the Dnieper at Prudishchevo, eight *versts* from Smolensk), they could have occupied the most important of our lines of communication – the Moscow road. To maintain it, we would have to retreat, with the objective of taking up positions better secured from being outflanked, but as we could not suddenly accustom ourselves to the idea of abandoning Smolensk, our Commanders-in-Chief decided, by mutual agreement, that First Army would defend this city, and Second Army would protect the Moscow road. Such a division of forces, in view of Napoleon's large army, in depriving us of the opportunity to operate decisively, would certainly lead to a further retreat, consistent with the course of action that we had been following since the beginning of the war. In all likelihood, Barclay de Tolly, in taking on the defence of Smolensk, already had a further retreat in mind; on the other hand, Prince Bagration believed that he had to defend Smolensk to the bitter end. He wrote to the Tsar: 'I hope that the Minister of War, having the entire First Army ready for action in front of Smolensk, will hold Smolensk. While I, in the event of an attempt by the enemy to push further along the Moscow road, shall repel it.'[6]

On 5 (17) August, at four o'clock in the morning, VIII Corps and IV Cavalry Corps, from Second Army, set off along the Moscow road and, leaving a rearguard facing the village of Shein-Ostrog, four *versts* from Smolensk, carried on a further four *versts*, to the Kolodnya stream; VII Corps, which was to be replaced by troops from First Army, was ordered to join Prince Bagration's other corps. The following were assigned to the defence of Smolensk, in addition to VI Corps: Neverovsky's 27th Division; Konovnitsyn's 3rd Division (from III Corps) and 6th Jäger Regiment from Kolyubakin's 12th Division, left in Smolensk by Raevsky.

General Dokhturov had fallen ill with a fever during the Russian army's offensive towards Rudnya, and although his illness was treated, he felt very weak. He was in this state when the decision was made to defend Smolensk. It was necessary to select the main defender and the choice fell on Dokhturov. Barclay de Tolly enquired after his health – would it permit him to take over the defence of Smolensk? Dokhturov happily expressed his readiness. He said to his confidants: 'Brothers, if I am to die,

---

6   Prince Bagration's report to the Tsar dated 5 [17] August, No 475.

it is better to die on the field of honour than shamefully in bed!'[7] Cool-headed, the fearless warrior withstood the test with honour – to fight all day at the head of 20,000 Russians against 140,000 of Napoleon's troops, of whom, according to the French themselves, at least 45,000 men were committed to battle.

General Dokhturov, located at the village of Divasy, near Rakitnya with VI Corps on the evening of 4 (16) August, received orders at very short notice – to go to Smolensk and replace Raevsky's VII Corps before dawn. All the baggage was ordered to be left on the right bank of the Dnieper. The posts occupied by the troops of VII Corps were handed over by General Paskevich and officers of His Majesty's Suite in the Quartermaster's Department (of the General Staff) to the Quartermaster in Chief of VI Corps, Liprandi [Ivan Petrovich Liprandi], with an explanation of the strengths and weaknesses of each location. Thereafter, still before dawn, the troops assigned for the defence of Smolensk settled into their designated locations, and VII Corps moved out of the city gradually, as its units were replaced by Dokhturov's force, which was deployed as follows:[8] Likhachev's 24th Division were on the right wing, holding the Krasnensk suburbs and Royal Bastion; Kaptsevich's 7th Division were in the centre, assigned to defend the Mstislavl and Roslavl suburbs; Neverovsky's 27th Division and 6th Jäger Regiment stood on the left wing in the Nikol and Rachenka suburbs; the Irkutsk Dragoons, Siberia Dragoons and Orenburg Dragoons with a small number of Cossacks were in front of the left flank, close to the Dnieper, under Major General Skalon's command; Konovnitsyn's 3rd Division were held in reserve, close to the Malakhov Gate. Some of the artillery was positioned with the forward troops as follows: in the Royal Bastion, on the terrace at the Malakhov Gate, in the towers of the walls and in the Mstislavl suburbs. For communications with the right bank of the Dnieper, in addition to the permanent bridge, two more pontoon bridges were set up. On Barclay de Tolly's orders, powerful batteries were placed on the right bank of the Dnieper, upstream and downstream of Smolensk, to provide enfilade fire on enemy troops in the event of an assault against the western or eastern extremities of the city.[9]

By the evening of 4 (16) August, following the battle endured by Raevsky, the enemy troops were positioned as follows: Ney's three divisions on the left wing, facing the Krasnensk suburbs; Davout's five divisions were in the centre facing the Mstislavl and Nikol suburbs; Poniatowski's two divisions on the right wing facing Rachenka, and further to the right, close to the Dnieper, were Murat's three cavalry corps. The *Garde* stood in reserve behind the centre. The total strength of their force approached some 140,000 men.[10] The Viceroy's *4e Corps* was still located between Krasny and Korytnya; while Junot's *8e Corps*, assigned in support of Poniatowski's *5e Corps*, had lost their way and arrived at Smolensk late in the evening: in these two corps there were 40,000 men.[11]

---

7   Extracted from Dokhturov's biography, found in the work: Tsar Alexander I and his
     contemporaries in 1812, 1813, 1814 and 1815, Vol. II.
8   See Plan of the Battle of Smolensk, 5 (17) August 1812.
9   Buturlin, *Hist. milit. de la campagne de Russie,* I, 263-264.
10   Thiers, XIV, 236. Buturlin believes that at Smolensk, not counting the corps under the
     Viceroy and Junot, Napoleon had 185,000 men, which is obviously an over-estimation.
11   Thiers, XIV, 237-238.

At dawn on 5 (17) August, a firefight broke out in the suburbs; as the French strengthened their advanced screen, ours also grew in strength; the fire gradually became more deadly. At eight o'clock in the morning, Dokhturov made a relatively strong sortie from the city into the suburbs and bundled the enemy out from there, almost without resistance, back into the open. Napoleon limited himself to the fire-fight, hoping to lure more of the Russian army onto the left bank of the Dnieper.[12] At ten o'clock, Barclay de Tolly, having arrived in Smolensk, stayed for about an hour on the terrace at the Malakhov Gate, where Dokhturov was also; from there it was possible to observe the surrounding area for a fairly long distance. The regiments of Likhachev's 24th Division, stationed to the right of this location, were made up of Siberians who were fighting the French for the first time, kept pressing forwards, despite repeated orders not to leave the suburbs. As soon as the enemy skirmishers closed in, our men ran out to engage them, shouting 'Hurrah!' and all the efforts by the commanders to moderate the enthusiasm of the soldiers were in vain.

The battle was restricted to skirmishing and a cannonade until three o'clock in the afternoon. Occasionally, from our side, on noticing a cluster of enemy here or there, round-shot and shell were fired at them from the city walls; from the French side, they did not fire into the city at all, and therefore perfect calm reigned there. Napoleon still hoped that the Russians, in holding onto Smolensk and maintaining the ability to cross the Dnieper under the protection of strong walls, would cross the river and offer a general battle in order to spare the city. Indeed, on the left wing of our position there was a flat hill (plateau), protected by a ravine and highly conven-ient for forming troops up in battle order upon it. Napoleon had intended to deploy cavalry there, but left it unoccupied with the intent of luring the Russian army into this space. His expectations did not come about. Barclay de Tolly would not engage in a decisive battle to save Smolensk, but sacrificed it at a high price.

At about noon, Napoleon, having received a report from the right flank of his position about the movement of significant elements of the Russian army along the Moscow road, went to the village of Shein-Ostrog and was convinced of the retreat of Prince Bagration at first hand. Thus, having made certain that we had no inten-tion of offering a general engagement, he intended to cross the Dnieper upstream of Smolensk and envelope us from the left flank. But in order to achieve this it would be necessary to cross the river with the entire army across a ford, because if the French began to build bridges anywhere, the Russians could counter them with significant forces at the places chosen for the crossing, or, by passing through Smolensk, they could get behind the flank and rear of the French army: in any case, the construc-tion of bridges would have taken so long that we could have avoided this battle and retreated along the Moscow road. Napoleon, understanding all these factors, sent several patrols to find fords, but the French could not find them. All that remained was to seize Smolensk.

Meanwhile, as the skirmishing continued ahead of the suburbs, Dokhturov, having dined on the terrace, immediately lay down to rest under a canopy made from some kind of door found by the gunners who were stationed at this post with

---

12   Condensed War Diary of First Army.

four guns. The entire VI Corps headquarters staff, surrounding their commander, passed the time in cheerful conversation, not thinking about the impending danger. Among the officers who were there was a captain late of the Prussian service, who had just joined our General Staff, Baron von Luce, who, from time to time, looking through a telescope, suddenly noticed an unusual movement in the undergrowth beyond the suburbs. At this very moment, at about three o'clock in the afternoon, Colonel Monakhtin [Fëdor Fëdorovich Monakhtin] returned to the Malakhov gate from the front line of the right wing. 'The French appear to be stirring themselves,' he said. No sooner had the words left his lips than a rocket shot up from the enemy facing our right flank, and thick clouds of French troops appeared on the horizon. A few minutes later, another rocket took off, then a third, and, at the same time, about two hundred round-shot and shells from a battery of guns fell into the city; several of them fell onto the terrace. This cannonade was the precursor to a French advance.

The action began with an attack by Bruyère's *1re Division de cavalerie légère* on our dragoons, who, having been overwhelmed, retreated in disorder through the Malakhov gate into the city. General Skalon was killed here. Subsequently, Poniatowski moved his infantry into the front line facing the Nikol and Rachenka suburbs, with their right flank on the Dnieper, and placed a battery of 60 guns right on the bank of the river, to shell the bridges set up by the Russians and to counter the Russian battery under Lieutenant Colonel Nilus, operating on the right bank of the Dnieper. The suburbs of Rachenka and Nikol caught fire in several places from the multitude of shells fired by the enemy. Poniatowski's troops, taking advantage of this, burst into the blazing suburbs; the Polish General Grabowski [Michał Grabowski] was bayoneted here in hand-to-hand combat.[13] The Poles, having reached the base of the city walls, attempted an assault, but having no ladders, they were repulsed with enormous casualties. General of Division Zajączek, who was marching at the head of his columns, was wounded.

During the course of these actions, Ney had taken possession of the Krasnensk suburbs and formed up Marchand's Division facing the Royal Bastion, but did not attack this fortification, considering it much stronger than it really was.

Meanwhile, Napoleon was preparing to direct the main attack on the Malakhov Gate with Davout's force, in the centre of our position. Morand's, Gudin's and Friant's divisions, immune to the enfilade fire from our batteries, arranged on the right bank of the Dnieper, after a bitter fight, had captured most of the Mstislavl and Roslavl suburbs, from where Kaptsevich and Konovnitsyn retreated into the city. Major General Balla [Adam Ivanovich Balla] was killed here in the skirmishers' screen. The defence of the city wall presented the enemy with an almost insurmountable barrier; but we could not operate here to full effect, because the walls were not at all adapted either for the positioning of guns behind them, or to the occupation of them by infantry.

---

13 We have taken the account by Sołtyk (*Napolèon en 1812*) at face value here, as he would have known the truth as it relates to Polish forces better than any other. In the work by Prinz Eugen von Württemberg, it states that Grabowski was killed when Prinz Eugen's 4th Division entered the battle.

The persistence of the enemy attacks forced Dokhturov to request assistance from Barclay de Tolly, who was on the right bank of the river. Barclay gave the following response to the messenger, the Quartermaster in Chief of VI Corps: 'Tell Dmitry Sergeevich that the salvation of the entire army depends on his courage' and sent Prinz Eugen von Württemberg's 4th Division and the Lifeguard Jäger Regiment to reinforce Dokhturov. But in the meantime, the enemy launched a new attempt to capture the city: Napoleon ordered General Sorbier to bring 36 heavy guns from the *Artillerie de la Garde* reserves up to the walls of Smolensk; overall, more than 150 guns were positioned facing the city walls. Their fire, directed against the strong walls of Smolensk, had little effect. If the enemy had concentrated their fire against the towers, which were incomparably less robust, they would have had a chance to punch breaches. Infinitely greater harm was done to us by the shells that struck the top of the wall, or flew over it into the city: the former smashed the battlements and showered the troops outside the wall with masonry fragments; while the latter ignited fires in the city, or fell among our columns, standing in the streets and squares, and killed the civilian populace. At five o'clock in the afternoon, Napoleon ordered Marshal Davout to storm the city. The French courageously attacked and almost captured the Malakhov Gate; but at that very moment, Prinz Eugen von Württemberg arrived to help Dokhturov.

While Prinz Eugen was with Barclay de Tolly, on the right bank of the Dnieper, in the course of the desperate defence of the Smolensk suburbs, he persuaded the Commander-in-Chief to dispatch 4th Division to the city and volunteered to go there immediately to assess the situation for himself.[14] He had barely crossed the bridge when he was caught up in a dense crowd of wounded leaving the scenes of carnage through the city; thousands of injured with lacerated faces, with mangled limbs, whose path was marked by trails of blood, filled the streets between burning buildings; while enemy round-shot and shell, striking those seeking salvation and covering the city with their corpses, increased the general confusion. Reaching the Malakhov Gate, the Prince found Dokhturov there, under a most severe hail of shells falling in dense swarms. Konovnitsyn, who was in the same place, acted with extraordinary energy, but expressed the hopelessness of holding in the city. Prinz Eugen raced back to meet his Division and, upon arriving in the city, immediately dispatched the Tobolsk Infantry and Volhynia Infantry to Rachenka, where they were intended, together with the Lifeguard Jägers who were in the left wing reserve, to hold back Poniatowski, also with the men of 12th Division and 27th Division. The Kremenchug Infantry and Minsk Infantry were directed to the right flank of our position, to assist Likhachev's 24th Division, and plunged into the heated fight. The Prince von Württemberg himself with the 4th Jägers and General Konovnitsyn with part of his Division charged at the enemy who were approaching the Malakhov Gate and drove them off. At this location, the fierce fire continued; the crews and horses of our four guns stationed there were wiped out and replaced several times;[15] few of

---

14   [This is at odds with the earlier paragraph, stating that Barclay had ordered Prinz Eugen to assist Dokhturov].

15   [Mikhailovsky-Danilevsky states this happened four times (Vol. I, page 103). Liprandi informs us that the commander of these four guns was Staff-Captain Sinelnikov; 'having

those who were with Konovnitsyn remained unscathed; he was wounded himself by a bullet in the arm, but did not leave the battlefield and did not even allow his wound to be dressed until the very end of the battle. His worthy companion, Prinz Eugen, raced from the Malakhov Gates with his jägers onto the covered way, held by the French; the front rank of his column fell under the bullets from a thick enemy screen; but this did not stop the brave men: the battalion under Major Heidecke's command, marching at the head of the regiment, drove the enemy out of the covered way with fixed bayonets. The Russian troops were equally successful in repelling the repeated attacks by the Poles in Rachenka.

Napoleon, convinced of the impossibility of taking the city by storm, limited himself to a powerful bombardment. More than a hundred guns, mostly howitzers lobbing explosive shells, operated for several hours around the city, spreading fires and devastation within it. The Russian troops, engulfed in flames from the front and behind by the enemy, courageously continued to defend the ruins of their native city. At seven o'clock in the afternoon, the French attempted an assault again and were repulsed once more. On the right wing of our position, in the Krasnensk suburbs, they operated with most success, but, finally, they were driven out from there by 30th Jägers and 48th Jägers from Olsufiev's Division, sent by the Commander-in-Chief to assist Likhachev. At nine o'clock the bombardment fell silent at all locations. Our troops settled outside the city wall, sending skirmish screens into the covered way and suburbs.[16]

Throughout the course of the battle, on 5 (17) August, Smolensk presented a terrible and moving spectacle. The people of Smolensk had considered themselves completely secure, having been reassured by Barclay de Tolly's reminder to the Governor of Smolensk, Ash [Kazimir Ivanovich Ash], a few days before about his intention to defend Smolensk to the bitter end, and the unification of both Russian armies, and then their offensive movements.[17] The defence of the suburbs by Raevsky, during which not a single enemy round-shot was fired into the city, obliged only a few of its inhabitants to leave, alarmed at the approach of Napoleon's army; all the

---

had his guns knocked out and having lost many men, he asked for Dokhturov's permission to remain at his post following the replacement of the guns and men, and received this permission, remaining in command on the terrace for the whole time that the battery was repeatedly replenished with guns and men.'].

16   Description of the battle of Smolensk compiled by von Toll. Chambray, I, 315-318.

17   Although Barclay de Tolly had secretly given permission to the civilian Governor of Smolensk, Baron Ash, to send sums of money, documents and maps, from which the enemy could have gleaned some intelligence about the state of the region, to Yukhnov by night and under the most covert means, however, the Commander-in-Chief, in conclusion of his review to the governor, wrote: 'I assure you that the city of Smolensk is not yet facing the slightest danger, and it is unlikely that it would come under threat. With myself on the one side, and Prince Bagration on the other, we are going to unite in front of Smolensk, which will take place on the 22nd [3 August], and both armies will jointly defend their compatriots in the province entrusted to you, until their efforts remove the foes of the fatherland from there, or until they are destroyed in their brave ranks to the last warrior. You may see from this that you have a perfect right to reassure the inhabitants of Smolensk, for whoever defends with two such brave forces can be assured of their victory.' Barclay de Tolly's instructions to the civilian Governor of Smolensk, Baron Ash dated 20 July 1812.

rest would not abandon their homes, having faith in the strength of the defenders of the city. When the thunder of war suddenly fell upon Smolensk, once houses were on fire, as the inhabitants, their wives and children, became the victims of war, fear and despair seized the citizens of Smolensk: some of them fled, not knowing where to look for refuge; others, having gathered in the houses of God, resorted to the source of strength and consolation – fervent prayer. In the midst of the thousands of deaths hovering over Smolensk, an all-night vigil was celebrated in every church on the eve of the feast of the Transfiguration of the Lord. At dusk, the miraculous icon of the Smolensk Madonna was taken out of the city and handed over to the troops as a sacred pledge of their victorious return to the ancient city temporarily doomed as a sacrifice.[18]

After a day marked by the deaths of many thousands of people and the devastation of the capital of the ancient Russian principality, the night that followed was no less terrible. Barclay de Tolly, unable to continue the defence of the blazing ruins of Smolensk, ordered Dokhturov to evacuate the city. It was alleged that our troops, the very troops that were ready to shed the last drop of their blood defending it, intensified the fire with arson during the retreat. In windless conditions, the flames were seen as a tall pillar, over which huge clouds of smoke swirled, presenting, in the words of Napoleon, a spectacle similar to the eruption of Vesuvius.[19]

Dokhturov's troops fell back through the city two hours before dawn, taking their artillery with them through the flames of the streets, and destroying the bridges on the Dnieper. The ferocity with which our soldiers fought on that memorable day of 5 (17) August surpassed all credibility: the wounded, not feeling pain from the lacerations inflicted upon them, remained in the heat of battle, shed their blood and fell from exhaustion. Napoleon was forced to commit a significant part of his force to battle against Dokhturov's VI Corps, which, with all the reinforcements that arrived

---

18   There are two miraculous icons of the Madonna in Smolensk. One of them, located in the Cathedral of the Assumption, is the icon of the Smolensk Madonna Hodegetria, painted by Luke the Evangelist, which the Greek Emperor Constantine IX Monomachos bestowed upon Princess Anna in 1046, upon her marriage to the prince of Chernigov, Vsevolod Yaroslavich. A copy of this icon is in the Moscow Cathedral of the Annunciation. Another icon in the church at the Dnieper Gate, copied from the first, performed miracles during a plague in Smolensk, at the time of Boris Godunov. Both of these icons were evacuated during the enemy occupation of Smolensk: the first by His Eminence Bishop Irenaeus, while the other, which was at that time, on the occasion of the restructuring of the church at the Dnieper Gate, in the parish Church of the Annunciation, was taken from there, on the evening of 5 [17] August, by order of Barclay de Tolly, and handed over to General Konovnitsyn, who gave orders for it to be given to Colonel Glukhov's 1st Battery Company (currently 1st Heavy Battery, 13th Artillery Brigade). From that time on, this miraculous icon was constantly with the troops of 3rd Infantry Division, who considered it a sacred pledge of God's mercy, until on 6 [18] November, following the victory at Krasny, it was escorted by General Konovnitsyn to the senior clergyman in Smolensk and was again placed in the church at the Dnieper Gate. 'And like Miriam, dwelt with them for three months, and returned to her home.' Throughout the entire time, while the icon was in the camp, thanksgiving prayers were offered before it, after each success won over the enemy (extracted from information delivered by the local authorities of the Smolensk Governorate).

19   *Au milieu d'une belle nuit d'Août, Smolensk offrait aux Français le spectacle qu'offre aux habitants de Naples une éruption de Vésuve. (Treizième bulletin).*

with him, counted no more than 30,000 men in his ranks. On the part of the enemy, the Polish troops under Poniatowski distinguished themselves with particular courage and suffered heavy losses. In general, the losses on both sides were heavy, but there is no way to show them exactly due to the extreme divergence of the sources that might serve as a foundation. Ségur, Larrey [Dominique-Jean Larrey] and Thiers estimate the casualties to Napoleon's troops at 6,000 to 7,000 men; Chambray at 12,000; Prinz Eugen von Württemberg at 10,000 to 12,000; documents captured from the enemy show more than 14,000. Buturlin suggests that about 20,000 men were withdrawn from Napoleon's service during the fighting at Smolensk. Among those killed was (as has been mentioned) General Grabowski. Among the wounded: generals Zajączek, Grandeau [Louis Joseph Grandeau] and d'Alton [Alexandre d'Alton].[20] On our side, in Barclay de Tolly's report to the Tsar, the number given for dead and wounded was 4,000 men; among the total for the former was (as has been mentioned) generals Skalon and Balla. Buturlin, in agreement with Toll, wrote that our losses on 5 [17] August extended to some 6,000; while in the returns showing dead, wounded and missing in action against the French in 1812, compiled by Duty General Kikin [Pëtr Andreevich Kikin], the casualties are shown in general for the actions on 4, 5, 6 and 7 [16, 17, 18 and 19] August, and therefore it is impossible to say for sure how great our losses were in the defence of Smolensk. But, judging from the course of the campaign, one may doubtless conclude that the enemy, operating for the most part on the offensive against Russian troops protected by buildings and walls, would have suffered no fewer casualties than ours.[21]

Meanwhile, as the Russian troops were marching out of Smolensk, Napoleon, not knowing about this, was preparing to storm the city once more on the following day; the main attack was assigned to Friant's Division, from Davout's *1er Corps*. Thus, having already lost a significant number of troops, on 4 and 5 (16 and 17) August, Napoleon intended to continue the bloody struggle to capture this devastated city. It is unclear how important Smolensk could have been to him. The only reason that prompted Napoleon to renew the assault was the fear of the unfavourable influence that a failed attempt to capture the city might have had on the French. Eyewitnesses have stated that on the evening of 5 (17) August, in the bivouacs, senior officers who had been on the Egyptian expedition compared Smolensk with Saint-Jean-d'Acre, where Napoleon had his first failure.[22] Napoleon's star shone brightly, but the slightest dimming of its brilliance revealed to the personalities of the world the possibility of its fall and destroyed the magic to which the conqueror owed so much of his success.

Barclay de Tolly was criticised for the fact that, having taken on the defence of Smolensk, without any likelihood of holding it, had suffered heavy losses and had given the enemy the opportunity to cut First Army off from its most important

---

20 Ségur, *Hist. de Napoléon et de la grande armée, 4 édit*, I, 280. Thiers, *Hist. du Consulat et de l'Empire*, XIV, 248. Chambray, *Hist. de l'expédition de Russie*, I, 332. *Erinnerungen aus dem Felzuge des Jahres 1812 in Russland, v. dem Herzog Eugen v. Wütemberg*. 26. Buturlin, *Hist. milit. de la campagne de Russie*, I, 268.

21 Barclay de Tolly's report to the Tsar dated 9 [21] August, No 661. Buturlin, I, 268.

22 *Journal de la campagne de Russie en 1812, par Fezensac*, 32.

line of communications. All of this is true; but could he have acted differently? In defending Smolensk, he was defending a shrine of the Russian nation. After a long retreat, the reason and benefits of which very few understood, it was necessary to give some satisfaction to national pride, love for the fatherland, readiness for sacrifice – those noble sentiments of the people and the army. Despite the important services rendered to Russia by Barclay de Tolly, who had preserved the army in order to save the State, his position at this point was such that he could no longer remain Commander-in-Chief without the authority and wavering approval of his troops. To that end, the two-day battle around Smolensk was offered, and none of the Russians, then or later, criticised Barclay de Tolly for this; while, on the contrary, many believed that it was necessary to continue to defend Smolensk.[23] Without a doubt, we could more surely achieve our objective of weakening the enemy army by retreating even further inland, rather than subjecting the fate of the war to the dubious outcome of a battle with Napoleon. But if we had retreated without fighting at Smolensk, we would have revealed our course of action in its entirety, and then it could easily have happened that Napoleon, forewarned of our intent, would have fully appreciated the danger of further pursuit and would not have gone further. On the contrary, the efforts and sacrifices we made to defend Smolensk gave Napoleon a reason to conclude that we would spare nothing to prevent his access to Moscow, and thus give him an opportunity to win one of the victories with which he usually decided the outcome of his wars.

Barclay de Tolly's actual course of action, who hesitated between the measures inspired by his own caution and the general urging of the army to take decisive action, was to bewitch – and indeed bewitched – Napoleon more than it should have. Noticing the Russians' thirst for combat, which more than once put us in a very dangerous situation, he never lost hope of taking advantage of any careless steps on our part in order to deliver a decisive blow.

The reasons that prompted Barclay de Tolly to end the defence of Smolensk were completely sound. By persisting in holding on to this location any longer, we were in danger of being driven back from the Moscow road, which Bagration's 30,000 man army could not defend. The enemy, after occupying the suburbs of Smolensk, had the

---

23   *La 1re armée, se trouvant établie sur la rive droite du Dnieper, qui est dominante, pouvant à son gré réunir ses forces et rafraichir ses troupes, qui defendaient la ville, occupait une position, que toute l'armée de Napoléon n'aurait pu forcer, et il n'y a pas de doute, que les Français n'auraient pu s'emparer de la ville qu'en y perdant un monde infini. Telle était du moins l'opinion de toute l'armée et il faut que le Ministre de la guerre aye eu des motifs, que je ne puis pénêtrer, pour avoir, contre l'avis de tous les généraux et contre l'opinion du Prince Bagration, donné l'ordre d'évacuer Smolensk et de se retirer sur la rive droite pour marcher ensuite sur Dorogobouje.* (First Army, being established on the right bank of the Dnieper, which is dominant, being able to unite its forces and refresh its troops, which defended the city at will, occupied a position, which Napoleon's entire army could not have forced out, and there is no doubt, that the French could only have seized the city by losing the infinite world. Such at least was the opinion of the whole army and the Minister of War must have had reasons, which I cannot fathom, to have, against the advice of all the generals and against the opinion of the Prince Bagration, given the order to evacuate Smolensk and to withdraw to the right bank to then march on Dorogobuzh). Extract from a letter by Saint-Priest to the Tsar dated 8 [20] August 1812.

opportunity to enfilade the bridges on the Dnieper and threatened to completely cut off both the communications between the army and the city and the line of retreat for its defenders.[24] In addition, only ruins remained on the site of Smolensk: out of 2,250 common dwellings, only 350 survived. It is much more difficult to understand why Napoleon was preparing to storm a city, which was of no particular importance to him. If he, after waiting for the arrival of 40,000 men under the Viceroy and Junot, and having concentrated some 180,000 troops near Smolensk, had sent most of them upstream to Prudishchevo, then we would have been forced to evacuate Smolensk, or we would lose our communications with Moscow.

During the night of 5 to 6 (17 to 18) August, the troops of First Army, located directly behind Smolensk, withdrew to a position where the whole army was located along the direction of the Porechye road, with the left flank towards the village of Krakhotkina [Korokhotkino]. At the same time, the troops defending Smolensk began to gradually withdraw from the locations they had been holding and cross the river; the last of them, under the command of Prinz Eugen von Württemberg, crossing at four o'clock in the morning, dismantled the floating bridges and burned the permanent one. Barclay de Tolly did not manage to draw up a disposition for the evacuation of Smolensk, and as a result it happened that no rearguard was left to secure the crossing for the final defenders of the city in the Petersburg suburbs and on the right bank of the Dnieper. But the composure and resourcefulness of the formation commanders sorted the issue. Konovnitsyn, upon leaving Smolensk, was concerned, at the same time with maintaining order among the retreating troops, and the fate of the citizens of Smolensk, who were abandoning their city with cries of despair; it was here that the hero Konovnitsyn became the comforting angel of these unfortunates: he gave money to one of them, encouraged others with words of sympathy, ordered the elderly and children to be put on carriages. The equally courageous defender of Smolensk, Dokhturov competed with him in the cause of charity.[25]

---

24 'If I had intended to hold the city behind me any longer, then I would have relieved the troops at Smolensk, which, on the 5th [17 August] had been under continuous fire for twenty-four hours, with the remnant of the army, that is, the selected part of this, which was in reserve and was being saved for a general battle; it would also have been necessary to expose them to the loss of several thousand men, and in a most difficult action as that of 5 [17] August, as the enemy occupied the high ground also on the right flank of the army's lines of communication with the city, but assuming that I would hold the city on the 6th [18 August] the enemy only had to cross the Dnieper downstream of Smolensk with a part of their army to threaten my right flank in order to force me to withdraw troops from the city, but this would abruptly have fallen into the hands of the enemy, and then, having lost between 8,000 to 10,000 men completely uselessly, I would have seen myself in need of fighting a superior enemy, or retreating in full view of them, both unpalatable to me. Second Army could conveniently have distracted the enemy by crossing the Dnieper upstream of Smolensk, but it was impossible to trust in the coordination of these movements, especially when the two armies, with two independent commanders, had to operate in unison, as was evidenced by the actions on 7 [19] August.' Depiction of the operations of First Army. Extracted from the note by Barclay de Tolly.

25 Extracted from the biographies included in the work: Tsar Alexander I and his contemporaries in 1812, 1813, 1814 and 1815.

Konovnitsyn, upon leaving the Petersburg suburbs, left his 20th Jägers and 21st Jägers there in order to cover the retreat of 4th Infantry Division under Prince von Württemberg; they were joined by 30th Jägers and 48th Jägers from 17th Division. Having let 4th Division pass, Konovnitsyn ordered his jägers to fall back behind his other troops. Meanwhile, the troops of 12th Division and 27th Division, fulfilling the orders given to them, turned to the right onto the Moscow road and went to link up with Prince Bagration. In other words, each of the formation commanders, left to their own devices, sent the regiments entrusted to them by the most direct route towards the forces with whom they were located; while for the defence of the suburbs and the banks of the Dnieper, only 30th Jägers and 48th Jägers, from 17th Division remained, and even those, not at all expecting to be engaged by the enemy, were mistaken.

At that very moment, Ney, believing the Petersburg suburbs to have been completely abandoned sent a single Württemberg battalion, followed by two Portuguese companies, wading across the river. The jägers from 17th Division, who had occupied the crown work and the suburb, were pushed out into the open. Whereupon Barclay de Tolly, who was close by, ordered Konovnitsyn's Jäger Brigade to counter attack; in the meantime, the enemy troops had been reinforced with four Württemberg battalions, but our jäger regiments from both 4th Division and 17th Division, under Konovnitsyn's and Toll's command, who raced forwards with the battalions closest to the enemy, closed with fixed bayonets and pushed the enemy back across the Dnieper. At the same time, a new rearguard, made up of 14 jäger battalions, from II Corps and IV Corps, and 16 squadrons from the Sumy Hussar and Mariupol Hussar regiments, under the command of Adjutant General Baron Korf,[26] retook the suburbs and tangled with the enemy light infantry who held the left bank of the Dnieper in skirmishing that lasted until nightfall. French light cavalry also attempted to ford the river downstream of the city, but were forced back by the troops of II Corps. This success was greatly assisted by the artillery, very skilfully sited on the high ground of the right bank. By evening, the entire suburb was engulfed in flames; our soldiers took refuge in the gardens, but even there the heat increased to the point that the fruit on the trees was completely baked. The soldiers, feasting on them, commented among themselves: 'They won't believe us back home when we say that in Smolensk we picked baked apples straight from the tree.'[27] The French, exploiting the fiery barrier separating them from the Russian

---

26   1st Jägers, 4th Jägers, 18th Jägers, 30th Jägers, 33rd Jägers, 34th Jägers, 48th Jägers, several regiments of regular cavalry, many Cossack regiments and 24 guns. *Erinnerungen aus dem Feldzuge d. Jahr 1812, v. d. Herzog v. Württemberg.* 31. Bernhardi, *Denkwürdigkeiten des Grafen v. Toll,* I, 373-375. *Darstellung des Feldzugs der französischen verbündeten Armee gegen die Russen im Jahr 1812, v. M. v. Miller,* I, 80-82.

27   Count Nikitin's papers. [Liprandi casts doubt on the veracity of the source, stating: 'But suppose that, were there really something of this sort in the indicated papers, then, of course, this story should in any case have no place in the text, but as an anecdote it could perhaps be placed in the footnotes, all the more so since the said papers have not been published, and, it seems, they are not in the archive either, otherwise it should be noted, that Nikitin was distinguished by common sense, and therefore that this obscure statement attributed to him is somewhat curious; but nobody knows what was written in these papers! One must get to the heart of this story...'].

troops defending the suburbs, established themselves in the crown work, and that night they repaired the destroyed bridge and built two bridges of boats.[28]

The situation for the last defenders of Smolensk, concealed in the burned out buildings of the suburbs, was very difficult; but it seemed enviable to the other troops who were leaving the city in deep distress. In particular, those who were unable to participate in the defence of sacred Smolensk did not hide their desire to continue the work started by their colleagues. Bagration himself wrote to Barclay the day before, demanding that First Army not only hold Smolensk, but also switch from defence to the offensive. According to Bagration, with the enemy having suffered attrition through unsuccessful attacks, it was essential to move forces across the river, to pass through the city and complete the victory with a decisive blow. Unfortunately, the contents of this letter were not kept secret, and therefore the orders by Barclay – to evacuate the city and destroy the bridges – aroused discontent in the army headquarters. Many of the generals expressed their opinion publicly regarding the need to continue the defence of Smolensk; others believed that the enemy had already been sufficiently weakened and that it was time to take advantage of the enthusiasm of our troops and attack Napoleon's army. It got to the point that some of the senior generals (including Bennigsen) decided to go to the Commander-in-Chief and demand that he cancel the orders he had issued. Although the cool-headed, unshakable Barclay de Tolly was able to maintain the discipline violated by his closest associates, it was easy to foresee that the force of circumstances would soon require the appointment of a new Commander-in-Chief.[29] Barclay de Tolly himself pinned his hopes mainly on diversions by Tormasov and Count Wittgenstein.[30]

Let us turn to the presentation of further events.

On the morning of 6 (18) August, at the same time that First Army, having evacuated Smolensk, was located to the north of the Petersburg suburbs, Second Army, upon linking up with the troops that had remained in the city, set out from the Kolodnya River, along the Moscow road, towards the Solovieva crossing. By agreement of both Commanders-in-Chief, it was decided that Prince Bagration would leave a strong rearguard at Zabolotye, facing the Prudishchevo ford, to shield the Moscow road. But, instead of that, only four Cossack regiments had been left at Prudishchevo, under the command of Major General Karpov; behind them – even further from Smolensk – Prince Gorchakov was stationed with the grenadiers under Count Vorontsov and with Vasilchikov's hussars, who had been ordered: 'to conform with the movements of Second Army as soon as the leading troops of First Army have arrived.'

After the enemy occupied Smolensk, on the morning of 6 (18) August, Napoleon, having entered the city through the Nikol Gate, stopped at the house of the Kakhovsky family, and immediately set off through the back streets to the Dnieper Gate. Entering the church by the gate, from the locked glass doors he surveyed the opposite bank, from where two Russian cannon, firing at the city, were inflicting

---

28   Bernhardi, I, 376.
29   Bernhardi, I, 368-370.
30   For Barclay de Tolly's letter to the Tsar dated 9 [21] August 1812, see Appendix XV.

considerable harm to the enemy. Napoleon, at the same moment, ordered two guns to be dragged into the church and, placing them in the doorway, opened fire on our guns and silenced them. Noticing that our marksmen continued to shoot from the right bank of the river, he left the church and ordered four more guns to be put on the earth rampart a short distance from there, while French infantry scattered behind the walls along the river bank and exchanged fire with our jägers. Having surveyed the banks of the Dnieper and ordered General Éblé to build bridges, Napoleon retired to his quarters.[31] The city presented a terrible spectacle: among the blazing buildings and burned out ruins, every street was littered with corpses and the wounded; some of the sufferers, with the final exertions of their strength, managed to find refuge, together with women, the elderly and children, in the Smolensk Cathedral. The French entered Smolensk differently from the way they entered cities conquered by force of arms previously: they experienced an uncomfortable sensation, convinced that we had left them essentially only ruins as booty and that Russia would be their second Spain.[32]

Meanwhile, as Napoleon, having occupied Smolensk, was forced to pay full attention to meeting the needs of his large army, Barclay de Tolly, seeing the enemy preparations for the construction of bridges over the Dnieper, could no longer remain in the position he occupied north of Smolensk, but would have to transfer his troops from the St Petersburg road to the Moscow road as swiftly as possible. To achieve this objective, he would have to take advantage of the moment before the French had chance to build bridges, namely: to carry out a flanking march by the army during 6 (18) August. If, having withdrawn from his position on the Porechye road, he could have immediately switched to the Moscow road, then the retreat of the army entrusted to him would have been much less difficult. But as the enemy had already occupied Smolensk and the left bank of the Dnieper in the vicinity of this city, and the road from Smolensk to Moscow at the beginning runs along the right bank for five *versts*, so as not to expose the troops to interference from enemy artillery on the left bank, during their march through this area, Barclay de Tolly decided to carry out the movement of his army from the St Petersburg road to the Moscow road, along country roads, in two columns: one was intended to emerge onto the Moscow road near Lubino, while the other, after two stages, was to emerge at the Solovieva crossing, where it was intended to reunite the two columns.

At first glance, it appears that we could have started the retreat from Smolensk immediately after leaving this city, that is, exploiting the darkness of the night from 5 to 6 (17 to 18) August, or, at least, the next day, because the enemy, separated from us by a river with fords as yet unknown to them, could neither discover our retreat in time, nor pursue us with significant forces. But the following must be taken into account: firstly, the Russian army had executed a forced march on 4 (16) August; secondly, that during the following night of 4 to 5 (16 to 17) August, Dokhturov's VI Corps had relieved Raevsky's VII Corps in Smolensk; thirdly, that during the entirety of 5 (17) August more than a third of the army had been committed to a bitter, exhausting battle, and fourthly that these troops had not been able to depart

---

31   Information provided by the local authorities of the Smolensk Governorate. Thiers, XIV, 252.
32   Thiers, XIV, 250-251.

Smolensk before four o'clock on the morning of 6 (18) August. Having understood all these factors, one cannot help but admit that if Barclay had begun his retreat on 6 (18) August, immediately after the evacuation of Smolensk, he would have exhausted and completely disordered his army. Such exertions by the troops may be demanded during offensive operations, and we find an example of this in Suvorov's advance to engage MacDonald before the battle of Trebbia. But after a long, bitter battle, having surrendered the battlefield to the enemy, one should not subject the troops to such a trial, which could entail a decline in their morale. There is no doubt that Barclay de Tolly could have taken the Moscow road in advance with that part of his army which had not been in the battle of Smolensk, but he considered this precaution unnecessary, because Bagration had been entrusted with the protection of this route.

Napoleon did not take advantage of Barclay de Tolly's enforced inaction during 6 (18) August. The reason for this was a complete lack of intelligence about the ground and about the Russian troops. Having invaded a hostile country, where, as soon as they appeared, the entire population vanished, the French had neither informants nor guides, and therefore, not knowing the advantages of their position, could not exploit them. The foe had not found the fords on the Dnieper upstream of Smolensk, despite the fact that during the dry spell that began in early August, there were plenty of them. Finally – Napoleon did not know exactly in which direction our troops were retreating, and, noticing Bagration's movement along the Moscow road, had assumed that First Army was following Second Army. The lack of this intelligence prevented the French from operating at the appropriate pace. Napoleon was forced to wait, to hesitate, to operate as if feeling his way, and thus gave Barclay time to evade the danger that threatened him.[33]

---

33   Bernhardi, I, 376-379.

11

The Battle of Lubino (or Valutina Gora)

The deployment of the Russian armies after the battle of Smolensk. – The flanking march by First Army between the St Petersburg and Moscow highways. – Tuchkov 3rd's advance towards the river Kolodnya. – The perilous situation of First Army. – The action at Gedeonovo. – Napoleon's orders. – The action on the river Kolodnya (at Valutina Gora) and Tuchkov 3rd's retreat to the Stragan. – The action on the Stragan (at Lubino). – The outcome of the entire general battle in the Smolensk area. – The retreat of the Russian armies along the Moscow road. – Napoleon's stay at Smolensk. – His views. – The conversation between Napoleon and Tuchkov 3rd. – Napoleon's orders in Smolensk.

After the battle at Smolensk, by the evening of 6 (18) August, First Army was located in several echelons along both sides of the Porechye road; II Corps and IV Corps were stationed in the first echelon, about two *versts* from the outermost buildings of the Petersburg suburbs; Stroganov's Grenadier Division (Tuchkov's III Corps), a *verst* behind the first echelon; finally – even further back – V Corps; I Cavalry Corps, II Cavalry Corps and Platov with most of the Cossack regiments were behind the right flank of II Corps or in front of it; III Cavalry Corps with several Cossack regiments was near the Pezovnya manor, in order to guard communications with Second Army. Korf's rearguard stayed in the Petersburg suburbs all day. Bagration set out from the Kolodnya river along the Moscow road with Second Army, towards the village of Pneva-Sloboda, near the Solovieva crossing, leaving the detachment under Lieutenant General Prince Gorchakov facing Shein-Ostrog with three of Karpov's Cossack regiments, six *versts* from Smolensk, with orders to stay there until relieved by troops from First Army.[1]

On the part of the French, the whole day of 6 (18) August was spent in attempts to ford across to the right bank of the Dnieper and establish themselves in the suburbs; eventually, after darkness had already fallen, overnight on the 6th to the 7th [18 to 19 August], they managed to build bridges and begin the crossing.[2]

Barclay de Tolly, intending to take advantage of the darkness of the night to conceal the initial retreat of our troops closest the enemy, issued a disposition according to

---

1 Buturlin, *Histoire militaire de la campagne de Russie en 1812,* I, 262-263 & 270. Handwritten notes by General Yermolov.
2 Thiers, *Histoire du Consulat et de l'Empire, Ed. de Brux,* XIV, 295.

which the corps of First Army were assigned to march from their locations, on the St Petersburg road, on the evening of 6 (18) August. The Commander-in-Chief, wishing to facilitate the flanking march by the army onto the Moscow road, divided the force into two columns, which, having completed two stages, were to rendezvous at the Solovieva crossing.[3] The first column, under General of Infantry Dokhturov, consisted of V Corps, VI Corps, II Cavalry Corps, III Cavalry Corps and all the reserve artillery. As these troops were to follow a more roundabout route than the other column, they were assigned to set off earlier in two groups, at seven o'clock in the evening precisely, along the St Petersburg road to Stabna, and then turn along the country road, to Zykolino, Poisklovo [Perfilovo] and Sushchovo, to Prudishche [Gorodok], stop there for the night and arrive, the next day at Pnevo-Sloboda near the Solovieva crossing. The second column under Lieutenant General Tuchkov 1st, accompanied by the Commander-in-Chief himself, consisted of II Corps, III Corps, IV Corps and I Cavalry Corps and was to follow the St Petersburg road only as far as Krakhotkina, and then turn via Poluevo, Gorbunovo, Zhabino and Koshaevo, onto the Moscow road and continue on the same day towards Bredikhino, and on the next – to the Solovieva crossing. The troops under Tuchkov 1st were assigned the following marching order: I Cavalry Corps at the head of the column; behind them III Corps and IV Corps; II Corps was initially ordered to set off along the direct route to the Moscow road; but later these troops also proceeded behind IV Corps, via Gorbunovo. The rearguard, under Adjutant General Korf, consisting of the Sumy Hussars, Mariupol Hussars, Poland Ulans, seven jäger regiments from II Corps and IV Corps and with one foot artillery company, was ordered to withdraw all their forward outposts before dawn, and to retreat behind the second column; while Platov was to detach some of his Cossacks to Korf's rearguard and form a screen of outposts across the sector from Smolensk to Porechye, which, once both columns of First Army had closed up to the Solovieva crossing, were intended to converge on the left towards the Dnieper and form the main rearguard of the army. Although Barclay de Tolly might have considered the Moscow road completely secured by the force under Prince Bagration, he ordered an independent vanguard made up of the Yelisavetgrad Hussars, Reval Infantry, 20th Jägers and 21st Jägers, three Cossack regiments and a company of horse artillery, under the command of Major General Tuchkov 3rd to set off at eight o'clock in the evening and march ahead of Tuchkov 1st's column, through Gorbunovo and onto the Moscow road.[4]

This detachment set out from its location by the Porechye road at the designated time; a small vanguard, made up of the Yelisavetgrad Hussars with two horse artillery guns moved ahead of them, under the command of Major General Vsevolozhsky. The country roads along which the detachment and the column

---

3   See Map illustrating operations in the vicinity of Smolensk.
4   In Tuchkov 3rd's notes (Active Privy Councillor and member of the State Council) it states that, on the basis of the disposition signed by the Chief of Staff of First Army, he received orders: to march via Gorbunovo and onwards towards Bredikhino, while in the First Army War Diary, compiled by Quartermaster General von Toll, of this army, it mentions that General Tuchkov 3rd was ordered: 'to execute a forced march and not only occupy the road junctions, but also move as far forward as possible, along the highway to Smolensk, in support of Major General Karpov.' (Condensed War Diary of First Army, compiled by Colonel von Toll).

that followed it had been assigned to follow, in many places running through hills, forests and over swampy streams, were very poor; while the bridges, which until that time had only to cope with the passage of peasant carts, were so dilapidated that after the first passage of artillery and cavalry over them, had to be repaired or even completely rebuilt, dismantling nearby peasant huts for this. Tuchkov's 3,000 strong detachment took 12 hours to cover a march of less than 20 *versts* and did not emerge onto the Moscow highway before eight o'clock on the morning of 7 (19) August. It was obvious that the troops marching at the tail of Tuchkov 1st's column could not arrive at this location before evening.

Just as the troops under Tuchkov 3rd were emerging from the forest near the village of Tychinino, and were nearing the highway, Prince Gorchakov, without waiting for his detachment to be relieved by troops from First Army, set off for the Solovieva crossing. Three Cossack regiments, under the command of Major General Karpov, had been left to monitor this highway in the direction of Smolensk. If Tuchkov, having emerged onto the Moscow road, had gone on to Bredikhino, he would have exposed the junction with the country road from Krakhotkina, and would have given the French the opportunity to cut off the entire force and trains moving along it. The situation in which Tuchkov was so unexpectedly placed gave him the opportunity to demonstrate the determination and quick wits demanded by the circumstances: the enemy was close by and in considerable numbers; while the detachment entrusted to Tuchkov was isolated from the army and could not expect any assistance. But, not paying this any heed, Tuchkov decided to protect the point at which the army was supposed to emerge onto the highway, and to that end, he sent orders to Major General Vsevolozhsky, who had left with the vanguard for Bredikhino, to return down the road towards Smolensk, while he, having marched about two *versts* along the highway towards Smolensk with the detachment himself, halted near the village of Latishino, where, having given the troops a rest as they were exhausted from the difficult march without any kind of halt, went forward with Quartermaster General von Toll, who had just reached the detachment, to conduct a reconnaissance towards Karpov's outposts at the front, which, meanwhile, had been pushed back to the village of Valutina Gora. Upon arrival at the Cossacks' location, Tuchkov and von Toll noted the advance of strong enemy columns made up of infantry and cavalry, and personally checked to ensure that, except for the three Cossack regiments, no troops had been left by Second Army in order to monitor the enemy. At the same time, a report arrived from General Karpov's forward outposts regarding the construction of bridges by the enemy upstream of Smolensk at Prudishchevo, from which it was possible to conclude that their intention was to move from there onto the Moscow road. Subsequently, a Westphalian deserter who had come over to us confirmed this report, announcing that Marshal Junot's *8e Corps* was indeed crossing at Prudishchevo. Having received this intelligence, General Tuchkov hurried back to his detachment, moved it forward and at ten o'clock in the morning deployed his troops behind the Kolodnya river, setting up a small vanguard in front of the village of Valutina Gora; the Cossack regiments under the command of Major General Karpov, moved to the left towards the Dnieper.[5]

---

5   Tuchkov's notes. Condensed War Diary of First Army, compiled by Toll. General Yermolov's handwritten notes.

Meanwhile, as Tuchkov 3rd was preparing to defend the position on the Moscow road with a detachment of 3,200 men on which the unimpeded retreat of First Army depended, at another point – in the vicinity of Smolensk – a bitter action was already underway. The circumstances giving rise to this were as follows. Of the troops closest to the enemy from Tuchkov 1st's column, only the two corps at the front, I Cavalry Corps and III Corps, had set out from their assembly areas in accordance with the disposition, at nine o'clock in the evening on 6 (18) August, and moved in the required direction via Gorbunovo; on the other hand, IV Corps, under Count Osterman, was late and delayed II Corps such that Prinz Eugen von Württemberg's Division, which was moving in the tail, did not move off from its assembly area until an hour after midnight. A large gap emerged between III Corps and IV Corps; while the regiments of IV Corps became strung out and separated from one another; some of them moved away from the proper direction and followed other routes. Crossing the many rickety bridges and having to fix them slowed down the pace of the column, which became stretched out in the extreme. No one could describe exactly where the troops had wandered, neither then nor later; it is only known that some of IV Corps and all of II Corps that was following, lost their way from the road leading from Krakhotkina to Gorbunovo, moved to the right along country roads through the forest, circled around Smolensk and, leaving the forest at six o'clock in the morning, found themselves near the village of Gedeonovo, a *verst* and a half from the outermost buildings of the Petersburg suburbs. At this very moment, Ney's troops had just managed to cross the Dnieper and were forming up in columns in front of the Petersburg suburbs; the French troops were at such short range from ours at that point that one could clearly hear the signals from their skirmishing screen, as well as the drums and music of the approaching regiments.

Fortunately, Barclay appeared at this point, quite by accident. In the midst of the general confusion resulting from the entanglement of the columns heading away from the proper direction, he did not lose his presence of mind, despite the obvious danger threatening his army: it would take some of the regiments lost in the forest, three of four hours to extract themselves, and their line of retreat would be severed if the enemy occupied Gorbunovo; Korf's rearguard, proceeding towards Krakhotkina, in order to disguise the direction in which our main force was retreating, could just as easily be cut off.[6]

Barclay de Tolly, halting at Gedeonovo in order to engage the enemy at this point, instructed the army's Chief of Staff, General Yermolov, to speed up the pace of the column proceeding along the country road to Gorbunovo. Barclay's orders were to hold the enemy at Gedeonovo with the nearest troops and send all other units from II Corps to Gorbunovo, while Korf was initially to go to Gedeonovo, and then also to Gorbunovo.[7] To that end, Barclay halted the first regiments of 17th Division, the Belozersk Infantry and Vilmanstrand Infantry, which were under the command of Colonel Kern [Yermolay Fëdorovich Kern], two platoons of the Izyum Hussars with four guns, and, placing this detachment, supported by the Tobolsk Infantry from 4th Division, on the high ground near the village of Gedeonovo entrusted

---

6   Bernhardi, I, 383-385.
7   See Plan of the Battle of Smolensk, 5 (17) August 1812.

this formation to Prinz Eugen von Württemberg, with orders to hold on until Korf arrived there. 'Even more energy is needed today than yesterday; it is a matter of saving the army.' The Commander-in-Chief told Prinz Eugen.

Fortunately, it was impossible for the enemy to know exactly what a state our army was in at that moment, and therefore they remained inactive. Ney, having crossed the Dnieper at dawn, waited for several hours in front of the Petersburg suburbs, between the Porechye and Moscow roads, and did not go further, waiting for definitive intelligence about the movements of the Russian army. And it truly was difficult to come to a conclusion as to where our main force was retreating: Korf's rearguard was retreating to the north, along the Petersburg road; to the east, on the route to Moscow, Karpov's forward outposts were visible; while in the interval between the highways, near Gedeonovo, a force appeared whose strength and mission could not be discerned by the enemy. Some time later, Murat, crossing the Dnieper via a ford with Nansouty's *1er Corps de cavalerie* and Montbrun's *2e Corps de cavalerie*, went to investigate the positions held by the Russian troops, to the right of Ney, along the Moscow road; while Grouchy's *3e Corps de cavalerie* moved to the left, along the St Petersburg road; he had been ordered to turn to the right towards Dukhovshchina, in order to block the path of the Russian troops, should they move in this direction.[8]

Ney's inaction made it possible for Prinz Eugen to prepare for the defence of his position, while Barclay himself, standing on the high ground behind Gedeonovo, followed his orders in person. Major Lüdinghausen-Wolff [Peter Johann Paul Wilhelm von Lüdinghausen genannt Wolff] (later Major General and Commander of 18th Division, mortally wounded in the assault on Brailov [Brăila] in 1828), with one of the battalions of the Tobolsk Infantry, occupied the slope in front of the village, successfully using the half-derelict parapet of an ancient earthwork; the rest of the detachment's troops were deployed between the village and the Moscow road, in the bushes, and behind the course of a seasonally dried up river bed. The bridge over this river on the highway was set alight.

The enemy remained static place, in full view of our position, until eight o'clock; at this time, a skirmish began, and at about nine o'clock French columns emerged from the brush, and attacked Wolff's battalion, enveloping it; Colonel Kern charged at the French skirmishers who were engaging Wolff from the rear, with the Belozersk Infantry; but being counter attacked by an overwhelmingly strong enemy, he was forced to retreat. The French, pursuing him, broke into the village, and although they were driven out of there by Major Reibnitz [Karl Pavlovich Reibnitz] with 1st Battalion, Tobolsk Infantry, they had managed to cut off Wolff's battalion. Thereafter, Ney led the troops forward that had remained in reserve by the suburbs; and a strong cavalry column, turning to face our left wing, launched an attack on the Vilmanstrand Infantry, which was stationed near the Moscow road. At this decisive moment, as some of our regiments were still wandering through the forest, it seemed there was no longer any way to hold fast in Gedeonovo, and with the occupation of this location, the enemy would have the opportunity to cut off Korf's rearguard and the other troops straggling behind the columns. But at that

---

8   Chambray, *Histoire de l'expédition de Russie*, I, 324.

very moment, from one side, the cavalry of Korf's rearguard, consisting of the Sumy Hussars and Mariupol Hussars, while from the other, Dokhturov[9] with some of the Yelisavetgrad Hussars, sent for reconnaissance from Tuchkov 3rd's detachment, and the Izyum Hussars, who had arrived via Gorbunovo from IV Corps, arrived at the scene of the battle; their successful attack slowed down the French advance and rescued the Vilmanstrand Infantry, and meanwhile Korf's infantry had arrived at Gedeonovo. Colonel Kern and Major Reibnitz fought their way through the enemy troops that had surrounded Wolff, drove them off, and then returned to Gedeonovo all together. Prinz Eugen, who personally participated in the attack by the Izyum Hussars, returning to the right flank of his detachment in Gedeonovo, received orders from the Commander-in-Chief to retreat to the nearby high ground (behind the village of Galionshchina) and, having taken a position there, was to cover Korf's withdrawal towards Gorbunovo. Moving towards Galionshchina, the prince found the Volhynia Infantry from his division and a foot artillery company there, the Volhynia Infantry relieved both regiments from 17th Division, who had used all their cartridges at Gedeonovo, and ordered them to follow the other troops of II Corps, along the Moscow road, towards Lubino. A little later, all Korf's troops passed through the position occupied by the prince, except for two battalions of 30th Jägers, which remained within sight of the enemy with a small number of Cossacks, between Gedeonovo and Galionshchina. These jägers, being attacked by Ney's superior numbers, retreated having taken casualties; while Prinz Eugen, letting them pass his troops and noticing that the French had suspended their advance, followed behind Korf's detachment towards Gorbunovo, and from there along country lanes towards the Moscow road.[10]

Napoleon, having learned of Ney's clash with a Russian force, ordered Davout's *1er Corps* to follow Ney's *3e Corps*, while Junot's Westphalian *8e Corps* was to cross the Dnieper at Prudishchevo. The *Garde* were left in Smolensk; the Viceroy's *4e Corps* had arrived there as well; Poniatowski's *5e Corps* remained on the left bank of the Dnieper, upstream of Smolensk. Napoleon himself, impatiently wanting to know the progress of the fighting, went to Davout's Corps, which, having detached Morand's Division to assist Ney, was located with his remaining four divisions near the village of Vyazovenka, between the Moscow and St Petersburg roads, two *versts* from Smolensk. Having received the news there, from orderlies who had arrived from the battlefield, of the appearance of Russian troops on the Moscow road, Napoleon, although he did not know that it was in fact a flanking march by the entire Russian army along this road, nevertheless ordered Ney to move to the right; while Morand's Division, from Davout's *1er Corps*, detached a short while earlier by Ney to the left, in order to envelope Prinz Eugen's right flank, was to return to Smolensk; Gudin, with another division from Davout's Corps, was sent to assist Ney to attack the Russian troops stationed on the Moscow road from the front, while Murat and Junot were to envelope the left flank of our position. The cannonade on

---

9   [Liprandi points out that Dokhturov was at the Solovieva Crossing at this time, with VI Corps].
10   *Erinnerungen aus dem Feldzuges des Jahres 1812 in Russland, v. Herzog Eugen v. Würtemberg,* 31-41.

the Moscow road, which began again at about noon, intensified more and more; but Napoleon, attributing it solely to the desire of the Russian commanders to cover the retreat of their trains and not knowing how vital it was for us to hold on to Tuchkov 3rd's position, returned to Smolensk at about five o'clock in the afternoon.[11] General Gourgaud [Gaspard Gourgaud], who was then an orderly officer (*officier d'ordonnance*) under Napoleon, stated that, before his departure, he was instructed to accompany the advancing troops and to coordinate the movements of Ney, Murat and Junot.[12]

Meanwhile, the troops under Tuchkov 3rd, at ten o'clock in the morning, in anticipation of the enemy, had taken up positions on the Moscow road, behind a river. It is rather difficult to say, with complete accuracy, where precisely these troops were located: behind the river Kolodnya or another river, between the villages of Toporovshchino and Latishino. Both of these rivers cut across the highway, almost at right angles, and then, having made a sharp turn, flow parallel to this road until their actual confluence with the Dnieper. Other rivers, including the Stragan, also cut across the Moscow road and, turning sharply, merge together and join the Kolodnya. All these rivers, where the left banks almost always dominate the right, would form fairly good positions against an enemy advancing from the direction of Smolensk, as long as these positions were not subjected to an envelopment of the left flank.

The troops under Tuchkov 3rd were initially located in position behind the river (Kolodnya) as follows: an horse artillery company across the highway on the forward slope of the high ground; 20th Jägers and 21st Jägers, under General Prince Shakovskoy's [Ivan Leontievich Shakovskoy] command, dispersed in the brush along the roadside; the Reval Infantry under Tuchkov 4th with several squadrons of Yelisavetgrad Hussars under Major General Vsevolozhsky were stationed in reserve; the Cossack regiments had been detached to the left as far as the Dnieper.[13]

The enemy appeared in front of our position at about noon. At first, Ney committed only Razout's division; behind them, the regiments of the other two divisions gradually arrived, moving to the left of the main road, across very rugged terrain. The deployment of the troops into battle order and preliminary measures for a reconnaissance of the location of our detachment took so long that by the time the enemy had deployed their troops and their superiority in numbers became beyond doubt, our first reinforcements had already arrived. General Yermolov, convinced of the danger that threatened us in the event of a further advance by these enemy troops along the Moscow road, used all means to quicken the pace of Tuchkov 1st's column and convinced him of the need to support his brother's detachment.[14] About an hour into the afternoon, as the last troops of III Corps, having crossed the junction onto the main road, moved towards Bredikhino, Colonel Zheltukhin [Pëtr Fëdorovich Zheltukhin] was immediately ordered to turn back to the Kolodnya river with the Leib-Grenadiers and Count Arakcheev's Grenadiers and with six guns from 1st

---

11   Fain, *Manuscrit de 1812*, I, 318-321. Sołtyk, *Napoléon en 1812*, 161-163.
12   Gourgaud, *Examen critique de l'ouvrage de M. le Comte de Ségur, Livre 6*, Chap. VII.
13   See Plan of the Battle at Lubino, 7 (19) August 1812.
14   Condensed War Diary compiled by Colonel von Toll. Buturlin, I, 275.

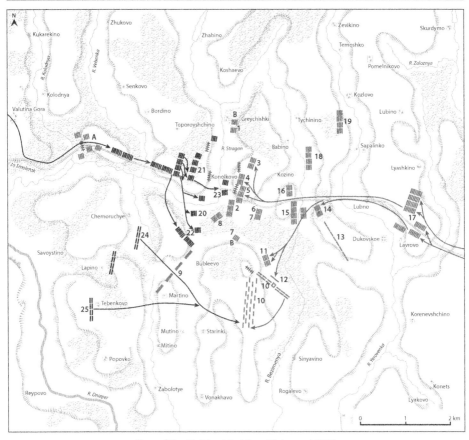

Plan of the Battle at Lubino, 19 August 1812.

Legend

Russian Forces

A. Tuchkov 3rd's initial position.

B.B. Second Russian position.

1. Reval Infantry.

2. 20th & 21st Jägers.

3. Leib-Grenadiers.

4. Yelets Infantry.

5. Yekaterinburg Infantry.

6. 3rd Division combined grenadiers.

7. Count Arakcheev's Grenadiers.

8. Rylsk Infantry.

9. Karpov's Cossacks.

10. Hussars.

11. Polotsk Infantry.

12. Pernov Infantry.

13. I Cavalry Corps.

14. Kexholm Infantry.

15. Murom, Chernigov, Kaporsk Infantry.

16. Yekaterinoslav Grenadiers.

17. Pavlov, Tauride, Petersburg Grenadiers.

18. Prinz Eugen's 4th Division.

19. General Korf's rearguard.

French Forces

20. Razout's division.

21. Ledru's division.

22. Marchand's division.

23. Gudin's division.

24. Murat's cavalry.

25. Junot's corps.

Battery Artillery Company, moving at the tail end of III Corps. The first of these regiments remained on the high ground by the highway, while the latter occupied the edge of the forest to the left of the road. This support, reaching a total of 2,200 men, made it possible for the detachment to hold on to the first position until three o'clock in the afternoon, when the significant superiority of the enemy troop numbers finally forced Tuchkov 3rd to retreat behind the Stragan River.[15] These were the measures taken by Chief of Staff, First Army, General Yermolov in anticipation of the arrival at the battle site of Barclay de Tolly, in order to support the detachment on whose courageous defence the salvation of a significant part of the force and trains, strung out along the country lanes, depended.[16] In addition to the heroic bravery of our detachment, the fact that the enemy did not have their supreme commander present, contributed greatly to their stubborn resistance. Napoleon, who had not expected bitter fighting on this day, because the Russians, after the bloody battle that had cost both sides so dearly, had just ceded Smolensk, had appeared in the vicinity of the troops in action for a short time and, considering the engagement at Valutina to be a simple rearguard action, left to go back to the city. Ney was directing the actions of only three divisions from his *3e Corps* and two divisions from Davout's *1er Corps* that had arrived towards the end of the battle. Murat, who deployed his cavalry to the right of the highway, and Junot, who had crossed the Dnieper at Prudishchevo, also commanded only those troops directly subordinate to them. All three acted independently of one another and, therefore, could not direct their efforts with appropriate coordination towards the achievement of a common objective.[17]

By four o'clock in the afternoon, our side had managed to gather 17 battalions, totalling some 8,000 men in positions behind the Stragan river. Firstly, at about three o'clock in the afternoon, one of the combined battalions, sent by Tuchkov 1st from III Corps, arrived, while the remaining troops from this corps continued to withdraw towards Bredikhino; then, at about four o'clock, the leading regiments of IV Corps (Yekaterinburg Infantry, Yeletsk Infantry and Rylsk Infantry) arrived, which, emerging from the forest near the village of Tychinino, were ordered to go to the right of the road to support Tuchkov 3rd's detachment. Due to navigational errors and unscheduled halts, IV Corps lagged behind III Corps by a considerable distance and came out onto the main road four hours later than the last troops of III Corps.

The position on the Stragan river, which directly protected the entry of Tuchkov 1st's column onto the main road, was so strategically important that it was essential to hold on to it to the last man. Its right wing stretched across the high ground, covering the junctions on the Moscow road with several country lanes; in the centre was a low-lying, somewhat marshy area; on the left wing protruded a rather dense but not extensive forest, and even farther to the left – a vast open area, convenient

15   In the Condensed War Diary compiled by Colonel von Toll, it states that Tuchkov retreated behind the Piravnits River at three o'clock in the afternoon.
16   Despatches regarding the fighting on 7 [19] August, submitted to Barclay de Tolly by Yermolov dated 22 August [3 September], No 501.
17   Tuchkov's notes. Bernhardi, I, 388.

for cavalry operations, which sloped down towards the marshy river. Consequently, behind the left wing was terrain that prevented a retreat by the troops, and in addition, this part of the position was separated from the right wing by marshy levels. Despite these important obstacles, however, it was impossible either to concede this position to the enemy, nor to confine ourselves to a defence of the highway and the high ground on the right wing, because in the former case, the enemy could seize the junction to Gorbunovo on the Moscow road, and in the latter, they could get around the left flank and into the rear of the position.

The troops assembled on the Stragan river were positioned by General Yermolov as follows: eight heavy guns (from III Corps and IV Corps) on the high ground by the highway; a horse artillery company also on the high ground to the right of the foot artillery; six battalions of the Leib-Grenadiers, Yekaterinburg Infantry and Yelets Infantry were stationed behind the artillery; the Reval Infantry (two battalions) was deployed farther to the right holding the woods at the village of Greychishki; 20th Jägers and 21st Jägers (four battalions) were holding a swampy, brush filled valley to the left of the highway, with a combined grenadier battalion from 3rd Division and one of the battalions from Count Arakcheev's Grenadiers in reserve; the other battalion of this regiment stood on a hill, behind the woods occupied by the Rylsk Infantry (two battalions). Major General Karpov was positioned in front of the left flank with the Cossack regiments, near the villages of Gumnichino and Mitino.[18] Meanwhile, Yermolov, having received intelligence from two Württemberg hussars sent to him by General Tuchkov 3rd, regarding twelve infantry and cavalry regiments under Junot and Murat enveloping our left flank, with the authority of the Commander-in-Chief ordered Adjutant General, Count Orlov-Denisov to hasten at the trot with I Cavalry Corps from Bredikhino to Zabolotye, and upon arrival there to position the corps on high ground, without crossing the swamps. The Sumy Hussars, Mariupol Hussars, two squadrons of Izyum Hussars and the Yelisavetgrad Hussars (a total of 26 squadrons with four horse artillery guns), who had arrived at Tuchkov's position from Korf's Detachment, were assigned to him [Orlov-Denisov] by General Yermolov. Count Orlov-Denisov placed them in front of a large swamp, with their front towards the forest so as to protect Tuchkov 3rd's position from envelopment from the left flank; wanting to convince the hussars that there was nowhere to retreat, he ordered several men from each squadron to be sent to scout routes that would permit a retreat beyond the swamp, and when it turned out that it was completely impassable, then Orlov-Denisov rode around the troops, exhorting them to fulfil their duty because they had no choice but to triumph or die. Anticipating an attempt by the enemy to emerge from the forest, he placed the Mariupol Hussars, Sumy Hussars and Yelisavetgrad Hussars in four lines, in a chessboard pattern, with squadron intervals between squadrons, anchoring the right flank to a knoll above the swamp that separated our cavalry from the highway. The four horse artillery guns were placed on this knoll. Five Cossack regiments and two squadrons of Izyum Hussars made up the left wing, anchoring their left flank to a swamp. The troops of I Cavalry Corps were deployed on high ground behind the swamp, to the rear

---

18   Condensed War Diary compiled by Colonel von Toll.

of the position. Count Orlov-Denisov, intending a show of strength for the enemy, took advantage of the small bushes that covered the high ground, and placed all this cavalry along their edge in a single line.[19]

The enemy, approaching the positions occupied by our infantry on the Stragan river, limited themselves to cannon fire and skirmishing for an hour, with the aim of allowing time for the reinforcements they expected. Gudin's division, on arriving at the site of the battle at about five o'clock in the afternoon, was sent by Ney towards the battery on the highway in two columns; Razout's division, also in two columns, moved across the low ground towards our left wing; the remaining two divisions from Ney's *3e Corps* were held in reserve: Ledru's division on the highway, Marchand's division facing Bubleevo woods. The French charged the battery four times, but each time they were repulsed by our troops; the Leib-Grenadiers in particular distinguished themselves here, losing five officers and 42 lower ranks killed and 286 men wounded on this their day of glory. The enemy, having been unable to seize our battery, turned their efforts to another point of the position: Razout's troops marched across the valley, avoiding the artillery, drove the Rylsk Infantry out of the forest and pushed the 20th Jägers and 21st Jägers back; but were themselves pushed back by the battalions in reserve, the combined grenadiers and Count Arakcheev's Grenadiers. Thus, 14 Russian battalions, numbering about 7,000 men, held out against Gudin's and Razout's 14,000. Gudin rode up to the dilapidated bridge on the Stragan river himself, dismounted from his horse and, standing at the head of *7e Légère*, led them across the bridge without firing a shot, and stopping on the opposite bank, watched the movement of his other regiments passing by him with exclamations of '*Vive l'Empereur*' (long live the Emperor!), but at the very moment that the last of his troops were already across the river, he was mortally wounded by round shot that shattered his leg. Gérard [Étienne Maurice Gérard] took over command of his division. Every enemy attack on our battery on the highway was repulsed with significant losses.[20]

But in the meantime the French had deployed powerful artillery facing the front of Tuchkov's position; at the same time, the positioning of significant forces facing our left wing threatened us with being outflanked. Junot, who had crossed the Dnieper with his *8e Corps* a few hours earlier, numbering 14,000, was near the village of Tebenkovo, during the period that Tuchkov's detachment was still defending its initial position. There had been nothing to prevent Junot's troops from moving onto the Moscow road, which, without any doubt, would not only have forced us to abandon the defence of the position behind the Stragan, but would also have put our detachment in a very dangerous position. But Junot, already suffering from

---

19   Description of the battle of Lubino, from the notes by Count Orlov-Denisov. Despatches regarding the fighting on 7 [19] August, submitted to Barclay de Tolly by Yermolov, dated 22 August [3 September], No 501.

20   *Das Buch vom Jahr 1812*, II, 189-190. The author cites the words of an eyewitness who assured him that Gudin's troops had driven the Russians out of their positions. On the other hand, in the Condensed War Diary compiled by von Toll, it states: 'the enemy's left wing, being reinforced with a new division by Davout, continued its rapid attacks to capture the high ground and our battery, but they were always repulsed with losses that were significant for the enemy.'

bouts of mental instability according to the assertions of some historians, instead of decisively taking the highway, concealed his troops in the Tebenkovo forest and went no further. Murat, galloping up to him with several horsemen, fruitlessly tried to persuade him to go into action; Junot remained where he was, making the excuse that he did not have orders from the Emperor. Finally, after great efforts, he decided to send forward a single battalion with a company of light infantry.[21] This company, inadvertently emerging from the scrub into the open, was cut down by the Mariupol Hussars. Some time later, once Ney had already launched a decisive attack on our position, Junot, at Murat's insistence, sent forward his cavalry,[22] which drove the Cossacks back onto the Sumy Hussars standing behind them and threw them into disorder; but then, Count Orlov-Denisov struck the flank of the enemy with the Mariupol Hussars and Yelisavetgrad Hussars and, making successive attacks in waves passing through one another, prevented the French cavalry from turning against the left wing of our position.

During the time of these actions on our left wing, the enemy again attacked the woods held by the Rylsk Infantry, but were repelled by them with the assistance of a battalion from Count Arakcheev's Grenadiers. Barclay de Tolly, having arrived at the scene of the battle himself, issued orders with his usual composure.[23] Having become aware of the need to shore up the detachment with fresh troops, the Commander-in-Chief ordered Konovnitsyn to reinforce the centre with the Murom Infantry, Chernigov Infantry and Koporye Infantry from his division (by prior orders from Chief of Staff, First Army, arriving from III Corps from the direction of Bredikhino); the Yekaterinoslav Grenadiers (which also came from III Corps), under the command of Major General Tsvilenev [Alexander Ivanovich Tsvilenev], moved into the front line on the right wing; while the Pernov Infantry and Polotsk Infantry (from IV Corps), under the command of Major General Choglokov, with a company of horse artillery, emerged onto the highway at Tychinino, and went to support the cavalry operating on the left wing. The Kexholm Infantry (also from IV Corps), moved to the right of I Cavalry Corps, on the high ground in the woods. Thereafter, on Barclay's orders, all the other regiments of III Infantry Corps (Pavlov Grenadiers, Tauride Grenadiers and St Petersburg Grenadiers), with three artillery companies, arrived at the detachment, at about six o'clock in the afternoon, and formed a general reserve at the village of Lubino.[24]

At this precise moment, the enemy renewed their intensive attacks on the centre of our position and forced the Leib-Grenadiers, Yelets Infantry and Yekaterinburg Infantry to pull back. Colonel Kikin, who held the office of Duty General, Lieutenant

21   In his History of the Patriotic War of 1812, General Mikhailovsky-Danilevsky states: 'two French infantry regiments.'

22   In the work Denkwürdigkeiten des Grafen v. Toll, I, 391-392, it states that the attack was carried out by twelve of Junot's squadrons. But in all likelihood, several of Murat's squadrons were committed to battle together with Junot's cavalry. This assumption is reinforced by the fact that Murat led the cavalry there himself.

23   In the work Denkwürdigkeiten des Grafen v. Toll, and in the Condensed War Diary, compiled by Colonel von Toll, it states that Barclay de Tolly joined Tuchkov 3rd's force at the time when they were still holding their initial positions.

24   Condensed War Diary, compiled by Colonel von Toll.

Grabbe, General Yermolov's aide de camp from the Guards Artillery, and General Miloradovich's aide de camp Captain de Juncker [Alexander Logginovich de Juncker], rallied the scattered men and counter attacked with drums beating and bayonets fixed, and cleared the road; meanwhile, Barclay de Tolly concentrated the fire of the battery stationed on the highway, reinforced with 12 heavy guns from Colonel Voeikov's [Alexander Ivanovich Voeikov] company, against the advancing troops, while General Konovnitsyn, with six fresh battalions from his division, struck with bayonets fixed, pushed the enemy back and restored communications between the right and the left wings of the detachment. Whereupon the French, having had no success attacking the centre, turned their efforts to our right flank. One of our batteries was forced to pull back, but General Yermolov led the Leib-Grenadiers against the enemy and cooled their ardour.[25]

At around seven o'clock in the afternoon, Lieutenant General Baggovut's II Corps emerged onto the Moscow road. The 17th Division, which was marching at the head of the corps, became the reserve for the Leib-Grenadiers, Yelets Infantry and Yekaterinburg Infantry, to the right of the highway; the Prince von Württemberg's 4th Division and Korf's rearguard, who arrived at the battle site as dusk was already falling, settled behind the villages of Kozino and Tychinino, as the reserve of the right wing and centre.[26]

Meanwhile, on our left wing, the enemy cavalry, moving to the right of the forest and scrub, was preparing to outflank the position occupied by our hussars on their left. Count Orlov-Denisov, noticing this movement, ordered all four of his lines to refuse their left flank, and by thus reducing the length of his frontage between the two swamps, he was able to detach some of the troops to form a reserve. The Yelisavetgrad Hussars were in column behind the right flank; while two squadrons of Izyum Hussars and one of the Cossack regiments were behind the left flank of the battle line. The troops sent to support them, at the request of Orlov-Denisov, were positioned as follows: the Polotsk Infantry stood on the right flank, in the scrub on the knoll; the Pernov Infantry were in square, positioned in the centre; 12 guns, together with the original four, were placed on the knoll masked by the front line of the right wing.[27]

At half past six o'clock (according to other sources, at seven o'clock), the troops of Ochs' division (Junot's *8e Corps*), emerging from the scrub, passed through Bubleevo woods and headed against the right wing of the position occupied by Orlov-Densov. The battery of sixteen guns stationed there, having allowed the enemy to close to canister range, opened a rapid cannonade, supplemented by the musketry of the Polotsk Infantry and Pernov Infantry. The enemy troops were repulsed with heavy losses and pursued towards the village of Gumnichino by the Sumy Hussars and

25   Despatches regarding the fighting on 7 [19] August, submitted to Barclay de Tolly by Yermolov, dated 22 August [3 September], No 501. Condensed War Diary, compiled by Colonel von Toll. Bernhardi doubts this event, based on the testimony of French historians, and believes that the French managed to cross the Stragan, but that their further advance was blocked by Russian troops, *Denkwürdigkeiten des Grafen v. Toll*, I, 393.
26   Condensed War Diary, compiled by Colonel von Toll.
27   Description of the battle of Lubino, from Count Orlov-Denisov's notes.

Cossacks. It was here that Major General Filisov [Pavel Andreevich Filisov] was seriously wounded in the torso by canister shot. By eight o'clock in the evening, the battle had died down completely on our left wing.[28]

At nine o'clock, once it was already completely dark, Gudin's division, under the command of General Gérard (later Marshal of France), crossing the Stragan, charged at our positions. Tuchkov 3rd, intending to ensure the safety of the wounded, led the Yekaterinoslav Grenadiers to engage the enemy; but he barely had chance to approach the French before his horse was killed under him. Wanting to encourage the soldiers, he went ahead of the front rank, charging with fixed bayonets, but our grenadiers were driven back while Tuchkov himself, wounded in the side by a bayonet and receiving several wounds to the head, remained in the hands of the French. The regiments of II Corps (Ryazan Infantry and Brest Infantry), having just reached the highway, under the command of General Olsufiev, blocked the enemy and prevented them from going further. Konovnitsyn, setting up a strong screen force, sent the artillery back along the Moscow road. Our troops were ordered to retreat the next day, 8 (20) August, at four o'clock in the morning.[29]

The action at Lubino was very bloody: the enemy lost on this day overall (including the casualties from Gedeonovo) 8,768 front line troops.[30] On our side, according to Buturlin, the losses reached some 5,000 men.[31]

The battle of Lubino (also known as the battle of Valutina Gora) was the final act of the bloody drama that began at Krasny on 2 (14) August. The consequences of all the fighting in the vicinity of Smolensk was the occupation of this city and the area in which the fighting on 7 (19) August took place by enemy troops, but Napoleon had not achieved his objective, which was to entangle our army in a general battle and win a decisive victory over it. The French have portrayed themselves as victors in all of these actions. But taking into account, on the one hand, those advantages they derived from their significant superiority in numbers, from the precarious situation of our armies near Smolensk, while on the other hand, how much Napoleon sacrificed in order to obtain possession of a destroyed city, it emerges that although the defence of Smolensk was not undertaken as a result of carefully considered assessments, it nevertheless brought us significant benefits, serving to weaken the enemy army. From the time of the river crossing at Rossasno to the battle of Lubino inclusive, Napoleon permanently lost more than 20,000 front line soldiers; on our side, the casualties were 14,000 men: hence they were one and a half times fewer than the enemy; besides, we could sooner replenish our losses to the force than the French, who were far from the sources of the means to replenish their army.

The troops of both sides covered themselves with glory; each of them fought with equal courage, but one cannot fail to notice that in all the actions that took place

---

28   Condensed War Diary, compiled by Colonel von Toll. Description of the battle of Lubino, from Count Orlov-Denisov's notes. Some foreign historians, based on Ochs' account, state that he stayed in the woods, Bernhardi, I, 394-395.

29   Tuchkov's notes. Condensed War Diary, compiled by Colonel von Toll. *Erinnerungen aus dem Feldzuges des Jahres 1812, v. d. Herzog Eugen v. Würtemberg*, 59.

30   According to documents captured from the French in 1812. In Buturlin the French losses are given as 9,000 men.

31   Buturlin, I, 285.

in the vicinity of Smolensk, on the part of the French there was a superiority in numbers of troops: Neverovsky with 6,000 infantry fought against Murat's 15,000 cavalrymen, supported by Ney's 7,000 infantry; Raevsky with 13,000 men held off Ney's 22,000; Dokhturov, having 20,000 initially, later increasing to 30,000 men, defended Smolensk for a whole day facing 45,000 men supported by Napoleon's 90,000. Prinz Eugen von Württemberg with a handful of troops, held his position at Gedeonovo against Ney's *3e Corps*; finally, Tuchkov 3rd covered his brother Tuchkov 1st's retreating columns in the position on the Kolodnya, initially with 3,000, later, with the arrival of assistance from Zheltukhin's Grenadier Brigade, with 5,000 men, facing Ney with 20,000; later, having withdrawn to the second position on the river Stragan, Tuchkov 3rd's detachment was gradually reinforced to 22,000 men, of whom about 17,000 men were actually committed to action, and held out for another six hours, against Ney's *3e Corps*, Gudin's division and some of Junot's troops, who were not less than 32,000 strong, supported by reserves numbering 17,000 men.[32] The extraordinary courage of the Russian troops made it possible for their commanders, placed in a dangerous position, to accomplish great feats. Neverovsky's retreat was glorious. Raevsky bought time for both our armies to reach Smolensk. Dokhturov, with the support of Konovnitsyn and Prinz Eugen von Württemberg, defended Smolensk against Napoleon and his *Grande Armée*, and retreated only once he had received orders from Barclay de Tolly. Prinz Eugen held back Ney's overwhelmingly superior numbers, for several hours, preventing him from cutting off a significant part of the army and gave Tuchkov 3rd time to shield the emergence of our column nearest to the enemy onto the Moscow road and secure its withdrawal.

On the other hand, the enemy commanders, although they held the battlefields from the actions at Smolensk and Lubino, had not done everything they could have. Murat did not manage to cut off and destroy Neverovsky's detachment; Ney did not take advantage of the limited number of Russians on the first day of the battle at Smolensk and did not take possession of this city; Napoleon, hoping to involve the Russian army in a general battle, stormed the fortified city, and his troops suffered incomparably greater casualties than ours; Junot, having crossed the Dnieper, instead of moving out onto the Moscow road into the rear of Tuchkov's position and paving the way for Murat's cavalry and assisting Ney's attack, remained inactive. We have already had occasion to note that many of these misunderstandings and mistakes were a consequence of ignorance of the topographic details of this theatre of war; but the experience and skill of the French generals should have mitigated against this disadvantage, which is always encountered in war, most especially in offensive operations. In general, while waging war, one rarely has accurate information about the terrain that will become the field of action; it is even less common to have such intelligence on the enemy forces. Military commanders find it essential at every step to deduce the truth from an assessment of insufficient and contradictory intelligence, and their skill is mainly evident from their conclusions.

---

32   For a breakdown of these numbers, see Appendix XVI.

After the battle of Lubino, the troops of Tuchkov 1st's column, having set off after an overnight stay on the Yarovenka river, at 4 o'clock in the morning on 8 (20) August, advanced to the Solovieva crossing, linked up there with Dokhturov's troops and crossed the Dnieper together with them over three pontoon bridges, some on the evening of that same day, some on the morning of 9 (21) August. Platov remained on the right bank of the Dnieper with Korf's rearguard, consisting of 32 squadrons (Sumy Hussars, Mariupol Hussars, Yelisavetgrad Hussars and Poland Ulans) together with most of the Cossack regiments; while in support was Major General Baron Rosen located on the left bank with six jäger regiments, a horse artillery company under Colonel Zakharzhevsky [Yakov Vasilevich Zakharzhevsky] and a half company of foot artillery.[33] All the remaining troops from First Army withdrew to Usvyatye on the Uzha river on 9 and 10 (21 and 22) August. As the bridges on the Dnieper had already been dismantled, the cavalry of the rear guard crossed to the left bank of the river by fording. The enemy hurried up to pursue them, but were restrained by the fire from batteries and marksmen who occupied the left bank of the Dnieper. On that same day, the 9th (21 August), Second Army was located on the left flank of First Army.[34]

Meanwhile, on 7 (19) August, as the battle of Valutina was taking place, Napoleon remained in Smolensk for almost the entire day. In the morning he rode to the cathedral with many of his generals. A terrible sight awaited him there as the inhabitants of Smolensk, crippled old people, women, children who had sought refuge under the sacred roof of Our Lady were dying of hunger with cries of despair. Reaching the centre of the cathedral, Napoleon took off his hat; all his retinue followed the example of their master. Glancing at the unfortunate citizens of Smolensk and not honouring them with a single word, Napoleon left the church and rode along the main street, where at every step he saw how his multi-national soldiery had robbed and murdered the defenceless inhabitants. Returning to his quarters, at five o'clock he left again with a large retinue and, meeting a priest who was leaving the Church of the Transfiguration, ordered him to be summoned and through an interpreter told him: 'Take me to the Dnieper Gate along such a route that none of the inhabitants of the city will meet me.' The priest led him through back streets and received a *Napoléon-d'Or* for his trouble. Napoleon rode through the Dnieper Gate, went to the Petersburg suburbs and from there (as already mentioned) to Davout's troops, but remained there for a very short time and returned to the city.[35]

In the evening, Napoleon, having learned about all the events of the Valutina battle, was dissatisfied with its outcome, and especially by the inaction of the Westphalian *8e Corps*. In the initial outburst of his anger, he gave orders for Junot to be stripped of command over the corps, to be replaced by Rapp, who had just arrived from Danzig; but his loyalty to an old military comrade forced him to

---

33   Condensed War Diary, compiled by Colonel von Toll. This gives the following regiments as being under Rosen's command: 4th Jägers (from II Corps), 1st Jägers, 18th Jägers and 33rd Jägers (from IV Corps), 19th Jägers and 40th Jägers (from VI Infantry Corps). Buturlin, I, 287.
34   Buturlin, I, 286.
35   Extracted from information provided by the local authorities of the Smolensk Governorate.

cancel the given order. Wanting to be reassured personally of the state of affairs, he set off for the battlefield at three o'clock in the morning on 8 (20) August. But the Russians were already preparing to retreat further. After examining the field of battle and showering the fighting men with awards, most especially the regiments from Gudin's division, Napoleon returned to Smolensk.[36] There, having weighed up all the factors of his situation, for the first time he doubted the success of his enterprise and expressed his intention to stay in Smolensk.[37] Some of his entourage, the Viceroy, Berthier, Davout, Caulaincourt, believed that at such a time of the year it would be unnecessary to start a new campaign, but it would be much better to establish themselves on the Dnieper and engage in the restoration of Poland during the winter. But many remained confident that Napoleon, through the power of his genius, would triumph over the Russians; that one decisive battle would bring the French to Moscow and that their master would dictate terms of peace to Russia as glorious as it would be lasting.[38] Napoleon himself was on the horns of a dilemma – should he halt in Smolensk, or go further? The first news he received in Smolensk about the action of his flanking corps on the Dvina and on the Bug prompted him to caution; but after that, having received information, on the one hand, about Tormasov's retreat to Volhynia, after the engagement at Gorodechno, and on the other, about the successful action by Saint-Cyr at Polotsk, meanwhile, Murat and Davout informed him that the main Russian army was retreating in a state of urgency and, apparently, was ready to offer a decisive battle. Napoleon, who wanted most of all to hasten the outcome of the issue, set out to continue the pursuit with all his own forces, except for Sebastiani's *2e Division de cavalerie* and Pino's infantry (*4e Corps*), detached to Velizh and Surazh facing Wintzingerode. Napoleon knew that many of his closest associates were critical of his expedition to Russia, but he did not pay the slightest attention to them, hoping that the eventual success would justify his decisions. Just as, in the past, they had been critical of his rapid march into Moravia in the same manner, until he ended all debate through the victory at Austerlitz; also previously, all had been considered lost after the battle of Essling, until the victory won at Wagram. Napoleon was confident of the probability of defeating the Russian army; he hoped that the glory of the success achieved would make the French forget – both the calamities they had endured and the sacrifices that the victory might cost. But these hopes were not destined to be realised.[39]

Napoleon had mistaken the nature of Tsar Alexander I and the spirit of the Russian people, hoping to break Russia with one decisive blow and subjugate our fatherland to his will. But this delusion of the man of genius was short-lived. Having encountered abandoned cities and villages from his first steps into the indigenous regions of Russia, reduced to ruins by their inhabitants, Napoleon, instead of his previous ambitious plans to dominate Russia, began to think about ending a struggle that could not guarantee a successful outcome, and his inclination towards peace was

---

36   Fain, *Manuscrit de 1812*, I, 323-329. 12e Ligne, 21e Ligne, 127e Ligne, and 7e Légère received 87 awards and promotions.
37   Fain, 330.
38   Baron Denniée, *Itinéraire de l'Empereur Napoléon pendant la campagne de 1812*, 58-59.
39   Fain, *Manuscrit de 1812*, I, 331-338.

clearly expressed when he met with General Tuchkov 3rd, captured in the battle of Lubino.

Having been introduced to Murat, immediately after the battle, Tuchkov was treated kindly by him. In his notes, Tuchkov states: 'The King of Naples ordered his surgeon to examine and dress my wounds then he asked me: how strong was your detachment that was in action with me, and when I answered that there were 15,000 of us in the fight, then he said with a grin: and the rest! and the rest! You were much stronger (*à d'autres, à d'autres! Vous étiez bien plus fort que cela*).' Murat's respect for Tuchkov made him fulfil the wishes of our general, who asked not to overlook an award for the officer who had introduced him to the King. The request was honoured and Lieutenant Etienne, on the very next day, received the Order of the *Légion d'Honneur*. General Tuchkov was brought from the battlefield to Smolensk at midnight, where he was assigned a room in the same house where Marshal Berthier's quarters were located. Tuchkov stated:

'A few days later, Napoleon gave orders to find out if my health would allow me to visit him, and receiving in reply that although I was still very weak, I could be introduced to him, at ten o'clock in the morning of the following day he sent Berthier's aide de camp, Colonel Baron Flahaut [Auguste Charles Joseph, comte de Flahaut de La Billarderie], who, on entering my room, asked me to go with him to the Emperor.

At the time, Napoleon was accommodated in the house which had previously been the residence of the Smolensk Military Governor. A crowd of officers and soldiers pressed around the house, and there were mounted cavalry sentries on both sides of the entrance; the staircase and front rooms were filled with generals and various military officials. Passing them, we entered a room where there was no one but a footman, who, opening the door to Napoleon's study, let me in alone. There I found the Emperor with his Chief of Staff. In the room, an unfolded map of Russia lay on the table by the window; the dispositions of the troops were marked with pins of various colours. In the corner, near the window stood Marshal Berthier, while Napoleon was in the middle of the room. His first words were: 'From which Corps are you?' – 'The Second,' I replied. – 'Ah! Baggovut's II Corps?' – 'Exactly that.' – 'Are you related to Tuchkov, the corps commander?' – 'He is my brother.' – 'I shall not ask,' Napoleon continued, 'about the numbers in your army, but I will tell you that it consists of eight corps, each corps of two divisions, each division of six infantry regiments, each regiment of two battalions. I can even tell you how many men are in a company.' – 'I see,' I replied, 'that Your Majesty is very well informed.' – 'It is nothing remarkable,' Napoleon said. 'Almost every day we take prisoners and there is almost none of your regiments from which we have not had any soldiers; they are interrogated, their answers are written down and thus information about the strength of your forces is obtained.' Then, after a pause, Napoleon continued: 'You wanted war, sir, not me; you say that I am the instigator of it, but that is not true, and I shall prove to you that I did not want war at all, but you forced me to do so.' Whereupon he outlined his relationship to Russia, from his point of view, since the signing of the Treaty of Tilsit. Then, turning to me, he asked: 'Will you soon offer a general engagement, or will you all retreat?' I replied that the intentions of the Commander-in-Chief were unknown to me. 'Trust me,' Napoleon said, 'his German tactics won't do you any good. Your nation, brave, noble, loyal to the Tsar, crave a fair fight, and not to follow stupid German tactics. If you were already determined to fight, why did you not seize Poland? It would have been very easy, and then instead of a war at home, you would be waging it on foreign soil. And the Prussians, who are against you now, would have been with you then. Your Commander-in-Chief did not know how to do any of this, and now, retreating incessantly, he is devastating his own territory. Why did he abandon Smolensk? If he wanted to defend it, then why did he not defend it for longer? If he did not have this intention, then why did he fight in Smolensk at all? Was it just to raze this city to the ground? Smolensk, such a beautiful city! For me it is better than the whole of Poland; it was always Russian and shall remain Russian.

I love your emperor. He is my friend, despite this war; the war means nothing. The interests of State can divide even siblings. Tsar Alexander was and shall remain my friend.' Then Napoleon permitted himself to criticise our Tsar for his predilection for foreigners. 'Could he not' asked Napoleon, 'choose worthy men from this brave people loyal to its Tsars such as yours, who, by accompanying him, would bring respect to his reign?'

When Tuchkov replied that, as a subject of his Tsar, he would never dare to judge His actions, then Napoleon was not angry, but even, as if affectionately, lightly touching his shoulder, said: 'You are absolutely right. I am very far from condemning your opinions; but I expressed my thoughts only because we are now face to face. Does your emperor know you personally?' – 'I hope so,' Tuchkov replied: 'I once had the good fortune to serve in the Guard.'

'Could you write to him?' – 'I would never dare to bother Him with my letters, and especially not in my present situation.' – 'But if you dare not write to the Emperor, then you could write to your brother, what more can I say?' – 'To my brother, that's another matter. I could write to him about anything.' – 'And thus, you would oblige me very much if you wrote to your brother that you have seen me and that I instructed you to write to him, that it would give me great pleasure if he himself, or via the Grand Duke, or the Commander-in-Chief, however it suits him best, would bring to your Tsar's knowledge that I wish nothing more than to peacefully end our military operations. We have already burned enough of our gunpowder and spilled enough blood; after all, it is necessary to end it at some point! What are we fighting for? I have no enmity towards Russia. Now, if I were dealing with the British (*parlez moi de cela*). That would be a different matter (with these words, Napoleon, clenching his fist and raised it upward threateningly). But the Russians are not my enemies at all. If you want coffee and sugar; you shall have them. But if you think that I can be easily defeated, then I propose: let those of your generals who are most respected among you, such as: Bagration, Dokhturov, Osterman, your brother and others, let them make up a council of war and assess the situation and strengths, mine and yours, and if they find that there is more chance for success on your side, then let them designate where and when they want to fight; if they find that all the advantages are on my side, as they truly are, then why should we shed blood for no reason? Is it not it better to negotiate before losing a battle than after? And what would be the consequences for you of a battle lost? I would occupy Moscow and whatever measures I might take to save it from ruin, it would all be in vain. A capital occupied by the enemy has the appearance of a girl who has lost her honour;

do whatever you wish afterwards, but you cannot return her honour. You say that Russia is not just Moscow; the Austrians said the same thing when I approached Vienna, but once I had occupied their capital, they spoke quite differently. And it will be the same with you. Your real capital is not St Petersburg, but Moscow.'

Whereupon, Napoleon, repeating his proposal to Tuchkov to write everything he had heard to his brother, also asked him to put in the letter that our Commanders-in-Chief were doing very badly, that as they retreat, they were taking all the local authorities with them. 'Because of this,' Napoleon continued, 'the country suffers more harm than do I; we have no need for them,' etc. After detaining Tuchkov for more than an hour, Napoleon dismissed him, gave orders for his sword to be returned to him and advised him not to be downhearted. 'Your captivity,' he said, 'does you no dishonour; due to the way you were taken, only those who are in front are taken, and not those who remain in the rear.' Tuchkov described his entire conversation with Napoleon in the letter to his brother and showed this letter to Marshal Berthier, which was sent to our headquarters and presented to the Tsar. There was no response for Napoleon, indeed how could it be possible for him to expect an answer from a great enemy who had given his word not to lay down his arms while at least a single foe remained on Russian soil.[40]

During his stay in Smolensk, Napoleon appreciated all the disadvantages of the French army's quartering locations on the Dvina and Dnieper. It was not easy to secure such quarters, especially in winter, once the rivers in Russia do not constitute obstacles to troop movements; it was even more difficult to provide food in this place, throughout all the winter months, for a large army that had moved a considerable distance from the sources of its rations. Was it possible to expect consistency in the endurance of hardship from an army of twenty nations, some of whom were hostile to Napoleon and France? Was it realistic to hope for the loyalty of Prussia, Austria, Germany? Such were, in all likelihood, the factors that caused this decisive military leader to hesitate doubtfully. If Napoleon really could get out of the predicament into which his limitless ambition had thrust him, then no one could have found a better means than himself, and Napoleon's own orders during his five-day stay in Smolensk serve as a proof of this. In this short time it was necessary: to take measures to supply provisions to a huge army in a devastated countryside abandoned by the inhabitants; to arrange hospitals for the many thousands of wounded; to secure the lines of communication with Lithuania for the army. Napoleon gave orders for the conversion of monasteries and public buildings into magazines, for the establishment of 24 bakeries and extensive hospitals in Smolensk, for the disposal of several thousand corpses, both in the city itself and in its environs; for the building of a sturdy bridge on piles across the Dnieper. Not all of these orders could be carried out: the establishment of magazines of the capacity which Napoleon demanded, was impossible; in the huge hospitals, overwhelmed by many thousands of wounded, the most essential needs were lacking, such that they even had to replace dressings with paper from the archives of public institutions; there was a shortage of resources

---

40   From Tuchkov's notes.

at every stage. In addition, in order for the administrative orders to be carried out, good executives were needed, which were lacking in the French army.

Napoleon, considering Smolensk to be a point of paramount importance for subsequent operations, left one division of *Jeune Garde* there, under the command of General Delaborde [Henri François Delaborde], while some of the various formations were located in Vitebsk. To shorten the route up which the march battalions were moving to the army, instead of the post-road that ran from Vilna, via Glubokoe and Vitebsk, to Smolensk, another was established through Smorgon, Minsk, Borisov and Orsha. The troops left to the rear of the main force, namely, Macdonald's *10e Corps*, Oudinot's *2e Corps*, Saint-Cyr's *6e Corps*, Schwarzenberg's Corps, and Reynier's *7e Corps* and Dąbrowski's detachment, were ordered to take great care to shield the flanks of the *Grande Armée*. Victor, who was on the Vistula with *9e Corps*, was ordered to be ready to move to Vilna, in order to support the troops operating to the rear of the *Grande Armée*, as necessary.[41]

After the Battle of Lubino the troops of the *Grande Armée* proceeded behind the Russians, who were retreating along the Moscow road. Murat and Davout were charged with the direct pursuit of our army; Ney's *3e Corps* and Junot's *8e Corps* were ordered to proceed in the same direction; the Viceroy, with the troops of *4e Corps* (with the exception of Pino's division, dispatched to Surazh together with Sebastiani's *2e Division de cavalerie*), and with Grouchy's *3e Corps de Cavalerie*, proceeded to the left of the main body towards Dukhovshchina; Poniatowski initially moved from Smolensk up the left bank of the Dnieper, and later, to the right of the main body. Having sent the *Garde* from Smolensk on the morning of 12 (24) August, Napoleon left that night himself and rejoined his troops at dawn on 13 (25 August), who were just a short march from Dorogobuzh, whence both of our Western Armies had retreated.[42] The number of troops with the *Grande Armée*, following the detachment of Delaborde with 4,500 men to Smolensk, and Pino with 8,000 to Vitebsk, at this point reached 148,000 to 150,000 men.[43] The number of troops with the Russian army, including the Cossacks who were with it, was slightly more than 100,000.

Thus, the strengths of both sides, little by little, were coming to an equilibrium which could be destroyed by a single decisive victory. Napoleon believed – and was not mistaken in his opinion – that the Russians were retreating, as it were, reluctantly, and therefore was in constant hope of entangling them in a general battle. This hope gradually led him on to Dorogobuzh, to Vyazma, to Borodino; while from Borodino it was only four or five stages to Moscow. Napoleon took this final step; but the Russian army was not destroyed, and the formidable conqueror did not achieve his objective.

---

41   Thiers. *Histoire du Consulat et de l'Empire*, XIV, *Edit. de Brux.* 271-274 & 302-303.
42   Thiers, XIV, 275-276.
43   The author of *Das Buch vom Jahr 1812* calculated the number of troops with Napoleon's *Grande Armée*, on 11 (23) August, at 155,675 men, but in the returns presented (II, 443, *Beilage* III) it includes Pino's division in the troop total for *4e Corps*, which had been detached to Vitebsk by then.

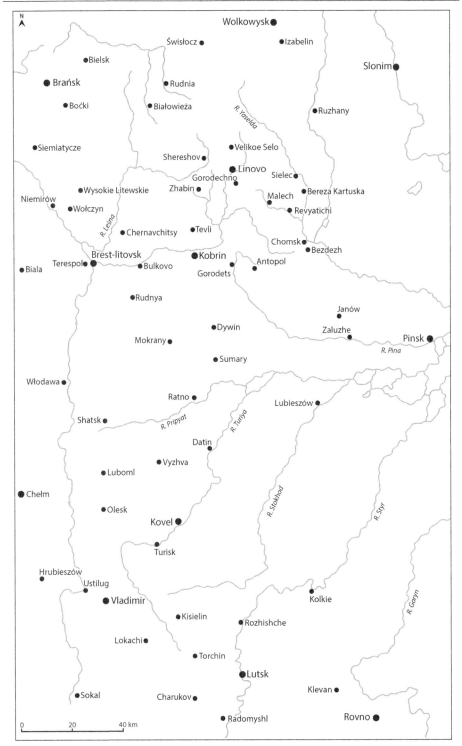

Map of the Area of Operations in Volhynia in 1812.

12

The Battle of Gorodechno

Deployment of Third Army of Observation before the outbreak of hostilities. – Tormasov and Count Lambert. – Reynier's advance towards Pruzhany. – Count Lambert's sweep into the Duchy of Warsaw. – The deployment of forces in Third Army. – Tormasov's advance to engage Reynier. – The action at Kobrin. – Reynier's retreat. – His unification with Schwarzenberg and the allied advance against Tormasov. – The Russian retreat to Gorodechno. – The battle of Gorodechno. – Third Army's retreat to the Styr. – Troop deployments by both sides in the second half of August. – Ertel's operations against Dąbrowski.

In early [mid] June 1812, simultaneously with the invasion by Napoleon's *Grande Armée* into Russia, Third Army was located in Volhynia under the command of General of Cavalry Tormasov, occupying the sector from Luboml to Stary Konstantinov and having its headquarters in Lutsk. Tormasov's army, as we have already had occasion to say in our review of the forces assigned to protect our western borders, was composed of 54 battalions, 76 squadrons, nine Cossack regiments, 14 artillery companies, one pioneer company and one pontoon company, in total 46,000 men with 164 guns.

General of Cavalry Tormasov, before his appointment as Commander-in-Chief of Third Army, was renowned as a skilful military administrator, possessing, at the same time, the talents of a politician, demonstrated by him during the war against the Turks and Persians a short while before. In the course of three campaigns, from 1809 to 1811, Tormasov, being Commander-in-Chief of the troops in Georgia and on the Caucasian Line, at the same time, had to face both Muslim powers and keep the highland peoples in obedience, and to achieve these aims he had no more than 42,000 men in the army. In such difficult circumstances, Tormasov, unable to defeat the enemy through brute force, resorted to cunning, both by stirring up discord between the pashas, then by preventing the conclusion of an alliance between the Turks and the Persians. Strict in his relations with his subordinates, Tormasov considered diligent service an obligation, and not a path to awards and distinctions; nevertheless, however, he knew how to appreciate and reward the merits of his associates: Lisanevich [Dmitry Tikhonovich Lisanevich], Kotlyarevsky [Pëtr Stepanovich Kotlyarevsky] and, subsequently, Count Lambert.

During the war of 1812, Count Lambert was constantly the commander of the vanguard – first for Tormasov, and then for Chichagov [Pavel Vasilevich Chichagov].

Forced to leave his fatherland, France, in his youth, Lambert dedicated his abilities to his adopted Russia and more than once sealed his vow with blood: to serve the Russian Tsars faithfully and truly. In the 1799 campaign, he fought like a hero and was badly wounded; while in the campaign of 1807 he received the Cross of St. George 3rd class and returned to Russia with the distinction of being an excellent cavalry general and an outstanding vanguard commander. This renown was crowned with new brilliance in the Patriotic War of 1812.

From Napoleon's side, the conduct of operations in Volhynia was entrusted to the Saxon *7e Corps* under Reynier, which, having already reached Nesvizh, was ordered to return to Slonim and move to Pruzhany, to shield the Duchy of Warsaw and to invade the Volhynia Governorate, while Prince Schwarzenberg was to go from Drohiczyn with the Austrian Corps, via Pruzhany and Slonim, to Nesvizh, and join the main force. The reason for these orders was Napoleon's distrust of his allies, the Austrians.[1] The number of troops in the corps dispatched to Volhynia was inadequate both for the importance of the objectives of their operations, and the forces against which they were advancing, and this was due to the lack of definitive intelligence regarding the strength of our army located in the southern theatre of operations.[2]

In early [mid] July, as Napoleon was attempting movements to outflank First Army along the Dvina, Reynier, having linked up with the Austrian Corps in Slonim on 7 (19) July, set off for Pruzhany. The number of troops in the Saxon *7e Corps* did not exceed 17,000. The objective of their operations was to protect the line of communications of Napoleon's *Grande Armée* from offensive operations by our Third Army. To achieve this objective, it would be necessary to block the three main approaches leading from Volhynia, through the swamps of Polesie into Lithuania, namely:

1.   From Zhitomir to Mozyr and onwards to Mogilev on the Dnieper.
2.   From Lutsk to Pinsk and onwards to Minsk.
3.   From Lutsk to Brest-Litovsk and onwards to Slonim.

Having occupied Mozyr, Pinsk and Brest, Reynier could block us from reaching Lithuania. But as his force was insufficient to protect all these points, he decided to guard the closest of them to the Duchy of Warsaw – Brest-Litovsk. To that end, in

---

1   Thiers. *Histoire du Consulat et de l'Empire*, XIV, *Edit. de Brux.* 203.
2   Chambray. *Histoire de l'expédition de Russie*, I, 209. This is proven by the following letter from Napoleon to Berthier: Glubokoe, 22nd July 1812. '*Mon cousin!* Write to General Reynier that I find the situation he is in is quite consistent with his mission, to operate in Volhynia; that I give him permission to invade Volhynia whenever he finds it convenient; that only 9th Division and 15th Division, commanded by General Kamensky, are fully operational, and even they, in all likelihood, will join Bagration's army in order to shield Moscow. That Tormasov's Corps cannot stop him: they are nothing but a rabble of third battalions, untrained recruits, which could only be used to keep the inhabitants of the countryside subdued. That General Reynier, by taking Warsaw officials with him, could invade Volhynia and stir up the local inhabitants to rebellion as soon as 9th Division and 15th Division have left. That the phantom force from the Crimea is a pure fiction; that the Sultan has refused to ratify the peace treaty, and that the Russians would be forced to strengthen their army in Moldavia and Wallachia, and so on.'

order to hold this location and Kobrin, Major General Klengel [Heinrich Christian Magnus von Klengel] was sent with four battalions, three squadrons and eight regimental guns, totalling about 3,000 men. One squadron was detached to Pinsk from the vanguard, which advanced to Janów [Ivanovo].[3]

Thus, there was a significant superiority in the ratio of forces in favour of Tormasov, although our Commander-in-Chief was forced to spread them across a significant area, to shield his line of communications with the internal regions of the Empire and with Chichagov's Army of Moldavia, and to secure the border with Austria. Despite repeated assurances from the Viennese Cabinet that their assistance to Napoleon would be limited to an agreed corps of 30,000, it would not be sound on our part, to rely on these promises and expose the border and thus give the Austrians an opportunity for the unhindered occupation of a country rich in resources for maintaining troops. These were the factors forcing our Commander-in-Chief to weaken the main body of his army. As First Army and Second Army had been operating against Napoleon for some time, General Tormasov decided to open offensive operations into the Duchy of Warsaw, taking advantage of the complete absence of enemy troops in the occupied areas. To that end, in early [mid] July the commander of the vanguard of the army, Adjutant General Count Lambert, moving across the Bug at several locations with part of the troops entrusted to him and marching on Hrubieszow, scattered the militia gathered there and captured some 100 of their men. Count Lambert proposed sending the entire vanguard to Lublin, to the Commander-in-Chief and, having taken possession of this city, to disrupt their mobilisation right from the start. But in the meantime, on 5 (17) July, Tormasov had received a Supreme command – to march into the rear of the enemy force operating against Prince Bagration.[4]

The protection of the Volhynia Governorate and Podolsk Governorate was entrusted to Lieutenant General Saken, who was stationed in Zaslav [Zasław] and Stary Konstantinov with six battalions from 36th Infantry Division and 12 replacement squadrons; the remaining six battalions from 36th Division had been sent to Mozyr to reinforce II Reserve Corps, which was under the command of General Ertel. Major General Khrushchev was stationed along the border with the Duchy of Warsaw with the Zhitomir Dragoons and Arzamas Dragoons and with two Cossack regiments, in order to monitor it and to maintain communications between Tormasov's main body and the troops stationed at Zaslav and Konstantinov. The Commander-in-Chief himself, with all his remaining troops, set off to engage Reynier.[5] Formations moved in various directions ahead of the main force: Adjutant-General Count Lambert proceeded from Vladimir [Volodymyr] along both banks of the Bug towards Brest Litovsk with four battalions from 10th Jägers and 14th Jägers, 16 squadrons from the Alexandria Hussars, Starodub Dragoons and Tver Dragoons, three Cossack regiments and six guns from 12th Horse Artillery Company;[6] Prince Shcherbatov also marched from Kovel towards Brest, via Ratno and Mokrany

3   Chambray, I, Table II.
4   War Diary of Third Army's vanguard (archive of the M.T.D. No 32,417).
5   Buturlin. *Histoire militaire de la campagne de Russie*, II, 67-68.
6   See Map titled Depicting the Area of Operations in Volhynia in 1812.

with six battalions from 18th Division, eight squadrons from the Tatar Ulans and Yevpatoria Tatars and 24 guns from 34th Light Artillery Company and 11th Horse Artillery Company; Major General Chaplits marched via Ratno and Dywin, along the direct route to Kobrin with 13th Jägers, Pavlograd Hussars and four squadrons from the Lubny Hussars, Barabanshchikov's Don Cossack Regiment, six guns from 12th Horse Artillery Company and Captain Kutsevich's Pioneer Company; they were followed by Tormasov's main force; Major General Melissino [Alexey Petrovich Melissino] was sent to Janów and Pinsk with an independent detachment consisting of 32nd Jägers, two combined grenadier battalions, Serpukhov Dragoons and three squadrons from the Lubny Hussars, in order to conduct a diversionary operation, while the rest of the army, having driven off the advanced enemy detachments, were to move into the rear of the main body of Reynier's *7e Corps*. To that end, Count Lambert and Prince Shcherbatov were ordered to arrive at Brest Litovsk on 13 (25) July and to attack the enemy troops located there with their combined forces; thereafter, having reported the success of this enterprise to headquarters, they were to turn on Kobrin for an attack on the enemy on 15 (27) July together with the main body of the army, which was assigned to march from Kovel to Kobrin on 10 (22) July.[7]

Tormasov's orders were executed successfully. The detachment under General Melissino captured one of the enemy outposts near Zaluzhe, crossed the Pina river and sent fighting patrols towards Pinsk and Janów.[8] Reynier, deceived by these diversions, moved towards Chomsk and sent the vanguard, under General von Gablenz's command, to Janów. Meanwhile, Tormasov's force was rapidly moving towards Brest and Kobrin.

On 12 (24) July, Shcherbatov, on the way from Ratno to Brest, having reached Rudnya, found out that Brest was occupied by a very weak Saxon detachment, and therefore, leaving his infantry halfway to the city, under the command of Major General Benardos [Panteleimon Yegorovich Benardos], he swiftly moved on with Colonel Knorring's cavalry brigade and two horse artillery guns. At three o'clock in the afternoon of the 13th (25 July), our cavalry, breaking into the city, scattered two Saxon squadrons stationed there, and more than forty men were taken prisoner; the remainder were almost all killed.[9] Thereafter, General Lambert arrived with his vanguard, which included Shcherbatov's troops.

On the following day, 14 (26) July, Count Lambert, leaving Major Baron Rosen in Brest, with one squadron of Alexandria Hussars and another of Tatar Ulans, in order to monitor the approaches from the Duchy of Warsaw, moved on towards Bulkovo.

On 15 (27) July, at one o'clock in the morning, Count Lambert set off on the road to Kobrin with the cavalry; the infantry were ordered to rest up for four hours, and then follow the path of the cavalry. At seven o'clock in the morning, our cavalry was approaching the town. The enemy, having been alerted to this, sent

---

7   For the March Disposition for the advance on the enemy forces located in Brest, Kobrin and Pinsk, see Appendix XVII.

8   Chambray, I, 281.

9   Prince Shcherbatov's notes. War Diary of Third Army's vanguard.

their cavalry along the Brest road and scattered skirmishers in the crops and in the ditches that intersect the open ground. Count Lambert, seeing the complete impossibility of deploying cavalry in such inappropriate terrain, attempted to lure the enemy into the open, but as the Saxons remained in their positions, our operations were limited to skirmishing, in anticipation of the appearance of Chaplits from the direction of Kovel and the arrival of the infantry left at Bulkovo. Once Count Lambert had received news of the approach of Chaplits towards the town, he immediately sent Lieutenant Colonel Prince Madatov [Valerian Grigorevich Madatov], with two squadrons of Alexandria Hussars and a *sotnia* of Cossacks, across the Mukhavets river to block the Pruzhany road. Madatov, after fording the river, charged two squadrons stationed on this road and drove them into the town. As there was no doubt that the enemy would make every possible effort to reopen their line of retreat to Pruzhany, two more squadrons of Starodub Dragoons, two squadrons of Alexandria Hussars and one squadron of Tatar Ulans were sent to assist Prince Madatov. Meanwhile, the Saxons, having placed two guns on the left bank of the river, were harassing our cavalry, and therefore Count Lambert sent two guns from Apushkin's [Alexander Nikolaevich Apushkin] 11th Horse Artillery Company across the river, which silenced the enemy. The Saxons, having lost hope of retreating along the Pruzhany road, charged at the Russian battery stationed on the left bank of the Mukhavets in order to open the route to Brest; but the successful actions of our artillery and the dismounted men of the Starodub Dragoons and Tver Dragoons forced the enemy to retreat.

Meanwhile, General Chaplits, moving ten *versts* ahead of Tormasov's main force with his detachment, learned about the location of Saxon General Klengel with 4,000 men in Kobrin from captured enemy patrols, and about Reynier's advance to assist him with 11,000 men, from Antopol. General Chaplits, meaning to cut off Klengel's lines of retreat, detached Major Ostrogradsky with a division [pair of squadrons] of Pavlograd Hussars along the direct route to Kobrin in order to distract the attention of the enemy, while he, using the forest lying close to the town, covertly moved over to the Antopol road himself with the rest of his force and sent some cavalry to ford onto the right bank of the Mukhavets, in order to block the routes from Kobrin to Slutsk. The enemy, having seen Chaplits' force, sent several squadrons with two guns to engage them along the Antopol road, but the Pavlograd Hussars drove them off, repulsed the guns and burst into the town on the heels of the enemy. The 13th Jägers were sent to support them. The enemy, who fought with extraordinary resolve, were finally forced to evacuate the town, which was burning in several places, and retreat behind the stone wall of the monastery and into the ruins of a small fort built by Charles XII back during the Great Northern War. Surrounded by our troops on all sides, the courageous Saxons were forced to submit to necessity and lay down their arms. The prisoners taken were: two generals, including the formation commander Klengel, 76 field officers and subalterns and 2,382 other ranks. Four Colours and eight guns remained with the victors. Russian casualties were: 77 killed and 182 wounded.[10] General Tormasov, out of respect for the courage shown by the Saxons,

---

10   Prince Shcherbatov's notes. War Diary of Third Army's vanguard. *Remarques sur la campagne de 1812, par le Général Czaplitz* (in the M.T.D. No 44,712). General Tormasov's report to the

ordered the swords to be returned to the captured officers. In the town, 548 houses burned down and only 82 survived.[11]

The action at Kobrin, remarkable for the precision of the movements made by the detachments under Count Lambert and Chaplits, who arrived at the enemy location at the appointed hour, was marked as the first victory won by Russian troops since Napoleon's invasion of our frontiers. Tsar Alexander granted Tormasov the Order of St George, 2nd class, and 50,000 roubles. Count Lambert received a sabre decorated with diamonds, with the inscription *За храбрость* [For Bravery].

Giving due justice to Tormasov's orders, which had the result of destroying the enemy vanguard, one cannot but notice that he did not fully exploit his success: if, immediately after the action at Kobrin, he had turned against Reynier's *7e Corps*, which had already passed Antopol and was located near the town of Gorodets, only twenty *versts* from our main force and at a distance of eight or ten stages from the Austrian Corps under Schwarzenberg, he could have caught him, and even cut him off from Slonim, which, in all likelihood, would have resulted in the complete destruction of this corps and would have given a most favourable turn to our operations in the southern theatre of war. The main reason for the slow pace of Tormasov's operations was the lack of provisions, which became evident immediately after the occupation of Kobrin by our troops. The train did not keep up with the movements of the army, and the enemy, during their retreat, tried to destroy the magazines they had established.

The inaction of our army after the action at Kobrin made it possible for the Saxons to evade the danger that threatened them. Reynier, having received news of the fate that had befallen Klengel's detachment, and having no more than 12,000 to 13,000 men under his command, immediately began to pull back from the vicinity of Antopol towards Pruzhany, on the route to Slonim, to link up with Schwarzenberg. From our side, on 17 (29) July, in the afternoon, Lieutenant Colonel Prince Madatov, with two squadrons of Alexandria Hussars and two *sotnia* of Cossacks and Kalmuks, was detached from Count Lambert's vanguard towards Pruzhany, where General Reynier had sent a squadron of dragoons to burn down a small magazine located there. Prince Madatov managed to capture this entire squadron, preventing them from destroying the stores, while Count Lambert moved initially to the town of Malech on 19 (31) July, from where he intended to go on to Sielec, hoping to catch up with the enemy rearguard there; but having learned about their departure for Mikhalin, he halted at Malech, holding the towns of Sielec and Bereza Kartuza [Byaroza] with advanced outposts. Chaplits' detachment was located in Chomsk, while the main body of Third Army was located at Antopol. Tormasov remained in this location from 20 to 28 July (1 to 9 August), directing strong raiding parties towards Białystok and Warsaw. The inhabitants of the Duchy of Warsaw, cut off from Schwarzenberg and Reynier, were horrified; their former self-confidence disappeared; mobilisation was halted. General Loison, commandant of the French troops in Königsberg, believing that the Russians had already managed to reoccupy Białystok, moved to Rastenburg [Kętrzyn] with 10,000 men, in order to assist

---

Tsar dated 2 [14] August, No 63.

11   Information provided by the local authorities of the Grodno Governorate.

Schwarzenberg and Reynier, and did not return to Königsberg before ensuring that our troops had withdrawn.[12]

While Tormasov remained at Antopol, Reynier retreated to Slonim, having previously informed Schwarzenberg about the danger of his position and asking for the assistance of the Austrian troops. Schwarzenberg, who had already issued orders for a march from Slonim to Nesvizh, cancelled the departure of his corps and as soon as he managed to establish communications with Reynier, on 22 July (3 August), on the day the Russian armies were united near Smolensk, immediately turned to face Tormasov on the road from Slonim to Chomsk, while Reynier, for his part, also began to advance on the route from Wołkowysk to Pruzhany. Having learned about this movement by the Saxon troops, on 25 July (6 August), Tormasov ordered Count Lambert to move from Malech to Pruzhany with the vanguard, to shield the army from being enveloped from the left flank; at the same time, Major General Prince Khovansky [Nikolai Nikolaevich Khovansky] relieved Count Lambert at Malech with Third Army's reserve, consisting of four combined grenadier battalions and the 38th Jägers with two artillery companies, while General Chaplits' detachment, consisting of eight battalions, twelve squadrons and four Cossack regiments, with three artillery companies, moved from Chomsk to Revyatichi in order to support Prince Khovansky. But the latter two detachments were attacked on 27th July (8th August) by the superior forces of the Austrian Corps and were forced to retreat to Chomsk. Taking advantage of this, Schwarzenberg undertook to outflank Count Lambert's vanguard, which was stationed at Pruzhany, via the Malech to Linovo road, meanwhile, Reynier was to move from the direction of Wołkowysk and around the left flank of our troops, towards the town of Shereshov [Šarašova]. Count Lambert, threatened with the same fate that had befallen Klengel, however, did not allow himself to be encircled like him, and immediately began to retreat towards Gorodechno, fighting off the enemy pursuing him every day. On this retreat, he was forced to endure a heated engagement at Kozi Brod, where our vanguard, pressed by superior forces, lost a gun. 'The enemy cost me dearly,' Count Lambert commented.

On 29 and 30 July (10 and 11 August), the vanguard and Corps under Markov and Kamensky, consisting of 24 battalions and 36 squadrons with three Cossack regiments, assembled in the position at Gorodechno. The reason for this weakening of the army was the detachment of 13,000 men to Pinsk and Chomsk, who were under the command of generals Melissino, Chaplits and Prince Khovansky, who had not had time to rejoin the main force.[13]

On 30 July (11 August), Bianchi's and Trauttenberg's Austrian infantry divisions and Frimont's cavalry division, having arrived at Gorodechno, settled down in front of the river covering Tormasov's positions; the Saxon *7e Corps* was stationed at Zhabin, while its leading elements were at Poddubno. Siegenthal's division, stationed at Malech, opposing the Russian troops retreating to Chomsk, leaving one battalion with some of the cavalry to observe them, joined Schwarzenberg's main

---

12   Chambray, I, 282-283. *Das Buch vom Jahr 1812*, II, 86. Napoleon, having received news of Reynier's defeat, ordered Schwarzenberg to march into Volhynia to oppose Tormasov taking the Saxon Corps under command in addition to the Austrian.

13   Buturlin, II, 81.

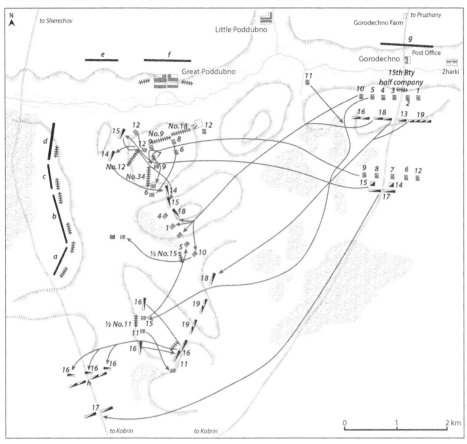

Plan of the Battle of Gorodechno, 12 August 1812.

Legend

Russians

1. Nasheburg Infantry.
2. Ryazhsk Infantry.
3. Vitebsk Infantry.
4. Kozlov Infantry.
5. Kura Infantry.
6. Dnieper Infantry.
7. Kostroma Infantry.
8. Vladimir Infantry.
9. Tambov Infantry.
10. 10th Jägers.
11. 14th Jägers.
12. 28th Jägers.
13. Tver Dragoons.
14. Taganrog Dragoons.
15. Starodub Dragoons.
16. Alexandria Hussars.
17. Pavlograd Hussars.
18. Tatar Ulans.
19. Irregular Troops

Austro-Saxons

a. Vanguard of the Saxon Corps.
b. Le Coq's Saxon Division.
c. Lilienberg's Austrian Brigade.
d. Funck's Saxon Division.
e. Hessen-Homburg's Austrian Brigade.
f. Siegenthal's Austrian Division.
g. Trautenberg's Austrian Division.
h. Polenz's & Hohenzollern's regiments.

force on the evening of the 30th (11 August) and was located near Zhabin, as reserve to the Saxon corps. Thus, the allied commanders managed to assemble some 40,000 troops against the position held by Tormasov, who could oppose them with no more than 18,000. If the detachments under Prince Khovansky and Chaplits had retreated from Malech and Revyatichi towards Gorodechno, rather than Chomsk, then our Commander-in-Chief, having concentrated more than 30,000 men at the position near Gorodechno, in all likelihood, could have halted the enemy.

This position was located on the high ground on the right bank of one of the tributaries of the Mukhavets river. The swampy ground, along the entire length of its course, made crossings possible only via a few narrow causeways, which were very convenient defiles for defence: one of them is on the route from Pruzhany to Kobrin, at Gorodechno; a second is four *versts* from Gorodechno, near the village of great Poddubno, between the roads from Pruzhany to Kobrin and from Shereshov to Tevli, leading into the rear of the position; a third is upstream of Poddubno, on the road from Shereshov to Kobrin via Tevli. The high ground of the right bank, which formed the position, reaches upstream and downstream of Gorodechno; at Poddubno, it forms a right angle from the river, almost parallel with the road that runs from Shereshov to Tevli, which in the vicinity of Poddubno passes through a forest for several *versts*.[14]

Tormasov's troops were deployed at Gorodechno on 30 July (11 August), such that Markov's Corps and the vanguard under Count Lambert stood facing the postal station, on both sides of the highway leading from Pruzhany to Kobrin, while Kamensky's Corps, which, due to his illness was under the command of Prince Shcherbatov, was in reserve; also on the main road, a *verst* behind the troops standing in line of battle.

Schwarzenberg, not daring to attack Tormasov's position frontally, preferred to envelope it from the left flank. To that end, Siegenthal's Austrian Division of was sent to the village of great Poddubno, to replace Reynier's Saxon *7e Corps*, which, having being reinforced with two Austrian formations, Lilienberg's infantry brigade [Wenzel Alois Vetter von Lilienberg] and Schmelzern's cavalry brigade [Johann Ritter Schmelzern von Wildmannsegg], received orders to pass covertly through the forest which lay on the allied right flank, and having bypassed the swamps, was to attack the Russian army.

On 31 July (12 August), at dawn, some of the Saxon infantry occupied the causeway at Poddubno and crossed the swamp. As soon as our patrols reported this to the command post, General Tormasov ordered Prince Shcherbatov to move to the left towards Poddubno with Kamensky's Corps, where our troops, pushing the Saxon outposts back across the river, settled down, at eight o'clock in the morning, on the high ground of the right bank, in two lines: the first consisting of the Vladimir Infantry and Tambov Infantry; while the second was formed by the Dnieper Infantry and Kostroma Infantry; one battalion of 28th Jägers was stationed ahead of the right flank while the other was ahead of the left flank of the front line; the Starodub Dragoons and Taganrog Dragoons, formed up on the left wing, at right

---

14   See Plan of the Battle of Gorodechno, 31 July (12 August) 1812.

angles with the infantry (*en potence*), facing towards the forest: forward of the front line were 9th Battery Artillery Company and 18th Battery Artillery Company in order to bombard the causeway.

At ten o'clock in the morning, Reynier's troops began to emerge from the forest and formed up on the left flank of Shcherbatov's Corps in a direction perpendicular to it. Although this movement had not been anticipated by Tormasov, nonetheless, he immediately took steps to counter the enemy: Shcherbatov made a change of front pulling the left flank back, with the exception of the Vladimir Infantry, who were left on the high ground facing Poddubno. The Tambov Infantry, Kostroma Infantry and Dnieper Infantry were deployed in a single line, facing the forest; the battalion of 28th Jägers that had been stationed on the left flank, was now in the space between the Vladimir Infantry and the other infantry. 12th Horse Artillery Company and 34th Light Artillery Company shored up the fighting line. The Taganrog Dragoons and Starodub Dragoons formed in echelon behind the left flank of the infantry.

Meanwhile, Reynier, constantly being reinforced by the rest of his divisions, moved to his right, threatening to envelope us from the left flank. General Tormasov, for his part, having been convinced that the enemy intended to direct their main effort at this location, decided to send all the rest of his troops there, except for the Ryazhsk Infantry and Tver Dragoons with six guns from 15th Battery Artillery Company, left to defend the causeway at Gorodechno. General Markov was ordered to redeploy his corps to the left flank of Shcherbatov's force, consisting of the Nasheburg Infantry, Vitebsk Infantry, Kozlov Infantry and 10th Jägers, four squadrons of Tatar Ulans and six guns from 15th Battery Artillery Company; at the same time, Count Lambert was directed further to the left with the Kura Infantry, 14th Jägers, Alexandria Hussars and Pavlograd Hussars with six guns from 11th Horse Artillery Company, in order to cover the flank of our position. These troops were engaged by 16 enemy guns stationed on the Saxon right wing; whereupon Count Lambert gave orders to direct two marksmen platoons from the Kura Infantry and 14th Jägers against the enemy battery. The close terrain allowed our skirmishers to approach the enemy to short musket range, which forced the Saxon battery to retreat and contributed to our artillery and 14th Jägers and Alexandria Hussars taking the high ground facing the flank of Reynier's troops. 'This shows,' states the War Diary of the vanguard of Third Army, 'how terrifying even a small number of marksmen were to the artillery.' A very remarkable conclusion, in an epoch when dispersed action by infantry was incomparably less effective than it is today.

The rest of Tormasov's force was deployed as follows: the Kura Infantry had been directed by Count Lambert to support Markov; four squadrons of Tatar Ulans and the irregular troops (Cossacks and Kalmuks) were stationed in the space between Markov's Corps and Count Lambert's detachment.

Reynier, whose entire force was already lined up facing our positions, detached the Austrian *Chevauxlegerregiment Prinz Hohenzollern* and Saxon *Chevauxlegerregiment von Polenz* to the right, completely isolated from the other troops, which, having passed behind their battle lines, raced along the Shereshov road, enveloping the left flank of our position. The Pavlograd Hussars, limiting themselves to skirmishing, retreated down the Kobrin road and, little by little, drew the cavalry pursuing them a considerable distance from Reynier's other troops.

Count Lambert, skilfully taking advantage of the enemy's negligence, raced into their rear with the Alexandria Hussars, while the Pavlograd Hussars attacked them from the front. The enemy *chevauleger*, cut off from their position and surrounded on all sides by our hussars, were completely scattered. Many of them ended up on the Kobrin and Brest roads, where they were rounded up by Major Rosen's cavalry detachment.

Reynier, having been unsuccessful in his enterprise against the left flank of the Russian force, sent Funck's division against our right wing, which, in several columns, swiftly attacked the high ground opposite Poddubno. This attack was supported by a crossfire from the Saxon batteries and the Austrian artillery stationed at Poddubno. But the Russian troops repulsed the enemy; and the Taganrog Dragoons pursued them and forced the Saxon *2. Regiment Leichte Infanterie* to form square. That evening, Funck's Division repeated their attack; Schwarzenberg, at the urgent request of Reynier, sent several more battalions from Bianchi's division to help him; the *Infanterieregiment Colloredo* managed to cross the swampy river upstream of Poddubno with great difficulty, but was repelled by the Vladimir Infantry. At the same time, a Saxon column, which appeared opposite the left flank of Markov's force, was engaged and pushed back by the 10th Jägers.

Meanwhile, Trautenberg's Austrian division, stationed at Gorodechno, limited itself to cannonade and offensive feints along the Pruzhany road, which allowed the Ryazhsk Infantry to hold out at the exit from the causeway until nightfall. The encroaching darkness put an end to the battle, which had lasted from ten o'clock in the morning until ten o'clock at night. It is rather difficult to make a precise comment on the casualties suffered by the fighting troops. According to Tormasov's official report, we lost some 1,300 men. The Saxons gave their losses at about 1,000 men; there is no accurate information about the losses of the Austrian force.[15]

Our troops, despite the huge superiority in numbers of the allies, managed to hold on to the positions they had occupied at the beginning of the battle. In his report to the Tsar, the Commander-in-Chief, outlining the progress of the action, wrote:

> All the efforts of the enemy were in vain. The troops of Your Imperial Majesty did not yield a single step to them, did not allow them to exploit anything and took 230 privates and four officers prisoner. The generals, officers and soldiers all fought courageously, and the enemy was forced to leave the battlefield, where the army of Your Imperial Majesty bivouacked.[16]

In spite of all this, however, the shortcomings of the position occupied by the Russian troops at Gorodechno did not allow Tormasov to continue to resist the incomparably stronger enemy, who, if they had repeated the flanking movement with all their troops, would have cut off our line of retreat. In addition, the resistance from

---

15   Buturlin calculated the enemy losses at around 5,000, and Russians from 3,000 to 4,000. The account of the battle at Gorodechno is from: the War Diary of Third Army's vanguard. Buturlin, II, 82-90. Vaudoncourt, *Mémoires pour servir à l'histoire de la guere entre la France et la Russie, par un officier de l'état major de l'armée française*, 136-140.

16   Tormasov's report dated 7 [19] August, No 67.

the inhabitants of Lithuania made it extremely difficult to supply the army with food; at the same time, intelligence had been received about the concentration of a large militia in the Duchy of Warsaw, assigned to invade Volhynia, where the enemy also hoped to start an uprising against the Russians.[17]

All these factors forced Tormasov to abandon the position at Gorodechno and retreat along the road to Kobrin, on the night of 31 July to 1 August (12 to 13 August). Although our retreat had not been forced upon us by enemy arms in any way, nevertheless they described themselves as victorious. Napoleon, reassured regarding the southern theatre of operations by the retreat of the Russians, which he had not expected so soon after the blow inflicted upon the Saxons at Kobrin, was extremely pleased with operations by Schwarzenberg, who, for the action at Gorodechno, was promoted to Field Marshal. In addition, Napoleon wanted to award the most distinguished Austrians with the Order of the *Légion d'honneur*, but Kaiser Franz rejected this proposal.[18] An impartial examination of the battle at Gorodechno shows that the allies had no right to consider it a victory. The circumstances themselves dictated the need to retreat to our commander, and it would have been even more advantageous for us, without giving battle at Gorodechno, to retreat beyond the Mukhavets, where Tormasov's troops would have been reinforced by the troops under Chaplits and Prince Khovansky.[19]

In considering the actions of Tormasov in the battle of Gorodechno, we find that although he took advantage of the indecision of his opponents and managed to change the facing of his position, nevertheless, he executed this movement rather slowly. As soon as the crossing by Saxon troops at Poddubno revealed the enemy intentions, he should have immediately stationed all the rest of his forces on the high ground facing the large forest, leaving the smaller part of the force in position, more to observe than to counter any attack (which would not be anticipated from the banks of the stream due to the impregnability of the position from this direction).

The enemy commanders did not know how to take full advantage either of the superiority of their numbers or of the weaknesses of the position occupied by the Russian troops. Schwarzenberg should have supported Reynier with much more significant forces; while Reynier, without moving troops across at Poddubno and without prematurely emerging from the forest with them, should have suddenly enveloped the left flank of Tormasov's position with his entire corps, reinforced by two Austrian divisions, and seized the Kobrin road to the rear of the Russian army. The indecision of the enemy commanders can be the only reason why, having 36 battalions and more than 60 squadrons on the battlefield, they committed only 23 battalions and 32 squadrons into action.

The retreat of the Russian army was entirely under the protection of Count Lambert's rearguard, who, slowly retreating to Tevli, were relieved there by Chaplits' detachment.[20] Upon reaching Ratno, Tormasov's Third Army was reinforced to 28,000 men with the addition of Prince Khovansky's detachment which became the

17   Tormasov's memo to Prince Gorchakov, head of the War Ministry.
18   General Mikhailovsky-Danilevsky's History of the war of 1812.
19   War Diary of Third Army's vanguard.
20   War Diary of Third Army's vanguard.

rearguard, relieving Chaplits' detachment. The enemy army pursued ours in two columns: one made up of Austrian troops marched on Kobrin, while the other, of Saxon troops, marched on Brest-Litovsk. From our side, on 8 (20) August, Chaplits' detachment was sent to Vyzhva [Vyzhhiv] while Count Lambert was directed on Turisk in order to shield the army from the Reynier's *7e Corps* and the Duchy of Warsaw; at the same time, General Melissino's detachment proceeded from Pinsk to Lubieszów [Liubeshiv] in order to link up with the main force.

On 12 (24) August, Count Lambert, having received orders to reconnoitre for enemy forces in the sector from Turisk to Luboml, left his infantry regiments and some of the artillery near Novoselok, while he moved to Luboml himself, with the cavalry (Alexandria Hussars, Tatar Ulans, Vlasov's Cossacks and Yevpatoria Tatars with 12 guns from 12th Horse Artillery Company) attaching the Starodub Dragoons and Dyachkin's Cossacks to his force on the way, and sent several *sotnia* of Cossack forwards to Luboml, supported by four squadrons of Tatar Ulans. On closing up to the town, our detachment struck up a successful action against the enemy vanguard, which was carrying out a reconnaissance under Reynier's personal direction; Count Lambert remained at Luboml the following day, returning to Turisk on 14 (26) August.[21] General Chaplits, having encountered an Austrian detachment advancing towards Vyzhva, held the enemy up for 18 hours.[22] The stubborn resistance by these detachments allowed Tormasov's main body to retreat from Ratno via Kovel, across the Styr river, to Lutsk. Count Lambert's detachment retreated from Turisk, to Torchin, and on to Lutsk; Chaplits' detachment moved off from Vyzhva, via Kovel, and over the Styr to the village of Rozhishche; Melissino's detachment moved from Lubieszów to the village of Kolki and came under Chaplits' command. The small detachment under Khrushchev, which had been stationed in Vladimir since 6 (18) July, retreated across the Styr and became part of Count Lambert's detachment.[23]

By 17 (29) August, Third Army was already on the right bank of the Styr. Tormasov's main body was located in the vicinity of Lutsk; Count Lambert's detachment along the Styr, from Lutsk to the Austrian border;[24] Chaplits' detachment also along the Styr, from Lutsk to Kolki.[25]

On the part of the enemy, the troops, halted by the sudden rising water level in the river Styr and intelligence of the approaching Army of the Danube, settled down between Styr and the Bug; the main body of the Austrian Corps at Kisielin, Siegenthal's division at Ratno; the Saxon *7e Corps* between Torchin and Lokachi; a brigade of Polish troops that had joined Reynier's Corps, was around Vladimir and Ustilug.[26]

---

21   War Diary of Third Army's vanguard.
22   Chaplits' notes (M.T.D. No 44,712).
23   War Diary of Third Army's vanguard.
24   Count Lambert's vanguard consisted of the Kozlov Infantry, Ryazhsk Infantry, Yakutsk Infantry, 10th Jägers, Alexandria Hussars (including its two replacement squadrons), Zhitomir Dragoons, Arzamas Dragoons, Tatar Ulans, four regiments of irregular cavalry, 11 guns from 12th Horse Artillery Company (War Diary of Third Army's vanguard).
25   War Diary of Third Army's vanguard.
26   Chambray, I, 289.

The troops of both sides remained in these positions until the arrival of the Army of the Danube on the Styr in early September.

To complete the overview of operations in this theatre of war, let us turn to a presentation of events in Polesia.

General Dąbrowski was detached from Napoleon's *Grande Armée* with his division on 11 (23) August, and sent to the Berezina river from Smolensk, in order to cover the main line of operations of this army and to monitor the Bobruisk garrison and the corps under General Ertel, stationed at Mozyr. His force, having replaced Latour Maubourg's *4e Corps de cavalerie*, which remained in the rear of the *Grande Armée*, was reinforced with elements from this corps and was composed of 16 battalions (*1 Pułk Piechoty, 6 Pułk Piechoty, 14 Pułk Piechoty* and *17 Pułk Piechoty*) and 12 squadrons (*2 Pułk Ułanów, 7 Pułk Ułanów* and *15 Pułk Ułanów*), totalling some 8,000 men with 20 guns.[27] The garrison of Bobruisk, under the command of Major General Ignatiev [Gavriil Alexandrovich Ignatiev], consisted of 12 weak battalions, 5,000 men in total; while II Reserve Corps under General Ertel, including six replacement battalions from 36th Division, had 17 battalions, 14 squadrons, three Don Cossack regiments and 13 *sotnia* of Malorussia Cossacks, having a total of some 12,000 men with 22 guns. Most of the troops from this corps consisted of recruits who had received no skill at arms training.[28]

General Dąbrowski, leaving four battalions and four squadrons (*17 Pułk Piechoty* and *15 Pułk Ułanów*), under the command of Colonel Małachowski [Kazimierz Małachowski] in order to cover Mogilev, settled down at the end of August [early September] with the rest of his infantry on the Berezina river near Svislach; while the cavalry, under the command of General Dziewanowski [Dominik Dziewanowski], he placed at Glusk [Hlusk] and Vilcha, where enemy magazines had been established. Once Polish patrols, having flooded the surrounding area, reached Mozyr, General Ertel, wanting to put a stop to these raids, which had caused disorder and unrest in the surrounding countryside, and in order to destroy the magazines established by the enemy, decided to engage the Polish detachment. Leaving three battalions, four squadrons and the Malorussia Cossacks to guard Mozyr and detaching Major General Zapolsky [Andrey Vasilevich Zapolsky] to Pinsk (seized by 5,000 Austrian troops under General Mohr [Johann Friedrich Freiherr von Mohr] upon Tormasov's retreat to the Styr) with eight battalions and two Don Cossack regiments, in early [mid] September, Ertel moved to Glusk with the remaining six battalions, ten squadrons and one Cossack regiment and, on 2 (14) September, ejected a Polish detachment under Captain Paradowski, consisting of two squadrons and three hundred unfit men, who had arrived there from Warsaw. Then, the following day [15 September new style], marching on Gorbatsevichi, Ertel defeated Paradowski, who had been reinforced by a march regiment (*régiment de marche*) and a battalion of the French *33e Légère* (Davout's *1er Corps*), who had arrived to support Dąbrowski. The

---

27   General Dąbrowski, in a memo he submitted to Marshal Victor on 5 January 1813 (new style), wrote that his detachment had no more than 5,000 infantry and 1,000 cavalry, but this statement is not in agreement with the total for these troops, at the opening of the campaign (reaching some 14,000), nor with the numbers given by Dąbrowski in other sources.

28   General Ertel's reports to the Tsar.

enemy losses, in this action, reached several hundred men, including 159 prisoners; 77 men were killed and 104 wounded on our side. Meanwhile, Dąbrowski, having received intelligence about the movement of the Chernigov *Opolchenie* towards Mogilev, sent four battalions (*1 Pułk Piechoty*) to help Małachowski, while he moved to Gorbatsevichi himself with two battalions (*6 Pułk Piechoty*), but being unable to hold our troops back, retreated to Svislach. General Ertel, having destroyed the enemy magazines, moved back to Mozyr and arrived there on 10 (22) September, while the troops under General Zapolsky caught one of Mohr's detachments, captured a gun and took about a hundred men prisoner, which forced the Austrians to evacuate Pinsk and retreat to Lubieszów, in order to be closer to Siegenthal's force, which was stationed at Ratno.[29]

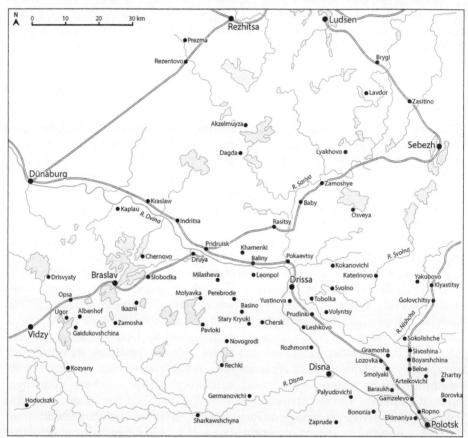

Map of Count Wittgenstein's Area of Operations, July and August 1812.

29   Buturlin, II, 96-100.

13

The Battle of Klyastitsy

The formation of I Corps. – Order of battle. – Count Wittgenstein. – The enemy corps operating along the Dvina. – The advance of MacDonald's force towards the Dvina. – Precautions taken by General Essen 1st in the event of the siege of Riga. – General Löwis' advance towards Eckau. – The action at Eckau. – The razing of the Riga suburbs. – MacDonald's advance towards Jakobstadt and Oudinot's towards Polotsk.

Wittgenstein's deployment at Pokaevtsy. – His precautions for the security of the flanks of I Corps. – His intention to launch an offensive along the left bank of the Dvina. – The move towards Pridruisk and from there towards Rasitsy. – MacDonald's crossing at Jakobstadt and Oudinot's advance towards Klyastitsy. – Wittgenstein's plan of action. – His advance towards Klyastitsy. – The crossing of the Svolna. – The action at Yakubovo. – The battle of Klyastitsy. – The action at Boyarshchina. – The death of Kulnev. – The action at Golovchitsy. – Oudinot's retreat towards Polotsk. – The outcome of Count Wittgenstein's operations.

MacDonald's advance towards Dünaburg. – The enemy attempt to besiege Riga. – General Essen's response.

On 5 (17) July, at the same time as the main body of First Army was leaving the Drissa camp, up the right bank of the Dvina, towards Polotsk, the commander of I Corps, Wittgenstein, received orders from Barclay de Tolly: to remain in the area currently occupied by I Corps, near Drissa, in order to cover the sector between Novogrodi and the Dvina, attempting to remain on this river, inflicting all manner of harm on the enemy while protecting Riga; if it became necessary to retreat, to withdraw via Sebezh to Pskov, where there were magazines with rations for his corps.[1]

The force entrusted to Count Wittgenstein, upon joining up with the replacement battalions and replacement squadrons, under the command of major generals Gamen and Prince Repnin, in early [mid] July (not including the ten replacement battalions and the Combined Hussar Regiment detached to Dünaburg), consisted

---

[1] War Diary of the independent I Corps. *Précis de la campagne du 1er corps de la 1e armée d'Occident pendant l'année 1812* (Archive of the M.T.D. No 19,200). For details of Wittgenstein's orders, see Appendix XVIII.

of 36 battalions, 27 squadrons, one Cossack regiment, nine artillery and one pioneer company, for a total of about 25,000 men with 108 guns. Magazines with rations for the corps were located in Sebezh, Ostrov and Pskov; while replacement parks were in Sebezh.[2]

Count Wittgenstein, who was then 44 years old, a vigorous, active warrior, was not blessed with multi–faceted knowledge, but he knew how to motivate the troops through personal example, inspired devotion to the Tsar and the fatherland in his subordinates and aroused their enthusiasm for the common cause. An affable, generous commander, Wittgenstein gave full justice to the merits of his colleagues: the Corps Chief of Staff, one of the most educated generals of the Russian army, d'Auvray [Fëdor Fillipovich Dovre]; the Chief of Artillery, the most gifted, ener-getic and brave Prince Iashvili; Chief Quartermaster, the ardent, ebulliently active, Diebitsch [Ivan Ivanovich Dibich], and the commander of the vanguard, the fearless Kulnev. The harmony that prevailed in the headquarters under Count Wittgenstein gave our commander a decisive advantage over the enemy generals, who were oper-ating against him without proper liaison between themselves.

From the very opening of hostilities, Napoleon had assigned one of his corps to capture Riga under the command of MacDonald. The seizure of this coastal fortress would provide support for his left flank and ensure the delivery of supplies to his army by sea. Subsequently, during the advance of the *Grande Armée* to Vitebsk, Oudinot's *2e Corps* was left to face Wittgenstein and to threaten St Petersburg, supported, a little later, by Saint-Cyr's *6e Corps*. Each of the corps commanders left on the Dvina operated independently of the other, at their own discretion. A Marshal of the French Empire, who had diligently carried out the will of his master, would be offended if he happened to serve under the command of one of his peers. Napoleon permitted such violations of military principles, and the consequences of this were often fatal to him.

At that time, as the main body of First Army was retreating towards Drissa, and Napoleon's troops, after occupying Vilna, had been sent from there in various direc-tions, partly to pursue First Army, partly to cut off Second Army, MacDonald's *10e Corps*, advancing on the left flank of the French, crossing the Neman at Tilsit, on 12 (24) June, arrived in Rossieny on 18 (30 June) and set out from there, on 26 June (8 July), in two columns: Grawert [Julius von Grawert] advanced through Schaulen to Bauske with his division, occupied Mitau [Jelgava] and sent his leading troops to the town of Eckau [Iecava]; while MacDonald went through Poniewież [Panevėžys] himself with Grandjean's division, where the enemy managed to capture one of our magazines, and on to Jakobstadt [Jēkabpils] arriving there on 9 (21) July.

Meanwhile, the military governor of Riga, Lieutenant General Essen 1st, at the first news of the crossing of our borders by enemy troops, placed Riga under martial law. The inhabitants were ordered to stock up on provisions for four months in case of a siege. Households who wanted to leave the city were required to leave two healthy people in each dwelling. At the same time, all necessary measures were taken for fire fighting, large stores of grain were established, and a significant amount of straw

---

2   For details of the strength and composition of Wittgenstein's I Corps, see Appendix XIX.

was brought from outside the city to line the streets in case of a bombardment. The procurement of various kinds of stores was entrusted to a commission composed of three merchants, three administrators, and three tradesmen. Due to a lack of artillerymen, some of the citizens were designated as crew for the guns. In the suburbs, houses were identified for demolition in the event of the appearance of enemy troops close to the city. Pitch soaked wreaths (*pekh–krantsy*) and other combustible materials were prepared. A telegraph was erected on the Lutheran Cathedral in order to communicate with the British squadron under Admiral Martin [Thomas Byam Martin], which had arrived off Dünamünde [Daugavgriva fortress] upon the opening of hostilities.

The fortifications of Riga and Dünamünde were garrisoned by regular troops; while eight British gunboats sent by Admiral Martin were deployed to prevent the enemy from crossing the lower Dvina; a larger flotilla subsequently arrived at Riga from Reval [Tallinn] and Sveaborg [Suomenlinna]. These boats also operated along the river Aa [Lielupe], in order to deny the Schlock [Sloka] district and harass the enemy.

From 6 to 11 (18 to 23) July, all the buildings that lay on the left bank and on the islands of the Dvina, in front of the fortifications laid out by us, were demolished or burned down. At the same time, most of the timber stocks that were on the left bank of the river, and all the boats measuring 30 to 40 feet long, were transferred to the right bank and placed at the disposal of the engineering department.[3]

General Essen, having some 18,000 men under his command, hoped to stay in the field to prevent the enemy from besieging the fortress. To that end, he sent Lieutenant General Löwis [Fëdor Fëdorovich Leviz] on the route towards Schaulen, with eight battalions, four squadrons and several Cossack regiments, a total of about 6,000 men.[4] General Löwis took up positions at Eckau.

On 7 (19) July, Grawert, having set out from Bauske with five battalions, attacked Löwis' force from the direction of Sorgen [Zorġi], while General Kleist [Friedrich von Kleist] was to move around the left flank of the Russian force with three battalions and six squadrons from the direction of Drächen [Vecumnieki]. Löwis' troops fought very stubbornly, but being outflanked on both sides, they retreated in disorder to Dahlenkirchen [Kekava], for the loss of up to 600 men. On the part of the Prussian troops, their casualties did not exceed 150 men.[5] The next day, Löwis' troops returned to Riga. An eyewitness to the events of that time, the chief pastor of Riga, Tile [Thiele?], wrote that 'the soldiers were as cheerful and carefree as if they were on a parade.' The Prussian troops deployed along the river Misa [Mūša], stretching a line of outposts to the left to Schlock on the lower reaches of the Aa, and to the right to the island in the Dvina, Dahlenholm, seized by them, on 10 (22) July.

As soon as the news came through to Riga about Löwis' retreat from Eckau to Dahlenkirchen, General Essen 1st ordered the civil governor and all government offices to go to Pernov [Pärnu] by sea. At the same time, it was announced to the residents of the quarters closest to the fortress, the Moscow and St Petersburg suburbs,

---

3   Information provided by the local authorities of the Livonia [Lifland] Governorate.
4   Buturlin, II, 3.
5   Buturlin, II, 3. Grawert's official report.

that they must evacuate their homes. After the occupation of Dahlenholm Island by the enemy and the appearance of Prussian troops on the right bank of the Dvina, near Kirchholm, 15 *versts* from Riga, General Essen, having received an exaggerated report about this from a field officer sent by him on reconnaissance, gave orders for the above mentioned quarters to be burned down.

On 11 (23) July, at ten o'clock in the evening, several reserve battalions were sent out of the fortress behind the esplanade; immediately all buildings condemned to be burned were checked and confirmed clear, whereupon teams with pitch soaked wreaths and other incendiary devices, under the direction of police officers, set fire to the suburbs at a number of points. Due to a strong, suddenly rising wind, the flames also caught on those buildings that were not supposed to be destroyed at all, and therefore, in order to save them, other reserve battalions were sent from the fortress. The troops were fighting the fires until four o'clock in the morning of 12 (24) July. In the midst of the flames that enveloped the suburbs, a church remained intact for a long time; the soldiers, who had been ordered to hang *pekh–krantsy* to it, said that they 'could not raise their hands to burn the house of God, and that it would burn by itself,' and in the mean time they were rescuing church implements. Eventually, once everything had already been taken out of the church, it also caught fire from sparks carried on the wind.

All together in both suburbs, this fire destroyed: four churches, 35 city and public buildings, 702 residential buildings and the Russian covered market with 36 shops. In addition, 117 houses were burned down in the Zadvinsk suburbs. The loss suffered by the city amounted to more than 17 million paper roubles.[6]

For the duration of these events, MacDonald moved the headquarters of his corps to Jakobstadt, ordered the construction of bridges there and sent one of his regiments to Dünaburg, along the left bank of the Dvina. At the same time, Oudinot was moving up the Dvina towards Disna and Polotsk.

Thus, facing Count Wittgenstein, who had some 25,000 men under his command, there were – on the one side, Oudinot's entire *2e Corps*, and on the other – MacDonald with Grandjean's division: according to statements by French soldiers, the former had at least 28,000 at that time, and the latter some 12,000 men, consequently both of them combined had more than one and a half times the strength of our corps.[7]

As soon as the orders to operate independently were received from Barclay de Tolly in the headquarters of I Corps, leaving his troops for the time being in their positions, that is, Gamen's detachment, amounting to 3,300 men, in Dünaburg, Kulnev's vanguard in Baliny, the main body of the corps along the Sariya river near Pokaevtsy, and the reserve opposite the Drissa camp, Count Wittgenstein established a screen of observation posts along the Dvina from Drissa to Dünaburg, where he established liaison points with the outposts of Gamen's detachment, which was monitoring the area downstream as far as Kreutzburg [Krustpils], opposite Jakobstadt; in order to gather the most accurate intelligence about everything happening on the left bank of the river, patrols were sent out, supported by small outposts.[8] At the same time,

6   Information provided by the local authorities of the Livonia Governorate.
7   Thiers, XIV, *Edit. de Brux.* 194. Chambray, I, 257.
8   See Map titled Showing the Area of Operations of Count Wittgenstein in July and August 1812.

Wittgenstein ordered the restoration of a bridge at the Drissa camp, on the exact spot where the bridges had been built before, but this work took a long time, because the pontoons belonging to I Corps had followed the army, and in order to restore a permanent crossing, Drissa had no other resources than to build a bridge of boats or rafts. As the bridgehead located there, in terms of its volume, required a significant number of troops for its defence, engineer Colonel Count Sievers [Yegor Karlovich Sievers] received orders to construct another, smaller one inside it. General Gamen was instructed to evacuate the Dünaburg bridgehead and send the artillery located there to Pskov, except for the six field guns left with the Dünaburg garrison, which, in the event of a crossing by significant enemy forces onto the right bank of the Dvina, were to retreat to Ludsen [Ludza].[9]

On 8 (20) July, Count Wittgenstein, having in mind the monitoring of the area of the Dvina upstream towards Disna, detached Major General Balk [Mikhail Dmitrievich Balk] to Leshkovo (where there was a ford) with two combined grena-dier battalions from 5th Division, the Riga Dragoons and six guns from 3rd Horse Artillery Company. The following day, a report was received in the corps headquar-ters from General Balk about the appearance of the enemy at Disna. These were the troops of Napoleon's *Grande Armée*, which at that time was moving up the Dvina; but since this situation was not known in our corps headquarters and it was assessed that the enemy might be crossing with significant forces at Disna, General Balk thereupon received orders to move the detachment entrusted to him to the right bank of the Drissa river and take up positions near the village of Volyntsy. Following which, Balk's force, having been reinforced with one battalion of 36th Jägers, two reserve grenadier battalions, two combined grenadier battalions from 14th Division, the replacement squadron of the Lifeguard Hussars and six guns from 28th Battery Artillery Company (seven battalions and five squadrons with 18 guns, including the original troops), formed an observation detachment on the left wing of the corps, which came under the command of Major General Kazachkovsky [Kirill Fëdorovich Kazchkovsky], who was ordered to withdraw towards Osveya [Asvieja], if pressed.[10]

Count Wittgenstein, intending to move across the line of communications of the enemy force which was passing the positions he occupied, in order to draw them away from First Army, ordered his vanguard to build a floating bridge near Druya. Indeed, all the intelligence received confirmed that MacDonald's *10e Corps* was stretched across 200 *versts* from the Gulf of Riga to Dünaburg, while Oudinot's *2e Corps* was at Disna at a distance of about 100 *versts* from MacDonald's nearest troops. Having assessed the situation, Wittgenstein intended to move into the gap between the enemy corps, at Druya, separate them completely and strike into the rear of Oudinot's Corps.[11]

To that end, on 11 (23) July, at noon, the vanguard of the corps moved to Pridruisk. A few hours later, the main body headed there along country roads from Pokaevtsy

---

9   *Précis de la campagne du 1er corps* (archive of the M.T.D. No 29,200). War Diary of the independent I Corps.
10   Buturlin, II, 4.
11   Lieutenant General Count Wittgenstein's report to the Minister of War dated 11 [23] July, No 74.

to Khamenki in order to avoid moving along the highway on the bank of the Dvina, which could have betrayed the aim of our operation. In the absence of pontoons, boats and the other materials necessary for the construction of a bridge were sent to Druya under escort by one battalion of 23rd Jägers with two horse artillery guns. The rearmost troops departed from Pokaevtsy upon the arrival of Kazachkovsky's detachment there, which, upon its departure from the village of Volyntsy, left Balk there with two combined grenadier battalions from 5th Division, three squadrons of Riga Dragoons and six guns from 3rd Horse Artillery Company. Both Kazachkovsky's and Balk's detachments were assigned to secure the left flank of the corps, while the troops of Gamen's detachment continued to hold in Dünaburg in order to provide cover on the right flank.

In making an advance across the enemy line of communications, Count Wittgenstein foresaw that Oudinot might move into the rear of our corps, along the St Petersburg road, and therefore ordered the detachments stationed at Pokaevtsy and Volyntsy, in the event of significant enemy forces crossing the Drissa river, to retreat towards Zamoshye and Osveya, destroying the crossings, cratering the roads and delaying the enemy at every step, while the main body was to head from Druya towards Ludsen and to attack the left flank of Oudinot's *2e Corps*.

On 12 (24) July, the construction of a bridge began at Druya, which was supposed to be completed by the following morning. Meanwhile, the main body under Count Wittgenstein managed to assemble at Pridruisk, while the reserve arrived at Rasitsy [Rositsa]. But at that very moment intelligence was received that forced Count Wittgenstein to postpone the proposed offensive. General Kazachkovsky reported to him that the enemy was advancing in considerable force towards the Drissa river, while General Gamen reported that enemy infantry had appeared on the right bank of the Dvina near Kreutzburg, and that, according to intelligence provided by informants, MacDonald had assembled some 6,000 men at Jakobstadt and was proceeding to build a bridge at this location.

The crossings by enemy corps on the flanks of the locations held by Russian troops led to the conclusion that the French commanders intended to unite their forces in the rear of our corps and, by severing its communications with St Petersburg, would put us in a most dangerous situation. Therefore, Count Wittgenstein, abandoning his original intention to launch an offensive with his main force on the left bank of the Dvina, decided to send only Kulnev's vanguard there, solely for the purpose of capturing transport and taking prisoners in the rear of the enemy army. Wittgenstein, exploiting the separation between MacDonald and Oudinot, proposed to assume a central position himself with the main body of the corps, to wait there for the enemy corps to cross to the right bank of the Dvina and attack the nearest of them with the main body, while the other corps could be held for a while by our small detachments.[12] This excellent plan, whose execution was facilitated by the inaction of MacDonald and the indecision of Oudinot, brought to the Russian commander all his subsequent successes.

---

12   Lieutenant General Count Wittgenstein's report to the Minister of War dated 13 [25] July, No 77. *Précis de la campagne du 1er corps.*

In order to concentrate the Russian force, a central position was chosen near the village of Rasitsy, and meanwhile, on 13 (25) July, Kulnev's vanguard, having been sent across the Dvina, pushed several detachments forwards: one of them destroyed an enemy convoy, which was under escort by 1,500 men, while the other captured an enemy outpost near the village of Chernovo [Chernevo]; in total, 434 men, including two officers, were taken prisoner by both detachments.

At the same time, Kazachkovsky, located at Pokaevtsy with his detachment, having learned about the advance by significant enemy forces towards the Drissa river and having no word from Balk's detachment stationed at Volyntsy, destroyed the magazines located in Drissa and retreated to Osveya, concerned about being cut off, which forced Balk also to retreat towards Sebezh. Count Wittgenstein, who, in the meantime had moved across to Rasitsy with the main body of the corps, on 14 (26) July, having learned about the retreat by Kazachkovsky's and Balk's detachments, ordered them to return to Pokaevtsy and Volyntsy, and entrusted the command of the former to Major General Helffreich [Bogdan Borisovich Gelfreikh 1st]. Balk's detachment, which was ordered to monitor the length of the Drissa river from Volyntsy to Sivoshina, was reinforced by three squadrons of the Lifeguard Combined Cavalry Regiment and one squadron of Pskov Dragoons.[13]

On 14 (26) July, the vanguard moved back to the right bank of the Dvina and moved towards Drissa, and on the following day [27 July new style] joined Balk's detachment on the Svolna. Count Wittgenstein, still remaining with the main body of the corps in its previous position at Rasitsy, received reports from Kulnev on the one hand, about the appearance of the enemy in significant numbers from Disna, and on the other hand, from Gamen, about the crossing by a strong detachment of MacDonald's troops at Jakobstadt and about Gamen's intention to retreat to Ludsen, in accordance with the instructions issued to him.[14]

Indeed, Oudinot, after several unsuccessful attempts to take possession of the Dünaburg bridgehead, had moved up the Dvina, destroyed the fortifications of the Drissa camp, left General Merle's infantry division and Corbineau's light cavalry brigade at Disna, in order to cross the Dvina at this point, and on 14 (26) July, had arrived at Polotsk, taking this city without opposition.

Fortunately for Wittgenstein, the French military commanders were operating without any liaison between themselves. MacDonald limited himself to probing attacks, in anticipation of reinforcements, without which he did not dare to proceed with the siege of Riga; while Oudinot, having received orders from Napoleon's État–major général to commence offensive operations against Wittgenstein, decided immediately after the occupation of Polotsk to get across the route to Petersburg. To that end, after giving his troops a rest day on 15 (27) July, he set out from Polotsk the following day [28 July new style], crossed the Drissa River by fording at Sivoshina and arrived at the village of Klyastitsy on the morning of the 18th (30 July). General Merle, having crossed the Dvina at Disna, on 16 (28) July, marched on Lozovka, in the direction of Sivoshina, while Corbineau, covering his advance on the left,

---

13   *Précis* etc. Lieutenant General Count Wittgenstein's report to the Minister of War dated 14 [26] July, No 80, from Rasitsy.

14   Reports by Wittgenstein, Kulnev and Gamen.

engaged in a heated fight with Kulnev's and Balk's cavalry near the village of Filipovo, five *versts* from Volyntsy.[15] From our side, four squadrons of the Grodno Hussars, a squadron of Lifeguard Hussars and Platov 4th's Cossack Regiment were brought into battle, while the French committed the *8 Pułk Strzelców Konnych, 7e chasseurs à cheval* and *20e chasseurs à cheval*. The enemy losses were much heavier than ours and included 167 prisoners alone, including three officers.[16] Merle's force, having arrived at Sivoshina, on 17 (29) July, were left there to protect the line of retreat of Oudinot's main body.[17]

Throughout the duration of these events, the arrival of one of MacDonald's regiments at the Dünaburg bridgehead along the left bank of the Dvina, together with intelligence on the construction of a bridge by the enemy at Jakobstadt, forced Gamen to evacuate Dünaburg on 15 (27) July, and retreat along the road to Rezhitsa [Rositten or Rezekne]. Major Bedryaga was left at Dünaburg with a small cavalry detachment in order to destroy the stores remaining there and to sweep up the detachments that had been left in Pridruisk, Krasław [Krāslava] and opposite Kaplau [Kaplava].

As all the intelligence collected during the 16th (28 July) and overnight from 16 to 17 (28 to 29) July confirmed that Oudinot's main body was advancing along the St Petersburg road, Count Wittgenstein decided to move to engage him, having ordered Gamen to delay MacDonald for as long as possible. In his report to the Minister of War dated 17 (29) July, Count Wittgenstein wrote: 'I have decided to march on Klyastitsy this very day and on the 19th [31 July], at dawn, to attack Oudinot with all my strength. If, with the help of the Almighty, I should be fortunate enough to break him, then I should be content to face MacDonald alone.' On 17 (29) July, at noon, the troops stationed at Rasitsy set off along the road leading from Kokanovichi to Klyastitsy, while Helffreich's and Balk's detachments were directed straight to Klyastitsy, having received orders to send fighting patrols along the right bank of the Drissa in order to protect the corps until the vanguard (marching from Volyntsy at two o'clock in the afternoon) had arrived on the St Petersburg road at Sokolishche. In the event that the enemy had already occupied this location before the arrival of our troops, the vanguard was to establish communications with the main body and move to Klyastitsy. The train was sent to Sebezh, under escort of three squadrons of the Combined Dragoon Regiment, which had been monitoring the course of the Dvina.

The troops were already on the march to Kokanovichi, when Major Neidhardt ([Alexander Ivanovich Neidgardt] later commander of the Independent Caucasus Corps), who had returned from a reconnaissance, reported that the enemy, having crossed the Drissa at Sivoshina, was moving towards Klyastitsy, and that there was no way to beat them to this location. The situation of the corps had become very precarious: the most convenient route to Sebezh having been severed by the enemy. There was only one of two options left: to head along country roads to Sebezh and give battle there, or to march on the flank of the enemy and attack them at

---

15   *Précis de la campagne du 1er corps.* War Diary.
16   *Précis* etc. Kulnev's report to Count Wittgenstein dated 16 [28] July.
17   Chambray, I, 259.

Klyastitsy, such that, in the event of failure, it was possible to retreat via Ludsen to Ostrov. Having realised that, as our corps was moving to Sebezh via country roads, Oudinot could forestall him at this location, Count Wittgenstein decided to attack the enemy at Klyastitsy. This course of action represented the best chance of success for the Russian force, both in terms of their method of fighting in rugged terrain, developed from the late war with Sweden, and the effect on morale that a surprise attack from the flank was expected to have on the enemy. In the event of a reverse, the retreat by our corps to Ludsen and on to Ostrov had been completely secured by Gamen's detachment, which, being located on the route leading from Dünaburg to Ludsen, where there are many defiles convenient for defence, could easily delay an advance by MacDonald.

During the night of 17 to 18 (29 to 30) July, the troops of I Corps moved to the village of Katerinovo, on the Svolna River. At this time, news was received from Barclay de Tolly, about his departure from Vitebsk towards Smolensk with the main body of First Army. The retreat by our army gave Napoleon the opportunity to detach part of his force to assist Marshal Oudinot, in order to give him the chance to break I Corps and move on St Petersburg. Under such circumstances, Count Wittgenstein felt it necessary to convene a council of war to discuss his proposed plan of action. The Chief of Staff, General d'Auvray, proposed to attack the enemy first, believing that we had no other means left to protect the northern regions of the empire, which was the primary mission of the corps. The Chief of Artillery, Prince Iashvili, supported this opinion, with which all the other members of the council were in agreement. It was decided to attack the enemy.[18]

On 18 (30) July, at dawn, the vanguard of I Corps, under Kulnev's command, assembled on the Svolna at the village of Katerinovo, consisting of: Platov 4th's Don Cossacks, the Grodno Hussars, 25th Jägers, 26th Jägers and Lieutenant Colonel Sukhozanet's 1st Horse Artillery Company, 3,730 men in total with 12 guns. The only means for crossing to the other side of the river there was a very rickety bridge, and therefore, under the leadership of engineer Colonel Count Sievers, they set about building a more reliable crossing made from house beams dismantled in the village. But as this work could not be completed quickly, and time was precious, the crossing was immediately started over the dilapidated bridge at Katerinovo. The infantry crossed by files; the hussars crossed singly, dismounting and leading their horses; the artillery was dismantled and moved piece by piece by hand. All this required extraordinary effort by the troops, but the keenness of the soldiers, encouraged in the highest degree by their commanders, overcame all difficulties, and by three o'clock in the afternoon the entire vanguard, having already managed to assemble for a rest halt on the far side of the Svolna, moved further along the road to Klyastitsy.[19]

Meanwhile, a strong bridge had been built, over which the main body of the corps (22 battalions, eight squadrons, one pioneer company and six artillery companies) crossed, totalling 13,065 men with 72 guns. The reserve (ten battalions, eight

---

18   *Précis de la campagne du 1er corps.* War Diary.
19   From Adjutant–General Sukhozanet 1st's notes.

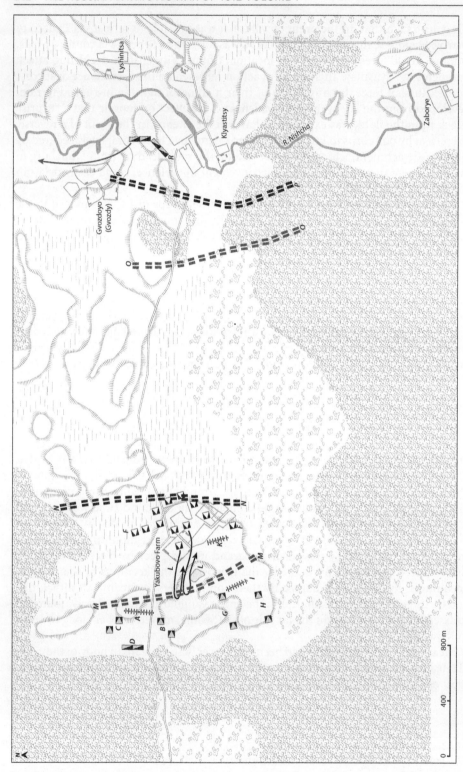

Plan of the Battle of Klyastitsy, 30–31 July 1812.

Legend

30 July 1812

Russian Forces		French Forces	
A.	1st Horse Artillery Company.	F.F.	56e, 19ᵉ Ligne & 26ᵉ Légère.
B.	25th Jägers.	K.	French battery.
C.	26th Jägers.	L.L.	Oudinot's attack.
D.	Grodno Hussars.	N.N.	Final Positions.
G.	23rd Jägers.		
H.	24th Jägers.		
I.	14th Battery Artillery Company.		
M.M.	Final Positions.		

31 July 1812

Russian Forces		French Forces	
M.M.	Initial Positions.	N.N.	Initial Positions.
O.O.	Subsequent Positions.	P.P.	Subsequent Positions.
R.R.	Cavalry flanking movement.		

squadrons and two artillery companies), totalling 6,165 men with 24 guns, received orders to remain in Katerinovo.

Overall, under Count Wittgenstein's direct command, on 18 (30) July, there were about 23,000 fighting men with 108 guns including the reserve.[20]

On the enemy side, under Marshal Oudinot's command, were the following troops: Legrand's division, Verdier's division and Merle's division, Doumerc's *3e division de cuirassiers* (from *3e Corps de cavalerie*) with Castex's and Corbineau's light cavalry brigades (in total, 51 battalions, 36 squadrons), making 28,000 men with 114 guns.[21]

At the same time as Kulnev's vanguard was crossing the Svolna, Oudinot halted the advance of his corps, having arrived at Klyastitsy with the troops of Legrand's division and Castex's cavalry brigade at 11 o'clock in the morning, and not having accurate intelligence about our forces, he sent one of the infantry regiments on the route towards Sebezh and placed the rest of Legrand's regiments at the village of Yakubovo, two *versts* from Klyastitsy, on the road to Katerinovo.[22]

At about two o'clock in the afternoon, two squadrons of Grodno Hussars, marching at the head of our vanguard, approached Yakubovo, while the other troops of the vanguard had halted at the entrance to the forest, near the village of Olkhovo. Count Wittgenstein, having received word of Kulnev's contact with the French, sent 23rd Jägers and 24th Jägers with 14th Artillery Company to support him and ordered the vanguard to attack the enemy without waiting for these reinforcements in order to deny them the chance to strengthen themselves. The remaining troops of the first fighting echelon were ordered to pick up the pace. At five o'clock in the afternoon,

---

20 Extracted from returns compiled for 18 [30] July 1812, in Katerinovo.
21 Extracted from returns presented in *Précis de la campagne du 1er corps*. The troop totals agree with those given in Thiers.
22 See Plan of the Battle of Klyastitsy 18 to 19 (30 to 31) July 1812.

Kulnev, having forced the enemy skirmishers out of the forest, on the road from Olkhovo to Yakubovo, repulsed a French attack on the flanks of our troops at the exits from the defile and positioned himself on the high ground facing the village of Yakubovo: Sukhozanet's 1st Horse Artillery Company was stationed in the centre; Colonel Denisiev's [Stepan Vasilievich Denisiev] 25th Jägers were to their right, while Colonel Roth's [Loggin Osipovich Roth] 26th Jägers were to the left of the battery; Lieutenant Colonel Rüdiger was in reserve with the Grodno Hussars. Legrand, noticing the small numbers of our troops, attacked the 25th Jägers with four battalions from *56e Ligne*, supported by eight battalions from *26e Légère* and *19e Ligne* regiments from Maison's [Nicolas–Joseph Maison] brigade; but the lethal cannister fire of our horse artillery, which constantly moved from one place to another and worked to enfilade the advancing enemy troops, helped the 25th Jägers to hold at the edge of the forest until the arrival of Count Wittgenstein with the 23rd Jägers and 24th Jägers under Colonel Frolov [Grigory Nikolaevich Frolov] and with the 14th Battery Artillery Company under Colonel Staden [Gustav Gustavevich Staden], which was immediately sent to the right wing of our line, while Frolov's jägers and some of the Grodno Hussars were directed to assist the 25th Jägers. The right wing of our vanguard moved forward; the Russian troops pushed the enemy back to Yakubovo, but could not capture this village, which was set on fire by the French; Meanwhile, on our left wing, the 26th Jägers also pressed forwards, but were forced to halt at Yakubovo. In the evening, Verdier's division managed to arrive, and formed the reserve for Legrand's force. The cuirassiers under Doumerc were left on the St Petersburg road, due to the impossibility of getting them into action in the wooded terrain on the battlefield. Oudinot, taking advantage of the arrival of reinforcements, pushed Kulnev's skirmishing screen back and launched an attack on the centre of our force. The position occupied by the French was constrained on the one side by dense forest, and on the other by the houses in the village of Yakubovo, which prevented them from getting any more than 12 guns up to support their attack; in contrast, we had the opportunity to engage the enemy with twice the artillery fire from 14th Battery Company and 1st Horse Artillery Company, which forced the French to retreat to Yakubovo with heavy casualties. Whereupon the screen of jäger regiments, supported by marksmen from the Kaluga Infantry and Sevsk Infantry regiments, pushed forwards and reoccupied their original positions. The French columns, falling back behind Yakubovo, left some of their infantry in this village. The cannonade continued until 11 o'clock at night. Its strength can be judged by the fact that Sukhozanet's horse artillery company lost 83 men on this day, out of an original strength of 216 men, therefore, more than a third of the available manpower.[23]

Count Wittgenstein, having decided to renew the attack the following day [31 July new style], drew his entire force up to Yakubovo, with the exception of Prince Repnin's cavalry detachment, which, due to the nature of the surrounding terrain, could not be brought into action, and therefore was left at Katerinovo. During the night, the troops of the vanguard and the first fighting echelon were placed in position

---

23   The description of the action at Yakubovo was compiled on the basis of the War Diary of I Corps, *Précis de la campagne du 1er corps*, and notes by Adjutant General Sukhozanet 1st.

in the following order: six battalions (24th Jägers, 25th Jägers and 23rd Jägers) with 14 guns (5th Artillery Company and one platoon of 9th Artillery Company) on the right wing; six battalions (Sevsk Infantry, Kaluga Infantry and 26th Jägers) in the centre; 12 guns (27th Light Artillery Company) and four battalions (Perm Infantry and Mogilev Infantry) on the left wing. The infantry were deployed in a single wave in battalion columns. The remaining troops of the corps stayed at Olkhovo, because the very limited depth of the area between the enemy position and the forest lying to our rear did not allow Count Wittgenstein to deploy a second wave directly behind the first. However, the troops left at Olkhovo were ordered to advance through the forest as soon as the first line had gone into action.[24]

On the part of the French, their troops remained in the places occupied by them at the end of the fighting on 18 (30) July: Legrand's division at Yakubovo, extending their left wing to the forest; Verdier's division forming the second line; Doumerc's cuirassiers, in reserve near Klyastitsy; Castex's light cavalry brigade at various point along the fighting line. Merle's division remained, as before, on the Drissa at Sivoshina, while Corbineau's brigade was near Volyntsy.[25] Thus Oudinot deprived himself of the use of 8,000 men, which could have given him a decisive numerical advantage over Count Wittgenstein's I Corps.

On 19 (31) July, at three o'clock in the morning, the Russian troops resumed their attack. Colonel Frolov, who had stationed himself facing the Yakubovo manor with 23rd Jägers, noticing that it was weakly held by the French, charged forwards with his columns and took possession of the manor house, but was driven out with losses by *26e Légère*, who were behind the farmyard in reserve: at the same time a firefight began, first on our right wing, and then along the whole line. Marshal Oudinot, exploiting the success of his *26e Légère*, led a determined attack on our centre, but was repelled by the crossfire from 5th Battery Artillery Company and 27th Light Artillery Company. Whereupon Oudinot, having reinforced his front line with part of the reserve, resumed the attack on the centre of our position and sent several battalions around the left wing. These attacks were also repulsed by the skilful operations of the Russian artillery.

Count Wittgenstein, noticing the wavering of the enemy columns, ordered Major General Berg, who was in command of the entire front line, to attack the French. Major General Kazachkovsky, with the Sevsk Infantry and Kaluga Infantry, supported by some of the Grodno Hussars, struck the centre of the enemy position; Prince Sibirsky [Alexander Vasilevich Sibirsky] was directed against the right wing with the Perm Infantry and Mogilev Infantry; Roth's 26th Jägers proceeded in echelon into the interval between the Kaluga Infantry and Perm Infantry; the other three jäger regiments attacked the French left wing through the woods. The second fighting echelon had advanced from Olkhovo, and was ready to follow the first. The Russian troops, spurred on by the example of their commanders, charged with fixed bayonets and drove back, initially the centre, and then the left wing of Oudinot's force. The French, forced to retreat at all points, attempted to hold on to the sandy hills on the right bank of the Nishcha river; but our troops attacked them again and

---

24   *Précis de la campagne du 1er corps.*
25   Chambray, I, 262.

forced them to continue their retreat. Oudinot, having sent back all his artillery, and wanting to gain the time necessary for them to cross the Nishcha, engaged our troops with his reserves, but this attack, being held off by the fire of Baikov's [Ivan Ivanovich Baikov] 27th Light Artillery Company which had moved up with Berg's infantry, brought no other benefits for the enemy, except for the retreat of Oudinot's force in good order behind the Nishcha and the French occupying a position on the left bank of this river, forwards of Klyastitsy.

By eight o'clock in the morning, the Russian troops, having captured the right bank of the Nischa, settled down facing the enemy position, along the river bank. Only the bridge at Klyastitsy could serve as a crossing point, and was under fire from French batteries and a dense screen of skirmishers who had settled in the houses of the village of Klyastitsy. Count Wittgenstein, intending to force the French out of their position by enveloping the enemy on their right flank, had sent cavalry to the village of Gvozdovo, at the same time as the latest attack by the infantry. General Balk was stationed in this village with the Riga Dragoons, while Kulnev went down to the bank of the Nishcha with the Grodno Hussars and Yamburg Dragoons, in order to cross upstream of Gvozdovo, but it emerged that, due to the swampy nature of the terrain at this point, there was no way to cross by fording, and therefore the engineer, Colonel Count Sievers, received orders to build a bridge there. As soon as Marshal Oudinot noticed this work commencing, he withdrew from his position and began to retreat towards Polotsk, ordering the bridge at Klyastitsy to be burned down. Count Wittgenstein, wanting to seize the crossing, in order to pursue the defeated French force immediately, sent the Replacement Battalion of the Pavlov Grenadiers there, which, having arrived from the second line was to support the skirmishing screen. The brave grenadiers, worthily maintaining the glory of their regiment, ran to the blazing bridge, crossed it under rapid fire from enemy marksmen and drove off any enemy they encountered, established themselves on the opposite bank of the river with the assistance of two guns from 27th Light Artillery Company, which had forded the river with Lieutenant Colonel Sukhozanet, who, on the occasion of the heavy losses suffered by his own company the day before, had left them in the rear. The Perm Infantry and Mogilev Infantry, following the Pavlov Grenadiers, occupied the houses of the village of Klyastitsy closest to the bridge; the remaining infantry regiments gradually also crossed the bridge, and meanwhile the cavalry crossed over via a ford found a little further downstream.

The exhaustion of the Russian troops, who had been fighting for two days, after a forced march from Rasitsy to Yakubovo, forced Wittgenstein to halt at Klyastitsy. Kulnev was directed to pursue the enemy with the Grodno Hussars, Yamburg Dragoons, some of the Riga Dragoons, 1st Combined Grenadier Battalion of 14th Division, four guns from 1st Horse Artillery Company with newly assigned crews, and the Cossacks. Skirmishers advancing at the head of our troops, while the Mogilev Infantry and Perm Infantry regiments,[26] advanced along with Kulnev's vanguard initially, but then halted six *versts* from Klyastitsy. Meanwhile, the enemy was retreating to Sivoshina, abandoning many vehicles and men along the way.

---

26   In the War Diary it states Sevsk Infantry and Perm Infantry.

The troops of our fighting echelons which remained at Klyastitsy settled down in bivouacs: the first line forwards of the town and the second line behind it. The reserve, under Major General Sazonov's command, which had not taken any part in the battle, repaired the damaged bridge at Klyastitsy and advanced in support of the vanguard, which continued to pursue the enemy and reached the Drissa river that night, meanwhile, Oudinot, having crossed this river at Sivoshina, attached Merle's division to his force there and stationed himself, four *versts* farther on, in a position near the village of Boyarshchina. The detachment under Prince Repnin was ordered to move by side roads from Katerinovo to Sokolishche, but finding this route completely impassable, he headed towards Klyastitsy following the other troops.[27]

The battle at Klyastitsy demonstrated both the valour of the Russian troops and the determination of Wittgenstein. The reserve of I Corps did not take part in the battle: consequently 17,000 Russians had defeated a 20,000 strong enemy corps. In this battle, success remained elusive for a long time; eventually, the advantage passed to the side with the most persistent commander, who, despite frequent setbacks, did not despair of success. It is impossible not to note that Count Wittgenstein managed to concentrate all the troops of his corps in the vicinity of Klyastitsy, except for a small detachment under Gamen, who had a very important mission, to hold off MacDonald's *10e Corps*. In contrast, Oudinot left between 8,000 and 10,000 men on the Drissa river. It is true that these troops could not be brought into battle at Yakubovo, due to the wooded nature of the terrain there, but if Oudinot had brought them to Klyastitsy, he could have held on at the Nishcha river and not allowed Wittgenstein to emerge onto the St Petersburg road.

After the battle of Klyastitsy, Kulnev received orders not to engage in a decisive action until the main body of the corps could close up to the vanguard, which was scheduled to depart from Klyastitsy on 20 July (1 August), at eight o'clock in the morning. But the dashing Kulnev, carried away by the courage that was a hallmark of his character, and by the success of the battle at Klyastitsy, crossed the Drissa at night and on 20 July [1 August], at dawn, moved on. His Cossacks encountered the enemy on the approaches to Boyarshchina. Whereupon Kulnev, believing that Marshal Oudinot meant only to buy time for a further retreat, sent the Yamburg Dragoons and four horse artillery guns to support the Cossacks; but noticing that the enemy was operating heavy guns, he sent a request to General Sazonov to bring similar artillery up to the vanguard, who, having sent Lieutenant Colonel Mewes' 27th Battery Artillery Company and the Tula Infantry ahead, followed them with the rest of the reserve force.

Meanwhile, Oudinot had deployed the main body of his *2e Corps* at the village of Boyarshchina, four *versts* from the Drissa, behind a long causeway.[28] As soon as Kulnev's troops had occasion to approach the causeway, having left the forest onto open ground, they were suddenly engaged in a crossfire from several French batteries placed on the high ground at the exit from the defile, and thereafter they were outflanked by superior numbers of enemy infantry, who had made their way through the swamp. The Russian cavalry, having been completely disordered by the

---

27 *Précis* etc. Count Wittgenstein's report on the battle of Klyastitsy.
28 See Plan of the Action at Boyarshchina, 20 July (1 August) 1812.

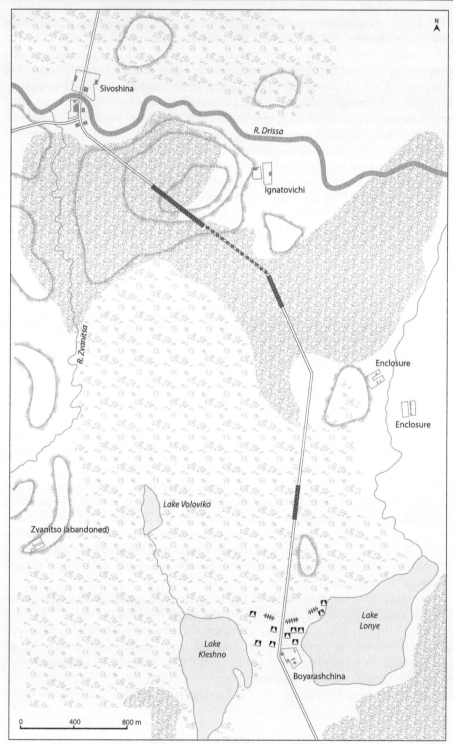

Plan of the Action at Boyarshchina, 1 August 1812.

artillery fire, was driven back across the Drissa river, with the loss of three guns from 1st Horse Artillery Company, knocked out at the beginning of the action. Some of our infantry, who did not have time to get to the bridge in the rush, were driven back into the river and drowned. Re–crossing the Drissa, Kulnev tried to restore order among the retreating troops under the covering fire of 27th Battery Artillery Company and the remaining eight guns of 1st Horse Artillery Company who had arrived on the orders of their battery commander. The heavy artillery was stationed on the dominant high ground on the right bank of the Drissa near the bridge, while the horse artillery was located to their right, in order to enfilade the advancing enemy columns. Meanwhile, the French, having crossed the river, began to infiltrate past our artillery on the flanks, which forced the battery company to retreat prematurely, precisely when its fire would have caused the greatest harm to the enemy. The French, exploiting this chance, captured six of 27th Battery Artillery Company's guns. The horse artillery, which was off to one side of the road, although they were in great danger, were nevertheless saved. Kulnev, not being able to hold on to any of the positions he occupied, was forced to retreat further to link up with the main body of the corps. Driven to despair by this reverse, which was the result of both his own negligence and the indecisiveness of General Sazonov, Kulnev dismounted from his horse, and moved back with the final ranks of the retreating troops, and just as he stopped by one of his guns, he was mortally struck by round shot that tore off both his legs. It was said that, as he was dying, he pulled the St George Cross from his neck and said to the soldiers who were carrying him away: 'hide this cross away so that the enemy does not know that they managed to kill a Russian general.'[29]

Such was the demise of one of the heroes of the Patriotic War, who had become a household name in Russia, perhaps because he showed many qualities of our national character in himself. His generosity reached the point of altruism, his courage to selflessness. Having almost no money, he constantly gave everything he had acquired through diligent service to his mother, while he himself went about in a soldier's uniform and was content with cabbage soup and porridge. *'Je me plais dans la grandeur de la pauvrété romaine'* (I delight in the grandeur of Romanesque austerity), he wrote to his brother. Kulnev told his colleagues: 'I live like Don Quixote, a knight–errant with a sad visage; no walls, no courtyard, but all are welcome: a beggars cunning for tales. I shall satisfy you with my home cooking, which God has sent us'. Sharing all the labour and hardships of his soldiers, Kulnev was adored by them, despite his extreme standards in his service. *'C'est Lasalle de l'armée russe'* (He is the Lasalle [Antoine Charles Louis de Lasalle] of the Russian army): such was the opinion expressed about him in the notes on our generals drawn up by the *État–major général* of the French army before the war of 1812.[30]

Count Wittgenstein was already on the march and had reached the village of Golovchitsy (ten *versts* from Klyastitsy) when he received news of the defeat of his

---

29   *Précis* etc. Biography of Kulnev, found in the work: Emperor Alexander I and his contemporaries. Adjutant–General Sukhozanet 1st's notes.

30   Biography of Kulnev, found in the work: Emperor Alexander I and his contemporaries. Notes on 60 Russian Generals (Manuscript held in the classified archive of the Chancellery of the Ministry of War).

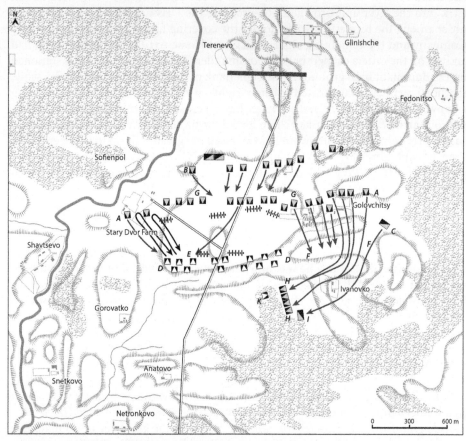

Plan of the Battle of Golovchitsy, 1 August 1812.

Russian Forces				French Forces	
A.A.	5th Division & jägers of 14th Division.	F.F.	General Kozachkovsky's advance.	D.D.	Verdier's division.
B.B.	Second Line.	G.G.	Advance of the Second Line.	K.	Detached column.
C.	Riga Dragoons.	H.H.	Sevsk Infantry & 24th Jägers.		
E.E.	General Berg's advance.	I.	Dragoons.		

vanguard. Having instructed Prince Iashvili and General Helffreich to rally the defeated troops, Wittgenstein placed the main body of his corps in position, with the right flank on the Nishcha, and the left flank at the village of Golovchitsy.[31] The front line consisted of 16 battalions from 5th Division and the Jäger Brigade from 14th Division with 48 guns; the second line was of nine battalions and eight squadrons of reserve cavalry under Prince Repnin; two squadrons were deployed to the left flank in order to monitor the area to the left of the position. All the infantry in general were deployed in battalion columns. Meanwhile, the vanguard, brought back under control by Iashvili, passed in the best order through the battle lines and formed the reserve,[32] with the exception of 1st Horse Artillery Company, which was placed in the front line, and one squadron of Riga Dragoons, which joined the two stationed on the left flank of the position.[33] Count Wittgenstein, having ridden around the ranks of troops from 5th Division and 14th Division standing in the front line, reminded them that they had decided victory at Klyastitsy and that they must maintain their glory. The troops, encouraged by the words of their beloved commander, were eagerly ready to fight, success was not in doubt.[34]

The French also approached with the confidence of victors. Verdier's division attacked our position having left the rest of Oudinot's force far behind. French skirmishers managed to take the Stary Dvor manor; but were driven out of there by the Perm Infantry Regiment. Meanwhile, on our left flank, the 24th Jägers and marksmen of the Sevsk Infantry also repulsed the advancing enemy.

Following this, Verdier's force reformed on the high ground facing our position. After a fierce cannonade, which lasted several minutes, the enemy columns headed against the centre and right wing of Wittgenstein's force, but being met by the fire of the Russian 1st Horse Artillery Company, 14th Battery Artillery Company and 27th Light Artillery Company, were thrown into disorder. Noticing the wavering in the French columns, Count Wittgenstein ordered his troops to attack. General Berg advanced against the enemy left wing with a line of the Perm Infantry, Mogilev Infantry, 25th Jägers and 23rd Jägers, while General Kazachkovsky attacked the French right wing with the Kaluga Infantry, Sevsk Infantry, 24th Jägers and 26th Jägers, supported by four squadrons. All the infantry of the first line advanced in battalion columns, with drums beating, while our artillery continued its lethal cannonade; and the infantry of the second line, following the first, headed towards the denuded centre of the enemy line. Verdier's force, driven in on both flanks, pulled back, and, in order to gain the time needed to retreat, occupied a small wood on their right wing, but were enveloped on the right by the Sevsk Infantry and 24th Jägers and pushed back frontally by the Replacement Battalion of Count Arakcheev's Grenadier Regiment; one of the French columns, which remained in the wood longer than the others, was cut off, and upon being attacked by two squadrons of Lifeguards and Riga Dragoons, some were killed and others laid down their weapons. Count Wittgenstein, who had personally directed this attack, was

---

31   See Plan of the Battle of Golovchitsy, 20 July (1 August) 1812.
32   *Précis de la campagne du 1er corps.* Count Wittgenstein's war diary.
33   Buturlin, II, 24. Count Wittgenstein's war diary.
34   *Précis* etc.

wounded by a bullet to the head, but did not leave the battlefield, and giving orders for his wound to be dressed quickly, he drafted orders for the pursuit of the French retreating at all points. Our troops quickly followed them and did not allow the enemy to rest until Sokolishche, where Verdier's troops positioned themselves in front of the manor behind a ravine and set fire to the bridge. This position, resting its right flank on the forest, and the left on the Nishcha, was attacked from the front by three battalions from the Sevsk Infantry and Mogilev Infantry regiments, under the command of Prince Sibirsky, supported by the fire of 5th Battery Artillery Company and 14th Battery Artillery Company, simultaneously with an attack by the 24th Jäger Regiment on the left flank of the enemy position, supported by fire from the 26th Jägers, with two guns, who had waded the Nishcha and moved along the right bank of this river. The successful bombardment by the two heavy batteries forced the enemy to abandon the other position occupied by them at the manor itself; the French, without waiting for the appearance of our columns, retreated non–stop to an open plateau between Sokolishche and Sivoshina, where they had deployed several squadrons of cuirassiers. Colonel Albrecht [Alexander Ivanovich Albrecht] received orders to attack them with the Lifeguard Ulan and Lifeguard Dragoon squadrons; but the cuirassiers pulled further back without waiting for our attack. 3rd Horse Artillery Company, with protection from the Kaluga Infantry, relentlessly pursued the enemy troops, seeing them off with round shot, while the jägers, racing into the forest down both sides of the road, enveloped the enemy from the flanks. Oudinot, noticing these movements, hastily retreated behind the Drissa and ordered the bridge at Sivoshina to be burned. 3rd Horse Artillery Company was stationed right on the river bank and forced the enemy to withdraw even further and retreat to Beloe, where the French camped for the night. Our light troops, having crossed the Drissa, halted at Boyarshchina, while the main body of the force stood in several echelons between Sokolishche and Sivoshina. The next day [2 August new style], Oudinot's *2e Corps* retreated to Polotsk. Our vanguard occupied Beloe, and then withdrew back behind the Drissa, to Sivoshina, while Count Wittgenstein's headquarters was moved to Sokolishche.[35]

The battles of 18 to 20 July (30 July to 1 August) cost us a total of 4,300 men; among the wounded, besides the Commander-in-Chief himself, were colonels Lukov [Fëdor Alexeevich Lukov] and Staden, Lieutenant Colonel Sukhozanet and Major Neidhardt, promoted to lieutenant colonel for his distinction in the battle of Klyastitsy. On the part of the enemy, according to French historians, the losses ranged from 3,000 to 4,000 men, but, in all likelihood, were much heavier.[36]

---

35   *Précis de la campagne du 1er corps.* Count Wittgenstein's war diary.
36   *Précis* etc. Count Wittgenstein's war diary. Buturlin, II, 29. Thiers, XIV, *Edit. de Brux*, 198. Buturlin gives the overall enemy casualties as some 10,000 men. Ker Porter writes that in all the actions of 18 to 20 July [30 July to 1 August], the casualties on our part did not exceed 2,000 men; and on the enemy side reached 8,000. *Histoire de la campagne de Russie pendant l'année 1812, contenant des détails puisés dans des sources officielles, ou provenant de récits francais interceptés*, 62.

In recognition of their outstanding performances over 18 to 20 July, Count Wittgenstein received the Order of St George, 2nd class, and a pension of 12,000 Roubles; Berg and Prince Iashvili were promoted to lieutenant general; d'Auvray received 5,000 Roubles and a pension

It is quite remarkable that both sides made similar mistakes on the same day. Firstly, Kulnev went into battle at Boyarshchina, having not taken into account either the superior enemy troop numbers, or the nature of the ground on which he happened to be fighting; thereafter Oudinot sent Verdier's division up to the Drissa, while he remained on the left bank of the river himself with the main body of the corps. The outcome of these rash actions were reverses for Kulnev and Verdier. But the mistake by the former is more forgivable, in the sense that, operating against a defeated enemy corps, he had hoped to exploit their disorder; in contrast, Oudinot had no good reason to assume that the defeat of Kulnev would have an unfavourable effect on Wittgenstein's main body.[37]

Meanwhile, MacDonald actively continued to build bridges on the Dvina: one at Jakobstadt, and the other about two *versts* downstream. Once a small enemy detachment, crossing by boat, had occupied Dünaburg abandoned by our troops and built a bridge of rafts on 23 July (4 August), to replace the one that was destroyed by Gamen, then MacDonald ordered a bridge to be constructed at Jakobstadt and halted the building of the other downstream of this location. Thereafter, leaving an outpost of 50 men in Kreutzburg, opposite Jakobstadt, on the right bank of the Dvina, communications with which were carried out by ferry, MacDonald moved into Dünaburg on 24 July (5 August) and began to destroy the fortifications there; huge stores of timber, spare gun carriages, entrenching tools and other materials were burned; cast–iron guns and ammunition were dumped in the Dvina. If MacDonald, instead of advancing on Dünaburg and destroying the stores there, which the French army could later have used, had kept his bridge at Jakobstadt, crossed the Dvina at this point and advanced on Sebezh, where Oudinot was heading at that same time, then Wittgenstein would have been forced to retreat beyond Sebezh, and the French corps operating on the Dvina could have united, or at least established communications with each other. In such an event, Grandjean's division, numbering 12,000 to 15,000 men, could have taken part in the fighting.[38]

The razing of the Riga suburbs clearly revealed the determination of the Russians to defend themselves to the bitter end. Nevertheless, however, the Prussian General Grawert demanded that the military governor of Riga surrender the city in a letter with the following content:

> Your Excellency knows as well as I do that the operations directed towards Vitebsk and the Dnieper have forced the Russian army, under the personal command of His Majesty the Emperor, to retreat from the fortified camp at Drissa. The immediate consequence of this retreat will be the siege of Riga; the siege artillery assigned for this purpose will not be slow to appear. The weakness of the fortress is as much known to me as you yourself must

---

equal to his salary; Kazachkovsky and Colonel Diebitsch received the Order of St George, 3rd class; Kakhovsky, the St Vladimir, 2nd class; Balk and Prince Sibirsky, the St Anna 1st class; Helffreich, a golden sword decorated with diamonds; Captain Krylov of the Pavlov Grenadier Regiment received the St George 4th class, etc.

37   Buturlin, II, 28.
38   Chambray, I, 255–258.

know. In spite of undaunted resistance, its surrender would be forced within a few days, or at most within a few weeks. But even this short time would be enough for the total ruin of a wealthy, trading city, which has already suffered a great deal from the latest fires, and a significant number of brave troops, led by commanders respected by all, would be sacrificed for a futile resistance.

It seems to me that in the present circumstances your duties, both in regard to humanity and duty in the service of your Tsar, demand that you deliver Riga from the disasters of a siege, which, as already said, due to the weak state of the fortress, cannot be prolonged, and, therefore, will only plunge thousands of innocent inhabitants into poverty, without bringing any benefit to your Monarch. If Your Excellency shares my way of thinking, based solely on humanitarian need, then I am ready to send an officer equipped with the necessary authority to conclude terms under which you may be pleased to surrender the city and fortress.

If, on the other hand, you do not accept my proposal, then at least I have expressed a desire to alleviate, as much as I can, the calamities of war and to reduce the number of its unfortunate victims.

I ask Your Excellency to rest assured that this demand is by no means based on any doubts about the courage of your troops, especially since at Eckau these warriors have proved their fearlessness. Rather, their courageous defence inspired all the more respect for them in me, I would regard the deaths of such brave men in the defence of poor fortifications with great regret.

In conclusion, I ask you to inform me as soon as possible of your intentions and to be assured of my unlimited respect.

In response to Grawert's demand, Count Essen wrote:

If I could concede that a Prussian general were in a position to write an account similar to the one I received from you on his own initiative, I would consider it unworthy of an answer. But as a foreign influence is clearly detectable in it, I interpret these lines from your letter, remaining confident that you are serving merely as the tool of an autocratic power, to which you consider yourself obligated to obey unconditionally. Please accept the assurance of my consideration.

If the Prussian troops in the war of 1812 had not been operating under duress, then Essen's proud response, albeit very appropriate to the circumstances, could have led to all kinds of reprisals against Riga. But Grawert, knowing the relationship between his fatherland and Russia, did not consider it necessary to shed the blood of his troops in a fight against the Russians, merely in order to satisfy insulted pride: the troops of both sides limited themselves to surveillance almost until the end of July.[39]

---

39   Buturlin, II, 30–33.

The First Battle of Polotsk

Count Wittgenstein's deployment on the Drissa following the battle of Klyastitsy. – His move towards Rasitsy. – Saint-Cyr supports Oudinot's *2e Corps*. – The composition of the Bavarian contingent. – The comparative strength of both sides. – Oudinot's advance towards the Svolna. – Wittgenstein's preparations for a crossing of the Dvina at Druya. – Intelligence on the advances by Oudinot and MacDonald. – The advance of the Russian corps towards the Svolna. – The action on the Svolna. – The arrival of Gamen's detachment. – Measures taken by Count Wittgenstein to supply his troops with rations and war supplies.

The pursuit of the enemy by Russian forces following the action on the Svolna. – The retreat of the enemy corps towards Polotsk. – The fighting on 5 (17) August. – Saint-Cyr's unexpected attack on the Russian force on 6 (18) August. – Count Wittgenstein's retreat to the Drissa. – The action at Beloe. – The deployments by both sides at the beginning of October.

Following the retreat of the enemy to Polotsk, on 21 July (2 August), Count Wittgenstein, in anticipation of offensive operations by MacDonald, remained on the right bank of the Drissa river near Sokolishche; the vanguard, consisting of six battalions, 11 squadrons and several *sotnia* of Cossacks, with 12 guns, under the command of Major General Helffreich, settled at Sivoshina, sending fighting patrols along the roads leading to Volyntsy, Polotsk and Nevel.[1]

The following day, 22 July (3 August), the Commander-in-Chief, having received intelligence of the enemy retreat to the left bank of the Dvina, moved his corps to Sivoshina, pushing the vanguard forwards to Beloe and detached Prince Repnin, with the Combined Cuirassier Regiment and one squadron of the Pskov Dragoons, to Volyntsy, in order to cover his right flank from the direction of Disna, where Oudinot had a bridge over the Dvina. But just as quickly a report arrived from Gamen, from Rybenishki [Robežnieki?], about the location of the French in significant strength in Dünaburg and about the construction of a bridgehead near Kreutzburg by the enemy, Count Wittgenstein decided to move to Rasitsy, from where he could conveniently counter any offensive by the enemy corps.

---

1   For details of the deployment of Wittgenstein's force, see Appendix XX.

To that end, the main body of I Corps marched to Volyntsy on 23 July (4 August); while Helffreich remained as before at Beloe with the vanguard; it soon became apparent that the enemy had no intention of operating from the direction of Disna and had even destroyed the bridge there, whereupon Wittgenstein, having absorbed Prince Repnin's detachment into his main body, moved along the route towards Rasitsy.

On 25 July (6 August), the troops of I Corps arrived at Kokanovichi. In order to shield the onward movement from the direction of the Dvina, Major General Balk was advanced in the direction of Druya, with a detachment consisting of four battalions, five squadrons and a *sotnia* of Cossacks, with 12 guns.[2] On the following day, the corps reached Rasitsy, where they camped, holding the reserve near the village of Baby. Helffreich's vanguard was moved towards Pokaevtsy in order to shield the left flank of the corps from the direction of the river Drissa; while Lieutenant Colonel Rüdiger was detached from there with four squadrons of Grodno Hussars and Cossacks towards Volyntsy, to monitor upstream of this river to Sivoshina and beyond. General Gamen was issued orders to join the main body of the corps with the rest of his force, having left the Combined Hussar Regiment in the vicinity of Kreutzburg in order to monitor MacDonald. The replacement battalions and batteries, marching from Pskov to reinforce Gamen's detachment, were ordered to turn towards Rasitsy.[3]

At the same time, Oudinot's corps was bolstered with significant reinforcements. Napoleon, having received reports regarding Oudinot's retreat to Polotsk, which came as a complete surprise to him, ordered Saint-Cyr, who was in Beshankovichi with the Bavarian *6e Corps*, to go to Polotsk immediately to assist *2e Corps*.

The troops under Saint-Cyr, from the very moment they crossed the Russian borders, had endured extraordinary hardship and privation. The Bavarians, having received orders from Napoleon to cross the Neman, at Preny, behind the troops of *4e Corps*, were forced to follow them along a road cluttered with stragglers and carts, lost 200 horses on the first stage and, having reached the village of Anuchishki, could go no further, and therefore stopped for six days, from 24 to 29 June (6 to 11 July). During this time, the troops had time to rest and stock up with bread. On 1 (13) July, *6e Corps* arrived in the vicinity of Vilna. On the following day [14 July new style], Napoleon, having reviewed them, detached all their cavalry; while the infantry and the artillery were directed to Glubokoe, where they were scheduled to arrive on 10 (22) July. On this march, the troops suffered a major disaster: having received a two-day issue of spoiled bread from Vilna on the eve of their departure, and being unable to forage for food in the country due to a lack of cavalry, the Bavarians left several hundred sick behind from this stage; all the surrounding manor houses were turned into hospitals. The troops of *6e Corps* were unable to arrive at Glubokoe by the appointed day and arrived there in such a miserable condition that

---

2   Balk's detachment consisted of: 26th Jägers, 24th Jägers (the latter had arrived from the vanguard at Beloe); Riga Dragoons, the Replacement Squadron of Pskov Dragoons; a Cossack *sotnia*; 9th Light Artillery Company.

3   *Précis de la campagne du 1er corps de l'armée d'Occident pendant l'année 1812.* (Archive of the M.T.D. No 29,200).

Napoleon cancelled the review scheduled for *6e Corps* and did not want to inspect them. Nevertheless, however, the Bavarian troops continued to advance towards Ostrovno, from where, after the occupation of Vitebsk by the French, they moved on to Beshankovichi. Saint-Cyr was ordered to forage for supplies for his troops on the right bank of the Dvina; but it was not easy to fulfil this order: the banks of the Dvina had been completely devastated, and the complete absence of cavalry did not allow the troops detached for foraging to travel any significant distance. On 20 July (1 August), one of the Bavarian divisions crossed to the right bank of the Dvina; the other remained on the left bank of the river, between Beshankovichi and Bui, where a bridge of rafts had been built. The sickness and death rates, which developed in the troops from exhaustion and hunger, continued as before. The Bavarian corps, which had counted more than 25,000 men in its ranks when it crossed the Neman, had been diminished to 13,000 in the course of five weeks, without being in a single battle. The Bavarian troops were in this situation when, on 23 July (4 August), Saint-Cyr received orders to march to Polotsk immediately.[4]

The arrival of Saint-Cyr at Polotsk was supposed to increase Oudinot's strength, according to the accounts of French historians, to 35,000 men (and indeed even more). On the other hand, Count Wittgenstein, although he expected the arrival of reinforcements, however, these could not reach his corps before 1 (13) August, the closest of them (Gamen's force), totalled no more than 3,000 men: consequently, the actual number of troops with Wittgenstein did not exceed 20,000. But, having said that, these troops were fresh, cheerful, provided in abundance with food supplies and were under the influence of the successes won in the battle of Klyastitsy; and, although the infantry of the independent I Corps, could not be regarded as skilled in marksmanship, in the absolute sense of the word, nevertheless shot better than the enemy, thanks to the activity of Count Wittgenstein, who, for several months before the opening of the campaign, had constantly engaged in marksmanship training and in target shooting.[5]

Despite the fact that some French historians (including the renowned Thiers) believed that success was on the side of their compatriots in the actions of 18 to 20 July (30 July to 1 August), Oudinot and Napoleon himself were convinced of the need to reinforce the French troops operating on the Dvina. We have already had occasion to note that before the battle of Klyastitsy, and even after this battle, the advantage in troop numbers was on the side of the French. Nevertheless, however, we see that Oudinot, instead of reporting on a victory over the Russians, expressed his despair of holding on along the Dvina; while Napoleon, instead of being reassured by Oudinot's (imaginary) success, urged Saint-Cyr to go to his aid, despite the fact that the Bavarian *6e Corps* was in dire need of rest. Saint-Cyr himself stated: 'The movement order was so urgent that the men seemed to fear that some disaster had occurred.' (*L'ordre de mouvement était si pressant, qu'on semblait craindre qu'il ne fût survenu quelque desastre*). As soon as the order to go to Polotsk was received in *6e Corps* headquarters, the troops set off without even waiting for the sub-units sent out

4   *Maréchal* Gouvion Saint-Cyr, *Mémoires pour servir à l'histoire militaire sous le Directoire, le Consulat et l'Empire*, III, 40-41, 45-47, 51-52, 54-56. Chambray, I 266-267. Thiers, XIV, 284.

5   *Précis de la campagne du 1er corps de l'armée d'Occident.*

for foraging; it was intended to move by forced marches, but the exhaustion of the troops forced them to abandon this intent and make the march from Beshankovichi to Polotsk (over a distance of 50 *versts*) in three stages: the Bavarians reached Ulla on 24 July (5 August), Turovlya by the 25th [6 August], joining Oudinot's force in Polotsk on the following day [7 August].[6]

As soon as these troops had crossed over to the right bank of the Dvina, then Marshal Oudinot, to whom both corps were subordinate, decided to resume offensive operations towards the Svolna river.

On 27 July (8 August), the day following the arrival of Saint-Cyr's *6e Corps* at Polotsk, Count Wittgenstein reached Rasitsy with his main body. Oudinot's inaction, which had lasted for several days, prompted our commander to return to his original plan of action against Macdonald. Count Wittgenstein had intended to build several bridges at Druya, but as all the materials that we had previously assembled there for the construction of a crossing had been abandoned during the movement of the corps to Klyastitsy and had been transported by the enemy to the confluence with the Druika river, then Colonel Albrecht was ordered to cross the Dvina with two squadrons and one jäger company and seize these materials. On 27 July (8 August), the courageous Albrecht crossed the river, drove off the enemy outposts, and having captured many boats, proceeded to construct a bridge. The commander of the vanguard on the left wing, Major General Helffreich, also sent a patrol of 12 Grodno Hussars from Drissa, under the command of Lieutenant Tsitlyadzev [Pavel Alexandrovich Tsitlyadzev]. This valiant officer, having forded the Dvina, attacked an enemy convoy, destroyed it and captured its entire escort, which consisted of 200 men, including two officers.[7] The next day, 28 July (9 August), the vanguard on the right wing, under the command of Major General Balk, having occupied Druya, began building a bridgehead; but soon thereafter, intelligence was received that forced Count Wittgenstein to abandon his offensive for a second time: several prisoners captured by our patrols during the French advance from Polotsk to Svolna showed that Oudinot had been reinforced by Saint-Cyr's *6e Corps*; at the same time, General Balk learned about the crossing of the Dvina near Kreutzburg by part of MacDonald force from informants and prisoners; in addition, the informants gave assurances that MacDonald was expecting the addition of 12 Spanish regiments, which, according to them, should have already reached Zamosha. Despite the improbability of this latest intelligence, it was impossible to doubt the advance by Oudinot's and MacDonald's significant forces. Count Wittgenstein, who was suffering from a wound received in the action at Golovchitsy, was forced to hand over temporary command of the force to the Chief of Staff of I Corps and left for Osveya. In the instruction given to General d'Auvray, he was ordered to move against Oudinot.

Assessing that the movement by enemy troops towards Svolna was made solely to shield the offensive by Oudinot's *2e Corps* along the route to Sebezh, General

---

6   *Mémoires de Saint-Cyr,* III, 56.
7   Major General Helffreich's report to Count Wittgenstein dated 28 July [9 August]. In recognition of the feats he accomplished Tsitlyadzev received the Order of St George, 4th class.

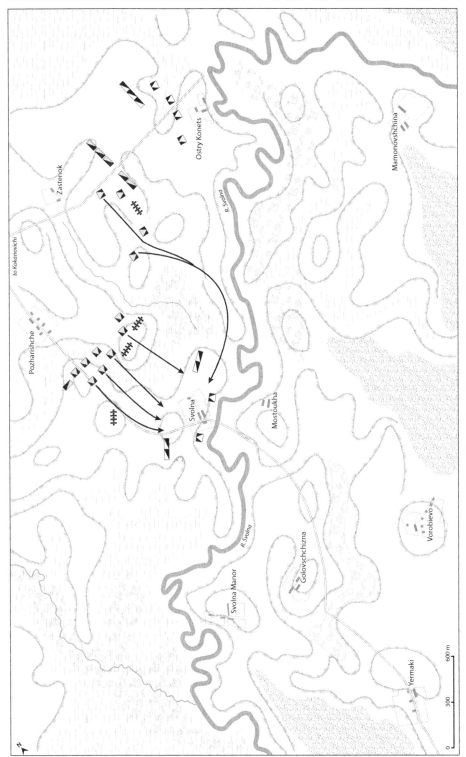

Plan of the Action at Svolna, 11 August 1812.

d'Auvray decided to march to Kokanovichi and ordered Helffreich to go there from Pokaevtsy and Rüdiger from Volnytsy, as well as Gamen from Rybenishki; Colonel Albrecht was also ordered to conduct a sweep to Belmont with two squadrons of hussars and a half *sotnia* of Cossacks, in order to collect intelligence on the enemy and to disperse a Polish mob that had gathered in the vicinity of this location.

On 29 July (10 August), the troops of I Corps marched towards Kokanovichi. Ahead of them moved the newly reorganised vanguard, of two squadrons of Yamburg Dragoons and 23rd Jäger Regiment, with nine guns from 1st Horse Artillery Company, under the command of Major General Kazachkovsky. They were followed by the main body of the corps, consisting of 25 battalions and five squadrons with 66 guns.[8]

Meanwhile, Oudinot's and Saint-Cyr's corps, having set out from Polotsk, on 27 July (8 August), moved along the road towards Osveya, in order to isolate the troops of I Corps. On 29 July (10 August), Saint-Cyr's *6e Corps*, having crossed the Drissa at Volyntsy, settled forwards of this location, while Oudinot's *2e Corps* marched to the Svolna River, to the village of the same name [Svolno], and seized the village of Kokanovichi with his advanced troops.[9] Helffreich's force, having arrived there almost at the same time as the enemy, attacked the French and forced them to retreat to the high ground lying on the right bank of the Svolna river. The main body of the corps and the reserve stood forwards of the village of Kokanovichi.[10]

On the following day, 30 July (11 August), the enemy remained static for the whole morning. D'Auvray, attributing this inaction to their expectation of reinforcements, decided to forestall their arrival by attacking the enemy position. To that end, a reconnaissance in force was carried out: the troops under Helffreich and Kazachkovsky, supported by the rest of the squadrons of the Yamburg Dragoon Regiment (eight battalions and 15 squadrons, with 21 guns in total), pushed the enemy back into the valley and occupied the high ground. Whereupon it emerged that the French main body was on the left bank of the river; on the right bank were their cavalry, supported by infantry, who occupied the village of Ostry Konets and the Svolno manor, near both of which were bridges that provided communications between the enemy vanguard and Oudinot's main body located behind the river.

General d'Auvray sent Lieutenant Colonel Rüdiger into action with the Grodno Hussars and Platov 4th's Cossacks, who forced the enemy cavalry to retreat onto their infantry, located right on the river bank, but upon encountering fierce fire from enemy artillery located on the high ground of the left bank of the Svolna, they

---

8   The composition of I Corps: First line, under Major General Berg's command: Combined Cuirassier Regiment; Perm Infantry, Mogilev Infantry, Sevsk Infantry and Kaluga Infantry; 5th Battery Artillery Company and 28th Artillery Company. Second line, under Major General Sazonov's command: Tula Infantry, Navaginsk Infantry, Tenginsk Infantry, Estland Infantry; Replacement Battalion of 11th Jägers; 14th Battery Artillery Company and 27th Light Artillery Company. The reserve, under Major General Kakhovsky: two Combined Grenadier Battalions from 14th Division; six replacement grenadier battalions; two squadrons of Yamburg Dragoons; 3rd Horse Artillery Company; six guns from 27th Battery Artillery Company.
9   Saint-Cyr, *Mémoires*, III, 59.
10   See Plan of the Action on the Svolna, 30 July (11 August) 1812.

were forced to retreat. Whereupon General d'Auvray advanced the artillery and infantry from Helffreich's vanguard and 5th Division onto the high ground near the village of Pozharishche; two squadrons of the Lifeguard Combined Cuirassier Regiment were sent to cover our right flank; the remaining two squadrons of the same regiment and the Yamburg Dragoons were sent along with two squadrons of Grodno Hussars to the left flank. The French left wing, which was stationed at the Svolno manor, was pushed back to the river bank itself, but during this attack, the commander of 25th Jägers, the brave Denisiev, was mortally wounded by round shot. The troops of our right wing dashed towards the bridge, but being engaged by lethal fire from the French batteries on the left bank of the river, they were forced to halt. In addition, a strong enemy column, which remained forwards of the village of Ostry Konets, threatened our vanguard with envelopment from the left flank. To hold them off, the Tenginsk Infantry and Estland Infantry regiments were detached with 14th Battery Artillery Company, under the command of Major General Kazachkovsky, who made up the left wing of our battle line. General Kazachkovsky masked the battery with cavalry until Staff Captain Nolde, who commanded them, closed up to the enemy and opened fire. The successful action of his guns forced the enemy to retreat with losses to the other side of the river, besides which, he set fire to the village of Ostry Konets and destroyed the bridge. Major General Kazachkovsky, having secured himself from the left flank, occupied the bank with skirmishers and detached Colonel Lyalin [Dmitry Vasilevich Lyalin], with two battalions of the Tenginsk Infantry and Estland Infantry regiments and with six guns from 14th Battery Artillery Company, to the right in order to capture Svolno manor, heavily garrisoned by enemy skirmishers. Having opened fire on the French, as soon as the artillery threw them into confusion, the valiant Lyalin, moving to the left of the manor, enveloping it from the direction of the river, charged with fixed bayonets and drove the enemy out of the buildings they had occupied; many Frenchmen were killed or drowned in the Svolna while more than 200 were taken prisoner. Meanwhile, the successful actions of 5th Battery Artillery Company, 28th Battery Artillery Company and 26th Light Artillery Company drove the enemy columns and artillery away from the opposite bank. Carried away by their success, our skirmishers, after taking possession of the manor, ran across the bridge after the defeated French and were attacked by Doumerc's cuirassiers. At this critical moment, Major Tarbeev of the Perm Infantry, having asked permission from General Berg to go across the bridge with his marksmen to the rescue of the skirmishers, called for volunteers to go into action; the first to step forwards was the senior officer of the 1st Flank Company, Lieutenant Druzhinin swiftly followed by the entire company. Major Tarbeev quickly led the grenadiers to the bridge at the village of Svolno and arrived there at the very moment that the French cuirassiers, having forced our skirmishers to recross the river, rushed after them over the bridge and were passing the manor. Taking advantage of the enemy's inattention, the grenadiers occupied the buildings and the palisade fence around the kitchen garden, and as the cuirassiers, engaged by Lieutenant Colonel Rüdiger with the Grodno Hussars, were driven back and forced to retreat, our grenadiers engaged them with musketry. The lethal fire of the artillery completed the destruction of the cuirassiers, of whom only a few managed to gallop back across the river. The troops of 5th Division and 14th

Division, supported by the destructive fire from 48 guns, lined up on the hills on the right bank of the river, while the enemy, retreating to the high ground on the left bank dominating the river valley, also established strong batteries; the troops of both sides attempted to cross the river, but each time they were repulsed by artillery fire, which was very advantageously located on both banks of the Svolna. This situation forced d'Auvray to accept the limits to his success and to postpone the pursuit of the defeated enemy until the next day.

In the action on the Svolna, overall, we lost some 700 men. On the enemy side, the casualties, in all likelihood, were incomparably greater, because the number of prisoners captured by the Russian troops alone reached 300 men.[11] In recognition for the action on the Svolna, General d'Auvray received the Order of St George, 3rd class.

The aggressive operations by the Russian forces made Marshal Oudinot believe that reinforcements had arrived, and was the cause of his retreat behind the Drissa. During the night of 30 to 31 July (11 to 12 August), Deroy's Bavarian Division set out for Lozovka, and at dawn Wrede's Division followed them; on the same day, both divisions retreated to Beloe on the route leading from Polotsk to Sebezh. Meanwhile, Oudinot's *2e Corps* retreated to Volyntsy.[12]

Throughout 31 July (12 August), the troops of I Corps remained in position near Svolno; the detachment under General Balk moved from the vicinity of Druya to Tobolka, in order to secure the right flank of the main body. Meanwhile, Colonel Albrecht had returned from the left bank of the Dvina, from Belmont (at a distance of more than 50 *versts* from Druya), capturing some 80 prisoners, among whom was the Braslav sub-prefect Manuzzi. On the following day, 1 (13) August, Count Wittgenstein arrived at the corps headquarters; taking back command over the force, he immediately issued orders for the pursuit of the French. In the evening, Gamen's detachment joined the main body, consisting of nine battalions; the tenth battalion of the Dünaburg garrison had been directed to Pskov with the guns previously located in the bridgehead. From among Gamen's troops, eight line battalions formed the 1st and 2nd Combined Infantry Regiments; while a battalion of 18th Jägers, together with those from 11th Jägers and 36th Jägers which had previously been attached to the corps, formed the Combined Jäger Regiment.[13] This reinforcement, which did not exceed 3,000 men, was of great benefit to us by making the enemy believe that I Corps had been reinforced by nine full strength battalions.

In the course of the ten days that had elapsed since the victory at Klyastitsy, Count Wittgenstein had displayed the extraordinary energy essential in the circumstances in which he had found himself. It had been necessary to ensure the rations and provision of military supplies to the force which was in constant motion. The Vitebsk Governorate, devastated by the enemy, presented very meagre resources; the local administration there had been completely disrupted. And therefore it was necessary

---

11   Sources for the battle on the Svolna were the reports by generals: d'Auvray, Prince Iashvili, Helffreich and Kazachkovsky (M.T.D. No 44,785, Vol. 7). In d'Auvray's report the enemy losses, based on statements by prisoners, is shown as 1,500 men.

12   Saint-Cyr, *Mémoires*, III, 60.

13   *Précis des opérations du 1er corps.*

to turn to the Pskov Governorate for the delivery of supplies, where there were quite large magazines; but the main difficulty was in bringing these supplies to the troops, and, in addition, it was necessary, in order to maintain strength and preserve the health of the soldiers, to supply them with meat and wine rations. It was also necessary to bring up the reserve parks in order to replenish the artillery ammunition, of which a huge amount had been expended. Fortunately, Wittgenstein found a diligent colleague in the head of the Pskov Governorate; Prince Shakhovskoy [Pëtr Ivanovich Shakhovskoy], taking advantage of the readiness of each of the classes of people of the governorate entrusted to him to sacrifice everything for the benefit of the fatherland, promptly fulfilled all the requirements of the military authorities. From the main magazines located in Ostrov and Pskov, a twenty-day supply of provisions (26,240 *Pud* of hard tack, 472 *Chetvert* of cereals and 7,200 *Chetvert* of oats) was immediately transported to the supply magazines established in Ludsen and Sebezh, which thereafter, gradually, as needed, delivered to all locations held by our troops, in such a way that they had everything they needed in abundance while being located close to an enemy exhausted by hunger. In order to replenish consumable supplies every ten days, it was intended to transport a ten-day supply of provisions and oats from the main magazines, which, in turn, were replenished by purchases, donations and the delivery of provisions from rural magazines. These same resources served to acquire oxen for meat rations, salt and wine in the Pskov Governorate. As for hay, it, as well as flour, cereals and oats, were obtained, in small quantities, in the districts of the Vitebsk Governorate liberated from the enemy, through requisition, according to a schedule of the number of souls, against receipts. But despite all the efforts by the *Proviant-Meister* General Laba and, despite the keen assistance of the local authorities, the supply of hay was very difficult due to the scarcity of transport resources, and there were almost no oats in the Vitebsk Governorate, on the occasion of the crop failure there in 1812, which forced them to levy a *Chetvert* of flour for every one and a half *Chetvert* of oats.[14]

The troops entrusted to Count Wittgenstein, being in constant contact with the enemy, had expended most of the ammunition held by the corps. A report by the commander of 25th Jägers, Colonel Denisiev, clearly shows how much live ammunition was fired by the regiment entrusted to him: on 12 (24) July, at Baliny, 6,438 rounds; on 18 (30) July, at Yakubovo and Klyastitsy, 87,300 rounds; on 20 July (1 August) 8,380 rounds, a total of 102,118 rounds.[15] The Chief of Artillery of I Corps, Prince Iashvili, reported to Count Wittgenstein (following the battle of Polotsk), regarding the expenditure of even more than a division's allocation of artillery ammunition and cartridges and about the lack of wagons and horses to move the reserve parks from Pskov up to the army, suggesting that they should be transported on peasant carts.[16] This proposal was immediately executed by Prince Shakhovskoy.[17] No less important services were rendered to them in terms of the delivery of medical

---

14   Report to Count Wittgenstein by the Pskov Civil Governor, Prince Shakhovskoy, and *Proviant-Meister* General Laba.
15   Colonel Denisiev's report to Count Wittgenstein dated 27 July [8 August], No 882.
16   Prince Iashvili's report dated 7 [19] August, No 392.
17   Prince Shakhovskoy's letter to Count Wittgenstein dated 12 [24] August, No 6,260.

supplies to the force and the establishment of postal stations, the supply of several hundred horses to the troops, and so on.[18]

Despite concerns about rations for the troops, about replacing the fallen, about keeping order in a region in which the civil administration had been completely disrupted, Count Wittgenstein did not take his eyes off the enemy. As soon as our commander was able to return to the headquarters of I Corps, he took steps to consolidate the successes gained in his absence. On 2 (14) August, the Russian troops set out from their bivouacs. Two vanguards moved ahead: Major General Helffreich's was initially directed towards Volyntsy with three *sotnia* of Cossacks, four squadrons of Grodno Hussars, four battalions from 25th Jägers and 26th Jägers and 26th Light Artillery Company; while Colonel Vlastov, advanced to Klyastitsy and on towards Sivoshina with two *sotnia* of Cossacks, four squadrons of Grodno Hussars, four battalions from 24th Jägers and the Combined Grenadiers of 5th Division, and six guns from 3rd Horse Artillery Company, in order to threaten the enemy right flank and their line of communications with Polotsk; the main body and reserve, consisting of 37 battalions and 15 squadrons, with 80 guns proceeded behind Helffreich's vanguard towards Volyntsy.[19]

The purpose of Vlastov's detachment was to induce the enemy to retreat behind the Drissa, and having occupied the course of this river with a small element of the force, to be ready in the event of an offensive by MacDonald, against them with his main body. Undoubtedly, splitting the force in this manner weakened I Corps, which was already inferior to the enemy in numbers, but the indecision evident in every operation by Oudinot gave Count Wittgenstein hope that his enemy, threatened simultaneously with an attack from the front and envelopment from the flank, would retreat to the river Drissa without a fight.

Indeed, Oudinot, noticing the advance of our troops, withdrew his *2e Corps* from Volyntsy to Filipovo and on to Lozovka, and ordered Saint-Cyr to retreat to Sivoshina with the Bavarians, in order to defend the route leading from Sebezh to Polotsk. On the morning of the following day, 3 (15) August, Helffreich's vanguard attacked the enemy in the village of Smolyaki and forced them to retreat. Meanwhile, Vlastov, having crossed the Drissa at Sivoshina without resistance, halted at Boyarshchina, facing Wrede's division, which was holding a position at the village of Beloe under the personal command of Saint-Cyr. Major General Prince Repnin was detached to

---

18   His letter to Count Wittgenstein dated 26 August [7 September], No 6,713.
19   The composition of the main body was: first line, under Major General Berg's command: Combined Cuirassier Regiment (four squadrons); 5th Battery Artillery Company; 23rd Jägers; four infantry regiments from 5th Division and 1st Combined Infantry Regiment (14 battalions); 28th Battery Artillery Company and 9th Light Artillery Company; two squadrons of Yamburg Dragoons; Lifeguard Combined Regiment (three squadrons). Second line, under Major General Sazonov's command: two squadrons of Riga Dragoons; Combined Jäger Regiment (three battalions); 27th Battery Artillery Company (six guns); four infantry regiments from 14th Division (eight battalions); 27th Light Artillery Company; two squadrons of Riga Dragoons. Reserve, under Major General Kakhovsky's command: two squadrons of Yamburg Dragoons; 14th Battery Artillery Company; two Combined Grenadier Battalions from 14th Division; six replacement grenadier battalions; 2nd Combined Infantry Regiment (four battalions); 1st Horse Artillery Company (nine guns) and 3rd Horse Artillery Company (six guns).

Disna in order to secure the right flank of the corps during the continuing offensive on Polotsk, with the Combined Cuirassier Regiment, two battalions of the Combined Jäger Regiment (11th Jägers and 36th Jägers) and two light guns, where he was ordered to destroy the bridge that the French had been using to cross the Dvina. These orders were executed to perfection: Prince Repnin, forcing the enemy to retreat to the left bank of the river, forded after them with the cuirassiers, occupied Disna, destroyed the arms depots located there, burned the bridge and rejoined the main body of I Corps.[20]

During the night of 3 to 4 (15 to 16) August, Oudinot continued his retreat to Gamzelevo and on towards Polotsk; Saint-Cyr was also ordered to retreat to Polotsk, turning onto the Nevel road via Arteikovichi. This retreat, which lasted all night, was extremely difficult: the troops of all arms were muddled up with the train, trudging slowly and arrived at Polotsk on the morning of 4 (16) August, in disorder, exhausted, weary and hungry. The Bavarian *6e Corps*, which up to that time had participated only in a few rearguard clashes, had lost some 2,000 lower ranks in a few days and counted no more than 11,000 men in the ranks.[21] The Russian troops, relentlessly pursuing the enemy, arrived in the vicinity of Polotsk: Helffreich's vanguard halted at Ropna; the main body of the corps halted at Gamzelevo; Colonel Vlastov's detachment arrived at the Borovka tavern in the evening. During the march from the Svolna to Polotsk, some 1,500 prisoners were taken by our troops.[22]

During the evening of 4 (16) August, Oudinot convened a council of war, which consisted, in addition to the corps commanders, of all the divisional commanders and the Chief of Artillery of *2e Corps*. The Marshal raised the question: was it better to give battle by remaining on the right bank of the Dvina, or move to the left bank of the river and hold Polotsk in the form of a bridgehead? After a rather lengthy discussion, Saint-Cyr's idea was adopted, believing that:

> if the enemy does not follow our retreating troops, then it might be possible to move to the left bank of the Dvina, holding Polotsk with a strong detachment; if the Russians, on the contrary, continue the pursuit and start an action, then we could not cross the river within their sight, both to avoid the losses associated with such a retreat, and in order not to weaken the morale of the troops.

Some of the generals participating in the military council hoped that Count Wittgenstein would not press the retreating troops and that the proposed crossing could be completed without any difficulty.[23]

But this assumption was erroneous: although Wittgenstein knew that the enemy had managed to assemble more than 30,000 men at Polotsk, whom we could oppose with no more than 20,000, nevertheless he decided to exploit the momentum of his

20   *Précis de la campagne du 1er corps de l'armée d'Occident*. Major General Prince Repnin's report to Count Wittgenstein, undated (from August), No 367.
21   Saint-Cyr, *Mémoires*, III, 64-65.
22   *Précis de la campagne du 1er corps*.
23   Saint-Cyr, *Mémoires*, III, 65-66.

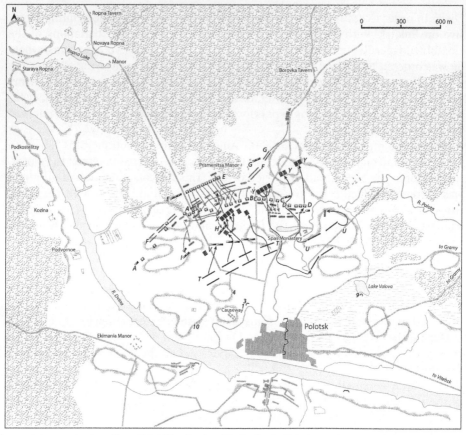

Plan of the First Battle of Polotsk, 17–18 August 1812.

Legend

Russian Forces on 17 August
A.A. First line, right wing

B.B. First line, centre
C.C. First line, left wing
D.D. Vlastov's detachment
E.E. Second line

Russian Forces on 18 August
F.F. Deployment at the start of the fighting
G.G. Vlastov's detachment at the end of the battle
H. Cuirassiers' attack
I. Hussars' attack

Franco-Bavarian Forces on 17 August
T.T. Legrand's Division, one regiment from Verdier's Division & part of Corbineau's Brigade
U.U. Bavarian Corps & Corbineau's Brigade

Franco-Bavarian Forces on 18 August
X.X. Valentin's Division & Legrand's Division
Y.Y. Deroy's Division & Wrede's Division

successes, to continue the offensive, with the objective of seizing the exits from the position at Polotsk and preventing the enemy from debouching onto the right bank of the Dvina. The council of war was still under way in the enemy headquarters when General Helffreich, having reached the village of Ropna, received orders to clear the forest defile to its very edge in the direction of Polotsk. The 25th Jägers under Major Vetoshkin's command, and Colonel Roth's 26th Jägers, supported by Prince Sibirsky's brigade were sent from the vanguard, after a fierce firefight that lasted about three hours, charged with fixed bayonets, driving the enemy out of the forest by dawn on 5 (17) August, capturing the Prismenitsa manor and established communications with Vlastov, who, for his part, having driven the enemy out of the forest, settled down at the Borovka tavern. During this action, General Verdier, one of the veterans of the French army, was seriously wounded. The enemy troops were forced to retreat to the town and settled forwards of it as follows:[24] Legrand's division, with one regiment from Verdier's division and part of Corbineau's light cavalry brigade attached, formed the left wing of the main battle line, on the right bank of the river Polota; the remaining troops of *2e Corps* (Verdier's division and Merle's division, Doumerc's cuirassier division, Castex's light cavalry brigade and all the artillery, except for a few light guns left with Legrand's division) had been transferred to the left bank of the Dvina with the entire train; the troops of the Bavarian *6e Corps* with the majority of Corbineau's brigade were stationed on the right wing of the general deployment, on the left bank of the Polota, their left flank being behind the Spas monastery, held by the Bavarian vanguard. Bridges had been constructed behind the monastery for communications between both corps. Thus Oudinot, in preparing to give battle, had weakened his force by more than 10,000 men and had no more than 19,000 in position ahead of Polotsk (11,000 from the Bavarian Corps, Legrand's 7,000 and 700 under Corbineau).[25]

The positions occupied by the enemy force gave their right wing an advantage by protecting them behind the Polota river; the left wing, although it had this river to its rear, nevertheless, this disadvantage was partly offset by the construction of several bridges that served as communications between both banks of the Polota. In addition, the ancient fortifications of Polotsk and the town itself could serve as very reliable strong points for the enemy.

As soon as our forward detachments, General Helffreich's and Colonel Vlastov's, had left the forest for the open ground stretching forwards of Polotsk on the morning of 5 (17) August, they were met with fierce fire from the enemy batteries. Count Wittgenstein, having intelligence on the significant superiority of the enemy troop numbers, did not want to operate decisively, but hoped to induce Oudinot to retreat behind the Dvina through feints.[26] To that end, the Chief of Engineers, Colonel Count Sievers, was ordered to build bridges on the Dvina, four *versts* downstream of Polotsk, and on the Polota, a little upstream of the town; the Chief of Artillery, Prince Iashvili, was instructed, having taken command of the left-flank vanguard, to

---

24   See Plan of the Battle of Polotsk, 5 to 6 (17 to 18) August 1812.

25   Major General Helffreich's report to Count Wittgenstein dated 10 [22] August, No 51. Saint-Cyr, *Mémoires*, III, 66-69.

26   Count Wittgenstein's report to the Tsar dated 30 August [11 September].

attack the enemy, while Wittgenstein himself, having extracted the main body of his corps from the forest, formed them up for battle in the area between the Dvina and Polota, in support of the vanguards. The right wing of the First Line, extending to the right beyond the Drissa road and to the left to the road from Sebezh, consisted of six battalions (23rd Jägers, 25th Jägers and 26th Jägers) and the Lifeguard Dragoons Replacement Squadron with six guns from 28th Battery Artillery Company; in the centre between the Sebezh road and Prismenitsa manor there were eight battalions (Kaluga Infantry, Sevsk Infantry and Combined Infantry regiments) and the Lifeguard Hussars Replacement Squadron with 33 guns from 1st Horse Artillery Company, 5th Battery Artillery Company and 9th Light Artillery Company; while on the left wing, from Prismenitsa to the Polota, there were four battalions (Perm Infantry and Mogilev Infantry) with six guns from 28th Battery Artillery Company and 12 from 26th Light Artillery Company, and Vlastov's vanguard (24th Jägers, two combined grenadier battalions from 5th Division, four squadrons of Grodno Hussars and the Lifeguard Ulans' Replacement Squadron). The Second Line, under General Sazonov's command, consisted of nine battalions (Tula Infantry, Navaginsk Infantry, Tenginsk Infantry and Estland Infantry and 11th Jägers' Replacement Battalion), almost all the cavalry and 42 guns (3rd Horse Artillery Company, 14th Battery Artillery Company, 28th Battery Artillery Company and 10th Light Artillery Company). In reserve, under General Kakhovsky's command, at Ropna, there were nine replacement and combined grenadier battalions with some of the Yamburg Dragoons and Riga Dragoons.[27]

Count Wittgenstein, having undertaken to attack the enemy with the actual objective of inducing them to retreat behind the Dvina, had assigned this mission to Vlastov's vanguard, as already mentioned, and intended to support him with just a part of the main body. The village of Spas, between the centre and the right wing of the enemy position, was chosen as the focus of the attack, because an attack on their left flank would expose the attacking troops to the fire of powerful batteries placed on the left bank of the Dvina by Marshal Oudinot; while enveloping the enemy position on their right flank would isolate us from our main line of operations – the Sebezh road.[28]

At seven o'clock in the morning, the Russian troops went into action. Prince Iashvili, having been ordered to take possession of the closest buildings of the Spas monastery, on the nearside of the ravine, sent Vlastov's vanguard and Prince Sibirsky's infantry brigade forwards (Perm Infantry and Mogilev Infantry). The marksmen of 24th Jägers and Perm Infantry ejected the enemy from several buildings and drove them back behind the ravine. Whereupon Oudinot, concerned that he might get separated from Saint-Cyr, sent Legrand's division forward and transferred some of Wrede's Bavarian division to the right bank of the Polota; at the same time, several enemy batteries placed on the left bank of the Polota river opened fire on the left flank of our leading troops. Count Wittgenstein, noticing the concentration of Oudinot's forces behind the Spas monastery, ordered General Berg to move to the

---

27 *Précis de la campagne du 1er corps.* Reports by formation commanders regarding the battle of Polotsk.
28 *Précis de la campagne du 1er corps.*

left to assist the vanguard with the Sevsk Infantry, Kaluga Infantry, 1st Combined Infantry Regiment and with six guns from 5th Battery Artillery Company, while he advanced one battalion of the Tula Infantry and 11th Jägers' Replacement Battalion from the Second Line to the centre of the First to replace these troops, and thereafter one battalion each from the Estland Infantry and Navaginsk Infantry. Oudinot, hoping to take advantage of the weakening of our centre, attacked it with Legrand's force, but the French were repelled by General Gamen, who had taken over command of this location after Berg's departure to the left wing. Our skirmishers charged at the enemy screen with bayonets fixed and drove them back to the suburbs. A second attack by the French was repulsed by Gamen with the assistance of another battalion of the Tula Infantry sent from the Second Line to assist him. It was here that Marshal Oudinot was seriously wounded in the shoulder.[29]

During this battle in the centre of our deployment, the Russian infantry, which was stationed on the left wing, was forced out of the buildings it had occupied in Spas; the Bavarians pressed forwards, but were met by fire from 3rd Horse Artillery Company sent from the Second Line, while 1st Horse Artillery Company under Lieutenant Colonel Sukhozanet, lining up somewhat to the right, opened fire on the enemy flank.[30] Meanwhile, on our left wing, the attack by two combined grenadier battalions from 5th Division, 24th Jägers and two battalions of Perm Infantry and Mogilev Infantry, under Berg's personal command, forced the Bavarians to retreat behind the ravine, whereupon Graf Wrede ordered the monastery buildings closest to us to be set on fire. Our skirmishers attempted to cross to the far side of the ravine, but were held back by heavy fire from enemy batteries and the thick skirmishing screen that occupied the buildings, hedges and gardens of Spas. Meanwhile, on our part, 5th Battery Artillery Company under Lieutenant Colonel [Ye.A.] Muruzi and 1st Horse Artillery Company under Lieutenant Colonel Sukhozanet worked very successfully against the columns continuously arriving from the town.[31] At this point, a very heated exchange of fire ensued, which lasted right up until nightfall.

In the centre of our line, the enemy, having been reinforced with fresh troops, renewed their attacks several times; enemy skirmishers closed on our batteries, but each time they were driven off by the supports; Count Wittgenstein, noticing the efforts of the French to break through our centre, ordered the Tenginsk Infantry to shore it up.[32] Thus, of the nine battalions that had been in the Second Line, seven had been brought up into the First; eventually, the Russian troops were able to hold their positions. And here, the darkness of the night put an end to the fighting.

The troops on our right wing had played almost no part in the battle at all. The enemy opened fire from 15 guns placed on the left bank of the Dvina on 23rd Jägers stationed opposite the Ekimaniya manor, where a significant part of their infantry

---

29   Count Wittgenstein's report to the Tsar dated 30 August [11 September], and to Barclay de Tolly (M.T.D. No 44,585 Vol. 7). General Sazonov's report to Count Wittgenstein dated 10 [22] August 1812.

30   Prince Iashvili's report to Count Wittgenstein dated 12 [24] August 1812, No 413.

31   Count Wittgenstein's report to Barclay de Tolly. Prince Iashvili's report to Count Wittgenstein dated 12 [24] August, No 413.

32   Count Wittgenstein's reports to the Tsar and to Barclay de Tolly.

and cavalry were also located; but the effect of this artillery, due to the considerable range to our right flank, was negligible. Count Wittgenstein, seeing that a small element of our force had diverted an incomparably superior French force, deliberately left his right wing inactive, while wanting in the meantime to launch a diversionary movement around the enemy army's left flank, he detached the Chief of Engineers, Count Sievers, with two battalions and a pioneer company, for the construction of a bridge on the Dvina, four *versts* downstream of Polotsk; once the bridge was ready by that evening, then Count Sievers, leaving both battalions that had arrived with him as protection and to threaten the enemy with a crossing, set off, on the night of 5 to 6 (17 to 18) August, by order of the corps commander, along the Dvina and Polota and proceeded to build another bridge on the latter river, four *versts* upstream of Polotsk, in order to threaten the enemy with envelopment from the right flank. Count Wittgenstein, resolutely following the plan of action drawn up by him, had no intention of attacking the enemy in the positions they occupied, because the capture of Polotsk by brute force would completely disrupt I Corps, already significantly weakened from five battles. The objective of our commander's operation was to induce the enemy to evacuate the right bank of the Dvina without committing to a decisive battle.[33]

The action on 5 (17) August had been indecisive, although it had cost a great deal to the participating corps. The troops of both sides remained in the same places that they had occupied at the beginning of the battle, except for our left wing, which had fought for and held the nearside of the Spas ravine. Count Wittgenstein's command post was in the Prismenitsa manor by the end of the fighting. The enemy headquarters remained in Polotsk. Marshal Oudinot, seriously wounded in the shoulder by canister shot, was forced to hand over command of his corps to Saint-Cyr, who had also been wounded, but rather lightly.[34]

During the night of 5 to 6 (17 to 18) August, Saint-Cyr assembled most of his generals to inform them of his intention to attack the Russian army with the full force of both corps located around Polotsk. Saint-Cyr, one of the most outstanding French generals, owed his rapid rise at the beginning of his service to the turbulent times of the revolution, and remained a republican at heart even during the Empire. This philosophy, together with Saint-Cyr's outspoken nature, was the reason for Napoleon's dislike for him, which, although he did reward his talents, nevertheless overlooked him in the general advancement of the Marshals of Empire and did not trust him with independent command of forces. The unforeseen departure of Oudinot, by handing Saint-Cyr command over the army assembled at Polotsk, opened the path to distinction for him. Saint-Cyr did not miss his opportunity: he had decided, as he himself stated at the council he had assembled, to launch an attack on Wittgenstein, because the position of the Russians at Polotsk was preventing the corps stationed at this city from either sending out detachments to collect provisions and fodder, or from giving any kind of relaxation to men exhausted by incessant marching and fighting. According to Saint-Cyr, the allies could not evade combat, even in event of the Franco-Bavarian army crossing to the left bank of the

---

33   Count Wittgenstein's reports.
34   Saint-Cyr, *Mémoires*, III, 74.

Dvina, and he was convinced of this by the persistence of Wittgenstein's attacks during the day of 5 (17) August, just as he was by the construction of Russian bridges over the Dvina and Polota. And therefore Saint-Cyr believed that only a decisive offensive could drag the allied army out of the difficult situation in which it found itself. All attendees of the council were aware of the need to attack the Russian army, but asked for the exhaustion of their troops to be taken into account, who, according to them, could not endure the exertions of combat if it, as it had on the previous day before, continued all day, and they assured Saint-Cyr that it would be impossible to keep the soldiers on their feet for even six straight hours. Saint-Cyr, yielding to necessity, proposed that the troops should fight for no more than four hours: finally, it was decided to send the troops into battle, the next day, at four o'clock in the afternoon, so that the onset of darkness would not force them to fight longer than the agreed time.[35]

We have already had occasion to mention that the total troops numbers of the French *2e Corps* and Bavarian *6e Corps* exceeded more than one and a half times the strength of our force. But many factors balanced out the advantage of the numerical superiority of the enemy army: chief among them was the influence of Count Wittgenstein's constant successes on morale; which was why our troops were fresh and cheerful, while the enemy were extremely weary and exhausted; Saint-Cyr was also very disadvantaged because, having no magazines, he was forced to send out significant detachments to obtain supplies (*envoyer à la maraude*), weakening the army by a whole quarter of the total number of troops.[36]

All these factors, together with the departure of the train and some of Oudinot's troops to the left bank of the Dvina on 5 (17) August, seen from our perspective, prompted Count Wittgenstein to remain in his positions for the following day. Judging from all previous operations by Oudinot (whose departure was not yet known in our corps headquarters), it could be assessed that, having failed in the fighting on 5 (17) August, he would retreat with all his forces behind the Dvina and leave only part of the force in Polotsk, for a temporary occupation of the town in the form of a bridgehead. Count Wittgenstein intended, in the event of a retreat by the enemy corps, to attack their rearguard, and, pushing them behind the Dvina, to clear the entire right bank of the river.[37]

The troops of I Corps were deployed in the same formation in which they were found during the night of 5 to 6 (17 to 18) August, namely: on the right wing: 23rd Jägers, 25th Jägers and 26th Jägers with six guns from 28th Battery Artillery Company and nine from 1st Horse Artillery Company; in the centre: Tula Infantry, Estland Infantry, 18th Jägers Replacement Battalion and a battalion from the Navaginsk Infantry, with six guns from 5th Battery Artillery Company, six from 27th Battery Artillery Company, 12 from 9th Light Artillery Company and six from 28th Battery Artillery Company; on the left wing: Perm Infantry, Mogilev Infantry, Kaluga Infantry, 1st Combined Infantry and 24th Jägers, combined battalions of 5th Division, with 12 guns of 26th Light Artillery Company, six from 3rd Horse

35   Saint-Cyr, *Mémoires*, III, 77-79.
36   Saint-Cyr, *Mémoires*, III, 79.
37   *Précis de la campagne du 1er corps.*

Artillery Company and six from 5th Battery Artillery Company. The cavalry and remaining infantry (which included those that had arrived overnight from Prince Repnin's detachment), were deployed in the Second Line. The reserve, under General Sazonov's command, had been moved from Ropna to the Nevel road, which lay behind the left wing of the position.[38]

The troop numbers under Count Wittgenstein, on 6 (18) August, did not exceed 18,000 men, but Saint-Cyr considered the Russian corps to be much stronger than it actually was: the stubborn resistance by Russian troops during any engagement with the enemy had misled them in their calculations of Wittgenstein's strength, and, in addition, the French, having intelligence on the arrival of Gamen with nine battalions (reported to Saint-Cyr as twelve), and Repnin with several battalions and squadrons with Wittgenstein's force, did not know the true strength of these battalions, some of which were calculated to have no more than 250 men in their ranks. Saint-Cyr, who was unaware of these circumstances (as can be seen from his notes), considered it necessary to reward the (imaginary) numerical superiority of our troops with a surprise attack. To that end, on 6 (18) August, at one o'clock in the afternoon, the significant trains and parks from both corps, stationed on the left bank of the Dvina, beyond Polotsk, were stretched out within sight of our troops along the road to Ulla; Valentin's division [François Valentin] (formerly Verdier's), also located on the left bank of the river the day before, near the point at which General Sievers was building a bridge, moved up the river, as if in order to escort the trains from behind, while Doumerc's cuirassier division and Castex's light cavalry brigade, having just returned from a foraging expedition, appeared to be preparing to escort the trains from the front and flanks. At half past three, the wagon train set off along the road to Ulla, enveloped in thick dust that made it impossible to observe the composition of the column, and at the same time Merle's division and most of the artillery of *2e Corps*, under the command of General Aubry [Claude Charles Aubry de La Boucharderie], crossed to the right bank of the Dvina.

At half past four, General Valentin's division crossed the Dvina following Merle's division, which was stationed on the left wing of the army; Legrand and behind him, at some distance, Valentin, moved to the right up the Polota valley with their divisions, screened by the high ground that prevented us from noticing this flanking movement around our positions, and the former was stationed on the right flank at Spas, while the latter was to their left; the cavalry formed up in the gap between Valentin's division and Merle's division; finally, both divisions of *6e Corps*, waiting for the signal to attack, were hidden in the Polota valley, behind the Spas monastery. The consequence of this skilful deployment by Saint-Cyr was that we paid full attention exclusively to the movements of the column beyond the Dvina, on the road to Ulla, not noticing the concentration of enemy forces in the Polota valley.[39]

At five o'clock precisely, all the Bavarian and French batteries closest to us opened fire on our troops stationed around the Prismenitsa manor, in which (as we have already mentioned) Count Wittgenstein's command post was located. Suddenly, a bombardment from more than 60 enemy guns was heard and one of the round

---

38   *Précis de la campagne du 1er corps.*
39   Saint-Cyr, *Mémoires*, III, 81-83.

shot struck the room where, at that very moment, Count Wittgenstein was having a meal with his staff. The enemy columns quickly attacked under the thunder from the battery that broke over the troops of our left wing and centre: Wrede's division, moving to the right around Spas monastery, charged at the left flank of our position; Deroy's division and Legrand's division advanced towards Prismenitsa, while Valentin's force was directed against our centre. In the first minutes of this completely unexpected attack, our troops were thrown into disorder; but quickly recovered. Saint-Cyr himself commented on the battle:

> The Russians have unshakable courage and fearlessness, of which few examples can be found in the troops of other nations. Their battalions, taken by surprise, separated one from the other, during our initial attack (because we had broken through their lines), were not disheartened and continued to fight, retreating extremely slowly and defending themselves from all sides with such courage, which, I repeat, is characteristic only of Russians. They performed miracles of courage, but could not withstand the simultaneous pressure of four divisions, which partially neutralised the troops against whom they were sent.[40]

Indeed, neither the surprise attack, nor the concentration of huge enemy forces against a single point of our position, shook Wittgenstein's battle-hardened soldiers. The Russian artillery (six guns from 28th Battery Artillery Company, 9th Light Artillery Company and six guns from 5th Battery Artillery Company), quickly opened fire and halted the initial dash by the enemy; while the regiments of 5th Division under Berg and the reserve battalions with three squadrons of Grodno Hussars charged towards the advancing columns and forced them to retreat, whereupon General Kazachkovsky suffered a gunshot wound to the leg. But the enemy, resuming the bombardment and thickening it with fire from batteries placed on the left bank of the Polota and operating in enfilade along our line, resumed the attack; bitter close quarter combat ensued, interrupted, from time to time, by exchanges of fire carried out at a very close range; eventually, 5th Division was forced to retreat to the Prismenitsa manor, while Vlastov's force had been committed from the reserve, supported by 1st Combined Battalion from 14th Division, retreated and occupied the edge of the forest. The battle resumed in this formation with even greater force; the entire area between Prismenitsa and Spas was littered with corpses. The enemy, seeing the failure of their attempt against our left wing, decided to turn their main body against the centre, with the aim of breaking through, in order to dash into the rear of the troops under Berg and Vlastov, while they were being attacked by the Bavarians from the other side. Legrand's division and Valentin's division charged our artillery, 9th Light Artillery Company, 28th Battery Artillery Company and 5th Battery Artillery Company, and pushed back their supports, but the brave artillerymen, fighting back with swords and rammers, managed to save their guns, with the exception of seven (five from 9th Light Artillery Company and two from

---

40   Saint-Cyr, *Mémoires*, III, 87.

28th Battery Artillery Company), which, being overrun and having lost almost all the horses with them, were captured by Legrand's troops, while the commander of 9th Light Artillery Company, Staff Captain Perrin [Pëtr Yakovlevich Perrin], had been wounded by a bullet in the leg.[41] Following this, Legrand took possession of Prismenitsa. It was necessary to stop the enemy advance, who, upon breaking through the centre, could cut off Berg's line of retreat to Ropna. General Gamen, with the Tula Infantry and Estland Infantry regiments and with the battalions of the Navaginsk Infantry and 11th Jägers, supported by one of the battalions of the Tenginsk Infantry, charged with fixed bayonets at the columns advancing against our centre and pushed them back with significant losses; at the same time, Colonel Protasov [Alexey Andrianovich Protasov], with two squadrons of Lifeguards from the Combined Cuirassier Regiment (Chevalier Guard and Lifeguard Horse), made several successful charges and drove back one of the brigades of Legrand's division, but was held back by Maison (later Marshal of France) with the *29e Légère*.[42] General Gamen, attacked several times in succession by superior forces, repulsed them successfully and remained with his troops, paying no heed to the two severe contusions he had suffered. General Sazonov, who commanded the Second Line, sent another battalion of the Navaginsk Infantry to assist him, under the command of Colonel Harpe [Vasily Ivanovich Garpe], who, charging the nearest French column with fixed bayonets, put it to flight. Despite these partial successes, however, the enemy, having pushed forward their powerful artillery, launched a general offensive against the centre and left wing of the Russian force: Legrand's division and Valentin's division pushed the centre and that part of the right wing closest to it into the large forest behind our position; the Bavarians forced Berg's 5th Division to retreat towards Ropna, while Vlastov's force was pushed up the Nevel road.

Vlastov's retreat exposed the observation posts set up by him to guard the left flank on the Polota river: one, consisting of a company of grenadiers, was covering the bridge built by Count Sievers four *versts* upstream of Polotsk, while the other, of a squadron of Grodno Hussars, was monitoring a ford at a distance of three *versts* from the former outpost. Colonel Vlastov, having learned about the appearance of the enemy across from the hussars, sent one of the combined grenadier battalions from 5th Division and the Pavlov Grenadier Regiment's Replacement Battalion detached from Major General Kakhovsky's reserves to support them. While they were still on the march, the enemy, distracting the hussars with cavalry skirmishers, sent four battalions with several squadrons of cuirassiers against the grenadiers guarding the bridge. These troops, driving off the grenadier company, moved into the rear of the second observation post and the two battalions sent to assist it, which, having gone quite far, were cut off, but cut their way back through the enemy force, capturing six officers and some 100 lower ranks and returned with them to Vlastov's

---

41   Count Wittgenstein's reports to the Tsar and to Barclay de Tolly.

42   Saint-Cyr, *Mémoires*, III, 89-90. In his report to the Tsar, Count Wittgenstein stated: 'Colonel Protasov charged at three enemy columns that were trying to envelope Major General Gamen's left flank with the Lifeguard squadrons of the Combined Cuirassier Regiment: the Lifeguard Horse drove back and destroyed two of them completely, while the third suffered the same fate at the hands of the Chevalier Guard squadron.'

detachment. Meanwhile, the Grodno Hussar squadron also began to retreat and barely managed to escape into the forest, as they was surrounded by enemy infantry, which opened heavy fire on them; but the hussars, under the command of their brave squadron commander, Lieutenant Mishkovsky, twice cut through the enemy blocking their path and joined the other three squadrons of the Grodno Hussars, which were with Vlastov's detachment.[43]

While the troops under Berg and Vlastov, yielding to the superiority of the enemy forces, were forced to retreat, our right wing was scoring brilliant successes. Saint-Cyr had intended to move his reserves along the Sebezh road, and then direct them to the left in order to sever the line of retreat of the Russian force which was stationed between this road and the Dvina; but was compelled to confine himself to defensive actions at this point. During the retreat by Gamen's force, the French advanced with more than 30 guns under cavalry escort, against Colonel Harpe who remained in position with the Tenginsk Infantry Regiment. The commander of our cavalry, General Balk, noticing the advance by the enemy column to the left, in order to protect our centre from the right flank, directed two Lifeguard Cuirassier Squadrons from the Combined Cuirassier Regiment, under the command of Colonel Yershov [Ivan Zakharovich Yershov], with two weak squadrons from the Grodno Hussars and Riga Dragoons, who, having ridden to the right in threes, raced to cut off the enemy column, consisting of *chasseurs à cheval*, formed up to the front and drove into the light brigade under General Corbineau. Panic stricken, the French *chasseurs à cheval* were driven back onto a Bavarian battery. The artillerymen, not daring to open fire on the cavalry of both sides rushing towards them, were cut down by our cuirassiers; lieutenants Vilamovich, Prince Shakhovskoy, cornets Veletsky and Okunev [Grigory Alexandrovich Okunev], were first to jump into the battery. Here, 15 guns were captured by the Russian troops, of which only two were taken away together with the battery commander, while the rest were all left in place, due to lack of time, however their carriages were smashed to pieces. Saint-Cyr, who could not ride due to the wound he had suffered, was thrown from a light cart (*petit wurtz*) in which he was being driven around the battlefield, in the confusion and almost fell into the hands of our armoured men himself. Meanwhile, the French *4e régiment de cuirassiers* rushed to the rescue of the captured battery, but were engaged by Her Majesty's *Leib* Cuirassier Squadron, under the command of Major Semek, was driven back and pursued into the streets of the suburbs. The confusion and disorder among the enemy was extraordinary; troops, artillery and carts were rushing towards the bridge and overcrowded it to the point that several wagons were shoved into the water. Only the arrival of Bavarian reserves and the nature of the ground, inappropriate for cavalry action, halted the brave charge of our grenadiers [*sic*]. Another squadron from the Combined Cuirassier Regiment, which charged after the departing enemy guns, was held up as it passed the cemetery by fire from infantry settled behind the wall. A Grodno Hussar squadron, under the command of Captain Dyadkov attacked the enemy no less bravely, and lost all its officers in this action.[44]

---

43   Count Wittgenstein's report to the Tsar dated 30 August [11 September].
44   Count Wittgenstein's report to the Tsar.

Meanwhile, the enemy sent up General Amey's Brigade [François-Pierre Joseph Amey] (Merle's division), consisting of seven battalions with 12 squadrons of *chasseurs à cheval* from Castex's brigade, with their artillery, against the tip of our right wing, where two battalions of 23rd Jägers, three squadrons of Grodno Hussars and 1st Horse Artillery Company were located. Such a huge superiority in numbers gave the enemy the opportunity to push our jägers back; but their success was fleeting. Lieutenant Colonel Sukhozanet dashed forward along the Disna road with 1st Horse Artillery Company, halted the enemy and disordered them with the fire from his guns, and assisted the brave Captain Kaempfert to charge decisively at Castex's cavalry with two squadrons of Grodno Hussars. This brilliant attack not only stopped the advance by Merle's infantry, but stunned Doumerc's cuirassier division into inaction, which had been standing to their right, and facilitated the success of the attack by the Combined Cuirassier Regiment preventing the enemy from persistently pursuing the troops of our centre. Once Saint-Cyr had eventually managed to restore order among his cavalry, then Doumerc's division was sent to pursue the retreating troops under Count Wittgenstein along with the infantry of the battle lines, while the Swiss infantry brigade under Candras [Jacques Lazare Savettier de Candras] (Merle's division) was brought up from the reserve to support the four battalions that had entered the forest on the road to Beloe; but this infantry, as exhausted as all the other enemy troops, lay down on the ground at the entrance to the forest and could move no further.

The troops under Berg and Gamen retreated to Ropna, under the protection of Helffreich's rearguard, which settled down for the night at the entrance to the forest, between Prismenitsa and Ropna. The detachment under Colonel Vlastov remained in the place he had occupied at the edge of the forest, near the Nevel road.

The Russian casualties, in the fighting at Polotsk, on 5 and 6 (17 and 18) August, overall extended to about 5,500 men, among whom were generals Berg, Kazachkovsky and Gamen; on the part of the enemy, according to official data, the losses shown for the fighting on 5 (17) August were 1,000, while on 6 (18) August were 2,000 men, but in reality there were twice as many, because at a review conducted by Saint-Cyr a few days later, the number of troops in both corps did not exceed 29,020 men.[45] Among the wounded were *généraux de division*: Deroy (soon to die), Valentin, Raglovich [Clemens von Raglovich] and *Général de brigade* Vincenti [Karl von Vincenti].[46]

Although the success gained by Saint-Cyr was not decisive, Napoleon, pleased that he had held out at Polotsk, promoted him to Marshal.

On 7 (19) August, the main body of the independent I Corps moved to Gamzelevo; the reserve was positioned at Beloe, where 4th Battalion of the Mogilev Infantry Regiment and 23rd Horse Artillery Company, which had arrived from Pskov, joined them. General Helffreich's rearguard was behind the Ropna defile, held by the leading troops of the detachment. Colonel Valstov's rearguard withdrew at dusk to the village of Arteikovichi.

The enemy remained around Polotsk for the entire day.

---

45   *Précis de la campagne du 1er corps*. Saint-Cyr, *Mémoires,* III, 105. General Buturlin gives the losses for each side as more than 2,000 men.
46   Saint-Cyr, *Mémoires,* III, 99.

On 8 (20) August, Wittgenstein's main body was deployed at Beloe; the reserve was on the Drissa at Sivoshina. The enemy attacked Helffreich's leading outposts and took the Ropna defile, from where our rearguard retreated towards Gamzelevo, which forced Vlastov to move back behind Arteikovichi.

On 9 (21) August, the Corps main body withdrew to the Drissa at Sivoshina, where the position immediately began to be fortified; the reserve was located at the village of Sokolishche-Eismont; the corps headquarters also moved there. Helffreich's and Vlastov's rearguards linked up at Beloe, taking up a quite advantageous position at the exit from the defile. The command of the rearguard, which included only a Cossack regiment, four squadrons (Grodno Hussars) and four battalions (24th Jägers and 26th Jägers) with eight guns (two from 14th Battery Artillery Company and six from 3rd Horse Artillery Company), was entrusted to Colonel Vlastov. The rearguard was ordered to hold out for as long as possible in the positions they had occupied and then to retreat to Boyarshchina, where Count Wittgenstein intended to engage the enemy with the main body at the exit of the defile; in the event of the numbers of enemy troops being significantly superior, it was intended to retreat behind the Drissa and accept battle in the fortified positions at Sivoshina.

On 10 (22) August, General Wrede, having received orders to drive the Russian rearguard out of Beloe with his division, marched there along the road from Gamzelevo. Vlastov's leading troops retreated in good order, while the enemy, following them, was halted by the fire from two heavy guns. Whereupon Wrede also set up a battery and sent thick screens of skirmishers along either side of the road. Our guns retreated, and the enemy, following them, was again engaged by fire from four horse artillery guns. The Bavarians were forced to halt; but in the meantime Wrede gathered the bulk of the force on his left wing, hurried them covertly through the forest and, having occupied Beloe manor, attacked our rearguard from the right flank. Lieutenant Colonel Silin [Vasily Mikhailovich Silin] was sent to counter attack the enemy with two squadrons of Grodno Hussars, who, having charged at the enemy column, drove the Bavarians back into the buildings; following which, Colonel Roth charged the enemy with the 26th Jäger Regiment with bayonets fixed and drove them out of the manor, while the hussars pursued the disordered column up to the forest itself; Colonel Rüdiger, with two more squadrons of Grodno Hussars, drove the infantry away that had been enveloping our detachment from the left flank. The enemy, who had not expected such resistance, retreated to Gamzelevo, losing 120 prisoners alone; among those killed were General Siebein [Justus Ritter von Siebein] and Lieutenant Colonel Gedoni [Joseph von Gedoni]. On our side, overall, there were 94 casualties. Vlastov's rearguard redeployed at Beloe, as before.[47]

A detachment was positioned at the village of Gramosha, in order to secure the right flank of the main body of the corps and to monitor the roads leading from Polotsk to Drissa and Disna, consisting of three companies from the Combined Jäger Regiment and two squadrons of Combined Cuirassiers, with two horse artillery guns; while Vlastov's detachment was reinforced with two battalions of 25th

---

47 *Précis de la campagne du 1er corps.* Saint-Cyr, *Mémoires*, III, 100.

Jägers. The Combined Hussar Regiment, located at Kamenets, near Dünaburg, was monitoring MacDonald's *10e Corps*. The main body of the corps, as before, remained partly in the fortified positions at Sivoshina, partly between Sivoshina and Sokolishche.

Saint-Cyr did not dare to attack our troops in this position; all his attention was turned to the regular supply of rations to the army through foraging and through the elimination of marauding. In order to collect supplies, the Bavarian troops were assigned the countryside on the left bank of the Dvina, *2e Corps* were assigned the right bank, while the cavalry had the area between the rivers Sosnitsa and Obol. Saint-Cyr's troops concentrated on the position at Polotsk, which was subsequently fortified; the vanguard was stationed at Gamzelevo.

Both sides remained in these positions from 11 (23) August to 4 (16) October, limiting themselves to guerilla warfare. During this time, the corps under Count Wittgenstein was strengthened by reinforcements that joined him, while Saint-Cyr managed to put his troops, exhausted by the campaigning and hardships, in some-what better order.[48] Postponing the presentation of individual actions in this theatre of war for the time being, during the course of almost two months' rest for Wittgenstein's main body, we turn to Napoleon's offensive following the battle of Valutino; but first we shall describe the actions of Emperor Alexander I, which had a paramount influence on the course of the war.

---

48   *Précis de la campagne du 1er corps.* Saint-Cyr, *Mémoires*, III, 101-103.

Appendix I

Terms of the Treaty of Tilsit for Prussia

No matter how painful the terms of the Treaty of Tilsit were for Prussia, they were only the foundations for further extortion by Napoleon, who changed these conditions at his own discretion, and, using the right of might, forced the Prussian government to agree to other, equally painful oppressive treaties. Thus, the following treaties were concluded, at various times:

1. The Convention of Elbing, 13 October 1807, new style, in which, in addition to free passage for Saxon troops through Prussian territory, from Saxony to the Duchy of Warsaw and back, it was decided to open three trade corridors from Dresden to Warsaw and Kalisz, with a most paltry payment of duties for goods imported.
2. The Second Convention of Elbing, 10 November 1807. It was decided that Prussia must cede the Michelau [Michałów] *Kreis* and New Silesia [Nowy Śląsk] in favour of the Duchy of Warsaw.
3. The Third Convention of Elbing, 6 December 1807. The area of the military city of Danzig was increased.
4. A Convention, concluded in Paris on 8 September 1808. In order to end the disputes that had arisen between the French intendant-general and Prussian local government, one of the brothers of the King of Prussia, Prince William, was sent to Paris on the account of the final payment of the indemnity imposed by Napoleon on Prussia. The final resolution of the issues in this case was extremely important: the evacuation of Prussia depended on him, occupied by a large number of French troops. In the opinion of the Prussian commission, 19 million francs remained to be paid, while according to Daru's calculations, it was 112 million. In March 1808 King Friedrich Wilhelm III had been forced to agree to pay the latter amount. But the matter did not end there: the duration for which the French army of 150,000 men had to be maintained by Prussia was extended for six months, and the French foreign minister announced to Prince William that the Prussian government remained indebted to the French to the tune of 154½ million. After lengthy negotiations, supported by threats from the French government and Napoleon, a convention was concluded on 8th September, 1808, on the basis of which it was agreed:

i.   For Prussia to pay France 140 million francs, within of 20 days of the exchange of ratification, half in cash, or bills of exchange guaranteed by the state treasury.

ii.   The other half in bank notes, secured against state property.

iii.   All revenues due to the Prussian government from the inhabitants of the Duchy of Warsaw were assigned in their favour, on the basis of the Treaty of Tilsit (nothing of the kind had been agreed at Tilsit).

iv.   The Prussian government had to repay revenues collected by them to the ceded provinces.

v.   French troops were to evacuate the King of Prussia's territory within 30 to 40 days (this condition was not fulfilled).

vi.   The fortresses of Glogau, Küstrin and Stettin would be occupied by French troops, totalling 10,000 men, until the indemnity was paid. Quartering, heating, lighting, food and fodder for these troops would be dependent on the Prussian government.

In Article XIII, the routes were agreed through Prussian territory for the movement of the French garrisons of the fortresses of Glogau, Küstrin and Stettin. In Article XIV, the area assigned to the Magdeburg citadel on the right bank of the Elbe was increased. In Article XVI, the King recognised Joseph Napoleon as King of Spain, and Murat as King of the Two Sicilies. Finally, according to a secret article – it was determined that Prussia should maintain no more than 42,000 troops for ten years.

In October 1808, during the Erfurt Congress, at the request of Tsar Alexander, the indemnity agreed in Paris was reduced by 20 million francs.

According to a convention concluded in Berlin, on 3 November, 1808, French troops were to evacuate Prussian territory, with the exception of three fortresses on the Oder.

According to a convention concluded in Bayonne, on 10 May, 1808, between Napoleon and Saxony, negotiations led at the time by Prince Wilhelm in Paris, Prussian subjects forfeited all their property in the Duchy of Warsaw, worth about 60 million francs.

Finally, Prussia was forced to join the continental system, to comply with each of the Berlin, Milan and Trianon decrees promulgated by Napoleon, and declare war on Sweden.

Despite all these sacrifices, the Prussian government did not manage to achieve the evacuation of those fortresses on the Oder occupied by the French, and was even forced to take part in the 1812 war by Napoleon against Russia in order to preserve its existence (*Hist. abrégée des traités de paix, par Koch, augm. par Schoell. 1838, III, 49-59*).

The total amount of indemnities and levies of all kinds, owed to Napoleon by Prussia, as a result of the war of 1806-1807, extended to over 600 million francs (150 million silver roubles [2,700 tonnes of pure silver]). *Hist. générale des traités de paix, par M. le comte de Garden. X, 301.*

Appendix II

The Tsar's Note to His Ambassadors Regarding Oldenburg

Sa Majesté Impériale de toutes les Russies a appris avec surprise que S.M. l'Empereur des Français; Roi d'Italie, son allié, donnant par un senatus-consulte, des nouvelles limites à son Empire, y a compris le Duché d'Oldenbourg. Sa Majesté a exposé à l'attention de l'Empereur, son allié, comme elle le fait à celle de l'Europe entière, que nommément le traitè de Tilsitt assure la paisible possession de ce Duché à son légitime Souverain.

Sa Majesté a rappelé à ce monarque et le fait à toutes les puissances, que la Russie, par le traité provisoire de 1767 et celui de 1773, abandonna au Roi de Danemark tout ce qu'elle possedait dans le Duché de Holstein, et reçut en échange les Comtés d'Oldenbourg et de Delmenhorst, qui par des transactions connues, aux quelles plusieurs puissances durent nécessairement prendre part, furent érigés en un Duché souverain en faveur d'une branche cadette de cette même maison de Holstein-Gottorp, à laquelle Sa Majesté Impériale appartient par le lien du sang le plus direct.

L'Empereur juge que cet Etat, créé par la générosité de son empire, ne peut être annulé sans blesser toute justice et ses droits. Il se voit par conséquent obligé d'user du droit de réservation, et de mettre à couvert, comme il le fait par le présent office, en son propre nom et celui de ses héritiers au trône à perpetuité, tous les droits et obligations qui dérivent des traités ci-dessus mentionnés.

Quel prix pourraient conserver les alliances, si les traités qui les fondent ne conservaient pas le leur? Mais Sa Majesté, afin de ne point donner sujet à aucune méprise, déclare ici qu'un grand intérêt politique a produit son alliance avec S.M. l'Empereur des Français; que cet intérêt subsiste, et qu'elle se propose par conséquent de veiller à la conservation de cette alliance, et s'attend à un soin pareil et réciproque de la part d'un monarque à l'amitié du quel elle a des droits.

Cette union de l'intérêt des deux empires, conçue par Pierre le Grand, et qui dès lors et depuis rencontra tant d'obstacles, a déjà procuré des avantages à l'empire de Sa Majesté, et la France de même en a recueilli de son côté.

Il parait donc de l'utilité des deux empires de s'appliquer à conserver cette alliance, es Sa Majesté y consacrera tous ses soins.

Appendix III

French Explanation for Their Mobilisation

On this matter, the Duc de Cadore gave our ambassador, Prince Kurakin, the following explanation:

Prince!
Vous avez desiré que je vous rappellasse dans ce billet ce que j'ai eu l'honneur de vous dire dans notre dernier entretien. Les lettres du Duc de Vicence de la fin de février et du commencement de mars m'apprennent que de faux bruits circulent à St. Pétersbourg et qu'ils y sont accueillis. L'Empereur Alexandre a paru persuadé, et lui-même l'a dit au Duc de Vicence, qu'un train considérable d'artillerie était entré à Dantzig, que les Princes de la Confédération avaient été requis de réunir leurs chevaux d'artillerie, et que sur leur réponse, énonçant que, sans les obliger à faire la dépense que cette réunion exigerait, leurs chevaux seraient toujours prets, quand on en aurait besoin, on avait insisté sur l'exécution de cette disposition. Ces assertions sont fausses; aucun train d'artillerie n'est arrivé à Dantzig; on n'a pas même songé aux troupes de la Confédération. On a fait grand bruit de quelques fusils achetés en France par la Saxe, mais le nombre n'en est que de vingt mille, au lieu de soixante mille qu'on a supposées. On a fait également grand bruit de quelques canons du petit calibre demandés par la Saxe pour ses régiments et que l'Empereur lui a donnés, parceque toute l'artillerie saxonne avait été prise à Jena. On n'accusera pas la Saxe d'avoir voulu mettre du mystère dans cette acquisition de fusils et de canons, puisque le transport des caisses de fusils et de canons montés sur leurs affûts s'est fait à travers toute l'Allemagne, sans aucune espèce de déguisement. Voila quels faits très simples ont été dénaturés et présentés sous un faux jour. Il est également faux qu'on ait fait à Dantzig des fortifications, ainsi qu'on a voulu le persuader à l'Empereur Alexandre. Lorsqu'on a vu des préparatifs sur la Dvina, la création de nouveaux régiments et de nouvelles places de guerre, le mouvement des troupes de Finlande et de Sibérie, s'avançant vers les frontieres occidentales de l'Empire, le retour de deux divisions qui étaient en Moldavie, circonstance si propre à retarder votre paix avec la Porte, tous ces faits n'ont-ils pas à prouver que l'Empereur Alexandre lui-même n'est plus dans les sentiments de Tilsitt? La facilité, avec laquelle on a accueilli à Pétersbourg des bruits sans fondement, fait assez prévoir l'exagération avec la quelle quelques mouvements que l'Empereur a jugé nécessaires seront rapportés. C'est pour prévenir ces inconvéniens

que je me suis empressé de Vous le faire connaître. L'annonce d'une escadre anglaise entrant dans la baltique a fait penser à l'Empereur qu'il devait mettre Dantzig en état de sureté. En conséquence Sa Majesté a fait demander deux régiments au Duché de Varsovie, un à la Saxe, un à la Baviére, un à la Westpahlie et un à Würtemberg. Il y a envoyé un millier de canonniers et un régiment de cavalerie française. La garnison de Dantzig pourra être de cette manière portée à quinze mille hommes. L'Empereur a ordonné la réparation des fortifications de cette Place et son approvisionnement pour deux ans. Ces mesures sont de précaution et purement défensives. Par ce mouvement, la Place de Stettin se trouvant sans garnison, Sa Majesté a ordonné au Prince d'Eckmuhl de la faire occuper par deux régiments français. Il manquait quelque approvisionnement à ce que les gens du métier avaient déterminé pour Dantzig, Sa Majesté en a ordonné l'envoi. D'ailleurs aucun contingent n'a été demandé à la Confédération, aucun mouvement extraordinaire n'a eu lieu dans l'intérieur de l'Empire. Les camps de Boulogne, d'Utrecht et de l'Escaut qui se forment, les grandes levées de marins dont on s'occupe, toutes les dépenses que l'Empereur fait faire dans ses chantiers et qui porteront à vingt cinq le nombre de vaisseaux lancés cette année, prouvent assez que les idées de Sa Majesté toujours fidèles au Traite de Tilsitt, n'ont pour but que l'accroissement de la marine et la poursuite de la guerre maritime. La réunion des villes anséatiques et du pays qui les embrasse n'a pas d'autre objet. Les circonstances lui sont favorables. Les débats de la Chambre de Communes en Angleterre et la triste situation du commerce de Londres annoncent assez le besoin de la paix et la lassitude de la guerre continentale qu'éprouve l'Angleterre. Tel est le but auquel on pourra se flatter d'arriver, si l'union entre la France et la Russie est constamment maintenue, et si toutes les deux, animées des mêmes vues et du même esprit dirigent contre l'Angleterre leurs efforts et leur puissnace.

Kurakin's Despatch to Rumyantsev of August 1811

Extrait d'une dépêche de l'Ambassadeur Prince Kourakin à S.E.Mr. le Chancelier Comte de Romantzoff, en date de Paris du 3 (15) Août 1811:

L'Empereur commença à me parler du mécontentement que lui avaient causé les dernières dépêches que j'avais reçues, et me dit que le Comte Lauriston à qui V.E. les avait communiquées n'avait pas manqué de lui observer qu'elles ne signifiaient rien, et qu'elles ne conduisaient nullement aux éclaircissemens et à la fin qu'on devoit tant souhaiter de part et d'autre; qu'il m'avait fait dire par le Duc de Bassano, que nous n'avions fait qu'un pas rétrograde, que nous ne voulons absolument pas nous expliquer et repondre aux avances qu'il nous a faites pendant six mois; que depuis six mois il propose de s'arranger sur l'affaire de l'Oldenbourg, qu'il a offert d'indemniser le Duc d'Oldenbourg par tout ce qui était à sa disposition, par Erfurth, par une population égale homme par homme, par un même revenu que celui qu'il avait, mais que la Russie se taisait sur ses propositions, qu'on ne m'avait pas envoyés les pleins pouvoirs qu'il avait desiré, pour que je puisse négocier et conclure l'arrangement qui était devenu nécessaire entre nous, que je ne pouvais pas soutenir que ces pleins pouvoirs me fussent superflus et que j'étais suffisamment accredité près de lui; qu'il savait fort bien que je n'avais pas la latitude qu'il me fallait pour négocier et pour finir s'il m'engageait à le faire; que le Duché d'Oldenbourg n'appartenait pas directement à la Russie, qu'il fesait partie des Etats de la Confédération du Rhin et que s'il était poussé à bout, toute négociation deviendrait desormais impossible, qu'il n'avait aucun compte à rendre de ses démarches envers les membres de cette confédération en étant le Protecteur et qu'il pouvait fort bien mettre le Duc d'Oldenbourg, comme on disait autrefois, au ban, puisqu'il ne voulait pas remplir ses obligations, comme membre de cette confédération, qu'il l'avait fait sommer trois fois pendant la guerre d'Autriche d'envoyer son contingent et qu'il ne l'avait pas fait, qu'il me le disait à présent quoiqu'il ne l'eut encore dit à personne, pas même à son ministre, que le Duc n'avait cessé de faire la contrebande avec les Anglais; qu'un grand intérêt politique l'avait forcé de reunir l'Oldenbourg, qu'en le faisant il n'avait pas du tout songé à faire de la peine à l'Empereur de Russie et à le blesser; que ce petit Duché qui ne rapportait que 500,000 francs par an, ne pouvait être une pomme de discorde et une raison de rupture entre deux grands Empires intéressés à être unis, comme la France et la Russie; que par égard pour l'intérêt que l'Empereur pouvait prendre au Duc, il lui avait fait proposer de l'indemniser complétement et que le silence que notre Auguste Maître gardait sur ses propositions, malgré qu'il les avait souvent repetées, prouvait que n'étant pas content de ses offres en Allemagne, il avait une arrière-pensée et que celle là était sans doute qu'il voulait avoir Dantzig; mais qu'il ne pouvait pas ceder cette ville pendant que la russie était armée, ou bien quelque district du Duché de Varsovie; mais que par les mêmes raisons il n'y consentirait jamais, que son honneur était engagé à soutenir et à conserver dans son intégrité ce nouvel état formé par ses soins, qu'il l'avait promis et qu'il tiendrait sa parole, qu'il n'en cederait pas un pouce de terrain, pas un village, qu'il l'avait remis au Roi de Saxe, dont la sagesse était si connue pour ôter toute inquiétude à la Russie, qu'il avait agrandi le Duché de Varsovie par la Gallicie parceque son honneur lui avait également prescrit de ne pas sacrifier à l'Autriche les Galiciens, qui pendant la guerre s'étaient revoltés en sa faveur, que malgré toutes mes assurances, il voyait fort bien et sans se tromper, que la Russie en voulait au Duché de Varsovie, qu'elle voulait l'engloutir, mais que son devoir lui prescrivait de s'y opposer; qu'il ne voulait certainement pas nous faire la guerre, mais que c'étaient nous qui l'y provoquions, que notre manifeste envoyé à toutes les Cours de l'Europe en était la plus grande preuve, qu'il savait fort bien que ce manifeste n'avait pû produire sur la Prusse et l'Autriche l'effet que nous attendions, parceque l'une et l'autre avaient à se rappeler, la Prusse, que nous avions pû prendre sur elle Bialystok, et l'Autriche, que pour arrondir notre frontière près de la Gallicie nous avions pû fort bien nous accommoder de quelques districts de cette province; que cete protestation n'était pas une simple déclaration pour mettre en reserve les droits de l'Empereur et de sa maison, comme j'ai continué de l'affirmer, que c'était un véritalbe manifeste et que cette manifestation des sentiments de l'Empereur pour lui et pour son alliance que je n'ai cessé de citer aussi, n'y avait été placée, que comme une simple formulaire d'habitude, que la réunion de Hambourg avait pû ne pas plaire à la Russie; qu'il le comprenait à cause de son commerce, mais que ce qu'il ne pouvait pas du tout comprendre – c'était le système actuel de la Russie et des combinaisons qu'elle pouvait avoir; qu'elle était en guerre avec l'Angleterre, en guerre avec les Turcs, et qu'elle se mettait mal avec la France, qu'il avait crû avoir payés tous les comptes envers la Russie à Tilsit, à Friedland et à Austerlitz, comme il l'avait fait envers l'Autriche, qui se le tenait pour dit, et qu'il n'avait qu'à se louer d'elle depuis sa dernière paix, qu'elle avait eu l'erreur de croire, que pendant qu'il était occupé de la guerre d'Espagne, elle pouvait regagner ce qu'elle avait autrefois perdu; mais qu'elle en était revenue, que quelques fussent mes argumens, il disait toujours que c'était nous qui avions armés les premiers, que l'Empereur avait dit lui-même au Comte Lauriston, qu'il était prêt à faire la guerre, qu'il l'avait donc été avant lui et tandis qu'il ne songeait pas à l'être, qu'àprésent la chose était différénte, qu'il cachait pas qu'il armait, qu'il avait dépensé 100 millions pour ses armemens, qu'ils étaient déjà très considérables, qu'il ne les *interromprait pas et les continuerait toujours pendant un an, pendant deux ans, pendant trois ans, tant que la Russie ne s'expliquerait pas franchement sur ce qu'elle veut et ne s'arrangerait pas avec lui sur ses griefs; que quoique je lui repetasse toujours qu'elle ne demandait rien, qu'elle ne désirait que la continuatin de son amitié et de son alliance, il ne pouvait y croire; que ses armemens prouvaitent autre chose; qu'elle s'était fair déjà le plus grand mal en se privant des moyens de faire sa paix avec les Turcs telle qu'elle la voulait, qu'elle y serait facilement pravenue en continuant l'offensive et les succès sur la rive droite du Danube, qu'elle avait eût l'année passée; que ce n'est qu'en avançant toujours qu'on peut forcer l'ennemi à la paix qu'on offre, qu'il ne concevait pas comment on avait pu fonder chez nous quelque espoir sur les négociatins de Bucarest et même comment on avait diminué dans le même temps nos armées sur le Danube dont l'emploi et les nouvelles victoires auraient dû seconder la négociation pour la paix; qu'en retirant par une vaine crainte et des articles des gazettiers 5 divisions de la Valachie, nous nous y sommes si fort affaiblis, que notre deffensive ne pourra être également suffisante sur tous les points; que la bataille de Rustschuk fait l'éloge de la valeur de nos troupes, mais que le général s'était trop avancé de la ville, que c'était une victoire militairement parlant entre généraux, comme nous le sommes, dit-il en regardant le Prince de Schwarzenberg qui se tenait à coté de moi; mais comme je vous parle d'objets politiques, je dirai que vous êtes politiquement battus, puisque vous avez abandonné Rustschuk, que vous vouliez et que vous deviez conserver comme une tête de pont; car c'est s'abuser que de croire qu'on peut empecher le passage d'un grand fleuve quand on n'a pas de tête de pont sur l'autre rive de ce fleuve. En ne cachant pas que je suis armé déjà, en avouant que je continuerai mes armemens, c'est que j'ai pû le faire et qu'ils me seront plus faciles et moins penibles qu'à la Russie, parceque j'ai plus d'argent et plus de moyens qu'elle. J'ai dit, que je ne veux point faire la guerre à la Russie et que je puis rester trois ans dans l'état armé où je suis, mais si dans cet intervalle la Russie ne s'explique pas sur ce qu'elle veut, sur son mécontentement, et que nos différends ne s'appaisent pas, je ne pourrai pas continuer toujours les mêmes sacrifices; les mesures que je prends et que je continuerai à prendre en restant armé m'enleveront mon argent et quand je me verrai sur le point de n'en plus avoir, je serai obligé malgré moi de tirer l'épée; je ne veux pas la guerre, je ne veux pas aller la chercher si loin dans le Nord, je ne veux pas rétablir la Pologne, je l'ai declaré positivements dans mes discours publics au Corps législatif et de toute manière, je l'ai dit au Prince Poniatowsky; les Polonais le savent; si je suis forcé à la guerre, je puis être battu aussi, mais si je ne le suis pas, le retablissement de la Pologne en sera le premier resultat. Je suis prêt encore à tranquiliser la Russie sur ce point par une convention, comme celle qui allait se conclure et qu'il ne m'a pas été possible de ratifier à cause d'un mot, d'une phrase, que le Comte Romantzoff a voulu y inserer et que je n'ai pû admettre, parceque'il est au dessus des forces humaines d'y souscrire de l'exécuter. Je suis prêt à cette convention pourvû que le Comte Romantzoff ne s'avise pas d'insister sur cette phrase, que la Pologne ne sera jamais rétablie, car j'aurai à y repondre toujours ce que j'ai repondu. J'ai levé une nouvelle conscription, je me suis armé, j'ai augmenté la garnison et les fortifications de Dantzig, mais je ne l'ai fait que quand les avis les plus détaillés me parvenaient de toutes parts sur les grands armemens de la Russie quoique le Duc de Vicence ne m'en disait rien et qu'à Pétersbourg on s'efforçait toujours à les lui contredire. J'ai créé de nouveaux bataillons dans les régimens de mon armée; au mois de novembre j'aurai 200,000 hommes, indépendament de 80,000 que j'ai envoyé cette année en Espagne. L'année prochaine je leverai encore une conscription qui me donnera de nouveau 200,000 hommes de plus contre vous, sans y compter les troupes de la confédération du Rhin et celles du Duché de Varsovie; dans deux ans je renouvellerai la même mesure et j'aurai alors 600,000 hommes à ma disposition; en continuant ainsi à augmenter progressivement mes forces contre la Russie, je continuerai à envoyer 25,000 hommes chaque année en Espagne et pour y finir la guerre, je ne ferai pas ce que vous faites pour finir la votre avec les Turcs; des fantomes chimériques ne m'effrayeront pas hors de propos. Comment pouvais-je ne pas croire aux informations qui me parvenaient sur vos armemens et à la direction que vous leur donniez contre moi, puisque vous les augmentiez au détriment de vos propres intérêts en y faisant servir les troupes que vous aviez en Finlande et en rappelant 5 divisions de votre armée contre les Turcs, ce qui à si efficacement changé l'état et la balance de votre guerre avec eux. L'Empereur Alexandre ne veut pas faire la guerre, il le dit, vous ne cessez de le repeter, je veux y croire; mais les faits ne sont pas conformes aux paroles. Le Duc de Vicence, revenu tout engoué de la Russie, a voulu me soutenir que ces 5 divisions n'avaient pas quitté la Valachie; mes nouvelles directes me le confirmaient pourtant et j'ai vu qu'il n'a pû qu'être abusé par tout ce qu'on lui fesait accroire à Pétersbourg. Le Comte Lauriston est également comblé de marques de faveùr de l'Empereur depuis les 5 mois qu'il y est. Un ambassadeur peut être fort sensible à de pareilles distinctions; mais il ne doit pas s'oublier en faisant sa cour au pays où il est envoyé; il y a des occasions où il doit agir avec énergie et developper la vérité toute entière. L'affaire de l'Oldenbourg doit finir, elle a commencée et alimentée seule nos différends; on n'a pas voulu vous envoyer les plein-pouvoirs que vous avez demandés; qu'on envoye donc ici des plénipotentiaires pour en traiter et la finir; je ne desire et je ne demande que cela. En attendant on vous ôte un bon secretaire auquel vous êtes accoutumé et on vous laisse dans l'embarras sans un bon aide pour vous soulager dans votre travail. J'ai repliqué que le Comte Nesselrode avait demandé un semestre pour retourner en Russie, qu'il y avait acheté des terres en commun avec le Prince Gagarine et que ses affaires domestiques l'y rappellaient pour quelque temps. L'Empereur Alexandre et le Comte Romanzoff vont être comptables des maux qu'ils feront éprouver à l'Europe par la guerre; on peut savoir quand on veut la commencer, mais on ne peut savoir comment et quand on peut la finir. La franchise doit-être toujours le langage des grandes Puissances et on ne s'observe pas chez nous; je ressentis la plus grande satisfaction quand le général Lauriston m'informa que l'Empereur lui avait dit qu'il aurait bien besoin de renvoyer sur le Danube les 5 divisions qu'il en a retirées et qu'il le ferait dès que je diminuerai de* moitié ma garnison de Dantzig. Je vis dans cette franchise un commencement de rapprochement et je m'étais flatté que tout allait finir entre nous; mais on en a fait un objet de reticence envers vous; on ne vous en a rien dit dans les dépêches que vous venez de recevoir, on n'a pas même voulu que vous me la confirmassiez officiellement; on ne vous repond rien sur le compte que vous avez certainement rendu de ma conversation et sur celle que j'ai eu avec Schouvaloff, où je lui ai repeté ce que je vous ai dis, on se tait sur toutes les représentations que vous avez du faire; ce silence n'indique-t-il pas clairement qu'ils ont à Pétersbourg une arrière-pensée et une intention qu'ils masquent encore par des protestations. Ils sont inconcévables dans leur aveuglement, on ne le comprends pas, ils agissent comme la Prusse l'a faite en courant d'elle-même à sa perte. Je ne suis pas comme le Comte Romanzoff qui s'amuse à rire et à faire des calembours de tout; moi, je ne sais pas en faire autant, je prends tout au serieux et j'agis d'après les conclusions que me présenterait mon devoir envers mes peuples et le véritable état des choses. Je sais que Vous voulez expédier un courrier; expédiez-le, informez l'Empereur Alexandre de tout ce que vous venez d'entendre de moi; je connais son bon ésprit et j'y compte beaucoup. C'est depuis un an que j'ai commencé à remarquer du changement dans sa manière e'être vis-à-vis de moi, ce n'est pas officiellement que je vous ai parlé, ce n'est que par forme de conversation, enfin je désire vivement que vos souhaits s'accomplissent et que vous puissiez voir bientôt, comme vous le croyez, toutes les difficultés applanies entre nous et nos rélations rétablies sur l'ancien pied.

L'Empereur a dit encore:

Ne concevant rien à la marche qu'on suit chez vous, je suis comme l'homme dans l'état de nature, qui, lorsqu'il ne comprend pas, se mefie. Il y a pourtant des talens en Russie, mais ce qui s'y fait prouve, ou, qu'on a perdu la tête, qui tourne et tourne sans savoir quelle direction il suivre, où il arrivera.

En parlant de la Pologne et qu'il ne soneait pas à la retablir, il a dit:

'Voulez-vous des assurances, des comventions, la garantie de l'Autriche, vous les aurez...'

Appendix V

Description of the Theatre of War

A Brief Description Of The Theatre Of War In 1812

The theatre of the war of 1812 was the western *Oblasts* of Russia and the area of land from the upper Dnieper to Moscow. In general, the entire western area of the Russian Empire, bounded on the north by the Baltic Sea, on the west by the Neman and the Western Bug, on the south by the Dniester and on the east by the Dnieper and the Western Dvina, according to the characteristics of the ground, it may be divided into three sectors (theatres of military operations):

1. Northern, from the Baltic to Polesia.
2. Central, comprising Polesia, including the swamps along the Berezina and the Białowieża Forest.
3. Southern, from Polesia to the Dniester and the Austrian border.

The northern part is undulating, intersected by rivers that do not present significant barriers to the movement of troops, partly covered with forests, lakes and small swamps; the coast of the Baltic Sea has alluvial soil, of clay, sand and Chernozem [loess-like loam], and is quite fertile; the area closest to Polesia is mostly sandy. The sector on the right bank of the Lower Dvina, between the sea and Lake Peipus, is covered with many lakes, swamps, forests, low hills and rivers flowing into the Dvina; of these rivers, the most important is the Drissa, which, with its direction parallel to the course of the Dvina, and the domination of the right bank over the left, it forms an advantageous defensive line against an enemy who had crossed the Dvina between the town of Drissa and the confluence with the Ula river. The area from Smolensk to Moscow, which served as the theatre of operations for Napoleon's *Grande Armée*, as we approach the capital city, becomes increasingly open; the land is fertile and well cultivated, providing abundant grain and other provisions necessary for an army.

Polesia, a land lying in the form of a triangle between Brest-Litovsk, Rogachev and the mouth of the Pripet, is a low-lying, swampy area covered with dense forests, among which there are small open spaces in the form of sandy hills, or plains suitable for agriculture, where there are occasional villages. All the rivers of this land flow between low-lying swampy banks and flood in spring and autumn for a considerable distance, whereupon crossing them becomes impossible, or must be carried out very slowly on flat-bottomed boats or ferries. From all that has been said, it follows: firstly, that Polesia separates the northern and southern parts of the western border areas of the Empire, and secondly, that this region is especially appropriate for operations by partisan detachments, especially since the sparse population and scarcity of the country's resources prevent the deployment of significant forces.

Finally, the southern part of the western border area of Russia is low-lying, partially swampy, or undulating and covered with forests; the rivers flowing through it into the Pripet, of which the most important are the Styr and Goryn, mostly have low-lying banks, but they present quite advantageous defensive lines, which in 1812 were secured on the left flank through the neutrality of Galicia, on the basis that although the Austrian government had provided an auxiliary corps in obligation to Napoleon, they had not declared war on Russia. The land south of Polesia comprises Volhynia and Podolia, which are among the most fertile regions of the Empire.

When Napoleon advanced through the north of the western part of Russian territory, which constituted the main theatre of operations, the Neman river was the first natural barrier; but this defensive line was unfavourable for us in that along almost the entire course of the river downstream of Grodno, its left bank dominates the right. The width of the Neman upstream of Kovno is between 250 to 300 paces, while downstream of Kovno, at the confluence of the Viliya with the Neman, it is between 350 to 400 paces. Bridges on the Neman were located in Novy-Sverzhen, Belitsa, the town of Mosty, Grodno and Tilsit; there were ferries at Kovno, Jurburg, and so on. The second significant obstacle in the direction of St Petersburg was the Western Dvina river, while in the direction of Moscow it is the Berezina and Upper Dnieper: the Western Dvina forms a very advantageous defensive line, reinforced on the lower reaches of the river by the Riga fortress (the fortifications of Dünaburg were barely begun). In addition, a fortified camp had been established 100 *versts* upstream of Dünaburg, on the left bank of the Dvina, in which it was intended to concentrate the main body of our army. Upstream of Dünaburg, the Dvina does not constitute a significant barrier, because its banks there are rather low and the depth is not great, such that in dry summers it is fordable. From Vitebsk to Drissa and a little downstream of this latter location, the left bank dominates the right; nevertheless, as far as Riga itself, the right bank is higher than the left. The width of the river between Vitebsk and Dünaburg is between 180 to 230 paces, while at Riga it is some 800. There were bridges at Velizh, Surazh, Vitebsk, Dünaburg and Riga; while ferries were at Budilovo, Beshankovichi, Ulla, Polotsk, Disna, Drissa, Leonpol, Druya, Krasław, Jakobstadt and Friedrichstadt [Jaunjelgava].

The Berezina River is useful as a defensive line to cover the area between the Dvina and the Dnieper. This area is 60 *versts* in length from Vitebsk to Orsha; while its width forms a swampy forest-covered strip, which runs to Senno in one direction, and to Porechye and Smolensk in the other. The area between the Berezina and the Dnieper is even more intersected and has similar characteristics to Polesia. The strongholds of the defensive line along the Berezina in 1812 were provided by the fortresses of Bobruisk and Borisov, but the former of these locations lay off the main routes leading to the interior, and therefore would not have a decisive influence on military operations; the fortification of Borisov, due to lack of time, could not be carried out, and therefore engineering work at this point was limited to the construction of a bridgehead. The width of the Berezina from the canal to the confluence with the Dnieper extends between 60 to 120 paces. The right bank dominates the left, except for locations near Veselovo, Studyanka, Borisov and Nizhny Berezino, where the left bank is higher than the right. It is fordable in summer, and sometimes in autumn, but in general crossing is obstructed by marshes that stretch along both banks of the river. There were bridges at Borisov and Bobruisk; ferries: at Veselovo, the village of Nizhny Berezino and so on.

The Dnieper River, flowing almost in parallel with the Western Dvina from Dorogobuzh to Orsha, while turning sharply to the south downstream of Orsha, although it is navigable throughout its entire length from Dorogobuzh to its mouth, however, it cannot serve as a reliable defensive line against an enemy advancing towards Moscow, both due to the dominance of the right bank over the left at many points, and because in the summer it is fordable upstream of Smolensk: and at Lyady, Khomino, Mogilev, Vorkolabovo, Novy Bykhov, and so on. The width of the river at Dorogobuzh is 90 paces, from Smolensk to Stary Bykhov between 100 to 150 paces, while downstream of Bykhov to the confluence with the Pripet it gradually increases to 500 paces. Bridges were located at Smolensk, Mogilev and Kiev; there were ferries at many locations. The fortified city of Smolensk lies on the junction of the roads from Porechye, Vitebsk, Orsha, Mstislavl, Roslavl, Dorogobuzh and Dukhovshchina, and presented the means for a stubborn defence.

The Western Bug river served as the first defensive line against an enemy invading the southern part of the border area. Its width at Ustilug is about 40 paces, while at Drohiczyn it is 120 paces. In the summer, in the area between Włodawa and Brest, there are many fords. In general, the left bank of the river commands the right, except for the following locations: Ustilug, Opalin, Brest, Niemirów and Drohiczyn, where the right bank dominates. Much more reliable defensive lines were formed by the courses of the Styr and Goryn rivers.

In general, in the areas north and south of Polesia, there were many roads that intersected each other in all directions; but their quality varied according to the weather and the season. It was impossible to use such wagons as had been used to transport supplies by Napoleon's armies with constant success in Germany and Italy on these roads; while the lighter peasant carts required many more horses to deliver the necessary amount of supplies necessary for the troops, which, in turn, was hampered by the difficulty of obtaining fodder, which was nowhere near enough to feed not only the draught horses, but also the war horses accompanying the half million man enemy army.

As far as Polesia is concerned, the number of roads in this country were very limited, and in general communications passing through it were difficult, most especially in spring and autumn.

Appendix VI

Russian Holdings of Military Stores in Early 1812

In the Archive of the Chancellery of the War Ministry is the following data on the stores prepared for the troops at the beginning of the war of 1812:

> Return for the ration stores, prepared at the start of the war in the bases and on the lines leading to the interior.
>
> In Riga for: eight infantry divisions & four cavalry divisions for one month.
>
> In Dünaburg for: eight infantry divisions & four cavalry divisions for one month.

These reserves comprised:

Location	Flour	Grain	Oats	Remarks
In Dünaburg:	18,934	1,300	32,739	Rations for 12½ days, fodder for 18 days.
In Disna:	19,518	1,828	18,369	Rations for 13 days, fodder at least ten days.
In Drissa:	5,583	928	–	Rations for four days at most.
In Polotsk:	–	–	3,000	Fodder for two days at most.

It was intended to re-stock these magazines, as follows:

From Velikye Luki for: eight infantry divisions and four cavalry divisions for two months.

But after the changes it actually contains:

Flour	Grain	Oats	Remarks
10,000	937	15,000	Rations for seven days at most, fodder for eight days or more.

From Novgorod for: eight infantry divisions and four cavalry divisions for two months.

But actually containing:

Flour	Grain	Oats	Remarks
10,000	937	15,000	Rations for seven days at most, fodder for eight days or more.

From Bobruisk for: two infantry divisions and one cavalry division for 1 month. To re-stock this magazine, the following was intended:

From Mogilev for: two infantry divisions and one cavalry division for 2 months. But due to low water levels, the bread made in Kiev in preparation for this magazine could not get further than Rogachev, and therefore as a result supplies are found:

Location	Flour	Grain	Oats	Remarks
In Rogachev	19,518	1,828	23,688	Rations for two months, fodder for one month and 23 days.
In Mogilev	–	–	300	Fodder for seven days.

In Kiev for: nine infantry divisions and four cavalry divisions for one month.

It was intended to re-stock this magazine, as follows:

From Sosnytsia for: nine infantry divisions and four cavalry divisions for two months.

However, these supplies have not yet been prepared. Reserves for a similar number of troops and period of time were required in Trubchevsk as in Sosnytsia; but this has also not been completed.

Ahead of the baseline and along the lines of operations:

In Schaulen for: one infantry division and half a cavalry division for one month.

In Vilna for: eight infantry divisions and four cavalry divisions for one month.

In Sventsiany for: eight infantry divisions and four cavalry divisions for half a month.

These reserves are located half in Sventsiany and half in Kołtyniany, for seven days in each location.

In Grodno for: two infantry divisions and one cavalry division for one month.

In Brest for: two infantry divisions and one cavalry division for one month.

In Slonim for: two infantry divisions and one cavalry division for one month.

In Slutsk for: two infantry divisions and one cavalry division for one month.

In Pinsk for: two infantry divisions and one cavalry division for one month.

In Mozyr for: two infantry divisions and one cavalry division for one month.

In Lutsk for: nine infantry divisions and four cavalry divisions for two months.

But once it was necessary to transport grain from the Podolsk Governorate to these, then, according to the opinion of the State Council, these stores were to be located and stocked as follows:

Location	Flour	Grain	Oats	Remarks
In Lutsk:	39,191	3,626	49,020	Rations for 27 days or more, fodder for at least 27 days.
In Stary Konstantinov:	10,451	979	16,369	Rations for 7½ days, fodder for at least eight days.
In Zaslavl:	27,760	2,657	25,007	Rations for at least 19 days, fodder for 13½ days.
In Dubno:	13,451	1,261	16,369	Rations for at least nine days, fodder for at least eight days.
In Kovel & Luboml:	1,449	274	2,900	Rations for one day, fodder for 1½ days.

In Ostrog for: nine infantry divisions and four cavalry divisions for ½ month.
In Zhitomir for: nine infantry divisions and four cavalry divisions for ½ month.

Appendix VII

Correspondence Between Tsar Alexander and Napoleon

Correspondance Officielle
Entre L'Empereur Alexandre Ier et Napoléon[1]

1

Monsieur mon Frère. Caulincourt me fait connaitre tout ce que V.M.I. a bien voulu lui dire d'aimable à l'occasion de mon mariage. J'y ai reconnu les sentimens qu'Elle veut bien me porter: Je la prie d'en agréer mes remercimens. Mes sentimens pour Elle sont invariables comme les principes politiques qui dirigent les relations de mon Empire. Jamais V.M. n'aura à se plaindre de la France. Les déclarations que j'ai faites en Decembre dernier font tout le secret de ma politique. Je les réitérerai toutes les fois que l'occasion s'en présentera. Je prie V.M. de ne jamais douter de mon amitié et de la haute estime que je lui porte.
(signé) Napoléon.
De notre Palais impériale
de Lacken, le 16 Mai 1810.

2

Monsieur mon Frère! Le Prince Alexis Kourakin partant pour se rendre auprès de V.M.I. je ne veux pas laisser passer cette occasion sans lui réitérer tous mes sentimens. Ceux que je porte à V.M. come les considérations politiques de mon Empire me font désirer chaque jour d'avantage la continuation et la permanence de l'alliance que nous avons contractée. De mon coté, elle est à l'épreuve de tout changement et de tout évènement. J'ai parlé franchement au Prince A. Kourakin sur plusieurs questions de détails, mais je prie V.M. de m'accorder surtout confiance, lorsqu'il Lui parlera de mon amitié pour Elle, et de mon desir de voir eternelle l'alliance qui nous lie. Je prie Dieu etc.
(signé) Napoléon.
à St-Cloud, le 29 Août, 1810.

---

1   The original letters and copies of letters are kept in the Archive of the Ministry of Foreign Affairs.

3

M. mon Frère! Je remercie V.M.I. pour sa lettre de Lacken du 16 Mai et pour l'envoie de M. de Watteville. Les assurances de son amitié me sont bien chères. Celle, que je porte à V.M. est aussi sincère qu'inaltérable. L'union de nos deux Empires assure la paix de continent. Plus elle deviendra intime et plus le système que V.M. à adopté pour reduire l'Angleterre ecquerera de force. De mon cotéje ne néglige rien pour la constater et prouver combien j'y tiens par principe, independamment même de toute l'affection et de la tout éstime que je porte personnellement à V.M.

(signé) Alexandre.
1810. (Sans date).

4

M. mon Frère! J'ai à remercier V.M.I. pour deux lettres par le Pr. Kourakin et le colonel Tchernicheff. Ce que V.M. veut bien m'y exprimer de sa politique, comme de ses sentiments personnels pour moi, m'a causé le plus grand plaisir par la conformité que j'y retrouve, avec ceux que j'ai voué à V.M. qui sont inalterables. Comme Elle, je n'ai rien de plus à coeur que la continuation de l'alliance qui lie les deux empires, qui assure la tranquilité de l'Europe. Aussi V.M. a pu se convaincre, que rien de mon coté n'a été négligé pour prouver en toute occasion le principe que je professe pour l'union la plus étroite entre nous. La Russie n'a rien à convoiter, vu que la paix avec la Turquie se trouvera conclue. V.M. connait les conditions aux quelles je la veux; je n'en ai jamais exigé d'autres. Les mesures contre le commerce anglais se poursuivent avec vigueur; les nombreuses confiscations exercées dans mes ports en font foi. Depuis, à peine 30 batimens de différentes nations s'y sont présentés. Il est peu probable que d'autres arrivent encore, plusieurs des ports se trouvant déjà fermés par les glaces; du moins le nombre ne pourra être que très petit; la même severité s'observera envers eux. Ainsi les 100 batiments dont Votre M. me parle retourneront en Angleterre. Les politiques de l'Allemagne se plaisent à repandre des bruits alarmants et à entretenir l'inquietude dans les ésprits. Je n'y ajoute aucune foi, car je place ma confiance dans les assurances de V.M. Le colonel Tchernicheff m'ayant paru mériter le contentement de V.M. c'est lui que j'envoie porter cette lettre. Je le fais passer par Stockholm pour faire connaitre au gouvernement le desir que V.M. a eu, que j'appuye les démarches qu'Elle a faites pour que la Suède rompt avec l'Angleterre, quoique j'ai déjà la nouvelle que cela se trouve fait. Tchern pourra rendre compte à V.M. de l'état des choses en Suède. Je prie V.M. de croire que mes sentiments pour Elle sont inalterables à l'abri du temps. Sur ce etc.

(signé) Alexandre.
1810. (Sans date, Novembre).

5

M. mon Frère! V.M.I. m'a envoyé de si beaux chevaux que je ne veux point tarder à lui faire mes remerciments. Les Anglais souffrent beaucoup de la réunion de la Hollande et de l'occupation que j'ai fait faire des ports du Mecklenbourg et de la Prusse. Il y a toutes les semaines des banqueroutes à Londres, qui portent la confusion dans la cité. Les manufactures sont sans travail: les magasins sont engorgés. Je viens de faire saisir à Francfort et en Suisse d'immenses quantités de marchandises anglaises et coloniales. Six cents batiments marchands anglais qui erraient dans la Baltique ont été refusés dans le Mecklenbourg, en Prusse, et se sont dirigés vers les états de Votre M. Si Elle les admet, la guerre dure encore, si Elle les sequestre et confisque leur chargement, soit qu'ils soient encore dans ses ports, soit que même les marchandises soient débarquées, le contre-coup qui frappera l'Angleterra sera terrible: toutes ces marchandises sont pour le compte des Anglais. Il dépend de V.M. d'avoir la paix ou de faire la fuerre. La paix est et doit être Son désir. V.M. est certain que nous y arrivons si Elle confisque ces 600 batiments ou leur chargement. Quelques papiers qu'ils aient, sous quelques noms qu'ils se marquent, français, allemands, espagnols, danois, russes, suédois, V.M. peut être sûre que ce sont des Anglais. Le colonel Tchernicheff qui retourne près de V.M. c'est fort bien conduit ici. Il ne me reste qu'à prier V.M. de compter toujours sur mes sentimens inaltérables qui sont à l'abri du temps et de tout évènement. Sur ce etc.

Napoléon.

à Fontainebleau, le 23 Octobre 1810.

6

Monsieur mon Frère. La mauvaise santé du Duc de Vicence m'oblige à lui envoyer des lettres de récréance. J'ai cherché près de moi la personne que j'ai supposé pouvoir être la plus agréable à V.M.I. et la plus propre a maintenir la paix et l'alliance entre nous; j'ai fait choix du général Comte Lauriston.

Je suis fort empressé d'apprendre si j'ai recontré juste. Je charge le colonel Tchernichef de parler à V.M. de mes sentiments pour Elle. Ces sentiments ne changeront pas, quoique je ne puisse me dissimuler que V.M. n'a plus d'amitié pour moi. Elle me fait faire des protestations et toute espèce de difficultés pour l'Oldenbourg, lorsque je ne me refuse pas à donner une indemnité equivalente, et que la situation de ce pays qui a toujours été le centre de la contrebande avec l'Angleterre me fait un devoir indispensable pour l'interet de mon Empire et pour le succès de la lutte où je suis engagé, de la réunion de l'Oldenbourg à mes états. Le dernier ukase de V.M. dans le fond, mais surtout dans la forme, est spécialement dirigé contre la France. Dans d'autres temps, avant de prendre une telle mesure contre mon commerce, V.M. me l'eut fait connaitre, et j'aurai pu, peutêtre, lui suggérer des moyens, qui en remplissant son principal but, auraient cependant empêché que cela ne parût aux yeux de France un changement de système. Toute l'Europe l'a envisagé ainsi, et déjà notre alliance n'existe plus dans l'opinion de l'Angleterre ed de l'Europe: fut-elle aussi entière dans le coeur de V.M. qu'elle l'est dans le mien, cete opinion générale n'en serait pas moins un grand mal. Que V.M. me permette de lui dire avec franchise, Elle a oublié le bien qu'Elle a tiré de l'alliance et cependant qu'Elle voie ce qui s'est passé depuis Tilsit. Par le traité de Tilsit, Elle devait restituer à la Turquie la Moldavie et la Valachie; cependant au lieu de restituer ces provinces V.M. les a réunies à son Empire. La Valachie et la Moldavie sont le tiers de la Turquie d'Europe, c'est une acquisition immense qui, en appuyant le vaste Empire de V.M. sur le Danube, ôte toute force à la Turquie, et on peut même le dire, anéantit cet Empire, mon plus ancien allié. Cependant au lieu de tenir à l'exécution du traité de Tilsit, de la manière la plus desinteressée et par pure amitié pour V.M. j'ai reconnue la réunion de ces belles et riches contrées; mais sans la confiance dans la continuation de Son amitié plusieurs campagnes très malheureuses n'eussent pu amener la France a voir depouiller ainsi son ancien allié. En Suède, dans le tems que je restituais les conquêtes que j'avais *faites sur cette Puissance, je consentais a ce que V.M. gardat la Finlande, qui est le tiers de la Suède, et qui est une province si importante pour V.M. qu'on peut dire que depuis cette réunion il n'y a plus de Suède, puisque Stockholm est maintenant aux avant-postes du Royaume. Cependant la Suède, malgré la fausse politique de son Roi, était aussi un des anciens amis de la France. Des hommes insinuans et suscités par l'Angleterre fatiguent les oreilles de V.M. de propos calomnieux. 'Je veux – disent ils – retablir la Pologne.' J'étais maitre de le faire à Tilsit: douze jours après la bataille de Fridland, je pouvais être à Vilna. Si j'eusse voulu rétablir la Pologne, j'eusse désinteressé l'Autriche à Vienne; elle demandait à conserver ses anciennes provinces et ses communications avec la mer, en faisant porter ses sacrifices sur ses possessions de Pologne. Je le pouvais en 1810, au moment où toutes les troupes russes étaient engagées contre la Porte. Je le pourrais dans ce moment encore, sans attendre qu V.M. terminât avec la Porte un arrangement qui sera conclu probablement dans le cours de cet été. Puisque je ne l'ai fait dans aucune de ces circonstances, c'est donc que le rétablissement de la Pologne n'était pas dans mes intentions. Mais si je ne veux rien changer à l'état de la Pologne, j'ai le droit aussi d'exiger que personne ne se mele de ce que je fais en de çà de l'Elbe. Toutefois il est vrai que nos ennemis ont reussi. Les fortifications que V.M. fait élever sur vingt points de la Dvina, les protestations dont a parlé le Pr. Kourakin pour l'Oldenbourg et l'ukase le prouvent assez.*

Moi, je suis le même pour Elle, mais je suis frappé de l'évidence de ces faits et de la pensée que V.M. est toute disposée aussitôt que les circonstances le voudront, à s'arranger avec l'Angleterre, ce qui est la même chose que d'allumer la guerre entre les deux Empires. V.M. abandonnant une fois l'alliance et brulant les conventions de Tilsit, il serait evident que la guerre s'ensuivrait quelque mois plutôt ou quelques mois plus tard. Cet état de méfiance et d'incertitude a des inconveniens pour l'Empire de V.M. et pour le mien; le résultat doit être de part et d'autre de tendre les ressorts de nos Empires pour nous mettre en mesure. Tout cela est sans doute bien facheux. Si V.M. n'a pas le projet de se remettre avec l'Angleterre, Elle sentira la necessité pour elle et pour moi de dissiper tous ces nuages. Elle n'a pas de securité puisqu'Elle a dit au Duc de Vicence qu'Elle ferait la guerre sur ses frontières et la securité est le premier lien des deux grands Etats. Je prie V.M. de lire cette lettre dans un bon esprit, de n'y voir rien qui ne soit conciliant et propre à faire disparaitre de part et d'autre toute espèce de méfiance et a retablir les deux nations, sous tous les points de vue, dans l'intimité d'une alliance qui, depuis près de quatre ans, est si heureuse.

Sur ce je prie Dieu, M. mon Frère, qu'Il veuille avoir V.M.I. en sa sainte et digne garde.

De V.M.I.
Le bon Frère
(signé) Napoléon.
à Paris, le 28 Février 1811.

7

M. mon Frère. Je m'empresse de répondre à la lettre de V.M. du 28 Février. Je regrette beaucoup que la santé du Duc de Vicence l'empêche de continuer sa mission auprès de moi. J'ai été extremement satisfait de lui, parceque en toute occasion j'ai reconu en lui la plus grand dévouement pour V.M. et un soin constant a resserer les liens qui nous unissent. Je remercie V.M. du choix qu'Elle a fait du G-l Lauriston; celui qui a Sa confiance est sûr de m'être agréable.

Tchernicheff s'est acquitté de mes ordres. Je vois avec regret que je suis méconnu par Elle. Ni mes sentiments, ni ma politique n'ont point changés et je ne desire que le maintien et la consolidation de notre alliance. Ne m'est-il pas plutôt permis de supposer que c'est V.M. qui a changé à mon égard? Je crois devoir lui parler avec la même franchise qu'Elle l'a fait dans sa lettre. V.M. m'accuse d'avoir protesté contre l'affaire d'Oldenbourg, mais pouvais-je ne pas le faire? Un petit coin de terre que possedait l'unique individu, qui appartient à ma famille, qui a passé par toutes les formalitès qu'on a exigées de lui, membre de la conféderation, et par la même, sous la protection de V.M. dont les possessions se trouvent garanties par un article du traité de Tilsit, s'en trouve dépossedé sans que V.M. m'en aye dit un mot préablement. De quelle importance ce coin de terre pouvait être pour la France, et ce procédé prouvait-il à l'Europe l'amitié de V.M. pour moi? Aussi – toutes les lettres écrites partout a cete époque prouvent qu'on l'a envisagé comme un désir que V.M. a eu de nous blesser. Quant à ma protestation, la manière dont elle est redigée sert de preuve irrécusable que je mets l'alliance de la France au dessus de toute autre considération, et j'y enonce clairement qu'on s'y tromperait beaucoup si on déduisait que mon union avec S.M. se trouve relachée. V.M. suppose que mon oukaze sur le tarif est dirigé contre la France. Je dois combattre cette opinion comme gratuite et peu juste. Ce tarif a été impérieusement commandé par la gêne extrême du commerce maritime, par importation enorme par terre de marchandises étrangères de prix, par les droits excessifs mis dans les états de V.M. sur les produits russes et par la baisse effrayante de notre change. Il a deux buts en vue: le 1er, c'est qu'en prohibant avec la plus grande sévérité le commerce Anglais, d'accorder quelques facilités au commerce américain comme le seul par mer dont la Russie puisse se servir pour exporter ses produits trop volumineux pour pouvoir l'être par terre. Le 2d, de restreindre autant que faire se peut l'importation par terre, comme la plus desavantageuse pour notre balance de commerce, introduisant une quantité d'objets du luxe très riches et pour les quels nous déboursions notre numéraire, tandis que notre propre exportation est si extremement genée.

Telles sont les raisons toutes simples de l'oukaze du tarif. Il n'est pas plus dirigé contre la France que contre tout autre pays de l'Europe et se trouve entièrement dans le système continental par la prohibition et la destruction des objets de commerce ennemi. V.M. trouve a redire de ce que préalablement je ne l'ai pas consulté sur cette mesure. N'étant que purement administrative, je pense que chaque gouvernement est le maitre d'en prendre chez lui d'après ses propres convenances, surtout quand elles ne se trouvent pas en opposition de traités existants. Mais que V.M. me permette une seule observation. Est-ce juste de sa part de me faire la remarque quand elle même a tenu la même conduite et m'a tout aussi peu averti des mesures qu'Elle a jugé devoir prendre sur le commerce non seulement dans son Empire mais dans toute l'Europe. Cependant ces mesures ont eu une réaction bien plus forte sur le commerce de la Russie que celles du tarif russe n'en auront sur celui de la France, et les nombreuses faillites qui en ont étaient la suite en servent de preuve. Je crois pouvoir dire à juste titre que la Russie a observé plus scrupuleusement le traité de Tilsit que la France et ce qu'Elle cite sur la Moldavie et la Valachie ne peut jamais être imputé à la Russie comme infraction des clauses de ce traité, car il statue que les Pricipautés resteront non-occupées par les troupes des Puissances belligerantes pendant l'armistice. Aussi mon armée avait fait quatre marches rétrogrades et ce n'est que quand les Turcs on fait une invasion, brulé Galatz et poussé jusqu'à Fokschani, que j'ai fait rebrousser chemin à mon armée. Depuis, la convention d'Erfourt m'assure la possession de la Moldavie et de la Valachie; par conséquent je me trouve entièrement en règle. Quant à la conquête de la Finlande, elle n'était pas dans ma politique et V.M. doit se rappeler que je n'ai entrepris la guerre contre la Suède qu'à la suite du système continental. Le succès de mes armes m'a valu la possession de la finlande comme des revers auraient pu me priver de mes provinces. Ainsi je crois être encore en regle sur ce second point. Mais si V.M. cite les avantages que la Russie a retiré de son alliance avec la France, ne puis-je pas citer à mon tour ceux retirés par la France et les immenses réunions qu'elle a faites d'une partie de l'Italie, du Nord de l'Allemagne et de la Hollande?

Je crois avoir prouvé plus d'une fois à V.M. que j'étais peu sensible aux insinuations fomentées par ceux qui ont intérêt à nous brouiller, et le meilleur témoignage que je puis en donner c'est de les avoir communiquées chaque fois à V.M. en m'en rapportant toujours à son amitié.

Cependant – quand des faits sont venus à l'appui des bruits qui circulaient, le moins que je pouvais faire était de prendre des mesures de prudence. Les armements du Duché de Varsovie sont suivis sans relache. On a augmenté le militaire de ce duché hors de proportion même avec sa population. On n'a pas cessé de travailler a de nouvelles fortifications. Celles par-contre que je fais élever, sont sur la Dwina et le Dnièper. V.M. est trop militaire pour ne pas reconnaitre que quand on établit des nouvelles fortifications à une distance de la frontière égale à celle qu'il y a entre Paris et Strasbourg, ils ne sont certainement pas des mesures aggressives mais purement defensives. Mes armements sont bornés à donner une meilleure organisation à des régiments déjà existans. C'est que V.M. n'a pas cessé de faire chez Elle. Au reste, tout ce qui se passe dans le Duché de Varsovie, comme l'augmentation toujours croissante des forces de V.M. dans le Nord de l'Allemagne, m'en a certainement fournie l'obligation. Tel est l'état exact des choses. Par consequent mes fortifications servent plutôt de preuve combien peu je me dispose à être agressif. Mon tarif, n'établi que pour une année, n'a eu d'autre but que de diminuer la défaveur de mon change et me fournir les moyens de persévérer dans le systême que j'ai embrassé et suivi avec tant de persévérance, et une protestation, commandée par ce que je dois à l'honneur de mon pays et celui de ma famille, motivée par une violation directe du traité de Tilsit, poret cependant la preuve la plus manifeste de mon désir de conserver l'alliance de V.M. Au reste ne convoitant rien à mes voisins, aimant la France – quel interet aurais-je a vouloir la guerre? La Russie n'a pas besoin de conquetes et peut être ne possede que trop de terrain. Le génie si superieur que je reconnais à V.M. pour la guerre ne me laisse aucune illusion sur la difficulté de la lutte qui pourrait s'élever entre nous. D'ailleurs mon amour-propre est attaché au systême d'union avec la France. L'ayant établi comme un principe de politique pour la Russie, ayant dû combattre assez longtemps les anciennes opinions qui y étaient contraires, ils n'est pas raisonnable de me supposer l'envie de detruire mon ouvrage et de faire la guerre à V.M. et si Elle la désire aussi peu que moi, très certainement elle ne se fera pas. Pour lui en donner encore une preuve j'offre à V.M. de m'en remettre à Elle même ce qu'Elle aurait désiré en pareil cas. V.M. a tous les moyens d'arranger les choses de manière à unir encore plus étroitement les deux Empires et à rendre la

rupture impossible à toujours. De mon coté je suis prêt à le seconder dans une inten-
tion pareille. Je répète, si la guerre aura lieu, c'est que V.M. l'aura voulue, et ayant
tout fait pour l'éviter, je saurais alors combattre et vendre cherement mon existence.
Veut-Elle au lieu de cela reconnaitre en moi un ami et un allié, Elle me retrouvera avec
les mêmes sentiments d'attachement et d'amitié qu'Elle m'a toujours connues. Je prie
V.M. de lire pareillement cete lettre dans un bon esprit et de n'y voir qu'un désir très
prononcé à concilier les choses.
    (signé) Alexandre.

8

Monsieur mon Frère. Aussitôt que j'ai appris par le duc de Vicence que le choix du
comte de Lauriston était agréable à V.M.I. je lui ai donné l'ordre de partir. Je n'envoie
pas à V.M. un homme consommé dans les affaires, mais un homme vrai et droit,
comme les sentiments que je Lui porte. Et cependant, je reçois chaque jour des nouvelles
de Russie qui ne sont pas pacifiques. Hier j'ai appris de Stockholm que les divisions
russes de la Finlande étaient parties pour s'approcher de frontières du Grand Duché.
Il y a peu de jours j'ai été instruit de Bukarest que cinq divisions ont quittées les prov-
inces de Moldavie et de Valachie, pour se rendre en Pologne, et qu'il ne reste plus que
quatre divisions des troupes de V.M. sur le Danube. Ce qui se passe est une nouvelle
preuve que la repetition est la plus puissante figure rhetorique. On a tant répété à
V.M. que je lui en voulais, que sa confiance en a été ebranlée. Les Russes quittent une
frontière où ils sont nécessaires, pour se rendre sur un point où V.M. n'a que d'amis.
Cependant, j'ai dû penser aussi à cette affaire, et j'ai dû me mettre en mesure. Le
contre-coup de mes préparatifs portera V.M. à accroitre les siens, et ce qu'Elle fera
retentissant ici me fera faire de nouvelles levées: et tout cela pour des fantômes. Ceci
est la répétition de ce que j'ai vu en 1807 en Prusse et en 1809 en Autriche. Pour moi je
resterai l'ami de la personne de V.M. même quand cette fatalité qui entraine l'Europe
dévrait un jour mettre les armes à la main à nos deux nations. Je ne me reglerait que
sur ce que fera V.M. Je ne l'attaquerai jamais, et mes troupes ne s'avanceront que
lorsque V.M. aura dechiré le traité de Tilsit. Je serai le premier à desarmer et à tout
remettre dans la situation où étaient les choses, il y a un an, si V.M. veut revenir à la
même confiance. A-t-Elle jamais eu à se repentir de la confiance qu'Elle m'a temoi-
gnée? Je charge bien spécialement le comte Loriston de Lui dire combien je Lui désire
de bonheur, combien je suis contrarié de m'imaginer qu'Elle éprouve des embarras
et de la peine par les fausses notions qu'Elle c'est laissé donner de ma politique et de
mes sentiments, et combien je serais heureux de la voir remplacée dans la même route
qu'à Tilsit et à Erfurt. Je prie V.M. d'accorder au C-te Lauriston une foi entière, quand
il Vous dira que je veux la paix, que je n'envie rien à la prospérité de son Empire, et
qu'au contraire je me complaisais à penser qu'Elle s'était aggrandie et avait rétiré des
avantages de mon alliance. Sur ce je prie Dieu etc.
    Napoléon.
    à Paris, le 6 Avril 1811.

9

Monsieur mon Frère. Le Comte Lauriston est arrivé depuis quelques jours et m'a remis
la lettre de Votre M.I. du 6 Avril. Les paroles pacifiques qu'elle contient, de même

que le langage de son ambassadeur, m'auraient fait le plus grand plaisir s'ils étaient appuyés par des faits. Les nouvelles que V.M. me cite sur le mouvement de mes troupes sont complettement fausses. J'en ai convaincu son ambassadeur en lui montrant en détail toute la dislocation de mon armée et en lui proposant même d'envoyer son aide-de-camp verifier les choses sur les lieux. Les divisions cantonnées en Finlande ne l'ont jamais quittées et trois s'y trouvent comme par le passé. Des cinq divisions de l'armée de Moldavie, dont V.M. me parle, trois sont encore dans cette province et ce ne sont que deux que j'ai mis à cheval sur le Dniester et non sur les frontières du duché de Varsovie, comme on l'avait mandé à V.M. Par consequent mon armée de Moldavie n'est pas reduite à quatre divisions, mais se trouve composée de sept divisions. Aucun rassemblement de troupes de ma part n'a eu lieu, sur la frontière du duché de Varsovie, aucune troupe même ne s'est rapprochée de cette frontière. Très certainement cet ordre, qui m'est commandé par la prudence, m'est très désavantageux, en paralysant l'activité que j'aurais donné à une opération sur le Danube. Tel est l'état des choses de mon coté, tandisqu'au moment où Lauriston me remettait à son audience la lettre de V.M. et en donnait de sa part les assurances les plus tranquillisantes, je venais de recevoir la nouvelle positive de la mobilisation et du rassemblement de l'armée saxonne par order de V.M. ainsi que de la marche de la division de cuirassiers de son armée. Qui de nous deux est donc celui qui arme? Mon armée est dans ses cantonnements habituels et celle de V.M. est en pleine marche. tous ces faits prouvent, si les griefs que contiennent la lettre de V.M. sont fondés et si j'ai donné lieu au mouvements qui se font. V.M. me cite ce qu'elle a vu en 1807 avec la Prusse et en 1809 avec l'Autriche. Qu'elle me permette de lui observer que ces époques ne ressemblent en rien à celle dans la quelle nous nous trouvons. La Prusse et l'Autriche voulaient la guerre; moi − je ne la veux pas, je ne convoite rien à personne et n'aye envie d'aucun agrandissement. Je ne desirais que la conservation intacte du traité de Tilsit. V.M. seul a rompu une clause de se traité en depouillant ma famille d'un patrimoine qu'elle possedait deduis plus de neuf siècles. Malgré cela j'ai déclaré à V.M. par le Duc de Vicence, que je me contenterai du retablissement du traité dans son intégrité. J'ose croire que c'est être assez modéré. Je devais espérer qu'après six mois d'attente le comte Lauriston m'instruirait des intentions de V.M. sur cet objet, mais je me suis convaincu du contraire.

Je ne puis assez répéter à V.M. que je n'ai aucune vue ici d'ambition, ni d'agrandissement, mais je désire être rassuré. Ce qui s'est passé depuis quelque temps m'en fait besoin et V.M. conviendra que j'ai droit de m'attendre à tant de sécurité qu'il y en a eu toujours dans notre alliance, comme dans tous nos rapports. Je charge de cette lettre le Duc de Vicence; il a été à même de voir de près ma marche et du juger des sentiments que je porte à V.M. et à la France.

Toute ma conduite a dû prouver à V.M. que ceux-là sont inaltérables. Je dois lui rendre la justice d'avoir agi constamment dans le but de cimenter l'union des deux Empires et je l'ai surtout apprecié par le devouement que je lui ai toujours trouvé pour la personne de V.M. Enfin le Duc de Vicence est chargé d'assurer à V.M. que je veux l'alliance aujourd'hui comme je la voulais le jour de son arrivée. Sur ce je prie Dieu etc.

(signé) Alexandre.
6 Mai, 1811.

10

Monsieur mon Frère. Après l'arrivée du courrier que le Comte Lauriston a expedié le 6 de ce mois, je pris le parti de causer avec le colonel Tchernicheff sur les affaires facheuses survenues depuis quinze mois. Il ne depend que de V.M. de tout terminer. Je prie V.M. de ne jamais douter de mon désir de lui donner des preuves de la considéra-tion distinguée que j'ai pour sa personne.

(signé) Napoléon.

à Paris, le 24 février, 1812.

11

Monsieur mon Frère. Ayant lieu de penser que V.M. a quitté St.-Pétersbourg, et que le Comte Lauriston n'est plus auprès d'Elle, je charge mon aide-de-camp le Comte de Narbonne de cette lettre. Il sera en même temps porteur de communications impor-tantes pour le Comte Roumianzoff. Elles prouveront à V.M. mon désir d'éviter la guerre, et ma constance dans les sentiments de Tilsit et d'Erfurt. Toutefois V.M. me permettera de l'assurer que si la fatalité devait rendre la guerre inévitable entre nous, elle ne changerait en rien les sentiments que V.M. m'a inspiré et qui sont à l'abri de toute vicissitude et de toute altération. Sur ce etc.

(signé) Napoléon.

à St.-Cloud, le 25 Avril. 1812.

12

Monsieur mon Frère. J'ai écouté avec la plus sérieuse attention le compte que m'a rendu le colonel Tchernicheff de l'entretien que V.M. a bien voulu lui accorder en l'expédiant pour Pétersbourg. Les communcations que le Prince Kourakin est chargé de faire au ministre de V.M. de même que celles dont il c'est déjà acquitté précede-ment, prouveront au monde entier, combien j'ai toujours été prêt à tout terminer. Je resterai constamment dans ces sentiments et tout ne dépend que de V.M. Je la prie de croire à la considération la plus distinguée que je porte à sa personne.

(signé) Alexandre.

27 Mars, 1812 .

13

Monsieur mon frère. Le Comte de Narbonne m'a remis la lettre dont V.M. l'a chargée pour moi. J'y ai vu avec plaisir qu'elle se rappelle de Tilsit et d'Erfurt. Mes sentimens comme ma politique sont constamment les mêmes et je ne désire rien tant que d'éviter la guerre entre nous. Dans ce but unique j'ai sacrifié depuis un an tous les avan-tages militaires qui se sont présentés à moi. C'est la preuve la plus convaincante que je puis donner à V.M. de croire que dans aucune circonstance mes sentiments pour Sa personne n'éprouveront la moindre altération et qu'elle me trouvera toujours ce que j'étais à Tilsit et à Erfurt. Sur ce je prie etc.

(signé) Napoléon.

14

Monsieur mon frère. J'ai appris hier que malgré la loyauté avec la quelle j'ai maintenu mes engagements envers V.M. ses troupes ont franchis les frontières de la Russie et je reçois à l'instant de Pétersbourg une note par la quelle le Comte Lauriston, pour cause de cette aggression, annonce, que V.M. s'est considérée comme en état de guerre avec moi dès le moment où le Prince Kourakin a fait la demande de ses passeports. Les motifs sur les quels le Duc de Bessano fondait son refus de les lui delivrer n'auraient jamais pu me faire supposer que cette démarche servirait jamais de pretexte à l'aggression. En effet cet ambassadeur n'y a jamais été autorisé comme il l'a déclaré lui même, et aussitôt que j'en fus informé, je lui ai fait connaître combien je le desapprouvais en lui donnant l'ordre de rester a son poste. Si V.M. n'est pas intentionnée de verser le sang de nos peuples pour une mésentendue de ce genre et qu'elle consente à retirer ses troupes du territoire russe, je regarderai ce qui s'est passé comme non avenu, et un accomodement entre nous sera possible. Dans le cas contraire, V.M. je me verrai forcé de repousser une attaque que rien n'a provoquée de ma part. Il depend encore de V.M. d'éviter à l'humanité les calalmités d'une nouvelle guerre.

Je suis etc.

(signé) Alexandre.

Correspondence
Between Emperor Alexander I and Napoleon

PRIOR TO THE WAR OF 1812.

1

Sir my brother. Caulaincourt has let me know all that Y.I.M. wished to say in congratulations to him on the occasion of my wedding. I acknowledge in it the feelings that he wants to show to me: I beg him to accept my thanks. My sentiments for Him are unchangeable like the political principles which direct the relations of my Empire. Y.M. will never need to complain about France. The statements I made last December are the whole secret of my policy. I shall reiterate them whenever the opportunity arises. I beg Y.M. never to doubt my friendship and the high esteem I have for him.

(signed) Napoleon.

From our Imperial Palace of Lacken, May 16, 1810.

2

Sir my brother! Upon Prince Alexis Kurakin leaving to go to Y.I.M. I do not want to let this opportunity pass without reiterating to him all my sentiments. Those that I bring to Y.M. such as the political considerations of my Empire make me desire the continuation and the permanence of the alliance which we have contracted more each day. For my part, it is proof against any change and any event. I spoke frankly to Prince A. Kurakin on several questions of detail, but I pray Your Majesty will grant me confidence above all, when he speaks to him of my friendship for Him, and of my desire to see the eternal bonds of the alliance. I pray to God etc.

(signed) Napoleon.

in St Cloud, on August 29, 1810.

3

Sir my brother! I thank Y.I.M. for his letter from Lacken dated May 16 and for sending it from Mr. de Watteville. The assurances of his friendship are very dear to me. That which I convey to Y.M. is as sincere as it is unalterable. The alliance of our two Empires ensures continental peace. The more intimate it becomes, the more effective the system that Y.M. has adopted to reduce England will become. For my part, I do not neglect anything to enforce it and prove how much I care about it in principle, even independently of all the affection and esteem that I personally have for Y.M.

(signed) Alexander.

1810. (undated).

4

Sir my brother! I have to thank Y.I.M. for two letters via Pr. Kurakin and Colonel Chernyshev. That which Y.M. wishes to express regarding his policy to me, as well as his personal feelings for me, caused me the greatest pleasure through the conformity that I find there, with that which I have dedicated to Y.M. which are unchanging. Like Him, I have nothing more at heart than the continuation of the alliance which binds the two empires, which ensures the tranquillity of Europe. Also Y.M. was able to reassure himself that nothing on my side has been neglected to prove on all occasions the principle that I profess for the closest union between us. Russia has nothing to covet, as peace with Turkey will be concluded. Y.M. knows the conditions on which I want it; I never demanded more. Measures against British commerce continue with vigour; the numerous confiscations executed in my ports bear witness to this. Since then, barely 30 vessels from various nations have visited. It is unlikely that more will arrive, several of the ports being already closed by the ice; at least the number can only be very small; the same severity will be observed towards them. So the 100 ships Your M. tells me about will return to Britain. Germany's politicians like to spread alarming rumours and keep the people worried. I place no faith in them, as I place my confidence in Y.M.'s assurances. Colonel Chernyshev having seemed to me to deserve Y.M.'s satisfaction, it is he whom I am sending to carry this letter. I am sending it via Stockholm to make known to the government the desire that Your Majesty has, that I support the measures that He has taken for Sweden to break with Britain, although I already have the news that this has been done. Chernyshev will be able to report to Y.M. on the state of things in Sweden. I pray Y.M. will believe that my feelings for Him are unalterable over time. On this etc.

(signed) Alexander.

1810. (undated, November).

5

Sir my brother! Y.I.M. sent me such beautiful horses that I did not want to delay in sending him my thanks. The British are suffering greatly from the reunion of Holland and from the occupation that I caused to be made of the ports of Mecklenburg and Prussia. There are bankruptcies every week in London, which brings confusion to the city. The factories are out of work: the warehouses are packed. I have just had immense quantities of British and colonial merchandise seized in Frankfurt and

Switzerland. Six hundred British merchant ships that plied the Baltic were refused in Mecklenburg, Prussia, and proceeded to the states of Your M. whether they are still in its ports, or whether even the goods were unloaded, the repercussion which will strike Britain shall be terrible: all these goods are at the cost of the British. It depends on Y.M. to make peace or to make war. Peace is and must be His desire. Y.M. may be assured that we shall succeed if He confiscates these 600 vessels or their cargoes. Whatever documentation they have, under whatever names they brand themselves, French, German, Spanish, Danish, Russian, Swedish, Y.M. may be sure that they are British. Colonel Chernyshev, who returns to Y.M., has acted very well here. It only remains for me to pray Y.M. to always count on my unalterable feelings which are protected from time and from any event. On this etc.

Napoleon.

in Fontainebleau, October 23, 1810.

6

Sir my brother. The poor health of the Duc de Vicence obliges me to send him letters of recognisance. I searched about me for the person I supposed would be the best for Y.I.M. and the most suitable to maintain peace and alliance between us; I chose General Comte Lauriston.

I am very keen to learn if I have judged correctly. I have instructed Colonel Chernyshev to speak to Y.M. about my feelings for him. These feelings shall not change, although I cannot deceive myself that Y.M. no longer has any friendship towards me. It causes me to make protests and all kinds of difficulties for Oldenburg, since I do not refuse to grant an equivalent indemnity, and when the situation of this country which has always been a centre for smuggling with Britain makes it an indispensable duty to annex Oldenburg to my states in the interests of my Empire and for the success of the struggle in which I am engaged. The last *ukase* by Y.M. in substance, but above all in form, is specifically directed against France. On other occasions, before taking such a measure against my business, Y.M. would have made it known to me, and I could, perhaps, have suggested methods to him, which, while fulfilling his main aim, would nevertheless have prevented what appears to France to be a change of system from happening. All Europe has looked upon it thus, and already our alliance no longer exists in the opinion of Britain and of Europe: were it as perfectly in the heart of your Majesty as it is in the mine, this general opinion would none the less be a great evil. Let Y.M. allow me to tell him frankly, He has forgotten the benefits He has gained from the treaty and yet He sees what has happened since Tilsit. According to the Treaty of Tilsit, He was to restore Moldavia and Wallachia to Turkey; however, instead of restoring these provinces Y.M. has annexed them to his Empire. Wallachia and Moldavia constitute a third of European Turkey, it is an immense acquisition which, upon joining the vast Empire of Y.M. on the Danube, removes all power from Turkey, and dare one say it, destroys this Empire, my oldest ally. However, instead of holding to the execution of the Treaty of Tilsit, in a most disinterested way and out of pure friendship for Y.M., I accepted the annexation of these beautiful and rich countries; but without confidence in the continuation of His friendship several very unfortunate campaigns could not have led France to see her former ally despoiled in this way. In Sweden, at the time that I restored the conquests that I had made on this Power, I consented to Y.M. keeping Finland, which is one-third of Sweden, and which is a province so important for Y.M. that we can say that since this annexation Sweden is no longer a Power, since Stockholm is now on the front line of the Kingdom. However Sweden, in spite of the false policy of its King, was also one of the old friends of France. Intriguers and British-influenced men weary Y.M.'s ears with slanderous remarks. 'He wants – they say – to restore Poland.' I had been able to do that at Tilsit: twelve days after the battle of Friedland, I could have been in Vilna. If I had wanted to re-establish Poland, I could have distracted Austria in Vienna; she asked to preserve her ancient provinces and her communications with the sea, by making her sacrifices bear on her possessions in Poland. I could have done it in 1810, when all the Russian forces were engaged against the Porte. I could do so even now, without waiting for Y.M. to ratify the treaty with the Porte which will probably be concluded during the course of this summer. Since I did not do it under any of these circumstances, it must be therefore that the restoration of Poland was not my intent. But although I don't want to change anything in the state of Poland, I also have the right to demand that no one meddle with what I'm doing on this side of the Elbe. However, it is true that our enemies have succeeded. The fortifications which Y.M. has erected at twenty locations along the Dvina, the protests of which Pr. Kurakin has spoken in favour of Oldenburg and the *ukase* are sufficient proof of this.

It is all the same to me, but I am struck by the evidence of these facts and by the thought that Your Majesty is quite disposed as soon as circumstances will require it, to make peace with Britain, which is the same thing as declaring war between the two Empires. Y.M. in abandoning the alliance at one go and burning the Treaty of Tilsit, it would be obvious that a war would ensue within a few months sooner or later. This state of distrust and uncertainty has disadvantages for the Empire of Y.M. and for mine; the result must be to put us in a position to stretch the resources of our Empires on both sides. All of this is undoubtedly unfortunate. If Y.M. has no plans to restore relations with Britain, He must feel the need for him and for me to dissipate all these clouds. He has no security since He has told the Duc de Vicence that He would make war on his borders and security is the first priority between the two great States. I beg Your Majesty to read this letter in a good spirit, to see nothing in it that is not conciliatory and likely to eliminate any kind of mistrust on both sides and to restore the two nations, from all points of view, to the intimacy of an alliance which, for nearly four years, has been so happy.

Whereupon I pray to God, Sir my Brother, that He will have Y.I.M. in his holy and worthy keeping.

From Y.I.M.

The Good Brother

(signed) Napoleon

in Paris, 28 February, 1811.

7

Sir my brother. I hasten to reply to Y.M.'s letter of February 28. I very much regret that the health of the Duc de Vicence prevents him from continuing his mission with me. I was extremely satisfied with him, because on every occasion I recognised in him the greatest devotion to Y.M. and a constant care to strengthen the ties that unite us. I thank Y.M. for the choice He has made of Lt Gen Lauriston; he who has His confidence is sure to please me.

Chernyshev has carried out my orders. I see with regret that I am misunderstood by Him. Neither my feelings nor my policy have changed and I only desire the maintenance and consolidation of our alliance. Am I not rather permitted to assume that it is Y.M. who has changed towards me? I think I should speak to him with the same frankness as he did in his letter. Y.M. accuses me of protesting the Oldenburg affair, but how could I not? A small piece of land owned by the only individual, who belongs to my family, who went through all the formalities that were required of him, a member of the confederation, and as a result of this, under the protection of Y.M. whose territories are guaranteed by an article of the Treaty of Tilsit, is dispossessed of them without Your Majesty having said a word to me beforehand. Of what importance could this corner of the earth be to France, and did this process prove to Europe the friendship of Y.M. for me? Also – all the letters written everywhere at this time prove that it was considered as a desire that Y.M. had to hurt us. As for my protest, the manner in which it is worded serves as irrefutable proof that I put the alliance with France above all other considerations, and I state clearly that it would be very much mistaken if it were deduced that my union with Y.M. is breached. Y.M. supposes that my *ukase* on tariffs is directed against France. I must oppose this opinion as gratuitous and unfair. This tariff is the subject of Supreme Orders by the extreme disruption of maritime commerce, by the enormous importation overland of luxury foreign goods, by the excessive duties imposed in the states of Y.M. on Russian products and by the frightful drop in our exchange rates. He has two aims in mind: the first is that by prohibiting British trade with the greatest severity, to grant some facilities to American trade as the only sea trade which Russia can use to export its products too bulky to be moved overland. The second, is to restrict as much as possible imports overland, as the most disadvantageous for our balance of trade, introducing a quantity of very rich luxury articles and for which we spend our money, while our own exports are so severely disrupted.

These are the very simple reasons for the *ukase* on tariffs. It is no more directed against France than against any other country in Europe, and is entirely within the Continental System by the prohibition and destruction of objects of enemy commerce. Y.M. finds fault with the fact that I did not consult him beforehand on this measure. Being only purely administrative, I think that each government is free to make them domestically according to its own conveniences, especially when they are not in violation of existing treaties. But let Y.M. allow me a single observation. Is it fair on his part to point out to me when he himself took the same methods and gave me just as little notice of the measures he deemed necessary to take on trade not only in his Empire but throughout Europe. Moreover, these measures had a much stronger impact on Russian trade than those of the Russian tariff will have on that of France, and the numerous bankruptcies which followed serve as proof of this. I believe I can rightly say that Russia observed the Treaty of Tilsit more scrupulously than France and what he quotes on Moldavia and Wallachia can never be imputed to Russia as a breach of the clauses of this treaty, because he decrees that the Principalities shall remain unoccupied by the troops of the belligerent Powers during the armistice. Also my army had made four retrograde marches and it was only when the Turks invaded, burned Galati and pushed to Foksani, that I made my army turn back. Since then, the convention of Erfurt assured me of the possession of Moldavia and Wallachia; consequently I find myself entirely in order. As for the conquest of Finland, it was not in my policy and Y.M. must remember that I undertook the war against Sweden only following the Continental System. The success of my armed forces has earned me the possession of Finland just as reverses could have deprived me of my provinces. So I believe I am still in order on this second point. But if your Majesty cites the advantages that Russia has derived from her alliance with France, can I not in turn cite those derived by France and the immense annexations that she has made from parts of Italy, from northern Germany and Holland?

I believe I have proved more than once to Y.M. that I was insensitive to the insinuations fomented by those who have an interest in embroiling us, and the best evidence that I can give is to have communicated them each time to Y.M. in always relying on his friendship.

However – when facts emerged to back up the rumours that were circulating, the least I could do was take precautionary measures. The mobilisation of the Duchy of Warsaw was followed relentlessly. The military of this duchy has also been increased out of proportion to its population. We have not stopped working on new fortifications. Those, on the other hand, that I have raised, are on the Dvina and the Dnieper. Y.M. is too militarily aware not to recognise that when new fortifications are established at a distance from the border equal to that between Paris and Strasbourg, they are certainly not aggressive measures but purely defensive. My mobilisation is limited to executing a reorganisation of already existing regiments. This is what Y.M. has not stopped doing with His. Moreover, everything that is happening in the Duchy of Warsaw, such as the ever increasing strength in the forces of Y.M. in the North of Germany, has certainly given me the obligation to do so. This is the exact state of affairs. My fortifications, therefore, serve rather as proof of how unwilling I am to be the aggressor. My tariffs, established only for one year, had no other purpose than to diminish the disfavour of my change and to provide me with the means of persevering in the system which I embraced and followed with so much persistence, and a protest, ordered by what I owe to the honour of my country and that of my family, motivated by a direct violation of the Treaty of Tilsit, and yet the most manifest proof of my desire to preserve the alliance with Y.M. Besides, coveting nothing from my neighbours, loving France – what interest would I have in wanting war? Russia does not need conquests and perhaps has too much territory. The superior genius that I recognise in Y.M. for warfare leaves me no illusions about the difficulty of the struggle that could arise between us. Besides, my self-esteem is attached to the system of alliance with France. Having established it as a principle of policy for Russia, having had to combat long enough the old opinions which were contrary to it, it is unreasonable to assume in me the desire to destroy my work and to make war on Y.M. and if He desires it as little as I do, most certainly it will not happen. To give him further proof of this, I offer Y.M. to rely on Himself for what He would have desired in such a case. Y.M. has all the means to arrange things in such a way as to ally the two Empires even more closely and to make a breach impossible forever. For my part, I am ready to support him in such an intention. I repeat, if a war were to take place, it would be because Y.M. will have wanted it, and having done everything to avoid it, I would then know how to fight and sell my existence dearly. Should he wish instead to recognise a friend and an ally in me, he will find me with the same feelings of attachment and friendship that he has always known in me. I beg Y.M. to read this letter in the same way in a good spirit and to see only a very pronounced desire to reconcile things therein.

(signed) Alexander.

8

Sir my brother. As soon as I learned from the Duc de Vicence that the choice of the Comte de Lauriston was agreeable to Y.I.M. I ordered him to set off. I do not send to Y.M. a man consummate in this business, but a true and upright man, like the feelings I have for Him. And yet, every day I receive news from Russia which is not peaceful. Yesterday I learned from Stockholm that the Russian divisions in Finland had left to move up to the borders of the Grand Duchy. A few days ago I was informed from Bucharest that five divisions have left the provinces of Moldavia and Wallachia, to go to Poland, and that only four divisions of the troops of Y.M. remain on the Danube. What is happening is further proof that repetition is the most powerful rhetorical figure. They repeated so much to Y.M. that I resented him, that his confidence was shaken. The Russians leave a border where they are needed, to go to a point where Y.M. has only friends. However, I had to think about this case too, and I had to put myself in a position. The response to my preparations will lead Y.M. to increase his, and what He will do resoundingly here will make me raise new means: and all for a phantom. This is the repetition of what I saw in 1807 in Prussia and in 1809 in Austria. As for me, I shall remain the friend of the person of Y.M. even should this fatality which involves Europe one day put weapons in the hands of our two nations. I will only respond to what Y.M. will do. I shall never attack him, and my troops will only advance once Y.M. has torn up the Treaty of Tilsit. I will be the first to disarm and put everything back in the situation where things were a year ago, if Y.M. wants to return to the same confidence. Has He ever had to repent of the confidence He has shown in me? I especially charge Comte Lauriston to tell Him how much I wish Him happiness, how vexed I am to imagine that He feels embarrassed and distressed by the false notions He has allowed to be given regarding my policy and my feelings, and how happy I would be to see it restored to the same foundations as at Tilsit and Erfurt. I pray Your Majesty to grant Comte Lauriston complete faith when he tells you that I want peace, that I envy nothing of the prosperity of his Empire, and that on the contrary I take pleasure in thinking that He has grown bigger and had taken advantage of my alliance. On this I pray to God etc.

Napoleon.

in Paris, April 6, 1811.

9

Sir my brother. Count Lauriston arrived a few days ago and gave me Your I.M.'s letter of April 6. The peaceful words it contains, as well as the language of its ambassador, would have given me the greatest pleasure if they were supported by facts. The news that Y.M. quotes to me about the movement of my troops is completely false. I convinced his ambassador of this by showing him in detail all the deployments of my army and even offering to send his aide-de-camp to check things on the ground. The divisions stationed in Finland have never left it and three are there as in the past. Of the five divisions of the army of Moldavia, of which Y.M. speaks, three are still in this province and it is only two that I put astride the Dniester and not on the borders of the Duchy of Warsaw, as it was stated. I had sent word to Y.M. Consequently my army of Moldavia is not reduced to four divisions, but is made up of seven divisions. No concentration of troops on my part took place on the border of the Duchy of Warsaw, no troops even approached this border. Most certainly this order, which is commanded by prudence, is very disadvantageous to me, by paralysing the activity which I could have given to an operation on the Danube. Such is the state of things on my side, whereas at the moment when Lauriston handed me the letter from Y.M. at my audience and gave the most reassuring promises of it on his part, I had just received the confirmed news of the mobilisation and the assembly of the Saxon army by order of Y.M. as well as the advance by the cuirassier division of his army. Which of us, then, is the one who mobilises? My army is in its usual cantonments and that of Y.M. is in full march. All these facts prove if the grievances contained in Y.M.'s letter are founded and if I gave rise to the movements that are taking place, Y.M. tells me that he saw in 1807 with Prussia and in 1809 with Austria. Let him allow me to observe that those times were in no way similar to the one in which we find ourselves. Prussia and Austria wanted war; me – I don't want it, I don't covet anything from anyone and don't want any aggrandisement. I only wanted the Treaty of Tilsit to be preserved intact. Y.M. alone broke a treaty clause by stripping my family of an inheritance that has been handed down for more than nine centuries. Despite this, I declared to Y.M. through the Duc de Vicence, that I would be satisfied with the restoration of the treaty in its entirety. I dare to believe that is being quite moderate. I would have hoped that after six months of waiting Count Lauriston would inform me of Y.M"'s intentions on this subject, but I have assured myself of the opposite.

I cannot repeat to Y.M. enough that I have no ambitions here, nor expansion, but I want to be reassured. What has happened for some time makes me require it and Y.M. will agree that I have the right to expect as much security as there has always been in our alliance, as in all our relations. I entrust this letter to the Duc de Vicence; he was able to see my progress in person and judge the feelings I have for Y.M. and for France.

All my conduct must have proved to Y.M. that these are unalterable. I must do him justice for having acted constantly with the aim of cementing the alliance of the two Empires and I especially appreciate him for the devotion that I have always found in him for the person of Y.M. Finally the Duc de Vicence is responsible to assure Y.M. that I want the alliance today as much as I wanted it the day it was made. On this I pray to God etc.

(signed) Alexandre

May 6, 1811.

10

Sir my brother. After the arrival of the courier sent by Count Lauriston on the 6th of this month, I made up my mind to talk with Colonel Chernyshev about the unfortunate affairs that have arisen over the past fifteen months. It only depends on Y.M. to complete everything. I beg Y.M. never to doubt my desire to give him proof of the distinguished consideration I have for his person.

(signed) Napoleon,

in Paris, February 24, 1812.

11

Sir my brother. Having reason to think that Y.M. has left St. Petersburg, and that Comte Lauriston is no longer with him, I charge my aide-de-camp the Comte de Narbonne with this letter. At the same time, he will carry important communications for Count Rumyantsev. They will prove to Y.M. my desire to avoid war, and my constancy in the sentiments of Tilsit and Erfurt. However, Y.M. will allow me to assure him that if fate were to make war between us inevitable, it would in no way change the feelings that Y.M. has inspired in me and which are immune to all vicissitudes and all changes. On this etc.

(signed) Napoleon,

at St.-Cloud, April 25, 1812.

12

Sir my brother. I have listened with the most serious attention to Colonel Chernyshev's account of the interview which Y.M. was good enough to grant him when sending him to Petersburg. The communications that Prince Kurakin is responsible for making to the Minister of Y.M. as well as those which he has already acquitted himself of previously, will prove to the whole world how much I have always been ready to complete everything. I will constantly remain in these feelings and everything depends only on Y.M. I beg him to believe in the most distinguished consideration I have for his person.

(signed) Alexander,

March 27, 1812.

13

Sir my brother. The Count of Narbonne handed me the letter with which Y.M. charged for me. I saw with pleasure that he remembers Tilsit and Erfurt. My sentiments, like my policy, are constantly the same, and I desire nothing so much as to avoid war between us. For this sole purpose I have sacrificed for a year all the military advantages which have presented themselves to me. This is the most convincing proof that I can give Y.M. to believe that under no circumstances will my feelings for His person experience the slightest alteration and that He will always find me as I was at Tilsit and Erfurt. On this I pray etc.

(signed) Napoleon.

14

Sir my brother. I learned yesterday that in spite of the loyalty with which I have maintained my engagements towards Y.M. his troops have crossed the borders of Russia and I have received just this moment in Petersburg a note by which Comte Lauriston, because of this aggression, announces that Y.M. considers himself in a state of war with me from the moment that Prince Kurakin requested his passports. The reasons for which the Duc de Bessano based his refusal to deliver them to him could never have led me to suppose that this step would ever serve as a pretext for aggression. Indeed this ambassador was never authorised to do so as he declared himself, and as soon as I was informed of it, I made known to him how much I disapproved of him by ordering him to remain at his post. If your Majesty has no intention of shedding the blood of our peoples for a misunderstanding of this kind and agrees to withdraw his troops from Russian territory, I shall regard what happened as null and void, and an accommodation between us would be possible. Otherwise, Y.M. I shall be forced to repel an attack that was not provoked on my part. It still depends on Y.M. to save humanity from the calamities of a new war.

I am etc.

(signed) Alexander.

Appendix VIII

Numerology of 'The Antichrist'

We attach the numerology derived from the apocalypse of St. John the Evangelist, where the following prophecy is found:

In chapter 13, verse 18: 'Here there is wisdom, who has the wit, let the number honour the beast: it is a human number and its number is six hundred-sixty-six.'

And in the same chapter, in verse 5: 'and it was given to him to create a month four-ten-two.'

As for the name and title of the beast, in French they are depicted with these words: *L'Empereur Napoléon,* and for the number of four-ten-two, which in that language is written with the words: *quarante deux,* both times the number 666 is found, which is defined in the aforementioned chapter, verse 18 of the Apocalypse.

In French characters, imitating the Hebrew number of the image, according to which the first ten letters are units, and the rest tens, have the following meaning:

a	b	c	d	e	f	g	h	i	k	l	m	n
1	2	3	4	5	6	7	8	9	10	20	30	40
o	p	q	r	s	t	u	v	w	x	y	z	
50	60	70	80	90	100	110	120	130	140	150	160	

from that, the following emerges:

L	20	Q	70
e	5	u	110
E	5	a	1
m	30	r	80
p	60	a	1
e	5	n	40
r	80	t	100
e	5	e	5
u	110	d	4
r	80	e	5
N	40	u	110
a	1	x	140
p	60	Total:	666
o	50		
l	20		
e	5		
o	50		
n	40		
Total:	666		

Appendix IX

Comte d'Allonville's Plan

Extracted from a draft drawn up by Comte d'Allonville, entitled: *Mémoire politique et militaire sur les circonstances présentes (janvier 1811).*

Moyens subsidiaires.

Les opérations propres à appuyer le plan proposé consistent à:

1. *se lier avec l'Angleterre plus généreuse à l'égard de la Russie durant la guerre que d'autres ne se le sont montrés. Malgré l'utilité de son alliance et dont le commerce seul vaut mieux à cet empire que les secours qu'elle pourrait esperer de quelque part que ce fût, il ne faudrait jamais compter sur une intervention militaire prompte et à point nommé, la nature de son gouvernement et de son armée entrainant nécessairement des lenteurs, et l'incertitude des vents produisant d'inévitables retards. Il ne faudrait pas d'avantage se piquer, à son propre détriment, des torts vrais ou apparents d'un tel allié. Frédéric II a donné sur cela, dans la guerre de sept ans, un bel et utile exemple.*
2. *faire cause commune avec l'Espagne et lui garantir son indépendance, à condition de ne point faire la paix sans concours de la Russie.*
3. *conclure une paix prompte et généreuse avec la Turquie, au prix, soit d'une rupture avec l'Autriche, à qui elle a toujours été rédoutable, dans le cas où cette dernière s'unirait à l'ennemi; soit d'une diversion puissante en Dalmatie, et d'opérations maritimes combinées, dans la Méditeranée, si l'Autriche concourait aux plans de la Russie.*
4. *obtenir l'accession de l'Autriche, qui a tout à craindre de la France, tout à ésperer de la Russie, ou du moins sa neutralité; dans le premier cas, éxciter les rivalités des généraux, la laisser agir seule en Lombardie et en Souabe, comme sur les derrières de l'armée française tenue en échec par les Russes, à l'aide des insurrections probables du Tyrol et de la Forêt Noire, en l'aidant par une diversion sur Naples; dans le second, s'en assurer par une armée d'observation sur la frontière de la Galicie; dans le cas enfin d'une rupture avec elle, l'attaquer simultantment avec les Turcs.*
5. *envoyer un corps auxiliaire russe dans la Prusse, menacée tant par le Royaume de Westphalie que par les cinq nouveaux départements français; l'aider à insurger le nord de l'Allemagne, qui y était si bien disposée lors de la guerre de 1809, affranchir toutes les côtes de la Baltique et l'Océan germanique, en ouvrir les ports aux*

Anglais, separer la France de la Suède et du Danemark et déterminer cette dernière puissance à s'unir à la ligue continentale pour eviter la ruine qui la ménace
doublement par l'extension de ses forces et la destruction de son commerce; mais
subordonner ses opérations à celles du centre où les grands coups doivent être
portés.

6. Engager la Suède par tous les moyens d'intérêt, de persuasion et de crainte à
rentrer dans l'alliance de l'Angleterre, qui peut seule la ruiner ou l'enrichir,
détruire ou raviver son commerce, insluter ou proteger ses côtes, et dans le cas
d'une révolution possible, faire tomber la couronne sur la tête des héritiers légi-
times de la maison Royale, dont un se trouve doublement lié à la Russie par le
sang et par alliance.

7. Ranimer en France le royalisme si utile aux Autrichiens dans la campagne de
1793 et aux Anglais à Toulon; ce qui forcerait l'ennemi à garnir de troupes les
provinces occidentales de la France, à accroitre la rigueur de son gouvernement,
et à faire désirer à ennemis et à une partie même de ses partisans, mais certainement à la plus part de ceux qui ont abattu le gouvernement diréctorial, de détruire
celui de Napoléon.

8. Enfin, pour mettre la France dans la nécessité de développer des forces supérieures à ses moyens en hommes et en argent, depuis le fond de l'Espagne et de
l'Italie jusqu'à la Vistule et aux côtes de l'Océan, opérer des diversions, comme
par exemple, soit dans la Dalmatie par les Grecs et les Albanois, soit à Naples, à
l'àide des Anglais, des Siciliens et des fidèles Calabrois; dix à quinze mille Russes
pourraient ainsi balayer rapidement cet état jusqu'à sa frontière, qui naturelle-
ment défendue, de Gaëte à Chietti, par des montagnes ouvertes seulement par
deux défilés, longs, ètroits et tortueux, à Itri et à Aquilée et par le vallon à fond
tourbeux de St.-Germano, ne laisse d'accessible qu'une plaine peu étendue près
de Chietti, frontière où dix mille hommes peuvent facilement en arrêter cent
mille, diversion qui occuperait de grandes forces à l'ennemi, ou le contraindroit à
évacuer entièrement la péninsule, ce qui retrancherait douze millions d'hommes
à son Empire.

Une autre diversion utile serait sur la Poméranie, le Hannovre, la Hollande, la
Brétagne ou les environs de Bayonne, pour seconder les opérations de l'armée prussi-
enne, des Anglais et reveiller le royalisme ou insurger les habitans des Pyrénées, partisans de l'Espagne, et faciliter ainsi les opérations projettées du Duc d'Orléan sur le
Roussillon; si les Anglais avaient substitué cette dernière expédition à celle de Flessing,
l'Espagne serait peut-être libre aujourd'hui.

Opérations militaires.
Il serait peut-être témeraire d'indiquer ici militairement les opérations à faire, et topo-
grafiquement, les positions à occuper; mais il est indispensable d'appuyer sur la nécessité:

1. de prendre l'offensive en se portant vivement sur le Duché de Varsovie, et gagnant
s'il était possible la Silésie, d'occuper, de concert avec la Prusse, la ligne de l'Oder,
pour faire déclarer les Princes de l'Empire, ou exciter des insurrections dans le
Nord de l'Allemagne et appuyer sa gauche soit par l'accession de l'Autriche, soit

par un corps d'observation et une rupture des Turcs avec cette puissance (voyez Moyens Subs. No 3 et 4).

2. de dissoudre le gouvernement Polonais, de dissiper ou d'enrégimenter ses corps armés, en les envoyant sur les derrières; mais devaster impitoyablement le Duché, si on se trouvait contraint de l'évacuer, afin d'oter à l'ennemi les moyens d'y subsister.

3. d'avoir ses deux flancs protegés par deux corps, l'un réuni comme auxiliaire au Roi de Prusse, l'autre menaçant la Galicie, tandis que la Hongrie serait attaquée par les Turcs dans le cas de la non-accession de l'Autriche, et dans le cas contraire agissant simultanement avec l'armée principale.

4. de former deux armées de reserve, stationnées, l'une à Kieff, l'autre à Smolensk, et pourvues de vivres, de munitions, d'armes et de moyens de transport, afin de pouvoir être vivement portées en tout ou en partie, sur les points où les circon-stances pourraient l'éxiger.

5. de tenir toujours, autant que ses mouvements le rendrait possible, l'armée prin-cipale réunie en grands corps qui peuvent être repoussés, mais non pas detruits; d'éclarirer le pays par des nuées de cosaques, propres à le dévaster si l'on était obligé à un mouvement retrograde, comme à harceller l'ennemi, à enlever ses convois, à inquiéter ses fourageurs et à retarder ainsi sa marche.

6. de fortifier les postes qu'on occuperait par la rupture des chemins ed des ponts qui y conduiraient l'ennemi, par des batteries de position, des retranchemens passagers et des abattis, d'employer alors l'état-major à reconnaître ceux qu'on pourrait être forcés d'occuper, ainsi que les moyens de les rendre formidables, et les routes qui y meneraient.

7. de couvrir soigneusement les magasins et les convois, en entretenant toujours ses communications avec les corps russes ou alliés, appui de ses flancs, ainsi qu'avec les deux armées de réserve, comme celles de ses derrières, avec les corps susdits par des postes intermédiaires ou un mouvement en avant, si l'ennemi venait à tourner l'armée principale.

8. de forcer l'ennemi soit à l'inaction, soit à des attaques hasardeuses et où il dut nécessairement éprouver des pertes considérables, en cas même de succès.

9. de ne l'attaquer qu'avec une supériorité accablante de forces et de situation.

10. de chercher, tandis qu'on le tiendrait en échec, à jetter sur ses derrières des corps mobiles et rapides qui pourraient enlever ou détruire ses convois, ou le forcer à s'affaiblir par des escortes.

11. de ne point ralentir pendant l'hiver, saison plus favorable aux Russes, qu'aux Français, ces expéditions actives et continuelles.

12. d'éviter toutes les actions décisives, qui procurent moins d'avantage dans le succès qu'elles n'entrainent de prejudice dans un échec.

13. de subordonner toutes les opérations auxiliaires aux opérations principales.

14. de combiner avec les armées de reserve, dans le cas où l'ennemi manoeuvrerait de manière à tourner l'armée agissante, les moyens de le menacer à la fois en tête et en flanc, de l'isoler de ses ressources et de le ruiner en détail ou de le mettre dans la nécessité de se battre dans une position hasardeuse.

15. *de s'assurer dans toutes les positions occupées des moyens de retraite et de trans-ports, comme des positions nouvelles, toujours liées avec les situations des corps auxiliaires et de réserve.*

16. *de defendre ainsi et successivement, s'il est nécessaire, les lignes de l'Oder, de la Vistule et même du Dnieper, à l'aide des positions intermédiaires, bien sûr qu'un succès définitif et complet rendrait et assurerait solidement ce qu'on aurait été momentanément forcé d'abandonner.*

17. *d'observer la Suède avec un corps dont les attaques pourraient, selon les occurences, être combinées avec les opérations maritimes des Anglais.*

18. *d'opérer deux diversions, l'une sur la Dalmatie ou sur Naples, l'autre sur les côtes françaises ou devenues telles; mais préférablement en Bretagne, où l'on peut à l'aide des joles de Jersey et de Guernesey, faire un débarquement, qui au nom loyalement prononcé du Roi serait le moyau d'une armée nombreuse, si l'on y portait de l'argent et des armes, car les Russes, n'inspirant aucune défiance, alli-eraient bientôt tous les ennemis du gouvernement dans un pays dont il n'est pas sûr et le forceraient, en lui ravissant des ressources, à y porter des forces consi-dérables aux moment où il en a le plus de besoin ailleurs, l'armée débarquée se trouvant nécessairement en Bretagne dans la même situation où les Anglais sont en Portugal.*

19. *d'employer, enfin, tout les moyens de prolonger la guerre, en obligeant l'ennemi à diviser ses troupes par la nécessité de les diriger sur un grand nombre de points très éloignés les uns des autres.*

Il faut que le gouvernement Russe ne perde point de vue, quel doit être le but de la guerre, et qu'il en proportionne toujours les moyens à ce but important; il faut que son militaire, accoutumé aux opérations brillantes des Roumanzoff, des Souvoroff et des Kamensky, songe qu'ici il n'est plus question de ces campagnes faites contre un ennemi soumis aux loix de la guerre et des gens; mais du débordement d'une nation, qui ne cherche la gloire que dans le bouleversement des Empires et ses moyens dans leur dévastation. Que la valeur peut être trompée par la fortune, mais que la sagesse et la patience la gouvernent ou la reparent; qu'aujourd'hui le destin du monde civilisé est entre les mains des Russes; que le sort d'un combat est incertain, celui de la tempo-risation sûr, principalement devant une armée sans argent si elle ne pille, sans alliés si elle ne bat, et qui entreprenante par caractère l'est encore plus par ncessité, enfin il ne faut pas perdre de vue que l'homme qu'on a en tête joint aux forces de l'ancienne France, accrue des conquêtes de la France nouvelle et celles du Jacobinisme organisé qui fait l'éssence de son gouvernement, la disposition des moyens hostiles de l'Italie, de la Suisse, du Danemark, de la Suède, de la Pologne et d'un tiers de l'Allemagne, supposé même que l'Autriche ne s'unisse point avec lui, que le but de la guerre est l'affranchissement de l'Europe, chose incompatible avec son existence; il ne suffit donc pas d'élever une digue fragile contre les efforts d'une aussi rédoutable puissance, mais de le détruire, mais de briser un instrument de destruction universelle si l'on ne veut point être broyé par les effets du mouvement accéléré imprimé à ses ressorts.

Forces nécessaires.

Les forces nécessaires à ces opérations seraient une armée centrale et agissante de 80 à 100 mille hommes tout au plus; un corps de 30 à 40 mille hommes, pour menacer la Galicie et la Hongrie simultanément avec les Turcs, dans le cas où l'Autriche méconnaitrait ses vrais intérêts; pour observer cette puissance dans l'hypothèse de sa neutralité, ou être plus utilement employé dans celle de son accession; un de 20 à 30 mille hommes auxiliaire de la Prusse; deux armées de reserve de 40 à 50 mille hommes, chacune stationnées à Kieff et à Smolensk. Une expédition de 10 mille hommes vers Naples, une seconde combinée avec les Anglais contre la France, occupant un nombre de troupes égal ou plus considérable si l'Autriche prenait part à la ligue; de 20 à 30 mille hommes en garnison, camps volans, éscortes de convois etc, en tout de 250 à 320 mille hommes. 285 mille hommes pour terme moyen, y compris les troupes légères, pionniers, artillerie etc, forces très imposantes quoique infiniment inférieures à celles que possède la Russie, et qui sagement dirigées sont suffisantes, dans le cas même où l'Autriche ne profitera pas des circonstances pour affranchir sa couronne, car la France ne pourrait leur opposer que celles qu'elle serait capable de mouvoir et de nourrir dans un pays ruiné et mécontent, ce qui rétranche beaucoup au calcul qu'une crainte éxagératrice en présenterait. Il est à observer ici que la population de la Russie est encore intacte; que ses impositions sont proportionnellement les plus faibles qui soient payées par aucun peuple Européen; que le retour du commerce Anglais, si utile par sa balance favorable aux Russes et par l'enlèvement de leurs denrées, enrichirait à la fois l'état et les propriétaires; que la suspension de celui de la France, qui emporte beaucoup, exporte peu, ne fournit que des objets sans valeur et se fait en grande partie par contrebande, réléverait son change, ce qui offre des moyens immenses pour soutenir une guerre longue et couteuse; joignez y l'abondance des vivres produit de l'interruption momentanée de leur exportation, et le sentiment universel qui ferait de la rupture avec la France une guerre vraiment natiionale.

Pour agir néanmoins avec autant de célérité que de prudence, il serait à propos d'employer des moyens télégraphiques et de faire de Moscou un grand dépôt de recrues, où seraient réunis, exercés et formés les soldats destinés à réparer les pertes éprouvées par les differentes armées.

Dispositions préliminaires.

Pour ranimer l'espérance de l'Europe et en rallier les intérêts à ceux de la Russie, il faut exposer qu'on ne prend les armes qu'en raison d'une nécessité irresistible et qu'on ne les posera qu'après l'affranchissement du Continent; opposer la franchise à la dissimulation, les projets de protection à ceux d'envahissement; promettre sureté et intégrité à tous les états qui adopteraient ce plan conservateur, guerre à mort à ceux qui s'y opposeraient en ouvrant néanmoins la porte au repentir et en offrant des avantages à un retour loyal, comme à une intervention utile.

Résultat.

Le plan conçu sur ces principes de loyauté, de sagesse et de fermeté, d'une guerre que la Russie pourrait entreprendre presque sans alliés, bien certaine de la continuer et de la terminer avec l'approbation et le concours de l'Europe entière, conduirait aux résultats les plus glorieux qui puissent jamais exciter la noble ambition d'un Souverain:

ce serait l'indépendance des couronnes, l'affranchissement de peuples, la réstauration du commerce, de l'industrie, des arts; la paix, la sécurité, la prospérité de l'Europe, la reconnaissance universelle et celle particulièrement de la part la plus saine d'une nation, que la criminelle imprévoyance de quelques novateurs a condamnée au joug d'un homme, qui la ruine par des entreprises extravagantes, étrangères à ses intérêts. Enfin le lustre indicible et immortel de la Russie.

Je n'ai exposé dans ce mémoire que des faits et des vérités incontestables; j'en ai déduit les résultats nécessaires en indiquant et les obstacles à craindre, et les moyens de les surmonter. Mon sujet eut été susceptible d'un plus vaste dévéloppement, mais peu de mots suffisent à l'expérience qui saisit tout avec rapidité et aux regards de la quelle je le soumets, en remarquant ici que si le rôle de Pierre Premier fut réellement grand, celui de Sa Majesté l'Empereur Alexandre peut être infiniment d'avantage, parcequi'il serait incomparablement plus utile, que celui du premier de ses souverains n'interessait que la Russie et que celui du dernier interesserait à la fois et cet Empire et le système général de la civilisation.

Appendix X

Von Toll's Plan

Military preparations on the part of Russia and our *opolchenie*, assembled at various locations, preparatory to the imminent war between us and France.

The current disposition of Russian forces along the western border, starting from the outskirts of Schaulen to the outskirts of Lutsk, encompassing about 800 *versts* of frontage, and the various magazines established in this area give rise to the conclusion that this arrangement simply has convenience for the provisioning of our army as its objective; but it is not the most advantageous position for conducting military operations, because the distance from one army to another is so vast (although Lt Gen Essen's observational corps is located between the armies), that the enemy, intending to open hostilities, having concentrated his main forces at Warsaw (moreover, having two flanking corps), can exploit interior lines of operations, and, through that sever all communications between the armies and smash each separately, having superior forces to oppose each.

I do not need to explain how an offensive war is more advantageous; but to my regret, I must note that the favourable moment for offensive action has passed for us: firstly, because the French have managed to corner every provisioning resource in the region between the Russian border and the Vistula and transport all food and fodder to fortified locations along the Vistula and beyond the Vistula, such as: into Warsaw, Modlin, Thorn, Graudenz, Marienwerder and Danzig, also arranging the restocking of the fortress of Zamość; secondly, because they have managed to muster a force of about 220,000 men who could unite in superior numbers against one of our armies, which must operate, according to their present location, along two lines of operation, namely: from Vilna, via Grodno to Warsaw, and from Lutsk, via Vladimir to Warsaw. Realising this, I believe that no other course remains to us but to wage, in the first instance, a defensive war, and to that end I intend to draw up the following plan of operations.

Redeployment of the army before the opening of hostilities.

The present situation of the army has the advantage that the enemy cannot anticipate our actual operational plan, and it is likely that, based on the present extended deployment of our troops, they will concentrate their main forces (*la masse de ses forces*), totalling 160,000, in the vicinity of Warsaw, from where, by the shortest and most advantageous line of operations for them, they will begin to operate towards Brest-Litovsk, or towards Brańsk, Slonim and onwards, and by this movement, forcing VI Corps under Lieutenant General Essen to retreat, sever all communications between First Army and Second Army. To prevent the disastrous consequences that the armies would then be subject to, it is necessary to bring them closer together in the following arrangement:

I Corps, under Graf von Wittgenstein, numbering 18,000 men, is to manoeuvre around the vicinity of the city of Kovno. This corps' mission is the observation of enemy movements along the Neman and the protection of Lithuania by its positioning, as well as efforts to destroy any enemy invasion of Courland (should they decide, after crossing the Neman, to move on Libau or Mitau), operating against their lines of communication to the Neman.

First Army, consisting of II Corps, III Corps, IV Corps, V Corps, I Cavalry Corps and II Cavalry Corps, totalling 80,000 troops, is to emerge from its current locations as follows:

II Corps, having assembled at the town of Boguslavishki, in three days, is to set out via the town of Podvarishki, the town of Sumelyzhki, Dlugi, Merecz, towards Grodno, where, having arrived without rest days after nine days, makes camp.

III Corps, having assembled at the town of Troki, in two days, will take the route through Orany, Mortsikantsy, Eziori, to the village of Komotov, where, having arrived after six days, makes camp.

IV Corps, excluding 1st Jägers and 18th Jägers, quartered in Odelsk and Krynki, is to camp at Mosty, where they should arrive in five stages.

V Corps, having assembled at Vilna in six days (excluding the troops located in Oshmyany, Smorgon, Vileyka, Kurzhenets, Holszany, Dziewieniszki, Sloviansk and Valozhin, who will assemble in Oyshyshki and await the arrival of V Corps), is to set out from Vilna via Paradomin, Oyshyshki, Kamenka, to the village of Dubno, where, having arrived after seven days, makes camp.

I Cavalry Corps, having assembled in Otsiany in one day, is to set out via Wiłkomierz, Boguslavishki, Podvarishki, Dlugi towards Grodno, where it will join II Corps after 13 days.

II Cavalry Corps, having assembled at Belitsa in three days, is to set out via Zelwa to the city of Wołkowysk, where, having arrived after four days, makes camp.

Of all the camps mentioned, along the right bank of the Neman and at Wołkowysk, the entire First Army, acting, according to the estimated time, by various routes, may arrive on the appointed day in the fighting positions chosen in the Białystok Oblast.

Namely: II Corps and I Cavalry Corps from Grodno to the village of Suchowola in two stages; III Corps and V Corps from the village of Komotov and the village of Dubno to the town of Korycin in three days.

IV Corps and II Cavalry Corps from the town of Mosty and the town of Wołkowysk to the town of Wasilków in four days.

The headquarters of First Army will be in Sokółka. The above-mentioned positions, at Suchowola, Korycin and Wasilków, represent the most advantageous fighting positions, where some 40-60,000 troops may be located in each; and as the distance from Wasilków to Suchowola is not more than 45 *versts*, therefore, in order for the army to concentrate on either flank of this local line, it would take 12 hours of time; or to be in the Korycin position, as the central one, no more than six hours.

The army, having positioned its corps, is to send out strong detachments: to the Vygoda Inn near Goniądz; to the Tatars tavern, which faces Tykocin, to Choroszcz and towards Suraż. These four posts are to liaise with the Cossack outposts along the border.

VI Corps, numbering 18,000 men, having assembled around Pruzhany, is to set off via Kamieniec, Wysokie-Litewskie and Siemiatycze towards the towns of Granne and Drohiczyn, where it is to make camp, here it will form the common vanguard for both armies. From this corps, it will be necessary to detach a strong outpost to Czekanów.

Second Army, numbering 50,000 men, at the same time as the First, is to close up to the border, namely:

VII Corps and III Cavalry Corps towards the town of Siemiatycze, where they are to make camp.

VIII Corps and X Corps, to the town of Niemirów.

IX Corps and IV Cavalry Corps to the city of Brest-Litovsk.

The whole of Second Army must be able to arrive in the aforementioned locations in 15 days, not taking rest days.

The headquarters of this army will be in the town of Wysokie-Litewskie.

The Reserve Army under General of Infantry Tormasov, numbering 40,000 men, is to deploy around the city of Dubno, in order to monitor the movements of the Austrian army.

First Reserve Army, numbering 40,000 men, to the town of Borisov, on the river Berezina.

Second Reserve Army, numbering 40,000 men, to the town of Mozyr, on the river Pripet.

The locations for the latter two reserve armies are designated as temporary assembly areas, as most of the troops joining the army are arriving from various recruitment depots located in Russia. Upon the arrival of all the troops at the assembly areas, these armies must move: First Reserve Army from Borisov towards Nesvizh, while Second Reserve Army moves from Mozyr towards Davyd-Gorodok, where they are to make camp.

The aforementioned positions of the various corps of the field armies cannot remain in the selected positions except once the enemy has reached Warsaw; otherwise, being closer, the armies would be exposed to being defeated in detail. To prevent this, I intend to determine, in accordance with the changing circumstances that we may encounter, assembly areas in which, having united, we will be able to give battle to the enemy.

One must know beforehand the areas across which marches by both sides may be undertaken.

On our side, from Brest-Litovsk (that is, the local line occupied by us from the left flank to the right), to the town of Suchowola is 176 *versts*.[1] Assuming forced marches, it takes 70 hours duration to cover this distance. This case can only be assumed if we do not have any intelligence about enemy movements, and they, with combined forces, having appeared near Szczuczyn, would threaten to attack the corps located at Suchowola; to avoid this clear threat, II Corps and I Cavalry Corps must immediately join III Corps and V Corps at Korycin. The detachment at the Vygoda Inn must hold firmly and defend the defile where it is located, and thus keep the enemy from trying to cross the Biebrza river; an equal effort must be made at the Tatars Inn, as this outpost is of a similar value as the Vygoda Inn. At the same time, it should be noted that to hold these places it is not necessary to detach entire divisions, but for this mission it would be enough for 2,000 light infantry with Cossacks and several horse artillery guns.

If II Corps, III Corps and V Corps with I Cavalry Corps consider it detrimental to fight the enemy in the Korycin position, in this case, in spite of losing communications with Grodno, they should go towards the town of Wasilków and take up a strong and advantageous position there on the left bank of the marshy Suprasl river (I do not mind mentioning that there are favourable positions on both banks of the Suprasl river, but the banks are so far apart that artillery operations from one to the other can do no damage).

At the same time, the detachments at the Vygoda and Tatars taverns are to retreat by the shortest routes to Białystok, and, upon crossing the Suprasl river downstream of Wasilków, take up positions at the village of Fasty, which completely secures the left flank of the army. It is likely that, in accordance with the steps taken to unite with First Army, Second Army, having closed up, will be in communications with them and, in conjunction with its movements, can operate together with VI Corps against the enemy lines of communication.

The above case may also be applied to the left wing of our local line; if the enemy should appear with combined forces near Konstantinow, then the armies must concentrate their forces between Brest-Litovsk and Niemirów.

Points to Note: If Second Army manages to reach Wasilków by forced marches just as the enemy is threatening to attack the corps united at Korycin, in this case, the position at Sokółka would be preferable to Wasilków, as the enemy could not prevent

---

1   Any right-minded person would be surprised at this large distance of 176 *versts*; but it should be noted that the army was taking this position so as not to reveal the actual objective of its operations and, considering the enemy advance from Warsaw, to join forces at whatever point it wishes according to the circumstances.

the unification of both armies, arriving from Korycin and Wasilków, together and from this position our line of operations to Slonim would be better secured.

The shortest route leading the enemy towards our occupied local line is from Warsaw via Węgrów, Granne and Bielsk. But in order for them to reach the latter location by forced marches, including all the delays that they may encounter during this stage from water crossings and the route, it would be necessary to plan for at least 80 hours duration. We, however, need only 25 hours to unite both armies at the village of Wojszki with an unimpeded march.

There is no doubt that the enemy, if they dare to fight in this position near the village of Wyszki on the right bank of the Narew (which needs to be examined in detail), could be defeated, as we, having in our combined force, some 148,000 regular troops and 25,000 Cossacks, could deliver a proper rebuff to them at all points.

The Russians have always defeated the French in those cases where they fought them with united and combined forces, and if the French could not cross our borders in the campaign of 1806 and 1807, then it was solely that our army was united and ready to meet the enemy everywhere to thank for that fact.

The main skill on the day of battle is to preserve as strong reserves as possible. These resources would be provided by a single concentrated army. Resounding victories have been won over an enemy from the blows inflicted on them by the reserves. Should the reserves not need to take part in these actions, then, having been preserved from damage, they may pursue the disordered enemy with tireless strength, and, bringing them to a desperate state, they often decide the outcome of the war through an advantageous peace, in favour of the victor.

The line of operations that is preferred above others.
The success of an entire campaign often depends on the selection of a good line of operations. The planned position of our armies above presents to us that from the Białystok *Oblast* through Slonim, Nesvizh, Minsk, Borisov, and onwards via Smolensk to Moscow: equally from Nesvizh via Slutsk, Bobruisk, Rogachev and Chernigov.

Along this simple operational line, the army is in the closest communications with the grain-growing governorates of Russia, such as: Vitebsk, Smolensk, Mogilev, Chernigov and Kiev, from which any rations can be easily delivered to the army along the existing water communications, namely: along the Dvina from Vitebsk, Smolensk and Mogilev and the Berezina as far as the town of Borisov, from where we drag 150 *versts* to the town of Stowbtsy; from this last place down the Neman to Grodno and onwards, depending on the circumstances, to Königsberg.

The river Pripet, which flows into the Dnieper, is another route for water communications from the governorates: Mogilev, Chernigov, Kiev and Volhynia. Although transport along this river would be more difficult than along the Neman, because it must be carried by rafts or by sail, it is no less advantageous to deliver bread from Volhynia from the neighbouring cities of Ostrog and Novgrad-Volynsky, along the rivers Goryn and Sluch (which are navigable until mid-June), to the city of Pinsk; and from this place along the Yaselda, the Oginsky canal and the Shchara river to Slonim. In the event of a retreat by our army to the border of the Minsk governorate, it would be possible, if time permits, to freely transport all supplies down the Pripet to Mozyr and onwards to Kiev.

This line of operations has equal benefits, relative to the shortest communications, both for all artillery stores located in Nesvizh, Bobruisk, Kiev, Smolensk, Bryansk and the Shostensky works, and for the recruitment depots located inside Russia. Malorussia offers us the resources to remount our cavalry and artillery.

Another potential line of operations.
It should be possible to notice from the enemy's movements if they want to wage war in Volhynia, whereupon the armies, joining together near Vladimir, have a line of operations, from this place, via Lutsk, Novgrad-Volynsky, Zhitomir, towards Kiev.

Only one of the proposed lines of operation should be chosen according to the circumstances, as the Pripet River, flowing into vast swamps, is located between them and makes it difficult for an army operating along two lines of operations to interact; therefore it is necessary to avoid the chance of straddling (*sa mettre à cheval*) the Pripet River, so that the enemy, having concentrated their forces against one of the armies, and having occupied the bottleneck passing through the Pripet, Pinsk and Kovel swamps with small detachments, would not be able to defeat one of these armies through superior numbers, while the other was racing to its assistance. It may be that some would raise an objection to this, that: 'at the very time when Napoleon moves on First Army, Second Army, by crossing the Bug, can operate along his line of communications and thus cut him off from Warsaw.' What might the outcome of this be?

1. As armies in isolation, they cannot maintain rapid liaison, therefore their operations cannot simultaneously strive towards a single objective.
2. The position of the defensive army is fairly well known, which, having barely acknowledged the operations of the offensive army, finds itself already attacked everywhere.
3. Suppose that one of these armies, in order to take advantage of an opportunity, switches from defensive to offensive operations; then one can imagine that these actions will barely have started before, as always Napoleon reaches the first army with his characteristic speed and its total defeat follows.

Suppose that Second Army succeeds in cutting Napoleon off from Warsaw; this will not in the least deprive him of communications along the Vistula, as his other reserves will be in Thorn, Graudenz, Marienwerder and Danzig, besides those that he has in Königsberg and Lyk. From this it follows that Napoleon, having defeated First Army and pursuing it with part of his force, returns, reuniting with his right-hand corps, towards Second Army, and having superior numbers for a second time, he would also defeat these.

In any case, however, it should be noted that the line of operations running through Volhynia represents a greater advantage for a defensive war, which can be seen by looking at the map; as the rivers Styr, Goryn and Sluch, flowing from south to north, provide strong barriers not far from one another, behind which there are many advantageous fighting positions. In spite of this, the first line of operation I proposed is preferred for the main combined forces; along the second, the army under General Tormasov can operate at their convenience.

The line of magazines belonging to the first line of operations.
Water communications, as mentioned above, between the Pripet and the Neman, via the Oginsky canal and the Shchara river, forms a natural line of magazines that can be conveniently resupplied, and for this I propose the main magazines to be: in Mosty, in the city of Slonim, in the village of Teleshany and the city of Pinsk. These should replenish the smaller magazines in front: in Grodno, Wołkowysk, Novy Dvor, Pruzhany and Kobrin; from the same magazines will be replenished: Sokółka, Velikoy Brestovits, Białowieża and Kamieniec. From this last line of magazines, the army located in the Białystok *Oblast* may be satisfied. Of course, in addition to these, there should be large reserves: in Belitsa, Novogrudok, Nesvizh, Minsk, Borisov, Bobruisk, Mozyr and Davyd-Gorodok.

Magazines belonging to the line of operations for I Corps.
Since the most advantageous line of operations for the corps under Lieutenant General Count Wittgenstein is from Kovno, via Janau, Wiłkomierz, to Dünaburg, then there are to be magazines: the main one in Wiłkomierz; smaller ones in Poniewież, Janau and Kovno; the main artillery parks to be in Wiłkomierz and Dünaberg.

Magazines for the line of operations of General Tormasov's Reserve Army.
The main ones should be in the village of Tuchin and the town of Ostrog. These are to resupply the smaller forward magazines, namely: in Klevani, Rovno and Varkovichi. The army should be supplied by these latter. In addition to the above-mentioned magazines, there should be large reserves; in Zaslavl, Stary-Konstantinov, Novgrad-Volhynsky, Zhitomir and Kiev. The artillery parks for this army: in Tuchin, Polonne, while the main one is in Kiev.

Since in all border governorates the breed of horses is very weak, then the replenishment of the magazines should be carried out by oxen; otherwise it will be delayed.

Regarding the Army of the Danube.
We should try to end the war against the Turks, in relation to the current political circumstances, by every possible means, and the most advantageous peace for us would be that if the Ottoman Porte agreed, remaining the mediator of the impending war between Russia and France, to yield to us Khotin, Bendery and Akkerman as a pledge of the inviolability of the peace. Having these three fortresses supplied with provisions, and in case of a breach of the treaty, adding a corps of 20,000 men to this local defensive line, it should be enough to frustrate all the efforts of the enemy from this direction.

In the light of these circumstances, it should be possible from four divisions, currently constituting the Army of the Danube, to detach three to join the reserve army under General Tormasov, while the fourth is to make up garrisons for the aforementioned fortresses.

Measures to be taken in the event of the proposed plan.

1. Make a note of all the grain that exists now in Samogitia and Courland, leaving only what is necessary to feed the population, transfer the rest to Libau and

Windau, from where it is to be sent to Riga by water. From the parts adjacent to Lithuania, direct it to Kovno, Poniewież, Janau and Wiłkomierz.

2.   The existing quantity of grain in the magazines in Slonim and Pinsk should be tripled, and again, I propose that the magazines be immediately replenished from it.

3.   Send the most outstanding officers of the Quartermaster's Department and Engineers with Pioneer teams, for a military survey of the region that lies between the Neman and Pripet, giving them the subjects: inspection of all roads, crossings, defiles, fighting positions, any intermediate positions and communication roads, as well as the establishment of communications along new roads, clearings in the forests; sever and destroy those that the enemy might exploit; draw plans of all fighting positions on a large scale, with an explanation in a dedicated description of their weak and strong points and what kind of man-made defences they require. In a word, each of the commanders of the state, who has an important role, is obliged to submit their opinion in writing about an offensive and defensive war in the proposed region.

Regarding the Volhynia Governorate, they have the best maps and plans, with detailed descriptions, made by Major General Mukhin, which are currently held by Second Army. In the event of them joining First Army, it will be necessary to deliver all this information to the army under General Tormasov.

Thoughts on the use of the Cossack forces.

Since the number of Cossacks in First Army and Second Army is 25,000 fighting men, then it will be necessary to leave the minimum necessary number of them with the armies to maintain forward outposts, along with light regular cavalry. However, this number should not exceed 5,000 men. The other 20,000 men are to be divided into raiding corps, from 1,000 to 3,000 men, so that, having the mission of inflicting powerful blows to the enemy, it may also be possible to recombine them into a single strong corps. The purpose of this order is to break into enemy territory and wage partisan war in it, such as: making night attacks on troops located in quarters; intercepting transport moving up to the army; capturing their couriers; in a word, to try to do all kinds of damage. If they notice that the enemy is concentrating great forces and intends to make an attack on us, then the raiding Cossack corps should also close up to our army, always threatening the rear and flanks of the enemy. These orders will bring us many advantages: firstly, Napoleon will find himself compelled to detach a significant part of his cavalry, which will never manage to gain ascendancy over the Cossacks, as the speed of their movements will forestall the enemy in any eventuality; secondly, in order to release the prisoners taken by the enemy, it will be necessary for him to detach a much larger escort than has happened before (the second case would be to weaken oneself), and wherever the Cossacks manage to break this escort (for example in the last war against the French), thereafter, having strengthened themselves with a certain number of infantry and having disarmed the enemy, they can more boldly strive for new attacks, without losing sight of one thing – the speedy and faithful reunion with our army as before.

Appendix XI

Barclay de Tolly's Plan

This note subsequently filed by Barclay de Tolly may serve as an expression of his thoughts on a plan of action for the war of 1812.

Extract from a note by Barclay de Tolly, entitled:

'Explanation of the Military Operations by First Army and Second Army in 1812.'

The beginning of the late war and its consequences are such events that will forever remain the astonishment of the whole world. They are all the more striking in that they turned on the errors of every calculation by deep politicians, betrayed the most experienced warriors to fortune-telling and surpassed, one might say, the expectation of each and every one. It is not surprising after this that they gave birth in the light of so many different interpretations, to so many diverse conclusions and so many strange inventions! A passionate person does not always view their most fortunate events without bias, even if they happened beyond their control; what should be expected of them when they fail, deceived by hope? In this case, any person born with failings may have those failings forgiven, and therefore it would be unfair to complain about wishful thinking this time.

There is no doubt that these very reasons, these very circumstances, have caused countless judgments among the Russian people, a whole century where their land had not been trampled by enemy feet, a whole century of terrifying their enemies from every country in the world. It is also quite natural that these judgments turned, for the most part, to the censure of those persons upon whom the security of the greater good lay. Unfortunately, caution did not allow the public to anticipate either the critical situation of the fatherland, or the acceptable measures to save it. A true son of the fatherland, in this case, would rather have decided to sacrifice his reputation than to disrupt the only means to repel the truly terrible thunderstorm with a premature justification of himself before the people! The brilliant consequences of this, in its way, singular war, fully justified the aforementioned persons, and a summary of the incidents of the 1812 campaign will prove this even more truly.

As early as the beginning of 1810 it was possible to penetrate the intentions of the Emperor of the French, covetous of Russia. It soon became known that he was preparing a war for us, and a war most terrible in intent, unique in its kind, and most important in its consequences, who had decided to terrify Russia and the whole of Europe also. To avoid it, or to postpone it until some more favourable time, only one means was required: to put oneself in all possible readiness to meet force with force. Any other means were pointless. The twists and turns of politics are not enough, where armed force could solve the issue: facing a sharpened sword, one must sharpen one's sword.

Thus, the government, finding itself needing to prepare for war, proceeded to do this with amazing activity and managed, in the course of 1810 and 1811, to almost double the army; bringing the most important old fortresses into a completely defensible state, and laying out, building and arming new ones; to prepare significant reserves of all kinds, to fill arsenals with weapons, to establish many parks with live ammunition and other necessities of all kinds, and to concentrate our forces in an almost imperceptible way on the assigned locations, bringing them together from the most remote corners of the state. In a word – just four years had elapsed since the Peace of Tilsit, which put an end to the devastating war in Prussia, the war with the Swedes had barely ended, and when the ongoing war with the Turks did not even give a shadow of hope for peace – Russia had already put itself in a position to resist this new disrespect from its foe.

This readiness, although it did not stop Napoleon's intentions, intransigent regarding the treaty, it had a great influence on his orders. Seeing for himself the impossibility of struggling with us with his own forces, he had to use every effort to entice many foreign and also friendly powers to his aid. Through intrigues, threats and subversion, he managed to move the forces of all almost every mainland European power against us. Given this state of affairs, was it really possible for us to launch an offensive war? From the very start of it, among the nations already hostile to us, we would have exposed ourselves to danger both from the flanks and from the rear, with regards to provisioning we would have exposed ourselves to a most difficult situation. There was nothing more to do than to wage a defensive war, and it was thus decided in general council. But a defensive war would also be useless and even fatal for us if its objective leaned solely towards the stubborn defence of our borders. Their extent and the unexpected superiority of the enemy forces up to half a million strong, also made this impossible. Successful resistance at a single point could in no way ensure another; and the fortunate repulse of the enemy in general on our borders would only extend new threats against us in the war; as, having the Allied Powers backing him up, he would have had all the most convenient means for reinforcing himself and renewing his assault. We could not choose to have a general engagement, which often determines the end of a war at its very beginning, because in that event, having concentrated our troops at one location, we would have opened up many routes for the most numerically superior enemy to attack us from all directions, and consequently ended the matter in their favour with a single step.

It is known from the movements of the enemy army themselves that from the opening of the campaign he mainly wanted and sought a general engagement.

So, in order to save the fatherland from the impeding tempest, and at the same time put an end to the disasters that had already oppressed the greater part of the World for twenty years, it was proposed by the general council to open the campaign with a retreat, and entice the enemy into the depths of the fatherland itself, force them to pay in blood to acquire every step, every means of support and for their very existence; and finally, having exhausted their strength with as little shedding of our blood as possible, inflict a decisive blow on them. It is true that, with such a plan, the devastation of some of our provinces would have to be expected, but of the two inevitable evils, the lesser had to be chosen: it is better to sacrifice a part for a time than to kill the whole forever.

With this plan, drafted with charitable care for the welfare not only of our own, but also of other nations, as a priority, the conqueror of the Turks was instructed to speed up the conclusion of peace with them. Upon the successful completion of this, the army operating there was assigned to join with Third Army, which was holding the Volhynia Governorate. Second Army, having crossed over to the northern bank of the Pripet River, settled down near Wołkowysk. General Platov with light irregular troops formed the forward screen in Grodno and Białystok. First Army and two independent corps, that is, VI Corps and I Corps, occupied the Vilna Governorate. The reserve corps were: I Reserve Corps, commanded by Lieutenant General Saken, in Zhitomir; II Reserve Corps, under Lieutenant General Ertel, in Mozyr; III Reserve Corps, under Adjutant-General Baron Meller-Zakomelsky, near Dünaburg. The fortresses of Riga, Bobruisk and Kiev were occupied with satisfactory garrisons. Only the fortress of Dünaburg, in terms of its size and the shortness of time, was not brought to completion; but its bridgehead was already in the best condition.

The deployment of troops over such a frontage was deemed necessary for the following reasons:

1. In order to hide our real intentions from the enemy, as the positioning of our troops had the appearance of an intention to operate offensively.
2. So that the premature exposure of the border areas did not make an unfavourable impression on the minds of their population.
3. In order to retreat from the borders for a general unification within the state, to divert the forces of the enemy, to deprive them of resources for food and to exhaust them in various ways throughout the entire areas of the provinces we had to abandon.

Napoleon, looking at this deployment by our army, convinced himself of two certainties: either to cut us into pieces with his columns and, destroying each in detail, triumph over us instantly, or to force us into a premature concentration close to the border, and force us to give a general battle when his forces, almost three times ours, were still in the best condition. But the swift and firm execution of our predetermined plan disabused him of both these hopes.

Appendix XII

Russian Army Order of Battle

Detailed depiction of the Russian armies located on the western borders of the empire at the beginning of the war of 1812.

First Army
Commander-in-Chief, Minister of War, General of Infantry Barclay de Tolly.
Chief of Staff, Lieutenant General Lavrov (from 21 June [3 July] this post was held by Lieutenant General Marquis Paulucci, while from 1 [13] July Major General Yermolov became Chief of Staff).
Quartermaster General, Major General Mukhin (from 29 June [11 July] Colonel von Toll was appointed to this post).
Duty General, Major General Kikin.
Chief of Artillery, Major General Kutaisov.
Chief of Engineers, Lieutenant General Truzson [Khristian Ivanovich Truzson].
Intendant General, Active State Councillor Kankrin (on 6 [18] June the main directorate for food supply for the army was entrusted to Privy Councillor Lanskoy [Vasily Sergeevich Lanskoy]).
Field *Proviantmeister* General, 5th Class Gove.
Field *Kriegscommissar* General, Major General Petrovsky.
Field Staff Surgeon General, Collegiate Councillor Gesling (on 29 June [11 July], the main management of the medical services for both Western armies was entrusted to Chief Medical Inspector Wylie [Yakov Vasilievich Willie or James Wylie]).
Waggon-master General, Colonel Cherpanov.
Provost General, Lieutenant Colonel Stellich.
Field Post Office Director, Collegiate Assessor Kanter.
Commandant of the Headquarters, Colonel Stavrakov.

I Corps
General Officer Commanding, Lieutenant General Count Wittgenstein.
Chief of Staff, Major General d'Auvray.
Over Quartermaster, Colonel Rennie.
Duty Field Officer, Colonel Baron Diebitsch.
Chief of Artillery, Major General Prince Iashvili.
Chief of Engineers, Colonel Count Sievers.

5th Infantry Division: Major General Berg.

Formation Commander	Units	Size
Major General Kazachkovsky (ordered on 2 [14] July to command the brigade of combined battalions from I Corps).	Sevsk Infantry	2 Bns
	Kaluga Infantry	2 Bns
Major General Prince Sibirsky	Perm Infantry	2 Bns
	Mogilev Infantry	2 Bns
Colonel Frolov	23rd Jägers	2 Bns
	24th Jägers	2 Bns
	Combined grenadiers	2 Bns
Lieutenant Colonel Muruzi	5th Battery Artillery	1 Coy
	9th Light Artillery	1 Coy
	10th Light Artillery	1 Coy

14th Infantry Division: Major General Sazonov.

Formation Commander	Units	Size
Colonel Harpe	Tula Infantry	2 Bns
	Navaginsk Infantry	2 Bns
Colonel Helffreich	Tenginsk Infantry	2 Bns
	Estland Infantry	2 Bns
Colonel Denisiev	25th Jägers	2 Bns
	26th Jägers	2 Bns
	Combined grenadiers	2 Bns
Colonel Staden	14th Battery Artillery	1 Coy
	26th Light Artillery	1 Coy
	27th Light Artillery	1 Coy

1st Cavalry Division: Major General Kakhovsky.

Formation Commander	Units	Size
Major General Balk	Riga Dragoons	4 Sqns
	Yamburg Dragoons	4 Sqns
Major General Kulnev	Grodno Hussars	8 Sqns

1st Reserve Artillery Brigade

Formation Commander	Units	Size
[Major General Prince Iashvili]	27th Battery Artillery	1 Coy
	1st Horse Artillery	1 Coy
	3rd Horse Artillery	1 Coy
	Pontoniers	2 Coys
	Pioneers	1 Coy

Don Cossack Regiments.

Formation Commander	Units	Size
	Rodionov's	1 Regt
	Platov's 4th	1 Regt
	Selivanov's	1 Regt

Total for I Corps: 28 battalions, 16 squadrons, three Cossack regiments, nine artillery companies, two pontonier companies and one pioneer company.

II Corps.
General Officer Commanding, Lieutenant General Baggovut.

4th Infantry Division: Major General Prinz Eugen von Württemberg.

Formation Commander	Units	Size
Major General Rossi [Ignatius Petrovich Rossi]	Tobolsk Infantry	2 Bns
	Volhynia Infantry	2 Bns
Major General Pyshnitsky [Dmitry Ilych Pyshnitsky]	Kremenchug Infantry	2 Bns
	Minsk Infantry	2 Bns
Colonel Pillar [Yegor Maksimovich Pillar]	4th Jägers	2 Bns
	34th Jägers	2 Bns
Colonel Voeikov	4th Battery Artillery	1 Coy
	7th Light Artillery	1 Coy
	8th Light Artillery	1 Coy

17th Infantry Division: Lieutenant General Olsufiev.

Formation Commander	Units	Size
Major General Count Ivelich [Pëtr Ivanovich Ivelich]	Ryazan Infantry	2 Bns
	Brest Infantry	2 Bns
Major General Tuchkov 3rd	Belozersk Infantry	2 Bns
	Vilmanstrand Infantry	2 Bns
Colonel Potëmkin [Yakov Alekseevich Potëmkin]	30th Jägers	2 Bns
	48th Jägers	2 Bns
Colonel Dietrichs 2nd [Ivan Ivanovich Dieteriks]	17th Battery Artillery	1 Coy
	32nd Light Artillery	1 Coy
	33rd Light Artillery	1 Coy
Major General Vsevolozhsky	Yelisavetgrad Hussars	8 Sqns
	4th Horse Artillery	1 Coy

Total for II Corps: 24 battalions, eight squadrons and seven artillery companies.

III Corps
General Officer Commanding, Lieutenant General Tuchkov 1st.

1st Grenadier Division: Major General Count Stroganov.

Formation Commander	Units	Size
Colonel Zheltukhin	Leib Grenadiers	2 Bns
	Count Arakcheev's Grenadiers	2 Bns
Major General Tsvilenev	Pavlov Grenadiers	2 Bns
	Yekaterinoslav Grenadiers	2 Bns
Major General Foch 1st [Boris Borisovich Fok]	St Petersburg Grenadiers	2 Bns
	Tauride Grenadiers	2 Bns
Colonel [V.A.] Glukhov	1st Battery Artillery	1 Coy
	1st Light Artillery	1 Coy
	2nd Light Artillery	1 Coy

3rd Infantry Division: Lieutenant General Konovnitsyn.

Formation Commander	Units	Size
Major General Tuchkov 4th	Murom Infantry	2 Bns
	Reval Infantry	2 Bns
Colonel Voeikov [in other sources; Ivan Mikhailovich Ushakov]	Chernigov Infantry	2 Bns
	Koporye Infantry	2 Bns
Major General Prince Shakhovskoy	20th Jägers	2 Bns
	21st Jägers	2 Bns
Colonel Tornov [Fëdor Grigorievich Tornov?]	3rd Battery Artillery	1 Coy
	5th Light Artillery	1 Coy
	6th Light Artillery	1 Coy
	Lifeguard Cossacks[1]	4 Sqns
	1st Teptyar Cossacks	1 Regt
Detachment from 1st Reserve Artillery Brigade	2nd Horse Artillery	1 Coy

Total for III Corps: 24 battalions, four squadrons, one Cossack regiment and seven artillery companies.

IV Corps
General Officer Commanding, Lieutenant General Count Shuvalov (by Supreme Command, on 1 [13] July, Lieutenant General Count Osterman-Tolstoy was appointed in his place).

---

1   In addition; the Lifeguard Black Sea *sotnia*.

11th Infantry Division: Major General Bakhmetiev 2nd.

Formation Commander	Units	Size
Major General Choglokov	Kexholm Infantry	2 Bns
	Pernov Infantry	2 Bns
Major General Filisov	Polotsk Infantry	2 Bns
	Yelets Infantry	2 Bns
Colonel Bistrom 1st [Adam Ivanovich Bistrom]	1st Jägers	2 Bns
	33rd Jägers	2 Bns
Colonel [A.] Kotlyarov	11th Battery Artillery	1 Coy
	3rd Light Artillery	1 Coy
	4th Light Artillery	1 Coy

23rd Infantry Division: Major General Bakhmetiev 1st.

Formation Commander	Units	Size
Major General Okulov	Rylsk Infantry	2 Bns
	Yekaterinburg Infantry	2 Bns
Major General Aleksopol [Fëdor Panteleimonovich Aleksopol]	Selenginsk Infantry	2 Bns
	18th Jägers	2 Bns
	Combined grenadiers[2]	3 Bns
Major General Dorokhov	Izyum Hussars	8 Sqns
Lieutenant Colonel [L.L.] Gulevich	23rd Battery Artillery	1 Coy
	43rd Light Artillery	1 Coy
	44th Light Artillery	1 Coy

Total for IV Corps: 23 battalions, eight squadrons, six artillery companies.

V Corps

General Officer Commanding, His Imperial Highness, Grand Duke Konstantin Pavlovich.

Lifeguard Infantry Division: Major General Yermolov (by Supreme Command of 1 [13] July, Count Shuvalov replaced him, and was replaced in turn on 23 July [4 August] by Lieutenant General Lavrov).

Formation Commander	Units	Size
Major General Baron Rosen [Grigory Vladimirovich Rosen]	Lifeguard Preobrazhensky	3 Bns
	Lifeguard Semenovsky	3 Bns
Colonel Udom [Ivan Fëdorovich Udom]	Lifeguard Izmailovsky	3 Bns
	Lifeguard Lithuania	3 Bns

---

2   From 11th Division and 23rd Division.

Colonel Bistrom 3rd [Karl Ivanovich Bistrom]	Lifeguard Jägers	3 Bns
	Lifeguard Finland	3 Bns
	Lifeguard Marines	1 Bn

Two battery artillery companies, two light artillery companies, two horse artillery batteries, with two guns attached to the Lifeguard Marines.

1st Combined Grenadier Division.

Formation Commander	Units	Size
	Combined grenadiers[3]	7 Bns
	Pioneers	1 Coy

1st Cuirassier Division: Lieutenant General Depreradovich.

Formation Commander	Units	Size
Major General Shevich	Chevalier Guard	4 Sqns
	Lifeguard Horse	4 Sqns
Major General Borozdin 2nd [Nikolai Mikhailovich Borozdin]	His Majesty's Cuirassiers	4 Sqns
	Her Majesty's Cuirassiers	4 Sqns
	Astrakhan Cuirassiers	4 Sqns

Total for V Corps: 26 battalions, 20 squadrons, four artillery companies, one pioneer company, two horse artillery batteries.

VI Corps
General Officer Commanding, General of Infantry Dokhturov.

7th Infantry Division: Lieutenant General Kaptsevich.

Formation Commander	Units	Size
Colonel Lyapunov [Dmitry Petrovich Lyapunov]	Moscow Infantry	2 Bns
	Pskov Infantry	2 Bns
Major General Count Balmain [Karl Antonovich Balmen]	Libau Infantry	2 Bns
	Sofia Infantry	2 Bns
Major General Balla	11th Jägers	2 Bns
	36th Jägers	2 Bns
Lieutenant Colonel Devel [Daniil Fëdorovich Devel]	7th Battery Artillery	1 Coy
	12th Light Artillery	1 Coy
	13th Light Artillery	1 Coy

---

3   From 1st Grenadier Division, 3rd Division, 4th Division and 17th Division.

24th Infantry Division: Major General Likhachev.

Formation Commander	Units	Size
Major General Tsybulsky [Ivan Denisovich Tsybulsky]	Ufa Infantry	2 Bns
	Shirvan Infantry	2 Bns
Colonel Denisiev [Pëtr Vasilievich Denisiev]	Butyrsk Infantry	2 Bns
	Tomsk Infantry	2 Bns
Colonel Vuich [Nikolai Vasilievich Vuich]	19th Jägers	2 Bns
	40th Jägers	2 Bns
	Sumy Hussars	8 Sqns
Colonel [I.G.] Yefremov	24th Battery Artillery	1 Coy
	45th Light Artillery	1 Coy
	46th Light Artillery	1 Coy
	7th Horse Artillery	1 Coy

Total for VI Corps: 24 battalions, eight squadrons, seven artillery companies.

I Cavalry Corps
General Officer Commanding, Adjutant General Uvarov.

Formation Commander	Units	Size
Major General Chalikov	Lifeguard Hussars	4 Sqns
	Lifeguard Ulans	4 Sqns
	Lifeguard Dragoons	4 Sqns
Major General Chernysh	Nezhin Dragoons	4 Sqns
	Kazan Dragoons	4 Sqns
	5th Horse Artillery	1 Coy

Total for I Cavalry Corps: 20 squadrons, one artillery company.

II Cavalry Corps.
General Officer Commanding, Adjutant General Baron Korf.

Formation Commander	Units	Size
Colonel Davydov	Pskov Dragoons	4 Sqns
	Moscow Dragoons	4 Sqns
Major General Panchulidzev 2nd	Kargopol Dragoons	4 Sqns
	Ingermanland Dragoons	4 Sqns
	Poland Ulans	8 Sqns
	6th Horse Artillery	1 Coy

Total for II Cavalry Corps: 24 squadrons, one artillery company.

III Cavalry Corps.

General Officer Commanding, Major General Count Pahlen.

Formation Commander	Units	Size
Major General Skalon	Irkutsk Dragoons	4 Sqns
	Siberia Dragoons	4 Sqns
Colonel Klebeck	Orenburg Dragoons	4 Sqns
	Courland Dragoons	4 Sqns
	Mariupol Hussars	8 Sqns
	9th Horse Artillery	1 Coy

Total for III Cavalry Corps: 24 squadrons, one artillery company.

Light Troops.

General Officer Commanding, General of Cavalry, *Ataman* of the Don Host, Platov.

Formation Commander	Units	Size
	Don Cossacks	8 Regts
	Bug Cossacks	2 Regts
	Bashkir Cossacks	1 Regt
	Mounted Tatars	2 Regts
	Stavropol Kalmyks	1 Regt
	Don Cossack Horse Artillery	1 Coy

Grand total for the First Army: 149 battalions, 132 squadrons, 18 Cossack regiments, 49 artillery companies (16 battery, 22 light, 11 horse), two pioneer companies and two pontonier companies.

Second Army.

Commander in Chief, General of Infantry, Prince Bagration.
Chief of Staff, Major General Comte Saint-Priest.
Quartermaster General, Major General Vistitsky.
Duty General, *Flügel-Adjutant* Colonel Marin [Sergei Nikiforovich Marin].
Chief of Artillery, Major General Baron Löwenstern [Karl Fëdorovich Levenshtern].
Chief of Engineers, Major General Förster [Yegor Khristianovich Ferster].
Intendant General, Privy Councillor Lanskoy.
Field *Proviantmeister* General, 6th Class Dombrovsky.
Field Intendant General, 6th Class Bibikov.
Commandant of the Headquarters, Colonel Yuzefovich.

VII Corps.

General Officer Commanding, Lieutenant General Raevsky.

26th Infantry Division: Major General Paskevich.

Formation Commander	Units	Size
Colonel Liebhardt [Anton Ivanovich Lipgart]	Ladoga Infantry	2 Bns
	Poltava Infantry	2 Bns
Colonel Savoini [Yeremey Yakovlevich Savoini]	Nizhegorod Infantry	2 Bns
	Orël Infantry	2 Bns
Colonel Gogel 1st	5th Jägers	2 Bns
	42nd Jägers	2 Bns
Lieutenant Colonel [G.M.] Schulmann 2nd	26th Battery Artillery	1 Coy
	47th Light Artillery	1 Coy
	48th Light Artillery	1 Coy

12th Infantry Division: Major General Kolyubakin.

Formation Commander	Units	Size
Colonel Ryleev [Mikhail Nikolaevich Ryleev]	Narva Infantry	2 Bns
	Smolensk Infantry	2 Bns
Colonel Panzerbiter [Karl Karlovich Panzerbiter or Karl Friedrich Panzerbiter]	Novoingermanland Infantry	2 Bns
	Alexopol Infantry	2 Bns
Major General Palitsyn [Ivan Ivanovich Palitsyn]	6th Jägers	2 Bns
	41st Jägers	2 Bns
Major General Vasilchikov	Akhturka Hussars	8 Sqns
Lieutenant Colonel [Ya.I.] Sablin	12th Battery Artillery	1 Coy
	22nd Light Artillery	1 Coy
	23rd Light Artillery	1 Coy
	8th Horse Artillery	1 Coy

Total for VII Corps: 24 battalions, eight squadrons, seven artillery companies.

VIII Corps.
General Officer Commanding, Lieutenant General Borozdin 1st.

2nd Grenadier Division: Major General Prinz Karl von Mecklenburg-Schwerin.

Formation Commander	Units	Size
Colonel Shatilov [Ivan Yakovlevich Shatilov]	Kiev Grenadiers	2 Bns
	Moscow Grenadiers	2 Bns
Colonel Buxhoeveden [Ivan Filippovich Buksgevden or Johann Friedrich von Buxhoeveden]	Astrakhan Grenadiers	2 Bns
	Fanagoria Grenadiers	2 Bns
Colonel Hesse [Vladimir Antonovich Hesse]	Siberia Grenadiers	2 Bns
	Malorussia Grenadiers	2 Bns

Colonel Boguslavsky [Alexander Andreevich Boguslavsky]	2nd Battery Artillery	1 Coy
	20th Light Artillery	1 Coy
	21st Light Artillery	1 Coy

Combined Grenadier Division: Major General Count Vorontsov.

Formation Commander	Units	Size
	Combined grenadiers[4]	4 Bns
	Combined grenadiers[5]	6 Bns
	31st Battery Artillery	1 Coy
	32nd Battery Artillery	1 Coy

2nd Cuirassier Division: Major General Knorring.

Formation Commander	Units	Size
Major General Kretov [Nikolai Vasilievich Kretov]	Military Order Cuirassiers	4 Sqns
	Yekaterinoslav Cuirassiers	4 Sqns
Major General Duka [Ilya Mikhailovich Duka]	Glukhov Cuirassiers	4 Sqns
	Malorussia Cuirassiers	4 Sqns
	Novgorod Cuirassiers	4 Sqns

Total for VIII Corps: 22 battalions, 20 squadrons, five artillery companies.

IV Cavalry Corps.
General Officer Commanding, Major General Count Sievers.

Formation Commander	Units	Size
Major General Panchulidzev 1st	Kharkov Dragoons	4 Sqns
	Chernigov Dragoons	4 Sqns
Colonel Emmanuel	Kiev Dragoons	4 Sqns
	Novorossia Dragoons	4 Sqns
	Lithuania Ulans	8 Sqns
	10th Horse Artillery	1 Coy
	Pontoniers	1 Coy
	Pioneers	1 Coy

Total for IV Cavalry Corps: 24 squadrons, one artillery company, one pontonier company and one pioneer company.

---

4   From 7th Division and 24th Division.
5   From 2nd Grenadier Division, 12th Division and 26th Division.

Light Troops.
General Officer Commanding, Major General Ilovaisky 5th.

Formation Commander	Units	Size
	Don Cossacks	8 Regts
	Bug Cossacks	1 Regt
	Don Cossack Horse Artillery	1 Coy

Grand total for Second Army: 46 battalions, 52 squadrons, nine Cossack regiments, 18 artillery companies, one pontonier company and one pioneer company.
In addition, the following were moving up to join this army:

27th Infantry Division: Lieutenant General Neverovsky.

Formation Commander	Units	Size
Major General Knyazhnin 1st [Alexander Yakovlevich Knyazhnin?]	Vilna Infantry	2 Bns
	Siberia Infantry	2 Bns
Colonel Stavitsky [Maxim Fëdorovich Stavitsky]	Odessa Infantry	2 Bns
	Tarnopol Infantry	2 Bns
Flügel-Adjutant Colonel Voeikov [Alexei Vasilievich Voeikov]	49th Jägers	2 Bns
	50th Jägers	2 Bns

Third Army of Observation.
Commander in Chief, General of Cavalry Tormasov.
Chief of Staff, Major General Inzov [Ivan Nikitich Inzov].
Quartermaster General, Major General Rennie [Roman Yegorovich Renni or Robert Rennie].
Chief of Artillery, Major General Sievers [Ivan Khristianovich Sivers or Georg Joachim Johann Graf von Sievers].

General of Infantry Count Kamensky's Corps.

18th Infantry Division: Major General Prince Shcherbatov.

Formation Commander	Units	Size
Major General Benardos	Tambov Infantry	2 Bns
	Vladimir Infantry	2 Bns
Major General Prince Khovansky	Dnieper Infantry	2 Bns
	Kostroma Infantry	2 Bns
Major General Meshcherinov [Vasily Dmitrievich Meshcherinov]	28th Jägers	2 Bns
	32nd Jägers	2 Bns
[Lev Korneevich (Kornilievich) Pashchenko]	18th Battery Artillery	1 Coy
	34th Light Artillery	1 Coy
	35th Light Artillery	1 Coy

	Combined grenadiers[6]	6 Bns
Major General Chaplits	Pavlograd Hussars	8 Sqns
	11th Horse Artillery	1 Coy

Total for Kamensky's Corps: 18 battalions, eight squadrons, four artillery companies.

Lieutenant General Markov's Corps.

15th Infantry Division: Major General Nazimov.

Formation Commander	Units	Size
Major General Stepanov [Alexei Yakovlevich Stepanov]	Kozlov Infantry	2 Bns
	Vitebsk Infantry	2 Bns
Colonel Oldekop [Karl Fëdorovich Oldekop]	Kura Infantry	2 Bns
	Kolyvan Infantry	2 Bns
Major General Prince Vyazemsky [Vasily Vasilievich Vyazemsky]	13th Jägers	2 Bns
	14th Jägers	2 Bns
[Alexander Dmitrievich Zasyadko]	15th Battery Artillery	1 Coy
	28th Light Artillery	1 Coy
	29th Light Artillery	1 Coy

9th Infantry Division: Major General Udom.

Formation Commander	Units	Size
Colonel Reichel [Abram Abramovich Reichel]	Ryazhsk Infantry	2 Bns
	Apsheron Infantry	2 Bns
Colonel Seliverstov [Alexei Matveevich Seliverstov]	Nasheburg Infantry	2 Bns
	Yakutsk Infantry	2 Bns
Colonel Krasovsky	10th Jägers	2 Bns
	38th Jägers	2 Bns
	9th Battery Artillery	1 Coy
	16th Light Artillery	1 Coy
	17th Light Artillery	1 Coy
Colonel Prince Madatov	Alexandria Hussars	8 Sqns
	12th Horse Artillery	1 Coy

Total for Markov's Corps: 24 battalions, eight squadrons, seven artillery companies.

---

6   From 9th Division, 15th Division and 18th Division.

Lieutenant General Baron Saken's Corps

36th Infantry Division: Major General Sorokin.

Formation Commander	Units	Size
[Lieutenant Colonel Khristoforov]	Replacement battalions[7]	6 Bns
[Lieutenant Colonel Protopopov]	Replacement battalions[8]	6 Bns

11th Cavalry Division: [Major General Melissino].

Formation Commander	Units	Size
[Lieutenant Colonel Krasovsky]	Replacement squadrons[9]	4 Sqns
	Replacement squadrons[10]	8 Sqns
[Lieutenant Colonel Cherepov 2nd]	Replacement squadrons[11]	4 Sqns
Major General Melissino	Lubny Hussars	8 Sqns
	13th Horse Artillery	1 Coy
	33rd Battery Artillery	1 Coy

Total for Saken's Corps: 12 battalions, 24 squadrons, two artillery companies.

Major General Comte Lambert's Cavalry Corps.

Formation Commander	Units	Size
Major General Berdyaev	Starodub Dragoons	4 Sqns
	Tver Dragoons	4 Sqns
Major General Khrushchev	Zhitomir Dragoons	4 Sqns
	Arzamas Dragoons	4 Sqns
Colonel Knorring	Tatar Ulans	8 Sqns
Major General Chaplits	Vladimir Dragoons	4 Sqns
	Taganrog Dragoons	4 Sqns
	Serpukhov Dragoons	4 Sqns

Total for Lambert's Cavalry Corps: 36 squadrons.

---

7   From 15th Division.
8   From 18th Division.
9   From 4th Cavalry Division [combined dragoons].
10   From 5th Cavalry Division [combined dragoons and combined light cavalry]
11   From 2nd Cuirassier Division.

Light Troops.

Formation Commander	Units	Size
	Don Cossacks	5 Regts
	Bashkir Cossacks	1 Regt
	Mounted Tatars	2 Regts
	Kalmuk Cossacks	1 Regt

Reserve Artillery

Formation Commander	Units	Size
	34th Battery Artillery	1 Coy
	Pontoniers	1 Coy
	Pioneers	1 Coy

Grand total for Third Army of Observation: 54 battalions, 76 squadrons, nine Cossack regiments, 14 artillery companies (with 164 guns), one pontonier company and one pioneer company.

Appendix XIII

Grande Armée Order of Battle

The *Grande Armée* order of battle featured in the works by Chambray and Buturlin. This order of battle was captured from the French during their retreat from Russia:

Detailed depiction of Napoleon's army at the opening of the 1812 war.

Major général, Marshal Berthier, prince de Neuchâtel.

Réserve de cavalerie, Murat, King of Naples.

Etat-major de l'Artillerie, comte de Lariboisière [Jean Ambroise Baston de Lariboisière].

Etat-major du Génie, marquis de Chasseloup [François Charles Louis de Chasseloup-Laubat].

Commandant en chef des équipages de pont, baron Éblé.

Le service topographique, comte Sanson [Nicolas Antoine Sanson].

Intendant Général, Dumas (Mathieu Dumas).

Aide-major-général, Comte Monthion [François Gédéon Bailly de Monthion].

Grand prévôt de l'armée, Comte Lauer [Jean-Baptiste Lauer].

Grand écuyer Baron Caulaincourt.

Staff at Napoleon's Imperial Headquarters numbered around 4,000 men.

Garde impériale

Jeune Garde: Marshal Mortier Duc de Trévise.

Formation Commander	Units	Size
1er Division de la Jeune Garde Comte Delaborde	*1er Voltigeurs de la Garde*	2 Bns
	1er Tirailleurs de la Garde	2 Bns
	Flanqueurs de la Garde	6 Bns
	Bataillon de Neuchâtel	1 Bn
	Hesse-Darmstadt	6 Bns
2e Division de la Jeune Garde Baron Curial [Philibert Jean-Baptiste Curial]	*4e, 5e, 6e Voltigeurs de la Garde*	6 Bns
	4e, 5e, 6e Tirailleurs de la Garde	6 Bns

Vieille Garde: Marshal Lefebvre, Duc de Dantzig.

Formation Commander	Units	Size
Comte Dorsenne [*sic*]	*Grenadiers à pied de la Garde*	6 Bns
	Chasseurs à pied de la Garde	4 Bns

Cavalerie de la Garde: Marshal Bessières, Duc d'Istrie.

Formation Commander	Units	Size
Division comte Walther [Frédéric Henri Walther]	*Grenadiers à cheval de la Garde*	4 Sqns
	Dragons de la Garde	4 Sqns
	Chasseurs à cheval de la Garde	4 Sqns
	Lanciers polonais de la Garde	4 Sqns
	Mamelouks de la Garde	1 Sqn
	1er chevau-légers lanciers	4 Sqns
	2e Lanciers de la Garde	4 Sqns
	Gendarmerie d'élite	2 Sqns
	Chasseurs à cheval portugais	3 Sqns
Division Claparède	*Légion de la Vistule*	12 Bns
	Veliti della Guardia Reale Italiana	2 Bns
	Pionniers espagnols	1 Bn
	7 Pułk Ułanów	4 Sqns
	Gardes d'honneur	1 Sqn

Total for the *Garde impériale*: 54 battalions, 35 squadrons, numbering 47,000 men.

1er Corps: Davout, Prince d'Eckmühl.

Formation Commander	Units	Size
1er Division, comte Morand	*13th Légère*	5 Bns
	17th Ligne	5 Bns
	30th Ligne	5 Bns
	2. Infanterieregiment (Baden)	2 Bns
2e Division, comte Friant	*33e Ligne*	5 Bns
	48e Ligne	5 Bns
	Regimiento de José Napoleón	2 Bns
3e Division, comte Gudin	*7e Légère*	5 Bns
	12e Ligne	5 Bns
	21e Ligne & 127e Ligne	8 Bns
4e Division, Dessaix	*33e Légère*	3 Bns
	85e Ligne & 108e Ligne	10 Bns
5e Division, comte Compans	*25e Ligne & 57e Ligne*	10 Bns
	61e Ligne & 111e Ligne	10 Bns
	Infanterieregiment (Mecklenburg)	3 Bns
1er Brigade de cavalerie légère	*2e Chasseurs à cheval*	4 Sqns
2e Brigade de cavalerie légère, Girardin [sic]	*9 Pułk Ułanów*	4 Sqns
	1er Chasseurs à cheval	4 Sqns
	3e Chasseurs à cheval	4 Sqns

Total for *1er Corps*: 88 battalions, 16 squadrons, numbering 72,000 men.

2e Corps: Oudinot, Duc de Reggio.

Formation Commander	Units	Size
6e Division, comte Legrand	*29e Légère*	4 Bns
	19e Ligne & 56e Ligne	8 Bns
	128e Ligne	3 Bns
	3 regimento de infantaria portugueses	2 Bns
8e Division, comte Verdier	*11e Légère*	4 Bns
	2e Ligne	4 Bns
	37e Ligne & 124e Ligne	7 Bns
9e Division, baron Merle	*3e Régiment croates*	4 Bns
	1er régiment suisse & 2e régiment suisse	6 Bns
	3e régiment suisse & 4e régiment suisse	6 Bns
	123e Ligne	3 Bns
5e Brigade de cavalerie légère, Castex	*7e Chasseurs à cheval*	4 Sqns
	23e Chasseurs à cheval	4 Sqns
	24e Chasseurs à cheval	4 Sqns
6e Brigade de cavalerie légère, Corbineau	*20e Chasseurs à cheval*	4 Sqns
	8 Pułk Ułanów	4 Sqns

Total for *2e Corps*: 51 battalions, 20 squadrons, numbering 37,000 men.

3e Corps, Ney, Duc d'Elchingen.

Formation Commander	Units	Size
10e Division, baron Ledru	*24e Légère*	4 Bns
	46e Ligne, 72e Ligne & 129e Ligne	11 Bns
	1 regimento de infantaria portugueses	2 Bns
11e Division, baron Razout	*4e Ligne, 18e Ligne & 93e Ligne*	12 Bns
	Régiment d'Illyrie	3 Bns
	2 regimento de infantaria portugueses	2 Bns
25e Division (Württemberg), Marchand	*1. Infanterieregiment*	2 Bns
	2. Infanterieregiment	2 Bns
	4. Infanterieregiment	2 Bns
	6. Infanterieregiment	2 Bns
	7. Infanterieregiment	2 Bns
	Württemberg Jäger	4 Bns
Division de cavalerie légère, Wohlwart [sic]	*11e Hussards*	4 Sqns
	6e Chevau-légers lanciers	4 Sqns

	4e Chasseurs à cheval	4 Sqns
	1. Chevauxleger-Regiment Heinrich	4 Sqns
	2. Leib-Chevauxleger-Regiment	4 Sqns
	4. Jäger-Regiment zu Pferde König	4 Sqns

Total for *3e Corps*: 48 battalions, 24 squadrons, numbering 40,000 men.

4e Corps: Viceroy of Italy.

Formation Commander	Units	Size
Guardia Reale Italiana, Lechi	Guardie d'onore & Veliti della Guardia	2 Bns
	Granatieri & Cacciatori della Guardia	3 Bns
	Dragoni della Guardia	4 Sqns
	Dragoni Regina	4 Sqns
13e Division, baron Delzons	8e Légère	4 Bns
	1er Régiment croates	3 Bns
	84e Ligne, 92e Ligne & 106e Ligne	12 Bns
14e Division, comte Broussier	18e Légère	4 Bns
	Regimiento de José Napoleón	2 Bns
	9e Ligne, 35e Ligne & 53e Ligne	12 Bns
15ª Divisione, Pino	1º Leggero & 3º Leggero italiano	6 Bns
	2o Linea & 3o Linea italiano	6 Bns
	Reggimento Dalmata	3 Bns
Division de cavalerie légère, d'Ornano	9e Chasseurs à cheval	4 Sqns
	19e Chasseurs à cheval	4 Sqns
	2o Cacciatori a cavallo Italiano	4 Sqns
	3o Cacciatori a cavallo Italiano	4 Sqns

Total for *4e Corps*: 57 battalions, 24 squadrons, numbering 45,000 men.

5e Corps: Prince Poniatowski.

Formation Commander	Units	Size
16e Division, Zajączek	11 Pułk Piechoty & 13 Pułk Piechoty	8 Bns
	15 Pułk Piechoty & 16 Pułk Piechoty	8 Bns
17e Division, Dąbrowski	1 Pułk Piechoty & 17 Pułk Piechoty	8 Bns
	6 Pułk Piechoty & 14 Pułk Piechoty	8 Bns
18e Division, General Knyazhevich [sic]	2 Pułk Piechoty & 8 Pułk Piechoty	8 Bns
	12 Pułk Piechoty	4 Bns
Division de cavalerie légère, General Kamieński	4 Pułk Strzelców Konnych	4 Sqns
	1 Pułk Strzelców Konnych	4 Sqns
	12 Pułk Ułanów	4 Sqns
	5 Pułk Strzelców Konnych	4 Sqns
	13 Pułk Huzarów	4 Sqns

Total for *5e Corps*: 44 battalions, 20 squadrons, numbering 36,000 men.

6e Corps: Gouvion Saint-Cyr.

Formation Commander	Units	Size
19e Division, (Bavarian) General Deroy	*1. Infanterie, 2. Infanterie & 3. Infanterie*	6 Bns
	4. Infanterie, 5. Infanterie & 6. Infanterie	6 Bns
	Leichte Infanterie	3 Bns
20e Division, (Bavarian) Graf Wrede	*7. Infanterie, 8. Infanterie & 9. Infanterie*	6 Bns
	10. Infanterie & 11. Infanterie	4 Bns
	Leichte Infanterie	3 Bns
Cavalerie légère, (Bavarian) Graf Seydewitz [Curt Friedrich August von Seydewitz][1]	*3. Chevaulegers & 6. Chevaulegers*	8 Sqns
Cavalerie légère, (Bavarian) Graf Preysing[2]	*4. Chevaulegers & 5. Chevaulegers*	8 Sqns

Total for *6e Corps*: 28 battalions. 16 squadrons, numbering 25,000 men.

7e Corps: comte Reynier.

Formation Commander	Units	Size
21e Division, (Saxon) Lieutenant General Lecoq [Karl Christian Erdmann von Le Coq]	*Grenadierregiment von Liebenau*	1 Bn
	Infanterieregiment Prinz Friedrich	2 Bns
	Infanterieregiment Prinz Clemens	2 Bns
	Infanterieregiment Prinz Anton	2 Bns
	1. Regiment Leichte Infanterie	2 Bns
22e Division, (Saxon) Lieutenant General Gutschmidt [*sic*]	*Grenadierregiment von Brause*	1 Bn
	Infanterieregiment König	2 Bns
	Infanterieregiment Niesemeuschel	2 Bns
	Grenadierregiment von Anger	1 Bn
	Grenadierregiment von Spiegel	1 Bn
	2. Regiment Leichte Infanterie	2 Bns
Leichten Kavalleriebrigade, (Saxon) Lieutenant General Funck [*sic*]	*Chevauxlegerregiment Prinz Clemens*	4 Sqns
	Chevauxlegerregiment von Polenz	4 Sqns
	Husarenregiment	8 Sqns

Total for *7e Corps*: 18 battalions, 16 squadrons, numbering 17,000 men.

---

1   Attached to *4e Corps*.
2   Attached to *4e Corps*.

8e Corps: Initially under General Vandamme, then Tharreau and finally Marshal Junot, Duc d'Abrantes.

Formation Commander	Units	Size
23e Division, (Westphalian) baron Tharreau	*Leichte Infanterie*	3 Bns
	2. Infanterieregiment	2 Bns
	5. Infanterieregiment	2 Bns
	6. Infanterieregiment	2 Bns
24e Division, (Westphalian) General Ochs	*Grenadier-Garde*	1 Bn
	Carabinier-Garde & Jäger-Garde	2 Bns
	7. Infanterieregiment	2 Bns
	8. Infanterieregiment	2 Bns
General von Hammerstein	*1. Husaren-Regiment*	4 Sqns
	2. Husaren-Regiment	4 Sqns
Colonel Wolff	*chevauleger-Garde*	4 Sqns

Total for *8e Corps*: 16 battalions and 12 squadrons, numbering 18,000 men.

9e Corps: Victor, Duc de Bellune.

Formation Commander	Units	Size
12e Division, comte Partouneaux	*Régiment provisoire & 44e Ligne*	7 Bns
	125e Ligne & 126e Ligne	6 Bns
	10e Légère & 29e Légère	8 Bns
26e Division, (Berg & Baden) General Daendels	*1er Régiment & 2e Régiment de Berg*	4 Bns
	3e Régiment & 4e Régiment de Berg	4 Bns
	Linien-Regiments Nr. 1 (Baden)	2 Bns
	Linien-Regiments Nr. 2 (Baden)	2 Bns
	Leichte Infanteriebataillon (Baden)	1 Bn
28e Division, baron Girard	*4 Pułk Piechoty*	4 Bns
	7 Pułk Piechoty	4 Bns
	9 Pułk Piechoty	4 Bns
	Infanterieregiment von Low (Saxon)	2 Bns
	Infanterieregiment von Rechten (Saxon)	2 Bns
	4. Infanterieregiment (Westphalian)	2 Bns
	Füsiliere (Hesse-Darmstadt)	2 Bns
Cavalerie, Delaitre [Antoine Charles Bernard Delaitre]	*Chevau-légers de Berg*	4 Sqns
	chevauleger (Hesse-Darmstadt)	4 Sqns
Cavalerie, Fournier	*Husarenregiment* (Baden)	4 Sqns
	Chevauxleger Prinz Johann (Saxon)	4 Sqns

Total for *9e Corps*: 54 battalions, 16 squadrons, numbering 33,000 men.

10e Corps: Marshal MacDonald, Duc de Tarente.

Formation Commander	Units	Size
7e Division, baron Grandjean	5 Pułk Piechoty	4 Bns
	10 Pułk Piechoty	4 Bns
	11 Pułk Piechoty	4 Bns
	13. Infanterieregiment (Bavaria)	2 Bns
	1. Infanterieregiment (Westphalian)	2 Bns
27e Division, (Prussian) General Grawert	Six Prussian regiments	18 Bns
	Prussian Jägers	1 Bn
	Füsiliere 2. Ostpreußisches Regiment	1 Bn
Kavallerie-Division, (Prussian) General Massenbach	Kombiniertes Husaren-Regiment	4 Sqns
	Husaren-Regiment Nr. 3	4 Sqns
	1 & 2 Kombinierte Dragoner-Regimenter	8 Sqns

Total for *10e Corps*: 36 battalions, 16 squadrons, numbering 32,500 men.

11e Corps: Marshal Augereau, Duc de Castiglione.

Formation Commander	Units	Size
General Heudelet's Division	Régiments provisoires	18 Bns
General Loison's Division	Régiments provisoires	12 Bns
	Chevauxleger (Württemberg)	1 Sqn
General Durutte's Division	Régiment Belle-Isle	3 Bns
	Infanterieregiment (Würzburg)	3 Bns
	Régiment ile de Walcheren	3 Bns
	Régiments provisoires	6 Bns
	Régiment ile de Ré	3 Bns
General Detrès' [sic] Division	Veliti della Guardia Reale (Naples)	2 Bns
	Marinai della Guardia Reale (Naples)	2 Bns
	5º Reggimento Fanteria di Linea (Naples)	2 Bns
	6º Reggimento Fanteria di Linea (Naples)	2 Bns
	7º Reggimento Fanteria di Linea (Naples)	2 Bns
	22e Légère	2 Bns
	Cavalleria della Guardia Reale (Naples)	4 Sqns
General Morand's Division	3e Ligne, 29e Ligne, 105e Ligne, 113e Ligne	10 Bns
	Infanterieregiment (Frankfurt)	3 Bns
	Rheinbund Regimenter	7 Bns
	Infanterieregiment Prinz Max (Saxon)	3 Bns
General Cavaignac's Cavalry Division	2e régiment de dragons	4 Sqns
	5e régiment de dragons	4 Sqns
	12e régiment de dragons	4 Sqns
	13e régiment de dragons	4 Sqns

14e régiment de dragons	4 Sqns
17e régiment de dragons	4 Sqns
19e régiment de dragons	4 Sqns
20e régiment de dragons	4 Sqns

Total for *11e Corps*: 83 battalions, 37 squadrons, numbering 60,000 men. Of these, only Loison's and Durutte's divisions took part in the 1812 campaign, numbering about 27,000 men.

Austrian Corps, Prinz Schwarzenberg.

Formation Commander	Units	Size
General Bianchi's Division	Hiller's & Colloredo's Regiments	4 Bns
	Kirchenbetter's Grenadier Battalion	1 Bn
	Simbschen's & Alvincy's Regiments	4 Bns
	Przeszinski's Grenadier Battalion	1 Bn
General Baron Siegenthal's Division	7th Jäger Battalion	1 Bn
	Warasdiner, de Lin's, Czartoryski's, Davidovich's & Kottulinski's Regiments	10 Bns
General Baron Trautenberg's Division	5th Jäger Battalion	1 Bn
	St George's Croats	1 Bn
	Duka's & Würzburg's Regiments	4 Bns
General Frimont's Cavalry Division	Archduke Johann's Dragoons	6 Sqns
	Hohenzollern's & O'Reilly's Regiments	16 Sqns
	Kaiser's & Hessen-Homberg's Hussars	16 Sqns
	Blankenstein's & Kienmeyer's Hussars	16 Sqns

Total for the Austrian Corps: 27 Bns, 54 Sqns, numbering 33,000 men.

1er Corps de Cavalerie, comte Nansouty.

Formation Commander	Units	Size
1re division de cavalerie légère, Bruyère	*7e & 8e hussards*	8 Sqns
	9e chevau légers	4 Sqns
	16e chasseurs à cheval	4 Sqns
	6 & 8 Pułk Ułanów	8 Sqns
	2es Leib Husaren (Prussian)	4 Sqns
1re division de cuirassiers, St Germain	*2e, 3e & 9e cuirassiers*	12 Sqns
	1er chevau légers	4 Sqns
5e division de cuirassiers, Valence	*6e, 11e & 12e cuirassiers*	12 Sqns
	5th chevau légers	4 Sqns

Total for *1er Corps de Cavalerie*: 60 Sqns, numbering 12,000 men.

2e Corps de Cavalerie, comte Montbrun.

Formation Commander	Units	Size
2e division de cavalerie légère, Pajol (Sebastiani)	11e & 12e chasseurs à cheval	8 Sqns
	5e & 9e husards	8 Sqns
	10 Pułk Huzarów	4 Sqns
	3es Jäger zu Pferd (Württemberg)	4 Sqns
	1es Westpreussisches Ulanen	4 Sqns
2e division de cuirassiers, Wathier	5e, 8e & 10e cuirassiers	12 Sqns
	2e chevau légers	4 Sqns
4e division de cuirassiers, Defrance	1er & 2e carabiniers	8 Sqns
	1er cuirassiers	4 Sqns
	4e chevau légers	4 Sqns

Total for *2e Corps de Cavalerie*: 60 Sqns, numbering 10,400 men.

3e Corps de Cavalerie, comte Grouchy.

Formation Commander	Units	Size
3e division de cavalerie légère, Chastel	6e, 8e & 25e chasseurs à cheval	12 Sqns
	6e husards	4 Sqns
	1es & 2es Chevauleger (Bavarian)	8 Sqns
	Chevauxleger Prinz Albrecht (Saxon)	4 Sqns
3e division de cuirassier, Doumerc[3]	4e & 7e cuirassiers	8 Sqns
	12e & 14e chevau légers	8 Sqns
6e division de dragons, Baron La Houssaye	7e & 23e dragons	8 Sqns
	28e & 30e dragons	8 Sqns

Total for *3e Corps de Cavalerie*: 60 Sqns, numbering 10,000 men.

4e Corps de Cavalerie, comte Latour Maubourg.

Formation Commander	Units	Size
4e division de cavalerie légère, General Rozniecki[4]	2, 15 & 16 Pułk Ułanów	12 Sqns
	3, 7 & 11 Pułk Ułanów	12 Sqns
7e division de cuirassiers, Baron Lorge	Garde du Korps & Kürassier von Zastrow (Saxon)	8 Sqns
	14 Pułk Kirasjerów	4 Sqns
	1es & 2es westfälische Kürassierregimenter	8 Sqns

Total for *4e Corps de Cavalerie*: 44 Sqns, numbering 8,000 men.

---

3   Attached to Marshal Oudinot's Corps.
4   *2, 7* and *15 Pułk Ułanów* were in Dąbrowski's detachment.

Siege artillery and Engineer Parks and Transport, came to 21,500 men.

March brigades, regiments, battalions and squadrons, as well as newly formed regiments in Lithuania, came to a total of 80,000 men.

The list of the total of enemy troops who invaded Russia in 1812.

In Napoleon's *État-major général* – 4,000

Garde impériale – 47,000

1er Corps, Davout – 72,000

2e Corps, Oudinot – 37,000

3e Corps, Ney – 40,000

4e Corps, Viceroy of Italy – 45,000

5e Corps, Prince Poniatowski – 36,000

6e Corps, Saint-Cyr – 25,000

7e Corps, Reynier – 17,000

8e Corps, Vandamme – 18,000

9e Corps, Victor – 33,000

10e Corps, MacDonald – 32,500

11e Corps, Augereau (those which invaded Russia) – 27,000

Austrian Corps, Schwarzenberg – 33,000

1er Corps de Cavalerie, Nansouty – 12,000

2e Corps de Cavalerie, Montbrun – 10,000

3e Corps de Cavalerie, Grouchy – 10,000

4e Corps de Cavalerie, Latour Maubourg – 8,000

Siege Parks and Trains – 21,500

March units and newly formed regiments in Lithuania – 80,000

TOTAL: 608,000

Appendix XIV

The Tsar's Letter to Barclay Regarding Count Osterman

The gracious Alexander I, wishing to reassure Barclay de Tolly, who was upset by the unexpected appointment of Count Osterman, wrote the following review to him in his own handwriting:

J'ai reçu, Général, vos lettres de hier, je l'avoue, avec un sentiment d'afliction. Comment se peut-il qu'après avoir pris à tâche de vous prouver estime, attachement, confiance et, permettez moi d'ajouter, distinction, car dans chaque occasion je vous donné même le pas sur des personnes de ma propre qamille, comment se peut-il que vous trouviez plaisir à être injuste envers moi, et cela dans un moment où chacun ne doit avoir d'autre pensée que le salut de l'Etat? Permettez moi de vous le dire, Général, avec cette franchise que mon amitié pour vous m'autorise d'avoir vis-a-vis de vous, je ne vous reconnais pas dans cette demarche et j'aime mieux l'attribuer à un moment d'égarement. Le fait même vous en convaincra: j'en suis sûr.

Au moment de partir de Belmonte je reçois la lettre du C. Schouvaloff, dans la quelle il me dit qu'il est hors d'état moralement et physiquement de commander son corps, qu'il ne peut plus se tenir à cheval, et qu'il ne peut pas rassembler deux idées dans sa tête – voilà ses expressions. Il n'y avait pas un moment à perdre, je n'avais de disponible qu'Osterman qui se trouvait depuis Vidzy, comme vous l'avez vu vous même, à ma suite. J'ai commencé par rendre la lettre originale de Schouvaloff à Woltzoguen avec ordre de vous la présenter et en y ajoutant de ma part, que l'ennemi, pouvant attaquer à tout moment ce corps, je croyais utile d'y envoyer tout de suite Osterman. J'ai pensé que, lisant la lettre de Schouvaloff, vous trouverez que j'ai très bien fait.

Les formalités peuvent se remplir ensuite; à la guerre, il me semble, qu'il faut penser au plus pressé. Je voulais donc, quand nons nous reverrons la première fois, vous dire de le faire donner, comme de coutume, au Приказъ [order]. Je vous demande à présent – quelmanque de confiance y a-t-il dans tout cela? Pouvais-je deviner que Schouvaloff tomberait malade et m'écrirait cette lettre, pouvais-je deviner même qu'Osterman se présenterait chez moi deux jours plutôt avec la prière de le reprendre au service? Enfin – pour l'amour d'un Приказъ et des formalités d'usage, pouvais-je sacrifier la sûreté d'un corps dont le chef se trouvait hors d'état de le commander? En vous envoyant par Woltzoguen la lettre originale, c'était vous mettre au fait de toute la chose aussi bien que je l'étais moi-même. Vous voyez donc, Général, que votre soupçon a été complettement injuste dans cette affaire. Je vais vous prouver qu'il l'est tout autant dans celle des rapports du Général Essen. Tous ceux que j'ai reçu, je vous les ai envoyés. Un seul, faisant mention qu'il a arrêté un courrier de l'Ambassadeur de France et lui a pris ses dépêches, je l'ai envoyé chez le Chancelier, comme ayant rapport à sa partie. Au reste, dans tous ces papiers il n'y avait rien d'interessant. Pourqui irais-je vous chacher des rapports du Général Essen, quand vous avez en main tous les papiers militaires de l'Empire de Russie entier? Convenez que cela aurait été ridicule. Ainsi cela doit vous convaincre, Général, que de ma part il n'y avait pas le moindre manque de confiance, et que vous m'avez accusé bien injustement.'

Appendix XV

Barclay's Defence of His Operations up to August 1812

Barclay de Tolly's letter to the Tsar dated 9th [21st] August 1812, held in the classified archive of the General Staff Department.

> *Je crois de mon devoir de declarer à Votre Majesté Imprériale, que dans les differens combats les deux armées ont essuyé une perte considérable et exigent d'être complettées. J'ose par conséquent présenter à Votre Majeste Impériale, s'il n'était pas à propos d'employer pour cet effet les bataillons, escadrons et compagnies d'artillerie, qui se trouvent aux ordres du général Miloradowitsch, car la manière dont ils existent actuellement, étant composés de recrues et d'officiers trop peu expérimentés, ne sera pas d'une grande utilité. C'est surtout à présent le moment, où tous les efforts possibles doivent être faits pour retenir l'ennemi. Les meilleurs expediens sont pour cet effet les opérations de l'armée du Général Tormassow, pour le porter au flanc droit et au dos de l'ennemi depuis Wolynsk et Mozyr. L'heureux succès de cette entreprise n'est sujet à aucun doute dès que les trouppes de l'armée de Moldavie sont attirées sans delai, pour couvrir la Wolynie et servir de soutien à l'armée de Tormassow. Une diversion prochaine au flanc gauche de l'ennemi, faite par une descente dans la Prusse, la Courlande, ou même dans la Livonie, serait e'un effet salutaire...*

I believe it is my duty to declare to Your Imperial Majesty, that in the various battles the two armies have suffered considerable losses and demand to be reconstituted. I therefore dare to suggest to Your Imperial Majesty, if it were not advisable to employ the battalions, squadrons and artillery companies which are under the orders of General Miloradovich for this purpose, because the manner in which they are constituted, being composed of recruits and officers with little experience, would not be of much use. Especially as now is the time when all possible efforts must be made to hold back the enemy. The best expedients for this purpose are the operations by General Tormasov's army, to bring him behind the right flank and the rear of the enemy from Volhynia and Mozyr. The fortunate success of this enterprise will not be in doubt as soon as the troops from the army of Moldavia are moved up without delay, to cover Volhynia and to serve as support for Tormasov's army. A similar diversion on the enemy's left flank, made by a raid into Prussia, Courland, or even Livonia, would have a salutary effect...

Appendix XVI

Relative Strengths During the Fighting around Smolensk

For all the disagreements between historians of the war in 1812, there is no doubt that, in all the actions around Smolensk, the superiority in numbers lay with the French. In the fighting on the Stragan river, there were – partly in actual combat, partly in reserve:

Russians according to:	Buturlin	Prinz Eugen
III Corps	13,500	
IV Corps	9,500	
I Cavalry Corps	3,700	
Total:	26,700	23,000
On Napoleon's side, according to: Prinz Eugen		
3e Corps	19,500	
Gudin's Division	8,000	
1er Corps de Cavalerie & 2e Corps de Cavalerie	8,000	
8e Corps	13,600	
Total:	49,100	

Of these, some 32,000 Frenchmen and their allies were sent into action against 17,000 Russians. *Erinnerungen aus dem Feldz. des Jahres 1812 in Russland*, 56-57. General Buturlin presents the number of active combatants among the French infantry at 35,000, while ours were 15,000 men.

Appendix XVII

March Disposition for the Attacks on Brest, Kobrin and Pinsk

March Disposition for the advance on the enemy forces located in Brest, Kobrin and Pinsk.

Kovel, 8 [20] July 1812.

The army will proceed as a single column through Ratno; the detachment under Adjutant-General Count Lambert's command will move along the banks of the Bug towards Brest; a detachment will be sent out from Ratno under the command of Major General Shcherbatov to support him; it is to consist of the following units: Tatar Ulans, Yevpatoria Tatars, Vladimir Infantry, Dnieper Infantry, 28th Jägers, 11th Horse Artillery Company, 34th Light Artillery Company.

In battle order, the right flank is to be commanded by General of Infantry Count Kamensky, while the left flank will come under Lieutenant General Markov. In this event, the vanguard is to be drawn up under the command of Major General Chaplits from the following: Pavlograd Hussars, four squadrons of Lubny Hussars, 13th Jägers, six guns from 12th Horse Artillery Company, Captain Kutsevich's Pioneer Company, Barabanshchikov's Don Cossacks.

Corps de Bataille: Taganrog Dragoons, Vladimir Dragoons, Tambov Infantry, Kostroma Infantry, Ryazhsk Infantry, Apsheron Infantry, Nasheburg Infantry, Yakutsk Infantry, Vitebsk Infantry, Kura Infantry, Kolyvan Infantry, 2nd Battery Artillery Company, 16th Light, 17th Light and 35th Light Artillery Companies, 15th Battery and 18th Battery Artillery Companies, 28th Light and 29th Light Artillery Companies.

Reserve, under Major General Prince Khovansky's command: four grenadier battalions, 38th Jägers, 34th Battery Artillery Company, 13th Horse Artillery Company.

A detachment under Major General Melissino's command is to occupy Lubieszów and monitor the roads leading to Kobrin and Pinsk and movements by the enemy located in Pinsk, consisting of: three squadrons of Lubny Hussars, Serpukhov Dragoons, two grenadier battalions, 32nd Jägers.

According to the attached general march route, Major General Lambert is to reach Brest on the 13th [25 July], while Prince Shcherbatov's detachment is to reach the same location by the same date and operate in unison against the enemy, agreeing among themselves on the time to commence operations, for which, while advancing, they are to have uninterrupted communications with each other by means of liaison patrols. Upon the success of this attack on Brest, they are to deliver word to me immediately; thereafter both are to turn towards Kobrin for an attack on the enemy with combined forces on the 15th [27 July], for which a separate disposition will be issued.

Regiments are to have with them only the cartridge and office box carts, provisions wagons with ten-days supply of rations and two infirmary carts each; in the infantry and hussar regiments, two of each, while in the dragoon regiments, one of each; personal carriages are permitted, two for generals, and one for regimental colonels in chief; all the rest should be left in Kovel to be drawn up in laager, under the command of Wagon-Master-General Major Rusanov, 15th Infantry Division is also to move with the laager.

The sick from all regiments and units are to be sent immediately to the hospital at Olyk.

The regiments and artillery companies assigned to the detachment under Major General Prince Shcherbatov must set out today and reach Ratno on the 10th [22 July] without fail.

The regiments and artillery companies that make up the main column must set out tomorrow, that is, 9 [21] July.

I shall be located with the troops making up the *Corps de Bataille*.

Signed in original: General of Cavalry Tormasov.

In the M.T.D. No 32,417.

Appendix XVIII

Barclay's Orders to Count Wittgenstein

When First Army marched from Polotsk to Vitebsk, Barclay de Tolly gave Count Wittgenstein the following orders:

> All the circumstances and the intelligence we have received confirm that the enemy have turned themselves away to the right with their main force, in order to completely cut 1st Army off from 2nd Army and to penetrate the very heart of our fatherland. His inaction after the three stages which I executed to prevent this, confirmed me in my suspicions, and therefore I have decided to hasten in the direction of Vitebsk by forced marches with my army.
>
> Wishing to respond to enemy movements and to be able to reinforce you, I have left VI Corps facing Disna, by which means I have disguised my movements, and those of my rearguard, under the command of Major General Baron Korf, and thereby over extended my force somewhat; now, in order to bring them closer to me, I have halted today with the infantry in camp, while yesterday evening I had already sent a detachment of cavalry forwards, to Beshankovichi, to drive away and destroy any enemy patrols, which have begun to spread out towards Vitebsk.
>
> This morning I Cavalry Corps proceeded thence, and tomorrow morning I shall follow them with the whole army and, with the help of the Almighty, I hope to forestall the enemy intentions.
>
> Your Excellency must now remain independent with the corps entrusted to you, and our Most Gracious Tsar entrusts you with full authority for the protection of the area in which you will operate, and with the granting to you of full authority to act in every event at your own discretion. The baseline upon which your operations are founded is Sebezh, Pskov and Novgorod. The objective is to hold, and if possible, to defeat the enemy, whom you may oppose, in order at the same time to protect Riga from being besieged.
>
> In order to secure your movements in the event it becomes necessary to retreat, I ask Your Excellency to order the immediate evacuation of all hospitals and baggage to the interior Governorates. I also humbly ask Your Excellency to forward your dispatches to me most frequently, sending your couriers via Nevel to Vitebsk, using the route attached herewith.

I am pleased to add the news I received yesterday that the corps under General Platov, which constitutes the vanguard for Prince Bagration, who is on his way to join 1st Army, defeated and completely destroyed nine enemy cavalry regiments at the town of Romanovo. More than 50 field officers and subalterns and 1,000 privates were taken prisoner. Today, a prayer service to the Almighty was held in my army on the occasion of this victory.

Your Excellency, of course, may allow your corps and troops to participate in the general rejoicing.

No 493. 7 [19] July 1812. Polotsk.'

Appendix XIX

Fighting Strength of I Corps

Returns for troop strengths in the independent I Corps and its detachments under the command of Major Generals Prince Repnin and Gamen available for service upon joining I Corps as reinforcements.

Vanguard, Major General Kulnev	Bns & Sqns	Fighting Men	Remarks
Platov 4th's Cossacks		336	Selivanov 2nd's Cossacks were detached on 2 [14] June to protect the borders of Courland and came under the Riga garrison, while Rodinov 2nd's Cossacks came under 1st Army on Barclay's orders on 24 June [6 July].
Grodno Hussars	8 Sqns	1,044	
23rd Jägers	2 Bns	1,408	
25th Jägers	2 Bns	1,268	
28th Battery Artillery Company	6 guns	160	
9th Light Artillery Company	12 guns	179	

Vanguard Total: four battalions, one Cossack regiment, eight squadrons, 18 guns, numbering 4,395 men.

Corps de Bataille, First Line, Major General Berg	Bns & Sqns	Fighting Men	Remarks
Perm Infantry	2 Bns	1,215	
Mogilev Infantry	2 Bns	1,235	
Sevsk Infantry	2 Bns	1,160	
Kaluga Infantry	2 Bns	1,065	
24th Jägers	2 Bns	1,285	
Replacement Battalion, 11th Jägers	1 Bn	240	
Replacement Battalion, 36th Jägers	1 Bn	234	

Combined Dragoon Regiment	4 Sqns	501	Three squadrons were left in Pridruisk, Kreslav and facing Kaplau, and then escorted the headquarters trains to Sebezh.
5th Battery Artillery Company	12 guns	213	
27th Battery Artillery Company	12 guns	251	
27th Light Artillery Company	12 guns	141	
Second Line, Major General Kakhovsky			
Replacement Battalion, Leib Grenadiers	1 Bn	288	All the infantry of this line was under Major General Kazachkovsky's command. The replacement battalions came under Major General Gamen, the cavalry under Major General Balk.
Replacement Battalion, Tauride Grenadiers	1 Bn	302	
Replacement Battalion, Yekaterinoslav Grenadiers	1 Bn	363	
Replacement Battalion, Pavlov Grenadiers	1 Bn	304	
Replacement Battalion, Count Arakcheev's Grenadiers	1 Bn	267	
Replacement Battalion, St Petersburg Grenadiers	1 Bn	357	
Combined Grenadiers of 5th Division	2 Bns	1,016	
Combined Grenadiers of 14th Division	2 Bns	972	
Riga Dragoons	4 Sqns	500	
Yamburg Dragoons	4 Sqns	409	
1st Horse Artillery Company	12 guns	216	
3rd Horse Artillery Company	12 guns	213	

Corps de Bataille Total: 22 battalion, 12 squadrons, 60 guns, numbering 12,747 men.

Reserve, Major General Sazonov	Bns & Sqns	Fighting Men	Remarks
Tula Infantry	2 Bns	1,156	
Navaginsk Infantry	2 Bns	1,126	
Tenginsk Infantry	2 Bns	1,204	
Estland Infantry	2 Bns	1,228	
26th Jägers	2 Bns	1,243	
Combined Cuirassier Regiment	4 Sqns	533	Under Major General Prince Repnin's command.
Combined Lifeguard Regiment	3 Sqns	404	

14th Battery Artillery Company	12 guns	233	
28th Battery Artillery Company	6 guns	159	
26th Light Artillery Company	12 guns	160	

Reserve Total: ten battalions, seven squadrons, 30 guns, numbering 7,446 men.
Pioneer company – 93 men.
Total for the independent I Corps under Count Wittgenstein: 24,681 men with 108 guns.[1]

---

1   10th Light Artillery Company, even before the opening of hostilities, had been sent via Mitau to the force under General Essen. 28th Battery Artillery Company joined I Corps along with Gamen's force.

Appendix XX

Deployment of I Corps After July 1812

Count Wittgenstein's force, following the fighting on 19 – 20 July [31 July – 1 August], was deployed as follows:

Vanguard under Major General Helffreich's command: two battalions each of, 24th Jägers, 25th Jägers, combined grenadiers of 5th Division, three squadrons of combined Lifeguard cavalry, eight squadrons of Grodno Hussars, Platov 4th's Cossacks, 3rd Horse Artillery Battery under Captain Bistrom.

Main Body. First Line under Major General Beg's command: two battalions each of, 23rd Jägers, 26th Jägers, Perm Infantry, Mogilev Infantry, Sevsk Infantry, Kaluga Infantry, four squadrons of combined cuirassiers, replacement squadron of the Pskov Dragoons, 14th Battery Artillery Company, 26th Light Artillery Company, 27th Light Artillery Company.

Second line under Major General Kakhovsky's command: two battalions of combined grenadiers of 14th Division, six replacement battalions from grenadier regiments, four squadrons of Riga Dragoons, 28th Battery Artillery Company, 1st Horse Artillery Company.

Reserve under Major General Sazonov's command: two battalions each of, Tula Infantry, Tenginsk Infantry, Navaginsk Infantry, Estland Infantry, replacement battalion of 11th Jägers, four squadrons of Yamburg Dragoons, 27th Battery Artillery Company, 9th Light Artillery Company.

Index

From Reason to Revolution – Warfare 1721-1815

http://www.helion.co.uk/series/from-reason-to-revolution-1721-1815.php

The 'From Reason to Revolution' series covers the period of military history 1721–1815, an era in which fortress-based strategy and linear battles gave way to the nation-in-arms and the beginnings of total war.

This era saw the evolution and growth of light troops of all arms, and of increasingly flexible command systems to cope with the growing armies fielded by nations able to mobilise far greater proportions of their manpower than ever before. Many of these developments were fired by the great political upheavals of the era, with revolutions in America and France bringing about social change which in turn fed back into the military sphere as whole nations readied themselves for war. Only in the closing years of the period, as the reactionary powers began to regain the upper hand, did a military synthesis of the best of the old and the new become possible.

The series will examine the military and naval history of the period in a greater degree of detail than has hitherto been attempted, and has a very wide brief, with the intention of covering all aspects from the battles, campaigns, logistics, and tactics, to the personalities, armies, uniforms, and equipment.

Submissions

The publishers would be pleased to receive submissions for this series. Please contact series editor Andrew Bamford via email (andrewbamford@helion.co.uk), or in writing to Helion & Company Limited, Unit 8 Amherst Business Centre, Budbrooke Road, Warwick, CV34 5WE

Titles